THORSONS GUIDE TO PUBLIC SPEAKING

Explains how this invaluable skill can be learnt and refined so that it need not be a nerve-racking experience but can be practised with confidence and enjoyment – to the benefit of speaker and audience!

By the same author

THORSONS GUIDE TO MAKING BUSINESS PRESENTATIONS

THORSONS GUIDE TO PUBLIC SPEAKING

HOW TO MAKE YOUR SPEECH A SUCCESS

by

STUART TURNER

THORSONS PUBLISHING GROUP

Wellingborough · New York

First published 1986

British Library Cataloguing in Publication Data

Turner, Stuart
 Thorsons guide to public speaking: how to make
 your speech a success
 1. Public speaking
 I. Title
 808.5'1   PN4121

ISBN 0-7225-1227-9

Printed and bound in Great Britain

Contents

Introduction

Many of us have opportunities to speak at some time or another but refuse, mainly because of nerves. This is a pity because although really outstanding speakers are perhaps born not trained – I suspect the sense of timing which is so vital has to be inbuilt – most people can become proficient speakers with just a little application and practice. I hope this book will help in the process. You will find in it no special breathing exercises, throat diagrams or other attempts to make the subject sound complicated, because it isn't. All you need is common sense plus a willingness to make an effort to control those initial nerves.

Animals have the sense to lie down after a good meal. Humans have the curious habit of listening to speakers, and after-dinner speaking is certainly one of the most challenging forms of the art, which is why this book often uses it to illustrate particular points. If you can master it you will easily handle other types of public speaking where the principles are much the same.

Finally, 'he' may be read as 'she' at all times. I am well aware that women can be very fine public speakers and the use of the masculine is purely for convenience.

Stuart Turner

1
Controlling Nerves

Controlling nerves may seem an off-putting subject with which to start a book on public speaking, but it's a sensible one to tackle head on because it probably causes the most alarm among those invited to speak. Surveys show that the fear of speaking is greater than that of flying, spiders or visiting in-laws, and fear certainly leads many people to refuse opportunities to speak.

This chapter was originally called 'Conquering Nerves' but that is almost impossible; total control of nerves may in fact be undesirable because a certain amount of nervousness can add sparkle to a speech. And take comfort – the terror, the sweaty palms, the dry lips, the urge to run to the lavatory are all quite natural. Honestly. Nervous tension is a perfectly normal reaction with any strong emotion and is something of a throwback to uncivilized life thousands of years ago (slightly less if you are speaking at a rugby club dinner) when meeting an adversary meant that you had to put the maximum effort into either fighting or running away. The emotion starts adrenalin chasing about your body, your heart rate increases, your blood-pressure rises and sweat glands in the skin work overtime to carry away the excess heat produced. But hold on – don't put the book down yet. All that hyper-action is perfectly normal and is just your body getting ready to perform at maximum efficiency. And remember that it's not just confined to public speaking – actors and sportsmen among many others go through exactly the same process before performing.

Those are the scientific reasons (using scientific in the loosest sense of the word, I hasten to add) for your terror, but before you refuse an invitation to speak perhaps it's worth trying to identify the causes of your particular metabolic madness.

- Inexperience? Never spoken before? Well, recognize that you really should start some time; in a world which depends so much on communication it is silly to remain silent. Incidentally, if you haven't spoken before perhaps you should blame your parents for not encouraging you to do so as a child or teenager – school debating societies are useful for providing experience.
- You don't know anything about the subject? Then don't speak. (Would that more speakers would follow this advice.)
- You've been asked to propose a toast or vote of thanks and it all seems too important for humble old you? This should be the least of your worries. A toast is the easiest speech of all to make, particularly if it is not preceded by a long build-up, while a vote of thanks simply means that you are acting as a spokesman for the rest of the audience in saying 'thank you'. The biggest snag with the latter is that you may be the only member of the audience who has to stay awake while the speaker drones on.

The main reason for being inclined to refuse an invitation to speak is likely to be the fear of making a fool of yourself. Go back to an earlier point – do you know something about the subject? If you do then you needn't make a fool of yourself. So accept.

I recognize that you may be a naturally timid person who simply doesn't want the hassle of screwing yourself up to speak in public. But before you finally put this book down (and I'll be sorry to see you go) just think of some of the advantages. You will be able to present your case better if you are lobbying for or against something (such as Barnsley's first airport on your allotment) or trying to raise funds for a favourite charity.

You will be able to communicate better with others and, for instance, pass on enthusiasm for your hobby and perhaps encourage them to take it up. Confidence in speaking may even help you to a better job because you will perform better at interviews. The benefits are endless. You could even entertain people with a witty after-dinner speech – and don't let anyone tell you it isn't rewarding to get warm applause after a speech which has gone down well. It is. Go to work on an ego.

I hope I've convinced you that the rewards justify the effort.

And just for a moment, stop thinking of yourself – consider the audience instead. I don't know about you but if a speaker gets it all wrong I want to crawl under the table with embarrassment for them. Yes, an audience can get nervous too, either if you gabble away from the start or, worse, if they think you are going to drone on for so long that the bar will be closed. They will enjoy themselves much more if they sense that you know what you are doing and are confident.

Having considered why you get nerves and the benefits of controlling them, how can you exert that control?

First, vow not to use drugs or alcohol to steady your nerves. If you take drugs regularly for a specific complaint then you will obviously continue to do so when speaking, otherwise don't be tempted by even a tranquillizer; be wary too of taking simple medicaments without a doctor's advice – I heard one speech that was horrendous simply because a glass of wine had reacted with something and caused very strange speech patterns. In fact, everyone should be wary of taking alcohol when speaking. One glass may be fine, but two and the microphone will magnify the oh so small, but oh so noticeable, slur to your words.

So no drugs or alcohol. Let's try self-analysis instead. Can you talk to a group of friends at a coffee morning or cocktail party? Of course you can. Then you can also talk to an audience. A coffee morning isn't public enough to be a fair comparison? Then go and ask questions at a political meeting or at a local lecture. Get used to the sound of your own voice raised in public (not too stridently, mind). Even buying something at an auction will give you practice because you will have to shout out your name to the auctioneer. I remember feeling very nervous the first time I did that, now I buy what my family considers the most appalling junk with total aplomb.

Reading aloud, either to yourself or a masochistic friend, may help to develop your technique and put expression into your voice – although do choose an author who uses simple words and short sentences with no jargon. You could even go on a professional training course to improve your speaking skills, but be careful. They have a tendency to turn out everyone as if they've come from the same mould, perhaps because they are aimed mainly at businessmen facing similar situations. Also as you get to know the others on your particular course you will gain confidence in front of them and then be scared all over again when you face a new audience.

Now that so many people have home video equipment it may be simpler, and certainly cheaper, for a group of friends, perhaps from the same society, to run their own DIY training course. Several videos are available which illustrate the key points to keep in mind and, after watching one, individuals could be asked to stand up and give a two-minute speech to the rest of the group on a subject they have prepared beforehand. It is even better if these speeches can be filmed and played back on a TV screen while the group is encouraged to be mercilessly critical of one another. After their two-minute prepared speeches participants could be asked to ad lib for a minute or so on a subject pulled out of a hat. Having to speak off the cuff on, say, 'wheel clamps and their place in a welfare state' should give you so much to think about that you will forget your nerves.

You will have gathered by now that a key factor in success-ful speaking is preparation and then practice. I suspect that the acute sense of timing and feel of a great speaker must be born, but anyone can improve with practice and certainly you will be able to control your nervous tension with proper prepara-tion. So, if there is the remotest chance that you will be asked to make a brief speech, do a little preparation. You didn't think the breathless addresses from Oscar winners, thanking their agents and directors and praising motherhood and apple pies, were unrehearsed did you?

And we have agreed that you will try to avoid speaking

unless you know what you are talking about, haven't we? Confidence in your knowledge of the subject will help you to relax and control your nerves, but don't relax so much that you send your audience to sleep – a point which boffins or the very knowledgeable need to watch when addressing less erudite audiences.

To some extent your subject matter may affect your nervous tension. If you are raising an unpopular topic you may anticipate the going getting rough. As an extreme example, I wouldn't relish giving a speech in the defence of cigarette smoking to many audiences nowadays. I suppose the only hope would be to concentrate on the 'freedom of choice' angle, but even then I'd find a train to catch before there was time for any questions.

Now let me digress briefly to consider those who stutter or stammer. I do not have the knowledge or impertinence to offer a cure and anyway sufferers with the problem will no doubt have had all the skilled advice they need. But, if it is any consolation to stutterers and stammerers, out of my personal 'top ten' of speeches I've really enjoyed, two were given by speakers with speech impediments – speakers who had the confidence to make the problem work for them in making an impact.

Now back to the main body of my sermon. If you have accepted an invitation to speak, recognize that there comes a time to stop preparing and worrying. You've done all you can, so why get ulcers? Regard the occasion as something to be proud of, not nervous about. YOU have been chosen to speak, not someone else. Many people kid themselves that they could write a book; few believe that they could make a speech, so most of the audience would be equally nervous in your shoes and therefore you will have their sympathy from the start. I've listened to over 1,000 speeches or lectures and I've only heard one person dry up and that was because of the aforewarned mixing of alcohol and medicine.

Your nerves may still be there when you get to your feet of course, but you will be too busy to worry about them unless you go adrift, and even then a mistake will make you seem human. In fact, if you make a mistake in front of an audience which knows you and someone gently heckles or ribs you, they may actually help you to relax and perform better.

Incidentally, even if you have been nervous when making a speech or giving a lecture, you will be less so when answering questions afterwards because your brain will be too busy working out your replies. If you don't know an answer, say so. Don't waffle.

One final thought – public speaking isn't the end of the world. I've never actually heard anyone's knees knock with fright and, apart from occasional politicians, who deserve little sympathy, no one gets physically hurt when public speaking.

Try it!

2
The Invitation

If your nerves are under control and you get an invitation to speak, don't rush to accept it. Find out more about the occasion first. Who are the organizers? Are you in sympathy with them and their aims? Is it an important audience for you or your message? And why have you been asked? Is it because of your natural charm, or because they think you will have something worth while to say, or because someone in the inviting organization has heard you speak before? Or are they simply scraping the barrel?

Weigh up all these things before you agree to speak. In some circumstances you won't receive 'an invitation' because you may be the chairman of an association and left with little or no choice about speaking, but even so many of the points in this chapter are worth considering.

Having decided that the invitation to speak has come from a worthwhile source (and you shouldn't be too choosy while trying to build up experience) you need to know the day and date of the function to see if you can fit it in. Always ask for both day *and* date because this avoids any confusion. Be wary of using a clashing engagement as an excuse for saying 'no'; the organization may then offer alternative dates. If you don't want to speak, it is better to say so right at the start.

Having established 'who' and 'when', next you need to know 'where'. In your early speaking career it is unlikely your fame will have spread very far so travelling will not be a problem, but for functions further afield you need to establish if you can get there on time and, if you have no car, if you can do so by public transport.

However far the venue, get clear directions for finding it plus a phone number in case you break down on the way. Many people are bad at giving directions and few will know road numbers, but do at least coax them to give you the name of a major landmark, such as a pub, near to the venue. A good organizer will advise you of complicated one-way systems and the more thoughtful ones will reserve a parking space for you and will have someone on the lookout when you arrive to make you feel welcome. But don't bank on it – the chairmen of local branches of well-known national organizations some-times treat speakers as unwelcome interruptions to their chats with cronies.

During your discussions with the person inviting you to speak, find out what arrangements will be made for accommo-dation should you be travelling a reasonable distance to speak in the evening. Opt for a hotel if possible. A stay with one of the committee may be fine in the euphoria leading up to a function, less so the next morning when the family are fighting for the bathroom.

It's a bit early in the book to mention it perhaps, but if you become a seasoned speaker you may need to consider what, if any, fee to charge. To save your blushes this sordid topic is covered in the last chapter. However amateur you are, you should still be reimbursed with your expenses, unless of course you are anxious for the opportunity to speak in order to put over a particular point.

Other things you need to know about a function include:

- Arrangements for food. If you eat on the train travelling to a function and then find you are faced with a five-course meal, you may become too bloated to speak well. Find out in advance.

- What dress is to be worn? If it says 'dress optional' for a dinner, ask if the top table at least will be in evening dress and if in doubt tend to dress up not down when speaking. I fear I cannot advise you on dress if you are invited to speak at a nudists' function because, to my chagrin, I've never been invited to do so. They do say you at least get an apparent round of applause when they sit down after drinking a toast you have proposed.

- What time will it start? Organizers usually expect you there far too early, so try to establish a realistic start time – usually at least fifteen minutes after that stated on a ticket, i.e. 7.30 for 8.00 means people will start supping soup at around 8.15.

- How long will you be expected to speak? Almost all organizers *under*-estimate how long raffles, official business and so on will take, while they *over*-estimate how long an audience will want to listen to you. The time of day will affect the length of your speech. Breakfast meetings are dodgy affairs because few are at their best first thing in the morning. If you speak too long after lunch you may hear the sound of chairs being pushed back as people leave. Some associations have a tradition of ending the meeting at, say, 2.30 p.m. come what may, which may seem harsh on a speaker but does serve to concentrate the mind.

Having sorted out some or all of the above, it will help if the organizer puts it all in writing to you (efficient ones will do this anyway). You should have business and home telephone numbers for your contact in the association. Remember that you won't need much, if any, of the above detailed information if you are an honorary official speaking to your own association, and all the stress on attention to detail may also seem a bit over the top if you've just been asked to propose the loyal toast at a local association dinner. Nevertheless, for many functions you will need all of that information and for others you may need even more, for example:

- Who were the speakers at the last function held by the organization? How well were they received? This information will give you that all-important 'feel' for the audience and its expectations, particularly if they say, for instance, 'We had old so and so and he went on for far too long'.

- Who else is speaking and in what order? This will save you going into shock on the day if you suddenly find you are sandwiched between two household names.

- Will there be any auctions, raffles, prize-givings or traditional ceremonies held before you speak? I was once about to get to my feet at a Round Table dinner when a host of pretty girls danced in wearing skimpy underwear. I'm not complaining you understand, just pointing out the sort of thing that can happen; better to be forewarned. Similarly, it helps to know if any celebrities or even royalty will be present because they can distract an audience and disconcert you. (Try to close your mind to them.)

- How many will there be in the audience and of roughly what age and sex? A small audience may need a more intimate approach than a large one where you will have to 'pitch up' to make an impact.

- Who are the members of the audience? Do they all belong to the same association? Are they there willingly, or have they been coerced by an enthusiastic club secretary? All these things will help you when planning your Gettysburg Address. A reader can turn a page (not yet) but a listener is stuck with you and may be less than enthusiastic if he was dragooned into attending. If an association has had problems in selling tickets and forty per cent of those present are guests, that means that only six out of ten will know, or care, what you are talking about if you get too technical about a subject. If partners are invited then just thirty per cent or so may be remotely interested in what you are saying. See why all the background information is so important? You *must* have a feel for why an audience is there and what it is expecting of you. I still wince when I recall attempting a light-hearted address to a business lunch where the audience traditionally had a much more erudite 'lecture'. Not a success.

The final thing you need to know is on what subject are you supposed to be speaking? Don't settle for an organizer's invitation to 'Just give us twenty minutes or so on whatever you feel like'. Try to get a more specific brief. I've listened to a

Euro MP speak for twenty-five minutes on a totally inappropriate theme to a trade association simply because he hadn't
determined the subject matter. Defining the topic becomes
even more important for businessmen who are invited to give
a keynote speech to a conference. Incidentally, if you are
speaking at a conference, try to resist requests to submit your
speech weeks in advance. This is a sure way to extinguish any
life in it.

Having settled on the subject, give some thought to a title
for your address. The stronger the title, the bigger your
audience is likely to be. 'How I made a million' will attract
more people than 'How I founded Bloggs Builders'.

By making a nuisance of yourself to the organizer to find out
all you can about your audience (and I can't stress its importance too highly) you will know whether your aim should be
to inform them, to motivate them, or simply to entertain
them. If your objective is none of these but is to persuade them
about an idea or thing – such as to lobby for or against
something – then perhaps your speech should be only a part of
a concerted approach. For example, if you are trying to stop a
by-pass and a minister is present, he will be more convinced of
the depth of local feeling mentioned in your speech if he has
passed posters in everyone's garden on his way to the hall. So
do your spadework.

Footnotes for Organizers

If you are sufficiently interested in public speaking to be
reading this book (or is it just that you like great literature?)
then it is likely that you will be invited to help organize events,
so this short section looks at speaking 'from the other side'.
Obviously organizers need to worry about much more –
microphones, food, room heating, keeping out extraneous
noise and so on – but this isn't the book for it. However when,
as an organizer, you come to consider speakers, keep the
following in mind:

- Consider the balance of a list of speakers. Don't have
  three or four of the same type and style – vary them.

- Don't have an inordinately long list of speakers. My record is to rise to speak at 23.57; it was the only time the date has changed on my watch while I was speaking. As an organizer you should not over-estimate people's thresholds of boredom.

- Put your speakers in the best order. If you have a noted humorist place him at the end. Even if he isn't the most important speaker at least he (and remember the note in the Introduction that 'he' can be 'she') will send your audience away happy.

- Work out a timetable for your function and try to hold to it.

- Use word of mouth as the best way of finding speakers, but keep the circumstances in mind. If someone strongly recommends a speaker without mentioning that he heard him in action at a ribald rugby club dinner, the effect on a more genteel audience (and every audience is more genteel than a rugby one) may not be quite what you wanted.

- Don't forget members of your own association or club when looking for speakers, at least they will come cheap.

- If a speaker goes well don't, in your euphoria, immediately invite him to come again in a year's time. Leave a day or two at least to check that everyone else shared your view of his talents and, if possible, leave a gap of a year before inviting him back.

- Call a speaker you are considering inviting, because the way he handles himself on the phone may give you a guide as to whether he is right for you.

- Be wary of well-worn speakers. I've seen some very well-known names search in their pockets for a speech during the chairman's introduction and clearly they had made no attempt to tailor things to their audience. It's sad to see the sense of let-down in audiences on such occasions.

- If you are a bright-eyed and keen organizer, you may be tempted to invite people to speak over a year ahead. Totally unnecessary for most speakers and off-putting for those who have volatile schedules – they will almost certainly turn you down.

- Put your invitation to a speaker in writing.

- Read this chapter again and try to see things through speakers' eyes. Vow to do all you can to make things easy for them – you will get better speeches as a result.

Finally, if you are involved with foreign audiences, remember that interpreters cost money so keep this in mind in your budgeting. For 'twin-town functions' the struggles to grope with each other's languages will add to the warmth and fun with perhaps no formal interpreter needed. I've seen an audience greatly amused by a pretty girl translating a torrent of Finnish into 'He says yes'. However, business organizers should get the best interpreters they can afford and preferably with some knowledge of the subject/s under discussion. Position interpreters where they can see a screen if visuals are being used and don't expect them to operate efficiently for longer than half an hour or so; arrange changeovers at convenient points.

3
Planning

Having received an invitation to speak and analysed your audience as suggested in the previous chapter, you may be keen to sit down and write your golden words. Curb your enthusiasm. Constructing a speech is covered in the next chapter, but first spend some time on planning what you are going to say. As you gain experience you will develop your own plan of action but until then you could follow this sequence: clarify your objectives – have a 'free thinking' session – gather the information – sort it into a relevant order. You may find that you will go through the sorting stage more than once.

Clarify Your Objectives

Accept from the start that you are very unlikely to change people's minds in a speech; what you *may* do is persuade them at least to consider your point of view. You may find it equally difficult to correct a well-entrenched falsehood, the 'big lie', but you may at least make them think twice.

Take care not to get out of your depth when speaking. Because of the power of the media we tend to deify too easily. Those who may be skilled or famous in one area, such as sport, are solemnly asked for their views on politics; worse, they are unwise enough to pontificate and make fools of themselves in the process. Don't fall into the same trap. Stick to what you know. Knowledge of a subject, however badly presented, is better than well-delivered waffle.

'Free Thinking'

Once you have an idea of your overall objective in making a speech, take a notepad and 'free think' for a few minutes. While the adrenalin is running at having been invited to speak, your first rough ideas may prove to be the best you will have on the subject. Just note down your comments in no particular order. If you have been asked to speak on, say, 'Buying and selling antiques' you might jot down 'Treasures from attics' to remind you that a lay audience will be intrigued by a tale of someone who has stumbled on a valuable painting gathering dust somewhere. Similarly 'rings' will remind you to include a piece on auctions, either confirming or demolishing the commonly held idea that dealers get together to rig things. Let me stress that you do not need to go into great depth during this free thinking period – just make a note of general ideas.

Gather Your Information

The next stage is to gather the information which will help you draft your speech. If your free thinking session has indicated that some specific research will be needed, then put this in hand straight away even if your speech is not for some time.

Keep a box file or a desk drawer for all the various bits of information you will accumulate – press clippings, brochures, letters, etc.

The reference room at a local library will be a good source of information and should also be quiet enough for you to concentrate. If you are assembling facts and figures to support your case, do *not* be tempted to shade or distort them. Someone in your audience may know better and if they correct you in a question-and-answers session they may destroy your credibility. However, don't be timid. If, for instance, some well-known or locally respected people support your view and have been quoted in the press, then by all means use that as ammunition. Let's face it, lobbying for or against a by-pass could mean a lot to you so pull out all the stops.

As well as using your local library, you may also accumulate a few reference books of your own. A thesaurus will be

useful when you are trying to construct a deft turn of phrase
(don't make it too convoluted) and a dictionary and, perhaps,
an encyclopaedia will be worth having to hand. If you wish to
quote from the Bible – and why not if it is appropriate? – a
concordance will steer you to a suitable quote on almost any
subject. In assembling information for a speech you will
almost certainly acquire too much. If, for instance, the event
organizer sends you reams of brochures and back-up leaflets,
sift through for the really relevant material and throw the rest
away.

Sort Your Information

Having gathered your information you come to your 'first
sort'. Go through everything you have accumulated – the bulk
of which should be slips of paper with your own thoughts on
them – and then grade the information into:

1. Essential facts which your audience *must* have.
2. Information which they *should* know.
3. Material which it would be nice for them to know but
   is not essential.

Sorting the information in this way will clarify your thinking
and will help if you have to delete material because you are
over-running.
   At this point you will begin to appreciate that the hardest
part of making a speech is not getting to your feet to deliver it,
but putting your backside on a seat to plan it. Force yourself to
go through this planning process because it is the secret of
success.
   Keep your audience in mind at all times. Don't assume that
they will know you. A bit player on a long-running television
drama may be famous to part of an audience, but totally
unknown to the rest. If you come into this category, make sure
the chairman has enough biographical information to
introduce you properly.
   At this stage of your planning, you may find it helpful to jot
down the key points you plan to make onto cards – I use a
printer's cheap offcuts which are roughly postcard size. The
advantage with such cards is that you can shuffle the points

around to improve the flow of what you plan to say. You can of course use a sheet of paper and put numbers and lines on it as you settle your running order, but I think cards make it easier. Do not confuse the rough notes made at this stage with the memory aids you may use when delivering a speech (see Chapter 5).

Logically, you could sort your notes into the following order: an introduction; the points you want to make; arguments to support your case; perhaps a brief note of any opposition view (being careful to demolish it of course); a summing up.

I said 'logically', but of course no two occasions are the same. If you were lecturing on the life of the house sparrow you would hardly need to be 'arguing' too strongly about anything, save perhaps whether or not sparrows are pests. Equally, if you were making an after-dinner speech proposing the toast of an association, you would rarely be quoting opposition views; although if you were addressing, say, solicitors and wanted to wake them up you could refer to the growth of self-conveyancing before coming down in their favour (always supposing that is your genuine view – steer clear of the subject if it isn't).

Whatever the occasion, your planning must aim to make your speech *flow*, ideally with a theme to tie it all together; your audience will get confused if you bob about without any logical links. Having the information on separate cards will help you to sort things into a logical sequence and after a first canter through you may decide on a 'second sort' in which you re-jig the running order either mildly or entirely. For example, the 'first sort' for the aforementioned speech on 'Buying and selling antiques' might put the attic treasure reference towards the end. The 'second sort' might bring it to the front as an attention-grabbing introduction, perhaps along the following lines: 'Last week an old lady brought into my antique shop a bowl which she had found in an old suitcase in her attic. I gave her £4,000 for it.' No-one will go to sleep after that (not too many will believe you either, mind).

Perceptive as you are, I am sure you see the point that flows through all this preparation – *remember the audience*. They don't want a secondhand speech, they want your views so try to bring something fresh to the subject. Pinching other people's ideas and dressing them up as your own is really not the done thing, apart from jokes that is. It is quite common to see members of an audience writing down a witty speaker's jokes. I'm not sure what they do with them afterwards but it doesn't matter too much anyway. Humour, which rates a chapter of its own later in the book, is as much a matter of delivery and timing as content.

To summarize: you've found out all you can about your audience; you've dug out some facts and sorted them into roughly the right order; you've gone through again and put them into an even more attractive order to give a better flow. Now you are ready to construct the speech.

4
Constructing a Speech

If you have the time, it is no bad thing to take a break between planning a speech and writing it down because you may have useful second thoughts; while if there is anything in your notes which you cannot understand later then you will have to change it if your audience is to follow you.

At this drafting stage of a speech use the cards with jotted notes mentioned in the previous chapter, but add additional comments such as a link between one point and the next; we will look at the actual notes you will use 'on the day' in Chapter 5.

The quality of your speech results from the style you impart to it. There is little point in including 'set' speeches in a book like this because circumstances vary too much but there are some things to watch out for:

- Have something to say. Sounds obvious? Of course, but an awful lot of speakers just use words to fill up the time.

- Don't be stuffy. You may be deeply interested in the minutiae of your subject; don't assume others will be or you may have to fight to hold their attention.

- Don't pretend to be more knowledgeable than you really are. You won't be too audible if you talk through your hat.

- Don't string a series of platitudes and clichés together and expect it to rate as a speech. It will just be soporific.

- Try to bring light and shade to a speech. Too even a pace can be monotonous.

- Don't be a poseur. Be yourself and don't talk up or down to an audience.

- Don't be afraid to admit your mistakes, perhaps to illustrate a point. The audience will warm to you because you will seem more human.

- Involve your audience whenever you can. For instance, if you are lobbying for a by-pass, a comment that 'If traffic flow continues through the high street at the present rate, in eight years time one in three of the houses will need major repairs and we will *all* face doubled insurance premiums' will make people pay attention.

- Use case studies, i.e. actual examples, whenever you can. They will hold attention better than generalities.

- Take people behind the scenes of your job or hobby. For instance, if you are in the legal profession give your audience an insight into what fruity old judges do at the end of lengthy court cases. I've always assumed that they throw off their wigs and nip down to the pub for a pint with the lads, but it would be nice to have this confirmed by a speaker. If you are in television, tell them that a particular scene had to be shot several times because, well, I was going to say the female lead was drunk but you'd better say because she was so deeply immersed in the part that she was too overcome by emotion to continue. We mustn't destroy everyone's illusions must we? Just bear in mind that audiences do love a bit of gossip, although clearly you should not be slanderous or too indiscreet, especially if the media are present.

- Don't ride your hobby horse too long or too hard. You will make your audience saddle sore.

- Try to make your speech apt. If you are presenting school prizes don't talk for twenty minutes on land drainage or you will bore everyone. And, whatever you do, don't patronize the children.

With those points in mind, you should start building your speech by framing a strong introduction. To some extent as a speaker you will have to 'control' your audience and to do this you first have to get its attention, which is why a good introduction is so vital.

If you are unknown to the audience you may dare to try a shock approach to grab attention, although this needs some care. Although attitudes have changed, standing up and starting with 'I am a lesbian' would still take courage before some audiences. But to start a talk on gambling by announcing 'I won (or lost) £1,000 last week' would assure you of a close hearing.

Having got through your introduction, tell the audience what you are planning to do. For example, 'I would like to discuss the new by-pass and the damage it will do to valuable farmland. I will then explain how an alternative line would halve the wastage of land and still retain the playing fields.' Then proceed to do just that and end by re-capping your main points. (By the way, I am not obsessed with by-passes but they seem to generate a lot of emotion.)

If you have a very strong introduction, the let-down will be all the greater if it is followed by a poor speech. Nevertheless don't be tempted to put your key message right after the introduction. Gain their confidence and feel your way with the audience first.

When you do come to your 'message' (always supposing you have one) make quite sure that the audience follows it. Don't wrap it up so warmly that no one spots it, nor cloud a message just because it is a sad one. Don't waffle on about the benefits to a village of this or that if the real crux is that the playing field is to be dug up. Always assume that you will be found out and when you are you will be branded as devious.

As you draft the body of your speech you may need to re-jig your note cards yet again to improve the flow. Whatever the final running order include some 'signposts' between the sections so that you carry an audience with you. People are happier when they know what is going on, so say such things as 'so that is the effect on jobs, now I would like to look at the effect on housing'.

Although you should be as natural as possible when speaking, you may still need to move into a higher gear because after all you are putting on a performance. Few of us in general conversation give much thought to our choice of words or spend time 'orating' (our friends would look askance at us if we did) but for a speech try to add a rhythm, occasionally even 'a rhythm of three': 'We are going to do this, we are going to do that and we are going to do the other'. But watch that your attempts to add rhythm don't turn your speech into a sing-song or poem; it must sound natural. To strengthen a point you may decide to argue against your viewpoint: 'It may be said that the changes will improve the amenities in the village, but it can be argued that they will in fact destroy them because. . .'. However, don't labour the point and avoid too much of 'on the one hand . . . on the other'. The audience wants to hear *your* views, so sooner rather than later you should put them across.

To create shock waves and keep people awake, you may decide to butcher a few sacred cows. Addressing a bunch of boffins, you could say 'the computer is turning us into a race of soulless zombies and the idea that we need one in every home to record accounts and addresses is quite ludicrous'. If this is too bold for you, try a more cowardly approach: 'Some people argue that. . .' followed by what may be the unpopular view. If the audience jeers, quickly move on to the opposite view or, if there is no reaction, say 'and I agree with them!'

When taking a controversial approach, be wary of attacking the cherished traditions of an association and of over-strong attacks on famous people, even politicians, because you will almost certainly offend some of your audience. Mock yourself by all means, in fact it is far better to do this than to praise yourself or your company or association, unless you do this by way of obvious overstatement. For instance, if you get up at a Round Table and say that you represent table number such and such 'which is of course the best table in the area' you will get ribald jeers but they will be friendly ones.

After telling you what to do, it is time for a few things to guard against:

- Avoid superlatives, particularly in connection with your own efforts or products.

- Avoid long convoluted sentences. Short ones will be more readily understood and make a greater impact. If you have to use a long sentence try not to leave the verb until the end. The audience will lose your thread if it has to wait too long for the 'action' word.

- If you use a long word, get it right. Look it up in a dictionary if you are not sure. Even if you get it correct you are likely to get a sarcastic 'oooh' from someone as you may, deservedly, if you quote some utterly obscure historical figure; they'll know you looked it up.

- Steer clear of phrases like 'at this point in time' if you mean 'now'. I'm sure you've heard many similar examples but that one has the most currency and is the most jarring.

- When using a point made in a recent newspaper or magazine article acknowledge the source, particularly if it is a specialist audience because they will have read it too.

If you are privileged to receive an invitation to speak to a *foreign audience* (and with the growth of town twinning you may), find someone of that nationality to steer you clear of the obvious pitfalls and introduce you to their customs (provided they are not too disgusting). Obviously you should delete any 'in' references or comments about domestic television pro-grammes because they won't be understood, and be careful not to patronize foreigners. You and I know that our country is best but it is a bit tactless to let them know that we know.

What you *must* do is say a few words in their language, either of welcome or in proposing a toast. Write your words in English and get someone to translate them and say them into a tape recorder for you. Write a phonetic interpretation of what is on the tape. Your notes can be total gibberish provided they sound like the foreign language when you say them. Then rehearse. I followed these instructions for a fifteen minute speech in a language I don't speak and was congratulated on my excellent accent.

Except for specialist audiences you should avoid complicated figures or statistics. Use even numbers whenever you can – 1100 not 1099 or 1101 – but not if you are talking about a rate increase where a percentage point may be critical. Paint word pictures of statistics to make them more easily understood: 'four times the size of this room' is more readily grasped than so many square metres. Incidentally, for some years yet you should assume that metric figures will result in glazed looks among older members of your audience. Finally on statistics, if something seems totally unbelieveable, say something like 'Yes, I know that sounds impossible but I've double checked it and. . .'.

There's a lot to think about, isn't there? Try to remember the following advice too:

- Avoid clichés.

- Avoid giving undue offence. I once saw a function wrecked because a speaker unthinkingly referred to someone who had made a mistake as a spastic and a listener in a wheelchair made for the door. Apart from political meetings and the glorious rumbustiousness of Speakers Corner your audience will not expect to be offended, so take care not to do so.

- Beware of jargon, attempts at current slang, or in-talk. A middle-aged person wrestling with youngsters' language is as comical as an ageing disc jockey.

- Don't use foreign phrases unless you know the audience will understand them. They will either confuse or sound patronizing.

- A general audience will not undertand GNP, GRP, etc. Avoid them.

- Avoid name dropping. It will just make an audience wince, as Prince Philip was telling me only the other day.

- Ask a friend to tell you if you have the less than endearing habit of saying 'I mean' or 'Like', then try to stop yourself. The most common is 'you know' – if they know, why bother telling them?

Having avoided all those pitfalls and put your note cards in the right order with explanatory or linking comments on them, go through and delete any waffle or unnecessary distractions from the main theme of your speech. Then step back and take a detached view of whether you have a logical form to your speech with a thread running through it.

Now draft your final section. You may say, 'So let me sum up' and then hit the key points again. On the day, if you can think on your feet, re-state anything which you felt was misunderstood or which got an adverse reaction. Add something like: 'You jeered when I said such and such, well let me just remind you that. . .'. Incidentally, if you re-cap on your main points at the end, it may help to rephrase some of them to introduce a fresh line, although if you have a slogan to put across then obviously you should not tamper with it.

Having finished the notes for your concluding section, take one final detached look at it all, remembering that your message is not what you think you have said but what your audience takes away with it. If a person cannot understand something they have read they can look at it again, but they only have one chance with your spoken word, which is why the planning stressed in the last chapter and the constructing in this are so important. If you haven't assembled your thoughts properly you have little chance of being understood.

I mentioned earlier that you should include 'signposts' in a speech to carry the audience with you. As an example, here is a signpost to indicate where we are in this book. We have seen how important it is to learn all you can about an audience. We have considered how to assemble facts on rough note cards and how to sort them into the right order, and we've looked at how to construct a speech using those facts. Now let us look at what, if any, memory aids you will need.

5
Memory Aids

If you are a miraculously clear thinker, and tidy to boot, then the rough jotting notes suggested so far may suffice as memory aids for a speech, but this is unlikely. They'll probably be covered with scribbles. So let us examine what memory aids you could make using the rough notes as a basis, in descending order of complexity.

Write Down Every Word

If you are unsure of yourself, having it all written down will calm your nerves and get you through the ordeal without too much difficulty. If you do a lot of speaking you could even put your comments onto a word processor and select key bits for particular speeches, but be careful that this doesn't make your speeches sound stale.

Although reading a speech will certainly get you through it, there are pitfalls however. For example, it is difficult to write words to be spoken. Few people say 'it is raining'; they say 'it's raining', so use the shorter version when writing out a speech. Saying your words into a tape recorder and then writing them down from a playback may help. Incidentally, if you have the luxury of dictating your speech to a skilled secretary, abbreviating things to 'it's' and 'that's' will not come naturally, so explain why you want it written thus before you start. Typed notes should be double spaced in upper and lower case, not capitals throughout, which can be difficult to read. Consider a machine with a large type face if you have poor vision, and wish to avoid wearing spectacles while speaking. Don't worry too much about grammar. Your task is to be understood, which means speaking the language used in everyday life, so split infinitives if you wish and hang the purists.

If you are going to read your speech, watch page turnover points. When you are in full cry over a key point a turnover will disturb your flow and could, if you turn over two pages by mistake, wreck a point completely. You may decide to underline or mark key pieces in colour, but don't overdo it or the bouts of emphasis will sound too regular and forced.

Writing out a speech sounds easy and less nerve-racking than other methods. Maybe. But sheaves of paper can dismay an audience, especially if you take forever before turning over the first one. Above all, the snag with reading from a script is that it will be *very* difficult to make it sound natural. Work hard to use spoken, not written, phrases; delete any unnecessary words and smooth out any tortuous sections.

Cueing systems are increasingly being used, whereby a speaker looks at his audience through one or more sheets of glass (which for some speakers should really be bulletproof). The speech is typed onto a paper roll and then projected up and onto the glass in front of the speaker. Someone out of sight turns the roll at the right pace for the presenter. The result is that the speaker sees every word of his speech while looking at an audience which only sees clear glass. This method is obviously much better for eye contact than putting your head down to read a speech, although fluffs tend to look strange and a breakdown in the system becomes positively surreal-istic. Such systems are likely to be out of reach of social organizations and anyway are quite unnecessary for most of their functions. And at business meetings you will still be *reading* your words with the resultant lack of naturalness.

You may of course need to read your speech if you have a number of visuals which need cueing in and many conference presentations are read for just this reason. A further advantage is that the approximate length is known in advance for timing a meeting. However, if you really want to progress as a fluent and natural speaker then move on to one of the other systems outlined below.

Part 'Bullets', Part Written

Bullets are short key words or phrases to remind you what to say – I am not suggesting for one moment that you should actually fire anything at an audience. You must use other skills to keep them awake. As an example of this system you might write:

> Honoured: 5 years
> Village hall/ballroom
> Message same:

to remind you to say: 'I am honoured to be speaking to you tonight. It is five years since I was last here and I recall that then you met in the village hall, not in this magnificent ballroom. But my message is still the same. . .' Then read your key message. Even if your opening words are less elegant than if they had been carefully written out beforehand, they will still sound a lot more sincere. Similarly you could end your notes with a few key words to remind you to wish them well in their fund-raising and then to propose a toast.

If you decide to try this halfway stage of 'part bullets, part written in full', you may construct your notes by editing down from a fully written out speech. Caution: highlighting a few key words or phrases on a fully written out copy of your text to use as bullet points will probably confuse you. Better to prepare fresh notes.

Bullets Throughout

This is likely to give you a more spontaneous approach than any of the methods considered so far. How detailed the bullets should be will depend on your confidence and subject knowledge. If you were making a speech on 'making a speech' you might prepare bullets as follows:

> Define objectives
> Inform, lobby or entertain?
> Jot down points to make
> Collect supporting information
> Sort into logical order

Draft outline
Prepare notes

These bullets would enable you to take your audience through some of the stages in preparing a speech. With more confidence you could abbreviate even further:

Objectives
Inform, lobby, entertain?
Points to make
Backup info
Sort
Outline
Notes

If you go too far in your paring down you may stumble once or twice in your first delivery, but your speech will be sharper and more alive than if you'd read it. Space out your notes so that you can add afterthoughts. For example, if an earlier speaker mentions a point you would like to pick up. I often find that having prepared very scanty bullet points I then add more detailed comments just before I speak. I recognize that this is simply through nerves, but it does no one any harm and at least I now find I can speak without taking my teddy bear with me every time.

You may develop a system of using capitals for the key sections of your speech, with subheadings to cover back-up points. Do whatever turns you on (see my earlier point about how silly such slang sounds?) or, above all, calms you down.

Visual Aids

If you know your subject well and have a series of slides or flipovers to illustrate your presentation, you may be able to dispense with notes altogether and let the visuals remind you of what you want to say. This method can give a very relaxed air to a talk and demonstrates that the speaker is totally in command of his subject. If you start to dry up over a particular visual just move on to the next one as a memory jogger. It is worth having bullet notes to hand as a safety net until you are confident enough to use just the visuals as notes.

Learn By Heart

This may sound the most genuine way of making a speech, but *don't*. It is hard work and unless you are a trained actor the audience will still sense that you are 'reading' your speech, in the back of your mind not on a sheet of paper. Drying up or losing your way can be disastrous, while if someone else uses a point you planned to make it may be difficult to modify your carefully memorized words. Above all, you may be concentrating so much on what you are going to say that you will find it almost impossible to react to an audience. If, despite all this, you do decide to memorize a speech, at least have a copy of the script in your pocket or on the table. It may give you added confidence.

If you are repeating a speech you have given several times before and know your subject well, then by all means get up and do so without notes – provided you are doing it from the heart and using *fresh*, not carefully memorized, words each time.

To summarize: unless you plan to get your message across by thought transference or mass hypnosis I strongly recommend that you use bullet points as memory joggers when giving a speech or talk.

Mechanics

Use firm paper for notes. If you have flimsy paper and are nervous, your slightest tremble will show as the notes wave about. If this becomes too obvious, say that you are waving the paper about as a temporary measure because the air conditioning has failed. Some platitudinous (and there's a word you'd be foolish to use in front of many audiences) speakers could almost have packs of 'cliché cards' to be shuffled without noticeable effect on the results. However, you should avoid having so many cards that it looks as if you are going to do conjuring tricks or that the audience is in for a long haul.

Loose cards should be large enough to be handled easily, yet small enough to go into a pocket or handbag. They *must* be numbered, and ideally, strung together with a cord through

holes punched in the top lefthand corners. I dislike books in
which an author imposes too much of 'I' this and 'I' that on his
readers, but I ask you to bear with me here while I describe the
notes I use because I think they are better than loose cards.

I rarely speak for more than twenty minutes (I'm kind to
dumb animals as well as audiences) and work from very brief
bullet points. I use sheets of card (slightly thinner than
postcards) which are A4 width (21 cm) and about the same in
depth. I fold the sheets once so that in effect I have four
columns, 10½ cm wide by 21 cm deep. Why this size? Because
the card will slip easily into the inside pocket of a man's jacket
(or a handbag). With the card folded I write '1' at the top of one
sheet and jot my bullet points down and then (remembering
my point about turning at a convenient part of the speech) I
start the second column, being careful to number that too. I
try to find a suitable point or, if I'm lucky, a laughter pause for
the bottom of page 2 to give me time to refold the card so that
column 3 and 4 are now on the outside ready to be used. For a
speech of up to twenty minutes my bullets usually end about
halfway down the fourth column. I draw a line under my final
bullet (often the toast to be proposed) and then in the spare
space jot down points which I could substitute for any in my
speech used by a preceding speaker. I've never needed more
than one of the cards.

I hope you are still with me. The advantage with my
method, which I am sure countless others use too, is that even
if you drop such a card the 'pages' can't get out of order
because they are all on the same piece of card. Making a speech
fit on no more than four columns (preferably less) acts as a
useful discipline too.

When you've completed your notes, consider pencilled
brackets round points which can be deleted if you are not
making any headway with your audience. Consider colour
coding your notes: red for things you *must* say, yellow for
things you can skip, and so on. There is no recommended
system for this, just do whatever you feel happy with.

I carry a spare copy of my note card, written on ordinary
paper, just in case I hack the first one about so much before
speaking that it is convenient to make a more legible set of
notes by modifying the spare set. I hardly ever need to do this

and, yes, I know carrying a spare is a nervous mannerism but I can't stop.

Two final tips:

- Be wary of putting gesture cues in your notes because the results may look staged. We will cover delivering a speech later in the book, but if you need to put a note to tell you to turn to the chairman when you are speaking about him, then I reckon you've got problems as a speaker which this book won't cure.

- Having prepared your notes, add key information like the address of the venue, the name of the person to contact etc. and then either file or throw away supporting material you've accumulated. You won't be using it during your speech.

6
Humour

When you laugh you take in oxygen which helps to keep you awake. To a public speaker this sounds like a Good Thing for an audience. To some extent after-dinner speaking can be regarded as up-market music hall and a little humour is highly desirable, as it is on other occasions. Relaxing an audience with wit or humour may help you later when you come to make a heavy point.

The approach to humour is the same whatever the occasion and the first thing to keep in mind is that it needs *great care*. You are more at risk when trying to be funny. If you quote a particular statistic or make a telling point on a planning matter, then you are not seeking a positive reaction (although you may get one or two 'hear, hears' or a few nods). But if you tell a joke you are looking for a response from the audience by way of smiles and, if you are lucky, laughter. If you get neither then you have failed which may embarrass you or your audience (or both) and thus slightly dampen the occasion.

Remember there is no written or unwritten rule which says that you *have* to use humour in a speech. Yes, being witty or occasionally lighthearted will stop you sounding too solemn, but a string of stories is not a speech. Use anecdotes or personal illustrations to lighten your address instead and if in doubt, use wit rather than humour. The difference? Well, humour is more comic, broader if you like, and less intellectual. Wit relies more on combining or contrasting previously unconnected ideas. A joke usually comes into the category of humour, a dead pan one-liner or a quote from Coward or Wilde is wit.

Tempting though it may be to try to be humorous, fight the feeling if you know in your heart that you do not have the timing or delivery. However, if you *are* a humorist but have been invited to speak on a serious topic, don't let the humour swamp the message. You want them to remember your telling points about a by-pass rather than your jokes.

Despite my awful warnings, if you decide to tell jokes, where do you find them? Many joke books are available but take care. They may feature well worn material and, also, it is difficult to tell from the printed word whether the material would work for you. Does a joke suit you? Will you feel comfortable telling it? The president of a women's organization would sound foolish telling a story which is clearly more suitable for a womanizing young bachelor. Don't attempt to wade through a joke book at one sitting; you will get indigestion. Take a few pages at a time and consider if something can be adapted for your purpose.

Collect clippings from newspapers and magazines of things which amuse you. Browse through books of quotations. The show business journals often feature advertisements from script writers who offer batches of jokes on various topics for fairly small sums, but you may find this material as tired as that from any other source and some of it may be too strong for the groups you have been asked to address.

Why not try writing something funny yourself? Impossible? Of course not. Among the funniest occasions for social groups are a mock 'This is your Life' on a member, or some new, more relevant words to a popular song. The humour doesn't have to be of the finest quality, the simple fact that it is different will entertain people (with the caveat that such parodies always tend to go on just a shade too long; resist this).

You can still develop your own material for more general audiences. At the time when Nottingham police were prosecuting kerb crawlers, someone said: 'I got lost coming here and stopped to ask a girl the way . . . my case comes up next week. Well, I didn't know I was in Hyson Green' (the area affected by the police action). If that doesn't sound funny in print it illustrates the problem in trying to judge what is funny from books. Believe me, it got a big laugh and a round of applause at a dinner because it was apt and topical.

Still, if you don't feel able to add your own humour to a speech and have to fall back on jokes which have been the rounds, don't despair too much. To each new generation old jokes must be new ones. In fact I have seen a comedian speak two years running to the same organization where ninety per cent of the audience were the same each year and certainly ninety per cent of his material was, yet he went down better the second time. I suspect it was a combination of the food, wine and sheer chemistry, but it does illustrate what a difficult area you have strayed into when trying to entertain with humour.

Television shows use warm-up men to get an audience in the right mood before recording starts and something lighthearted fairly early on in a speech is desirable too to show that you are not such a dry old stick after all. At one function where the chairman had welcomed or introduced virtually everyone in the room, a friend of mine had the audience with him from the start by saying 'For those of you not mentioned by name, hello from me'. However, be cautious in starting with an hilarious five minutes and then switching abruptly into a serious quarter of an hour. Your audience may get confused because you will have struck a jarring note.

Turn a joke into a personal anecdote if you can. Instead of 'there was this man who fell off his bike', try 'I remember when I once fell off my bike'. Then lead into the joke as if it had happened to you, *provided* it is apposite. The worst words in any speech are: 'That reminds me of the story about . . .' because the stories are never relevant.

Beware of long complicated jokes. You are more likely to get them wrong; people's agony will be prolonged if they have heard them before or you tell them badly, and if you 'die' in telling a long joke you will die in a big way and your speech may perish with it. You are much less at risk with a crisp one-line comment. If you want something longer then a joke which builds up is better than one which is hopelessly involved. An old example of a build-up joke is to say, 'I am sorry that X (pick whoever is currently famous but not for his or her intellect) can't be with you tonight. He had a fire at his home last week and his library burnt down. Both books were destroyed.' Pause – some, if not all, of the audience will laugh

– then say, 'which was a pity because he'd only coloured in one of them'.

And that highlights two of the points I've made: it isn't funny in print and it is very old, but it is always well received.

Obviously with an example like that you would have to choose the right person to rib and don't mock the cherished traditions of the group you are addressing (especially regiments), unless you are able to do so very affectionately.

As well as build-up jokes, 'sting in the tail' comments may also be well received. For instance: 'Where would we be without our wives? (pause) . . . Gleneagles?' Or: 'The legal profession is part of our great tradition, like the stocks and the Bloody Tower . . . and some solicitors should be put in both'. Or perhaps write a very twee poem, with a sting in an unexpected last line. Or make the last line equally twee and then attribute it to a totally inappropriate figure, such as a trade union leader in current bad odour.

Avoid sarcasm, it is rarely funny. But do use topicality. It will show you are in touch with life and your audience will think what clever people they are for spotting the reference too. There are two provisos:

- Don't refer to news which broke at 7 p.m. if you are speaking at seven-thirty, because few in the room will have heard it.

- Avoid topical subjects which are only known to a few of those present, for instance at a professional meeting at which the majority are guests. The reference may irritate those not in the know because their lack of under-standing will make them feel just slightly ignorant, whereas your aim should be to keep people relaxed and entertained.

Perhaps the most important word on the subject of humour is 'timing'. The ability to time a joke or comment is inborn, as is the ability to be a good organizer. If someone doesn't sense intuitively that a room needs a microphone, then it shows a lack of basic feel for the subject.

As regards timing, you should learn by your own experience and try to judge whether, if you get a laugh, you should cut in and carry on (thus bringing some laughter to a premature end) or wait until it all dies down, which may mean that those who stopped laughing first have been waiting with their attention flagging.

Recognize that a joke will fail occasionally, however well told, because another speaker may have told it or it has been well used in the area. If one does fail, don't immediately plough straight into another. Get their confidence back with some general chat first.

Be grateful for any unexpected laugh – you may stumble into something unknown to you but known to the audience. But if a speech is going well *don't* add new material or go on too long. The finest sound you can hear as a speaker is 'more'.

It is easy to get carried away and mistake joke telling for public speaking (although there are occasions, like the much maligned rugby club, where the two may be synonymous) so to keep your feet on the ground, here are some 'don'ts':

- Don't read jokes, even if you are reading the rest of your speech. They will sound too forced and lack spontaneity.

- Don't put your punch line first. If you do, why bother telling the joke?

- Don't giggle or laugh at your own comments.

- Don't signal that something is supposed to be funny. 'Here's a good one' is guaranteed to turn people off.

- Tailor jokes to your audience, but remember that professional groups will almost certainly have heard all the jokes about their specialist world.

- Don't pun. Very occasionally a pun will amuse: more often, your audience will groan and their distress will be fairly genuine.

- Don't do impersonations unless you are very sure of yourself.

- Don't fall in love with a joke. If you think something is very funny but it never gets a reaction, drop it.

Remember that the order in which you narrate something may affect how humorous it is. As an example, a friend with four daughters planned to start a speech by saying: 'I'm delighted to be here because it is unusual for me to be able to get a word in edgeways as I've got four daughters'. He reversed the order to: 'I've got four daughters so it is a delight for me to come somewhere where I can get a word in edgeways' and it worked much better. Now, before women's groups start marching on my publishers shouting 'male chauvinist pig', let me point out that while no one is claiming that it was one of the great *bons mots* of our time, it was well received by a mixed audience and made a pleasant introduction. So always consider if you can improve something by re-arranging it.

Finally, consider the boundaries of taste when using humour. Four-letter words are regularly used on television, but I would not consider using them in this book and I don't think you should use them when making speeches. A comic or an actor playing a part may get away with them but you may not, not least because you will be uneasy using them.

Risqué stories are a different matter and one or two (not a string) will be enjoyed by most audiences, however starchy the organizer may have made them sound in his invitation to you. Best of all, if you can find them, are stories which appear as if they are going to be rather broad but turn out to be totally clean. If in doubt, don't go too far. Certainly you should eschew blue jokes in front of mixed audiences; they will irritate many male groups too, except for classic 'stag' functions where they are the norm.

It is puzzling that hen parties are growing in popularity (and saddens me that I've never been invited to star at one) because it seems to me that as women make their way in so many professions, the stag function must eventually die. Perhaps I'm wrong and it just illustrates that good honest vulgarity – on which after all, much of the world's humour is based – is healthily therapeutic.

There are a few other points on taste to remember:

- Be doubly cautious with foreign audiences. Use wit rather than broad humour and try to get a national to check that you are not going to blunder into *double entendres*.

- Avoid religious jokes, unless they gently illustrate a point or if you can honestly say, for instance about a Jewish story, that 'this was told to me by a rabbi'.

- Avoid ethnic jokes. Humour should not be taken too seriously but the growth of racist material is less than savoury. Don't join in.

And finally, just in case you've forgotten, you don't have to tell jokes when making a speech.

7
Visual Aids

Visual aids would be inappropriate to support after-dinner speeches, but they sometimes have a supporting role to play at talks and lectures. First ask yourself if visuals are really necessary. They should not be used as crutches to prop up a poor presentation. Polish up your words first and then decide whether to use them.

Visual aids can add interest and impact to a talk; as the cliché says, one picture is worth a thousand words. I wouldn't put it as high as one thousand, but it is certainly quite a lot. Even the lowering of lights to show films or slides may create excitement and/or intimacy, although the speaker will lose eye contact with his audience.

Here are a few general points to remember:

- ALWAYS concentrate on the words first before the visuals. Slides and charts will cost time and money, so be quite sure what you need before commissioning them. You don't have to go to elaborate type-setting for illustrations; a co-operative artist's free hand may be fine provided it is consistent.

- Tailor the lavishness of your visual aids to your audience and to the impression you hope to make. For a travel talk to a club by one of its members, a simple series of slides will be fine; a local or national company presenting to the same group should aim for a slightly more professional approach. Remember, the way you put your message across says something about your organization. If the slides are upside down or a projector fails, then it reflects adversely on you. Despite this advice, don't go absurdly over the top in your use of visuals. A massive sound and light show with dancing girls is not really necessary if you are telling people about a new carpet cleaning service.

- Don't cram too much information onto a slide or flipover, spread it over two or more.

- If you have to show columns of figures (and avoid them if you can), be consistent in the presentation. If years are shown across the top of the first illustration, don't put them vertically on the next.

- Most audiences will include people who have forgotten their glasses, so use large visuals, and vet them from the back of the room. In particular, check if they are high enough for people at the back to see.

- Visuals must be honest. Graphs should not show a distorted view and facts must be accurate. Obviously you do not have to point out the adverse side of anything, but if you try to cheat and mislead people your credibility will disappear.

- First aid lectures apart, be wary of gory visuals – some people may faint. I invariably do.

- Don't overdo the use of pointers. There are retractable ones which clip in your pocket like a pen, or beams of light, or simply good old billiard cues; but first ask why you need to point at all. Is your illustration not clear enough in the first place?

- Check any equipment in advance. Never rely on a promise from an hotel that they will have what you need, even a piece of chalk: check.

- Ensure that equipment has appropriate extension leads.

- Rehearse with, or at the very least chat with, whoever will be working the lights so that he knows when you want them on, off or dimmed.

- Extraneous light must be kept out for some visual aids (e.g. slides).

- Photographs of club officials or VIPs should be recent, not glamour shots taken years ago (otherwise they may receive a ribald welcome).

Visuals must be tailored to the words. If you are talking about one figure while another is showing on the screen you will confuse your audience. If you are going to say 480, don't show 478. Give people time to digest what they see and fit the style of the visuals to your theme. For example, cartoons should not be used to illustrate a serious subject. (Cartoons need special care anyway; what some find amusing others will consider tiresome.)

Try not to mix visual aids. Bobbing about from flipcharts to video to slides may perplex your audience and will do nothing for the projectionist's peace of mind. One change is fine, say to introduce a film sequence, but avoid too many.

Now for a few specific points on various types of visual aids, starting with *slides*. And no, we don't want to see the ones you took on holiday, thanks all the same. Holiday slides are eminently resistable unless the audience was present when they were taken. A local horticultural society's visit to a national show would be a suitable case for treatment.

Slides are the most widely used (and abused) visual aid, but to make the right impact with them, you need to remember a few basics:

- Avoid word slides where possible. Words should be heard, pictures should be seen. In particular, avoid word slides saying 'Objectives' or 'Good morning'. (Don't laugh, they've been seen.)

- When you have no specific slide to illustrate a section of your talk, use a general picture or, better, the organization's logo or badge.

- Use *a* consistent *style* for *slides* if *you* are *having* them *specially* made. *It* will *distract* an *audience* if, *for* example, *the* lettering *keeps* changing – *as* these *lines* have *probably* distracted *you*.

If you are giving a talk or lecture using slides, you will probably have a fully written out script, possibly with a second copy for the projectionist if you are not operating the equipment yourself. It is important that the script clearly shows the slide change points. There are many ways of doing this – for example, you could circle the words where you want a new slide, or put a line between the words – whatever makes you feel confident. It's not important what system you use. I break a script completely at a slide change point and write enough about the slide to tell me what should be on the screen, like this:

'Make your notes for a speech on

SLIDE – CARD FOLDED TO GO IN POCKET

a piece of fairly stiff card which is folded so that it will go into an inside jacket pocket or handbag.'

You soon get used to ignoring the capitals and reading through them. This method makes it easy to sort slides into the correct order before a talk, while a projectionist would have to be fairly absent-minded to miss one of the change points.

Avoid cramming in so many slides that the audience misses the message you are trying to convey. Eighty slides fit in a tray and you should try not to go above this figure. The growth of computer-generated graphic slides for business presentations means that complicated slides can now be prepared very rapidly and, with computers also used to operate multi-projectors, highly sophisticated presentations can result. But if you are ever told that you cannot react to circumstances and change a slide 'because it's in the computer' ease yourself out of the grip of technology next time and go back to a simpler system. You want people to remember your message, not the hi-tech methods used to put it across.

Although slides are the most used visual aids, *overhead projectors* will be ideal for many lecturers. They are low cost and a speaker can face his audience all the time, although the system doesn't really work for large audiences. The transparencies used are easily made by writing on acetate sheets with a felt tip pen and a slightly home-made air can be part of the charm of OHP.

If you use *films* or *videos* as visual aids you are unlikely to be speaking while they are showing, but you must let the projectionist know exactly what you are going to say as an introduction (and don't ad lib) so that the films or videos start on cue. When you say 'now let's see the film' a pause of only a few seconds will seem like an eternity.

Several sections of film to be shown one after the other may be spliced together with blank pieces between them so that the projector can be left running. Time the gap between each section, write suitable words to fit and rehearse the links carefully. Resist the desire to speed up the linking sections during your presentation because this will cause awkward pauses. Make sure your microphone will be switched on at the necessary moments.

At large venues you may find yourself projected onto a screen via a video system so that people at the back can see you. If so, guard against any distressing personal habits which might otherwise go unnoticed.

As we move down the audience size scale, *flipover charts* will be fine. Even large sheets of plain wallpaper will work, provided what is written or drawn on them is clear and legible. Put a blank sheet or a print of your organization's symbol over the first illustration so that the audience doesn't start reading until you want them to.

If you intend drawing on a chart during your talk, cheat a little and lightly pencil on the sheet what you want to illustrate, then boldy draw over the pencil marks with a felt tip during your presentation. You will be admired for your artistic, if not speaking, ability. With flipover charts, as with most other visual aids, use different colours to make the graphics clearer. For example, red to indicate dates of committee meetings, green to show social evenings, and a third colour giving film shows. Photographs rarely work well as flipovers – better to pin them around the walls for people to study later perhaps.

Instead of flipping over sheets of paper, you can put your visuals onto cards which are then stood on an easel. Plan them so that they will go under your arm, otherwise they will be awkward to carry around.

A hardened speaker becomes something of a survival expert and will carry such things as string, pins and sticky tape – the latter to tape pegs firmly onto easels.

Incidentally, don't neglect the dear old *blackboard* as a visual aid. It worked well enough for us at school. As with flipover charts, lightly chalk in things to be drawn later and then rub them out gently enough so that you can still see an outline to draw over. If you rub something out during a presentation, use a damp cloth which will avoid dreadful squeaks and your disappearance behind a cloud of chalk dust.

You may consider handing something round as a 'visual aid' during your talk. A 'Ming' vase which was made last week in Mablethorpe would certainly command attention if you were talking on fake antiques. However, handing things out needs care because it can result in a certain amount of shuffling and chatter as an object is passed along. Better to wait until an interval.

I once saw a crowd dive under their seats when a shotputter hurled what they thought was a heavy object at them. In fact it was a rubber ball painted to look like a shot. It was hilarious at the time, but on reflection perhaps a bit risky. One or two people looked ready to pass out with fright.

You've plenty of choice of visual aids. But remember, *concentrate on the words first.*

8
Rehearsing

Having constructed your speech and prepared memory aids, consider what rehearsing to do beforehand. As with so much in public speaking it is a question of striking the right balance. You should run through your speech enough to highlight any clumsy links or phrases that may need to be changed, but not over-rehearse so that all spontaneity slips away before your live performance.

I'm not an advocate of rehearsing in front of a mirror because this seems totally unnatural, but do say your speech aloud a time or two. Try to vary the pace so that it does not become monotonous. Tape recording may alert you to distressing mannerisms, like 'you know' and so on. But the main problem with any rehearsal is lack of audience reaction, which is why timing can be slightly misleading because you can't gauge the length taken up by applause or laughter. You may consider that, if you are not attempting to be humorous, a dry run will give you a complete feel for what it will be like on the day because you will not be looking for an audience reaction. Not so. The fact that there is an audience present *will* affect you. It may cause you to repeat a point or stress a particular section, or you may even decide to delete something altogether.

One exception to this rule about avoiding too much rehearsal is the fully written out speech or lecture which is to be given with a lot of visual aids, such as slides. Here you will have to rehearse the presentation, preferably with the projectionist present, until you are able to read it without stumbling, and almost inevitably you will have to edit it to make it flow. Even if you plan to read a speech right through, do remember to look up at frequent intervals to develop eye contact with your audience. Your rehearsal may show that some slides are on the screen for too short a time. Either delete them or add a few more words so that they can stay up longer.

When your speech or lecture has been assembled from material written by different people (as may happen to a chairman of an association who is delivering a report on several sections' work), the various sections should be 'tuned' to the deliverer's own style. In such a case the speaker should always ask himself if he really believes in what it is suggested that he should say; he will be less than persuasive if he doesn't.

Ask a long-suffering friend whose opinion you trust to listen to your rehearsal and tell you what message or messages he received from your words. The friend needs to be fairly typical of the members of your expected audience for this to work properly. For example, if you are a boffin preparing to talk to a general audience, don't rehearse in front of a fellow boffin. He will follow your abstruse references; find a less knowledge-able guinea pig.

It may sound like cheating but if you have a key speech which you really want to hammer home to an important audience you could consider a full-scale practice in front of a 'less important' audience in advance of your big day (in much the same way as plays tour the provinces before moving into the West End). The same applies to jokes. However hard you rehearse in private you need an audience to gauge the real reaction. Many comedians try out new material on sample audiences before using it in, say, a Royal Variety Show or television programme.

Whatever form your speech takes, when you have finished rehearsing sit back and have a final think. Have you held on to your message? Would your case be presented better if the running order was changed? Have you struck the right tone, or are you too hectoring or not forceful enough? Now is the time to change. Unhappily for audiences, not enough speakers go through this final analysis – either because they are just relieved to have cobbled at least something together or because they have run out of time.

When a series of lectures or talks is to be given, it is important that someone sits in on all the rehearsals to listen for any inconsistencies. Even if it is too late to change any of the individual presentations, a chairman may be able to improve things by carefully writing links between any jarring sections.

At the same time as you review what you plan to say, decide if you are happy with the memory aids you intend to use. If you just can't get to grips with bullet points as notes, either write more detailed bullets or go back to reading the whole thing.

Stand up when you are rehearsing. You will tend to project more when on your feet, but the main advantage will be to see if you can actually read the notes you have prepared. If you wear glasses for close work, you may need to adjust the size of the writing on your notes so that you can read them at a glance, perhaps without glasses. A beautifully flowing speech may be ruined if your speech binder is placed at the wrong height for you to read the words clearly.

Although you will be unable to time applause or laughter during a rehearsal, you should at least have an idea if your speech is roughly the right length. The most likely change you will need to make will be to shorten it. And do keep in mind all those earlier considerations about your audience. Yes, the secretary assured you that your audience will be a serious lot and, yes, your thoughts on the latest lunatic legislation to come out of Brussels are really terribly interesting. But don't you think fifteen minutes would be better than the twenty-five you've got now? (Particularly if you find on the day that the wine has flowed fairly freely before you rise.)

It is often the practice to run sweepstakes on the length of speeches. A senior policeman, who shall remain nameless, once said as I was about to stand up: 'These sweeps are of course illegal . . . but please speak for exactly thirteen minutes'. However, sweeps should not influence the length of your address as much as the thought that few professional entertainers can hold an audience for an hour, and even those that do may intersperse comic routines with songs. So why should a good after-dinner speaker think he is likely to hold an audience for half an hour? And, in turn, why should you even dream of going on for more than fifteen minutes? Some excellent after-dinner speeches I've heard have lasted forty minutes or so but, almost without exception, people said afterwards 'What a pity he went on a bit too long'.

The same concerns about timing apply to occasions other than dinners. A talk on jam-making or antique furniture to a broad audience should err on the side of brevity. If your audience is clearly expecting more when you finish, and the organizer is looking distraught because the next attraction is not yet ready, fill in by inviting questions.

While your long-suffering friend is sitting through your rehearsal, ask him to watch what you do with your hands. Some books on public speaking make much play of the importance of gestures, but I think such things should come naturally or not at all. However, while not planning deliberate hand movements you should avoid any habits which are positively distracting. If you have any, try to control them. It is very off-putting to watch a speaker constantly fiddling with his glasses or putting his hands in his pockets then immediately taking them out again. Gestures which are carried to excess may even leave you open to ribbing. One speaker wrung his hands so much that a voice asked 'Are you cold?'

Finally, as you use a rehearsal to break in a speech, use it also to try out new shoes. Squeaking may amuse some and distract others just as you are trying to command their attention. Also rehearse your reading glasses as previously forewarned, and even false teeth. Try saying 'Stress is a major source of suffering in single Siamese cats'. If in doubt, go back to your dentist.

Audiences can be very cruel.

9
Talks and Lectures

So far this book has been directed at those making *speeches* – such as at a social organization's annual dinner – but the same principles apply if you are giving a talk or lecture. Few dictionaries are clear on the difference between the two, but I guess if you were addressing a general audience on woodland mammals it could be described as a talk, whereas an address to biology students on the nervous system of small vertebrates would be a lecture. Talks are likely to be given to those who are interested, however mildly, in the subject; lectures are often directed at those who know something about a subject and want, or need, to know more. Lectures tend to be more formal and are expected to inform more than talks which may be quite general; both perhaps appeal more to the intellect than the emotions as in a public speech.

If talks and lectures are to inform, then it follows that if you are to deliver one you need to know your subject. Anyone can propose a toast to an association because anyone can dig out a few things to say before asking people to raise their glasses. Not everyone can, or should, stand up and talk or lecture on Renaissance Art. No one should talk or lecture without a reasonable knowledge of the subject. If they've only read a couple of books and try to bluff their way through, Sod's Law states that there will be someone far more knowledgeable in the audience who will be itching to air his knowledge by asking questions.

Lectures should not be considered in isolation. Consider what has gone before, either on the day or at the previous function held by the body. A series of lectures should be planned as a whole and an organizer should have briefed you that you are following Mr Jones who will be speaking on such-and-such. If your such-and-such is similar to his, you may need to contact him to avoid duplication. Ideally, an organizer should plan a series of lectures so that there is light and shade – a procession of very heavy topics will stupefy even the most learned audience. Lectures should be connected by 'bridges', either by a chairman linking the various speakers or by you, at the start of your address, saying something like 'Mr Jones looked at housing, I'd like to move outside and consider roads'.

If lecturing, try to sit at the back for the lecture immediately preceding yours in order to get a feel for an audience. That is also why I suggest that you should find out what has gone on at the previous function held by the organization. If someone went down well talking about a very obscure topic, it may give you a pointer as to how serious you need to be. If you know one of the previous speakers, ring him to get his views of the association – they may be very different from the secretary's.

You will have to pay even more attention to your preparation if you are billed to give a keynote speech or lecture. You are supposed to strike at the heart of the topic with other presentations being complementary to yours. Although you must obviously state your own views, check with the organizers to see if they are anxious to have particular points put across.

Many scientific bodies like to have lectures supplied well in advance; some even issue them and then the members sit politely while they are read through. If you find yourself in this strange situation, try to freshen your address with an occasional ad lib, although take care that you don't then lose your thread and find difficulty in returning to the main body of your address.

Frankly, many lectures regurgitate old information and some lecturers do get stale. Listen to what children say about their teachers. This even applies to business conferences where the audience has paid fees to attend, although this may not be totally disastrous because the exchange of views over coffee or lunch may be just as valuable to attendees as what they hear in the lecture hall. Nevertheless, if you are invited to lecture do try to bring something fresh or thought provoking to the subject.

10
Toasts and
Forms of Address

When asked to propose a simple toast people often get worried about protocol – how they should address the Lord Mayor, and so on. This concern is quite unnecessary because if a dignatory is present he, or an aide, will tell you the right form, as will any competent toastmaster. And even if you get it all wrong hardly anyone in the audience will know or care, so don't worry unnecessarily. If you ever find yourself on your feet in front of a bunch which includes Beefeaters, barristers, a Baron and the Dagenham Girl Pipers, just start by saying 'friends'.

However, despite my flippancy and the decline in traditions, you may feel happier if you have given just a little thought to the correct form.

Although graces are short thanksgivings rather than toasts it seems appropriate to include them here. Where possible, grace should be said before guests sit down so that they are not disturbed immediately they have settled in their seats. You don't *have* to stand for grace, but it would be a bold organizer who suggested otherwise because the convention is so strong that guests would be confused – folk are happier when they are comfortable with what is happening.

If you are asked to say grace try to come up with something more original than 'For what we are about to receive may the Lord make us truly thankful'. A clergyman once said: 'Bless the chef and all who serve us. From indigestion Lord preserve us', after which everyone sat down smiling. The Selkirk Grace, which is attributed to Robert Burns, always makes a nice start to a meal although it really needs the right accent to deliver it properly:

> Some hae meat, and canna eat,
> And some wad eat that want it,
> But we hae meat and we can eat,
> And sae the Lord be thankit.

In striving to be original, it is acceptable to say something like: 'Bless our food, our friendship and the aims of our association' but don't go too far in this direction. Don't include a plug for a product or ask people to pray for the downfall of an opposing team at a sports dinner for instance.

I saw a poster recently of a prayer found on the wall of an old inn:

> Give us, Lord, a bit o' sun,
> a bit o' work and a bit o' fun;
> give us all in the struggle and sputter
> our daily bread and a bit o' butter.

Those lines would make rather a nice grace.

Without wishing to overdramatize the saying of grace, it is the first thing said during an evening so remember that if you can produce something apt and original you will get things off to a fine start.

Next on the agenda is likely to be the *loyal toast*. No speech is required, in fact one would be quite wrong. Usually the chairman or president just says: 'The Queen'. The master of ceremonies, the toastmaster or the chairman himself should ask guests to 'be upstanding' before the toast is proposed. Patriotic guests may occasionally wish to sing the National Anthem after the loyal toast but this is rare – mercifully so, because the result is usually ragged and embarrassing. Contrary to popular belief, there is no formal connection between the loyal toast and smoking, although convention has it that people do not smoke until after the toast. It is usual for someone to announce that 'you now have your chairman's permission to smoke'. Increasingly people tend to smoke before the toast but, on the other hand, smoking is decreasing which balances things out. It can't be many years before formal dinners feature 'no smoking' tables.

Other toasts may occur during a meal before you get to the formal speeches and toasts. If the beef is piped in, it is customary for the senior person present to toast the piper, which means having a couple of glasses ready. Scots may wish to 'address the haggis'. My publisher tells me that he hopes to sell this book north of the border so I will refrain from further comment, save to say that such activities should be kept fairly brief. Sassenachs have a low threshold of boredom for Scottish tunes and customs. I really can't think why.

At some associations it is customary for the chairman (and his lady) to 'take wine with. . .' various sections of the audience. This is appropriate with, say, 'all the founder members' when an association is celebrating a significant anniversary but, as with all activities like this, it should not be so overdone as to become tiresome.

Eventually, you will arrive at the more usual toasts. Someone may propose a toast to an association, a senior member will respond, after which the chairman will propose 'the guests' with a response by a fourth speaker. Sadistic or over-enthusiastic organizers will prolong things with an extra couple of toasts, more caring ones (perhaps because they are unable to find enough speakers) will have the chairman respond to the first toast and continue to propose the guests so that there are only three speeches.

You will rarely need a long rigmarole as you start your speech, but you should acknowledge the senior person present by opening with: 'Mr Chairman (or Mr President), ladies and gentlemen'. If you refer to other people by name, either at this point or during your speech, make an effort to get things right. It is discourteous to call Mr Wilson, Watson or vice versa. If a 'Sir' is present and you wish to refer to him, drop the surname – call Sir John Smith, 'Sir John'; or if a Mayor is present, 'Mr Mayor' or 'Madam Mayor'. Incidentally, the chairman is always mentioned first unless Royalty is present. If you are speaking in front of the Queen (one can dream), begin: 'May it please Your Majesty, Mr Chairman. . .'. If other Royals are present, you should start: 'May it please your Royal Highness, Mr Chairman. . .'. In America, obviously, you would refer to Mr President (if he were there) before Mr Chairman, etc.

But this is all getting too high flown and blown. There are

other 'rules' for senior church figures and for Lords, Dukes and so on. Ask the toastmaster or others for advice on the day. A good organizer will even put a slip of paper in front of speakers with the suggested form of introduction on it. But above all, don't worry. If you get it wrong the audience won't notice. The only ones likely to be remotely peeved will be minor public officials whose sensitivity tends to be in inverse proportion to their importance.

11
Special Occasions

Most of the advice in this book applies to speech making on any occasion but this chapter discusses a few special functions where additional preparation or a different approach may be needed. Bascially it reinforces the earlier plea that you should always consider your audience when preparing a speech.

Family Get-togethers

Family occasions should, in theory anyway, be relaxed, friendly affairs at which to speak.

The star guest at a *christening* is unlikely to understand any of your mellifluous meanderings, but if you are proposing a toast to a baby you should wish it a long and happy life, add a comment about its splendid parents and then propose the toast. Don't go on too long otherwise the baby is likely to show its disapproval, even if everyone else is too polite.

Moving up the age scale, the next family occasion at which a toast is necessary may be a *birthday*. As there will probably be more outside guests than relatives at birthday parties you should not make too many family references which may not be understood. Expect some ribaldry if the audience is young and/or has been at the champagne too long before you speak. A ghastly tradition has it that some self-opinionated old uncle is supposed to get up and reminisce about how the birthday boy or girl used to do this, that and the other as a small child, but the guest of honour won't thank you for doing so. So don't. You could take a tongue-in-cheek approach and say something like 'It is traditional on these occasions to embarrass the guest of honour by reminiscing about how Margaret used to roll about on the floor, chuckling, with a bottle and no clothes on. . '. Then as the aunts start just that reminiscing, continue: 'but I'm not going to do that. What she did on her holidays last year is her own affair'.

Moving further up the ages of man, *wedding* toasts seem to cause more anguish than any others. And so they should because you are most at risk because of the latent tribal warfare which is only barely contained on some such occasions.

The theoretical running order at a wedding is that first an old acquaintance proposes a toast to the bride and groom. The groom replies on behalf of himself and his bride, pausing for applause as he says 'On behalf of my wife and I' for the first time. The groom then proposes a toast to the bridesmaids, to which the best man replies; who in turn proposes a toast to the parents. That's the theory anyway, but it may be difficult to stop others jumping on the bandwagon and the suffocating air of sentiment among older guests and the swill of booze among younger ones, means that above all you should *not* prepare a long erudite speech because you will lose your audience. Worst offenders are usually those proposing the first toast to the bride and groom. Obviously if you are a groom responding to such a toast you must be sincere and don't forget to mention your in-laws even if you usually only communicate with them through a solicitor.

Only one thing is certain about wedding speeches: you can safely assume that you will offend or upset someone. Don't let it worry you. My worst gaff at a wedding was to suggest that a relative lifted a veil so that I could give her a kiss, only to find that she wasn't wearing one.

Speeches at silver or golden *wedding anniversaries* should always be given by old friends who know the couple well. It is entirely forgiveable if they go on a shade too long.

Perhaps the most difficult speech you will have to make will be at the *funeral* of a relative or friend. Such occasions need great care and tact. In some places it is traditional to deliver a panegyric to the departed; they should be fairly brief. It may even be appropriate to tell jokes, or certainly anecdotes, at memorial services for well-known or particularly well-loved people – if it is done well.

Speeches will sometimes be called for at the gatherings which follow funerals; it may even be appropriate to mention that a memorial fund of some sort is to be started, but again great care is needed.

General Occasions

Retirement parties or presentations sometimes cause a disproportionate amount of embarrassment, paradoxically because they involve people who work together every day and probably never see each other 'on stage' making a speech. Be as natural as possible and relate one or two things that have happened to the retiree over the years which, with luck, will amuse and at the same time show what a fine fellow he is. Bear in mind that young members of staff won't respond to a long anecdote involving someone who left the firm twenty years ago. It is usual to say that you hope the retiree 'will keep in touch' (although no one is likely to remember him if he leaves it more than six months before coming back) and as there is often an awkward pause after the speeches, it helps if people then crowd round to gasp at the engraved clock or whatever other horror the poor devil has got to carry away.

If you are ever asked to propose a *vote of thanks*, then keep awake, listen to what the speaker says and in your speech just pick up one or, at most, two points to show that you were paying attention. Don't go on too long and don't grind your own axes. Even if you disagree with every word you should not go on the attack but instead should simply say something like 'I am sure we all found that unusual approach to the problem very thought-provoking'. Don't over-praise a speaker when he has clearly been totally out of touch with his audience, but do at least be polite.

When acting as toastmaster or master of ceremonies and you have to *introduce* something, such as a cabaret, pitch up your voice to command attention and be enthusiastic enough to take the mood of the audience up a gear so that the shift from a rather dull dinner to an entertainer will not be too sudden.

If you are making presentations at a *prizegiving* you will probably only be expected to say 'congratulations' to each of the prize-winners as they collect their awards. If more is expected, keep things short and relevant. If you have risen to the dizzy heights of presenting school prizes, assume you are addressing adults. Don't patronize the pupils by calling them kids or children and don't reminisce about what happened when you were a lad. And avoid suggesting that all that is needed to cure the ills of the world is the return of National Service. Don't ever think of trying to be 'with it' in your choice of words at a school prizegiving, unless you do so as a way of humorously confirming their view that you are on nodding terms with Methuselah.

(It occurs to me that you may think that I am being too flippant about weddings, prizegivings and so on, but I am only trying to impress on you that you *must* consider the audience. If you simply orate platitudes or try to deliver a stirring message to mankind, well, you may like the sound of your voice, but your audience won't.)

If you are asked to *open a fête* then recognize that your audience won't want to stand about for too long. Plug the cause for which funds are being raised with a telling phrase or two and by referring to things to which they can relate – a local comparison will produce a greater cash harvest than a lesson on macro-economics. After a short message, declare the fête, or whatever it is, open and then set off to buy your obligatory jar of jam.

When the purpose of your speech is *fund-raising* then you need to work closely with the organizer so that you are on your feet at the most propitious moment; for example people will donate more when they have had a glass or two of wine. Tell them what you are raising funds for and why. Incidentally, although you may be deeply involved with a particular project or charity, don't assume your audience is equally knowledgeable or enthusiastic but accept that you may have to sell your appeal to them. Under no circumstances berate people for not giving as generously as you had hoped.

This is one occasion when you should not read a speech. An

'appeal' must be just that, and preferably from the heart, so it should not be read. If there are tax advantages for your audience through covenants then say so and, if you plan an auction to raise funds, approach one or two key supporters beforehand and ask them to start the ball rolling.

Annual general meetings really call for more skill on the part of the organizers than the speakers because the choice of venue, drinks and food (if any) and, above all, attention to the rulebook are as important as the words. If organizations are hard pushed to get anyone to attend an AGM they should consider laying on something else to follow immediately afterwards, such as a film show. An AGM is one occasion when the speaker (who is likely to be the chairman) should not attempt to entertain or ad lib, but should simply concentrate on grinding through the business in hand.

If you are speaking at a *protest* meeting (you thought I'd given up on my by-pass, didn't you?) then you should not do so in isolation. You may be the spokesman for a group, but the planting of questions to be thrown at 'unfriendly' speakers or officials should be worked out in advance, as should the preparation of any banners to be waved and any stunts. Yes, stunts – in the weird media world in which we live, you may, reluctantly, have to resort to such things to get attention. The key is an organizing group with broad interests. If all the members share a deep-seated but narrow view of the problem to be tackled, they are likely to be seen as bloody-minded bigots.

Elected officers, or candidates hoping to be so, won't need any advice from me about *political meetings*. If you are attending in the hope of asking questions, then position yourself where you can be seen and speak in a clear voice. Don't turn a question into a speech; the audience will react against you. The best practice for political meetings is to play charades with young children. It's the closest analogy I can draw, albeit rather unkind to children.

Whether we like it or not we live in a media world. Politicians plan their activities with television exposure in mind, and it behoves even the smallest organizations to promote themselves whenever possible by holding *press conferences*. If bee-keeping societies or motor clubs don't tell local newspapers what they are doing, they are missing opportunities to recruit new members.

But dealing with the press does need care. Don't waste journalists' time. Your message may be simple enough to be written, rather than demand their presence at a press conference. If you do invite journalists to a conference, don't give a formal speech but simply take them through your plans and then invite questions. If the news you have to announce is bad, then dress it up as best you can but if you try to conceal it you can bet you will be found out.

The brightest journalists won't be satisfied with an open questions session but will want their own private discussion with you later. Remember that competition among newspapers and magazines for sheer survival, coupled with aggressive interviewing techniques seen on television, may lead to young reporters quizzing you harder than you expected. This may strike you as rather harsh when all you are trying to do is announce that you are starting to fund-raise for a new clubhouse, but don't let such an approach rile you. Just stick to the facts.

Never say that you 'expect' coverage, even if you've given journalists three free cups of coffee. And when, after all your efforts, a report appears with a mistake in it, don't charge round to the editor to complain. Write to him if it is an important error, otherwise let it lie. The best way of preventing mistakes is to have a simple press release spelling out your plans, e.g. where the clubhouse will be, how far you have got with planning permission, how much you hope to raise, etc.

Two final points on the press. Check if they are present whenever you are speaking and, if they are, guard against indiscretions you would not want to appear in print. If you are actively seeking coverage, make sure journalists have a copy of the relevant section of your speech.

By including *discussions and debates* I am perhaps straying away from public speaking pure and simple, but if you do get involved in either of these then prepare in advance but do not be too rigid in your approach. The whole purpose of these functions is for topics to be well aired and if, say, you open the batting in a debate and are too dogmatic in your views, you may dampen the occasion. For either discussions or debates you should be quite clear what the rules are and who speaks in what order. A good chairman is vital on such occasions. Most important of all, listen to other speakers so that you can, if necessary, modify your own comments accordingly.

There are countless other 'special' functions where you may be asked to speak, but if you treat *every* speaking engagement as special and always keep your audience in mind, you need have few fears.

12
Chairmanship

If you are sufficiently involved in an organization to be making speeches, then you may sooner or later be elected chairman. This chapter is devoted to the subject of chairmanship. (Yes, I know women are often in the chair, but I just can't bring myself to use the dreadful 'chairperson'.)

A good chairman will be a leader able to command respect and keep order; he will be fair and just, tactful and even tempered. Don't worry if you don't possess all those virtues, because neither do ninety per cent of chairmen. Speakers are continually swopping horror stories about bad chairmen. So accept the job if you are offered it; there is no reason why you shouldn't do it well, or at least as well as anyone else. The message for organizations is: don't elect a chairman on the 'your turn next' principle, but pick someone with at least a few of the required attributes.

A chairman should totally immerse himself in the rules of his organization. The secretary will, or should, have them at his fingertips, but it still behoves the chairman to understand them too. For example, how many members constitute a quorum? Does the chairman have a casting vote? At some events, such as a dinner dance, a master of ceremonies or toastmaster may in reality take control, but even so the chairman should keep an eye on things and keep in touch with what is happening back stage. For example, he should be told about any disaster in the kitchen which might require alteration to the timetable in order to conceal the problem from the guests.

A chairman should always arrive early so that he sets an example to the others. If he is chairing a committee meeting at which a particularly contentious matter is to be discussed, a wise chairman will do some lobbying beforehand and will certainly discuss with the secretary the best approach. I'm not suggesting direct manipulation you understand – just the normal procedures which form part of our muddled but glorious democracy.

Once a function begins a chairman must make it clear that he is in charge; not with whips and cattle prods, but by having a stout gavel to bang. And bang with confidence – a timid tap on the side of a glass with a spoon is not going to command anyone's respect.

Social functions, such as dinner dances, usually start fifteen minutes or thereabouts after the start time on the ticket. The chairman should obviously liaise with the catering manager over this. Functions such as committee meetings should *start on time* to show people that there is business to be done. This may seem a bit heavy-handed when a small social group with only three officials is meeting in someone's kitchen, but even so it is not a bad idea to discipline yourself. If you start a meeting on time and people turn up late do make them welcome. When a large group arrives late give a quick résumé of what has happened so far.

Having banged the gavel on time, the next thing is to set the scene. After a word or two of welcome, a chairman should ensure that members know what they are there for – to resolve something or launch a fund-raising appeal – and then his task is to keep to the agenda. Announce at the start if any printed material is to be given out, or if they need to take notes.

During the meeting remember the quality of fairness which is needed in a chairman. It is his job to keep the meeting on course by, for example, insisting that the committee decides *whether* to organize a particular function before discussing *when*. However, a chairman should not push things so fast that he rides roughshod over those who are trying to get a word in. People will only respect a dictator when he is a benevolent one. Keep your temper at all times. Cut out too much waffle. Don't let things constantly be put off to the next meeting and, at intervals, sum up 'so far' to keep members on the right lines.

After a committee meeting the chairman should ensure that minutes are circulated quickly.

Another role the chairman may play is that of host to any speakers. Appreciate that speakers may be in a worse nervous state than you are and calm them if you can. It is best to shield them from the general audience before they speak, because they may prefer to be left alone to concentrate on what they are going to say.

When drawing up your seating plan it makes sense to place speakers so that the microphone can be passed along the table in one direction, not backwards and forwards as various toasts are made. Ensure that serving staff do not disrupt speeches and keep waitresses out if speakers are likely to be robust. Most caterers will want to clear the tables before speeches start anyway, to avoid payment of overtime to staff who may be kept waiting.

At fairly formal functions the chairman will probably liaise with a toastmaster. In theory a toastmaster should ask a chairman's permission before calling on speakers to perform and the best of them will do so. But beware of those toast-masters who are too chatty and like giving speeches them-selves. Work closely with your toastmaster and go through *exactly* what he has to say.

As chairman, you will probably introduce the speakers. Give the audience enough information so that they know who is addressing them and why, but don't ramble into effusive over-praise. Pronounce names properly and if you use christian names for one speaker (which I strongly recommend, no matter how formal or pompous the occasion) use them for all speakers. Similarly if academic or professional qualifica-tions are given.

Make sure that any photographer present doesn't disrupt a speaker. If a speaker performs poorly and starts to get a rough ride from the audience, the chairman must step in, bang his gavel and ask for respect for the speaker. If things get really rough, the chairman may have to threaten to have people ejected (see Chapter 16).

One of the chairman's more delicate problems may be a speaker who drones on and on, far beyond the planned time. Don't tug at his sleeve, the audience will notice. Try handing him a slip saying 'Please end in five minutes' or words to that effect. A speaker in full cry who is totally fascinated with the sound of his own voice may take offence at this, but you are unlikely to invite him again anyway so no great harm will be done. Alternatively, tell a white lie and say that you had to ask him to end because the bar was closing.

If all goes well and a speaker draws to a sensible end, the chairman should lead the applause. This is particularly important if a speaker has proposed a toast. The audience may be unsure whether to applaud as they sit down again afterwards – lead them.

When a speech is followed by questions, the chairman should ask for them be put 'through the chair' if it seems likely that things may need to be kept under firm control; obviously someone taking questions from a friendly audience may not need this protective intermediary. The chairman should not allow one questioner to hog the limelight or grind a pet axe. When repeating questions from the audience before the speaker answers them, the chairman must not attempt to shade their meaning no matter how unfavourable the thrust may be to his own views.

A few other points for the chairman:

- If an audience has paid and a star speaker fails to turn up, make the excuse a convincing one. If in doubt, cancel and offer a refund rather than muddle on.

- Ask an understanding friend to have a speech in mind in case someone fails to turn up (say, to propose the guests at an annual dinner).

- A chairman should set the style of dress. He should invite gentlemen to take off their jackets if it is sweltering (perhaps with some comment about 'ladies will have to use their own discretion') but should stop short of undoing a collar button and pulling down his tie – it looks scruffy.

- Try to get the feel of how a function is going and, if necessary, amend the arrangements as they progress (e.g., delay a tombola if the speeches are running late).

- Decide whether to have what is euphemistically called a 'comfort break' during a function, for instance after a meal but before the speeches. Guests will welcome such breaks as they get older.

- Consider a simple signalling system to helpers which might indicate that you are going to wrap things up after one more question. An announcement of 'one more question' may trigger an unseemly rush to the bar.

- Draw up rough contingency plans in case something goes wrong. Don't lay detailed plans – the worst rarely happens – but do think in advance what to do if a speaker doesn't turn up. I suppose chairmen should also know about evacuation procedures in case of fire, but I suspect they rarely do.

Finally, if you have chaired a function to a successful conclusion, don't just relax and forget all about it afterwards. Remember to write to key people to thank them (only around five per cent of organizations bother to write to thank speakers by the way) and arrange a simple inquest so that your club or organization learns by its mistakes for the next time.

13
Venues

It is appropriate that unlucky thirteen should be the number of the chapter covering venues – they can be the bane of a speaker's life. To add to the sorrow, microphones too can cause much anguish. You may feel that venues and microphones are outside your control as a speaker. Well, not entirely as we shall see. Anyway as a speaker you may well be involved in organizing functions so you need to know something about them. In this area a little knowledge is not a dangerous thing but in fact a whole lot more than that displayed by many organizers.

Whether you are speaking at a conference where you have rehearsed in the actual venue, or if you simply arrive at a village hall a few minutes ahead of the audience, many of the things to consider are the same. Will the audience be able to see you? Maybe you will be speaking in an informal area, perhaps while people are having coffee or cocktails. Find a chair or table to stand on and then they will concentrate more than if they are peering at you across the heads of fellow guests.

Is the lectern at the right height for you? If necessary stand on a box because you will look faintly ludicrous if you can only peer over the top of the lectern. Check also that the height of the table or lectern on which your notes will be resting is correct for your eyesight. You may be able to do little about the seating arrangements except tactfully point out to the organizer anything which seems really hopeless. Never have your back to anyone when speaking. Preferably have your back to a wall and be seated roughly at the centre of one wall so that you have the best eye contact with your audience. The worst situation for a speaker is where a top table faces an empty dance floor with tables of guests at either side; most disconcerting. Incidentally, sometimes guests are unavoidably placed in an annex or even in another room altogether, with an extension speaker. If so, make some reference to their plight during your speech, perhaps something along the lines of: 'We've enjoyed our caviar here in the main hall, I hope you enjoyed your fish and chips in the overspill section'.

Organizers should not place speakers in front of windows: the light will distract an audience and may give a speaker an unwarranted halo. If you find yourself in this position when speaking during daylight hours, ask for the curtains to be drawn behind you, provided there is enough light from other windows. Otherwise a cheery window cleaner with his chamois leather or a pretty girl strolling by in the street outside will prove far more riveting to the audience than your words. At functions in darkened rooms, speakers should be lit enough to highlight their presence and put them 'on show', but they should not be blinded. There is no harm in 'dressing' the speaker's area a little, say with the association's badge or flag, although this should be kept in perspective. A dramatic company display in a village hall would look over-the-top, particularly if the rest of the walls were covered with the results of a children's painting competition.

Remember you will need a light on a lectern; cautious speakers will also have a torch near to hand. If you are sitting at a table on a stage then a modesty cloth over it is desirable. Male ankles are less than appealing, those of female speakers may be too much so – a modesty cloth solves both problems.

All the above considerations assume that you use your eyes when you arrive at a venue. Now use your ears. Is the air conditioning noisy? Is there a tannoy system? Is it playing muzak? Ask for them to be turned off before you speak. Even the hum of a fridge in a bar at the back of a room can distract. And if you spot a phone in the function room ask if it has been disconnected or, at least, if the operator has been told not to put calls through. If you don't do this, the one thing you can be certain about is that it will ring at a key moment in your speech. Some self-styled wag will shout out 'It's for yoo-hoo' and your dramatic impact will be lost forever.

Wise organizers will have 'noise marshals' whose job is to quell unwanted sound. It helps to have someone primed in advance to rush into an adjacent kitchen and stop the staff from chattering while someone is speaking. Obviously, as a nervous speaker approaching your first big moment, you will not wish to start over-organizing, but if intrusive noise does spoil your seech, *you* will be the one to suffer so make a mild fuss in advance if you feel it will reduce the risk.

Microphones

As you walk through an empty venue with an organizer before a function starts, you will be able to hear each other clearly and you may therefore be inclined to do without a microphone. Don't. If in doubt, *use one*. The rustle of movement from any audience and the chatter from ruder ones when people are speaking make this advice essential. If you have a microphone and find you don't need it you can always push it to one side. If you have to struggle to make yourself heard it will put a strain on you and may kill the flow of your delivery. Ideally, you should try out microphones beforehand but if this isn't possible then at least study how earlier speakers get on with the equipment. If you are following other speakers check how tall they are – this will act as a guide before you adjust the height of the microphone.

When speaking, don't touch or hold on to a microphone. Contrary to the usual advice, it is quite acceptable to tap one lightly before you speak while there is general chatter going on to see if it is live. The noise will hardly be noticed and, even if it is, it will alert your audience to the fact that you are about to start. What you should not do is tap a microphone, blow into it and then say 'One, two, three, testing'.

Even the sight of a technician present during a function doesn't mean that you can relax your vigilance about microphones – his presence may simply mean that the equipment is so unreliable that running repairs are usually necessary. However, he may at least be able to stop microphone howl which causes audiences so much hilarity and is often caused by the poor placing of speakers in relation to microphones.

If the public address system continually gives trouble while you are speaking, push the microphone aside and carry on without it, if necessary moving in among your audience to make yourself heard.

Many speakers swear by microphones worn on a cord around the neck because your voice will still be picked up if you move your head from side to side. Mikes clipped to a jacket collar can come adrift and both these and neck mikes do take a little getting used to. For most occasions a stand-mounted microphone is probably the best, preferably on a short stand placed on a table. Having to speak at a floor-standing microphone makes you look as if you are about to start singing 'My Way'. As a last resort you can use a hand-held mike, but this does tie up one hand, thus restricting your gestures and making it more awkward to cope with notes.

Whatever microphone you use, guard against off-the-cuff comments when the equipment may be live. If you say to the chairman 'They were a dim lot' as you sit down and it booms out over the address system, it could bring your applause to an abrupt halt.

14
On the Day –
Before You Speak

Your preparation to speak should start even before you leave home on the great day. Is your hair tidy? Although I keep stressing that you should be yourself, you may distract an audience if you look like Wurzel Gummidge, unless of course you are speaking on crop protection or conservation when it might be an advantage to be slightly unkempt.

Be over, rather than under, dressed – as a speaker you will to some extent be 'on stage'. Having received wrong instructions and spoken in flannels at an evening dress affair and in a monkey suit when the rest were in casual clothes, believe me, the latter is better. If you are wrong-footed in either direction you could make some lighthearted reference to it in your speech: 'I know your treasurer is always pleading for more funds, but I didn't think he'd extracted so much money from you that I'd be the only one here tonight able to afford evening dress'.

For informal functions aim to be slightly more formally dressed than the majority, say in a suit while most are in sports coats and flannels. Although if you are talking about sheep dog training presumably you could get away with the sort of tweeds which look as if they are made from chunky marmalade and, of course, if you take a dog along too the audience will forgive anything you do.

Your clothing should be comfortable without anything tight around the neck. This is one area where women are at a mild disadvantage. Their appearance is likely to be more critically examined than men's, who are able to shelter behind their anonymous penguin suits at formal functions. Both sexes should avoid an overt display of jangling jewellery, unless they want to look as if they are about to start reading palms.

Remember to take your notes with you when you leave. Pencil on the top any points to query when you arrive, e.g., do you need to refer to a council or a committee? For some functions you may need money for cloakroom tips or raffles. A freshening sachet as supplied with airline meals is worth taking to use shortly before you speak.

Leave home in ample time to reach the venue without being rushed. You will not be at your best if you've sweated through traffic jams to arrive as they are announcing your name.

Take a book with you in case you arrive too early and have travelled by car. It is better to sit in it quietly reading rather than get under the feet of the organizers or spend a long time chatting with officials before the start. Of course, you can use the time to browse through your notes again, but a book or magazine may calm you more.

On arrival check the room in which you will be speaking as soon as possible. If you foresee any problems - say the room is so big that the audience should be shepherded to the front - tactfully mention them to the organizers when you meet. Note 'tactfully'. Organizers will not relish neurotic busybodies trying to change everything, but they may welcome sensible suggestions learned by you from bitter experience as a speaker. Find out the answers to the pencilled points on the top of your notes and check people's names. If you are planning to refer to, or rib, someone it is worth mentioning it to the organizer - it would be in bad taste to mention someone who had recently been declared bankrupt or had a serious illness, for example.

As well as checking what you are going to say about others, try to find out what they in turn plan to say about you in their introduction. A club member may have assembled a long list of your outstanding achievements, but for heaven's sake persuade him to cut it down to just enough key points to establish your right to be addressing them. At a more mundane level, if you are expecting a lift back to the station establish from whom.

Make yourself known to the master of ceremonies or

toastmaster beforehand to check how they propose to introduce you. One MC asked me if I would signal when I was
within a couple of minutes of the end of a speech to a very
distinguished gathering. Helpfully I did so and to my surprise
was nearly bundled off the stage by the stripper who was due
to follow me. Memories are made of this.

Inquire if there are any presentations or raffles which are
likely to disrupt the flow of speeches and, if necessary, gently
ask if the running order can be changed. If fund-raising raffles
follow a lunch then the speaker coming later may find his
audience drifting out.

A speaker will often be invited into a VIP area for drinks
with senior officials. It would be discourteous not to join
them, but don't succumb to many offers for all the obvious
reasons.

If you are at a meeting to put across a message and a
television crew is there, make sure it knows which is your key
section and offer to do a separate interview if it will help your
cause. The same goes with radio.

Try not to be thrown off balance by an unforeseen happening which affects what you planned to say. If the chairman is
ill and the president is taking over his duties, go through your
notes deleting the references to Fred and substituting ones to
Arthur. The revisions may be more substantial if a major
event occurs, such as the resignation of a key politician or a
devaluation or a council changing its mind about a by-pass.
You will have to use your judgement at such times but just
recognize that, however rigidly you have prepared, you may
have to modify your notes under certain circumstances.

Have a supply of water available in case you dry up while
speaking; a carafe is better than a jug because there is less
landing space for flies. The water should not be too iced as this
can have an adverse effect on your throat.

Still before the function has begun, brush your clothes,
switch off the alarm on your wrist watch and . . . well, do any
other small things you may think of. You may develop a
pattern of behaviour before speaking that is really due to
nerves, but a routine helps to soothe them.

When the event has started, but still before your oration,
there may be a break before any speeches. If not it is still worth

nipping out around coffee time if it is a dinner (tell your neighbour whether you want black or white). Grab a breath of fresh air if you have been sitting in a stuffy smoky atmosphere during a meal. Use your freshening sachet or better still, if you have a room, slip up and have a quick wash and clean your teeth. This will liven you up.

Back at the table, clean your glasses if you wear them and empty your pockets of bulky items because your clothes will look smarter. By this stage you should have a clear idea of the mood of the audience, which at a dinner will depend on how freely the wine has flowed – too much and they may have become 'brittle' and mildly hostile. If they are throwing bread rolls by this time, you will be wise to cut any whimsical references from your speech.

You may not be making an after-dinner speech, but whatever the occasion the moral is to keep the audience in mind at all times. With experience you will 'feel' the atmosphere in a room and this will guide you whether, for example, to fillet out long, complicated anecdotes; you should do so if the room feels at all cold.

Listen to the other speakers while you are waiting to perform. It is a bit rude to sit writing down their jokes (although this seems to be the done thing) but you should listen to the points they make because you may want to delete the same ones from your speech, or rebut them, or simply add 'As Lizzy said. . .' before supporting the same view. As well as listening to what is said, listen for what is not said. If no one else has thanked the organizer for an excellent event then do so in your speech. It may be the only round of applause you will earn.

If you are a supporting speaker for a bigger 'star' tailor your notes accordingly. The audience certainly won't want you to drone on. Be prepared to cut too if you stand at the end of a long line of speakers. Some organizers seem to vie over the numbers of speakers they field, and such marathons ask too much of audiences. Similarly, if things are running late, cut if necessary and early in your address say that you plan to end by a certain time.

With luck, your organizer will have cleared the decks ready for any speeches and at a dinner staff will have cleared away coffee cups. In fact it is worth hinting that you will not be prepared to speak if staff are still wandering in and out or collecting drinks bills during speeches (it's been known). This sounds pernickety but an audience should be ready to listen before you begin and they won't be if they are distracted.

If you are to speak from a stage or platform, position yourself near to the front of the room before you are introduced, otherwise you will arrive to the chilling sound of your own footsteps. However, don't slink on stage as if you are ashamed of what you are going to say.

When your time comes (the deathly phrase is not entirely inappropriate) put out any cigarettes or cigars. Never smoke while speaking. Yes, I know some comedians use cigarettes as props for their acts. A cigarette may soothe your nerves, but it won't do your voice much good and you will look clumsy if you are also holding notes.

If you happen to follow a brilliant speaker, try not to be put off. Perhaps start with 'I've heard many brilliant speeches in my time, but that was the best. . .' and then carry on exactly as planned.

Be warned that some associations have friendly, but off-putting, traditions which may affect you as you are about to speak. Speakers may be introduced with a medley of tunes relevant to their professions, played by a military band. It has been known for a speaker's name to be greeted with a thunder flash and a deliberately over-elaborate trumpet fanfare. Your introduction to the noble art is likely to be less hectic but as you are about to be introduced *switch on*. If you have had a rough day and the world seems against you, well that is your problem – the audience won't want to know; it is there to be entertained or informed. Change up a gear when you are ready to perform and *concentrate*. No one said it would be easy but, if you've followed the advice so far, you've done all the preparation you can.

Now stand and deliver.

15
Delivering a Speech

Delivery is what public speaking is all about; no matter how thorough your preparations, you still have to put a speech across properly.

I don't plan to lay down too many hard and fast rules but there is one important law: be yourself. You are on show in front of an audience, so although you should not slouch, nor should you stand as if you are about to drill a squad of guardsmen. Be as natural as possible in all you do. Here are some of the specific areas which may affect how well your speech goes.

Voice

'Be yourself' means be sincere. An audience will quickly detect someone who is either lying or clearly hasn't much belief in what he is saying. Use your normal voice. Don't try to alter the pitch even if your voice is normally high and squeaky – straining to change it may make things worse – and if it reverts to its normal pitch in the middle of a key passage, it will amuse your audience no matter how serious your message.

You are more likely to speak naturally if you are using bullet points rather than a fully written-out speech because you will use spontaneous phrases rather than carefully honed words which may not really be 'you'; over-polishing can make things sound artificial. The best way to avoid running out of breath is to shun long sentences; short ones with well-timed pauses between them will be far more effective.

If your family or friends rib you for putting on a 'posh' voice on the phone, take care not to do this while speaking. Apart from the fact that you won't sound natural, a too formal or plummy accent is actually a disadvantage when public speaking. If you drop the occasional aitch don't waste time trying to pick it up, you will only draw further attention to your slip and may even tack it back onto the wrong word. Never drop aitches deliberately or 'talk common' to show you are one of the lads because this will be seen as offensively patronizing.

An accent or dialect may be an asset when speaking. A Frenchwoman speaking English with an accent can be devastatingly erotic, while a strong regional accent can add character to a speech provided it is understood. Avoid phrases which don't travel – a saying in common use in Cornwall could be incomprehensible in Clapham, or vice versa.

In being yourself, try not to orate other than as a direct parody of the genre. Aim to be clear not loud. Aim at the back of the room and try not to talk out of the side of your mouth. It will look underhand or as if you are a ventriloquist.

Content

A successful speech relies on its content. If you have nothing to say, why on earth are you on your feet? Your content should be well fixed in your mind whatever form of notes you are using. Don't apologize for any lack of speaking experience. You may have been overpraised in the introduction and, if so, it is worth gently deflating the praise by a little self-mockery. If you don't do this or, worse, seem to preen at the words, your audience will sense that you are a self-satisfied ass. Equally, you should not scatter undeserved praise around in your speech. If the meal was lousy, better not to refer to it than praise it.

Is your subject likely to be boring? If so, you may risk warning your audience, taking care to explain *why* the subject is dry but, equally, why it is so important. For example: 'I'm going to be throwing a lot of apparently boring figures at you as we look at the next five years. Please consider them carefully because they show that if we don't do something our club will be bankrupt well before the five years are up. Yes, bankrupt'.

If you get lost during your speech, recapping on the points you have made so far may bring you back on track. A highly charged subject when precision in the use of words is vital, such as in a planning matter or industrial relations negotiation, may require you to read a key piece. Better to seem a little formal during a section than to be misunderstood or misquoted later.

Don't forget to build in signposts during your speech so that you carry your audience with you – 'Having considered apples, now let us look at pears'. Preface occasional paragraphs with 'Mr Chairman, what we must do is. . .' or 'Ladies and gentlemen, I think it is important to remember. . .'. These will add a touch of courtesy to your speech and at the same time act as mild break points, worth using at the start of key sections for example.

Avoid making asides to the chairman or anyone on the top table while you are speaking. It is discourteous and treats part of the audience as outsiders, which they will resent.

Finally, on content, do have a good finish. Too many speakers pay great attention to their introduction and then tail away. It is better to do the reverse and concentrate on the finish because that will be the part people remember longest. Summarize what you have been saying and, if you are calling for action, stress *exactly* what you want to happen. Never leave people thinking 'Yes, what a shocking problem' without knowing what they can do to correct it.

Flavour

The flavour of a speech is less tangible than the content, but in your earlier planning you should have given some thought to the tone you hope to project. Are you trying to entertain, convince, motivate, or what? Pitch your approach and tone accordingly. You need to speak with enough conviction to control your audience without making authority sound like superiority. Don't be too intense. If you stare at your audience wild-eyed and thump the table too often in your attempts to convince them of the benefits of macrobiotic food, they may conclude that you are deranged and switch off to your message.

Occasionally, very occasionally, a judicious loss of temper will add impact to a speech, but generally it is better to keep calm and adopt a gentle approach. Some of our more extreme political figures realize this and are perhaps at their most dangerous when they are being sweetness and tolerance personified on radio and television question panels.

In being yourself, don't be afraid of a bit of sentiment or even an occasional tear, if it is an emotional subject about which you feel strongly. But such human touches must be spontaneous. For a similar reason you should avoid deliber- ately rehearsed 'mistakes', perhaps in an attempt to get a laugh, because they invariably sound false. As an example, a spontaneously lighthearted comment after someone has dropped a plate will amuse, but don't ask for one to be dropped deliberately because you will be waiting for it to happen and your response will sound forced. Take care if you decide to step out of character. People are conditioned to expect certain behaviour from certain people and may be confused if they do not get it – vicars stepping too far down market can make uneasy speakers, for example.

Be careful with your use of christian names. As a general rule it is more relaxed and friendly to talk about Jack Smith than Mr Smith in a speech (and I wish organizers would always put christian names on menus and place cards), but don't go too overboard. The cosy informality of radio disc jockeys when interviewing elderly statesmen can be quite ludicrous – the 'Brian and Jimmy' nonsense. Equally, if you are speaking in front of a High Sheriff, it could be a bit tactless to call him 'Alf'; and don't let us down by asking where he has left his bow and arrows, will you?

Pace

Don't attempt to maintain an even pace throughout your speech, you won't be able to do it. In any case, an even delivery can be monotonous if under-stated and exhausting if over-enthusiastic. Be enthusiastic, but don't gush. If your normal speech is slow and deliberate, perhaps you could speed up a shade. The audience hears much faster than you can speak because the endings of some sentences are predictable and the audience will have reached them before you have said them. They may use the time lag to let their minds wander. The use of pauses is a delicate area – you need them as punctuations, but they must be so timed that you keep the audience concentrating.

Once familiar with the outline of your speech, be careful not to digress or elaborate on one point too much as this may mar the rhythm and pace of your speech.

With experience, you will 'feel' the vibes from an audience and sense how your speech is being received. The initial mood of an audience of course will be beyond your control. If they have had a heavy day, followed by a large meal, they may be nearly asleep. It simply means that you will have to work that much harder to get a reaction from them.

Timing

Here we come back to those pauses, the most important of which is right at the start of your speech. As you are introduced, don't leap up and start gabbling away immediately. Instead, pause just long enough for them to look at you and for you to establish your presence before speaking, but not so long that someone shouts 'Get on with it'.

Never apologize for lack of time in preparing a speech; that is your problem not theirs. Absorbed though you may be with your words, you must have an awareness of real time while you are speaking. At a carefully planned series of lectures you may cause chaos if you promise to speak for forty-five minutes and stop after ten, but at a dinner where the meal has overrun be prepared to shorten your speech, particularly if dancing is to follow. The emphasis on timing is one of the reasons why in your planning you should have sorted your information into an order of importance and then marked your notes, perhaps with a colour code, so that you know what to delete.

Give your audience time to digest statistics before moving on to the next point. However, if the noise level starts to rise as you are speaking then you have lost them; shut up rather than try to shut them up. If you insist on ploughing on you will get perhaps the most insulting 'applause' of all – ironically loud clapping and shouts of 'more'.

It is almost unnecessary to point out that timing is the key to successful humour. If you haven't got it, go back and read again all the 'don'ts' in Chapter 7. You don't need a finely honed sense of timing to lobby for a by-pass, but you do if you are trying to tell jokes.

On some occasions it will be useful to have preplanned signals so that, for example, someone at the back can let you know that a film has arrived or the bar is ready to open and you can draw to a close. Next time you are at a dinner try to spot what the head waiter's signal is to staff to start them clearing a course away. Similarly, use a particular phrase or gesture to warn that you plan to finish in five minutes, so that bar staff can be alerted or papers got ready to be handed out.

Take care about overt signals to the audience itself. 'My last point is. . .' will alert some that an end to their agony is in sight, but it may also encourage others to nip out to be first for the loo or the hot pies, and the exodus will disrupt your speech. Worst sin of all for a speaker is to say 'Finally, ladies and gentlemen. . .' and then drone on for several more minutes. It is quite unfair to raise false hopes in your audience.

Gestures

If you are being yourself you will probably make spontaneous gestures while you are speaking. They certainly add warmth to an address but resist the temptation to create them deliberately, and never over-act.

There are no hard and fast rules about stance and posture. Stand naturally. Of course, if you rock from side to side while speaking you may put your audience to sleep. It works with babies. If you are using notes, don't be furtive about them. Audiences are used to seeing VIPs read speeches on television (often very badly), so they will not be surprised that you use notes.

The previous points in this chapter assume that all is going well with your speech but, of course, you may occasionally have problems.

Ad libs

These may come early in a speech if there are a lot of latecomers. Welcome them to show that you are aware of their arrival (your audience will be) and, if appropriate, quickly sum up where you are.

Don't fall into the trap of asking if people can hear at the back. Someone is likely to say 'Yes, but I'll gladly change places with someone who can't'. Better to have a friend at the back primed to signal if he can hear.

Try not to be thrown out of your stride by a clanger. The chill in a room if something goes wrong and embarrasses the audience will be unsettling but, when appropriate, you should keep going. (Obviously if someone is taken ill, you may have to break off.)

If you inadvertently use a word or phrase which has an unfortunate double meaning, be careful that in correcting the mistake you don't actually make it worse. Better to grin along with the audience and carry on.

You may need ad-libbing powers if you ask your audience questions, however rhetorical. In answer to 'what should we do about the Birth Control Bill', some wag may shout 'Pay it'! When such exchanges become too prolonged they may turn your speech into a double act.

At the intrusion of a police siren the comment 'Just let me make this point before they take me away. . .' will raise smiles, however unfunny it may look in print.

Perhaps the worst time for ad-libbing is when you are unexpectedly asked to say a few words at the last minute. If there is the remotest chance of this happening give a little thought to it before the function, otherwise *be brief*. Never attempt a long speech without proper preparation.

Incidentally, most of the points in this chapter apply to talks and lectures as well as pure speeches, although informative lectures may be less 'theatrical' than speeches which are simply intended to entertain.

Whatever the circumstances, once you are on your feet CONCENTRATE. It is possible to be in full cry and still find your mind wandering, but that means you are either coasting through your words through over-familiarity, or you are altogether too relaxed and heading for a fall. And consider, if you can't concentrate when you are saying the words, how on earth is your audience expected to when it is trapped into listening to them?

Before you get on your feet you should know what will happen at the end of your speech. Are you to propose a toast, hand the meeting back to the chairman, or introduce another lecturer? Be clear in advance so that there isn't an anti-climactic pause. Incidentally, if you are lecturing on a spotlit podium with the rest of the room in darkness, don't trip over the step as you walk away, otherwise you will get the biggest laugh of the day.

A final point. If you have been on an adrenalin 'high' through speaking, especially in a smoke-filled room, and you are due to drive home, it may be safer to wind down by walking a few yards in the fresh air first before setting off.

16
Hecklers, Questions and the Law

These three subjects can become interconnected, as this chapter will show.

Hecklers

Banner-waving protesters at mass marches and televised meetings have unfortunately tended to encourage similar stridency at less significant public occasions. Over-indulgence in alcohol may also lead to rather robust behaviour by audiences so, as a public speaker, you may have to cope with hecklers. Don't be too alarmed; only a very small minority of speakers encounter any problems. Nevertheless, it is worth being prepared.

To counter a rowdy audience, you can simply refuse to rise to your feet until the master of ceremonies, or whoever else is in charge, has quelled the noise. It is not *your* fault if they are noisy, so why should you bear the brunt of the problem? At most functions it will be enough for the chairman to say something like 'May we please have respect for our guest'. Laying the emphasis on *guest* may prick a few consciences.

On rising to your feet, you may be saddled with a heckler in your audience who has either had too much to drink or is blessed with an over-estimation of his own wit. He may have been active during earlier speeches, which will have given you time to consider how to handle him. If not, ignore the first heckle unless it is a friendly and/or amusing comment, in which case join in the laughter so as not to appear churlish. But don't respond to a more asinine remark, other than perhaps to smile in a way which indicates to the audience that you both know that there is an idiot present. Any further interruptions and you will just have to rely on your wits. If the heckler makes a telling point on an important issue you may have to respond, but don't turn it into a double act. Suggest instead that he leaves that point until the questions session.

For would-be humorous interjections you could perhaps try a rehearsed put-down. The following ripostes may be useful against interrupters:

> Would someone please keep that child quiet?
> Would someone please pour that man back in the bottle?
> You're getting over-excited now. There'll be tears before bedtime.
> One fool at a time please.

If you are expecting an 'exciting' time you could insert a few of these at the top or bottom of your notes for easy reference. Your response must be quick, but it doesn't have to be particularly funny or witty; the fact that you have made one at all will probably get a round of applause whereby the audience can indicate its views of the heckler and, with luck, shame him into silence.

Don't lose your temper with a heckler; the audience may swing round and support him. Similarly control an audience with wit and personality rather than with shouting. An imperious delivery of 'I will continue when you are quiet' will never get a raucous audience to hush.

Your own speaking style will, to some extent, influence whether you get heckled. To adopt a blunt 'I call a spade a spade' approach will get, and deserve, more heckling than a mellower, friendly manner.

Avoid making martyrs of hecklers. If you flatly refuse to give people a hearing at some functions, you may be playing into their hands. Their objective may simply have been to demonstrate that they were being denied a chance to speak, which may particularly apply at political meetings. However, those who have chosen to stray into this area can probably handle themselves without further advice.

Above all, don't be put off speaking by the thought of these interruptions. Problems rarely happen; just be on your mettle.

Questions

If, as a solo speaker, you plan or are prepared to take questions at the end of your address, say so near the start. Occasionally it may be appropriate to answer questions during your presentation, but avoid this if you can because it will disturb your flow.

In theory, questions should be put 'through the chair', but for many functions this will be quite unnecessary. If you have been chatting about stamp collecting it would obviously be absurd to bring the host up to join you on the platform just to formalize things. Even at those functions where questions should really be put through the chair, you could gently take control of events if the chairman is inept. Your audience is there to be entertained or informed and will not be too concerned with formalities.

Earlier it was stressed that you should use a microphone if in any doubt about accoustics; the same applies to questioners, but there are greater problems. People – not least the person answering them – must be able to hear the questions, otherwise the speaker's answers may be meaningless or, worse, misleading. Floor mikes are sometimes used but these slow things down unless people queue at them to avoid long pauses between questions. Other organizers have microphones on long leads which can be passed among an audience, but these are equally unsatisfactory for the same reasons. 'Gun' mikes (highly appropriate for some questioners) which a technician can point at a questioner from some distance away are the best system, but will be too hi-tech and expensive for most functions.

Where none of the above solutions appeal, either ask questioners to stand up and speak up, or have someone near the back primed to repeat questions in a loud voice.

You may reduce cross-examination by asking questioners to stand up and shout – questioners can be as nervous as speakers. Incidentally, it may sometimes be appropriate for

questioners to be asked to state their names and the associations they represent.

As the speaker, if you are in any doubt about whether
people have heard a question, repeat it without any change of
emphasis. If it was a nasty one, don't try to soften it. There is
some merit in deliberately arranging for any awkward
question to be raised early in the session. The audience may be
anticipating it and by raising the subject early it may help to
defuse things. It may be better coming from a 'plant' than from
someone who has simmered for some time before getting a
chance to ask it.

Always plant a few questions in the audience, not because
you expect your subject to be so dull that there won't be any,
but simply to recognize that people may be reluctant to be the
first to ask. A friendly, planted question will start the ball
rolling. Prime one or two people by giving them a broad
indication of suitable questions to ask. This will give you a
chance to stress one of the areas you have covered. However,
a planted question which has been written out in detail may
sound obviously staged. Planted questioners should not jump
in the moment you call for questions, but should pause just
long enough for spontaneous ones to be asked without waiting
so long that a chill settles on the room. Good timing is
important.

I am not suggesting that you should totally stage-manage
every function you attend, but if, for example, you have an
answer to a question which you know amuses audiences and
makes a good point on which to close, an appropriate signal to
a friend to ask the question is a sound tactic.

If you know that a member of the audience is an expert in a
particular area, don't hesitate to ask him to comment,
provided you know that he can be heard easily and won't go
on for hours.

Despite all your planning no questions may be forthcoming.
Instead of: 'Would you like to know more about X?' (some
wag may shout 'no'), try: 'Well, as we have some time left, I'd
like to tell you a little more about X'

In spite of all the previous emphasis on planning and bullet
point notes, by the time you get to this stage in your speech
you will be well through the nerve barrier. All you need do in

advance is list at the end of your notes one or two other points you could make if there is time. For example, 'other countries' would remind you to talk about aspects of your subject matter in other parts of the world.

A few other points on handling questions:

- Don't read more hostility into a question than is perhaps intended. Your questioner may be nervous and use words which sound sharper than are meant. 'What will happen to the interest on the funds deposited?', may not always imply that you plan to abscond with it.

- A question may be totally irrelevant to the subject of the meeting, in which case offer to discuss it privately afterwards or get it handled in some other way. Suppose you have spoken on 'motor racing' to an audience in a garage and someone persists in labouring on about the problem of getting a warranty claim fixed; refer him to the dealer and simply say: 'I'm sure the manager will discuss that with you during the break, now can I have another question on motor racing?'

- Don't stamp on a questioner if he asks a silly question. Let the audience come to its own conclusion about his foolishness; don't emphasize it. Of course, before you assume a questioner is a simpleton, ask yourself if the fault lies with you for not getting the points across clearly enough in your speech.

As a public speaker you may occasionally appear on a *panel*. If so, the following notes may be useful:

- Jot down questioners' names where given so that when it comes to your turn you can address them by name. The questioner and the audience will think what a thoughtful fellow you are. Remember to write down the question too of course, or they will be less impressed if you can't remember what was asked.

- Where questions are submitted to you or a panel in

advance, you or the chairman should group them so that related topics can be covered at the same time.

- If you have briefing papers with you, don't soak each questioner in a shower of statistics which you are obviously reading.

- Polite agreement with other panel members leads to a very boring function. A different view, preferably an opposing one, will make much better entertainment.

- Don't chatter to other panellists while someone else is answering a question. It will look very rude.

- Panels are far less nerve-racking than making speeches, but don't become so relaxed that your comments become slanderous.

The Law

Without suggesting that there are pitfalls along every path you take in public speaking, it would be irresponsible not to alert you to the laws of defamation if you make inaccurate remarks about others. You are likely to be most at risk when your guard is down during an informal questions and answers session, but you should avoid straying into danger at other times too.

A clearly humorous and lighthearted remark about someone who is present is unlikely to cause problems. 'I wouldn't buy even a new car from the club treasurer, let alone a secondhand one,' with a grin at him as you say it, will do you no harm. However, if your comment gets passed on secondhand you could find yourself being sued. The remark would be heard in the cold light of day away from the jovial atmosphere.

Of course an audience may relish a good old slanging match between speakers on a panel, while household names automatically become butts of jokes by amateur public speakers as well as professional comedians. It is unlikely that Hollywood lawyers will descend on you after an incautious remark in your speech to a train spotters' society, but you should be cautious when referring to people who may be more sensitive.

A vicious personal attack, however accurate, may offend your audience and turn it against you, as will swearing. Although blasphemy is still technically against the law, no legal action is likely to be taken against you, but why upset people unnecessarily?

You will almost certainly run into trouble if you break the Official Secrets Act when speaking, although I guess it is now safe to reminisce about the happy hours you spent behind the NAAFI with that WAAF in 1943.

Legal problems may sometimes stem not from your behaviour, but from members of the audience who decide to cause trouble. The organizers of a function are, temporarily at least, 'the occupiers' of the premises where it is held and can therefore decide who may attend. Even if people turn up in response to advertisements and are therefore legally present, an organizer can still ask them to leave if their behaviour justifies it. 'Threatening, abusive or insulting words' may amount to behaviour likely to cause a breach of the peace, which is an offence. It is also an offence if people are creating a disturbance to prevent the completion of business at a lawful public meeting. If they don't leave when asked they are trespassers and you are allowed to use 'reasonable force' to eject them. As this may lead to the creation of martyrs, try the softly, softly approach first.

Where trouble is forecast, an organization should have a tactful but strong chairman and firm but understanding stewards. If the trouble starts while you are speaking, try to calm the situation if you can; if you fail hand the meeting back to the organizer or chairman who can take more formal action. (If your attitude as a speaker started the trouble, then you deserve all you get, of course.)

17
Inquests

This chapter was originally to be called Post Mortem, but that implies that your speech has died. Let us be more optimistic about your efforts and consider whether you should hold an inquest after making a speech. I think you should. Unless you analyse how it went, it will be difficult for you to improve next time.

Immediately you sit down at the end of an address, the chairman or organizer is likely to say: 'Wonderful speech, old boy'. Well, he may just be being polite because he invited you in the first place. You need to get other opinions. The length of the applause, if any, will obviously be one guide to the success of your speech, as will the financial response if you have made an appeal for funds.

A friend in the audience may be willing to eavesdrop on the comments after your speech when people are really saying what they think. If one agrees to act as a sounding board ask him to look out for, at the same time, any unfortunate gestures or mannerisms you may have which distract an audience. As after-dinner speaking gets closer to up-market music hall, there is almost a case for critical reviews exactly as for other forms of show business.

Usually the main thing to consider is whether your message got across or if further action is needed: for example, a follow-up letter to the people attending pointing out, say, the perils of the by-pass scheme and what action they should take.

A tape-recording taken during your speech will help you to judge the reaction. In fact, some organizers record speeches and then sell them to club members. They should never do this without prior permission from speakers, because to some extent the process is stealing the material of professional speakers who do it for a living.

Make a note of how long your speech took for future guidance. Eventually you will be able to judge that X of your bullet points equals Y minutes.

Fairly soon after you have finished speaking, edit your notes so that they accurately reflect the points you made. If you left out a particular comment you may be able to use that point if you are invited to speak to the same audience again.

If the speech went all wrong, console yourself with the fact that they won't remember a thing you said the next day anyway. I once sat through a speech by a well-known politician who got a standing ovation at the end of a brilliant conference performance. As an experiment during coffee exactly thirty minutes after the speech, I asked six people if they could remember any two of the points that had been made in the speech. None of them could. Unhappily, of course, this lack of attention also means that they won't remember many of your messages either, so don't include too many of them. Never kid yourself that you are going to move mountains, or by-passes, with one passionate speech.

Incidentally, when you get home, remember to write a note of thanks if you have been put up for the night by one of the organizers.

Don't let your inquest turn you into a bundle of nerves about speaking again; just analyse things enough to make you better next time. You never know, you may become so good that people will be prepared to pay you to speak.

18
Getting Paid For Speaking

Don't laugh at the idea of getting paid for speaking. The demand for reasonable speakers seems inexhaustible and if you become competent then, yes, you may end up in that happy position. Consider, if you are entertaining a group of people, either by amusing or informing them, and you have had to travel or put yourself out to do so, then why shouldn't you be recompensed?

Obviously, if you are trying to sell an idea or lobby for action there may be no question of any fee, but there will be many other occasions when you can reasonably expect to get something – at the very least your expenses.

The first indication that you are about to break into the ranks of paid speakers may be a letter from an organizer with some delightfully vague phrase such as: 'Please let me know what arrangements you would like'. This probably means that they are expecting to pay, but remember: if you don't ask, you may not get.

However, if you are too modest to barter over your services, consider using an agent. The best way to find one is by asking organizers how they find their speakers. Toast-masters may be another source of information. I won't get many bookings for saying so, but the market for speakers isn't a particularly well-organized one; for example, many large companies still rely on word of mouth to find speakers. Not that this is a bad thing – better to rely on the opinion of someone who has heard a speaker than on an agent's hype about him.

An agent will act as a third party, which may make negotiations that much easier. He can say things in praise of your abilities which modesty would prevent you from doing. But, of course, he will want a percentage, which is likely to be negotiable depending on whether you provide the lead for a booking or he does. Some agencies will charge a minimum fee to handle a booking, which is not unreasonable because dealing with over-anxious organizers can be time-consuming.

An efficient agent will obtain most of the details a speaker needs, which were outlined near the start of this book but, even so, you should get the name and telephone number of a direct contact in the organization who you can call for background information when preparing your speech.

What to charge? I can't tell you. It will depend on your ability and subject matter and, frankly, on your star quality – some television names are able to command very high fees.

Remember that the Inland Revenue will be interested in what you are up to. If you are normally taxed on PAYE, don't rush out and spend your first fee without considering that tax will have to be paid on it many months later. You will be able to charge such things as travelling, typing, books and papers for research and so on as expenses against the fees you earn; maybe even the use of part of your home as an office; keep them all in mind when you do your tax return. A bright accountant will be a help at this hour.

It has been known (so I'm told) for fees to be offered in cash, perhaps out of raffle proceeds. Your approach to this and the Tax Man has to be between you and your conscience.

I should warn you that being paid does tend to change slightly the relationship you will have as a speaker with a few organizers. Some make quite a ceremony of the 'handing over of the envelope' with your cheque in it. If you are using an agent, it will usually come by post later.

If you found this chapter all too mercenary and sordid for you, I will leave you with one final thought. If you won't accept money for yourself, why not ask for a donation to your pet charity? That will solve any embarrassment and salve any conscience.

Index

Of further interest . . .

THORSONS GUIDE TO MAKING BUSINESS PRESENTATIONS
Practical Advice on Preparation and Delivery

Stuart Turner. Many people are likely to be called upon to make a business presentation at some point in their career. The author here shows that this need not be an insurmountable hurdle, but rather an invigorating challenge which can be met and overcome *provided adequate preparation has been made beforehand.* This excellent book fully explains how *you* can turn a challenge into a triumph! Includes: setting objectives; preparation and delivery; audience control – regardless of size; revealing the product, and post-mortems.

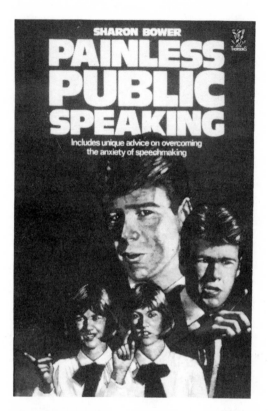

PAINLESS PUBLIC SPEAKING
Develop and Deliver Your Train of Thought Anytime, Anywhere

Sharon Anthony Bower. A unique programme for practising a speech step-by-step, with techniques for overcoming stage fright, remembering your train of thought, speaking in a compelling persuasive manner. *Includes:* Proven techniques for coping with anxiety: How to deal with difficult questions or people; Steps for organizing your train of thought; Light up your speech with attention getters; Polish your speaking style; How to confront difficult personalities; How to practise the progressive relaxation exercise; Routine warm-up exercises for performers.

Kenneth P. Brown

STAND & DELIVER

A Handbook for Speakers, Chairmen
and Committee Members

Shows how to:

- Give bright and to-the-point
  short speeches
- Deliver interesting talks
- Be a competent chairman
- Know correct meeting procedures

STAND AND DELIVER
A Handbook For Speakers, Chairmen and Committee Members

Kenneth P Brown. Based upon the author's courses on public speaking this book provides an invaluable guide to the art of delivering a speech successfully, and is aimed at both the absolute beginner and the more experienced public speaker. Advice is given on presentations, votes of thanks, introductions, toasts and the impromptu speech, organization of material, how to avoid disasters and many other aspects all illustrated with amusing examples.

CONTENTS

iii

NOTATION

A a constant

A area; for thin hollow torsion members see p. 26

a a length

b width or breadth

C torsional stiffness (equal to GI_p for a circular section)

C_1 a constant of integration

D plate constant, Eq. (64), p. 107

E modulus of elasticity, lb/sq in.

$F_{1,2,3,4}$ elastic foundation functions, Eqs. (88) and table, p. 146

G shear modulus, lb/sq in.

g gravitational acceleration

h height

I moment of inertia

I_p polar moment of inertia

j $\sqrt{-1}$, imaginary unit

k foundation modulus, lb/sq in., Eq. (84), p. 141

k spring constant, lb per inch deflection

L length of contour of thin-walled hollow torsion member, p. 27

l length

M moment

M_b bending moment

M_t torsion moment, torque

M_1 moment per unit length of cut through a plate; Fig. 75, p. 107

n the normal direction

n a number, usually but not always, integer

P force, lb

P^* Biezeno's "reduced" load, p. 320

p pressure, lb/sq in. on surface; lb/in. on line or beam

p_i, p_0 inside and outside pressure

q load per unit length on beam

R large radius, the largest one in the problem

R_m, R_t, R_x, R_y radius of curvature, meridionally, tangentially, in the x and y direction

r radius in general, usually a variable in the formula

r_i, r_0 inner and outer radius

S shear force, lb, beams

S_1 shear force per unit length of cut through plate

s stress, lb/sq in.

ds peripheral length element

s_n normal stress

s_t tangential stress

s_r radial stress

s_s shear stress; for sign convention in Cartesian coordinates see Fig. 115, p. 173; in polar coordinates, Fig. 121, p. 185

v

T tension of a membrane (lb/in.) or of a string (lb)

T_{xy} twist of a surface, Eq. (59a), p. 100

T_1 twisting moment per unit length of cut through plate

t thickness, in.

U stored energy

U^* complementary energy, p. 216

u displacement in x direction, or in the radial direction in problems of rotational symmetry

u (on pp. 231 to 233 only) small "variation"

V speed, sometimes peripheral speed of a disk

v displacement in y direction; tangential displacement in rotationally symmetrical problems

W weight, lb

w displacement in z-direction

w deflection of a plate in the normal (or z) direction

X force, unknown support reaction

y (subscript) yield

Z section modulus in bending $= I/z_{max}$

Z_1 section modulus per unit length of cut through plate

α coefficient of thermal expansion

α an angle

α_{12} an influence number, Eq. (120), p. 226

β an angle

β characteristic of beam on elastic foundation, Eq. (86), p. 143

β_{12} inverse influence number, p. 228

γ weight per unit volume $= \rho g$

γ an angle, the angle of shear

γ_{xy} angle of shear in the xy plane

δ deflection, in.

Δ an increment as in Δr, Δx, etc.

Δ ∇^2, the Laplace and del operators, see p. 110

ϵ strain; sometimes a small quantity generally

ϵ_x strain in the x direction

ϵ_r strain in the radial direction; ϵ_t = tangentially

λ a length, see Eq. (51), p. 66

λ curved pipe characteristic, Eq. (125), p. 243

μ Poisson's ratio, about 0.3 for steel

ρ density $=$ mass per unit volume

Φ a stress function; Saint-Venant's defined on p. 7; Airy's defined on p. 174; Jacobsen's defined on p. 42

φ an angle

Ψ stream function, p. 21; Jacobsen's equiangular function, p. 43

θ angle, angle of twist

θ_1 angle of twist per unit length

ω angular speed

CHAPTER I

TORSION

1. Non-circular Prisms. The most useful and common element of construction subjected to torsion is the shaft of circular cross section, either solid or hollow. For this element the theory is quite simple, and we remember that the shear stress in a normal cross section is directed tangentially and its magnitude is given by the expression

$$s_s = \frac{M_t r}{I_p} = \frac{M_t r}{\pi R^4/2} \tag{1a}$$

where R is the outside radius of the shaft, r (smaller than or equal to R) is the radius at which the stress is measured, and M_t is the twisting moment on the shaft. We also remember that the angle of twist θ is determined by

$$\theta = \frac{M_t l}{GI_p} \tag{1b}$$

In the derivation of these two equations it was assumed (or rather it was shown by an argument of symmetry) that plane cross sections in the untwisted state remain plane when the twisting torque is applied and also that these cross sections remain undistorted in their own plane.

We now propose to find formulae for the twisting of shafts that are not circular in cross section but that are still prisms, *i.e.*, their cross sections are all the same along the length. For such shafts it is no longer possible to prove that plane cross sections remain plane or that they remain undistorted in their own plane. In the proof of these properties for a circular cross section the rotational symmetry of that section about its central point is essential.

If plane cross sections remain plane and undistorted, it follows logically that the shear stress must be along a set of concentric circles, as in the round shaft. Now it can be easily seen that this cannot be true for a non-circular shaft, because then the stress (Fig. 1) would not be tangent to the boundary of the cross section, and would have a component perpendicular to that boundary. Such a component would be associated with another shear stress on the free outside surface of the shaft, which does not exist. The shear stresses on a cross section thus must be tangent

1

to the periphery of the cross section. As a special case of this we see that the shear stress in the corners of a rectangular cross section must be zero, because neither one of its two perpendicular components can exist.

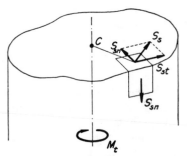

FIG. 1. If the shear stress s_s in a peripheral point of the cross section is perpendicular to a radius from the center of twist C, then it can be resolved into tangential s_{st} and normal s_{sn} components. The normal component must have a companion stress on the free outside surface, which does not exist. Hence the normal component s_{sn} must be absent.

Figure 2 shows a circular shaft and a square shaft being twisted. In both cases longitudinal lines on the periphery which were originally straight and parallel to the shaft's center line become spirals at a small angle γ as a result of the twisting. In the round shaft (Fig. 2a), an element $dr \, rd\theta \, dl$, in which all angles are 90 deg in the untwisted state, then acquires angles of $90 - \gamma$, as shown in Fig. 2c, because the plane cross section remains plane. This angle of twist γ of the particle is associated with the shear stress of twist. Now let us look at the corner particle $dx \, dy \, dl$ of the square shaft. Again the spiral effect of the twisting couple causes the small angle γ, and if plane cross sections would remain plane, then the angle γ would necessarily be associated with the shear stress of Fig. 2c. But, as we have seen, this is impossible because the shear stress s_{sn} on the free outside surface does not exist. Hence the only possibility is shown in Fig. 2d; the upper

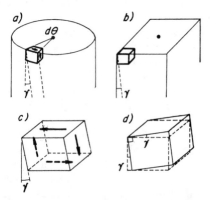

FIG. 2. If in a twisted bar of square cross section a plane cross section should remain plane, there would be shear stresses in the corner, as shown in (c); a zero shear stress in the corner is possible only when the upper surface of (d), that is, the normal cross section, tilts up locally. Only with a circle (a) is a plane cross section possible.

face of the cross section also must turn through an angle γ, to keep the angle at 90 deg, so that no shear stress occurs. This means that the corner element of area of the cross section is perpendicular to the spiraled longitudinal edge, and since this must be the case at all four edges, the plane cross section is no longer plane but becomes warped vertically.

For the circular cross section it was shown that plane cross sections remain undistorted in their own plane. This means that if we draw on that normal section a network of lines at right angles (such as a set of concentric circles and radii or also a square network of parallel x and y lines), then these right angles remain 90 deg when the torsional couple is applied. We cannot prove that this property remains true for non-circular cross sections. However, in Fig.

FIG. 3. If in a twisted shaft normal cross sections should distort in their own plane, there would be shear stresses on sections parallel to the longitudinals of the bar. Such stresses do not contribute to a twisting moment. In fact they do not exist, and normal cross sections do not distort in their own plane.

3 we see what a distortion of the normal cross section implies. With such a distortion shear stresses appear in sections parallel to the longitudinals, while no shear stress in a normal section is necessary. Only these latter stresses can possibly add up to a twisting torque, and the stresses of Fig. 3 are useless for resisting a twisting torque. Later, in Chap. VII we shall see that such useless stresses never appear. Nature opposes a given action (here a twisting torque) always with the simplest possible stresses: to be precise, the resisting stresses are so that they contain a "minimum of elastic energy." The stresses of Fig. 3 add to the stored elastic energy in the bar, while they do not oppose the imposed twisting couple. Although this argument does not constitute a proof, it makes it plausible that normal cross sections do not distort in their own plane.

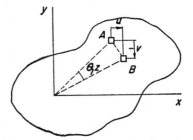

FIG. 4. Saint-Venant assumes that a cross section turns bodily about a center, without distortion. Thus a point A turns to B through an angle $\theta_1 z$. When the displacements are called u and v, this turning is expressed by Eqs. (2).

With this preliminary discussion we are now ready to start with the theory of twist of non-circular cylinders or prisms. This theory is due to Saint-Venant and was first published in 1855.

2. Saint-Venant's Theory. Let x and y be perpendicular coordinates in the plane of a normal cross section with their origin in the "center of twist," *i.e.*, in the point about which the cross section turns when twisting. Let z be the coordinate along the longitudinal center line, and at $z = 0$ we place our section of reference which is not supposed to turn. Then Saint-Venant's assumption for the deformation (Fig. 4) can be written as

$$u = \theta_1 z \cdot y$$
$$v = -\theta_1 z \cdot x \qquad (2)$$
$$w = f(x, y)$$

Here u, v, and w are the displacements of a point x, y, z from the untwisted state (A in Fig. 4) to the twisted state B, in the x, y, and z directions, respectively, and θ_1 is the angle of twist of the shaft per unit length. The expressions for u and v state that a cross section at distance z from the base turns about the origin through an angle $\theta_1 z$ in a clockwise direction. The sign of v is negative because for positive x, a point moves in the negative y direction when it turns clockwise. The third expression $w = f(x, y)$ states that a cross section warps by an amount w in the longitudinal z direction; that this warping is different for different points x, y, following an as yet unknown pattern $f(x, y)$. It further states that all cross sections warp in the same manner since w is independent of z.

The next step is to express the assumed displacements, Eq. (2), into "strains," which are displacements of one point relative to a neighboring point. There are two kinds of strains: direct strains ϵ, which are extensions or contractions, and shear strains γ, which are angular changes. The first two of Eqs. (2) express the assumption of no distortion in the normal cross section. Thus $\epsilon_x = \epsilon_y = 0$ and also $\gamma_{xy} = 0$. The third of Eqs. (2) states that all planes warp in the same manner; hence the z distances between two cross sections are the same for all points of that section, or $\epsilon_z = $ const. If we rule out longitudinal tension in the shaft, we have, in particular, $\epsilon_z = 0$. Thus there are only two strains left: γ_{xz} and γ_{yz}. In order to express γ_{xz} we study a section in an x-z plane ($y =$ constant) which is parallel to the longitudinals of the bar, shown in Fig. 5. An element $ABCD$ goes to $A'B'C'D'$ because of twisting, and the two originally plane sections z and $z + dz$ become the warped ones shown in dashes. The horizontal distance between A and A' we have called u. The horizontal

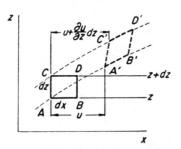

Fig. 5. Derivation of the expressions (3) for the strain γ_{xz}. An element $dx\,dz$ in the vertical xz plane has the contour $ABCD$ before the bar is twisted and goes to $A'B'C'D'$ when the bar is twisted.

distance between C and C' can be written as $u + (\partial u/\partial z)\, dz$, because point C differs from point A by the distance dz only, while A and C have the same x value. The horizontal distance between A' and C' then is $(\partial u/\partial z)\, dz$, and the (small) angle between $A'C'$ and the vertical is $\partial u/\partial z$. We now repeat this whole story for the vertical distances (instead of the horizontal ones) of the points A, B and A', B'. The reader should do this and draw the conclusion that the (small) angle between $A'B'$ and the horizontal is $\partial w/\partial x$. Hence the difference between $\angle\, C'A'B'$ and $\angle\, CAB$ is $(\partial u/\partial z) + (\partial w/\partial x)$, and by definition this is the angle of shear γ_{xz} in the xz plane. For the yz plane the analysis is exactly the same, only the letter x is replaced by y (and consequently u is replaced by v) in all of the algebra as well as in Fig. 5. Thus we arrive at

$$\epsilon_x = \epsilon_y = \epsilon_z = \gamma_{xy} = 0$$

$$\gamma_{xz} = \frac{\partial u}{\partial z} + \frac{\partial w}{\partial x}$$

$$\gamma_{yz} = \frac{\partial v}{\partial z} + \frac{\partial w}{\partial y}$$

Now Eqs. (2) state what the displacements are. Substituting Eqs. (2) into the above leads to

$$\gamma_{xz} = \theta_1 y + \frac{\partial w}{\partial x}$$

$$\gamma_{yz} = -\theta_1 x + \frac{\partial w}{\partial y} \tag{3}$$

With Hooke's law these strains are expressible in the stresses

$$(s_s)_{xz} = G\!\left(\theta_1 y + \frac{\partial w}{\partial x}\right)$$

$$(s_s)_{yz} = G\!\left(-\theta_1 x + \frac{\partial w}{\partial y}\right) \tag{4}$$

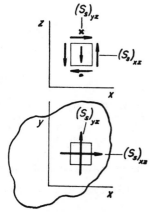

Fig. 6. Definition of the signs of the shear stresses $(s_s)_{xz}$ and $(s_s)_{yz}$. The z axis points upward; the three axes form a right-handed system, and the two subscripts xz mean that the shear stress chases around a small element in the xz plane. The $\times$ means that we are looking on the feather end of an arrow and • looks on the point of an arrow.

where the signs of the stresses are shown in Fig. 6.

The next step is the *derivation of the equation of equilibrium.* It is clear that the shear stresses are not constant across a normal cross section xy but differ from point to point. (In the circular section the stresses are zero at the center and grow linearly with the distance from it.) Thus the stresses on opposite faces of the $dx\, dy\, dz$ element of Fig. 7 are not exactly alike but differ from each other by small amounts. If, for example, the stress on the $dy\,dz$ face for the smaller of the two x values is denoted by $(s_s)_{zz}$, shown dotted in the figure, then the stress on the opposite $dy\,dz$ face (which is distance dx farther to the right) is somewhat different and can be written as

$$(s_s)_{zz} + d(s_s)_{zz}$$

or more precisely as

$$(s_s)_{zz} + \frac{\partial}{\partial x}(s_s)_{zz}\,dx$$

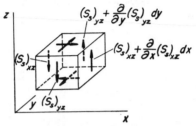

FIG. 7. Derivation of the equilibrium equation. Vertical equilibrium (in the z direction) of the element requires that Eq. (5) be satisfied. Horizontal equilibrium, both in the x and y directions, is automatically satisfied because the stresses are functions of x and y only and do not vary in the z direction by Eqs. (4) and the last of Eqs. (2).

The extra, unbalanced, upward stress on the pair of $dy\,dz$ faces thus is $\frac{\partial}{\partial x}(s_s)_{zz}\,dx$, and since this stress acts on an area $dy\,dz$, the unbalanced force is $\frac{\partial}{\partial x}(s_s)_{zz}\,dx\,dy\,dz$. The reader should now repeat this argument for the two $dx\,dz$ faces (fore and aft) and conclude that the upward unbalanced forces there is $\frac{\partial}{\partial y}(s_s)_{yz}\,dy\,dx\,dz$. There are no other vertical forces or stresses on the element, and an element in a twisted bar is obviously in equilibrium. Setting the net upward force equal to zero and dividing by the volume element $dx\,dy\,dz$ gives the *equilibrium equation*

$$\frac{\partial}{\partial x}(s_s)_{zz} + \frac{\partial}{\partial y}(s_s)_{yz} = 0 \tag{5}$$

This is a partial differential equation in terms of *two* unknown functions $(s_s)_{zz}$ and $(s_s)_{yz}$, both depending on two variables x and y. The problem of finding a solution would be very much simpler if we had to deal with *one* single function of $(x,\,y)$ instead of with *two*. Here we come to the vital step in Saint-Venant's analysis. He assumes that there is a function $\Phi(x,\,y)$, such that the stresses can be found from it by differentiation, thus:

$$(s_s)_{yz} = + \frac{\partial \Phi}{\partial x}$$

$$(s_s)_{zz} = - \frac{\partial \Phi}{\partial y}$$

(6)

The definition (6) of the new function Φ has been chosen cleverly: by substituting (6) into (5) we see that Eq. (5) is automatically satisfied for any arbitrary function Φ, provided that

$$\frac{\partial^2 \Phi}{\partial x\, \partial y} = \frac{\partial^2 \Phi}{\partial y\, \partial x}$$

which is always true if Φ is a continuous function. The function Φ is called the "stress function" of the problem; here it is "Saint-Venant's torsion stress function." Other examples of stress functions will be seen later, on pages 42 and 174.

Now we can begin to visualize the situation geometrically. The value Φ can be plotted vertically on an xy base and thus forms a curved surface. Then Eqs. (6) state that the $(s_s)_{yz}$ stress, $i.e.$, the stress in the y direction, is the slope of the Φ surface in the x direction, and vice versa, that the shear stress in the x direction is the (negative) slope of the Φ surface in the y direction. We shall now prove that this statement can be generalized and that the shear stress component in any direction equals the slope of the Φ surface in the perpendicular direction. Before we proceed to the proof, we notice that by Fig. 1 (page 2) the shear stress normal to the periphery of the shaft is zero; hence the Φ slope along the periphery must be zero, which means that the Φ height all along the periphery must be constant. The Φ surface then can be visualized as a hill, and if we cut this hill by a series of horizontal planes to produce "contour lines," then the shear stress follows those contour lines. For a circular cross section the contour lines are concentric circles, and the Φ hill is a paraboloid of revolution.

Now to the proof. Consider in Fig. 8 an element at point A with the stresses $(s_s)_{zz}$ and $(s_s)_{yz}$. Draw through A the line AB in an arbitrary direction α, and let AB be dn, the element of the "normal" direction. Perpendicular to AB is the line CD. When $AB = dn$, then $AE = dx$ and $EB = dy$, and we see from the figure that $dx/dn = \cos \alpha$ and $dy/dn = \sin \alpha$. Over all these points is the hilly surface of the stress function Φ, and we have in general

$$d\Phi = \frac{\partial \Phi}{\partial x}\, dx + \frac{\partial \Phi}{\partial y}\, dy$$

or

$$\frac{d\Phi}{dn} = \frac{\partial \Phi}{\partial x} \frac{dx}{dn} + \frac{\partial \Phi}{\partial y} \frac{dy}{dn}$$

Transcribing this by means of Eqs. (6) leads to

$$\frac{d\Phi}{dn} = (s_s)_{yz} \cos \alpha - (s_s)_{zz} \sin \alpha$$

Now, looking at Fig. 8 we see that

$$\frac{d\Phi}{dn} = AD - AC$$

or equal to the component of stress in the direction DAC, which is perpendicular to AB. But $d\Phi/dn$ is the slope of the Φ surface in the AB direction, which completes our proof.

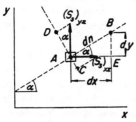

FIG. 8. Toward the proof that the slope of the stress function surface in any arbitrary direction α equals the total shear stress component in the perpendicular direction.

Now we possess the *single* stress function Φ, with which we shall operate instead of with the *pair* of stresses $(s_s)_{zz}$ and $(s_s)_{yz}$. The first thing to do is to rewrite all our previous results in terms of Φ. Turning back, we first find Eq. (5), which we have seen is automatically satisfied by the judicious definition of Φ. Next we find Eqs. (4), which now become

$$-\frac{\partial \Phi}{\partial y} = G\left(\theta_1 y + \frac{\partial w}{\partial x}\right)$$
$$+\frac{\partial \Phi}{\partial x} = G\left(-\theta_1 x + \frac{\partial w}{\partial y}\right) \qquad (7)$$

In these the quantity w is the warping of the cross section. We do not know what w looks like, but it is certain that w and its derivatives are continuous functions of x and y: the warping will have no sudden jumps or cracks in it. One mathematical consequence of this continuity is

$$\frac{\partial^2 w}{\partial x \, \partial y} = \frac{\partial^2 w}{\partial y \, \partial x}$$

We now operate on Eqs. (7) in two ways. First we apply $\partial/\partial y$ to the top equation, $\partial/\partial x$ to the bottom equation, and subtract them from each other, which gives

$$\frac{\partial^2 \Phi}{\partial x^2} + \frac{\partial^2 \Phi}{\partial y^2} = -2G\theta_1 \qquad (8)$$

Second we apply $\partial/\partial x$ to the first of Eqs. (7), $\partial/\partial y$ to the second, and add the results together, which leads to

$$\frac{\partial^2 w}{\partial x^2} + \frac{\partial^2 w}{\partial y^2} = 0 \qquad (9)$$

The last result is a partial differential equation for finding the warping function w. We shall postpone discussing it until page 31.

The result, Eq. (8), is a partial differential equation for the stress function Φ. From the previous derivations we understand that *any* arbitrary function Φ, whether it satisfies Eq. (8) or not, leads to stresses [by the process of Eqs. (6)] that satisfy the equilibrium equation (5). If the function *does* satisfy (8), it leads to stresses which correspond to continuous warping deformations w, whereas a Φ which violates (8) gives equilibrium stresses all right, but the corresponding warping function is discontinuous. Therefore Eq. (8) is an equation of continuity, or, by a special term used in the theory of elasticity, Eq. (8) is known as the equation of *compatibility*. If for a given cross section we can find a Φ function which satisfies Eq. (8), and which also satisfies the boundary condition $\Phi =$ constant along the periphery, then the stresses derived from that Φ are the true solution to the torsion problem.

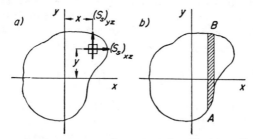

Fig. 9. The transmitted torque across the section is found by integrating the contributions of all elements $dx\,dy$ of the section.

Torque in the Shaft. Before we proceed to find a few solutions of this kind, we first derive one more result: for the torque transmitted by the shaft. The clockwise torque about the origin furnished by an element $dx\,dy$ (Fig. 9a) is

$$[+(s_s)_{zz}y - (s_s)_{yz}x]\,dx\,dy$$

To find the total torque, this expression must be integrated over the entire cross section. We first calculate the first term in the bracket, *i.e.*, the torque caused by the $(s_s)_{zz}$ stress alone.

Substituting Eq. (6), we find

$$+(s_s)_{zz}y\,dx\,dy = -dx\,\frac{\partial \Phi}{\partial y}\,y\,dy$$

Integrate this first along a strip of width dx parallel to the y axis (Fig. 9b). Then x is constant, and we can replace $(\partial\Phi/\partial y)\,dy$ by $d\Phi$ without ambiguity. Thus, integrating by parts,

$$-\int dx \left\{ \int y \, d\Phi \right\} = -\int dx \left\{ [y\Phi]_A^B - \int \Phi \, dy \right\}$$

The first term in brackets, when taken between the limits A and B, is $y_B \Phi_B - y_A \Phi_A$. Now we know that Φ must be constant along the boundary, so that $\Phi_A = \Phi_B$. We have not so far decided what absolute value we shall assign to Φ at the boundary. For simplicity we now decide to set Φ equal to *zero* at the boundary. We are allowed to do this, because Φ after all is only an auxiliary function, existing only for convenience. We are decidedly interested in the stresses, which follow from Φ by differentiation by Eqs. (6). Suppose we add a constant to Φ, that is, suppose we raise the entire Φ surface. Then the slopes remain the same everywhere, and hence the stresses remain the same. The Φ function has the nature of a potential function, such as gravitational height, electric voltage, or the velocity potential of hydrodynamics. Its absolute value has no meaning; only its differences are important. Hence we are free to assign a zero value to Φ at *one* location wherever we please; then the function is fixed at all other locations. We choose for zero Φ the boundary of the bar; then $\Phi_A = \Phi_B = 0$ (Fig. 9b), and the above integral becomes

$$\int dx \int_A^B \Phi \, dy = \iint \Phi \, dx \, dy$$

which is the volume under the Φ hill. The reader should now calculate the torque caused by the $(s_s)_{yz}$ stresses in the same manner, by integrating first over a strip dy parallel to the x axis. He should find the same result with the same sign. Thus it has been proved that the transmitted torque M_t equals twice the volume under the Φ hill, provided that Φ is taken equal to zero at the boundary:

$$M_t = 2 \iint_A \Phi \, dA \qquad (10)$$

3. Prandtl's Membrane Analogy.

Saint-Venant in 1855 found solutions of this torsion problem for a number of cross sections, such as rectangular, triangular, and elliptic sections. Those solutions were found by complicated mathematical methods, often involving infinite series. Many important practical sections such as channels and I beams cannot even be reduced to a mathematical formula, so that approximate methods of solution are desirable. The best method of this sort among the many that have appeared is due to Prandtl (1903). Prandtl observed that the differential equation (8) for the stress function is the same as the differential equation for the shape of a stretched membrane, originally flat, which is then blown up by air pressure from the bottom. This remark will give us an extremely simple and clear manner of visualizing the shape of the

Φ function, and the stress distribution. We therefore now derive the equation of a thin, weightless membrane initially with a "large" tension T (expressed in pounds per inch, and having the same value in all directions), blown up from one side by a "small" excess air pressure p (expressed in pounds per square inch). By a large initial tension T we mean such a tension that its value will not be changed by the blowing-up process. The membrane is an elastic skin, of rubber, for example. If in the unstressed state we draw on it a network of squares, then these squares have to be deformed into larger squares in order to get tension in it; in other words, there must be initial strain connected with the tension T. This initial strain must be the same in all directions, and hence T is also the same in all directions and is expressed in pounds per running inch of (imaginary) cut in the membrane. When the membrane is blown up from the flat shape into a curved surface, being held at the edges, obviously the lengths of lines drawn on it increase, so that the blowing-up process causes more strain. We now prescribe that the air pressure p must be so "small" and the initial tension T must be so "large" that the blowing-up strain is negligible compared with the initial strain and that consequently T remains constant during the blowing-up process.

Derivation of the Membrane Equilibrium Equation (11). Let in Fig. 10 such a membrane be shown, lying originally flat in the xy plane and then having air pressure p blowing it up to ordinates z. The periphery of the membrane is fixed so that the peripheral points remain at $z = 0$ when the interior is blown up. Since the pressure p is "small," the ordinates z likewise will be "small." The equation of the blown-up skin then will have the form $z = f(x, y)$, and the slopes of this shape, $\partial z/\partial x$ and $\partial z/\partial y$, will also be "small." Consider a small element $dx\ dy$ of the membrane. It will have acting on it two forces $T\ dy$ in the x direction on the two opposite cuts dy, two forces $T\ dx$ on opposite faces dx in the y direction, and finally a force $p\ dx\ dy$ perpendicular to it, practically in the z direction. Now we resolve these various forces into components in the x, y, and z directions. These components are the forces themselves, multiplied by the sine, cosine, or tangent of the slope. Since, for small angles,

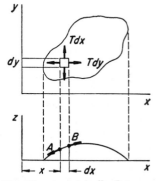

Fig. 10. An originally flat membrane with "large" tension T under the influence of a "small" air pressure p from the bottom assumes a shape z with "small" slopes, satisfying the differential equation (11).

$$\cos \epsilon = 1 - \tfrac{1}{2}\epsilon^2 + \cdots \qquad \text{and} \qquad \sin \epsilon = \epsilon - \tfrac{1}{6}\epsilon^3 + \cdots$$

we can say that the cosine of the slope equals unity and that the sine (or tangent) of the slope equals the slope itself. Then we are correct up to magnitudes of the first order small, neglecting quantities of the second and higher orders. In that case the horizontal equilibrium, either in the x or in the y direction, of the $dx\,dy$ element is automatically satisfied, because the horizontal components to the right and left are both equal to $T\,dy$, while the x component of the air-pressure force is two orders smaller than that and hence negligible. However, the z equilibrium gives a good equation, as follows: The z component of $T\,dy$ on face A (Fig. 10) is $T\,dy\,(\partial z/\partial x)$ downward. The z component on the opposite B face would be the same (upward) if the slope $\partial z/\partial x$ were the same, but in general it is not. That component can be written as

$$T\,dy\left(\frac{\partial z}{\partial x}+\frac{\partial}{\partial x}\frac{\partial z}{\partial x}\,dx\right)=T\frac{\partial z}{\partial x}\,dy+T\frac{\partial^2 z}{\partial x^2}\,dx\,dy$$

The net sum upward of the membrane tensions at A and B together thus is

$$T\frac{\partial^2 z}{\partial x^2}\,dx\,dy$$

and we see that it is proportional to $\partial^2 z/\partial x^2$, which is the curvature (for small slopes). Similarly we deduce that the net upward force resulting from the two dx faces is

$$T\frac{\partial^2 z}{\partial y^2}\,dy\,dx$$

The third upward force is the air pressure $p\,dx\,dy$, so that, after dividing by $T\,dx\,dy$, the z equilibrium equation becomes

$$\frac{\partial^2 z}{\partial x^2}+\frac{\partial^2 z}{\partial y^2}=-\frac{p}{T} \tag{11}$$

or, in words: The sum of the curvatures in two perpendicular directions is a constant for all points of the membrane.

Now, if we adjust the membrane tension T or the air pressure p so that p/T becomes numerically equal to $2G\theta_1$, then Eq. (11) of the membrane is identical with Eq. (8) of the torsional stress function. If, moreover, we arrange the membrane so that its heights z remain zero at the boundary contour of the section, then the heights z of the membrane are numerically equal to the stress function Φ; the slopes of the membrane are equal to the shear stresses (in a direction perpendicular to that of the slope); the contour lines $z=$ constant of the membrane are lines following the shear stresses, and the twisting moment is numerically equal to twice the volume under the membrane [Eq. (10)].

Practical Use of the Membrane Analogy. To *calculate* the shape of a membrane for a given cross section by integration of Eq. (11) is, of course, just as difficult as to calculate the stress function from Eq. (8). But with the membrane analogy we can do two things: we can measure experimentally, or, more important still, we can visualize intuitively.

Experiments have been made, using stretched rubber sheets or soap films for membranes. At first thought it would seem necessary to know the value of the tension T and to regulate the air pressure p of the membrane so that $p/T = 2G\theta_1$. This would be complicated and is usually avoided by taking a large membrane and by blowing up side by side two cross sections: the one to be investigated and a purely circular one. Since the p/T value is the same for both, because the same membrane is used, the corresponding $2G\theta_1$ is also the same. Then if we measure the volumes under the two hills and also the slopes in each, we conclude that in

$$\frac{\text{Volume}}{\text{Slope}} = \text{const} \frac{\text{torque}}{\text{shear stress}}$$

the constant is the same for both sections. Since we know all about the circular section, the constant is easily calculated and then we have the torque/stress ratio for the other section. Also,

$$\frac{\text{Volume of circular hill}}{\text{Volume of other hill}} = \frac{M_t/\theta_1 \text{ of circle}}{M_t/\theta_1 \text{ of other section}}$$

We now propose to calculate the stress and stiffness of a few simple sections by the membrane analogy. Before doing that, let us first see what happens to the circular section. On account of symmetry the height z of the membrane there does not depend on the *two* numbers x and y but can be said to depend on the single quantity r only. Cutting a concentric circle out of the membrane and setting the downward pull on the periphery $2\pi r$ equal to the upward push of the air pressure on πr^2 gives

$$-T \frac{dz}{dr} 2\pi r = p\pi r^2$$

$$-\frac{dz}{dr} = \frac{p}{2T} r$$

or, in words: The slope of the membrane is proportional to the distance r from the center, and hence the shear stress follows this law also. Translated from a membrane to a twisted shaft by $p/T = 2G\theta_1$, this reads

$$s_s = G\theta_1 r$$

which we know to be correct. We now find the shape of the membrane by integrating:

$$z = -\int \frac{pr}{2T} dr = -\frac{pr^2}{4T} + \text{const}$$

The constant follows from the fact that at the periphery $r = R$ the height z must be zero, so that

$$z = \frac{p}{4T} (R^2 - r^2)$$

The volume under the membrane hill is

$$\text{Volume} = \int_{r=0}^{r=R} 2\pi r \, dr \, z = \frac{p\pi}{2T} \int_0^R (R^2 - r^2) r \, dr = \frac{\pi}{8} \frac{p}{T} R^4$$

Translating this into the twisted shaft by means of Eqs. (8), (10), and (11), we have

$$M_t = \frac{\pi}{2} R^4 \cdot G\theta_1 = GI_p\theta_1$$

or

$$\frac{M_t}{\theta_1} = \text{``}C\text{''} = GI_p$$

the known result for the circular shaft. The letter C is commonly used for the torsional stiffness which is *not* equal to GI_p for any section other than the circular one.

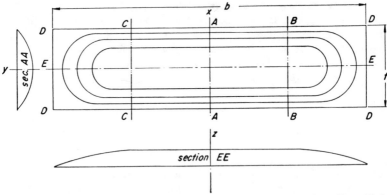

FIG. 11.   Membrane contour lines of a narrow rectangular cross section of breadth b and thickness t.

Thin Rectangular Section.   Next we consider a narrow rectangular cross section bt (Fig. 11). If b is very much larger than t, we see by intuition that the bulges of the membrane across AA, BB, or CC are all the same and that only near the ends DD the membrane flattens down to zero. Then the contour lines in the central portion are straight and parallel to the y axis. In this central portion, there being no curvature parallel to the y axis the membrane is held down by vertical tension components in the x direction only. Cutting out a central piece of membrane of dimensions $2x$ and l, the equilibrium equation is

$$-2Tl\frac{dz}{dx} = p2xl \quad \text{or} \quad \frac{dz}{dx} = -\frac{p}{T}x$$

Integrate:

$$z = -\frac{p}{T}\int x\,dx = -\frac{px^2}{2T} + \text{const}$$

Again the constant must be chosen so as to make $z = 0$ at the periphery where $x = t/2$, or

$$z = \frac{p}{2T}\left(\frac{t^2}{4} - x^2\right)$$

which is a parabola. The maximum slope obviously occurs at the edges $x = \pm t/2$ and is

$$\left(\frac{dz}{dx}\right)_{\text{max}} = \frac{p}{T}\frac{t}{2}$$

Translated from the membrane to the twisted rectangular shaft, this becomes

$$(s_s)_{\text{max}} = G\theta_1 t$$

Now, in calculating the volume under the membrane, we neglect the flattening out of the membrane near the edges $y = \pm b/2$, and since the area of a parabola is $\frac{2}{3}$ base $\times$ height, we find

$$\text{Volume} = \frac{2}{3}t\left(\frac{p}{2T}\frac{t^2}{4}\right)b$$

Translating to the twisted shaft [Eqs. (8), (10), and (11)], we find for the torsional stiffness C

$$\frac{M_t}{\theta_1} = C = G\frac{bt^3}{3} \tag{12}$$

Eliminating $G\theta_1$ from between this result and the one just found for the shear stress gives

$$s_s = \frac{3M_t}{bt^2} \tag{13}$$

These formulae are true only when $b \gg t$. For less narrow cross sections,

Saint-Venant has found the solution by a much more complicated method, the results of which are shown in the table below:

b/t	∞	10	5	3	$2\frac{1}{2}$	2	$1\frac{1}{2}$	1
$\dfrac{(s_s)_{\text{max}}}{M_t/bt^2}$	3.00	3.20	3.44	3.74	3.86	4.06	4.33	4.80
$\dfrac{M_t/\theta_1}{Gbt^3}$	0.333	0.312	0.291	0.263	0.249	0.229	0.196	0.141

There are two remarkable facts in connection with the results (12) and (13). First of all, the maximum stress occurs at that point of the periphery which is *closest* to the center of the section, whereas the peripheral point farthest away from the center, *i.e.*, the corner, has zero stress. This is in complete opposition to what happens in the *bending* of beams and in the torsion of a circular bar. The second point of importance is that by Eq. (12) the "stiffness" M_t/θ_1 grows with the first power of b only. The polar moment of inertia grows with the cube of b, and hence if we should extrapolate the simple formula for the circular cross section, where the stiffness is GI_p, to the narrow rectangle, we should be in complete error.

Now suppose we take our narrow rectangle of Fig. 11 and imagine a 90-deg bend in it in the middle, so that the section becomes a thin-walled angle. The membrane will not change its shape, except for local effects in the corner, to which we return later. The volume under the membrane

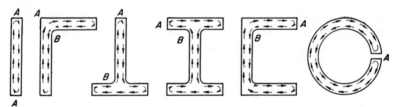

Fig. 12.　Cross sections to which Eq. (12) for the torsional stiffness applies, if t is the wall thickness and b is the total aggregate length of wall in the section. Equation (13) for the stress applies to all these sections except near corners. The corners marked A (90 deg of material and 270 deg of void) have zero stress; those marked B (270 deg of material and 90 deg of void) have a large stress concentration depending on the radius of the fillet.

for a given pressure does not change materially. Hence Eq. (12) is good for an angular section as well, if only we interpret b as the total length of both legs of the angle combined. The same remark is true (Fig. 12) for T shapes, I shapes, and slit tubes and in general for sections that can be built up of rectangles. It is *not* true for closed box sections, such as the hollow thin-walled (non-slitted) tube or a rectangular thin-walled box. We shall return to those sections on page 26. If in an I beam the flanges and web are not of the same thickness, Eq. (12) still applies, only now the torque M_t has to be calculated separately for the web and for the flanges, and these partial torques then must be added to give the complete torque for the entire section.

Stress Raisers and Dead Corners. The stress equation (13) was derived for the point A of Fig. 11, and thus it holds for peripheral points of the sections of Fig. 12 that are not in the vicinity of corners. There are two kinds of corners: *protruding* corners, which have less than 180 deg of material and more than 180 deg of open space; and *reentrant* corners, where there is more than 180 deg of material and less than 180 deg of open space. These have been marked A and B, respectively, in Fig. 12. In a protruding corner of type A the membrane is held down by two intersecting lines, and it cannot bulge up in that corner: it remains sensibly flat, hence no slopes and no shear stresses. The material in protruding corners has no shear stress: it is dead material. (This conclusion can be immediately verified by assuming a shear stress in the corner, by resolving that shear stress into components perpendicular to the two sides locally, and by remarking that both components must be zero by virtue of Fig. 1.)

On the other hand the stress at a reentrant corner is always greater than the shear stress in the general vicinity. At such a corner the membrane is held down locally by the boundary less than it would be by a straight 180-deg ruler, and it can bulge out more. This we cannot strictly prove at this point, but the stress concentration depends greatly on the local fillet radius of the reentrant corner: for a mathematically sharp corner (zero fillet radius) the stress becomes mathematically infinitely large, which in practice means very large, equal to the yield point of the material.

Elliptical Section. Now we shall discuss a shaft of elliptical cross section (Fig. 13), not because it is likely to occur in practice, but rather to show another beautiful example of the power of the membrane analogy. Let the two principal semiaxes of the ellipse be a and b, where $b > a$. Consider that this elliptical cross section grows out of a circular cross section of radius a, by letting all lengths in the y direction remain constant and by letting all lengths in the x direction be multiplied in ratio b/a. Imagine the membrane hill z erected over the circle a, and assume that this membrane hill also stretches in ratio b/a in the x direction while the heights z and the values y remain the same. By this stretching process all x base lines become b/a larger, while the heights z do not change; hence the slopes $\partial z/\partial x$ diminish in ratio b/a, in other words, are multiplied by a/b. The slopes in the y direction, $\partial z/\partial y$, remain unchanged. The curvature, or rate of change of slope, $\dfrac{\partial^2 z}{\partial x^2} = \left(\dfrac{\partial}{\partial x}\right)\left(\dfrac{\partial z}{\partial x}\right)$ then is multiplied by

$\frac{a^2}{b^2}$, while $\frac{\partial^2 z}{\partial y^2}$ remains unchanged. Thus, since for a circle $\frac{\partial^2 z}{\partial x^2} = \frac{\partial^2 z}{\partial y^2}$, the stretching process multiplies the sum of the two curvatures $\left(\frac{\partial^2 z}{\partial x^2} + \frac{\partial^2 z}{\partial y^2} \right)$ by $\frac{1 + (a^2/b^2)}{2}$, and since this sum was constant for the membrane over the circle, it is again constant when stretched out into elliptical shape and thus it can be the shape of a membrane blown up over an elliptic base. From Eq. (11) we conclude that if on the circle the air pressure is p, then for the ellipse it has to be $p \, \frac{1 + (a^2/b^2)}{2}$.

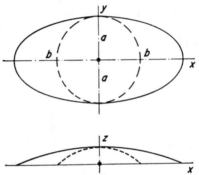

FIG. 13. A shaft of elliptical cross section with diameters $2a$ and $2b$ is generated from a circular shaft by stretching in the x direction. The same is done with the z membrane. The contour lines of that membrane are all ellipses. The analysis leads to the results Eqs. (14) and (15).

Since the height z remains constant, the volume of the elliptic hill is b/a times the volume over the circle.

Dividing these two results, we find

$$\left(\frac{p/T}{\text{Volume}} \right)_{\text{ellipse}} = \frac{1 + (a^2/b^2)}{2b/a} \left(\frac{p/T}{\text{volume}} \right)_{\text{circle}}$$

Translated from membranes to twisted bars,

$$\left(\frac{2G\theta_1}{M_t/2} \right)_{\text{ellipse}} = \frac{1 + (a^2/b^2)}{2b/a} \left(\frac{2G\theta_1}{M_t/2} \right)_{\text{circle}}$$

Now for the circle we know $M_t/\theta_1 = GI_p = (\pi/2) \, a^4 G$ so that for the ellipse

$$C = \frac{M_t}{\theta_1} = \frac{\pi a^4 G}{2} \frac{2b/a}{1 + (a^2/b^2)} = \frac{\pi a^3 b^3}{a^2 + b^2} \, G \tag{14}$$

Considering the slopes of the two membranes (which have equal central height), we see that the maximum slope in the ellipse membrane occurs at the end of the small semiaxis a and is equal to the slope of the corresponding circle membrane. Hence we write

$$\left(\frac{\text{Slope}}{\text{Volume}}\right)_{\text{ellipse}} = \frac{1}{b/a}\left(\frac{\text{slope}}{\text{volume}}\right)_{\text{circle}}$$

or, translated into twist,

$$\left[\frac{(s_s)_{\max}}{M_t}\right]_{\text{ellipse}} = \frac{a}{b}\left[\frac{(s_s)_{\max}}{M_t}\right]_{\text{circle}}$$

We know all about the circle [Eq. (1a)] so that for the ellipse

$$(s_s)_{\max} = \frac{2M_t}{\pi a^2 b} \tag{15}$$

Saint-Venant has found exact solutions not only for the ellipse and rectangle but also for triangles, semicircles, and several other figures that are easily brought into mathematical formulae. However, many practical sections, such as for example a shaft with a keyway cut into it, cannot be reduced to formula, and then the membrane experiment is useful. Figure 14 gives three examples of cross-sections with their stress function contour lines.

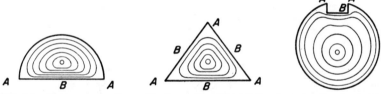

FIG. 14. Three cross sections with the contour lines of the stress function for twist. In the corner points marked A the stress is zero; these corners can be pared away without changing the stiffness of the section; the points marked B are those of maximum stress; the bottom of the keyway has a stress which depends vitally on the fillet radius, and is sure to reach the fatigue limit for even a small alternating torque in the case of a sharp corner.

Empirical Formula for Squatty Sections. Twenty-five years after the publication of his theory Saint-Venant came to a remarkable practical discovery. He noticed that Eq. (14) for the ellipse can be written in the following form:

$$\frac{M_t}{\theta_1} = \frac{1}{4\pi^2}\frac{GA^4}{I_p}$$

where $A = \pi ab$ is the area of the ellipse and $I_p = (a^2 + b^2)A/4$ is its polar moment of inertia. On comparing the results for the many sections he had calculated he found that all of them (except a few very elongated ones) fitted the above formula with an error of less than 10 per cent. In fact the mean error was a little smaller when the factor $\frac{1}{4}\pi^2$ was replaced by $\frac{1}{40}$. Hence

$$C = \frac{M_t}{\theta_1} = \frac{GA^4}{40I_p} \tag{16}$$

is an appropriate formula (with errors of the order of 8 per cent at the most) applicable to all cross sections that are not too elongated such as, for example, those of Fig. 14, but *not* applicable to those of Fig. 12.

Plastic Torsion. From all previous derivations it is clear that the membrane theory is based on Hooke's law [Eq. (4)], and that consequently it applies only when all stresses in the section are below the yield stress. As soon as one point of the section reaches the yield point, the membrane at that spot reaches its maximum slope of significance. If we blow up the membrane further, we get larger slopes, which can be interpreted only as stresses greater than the yield stress, which makes no sense. What actually happens is that plastic flow takes place at the spot of maximum stress. The usual idealization of the actual law of plasticity is that for strains greater than the yield strain, the stress remains constant and the strain increases further, without corresponding increase in stress. A beautiful extension of the membrane analogy to cover cases of plastic flow

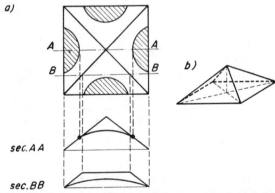

FIG. 15.   Nadai's extension of the membrane analogy to cases of plastic flow. Over the section is a solid roof of which the slope is equal to that corresponding to the yield stress. The membrane in certain places will be pressed against this roof: there the stress then equals the yield stress. Everywhere else the membrane is free with slopes less than the yield slope.

was found by Nadai in 1925. He noticed that the maximum stress always occurs at a point of the periphery, never at a point inside the section. So he erected over the section a solid roof having everywhere a slope equal to the yield slope. This roof (Fig. 15) for a rectangular section looks like a common house roof; for a circular section it is a cone. If the stress everywhere is below the yield stress, the membrane under this roof is unimpeded by it and Prandtl's analogy applies. As soon as yield is surpassed, the membrane will be pushed against the roof in certain places, shaded in Fig. 15. In those regions the slope and stress have the yield value; in the unshaded regions the material is still elastic, and the stress is found from the slope of the membrane.

4. Kelvin's Fluid-flow Analogy. More than thirty years before Prandtl conceived the membrane analogy, Lord Kelvin (then Sir William Thomson) interpreted Saint-Venant's pictures of Fig. 14 in terms of streamlines of a circulatory flow of an ideal fluid with constant vorticity over the cross section. With the usual notation of fluid mechanics let u and v be the components of velocity in the x and y directions [not to be confused with the displacements in elasticity of Eqs. (2), page 4]. Then a stream function Ψ of x and y is assumed, and in fluid mechanics we write

$$u = -\frac{\partial \Psi}{\partial y} \qquad v = +\frac{\partial \Psi}{\partial x} \qquad (a)$$

for the reason that then automatically we have

$$\frac{\partial u}{\partial x} + \frac{\partial v}{\partial y} = 0$$

which is the condition of incompressibility of the fluid. The incompressible fluid may or may not have vorticity at its various points. The expression for the vorticity ω is

$$2\omega = \frac{\partial u}{\partial y} - \frac{\partial v}{\partial x}$$

and substitution of Eq. (a) into this gives

$$\frac{\partial^2 \Psi}{\partial x^2} + \frac{\partial^2 \Psi}{\partial y^2} = -2\omega \qquad (17)$$

This differential equation is seen to be the same as Eq. (8) for the stress function, if we set the vorticity $\omega = G\theta_1$ constant over the entire cross section. It is shown in fluid mechanics that the lines $\Psi =$ constant are the streamlines, and then obviously the boundary condition is that $\Psi =$ constant along the boundary. This is the same boundary condition imposed on the stress function. Hence the analogy is complete. A comparison of Eqs. (6) for the shear stresses with Eq. (a) above shows that the stresses are analogous to the velocities of the fluid flow.

This analogy enables us to visualize certain aspects of the torsion problem even more easily than the membrane analogy. However, it is not particularly suited to experiments because drugstores usually have some difficulty in supplying a customer with a few pints of ideal fluid. Thus in an actual experiment we use water, which does have some viscosity. The apparatus consists of a horizontal table mounted rotatable about a vertical axis. A shallow tank of proper contour, painted black, is placed on the table, filled with water, and aluminum powder is put on the water surface. A camera placed above the tank, facing downward, is attached to the table, so that it can rotate with the tank only. To avoid the effects of viscosity (friction), the table is rotated through an angle of not more than 10 deg, starting from rest, and a photograph is taken during this motion. The fluid at rest certainly has zero vorticity all over. When set in motion from rest, the vorticity remains zero, according to a theorem in fluid mechanics. When the water in the tank, having zero vorticity, is photographed from a rotating camera, the picture shows the flow with a rotation equal (and opposite) to that of the camera. This can be understood easily for the case of a circular tank, mounted concentrically on the table. When the tank starts to rotate, the water remains still in space, because the friction from the tank walls has had no time yet to make itself felt. The still water photographed from the rotating camera will show a rotational flow. When the circular tank is replaced by a square one or by one of

FIG. 16. Photograph of small aluminum particles on the surface of water in a square tank. The camera rotates with the tank through a small angle, starting from rest. By Kelvin's analogy the streaks indicate the shear stress in direction as well as magnitude for the twisted bar of square cross section.

another shape, the water can no longer stand still in space when the tank is rotated but nevertheless its vorticity remains zero for a little while. In the photograph the individual aluminum particles will appear as streaks, having lengths proportional to the shear stress and being in the direction of the shear stress (Fig. 16).

The real value of Kelvin's analogy lies not so much in actual experiments as in the ease of visualization and also in the fact that numerous mathematical solutions of ideal fluid flow have been worked out during the past century, many of which can be usefully interpreted in the torsion problem. The first of these, shown in Fig. 17a, is that the flow past a cylinder shows two points of zero speed (the stagnation points) and two points of speed 2V_0, where V_0 is the speed of the undisturbed stream at some distance from the cylindrical obstacle. The torsional analogue of this case is shown in Figs. 17b and c. It applies to small circular holes all along the length of a twisted shaft. Semicircular notches at the periphery also have a stress concentration factor 2, because the local flow picture is half that of Fig. 17a

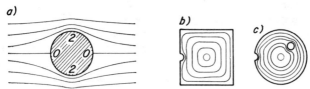

FIG. 17. The flow of ideal fluid past a circle shows a maximum velocity twice that of the undisturbed main stream. Hence the torsion stress-concentration factor at the edge of a small circular hole in the solid material or at the bottom of a small semicircular notch in the periphery is 2.0.

For the case of narrower and deeper notches the flow around an elliptical obstacle is of importance (Fig. 18). Here the stress concentration factor, as found by writers on fluid mechanics, is $1 + (b/a)$. A crack in the

FIG. 18. The flow around an elliptical obstacle shows two stagnation points S and two points M of maximum velocity $V_0(1 + b/a)$. Hence the stress-concentration factor in a twisted bar with a semi-elliptical notch of semi-axes a and b also is $1 + (b/a)$, which for a sharp and deep notch can become very high.

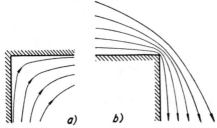

FIG. 19. The solutions for ideal fluid flow around corners show zero speed in the corner if the fluid occupies less than 180 deg and infinite speed at the corner if the fluid occupies more than 180 deg. Analogously the stress concentration in a reentrant corner of a twisted bar is serious, while there is zero stress in a protruding corner.

material, as it appears prior to a fatigue failure, can be regarded approximately as a semi-ellipse with $b \gg a$, and hence the stress concentration factor at the bottom of such a crack is extremely high.

Figure 19 shows the hydrodynamic solutions for the flow in a 90-deg corner and around a 270-deg one. In the first case the flow is stagnant in the corner; in the other case the velocity is theoretically infinite for a sharp corner. This again illustrates the fact, previously deduced from the membrane analogy, that protruding corners consist of dead material, while reentrant corners show serious stress concentrations. In particular, the stress concentration in the corner of a keyway in a shaft becomes "infinite" if the corner is "perfectly" sharp. In practice, almost every shaft that fails in torsion fatigue does so from the corner of a keyway.

Finally we return to the dangerous corners marked *B* in Fig. 12 (page 16), which occur in thin-walled structural sections. An approximate solution of this difficult problem was found by Trefftz in 1922 with the result that the stress concentration factor in the fillet is

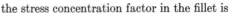

$$\frac{(s_s)_{\text{max}}}{(s_s)_{\text{Eq. (13)}}} = 1.74 \sqrt[3]{\frac{t}{r}} \tag{18}$$

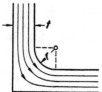

where *t* is the wall thickness of the webs and *r* is the fillet radius of the 90-deg corner. This is illustrated in Fig. 20.

Fig. 20. The flow around a 90-deg corner with a fillet radius *r* in a channel of width *t* shows a maximum velocity in the fillet approximately $1.74 \sqrt[3]{t/r}$ times the velocity at some distance from the corner. Hence the stress-concentration factor in the corresponding torsion cases *B* of Fig. 12 is given by Eq. (18).

5. Hollow Sections. The stress distribution in a solid circular shaft in torsion is such that, if we imagine this shaft to be cut up into a number of concentric cylindrical shells, all fitting snugly together, then no stress or force is transmitted from any of these shells to its neighbors. This remark is used for calculating the stress distribution and the stiffness of hollow shafts (with a concentric hole). The stresses in the hollow shaft for a given angle of twist per unit length θ_1 are exactly the same as in the corresponding portion of a solid shaft. The torque transmitted (for a given θ_1) by the hollow shaft is less than that transmitted by the solid one by an amount equal to the torque that would have been transmitted by the non-existent inner core if it had existed.

Now we look at this situation by means of the membrane analogy. In Fig. 21*b* the full line shows the membrane for the solid shaft. Since (for a given unit twist angle θ_1) the stresses remain the same when the central portion of the shaft is removed, the stresses in the remaining outer shell are obviously given by the slopes of the remaining ring-shaped portion of the membrane. The center portion of the membrane then has no meaning for us. Looking at that center portion, we know it is in vertical equilibrium by the up push of the air-pressure force $p \cdot \pi r^2$ and the down pull of the membrane tension forces. Now if the center portion of the membrane were replaced by a thin, weightless, stiff, flat circular plate, that plate would be in equilibrium at the same height as the periphery of the inner portion of the membrane, because the upward air push and the downward membrane pull from the annular part would be the same for the plate and for the center membrane.

Suppose some disagreeable person now proposes to locate that central plate at a different elevation (Fig. 21c) and remarks that the annular membrane still is a membrane, hence satisfies Eq. (11), and all boundary conditions Φ_{boundary} = constant are fulfilled. The slopes and hence the shear stresses from Fig. 21c obviously are different from the slopes and stresses, Fig. 21b, and since we know Fig. 21b to be correct, Fig. 21c must be wrong. The question why it is wrong is quite complicated, and its discussion will be postponed to page 32.

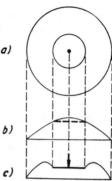

FIG. 21. The membrane analogy for a circular shaft with concentric hole in torsion. The membrane b, being a part of the membrane for a solid shaft, is the correct one. The case shown as c in which the central flat plate is pushed down somewhat gives an erroneous membrane, although the membrane equation (11) as well as the boundary conditions Φ_{bou} = constant are satisfied.

Now we go a step further and consider a circular shaft with an eccentric hole. Now there *are* stresses transmitted between the outer ring and the inner core, and we cannot cut out the core without disturbing everything. But we can still make a membrane test, replacing the hole by a stiff, weightless, flat plate and then blowing up the membrane. The plate, of course, will be pushed up obliquely in general, and the condition at the inner boundary requires that Φ is constant, so that the plate must be horizontal. We proceed to make it horizontal by applying a force and maybe a couple to it. But in that way we can push it up or down to any height, and now we really are in a quandary as to which height to choose.

It will be proved on page 33 (unfortunately in a rather involved manner) that the membrane analogy gives correct results if the plate is forced to be horizontal by the application of a pure couple only, without a resultant vertical force. The vertical upward force of air pressure then equals the downward pull of the membrane tension. This statement holds for more than one hole in the section. Every hole is simulated by a weightless, stiff disk glued to the membrane; the membrane is then blown up, and pure couples are applied to each disk till they are all horizontal, probably at different heights. The slopes of the membrane then indicate stresses, and the volume indicates half the transmitted torque. From the reasoning given with Fig. 21 it is clear that the "volume" under the membrane includes the part under the flat plate.

Thin-walled Hollow Sections. The most important practical sections with holes are thin-walled ones, such as steel box girders in building construction, thin-walled closed tubes, circular, elliptic, or square, made of aluminum in aircraft construction, and even entire airplane wings or fuselages, where the wall thickness consists of the aluminum skin only. The membrane theory for such thin-walled structures becomes particularly simple.

The general section with its membrane is shown in Fig. 22. The wall thickness is t, and while in almost all practical cases this t is constant, there are some cases where t varies along the periphery. The analysis for variable t is not much more complicated, so that we take t variable, although everywhere "small." This implies that the blown-up membrane must be sensibly straight across the gap of width t.

The height of the central plate must be constant, say h. Then the membrane slope is h/t, and since slope $\times t = h =$ constant, we find analogously

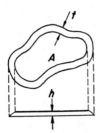

$$s_s \cdot t = \text{const}$$

or the stress is inversely proportional to the local wall thickness. The stress is directed tangent to the walls and is assumed distributed evenly across the thickness t (because we see intuitively that the slope of the membrane is about constant across t). This important result can also be easily visualized by Kelvin's analogy. There all walls are streamlines of an incompressible flow. Hence the fluid just cruises around the section through a channel of width t, and, being incompressible, its velocity (and analogously the shear stress) must be greatest when the channel width t is smallest.

Now we write the vertical equilibrium equation of the plate. Let A be the area of the plate. Then the upward push is pA. The downward pull is made up of the downward component of membrane pull integrated along the entire periphery:

Fig. 22. Single-cell thin-walled torsion section with its membrane. The height of the central plate above the outside boundary is h, and the volume under it is Ah.

$$pA = \oint (T \, ds) \frac{h}{t}$$

Translated to torsion by setting $p/T = 2G\theta_1$ and $h/t = $ slope $= s_s$, we have

$$2G\theta_1 = \frac{1}{A} \oint s_s \, ds \qquad (a)$$

On the other hand, the transmitted torque, about any point O, due to one area element $t \, ds$, is (Fig. 23)

$$s_s \cdot t \, ds \cdot n$$

where n is the normal or moment arm. But $n \, ds$ can be interpreted as twice the area of a small triangle with ds as base, n as height with its apex at O; further we have seen that $s_s t$ is constant all along the periphery. Thus the total torque is

$$M_t = \int (s_s t) n \, ds = s_s t \int n \, ds = 2A s_s t$$

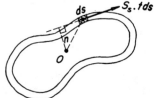

where A, the sum of all the little triangles of base ds and height n, is the total area of the plate (or, which is practically the same, the area within the outside perimeter of the section). This result, rewritten as

$$s_s = \frac{M_t}{2At} \tag{19}$$

is the first important equation for the single-cell thin-walled torsion member. For constant thickness t this stress is the

Fig. 23. Calculation of the torque transmitted by the shear stresses in a thin-walled tubular section by integrating the moment of a small force $s_s t \, ds$ about a center O. The final answer comes out independent of the choice of point O. It should; explain why.

same all around. We repeat that A is the area of the "plate," *i.e.*, the entire area enclosed by the thin-walled section, and it is *not* the cross-sectional area of the material.

The second equation, for the stiffness, is found by substituting Eq. (19) into Eq. (*a*) (page 26):

$$\theta_1 = \frac{M_t}{4GA^2} \oint \frac{ds}{t}$$

or:

$$C = \frac{M_t}{\theta_1} = \frac{4GA^2}{\int (ds/t)} \tag{20}$$

For the usual case of constant wall thickness this becomes

$$C = \frac{M_t}{\theta_1} = \frac{4GA^2 t}{L} \tag{20a}$$

where L is the peripheral length of the wall.

Equation (19) for the stress of course applies only where the "stress flow" or the fluid flow of Kelvin can take place without hindrance, *i.e.*, in smooth channels without abrupt curvature. If there are sharp corners, the general remarks on Fig. 12 (page 16) apply, and, in particular, for 90-deg reentrant corners the stress concentration factor of Eq. (18) must be applied to Eq. (19).

The practical consequences of Eqs. (19) and (20) sometimes are surprising. We shall discuss two examples. First consider a circular thin-walled tube. Let this tube then be flattened out first into an elliptic tube and finally into a double flat plate. What happens to the stress and to the torsional stiffness as a result of the flattening? We see that in Eqs. (19) and (20a) the quantities t and L remain unchanged, but the area A is diminished from a maximum for the circle to zero for the double flat. Hence the double flat cannot transmit any torque to speak of for a given maximum stress. Or, saying it differently, for a given torque to be transmitted, the shear stress becomes very large in the double flat. From Eq. (20a) we see that the double flat tube will twist through a large angle for a small torque: it has practically no stiffness. Since we know that among all closed curves of given peripheral length L the circle is the one enclosing the maximum area A, we conclude that of all tubes of given peripheral length a circular tube is the stiffest in torsion and will have the smallest stress for a given torque.

As a second example consider a square, thin-walled box section (Fig. 24a), and investigate what happens if it is replaced by another one of the same over-all size, but with two internal crimps in it (Fig. 24b). The answer is simple. In Eqs. (19) and (20a) the quantities A and t are the same for both sections; they differ only in the peripheral length L, which is $4a$ in the first and $16a/3$ in the second section, or 33 per cent greater. Hence we see from Eq. (19) that the basic stress for a given torque is the same in both cases,

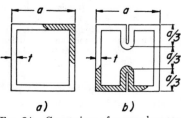

a)   b)

Fig. 24. Comparison of square box sections without and with crimps. In spite of the greater weight of the section (b) it has the same torsional shear stress as (a) for the same torque. Section (a) is stiffer torsionally than section (b) by a factor $\frac{4}{3}$, which is the ratio of the two L values [Eq. (20a)].

while from Eq. (20a) we see that the crimped section is 33 per cent more flexible than the square box. With a view to stress concentration the crimped section is worse than the square one, because it contains at the bottom of the crimps a 360-deg reentrant angle, which is about as bad a concentration as can be imagined. If all fillets were made alike, the section of Fig. 24b would be expected to show a fatigue failure at the inside bottom of the crimp at a torque which could be taken without trouble by the box of Fig. 24a.

Multicellular Sections. Now we turn to the investigation of the torsion of thin-walled sections consisting of several cells. The membrane analogy will involve several of the weightless stiff plates, which all have to be blown up to such heights as they will naturally take by the air pressure p. The individual plates are to be subjected to pure couples only to make them horizontal. The heights of the n plates are unknown, and we shall call them h_1, h_2, . . . , h_n. For the outside walls the slopes will be h/t, while for inside walls the membrane slopes will be $\Delta h/t$, where Δh is the difference in height of the two adjoining plates. Then we can write one equation of vertical equilibrium for each plate,

$$pA_n = T \oint \frac{\Delta h}{t} \, ds$$

where A_n is the area of the nth plate, the integral extends all around that plate, and Δh is the height of the plate in question less the height of the neighboring plate.

Now there are n such equations, linear in the n unknowns $h_1 \ldots h_n$, so that we can solve them for the heights. Once these heights are known, we translate the membrane problem to the torsion problem by setting $\Delta h/t = $ slope $\rightarrow s_s$ and by setting $p/T \rightarrow 2G\theta_1$. Finally the torque is twice the volume under the membrane, or

$$M_t = 2 \sum_n A_n h_n$$

For more than two cells this becomes rather complicated, but not basically difficult. Many papers have been published lately giving all sorts of short-cut methods of solution, and these papers are recommended to readers who expect to spend a good portion of their life solving multicell torsion problems. Most of us, however, do this but seldom and then it takes less time to do it as indicated above than to learn and understand the short-cut procedures.

We shall now illustrate the method by *an example*, and in order to bring out the principles more clearly we choose a case (Fig. 25) where the wall thickness is not the same everywhere. For the dimensions indicated we ask for the torque transmitted if the maximum shear stress $s_s = 5{,}000$ lb/sq in., disregarding stress concentrations in corners, and further we ask for the angle of twist per unit length θ_1 under that torque.

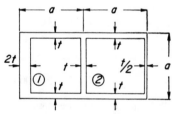

FIG. 25. Two-celled box beam of steel with $a = 6$ in., $t = \frac{1}{2}$ in., having wall thicknesses of $\frac{1}{2}$, 1, and $\frac{1}{4}$ in.

Numbering the cells 1 and 2 with heights h_1 and h_2, we write the vertical equilibrium equations of the plates 1 and 2 as follows:

$$pa^2 = Ta\left(\frac{h_1}{2t} + \frac{h_1}{t} + \frac{h_1 - h_2}{t} + \frac{h_1}{t}\right)$$

$$pa^2 = Ta\left(\frac{h_2 - h_1}{t} + \frac{h_2}{t} + \frac{h_2}{t/2} + \frac{h_2}{t}\right)$$

In the above equations we have started with the vertical leg at the left of each cell and then proceeded around the cell clockwise. These equations work out to

$$\frac{pat}{T} = 3\frac{1}{2} h_1 - h_2$$

$$\frac{pat}{T} = 5h_2 - h_1$$

Solving for the heights,

$$h_1 = \frac{4}{11} \frac{pat}{T} \qquad h_2 = \frac{3}{11} \frac{pat}{T}$$

The maximum slope is seen to occur in the thin leg $t/2$, and it is $h_2/(t/2) = 6pa/11T$. The volume under the membrane and plate is $a^2(h_1 + h_2) = 7pa^3t/11T$.

Now we translate from the membrane to torsion by the usual three-worded dictionary:

$$\frac{p}{T} \to 2G\theta_1 \qquad \text{slope} \to s_s \qquad 2\text{ vol} \to M_t$$

and we find

$$(s_s)_{\max} = 12\frac{6}{11} aG\theta_1$$

$$M_t = 28\frac{6}{11} a^3 t G\theta_1$$

Substituting numbers $(s_s)_{\max} = 5,000$ lb/sq in , $G = 12 \times 10^6$ lb/sq in., $a = 6$ in., $t = \frac{1}{2}$ in., we find

$$\theta_1 = 6.35 \times 10^{-5} \text{ radian/in.} = 0.044°/\text{ft}$$

$$M_t = 210,000 \text{ in.-lb}$$

This answers our question.

Some practical remarks are in order. Suppose in the above example the legs all have the same thickness t; then we can conclude from symmetry that the two plates will blow up to the same height and the central leg will have zero slope in its membrane and hence zero stress. We thus recognize that internal cross connections that subdivide a box section in a symmetrical manner will be without stress and will not affect the stiffness of the construction. If the internal connections are not too far from the center, their stress is small and they are all but useless. The example of Fig. 25 would not have been weakened materially by omission of the central leg. In many constructions such central stays are put in for other reasons, because the structure is subjected to other loads than the torsion.

The analysis of the example of Fig. 25 could have been carried out also by means of Kelvin's flow analogy. The fluid chases around each loop in the same direction; in the center leg the streams around the two loops are in opposition; hence the velocity in the central leg (and with it the torsional stress) is small.

6. Warping of the Cross Sections. Consider in Fig. 26a a thin-walled cylindrical tube. This is the simple case of Fig. 2a, where the shear stress distribution is linear radially and where plane cross sections remain plane. The membrane consists practically entirely of the stiff weightless plate lifted to a certain height *h* above ground level. Looking at the stress distribution in a section parallel to the longitudinal axis, we see that downward shear stresses must exist, as shown in the figure, because a shear stress on the top annular section is associated with an equal one in a perpendicular plane.

Now let us attempt to cut a slit in the tube of Fig. 26a while keeping the twisting torque on. By cutting we remove the downward shear stress on the face shown, and hence that face will spring up and its mating surface will spring down as shown in Fig. 26b. Thus considerable warping of the normal cross section of a slit tube takes place. From the shapes of the two membranes shown also in the figure, we conclude that for the same air pressure *p* its volume for the non-slit tube is far greater than that for the slit one. Hence the stiffness of the non-slit tube is enormously greater than that of the slit one. The membrane of Fig. 26b differs from that of Fig. 26a in that the central plate of Fig. 26b has been pushed down to the bottom. We see that the warping function *w* in Fig. 26b is continuous over the cross

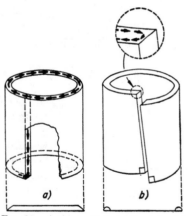

Fig. 26. A thin-walled circular tube (*a*) without and (*b*) with a longitudinal slit, with the corresponding shapes of membrane.

section, but that cross section is slitted. If we should try to apply the stresses that follow from the membrane of Fig. 26b to the tube of Fig. 26a, we should find that those stresses cause a discontinuity in the height *w* across the now non-existing slit. This obviously is impossible. Returning now to the unproved statement of page 25, we see that it is not sufficient to have a "continuous" *w* function, because a helical *w* surface like that of Fig. 26b is continuous analytically. That helix, properly extrapolated, is a multivalued function, and we can find ourselves at a certain *x*, *y* location on any of the z levels of the helical screw. Thus, in constructing a membrane for a cross section with a hole, we must demand that it leads to stresses and deformations so that if we start from a point in the material and proceed around the hole to the same point, we end up with the same value of w and not one screw pitch higher.

Mathematically this requirement can be written as

$$\oint dw = 0$$

stating that in proceeding around the boundary of a hole the increases and decreases of w must cancel out. The working out of this integral will give us the recipe of page 25 for fixing the proper height of the plate over the hole in the membrane.

The proof is as follows:

$$w = f(x, y)$$

Hence

$$dw = \frac{\partial w}{\partial x}\, dx + \frac{\partial w}{\partial y}\, dy$$

and, by substitution of Eqs. (7) (page 8), the integral is

$$0 = \oint dw = \oint \left[\left(-\frac{1}{G}\frac{\partial \Phi}{\partial y} - \theta_1 y \right) dx + \left(\frac{1}{G}\frac{\partial \Phi}{\partial x} + \theta_1 x \right) dy \right] = 0$$

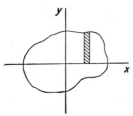

Of the four terms in this integral we first investigate the second one. Figure 27 shows an element $y\, dx$, and when we proceed counterclockwise around the curve we see that dx is negative, because x diminishes. Going entirely around the curve, we add up the various elemental areas and conclude that

$$\oint y\, dx = -A$$

where A is the area of the hole or plate.

Fig. 27. For the proof that $\oint y\, dx = -A$, when going around the curve in a counterclockwise direction.

The fourth term of the integral is treated in the same manner, now with horizontal strips instead of vertical ones, and we find

$$\oint x\, dy = +A$$

Substituting these results into the above condition,

$$\oint \left(\frac{\partial \Phi}{\partial y}\, dx - \frac{\partial \Phi}{\partial x}\, dy \right) = 2GA\theta_1$$

We intend to prove something about a membrane, and so far we have talked torsion only. Now we translate to the membrane of height z:

$$T \oint \left(\frac{\partial z}{\partial y} \, dx - \frac{\partial z}{\partial x} \, dy \right) = pA$$

The right-hand side is the upward force on the plate due to air pressure; we now have to prove that the left-hand side is the downward pull from the membrane forces, because then no extra vertical force is required on the plate. In the case of a rectangular membrane we see it right away. Take an element dx on the x side of the rectangular hole, dy being zero there. Then dz/dy is the slope perpendicular to that edge, and $T(\partial z/\partial y)$ is the downward pull per unit length. Integrating around, the first term comes in on two sides and the other term on the other two sides of the rectangle.

Now we prove it for a non-rectangular hole, with the help of Fig. 28, which shows an element of the boundary of the hole with points 1 and 2, while the point 3 lies inside the hole on the (extrapolated) membrane. Point 4 is on the normal to the boundary from point 3. We call

$$\overset{\frown}{1\,2} = ds \qquad \overset{\frown}{1\,3} = -dx \qquad \overset{\frown}{3\,2} = -\overset{\frown}{2\,3} = dy \qquad \overset{\frown}{3\,4} = dn$$

Let further dh be the height of the (extrapolated) membrane at point 3 above the common level of points 1, 2, and 4. Then we can write

$$dx = -ds \cos \alpha \qquad dy = ds \sin \alpha$$

$$dn = -dx \sin \alpha = ds \sin \alpha \cos \alpha$$

$$\frac{\partial z}{\partial y} = \frac{-dh}{ds \sin \alpha} \qquad \frac{\partial z}{\partial x} = \frac{dh}{-ds \cos \alpha}$$

$$\frac{\partial z}{\partial y} \, dx - \frac{\partial z}{\partial x} \, dy = dh \frac{\cos \alpha}{\sin x} + dh \frac{\sin \alpha}{\cos \alpha}$$

$$= \frac{dh}{\sin \alpha \cos \alpha} \frac{ds}{ds} = \frac{dh}{dn} \, ds = \frac{\partial z}{\partial n} \, ds$$

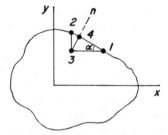

Fig. 28. To prove that
$$\frac{\partial z}{\partial y} \, dx - \frac{\partial z}{\partial x} \, dy = \frac{\partial z}{\partial n} \, ds$$

Hence the integral on the left-hand side is

$$T \oint \frac{\partial z}{\partial n} \, ds = \oint T_{\text{vert comp}} \, ds$$

which is the downward pull. Thus the proposition of page 25 is proved.

The case of the slit tube (Fig. 26b) is one of the few where the configuration of the warping function w can be visualized intuitively. For most other sections this is difficult to do. One might look at Eq. (9) for the warping and at Eq. (11) for the membrane and say that the warping function is represented by a membrane with $p = 0$, with equal air pressure on both sides. That is true and easy enough; the difficulty comes in the boundary condition. Whereas the membrane for the stress function can be visualized because it must have zero heights at the boundary, no such simple prescription exists for w. From Eqs. (7) (page 8), a boundary condition for w can be deduced (we shall not do it here); it states that the *slopes* of w at the boundary are proportional to the angle between the local tangent to the boundary and a line perpendicular to the radius to that point (which verifies that the w slope must be zero for a circular boundary and hence w must be zero over the entire section). This condition is so complicated that it is useless for visualization. A fluid-flow analogy exists for the w function, which is little better. Therefore, although Saint-Venant in his first analysis gave the w function great prominence, we do not now use it much any more.

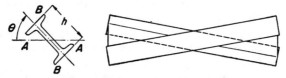

FIG. 29.   When twisting an I beam through a small angle, the flanges remain practically straight because of their large sidewise bending stiffness. The figure shows this; the cross section is the one of the left-hand end of the beam. It is seen that the points A have a longitudinal w displacement to the left, while the points B have a w toward the right.

We saw in Fig. 26 how a prevention of the warping of the ends can make a cross section much stiffer in torsion. This idea has been worked out for the case of some structural sections, particularly I beams, by Timoshenko (1905). The warping of a cross section of an I beam can be visualized by noticing that the flanges must remain straight (Fig. 29). Consequently one corner of the flange must come forward along the beam length, while the other corner must recede. Suppose now that this free warping of a cross section is prevented by building one end of the beam into a solid wall, or better still by the arrangement of Fig. 30a, where the bar is subjected to torques M_t at each end having the same sense of rotation, held in equilibrium by a torque $2M_t$ in the center. Then by symmetry the center section cannot warp, and this form of cantilever clamping is much more potent for the prevention of warping than any "solid wall."

Now if the bar of Fig. 30a should twist like the one of Fig. 29, with straight flanges, we should have the situation of Fig. 30b, where both the upper and the lower flange of the I section would suffer a discontinuity in slope, which of course is physically impossible. What really happens is that both flanges bend in their own (stiff) planes near the center (Fig.

30c) and become straight only at some distance from the center, where the cross sections can warp freely.

The bending of the flanges will involve bending moments and shear forces S in the flanges. Making a cut at distance x from the center (Fig. 30d) and applying M_t at the right-hand end, which is clockwise when seen end on from the right, this M_t is transmitted through the cut x in two ways:

a. By the usual twist stresses, distributed over the I section as in Fig. 12 (page 16)

b. By means of shear stresses having resultants S equal and opposite in the upper and lower flanges

so that

$$M_t = M_{\text{just torsion}} - Sh$$

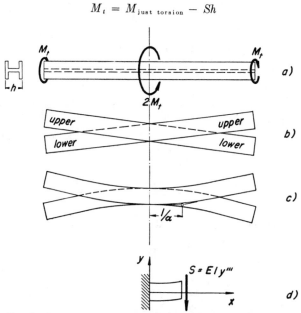

FIG. 30. Two back-to-back torsional cantilevers. The deformation (b) would occur if the cross sections could freely warp. This involves breaking the back of the flange in the center, which does not occur, so that the flanges must bend in their stiff plane (c).

where h is the height of the web. The minus sign for S holds, because we shall call S positive in the upper flange when it has the sense of Fig. 30d. For the first term at the right we may write $C\theta_1$ or rather $C(d\theta/dx) = C\theta'$, where C is the torsional stiffness of Eq. (12) (page 15). The shear force is $S = EIy'''$, where EI is of one flange and the reader should verify that the sign is correct with the conventions of Fig. 30d. But there is a relation between y of the upper flange and the angle of twist θ, because $\theta = y = 0$

at the center. The relation is simply $y = \theta(h/2)$. Therefore Timoshenko's differential equation for this case is

$$C\theta' - EI \frac{h^2}{2} \theta''' = M_t \tag{21}$$

This is a linear differential equation of order 2 in the variable θ' with a constant right-hand member. Its general solution is

$$\theta' = C_1 e^{\alpha x} + C_2 e^{-\alpha x} + \frac{M_t}{C}$$

where

$$\alpha = \sqrt{\frac{2C}{EIh^2}} \tag{22}$$

One boundary condition is that at $x = \infty$ the rate of twisting θ' must remain finite at least, so that the term $C_1 e^{+\alpha x}$ must vanish. Hence,

$$\theta' = C_2 e^{-\alpha x} + \frac{M_t}{C}$$

The next condition is that in the center, at $x = 0$, the slope $y' = 0$ and hence $\theta' = 0$, so that

$$\theta' = \frac{M_t}{C} (1 - e^{-\alpha x})$$

Integrating,

$$\theta = \frac{M_t}{C} \left(x + \frac{1}{\alpha} e^{-\alpha x} \right) + \text{const}$$

The constant is found by stating that $\theta = 0$ at $x = 0$, or

$$\theta = \frac{M_t}{C} \left[x + \frac{1}{\alpha} (e^{-\alpha x} - 1) \right] \tag{23}$$

and, in particular, for $x \rightarrow \infty$

$$\theta_{x \rightarrow \infty} = \frac{M_t}{C} \left(x - \frac{1}{\alpha} \right) \tag{23a}$$

Equation (23) gives the relation between the angle of twist and the distance from the center x and hence is the equation of the center line of a flange, Fig. 30c. Equation (23a) states that the torsional stiffness of a long cantilever I beam is equal to the torsional stiffness of a free beam of a length shorter than the cantilever by an amount $1/\alpha = \sqrt{EIh^2/2C}$. The significance of this can be seen graphically in Fig. 30c.

Now we investigate the stress picture. The bending moment in the flange is $EIy'' = EIh\theta''/2$. We find θ'' by differentiation: $\theta'' = M_t \alpha e^{-\alpha x}/C$, and the maximum value of this occurs at the center $x = 0$. Hence

$$M_{\text{bending max}} = \frac{EIh\alpha}{2C} M_t$$

and by substitution of Eq. (22)

$$M_{\text{bending max}} = \frac{1}{\alpha h} M_t \qquad (24)$$

The shear force $S = EIy''' = EIh\theta'''/2$. Differentiating θ'' and observing that the maximum value of θ''' also occurs at the center $x = 0$, we find

$$S_{\text{max}} = -\frac{M_t}{h}$$

Hence at the center $x = 0$ the entire twisting moment is transmitted by transverse shear forces in the upper and lower flanges, and nothing is transmitted there in the manner of Fig. 12.

We conclude by applying the theory to *a specific example*: the I section of Fig. 31. For one flange we have $EI = Eta^3/12$. For the torsional stiffness we have by Eq. (12)

$$C = G\frac{3at^3}{3} = Gat^3$$

Hence Eq. (22) leads to

$$\alpha = \frac{1}{a}\sqrt{\frac{2Gat^3}{Eta^3/12}} = \frac{t}{a^2}\sqrt{\frac{24G}{E}}$$

The length $1/\alpha$ by which the cantilever must be shortened to express the additional stiffness caused by the prevention of warping at the built-in end is, for steel,

$$\frac{1}{\alpha} = \frac{a^2}{a/12}\sqrt{\frac{30\frac{1}{12}}{24}} = 3.9a$$

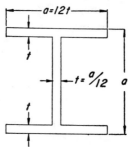

Fig. 31. Idealized I-beam section of equal base and height to which the results, Eqs. (21) to (24), are applied numerically.

By Eq. (24) the bending moment in the flange at the center is 3.9 times as large as the applied twisting torque M_t. The ratio of the stresses is

$$\frac{s_{\text{bending}}}{s_{s\text{ twist}}} = \frac{M_b/(ta^2/6)}{M_t/(3at^2/3)} = 3.9\frac{t}{a} \times 6 = 1.95$$

The bending stress occurs at the center, where the twist stress is zero, so that the two are not additive in any way. The bending stress, being tensile, at 1.95 times the twist shear stress is less dangerous than the twist stress. Thus in this typical numerical example we see that the stresses caused by the suppressed warping are inconsequential, and that the only significant effect is an apparent shortening of the cantilever by 3.9 section heights for purposes of torsional stiffness calculation.

7. Round Shafts of Variable Diameter. Most twisted shafts in actual practice are of circular cross section, but their diameter is usually not constant along the length, stepping from one diameter to another through a connecting fillet (Fig. 32). We have seen that in the torsion of a circular shaft of constant cross section two properties exist:

1. Plane normal cross sections remain plane.
2. Plane normal cross sections remain undistorted in their own plane.

These properties were deduced by a simple argument of symmetry. For non-round shafts of constant cross section along the length the symmetry reasoning fails, and neither property can be proved. We have seen on pages 2 to 10 that Saint-Venant found that property 1 is violated but that property 2 is retained for non-round shafts of constant section.

Now, for our new problem of a round shaft with a section variable along its length, again the symmetry reasoning breaks down. The solution that has been found to this problem shows that the situation is reversed with respect to the Saint-Venant problem: here property 1 is retained while property 2 is violated, according to the schedule below:

Property	Circular cylinder	Non-circular prism	Circular section of variable diameter
1. Plane normal sections remain plane	Yes	No	Yes
2. Normal sections remain undistorted in their own plane	Yes	Yes	No

Rather than prove this, we shall assume it and subsequently show that the assumption leads to a solution for the stresses and deformations which satisfies the conditions at the boundary and the conditions of equilibrium and continuity (which is called "compatibility" in this branch of science).

The shaft is shown in Fig. 32, and we choose for coordinates z, r, and θ, the longitudinal, radial, and angular (or tangential) locations of each point. In Saint-Venant's problem (page 4) we assumed that the displacements of an arbitrary point due to twist were tangential ($z\theta_1$) and longitudinal (w) only, while the radial displacement was zero. Here we assume that the radial as well as the longitudinal displacements of all points are zero and that the only displacement is tangential, called v. We see in Fig. 32 that $v/r = \Psi$ is an angle, which we might call the angle of twist at the point. Now, whereas in Saint-Venant's problem (Fig. 4, page 3) this angle of twist was $\theta_1 z$, independent of r, here we make no such assumption and leave Ψ a general function of r as well as of z. If Ψ varies with r, it means that a straight radius does not remain straight after twisting: the sections distort in their own plane.

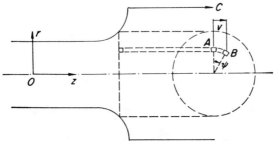

Fig. 32. Shaft of variable cross section in torsion. We assume that owing to twisting each particle displaces in a tangential direction only through distance v; we assume that the longitudinal and radial displacements are zero. The tangential displacement v is a function of z as well as of r. Point A is the unstressed location, which goes to B as a result of the torque.

The assumption of no longitudinal displacement (no w displacement in the z direction) means that all cross sections must warp exactly alike, and since the cross section at O or C (being in a cylindrical position far from the fillet) does not warp, all plane normal sections remain plane.

Now we shall *start the analysis*, which in all its essential steps is parallel to Saint-Venant's analysis of pages 2 to 10. The principal results to be obtained, Eqs. (25) to (32), correspond to Eqs. (3) to (10), so that to find Saint-Venant's corresponding formula we just subtract 22 from the equation number.

The *first step is to deduce the strains from the assumed displacements*. From $w = 0$ follows $\epsilon_z = 0$, and from $u = 0$ (in the radial direction) follows $\epsilon_r = 0$. From the fact that $v = f(r, z)$ is independent of θ, on account of rotational symmetry, follows $\epsilon_\theta = 0$. If in Fig. 32 we look at a small square element $dr\,dz$, we find that as a consequence of $u = w = 0$ this element remains square, so that $\gamma_{rz} = 0$. This leaves us with only two remaining strains: $\gamma_{r\theta}$ and $\gamma_{z\theta}$. To calculate the first of these, we look at an element $dr\,rd\theta$ in a normal cross section (Fig.

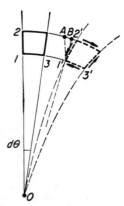

Fig. 33. An element $dr\,rd\theta$ in the untwisted state (full outline) and the twisted state (dashed outline). From this we prove that $\gamma_{r\theta} = (\partial v/\partial r) - (v/r)$, corresponding to a shear stress on face 21 directed toward O, which is in the negative r direction.

33). The distance $11'$ we have called v; then the distance $22'$ is $v + (\partial v/\partial r)\,dr$. From $1'$ we draw two lines: to A parallel to $O12$ and to B radially through

O. Then $2A = 11' = v$. By similarity of $\triangle O11'$ with $\triangle 1'AB$ we have

$$\frac{AB}{1'A} = \frac{11'}{O1} \quad \text{or} \quad \frac{AB}{dr} = \frac{v}{r}$$

Now

$$B2' = 22' - 2A - AB = \left(v + \frac{\partial v}{\partial r}\,dr\right) - v - \frac{v}{r}\,dr$$

$$B2' = \left(\frac{\partial v}{\partial r} - \frac{v}{r}\right)dr$$

Since $\angle B1'3'$ is 90 deg, the angle of shear of the element is

$$\frac{B2'}{B1'} = \frac{B2'}{dr} = \frac{\partial v}{\partial r} - \frac{v}{r}$$

From the figure we see that this angle of shear is associated with a shear stress pointing toward O on face $1'2'$ or 12. Since this is in the negative r direction and since we shall find it more convenient to have the positive shear stress point in the positive r direction, we reverse the sign and define

$$\gamma_{r\theta} = \frac{v}{r} - \frac{\partial v}{\partial r}$$

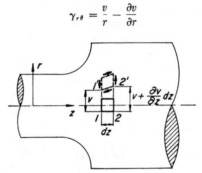

Fig. 34. The element $dz\,rd\theta$ is located at height r above the center line. The full outline is unstressed; the dashed outline is in the stressed state. The angle of shear is $\partial v/\partial z$, corresponding to a shear stress on face 12 directed to the left, which is in the negative z direction.

The other shear strain must be studied in another plane, Fig. 34, which should be self-explanatory. Again, for the same reason, we define $\gamma_{\theta z}$ with a negative sign, so that

$$\gamma_{\theta r} = \frac{v}{r} - \frac{\partial v}{\partial r}$$

$$\gamma_{\theta z} = -\frac{\partial v}{\partial z} \tag{25}$$

Next we apply *Hooke's law*. All stresses are zero, except $(s_s)_{r\theta}$ and $(s_s)_{z\theta}$, which, for short, we shall designate as s_{sr} and s_{sz}; they satisfy the equations

$$s_{sr} = G\left(\frac{v}{r} - \frac{\partial v}{\partial r}\right)$$

$$s_{sz} = -G\frac{\partial v}{\partial z}$$

(26)

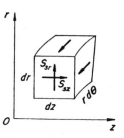

and they are directed in the positive r and z directions, respectively, when drawn on the $+r$, $+z$ half of a meridional section (Fig. 35 or 36).

Now we are ready to *derive the equilibrium equation* for the stresses, which are shown on an element $dr\,dz\,rd\theta$ in Fig. 35. From the rotational symmetry we understand that these stresses are functions of r and z only; they do

Fig. 35. An element of shaft with the shear stresses acting on it. From this the equilibrium equation (27) is derived.

not depend on the angle θ. On the block there are two forces in the r direction, on the fore and aft faces, and these forces are *exactly* equal and opposite, because the faces differ by $d\theta$ only, having the same r and z coordinates. Hence there is automatic equilibrium in the r direction. The same is true for the z direction, again with two equal and opposite forces on the fore and aft faces.

But in the θ direction, perpendicular to the paper, four forces are acting. Calling these positive when pointing into the paper, they are

On the bottom face: $+ s_{sr}\,dz\,rd\theta$

On the top face: $-\left[\text{same} + \dfrac{\partial}{\partial r}\,(\text{same})\,dr \right]$

On the left face: $+ s_{sz}\,dr\,rd\theta$

On the right face: $-\left[\text{same} + \dfrac{\partial}{\partial z}\,(\text{same})\,dz \right]$

Moreover, the up and down forces on the fore and aft faces, being $s_{sr}\,dz\,dr$, are equal in magnitude and almost opposite in direction, but not quite. They include the angle $d\theta$ between them, and hence their resultant is $d\theta$ times the forces, directed out of the paper, which is a negative force:

$$-s_{sr}\,dz\,dr\,d\theta$$

The sum of all these five forces in the $+\theta$ direction set equal to zero gives the equilibrium equation

$$r\frac{\partial s_{sr}}{\partial r} + r\frac{\partial s_{sz}}{\partial z} + 2s_{sr} = 0$$

which can also be written as

$$\frac{\partial}{\partial r} (r^2 s_{sr}) + \frac{\partial}{\partial z} (r^2 s_{sz}) = 0 \tag{27}$$

This is an equation in the two unknowns s_{sr} and s_{sz}, and to simplify the problem we *assume a single stress function* $\Phi(r, z)$ and derive the stresses from that new stress function by

$$r^2 s_{sz} = \frac{\partial \Phi}{\partial r}$$

$$\tag{28}$$

$$r^2 s_{sr} = -\frac{\partial \Phi}{\partial z}$$

By this definition we automatically satisfy Eq. (27), if only Φ is continuous, *i.e.*, if only $\partial^2 \Phi / \partial r\, \partial z = \partial^2 \Phi / \partial z\, \partial r$.

We can now visualize the stress function $\Phi(rz)$ as a surface erected perpendicularly on the meridional rz base of Fig. 32. Then Eq. (28) tells us that $r^2 s_{sz}$ is the slope of this surface in the r direction and $r^2 s_{sr}$ is the slope of the surface in the z direction. These are two special cases of the more general property, that if the two shear stress components s_{sr} and s_{sz} (lying in the rz plane of Fig. 32) are resolved along another pair of perpendicular directions through the same point, then the shear stress so found in any direction multiplied by the local value of r^2 equals the slope of the Φ surface in the perpendicular direction. The sign is so that when proceeding in the direction of the total shear stress the high bank is on the left hand. The proof of this is given on page 8, where xy is used instead of rz. The factor r^2 with the stress here is of no significance, because at each point r^2 is a constant.

Thus, in particular we recognize that when proceeding along the direction of the resultant stress, Φ must be constant, because the shear stress perpendicular to the resultant is zero and is equal to the slope of the surface in the first direction.

Thus the lines $\Phi =$ constant follow the stress direction. The boundary condition is that the shear stress shall be tangent to the boundary. Hence the boundary is a line $\Phi =$ constant. Along the center line ($r = 0$) the stress s_{sr} is necessarily zero from symmetry. Hence the center line also is a line $\Phi =$ constant. The absolute level of Φ has no meaning, because the stresses are expressed as slopes only. Thus we are free to choose the $\Phi = 0$ level anywhere we like, and we find it convenient to put $\Phi = 0$ at the center line. Then the lines $\Phi =$ constant show a stream of stress running to the right in the upper half of Fig. 36a and to the left in the lower half.

Following Saint-Venant's procedure (page 8) we now substitute Eqs.

(28) into Eqs. (26), but before doing this we rewrite (26) in terms of the "angle of twist" $\Psi = v/r$ rather than in terms of v. Since $v = \Psi r$, we have $\partial v/\partial r = \Psi + r(\partial\Psi/\partial r)$ and $\partial v/\partial z = r(\partial\Psi/\partial z)$. With this Eqs. (26) become

$$s_{sr} = -Gr\frac{\partial\Psi}{\partial r}$$

$$s_{sz} = -Gr\frac{\partial\Psi}{\partial z}$$

(26a)

Substituting (28) into this,

$$\frac{\partial\Phi}{\partial z} = Gr^3\frac{\partial\Psi}{\partial r}$$

$$\frac{\partial\Phi}{\partial r} = -Gr^3\frac{\partial\Psi}{\partial z}$$

(29)

On this set of equations we operate in two ways, eliminating first Ψ from between them, then Φ. Both operations are based on the fact that $\partial^2/\partial r\,\partial z = \partial^2/\partial z\,\partial r$ for Φ as well as for Ψ, because both functions must be continuous for physical reasons.

First then eliminate Ψ by dividing both equations of (29) by Gr^3, then differentiating the first one with respect to z, the second one with respect to r, and adding the two together:

$$\frac{\partial}{\partial z}\left(\frac{1}{r^3}\frac{\partial\Phi}{\partial z}\right) + \frac{\partial}{\partial r}\left(\frac{1}{r^3}\frac{\partial\Phi}{\partial r}\right) = 0$$

(30)

Then we differentiate the first of Eqs. (29) with respect to r, the second one with respect to z, and subtract, thus eliminating Φ:

$$\frac{\partial}{\partial r}\left(r^3\frac{\partial\Psi}{\partial r}\right) + \frac{\partial}{\partial z}\left(r^3\frac{\partial\Psi}{\partial z}\right) = 0$$

(31)

Finally we *calculate the torque transmitted* by a portion of the shaft around the center line up to a certain $\Phi = $ constant line, not necessarily the outer boundary. Making a normal section r, θ with $z = $ constant, the only stresses appearing in that circular section are the s_{sz} stresses, and they are directed tangentially. The total torque is calculated as the integral of the torque contributions by thin rings of width dr:

$$(M_t)_{\text{up to }\Phi} = \int_{r=0}^{r=r} s_{sz}2\pi r\,dr\,r$$

$$= [\text{by (Eq. 28)}]\,2\pi\int_0^r\frac{\partial\Phi}{\partial r}\,dr = 2\pi\int d\Phi = 2\pi(\Phi_{r=r} - \Phi_{r=0})$$

But we have agreed to let $\Phi = 0$ at the center line $r = 0$, so that

$$(M_t)_{\text{up to }r} = 2\pi\Phi_r$$

(32)

and particularly

$$(M_t)_{total} = 2\pi\Phi_{boundary} \tag{32a}$$

Now we are ready to sketch the picture Fig. 36a for a shaft stepping from a radius r to a radius $2r$ with a fillet radius $\frac{3}{4}r$. The Φ lines are spaced one unit apart; $\Phi = 0$ at the center line as agreed, and $\Phi = 5$ at the upper boundary. By Eq. (32) equal increments in Φ mean equal

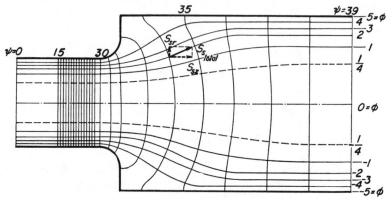

FIG. 36a. A shaft with its equimomental tube, spaced at equal Φ intervals, and its equiangular surfaces, spaced at equal Ψ intervals. These two networks are mutually perpendicular and obey the differential equations (30) and (31). The resultant shear stress is directed tangent to the Φ curves.

torques. Therefore by the Φ surfaces of revolution shown in Fig. 36a the shaft is cut up into tubes, which for equal increments in Φ are called the *equimomental tubes.* Each tube here carries one-fifth of the total torque; the center core has to be very thick in comparison with the outermost tube to do this. The figure is drawn to scale in this respect, and the reader is advised to check this detail numerically. The equimomental tubes are pure cylinders in the left and right positions; in between they are faired in by the eye of the draftsman; mathematically of course they have to obey Eq. (30). Now we proceed to sketch in $\Psi = $ constant lines. They form surfaces of revolution, perpendicular to the center line of the shaft at right and left and more complicated in the fillet region. On these surfaces the angle of twist is constant, and for better understanding we draw these *equiangular surfaces* at equal Ψ increments. Since the $2r$ shaft is 16 times as stiff as the r shaft, these surfaces must be spaced 16 times farther apart at the right than at the left. At right and left the two sets of curves obviously are everywhere perpendicular to each other; this is also the case in the fillet region as we shall prove presently. From the fact that *the equiangular curves and the equimomental curves form a mutually perpendicular network* we can sketch in the curves by draftsman's eye. Mathematically, of course, the Ψ lines have to obey Eq. (31).

From the fact that the equiangular Ψ surfaces are not flat we see that plane normal cross sections of the bar distort in their own plane. For if we draw such a normal cross section in Fig. 36a, it crosses several $\Psi =$ constant lines, so that for various radial distances in the section Ψ has different values, which means that straight radii in the section become curved.

We still have to prove that the Φ and Ψ lines are mutually perpendicular. In Fig. 36b two such lines have been drawn purposely non-perpendicular. Along the line $\Phi =$ constant we have

$$d\Phi = 0 = \frac{\partial \Phi}{\partial r}\, dr_1 + \frac{\partial \Phi}{\partial z}\, dz_1 = 0$$

In the same manner along the $\Psi =$ constant line,

$$d\Psi = 0 = \frac{\partial \Psi}{\partial r}\, dr_2 + \frac{\partial \Psi}{\partial z}\, (-dz_2) = 0$$

Rewritten,

$$\frac{dr_1}{dz_1} = - \frac{\partial \Phi / \partial z}{\partial \Phi / \partial r} \quad \text{and} \quad \frac{dz_2}{dr_2} = \frac{\partial \Psi / \partial r}{\partial \Psi / \partial z}$$

But, by Eqs. (29) the right-hand members of these two expressions are the same, so that

$$\frac{dr_1}{dz_1} = \sin \alpha = \frac{dz_2}{dr_2} = \sin \beta$$

Hence $\alpha = \beta$ in Fig. 36b, which means that the Φ and Ψ lines are perpendicular.

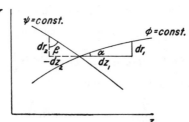

Fig. 36b. To prove that the Φ lines are perpendicular to the Ψ lines in Fig. 36a.

8. Jacobsen's Electrical Analogy.

Just as Saint-Venant's pictures (Fig. 14) suggested to Lord Kelvin the idea of a circulating flow, the diagram, Fig. 36a, started Jacobsen thinking (in 1924) of a flow from left to right in a channel. It might be that the equimomental Φ lines would be the streamlines and the equiangular Ψ lines the equipotential lines of some flow. (We notice that the letters Φ and Ψ as used here in an elastic problem are just the reverse of the usual hydrodynamic notation of Ψ for the stream function and Φ for the potential function.) However, the analogy does not work out correctly for the usual ideal flow motion, because among other things we remember that in the ideal fluid the Φ, Ψ network consists of little squares, whereas Fig. 36a shows rectangles of various side ratios. But Jacobsen reasoned that in the left and right portions of Fig. 36a one-fifth of the total half stream passes between each two adjacent Φ lines, so that if we want to keep equal velocities all across the shaft our hydrodynamic tank has to be made deeper near the outside of the shaft and very shallow at the center. This suggested trying an analogy based on ideal fluid flow in a tank of variable depth $h = f(r, z)$ or maybe $h = f(r$ alone). We shall derive the non-compressibility condition for such a flow, keeping the notations r, z of Fig. 36a, and calling the velocity in the z direction u and in the r direction v. The third velocity component w in the h direction we make zero simply by stating that our analysis is restricted to tanks so shallow that $h \ll r$ or z, so that the flow is considered two-dimensional.

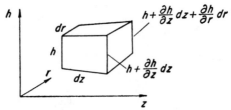

FIG. 37. To derive the equation of non-compressibility of fluid flow in a tank of variable depth h, resulting in Eq. (33).

In Fig. 37 the volume per second flowing in at left is $uh\,dr$ and out at right is $uh\,dr + \dfrac{\partial}{\partial z}(uh\,dr)\,dz$. The excess volume per second out is $dr\,dz$ $\dfrac{\partial}{\partial z}(uh)$. Similarly for the fore and aft faces, $dr\,dz\,\dfrac{\partial}{\partial r}(vh)$. The equation of non-compressibility of the fluid thus is

$$\frac{\partial}{\partial z}(uh) + \frac{\partial}{\partial r}(vh) = 0$$

If we insist in interpreting the Ψ lines of Fig. 36a as equipotential lines for this flow, we write the usual hydrodynamic equations,

$$u = \frac{\partial \Psi}{\partial z} \qquad v = \frac{\partial \Psi}{\partial r}$$

in which the reader should not be confused by the fact that in hydro-dynamics we usually write Φ, x, and y instead of the Ψ, z, and r used here. Substituting this into the non-compressibility equation,

$$\frac{\partial}{\partial z}\left(h\,\frac{\partial \Psi}{\partial z}\right) + \frac{\partial}{\partial r}\left(h\,\frac{\partial \Psi}{\partial r}\right) = 0 \tag{33}$$

This equation of the ideal fluid flow in a tank of variable shallow depth h coincides with Eq. (31) of the equiangular curves in a twisted round stepped shaft only if

$$h = Cr^3 \tag{34}$$

Thus we must construct our tank accordingly: deep toward the outside edges, very shallow near the center and with zero depth in the center line. The most convenient ideal fluid available for the purpose of actual testing

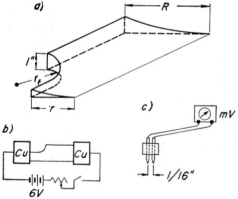

FIG. 38. Jacobsen's hollow ground razor-blade apparatus for the electrical analogy of the torsion of a circular stepped shaft.

is electricity. Jacobsen's experimental apparatus (Fig. 38) consisted of a steel piece of about 12 by 6 by 1 in., which was cut out in the machine shop to a cubic parabola $h = Cr^3$, the thick edge being about 1 in. Out of this block a piece was removed with the proper fillet radius as shown. The block is brazed at the ends to substantial copper blocks and a 6-volt battery is short-circuited through it, giving considerable current. On the flat back of the block a square coordinate network has been ruled. The field of voltage is explored on this back by means of a two-needled device wired to a millivoltmeter. By using the device as a compass, turning one point about the other, the angular position of zero voltmeter indication can be accurately found, and thus the lines of constant voltage (the Ψ lines of Fig. 36a) can be plotted. By measuring the voltage drop at that same point in a 90-deg direction, *i.e.*, the direction of maximum flow, the local current density is measured. The shear stress is proportional to this current multiplied by r^3.

Since at the dangerous point of the fillet the value of r^3 does not differ much from r^3 at the periphery of the small shaft the stress-concentration factor at the fillet can be visualized by noting the width of channel at the fillet (Fig. 36a) and comparing it with the width of the same channel elsewhere. The stress (for the same r^3) is inversely proportional to the width of channel. In Fig. 36a the fillet radius r_f, being 75 per cent of r, is extremely generous: there is very little stress concentration; for a sharp corner, however, the lines will crowd together at that corner, and the concentration is high.

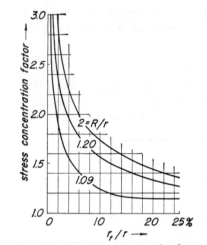

Fig. 39. The stress concentration factor of a twisted shaft stepped from a diameter $2R$ down to $2r$ through a fillet radius r_f. This is the factor whereby the torsional stress in the small shaft has to be multiplied to obtain the shear stress in the danger point of the fillet. From experiments by Jacobsen with the apparatus of Fig. 38.

The first test to be carried out with the apparatus of Fig. 38 is the one in which only a small amount is cut out of the plate (r nearly equal to R). For subsequent tests more and more material is cut away, so that we end up with a small r and a small fillet radius r_f. The results of a series of such experiments are shown in Fig. 39. From it we conclude that if the fillet radius r_f is made equal or better than ¼ of the small shaft radius the stress-concentration factor is about 1.35 or better, which is low. Therefore more generous fillets than ¼ are not practically justifiable. However, if the fillet corner is sharp, the stress-concentration factor becomes enormous. Thus the useful concluding moral of this chapter is again:

Round Your Corners!

Problems 1 to 32.

CHAPTER II

ROTATING DISKS

9. Flat Disks. The problem of the stresses and deformations in disks spinning at high speed is of vital importance in the design of steam and gas turbines, as well as many other pieces of apparatus, from gyroscopes to vacuum cleaners. Quite often the disks are not flat, being usually thicker near the hub than near the periphery, but flat disks *are* being used. The theory of flat disks, of course, is simpler than that for disks of variable thickness, so that it is always discussed first. The problem is very closely related to Lamé's problem of non-rotating flat disks under internal or external radial pressure, which is often treated in more elementary texts.

Figure 40 shows an element $dr\,rd\theta$ cut out of the disk which is spinning with angular speed ω in its own plane. This is a problem in dynamics which is reduced to one in statics by d'Alembert's theorem; in this case by the simple application of a centrifugal force. The element in Fig. 40 is supposed to be of unit thickness perpendicular to the disk. This saves us some writing, because if we should call the thickness t, every force would be proportional to t and the letter would cancel out of all equations. Physically this means, of course, that a 1-in.-thick disk acts exactly like a 2-in.-thick one, and a 2-in. solid disk is in the same

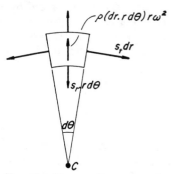

Fig. 40. Forces acting on an element of unit thickness and area $dr\,rd\theta$ in a flat spinning disk.

position as two 1-in. disks side by side, because no stresses are transmitted across the middle surface of the 2-in. disk. The centrifugal force then is $\omega^2 r\,dm = \omega^2 r\rho\,d\,\text{vol} = \omega^2 r\rho\,dr\,rd\theta$, where ρ is the density, which for steel is 0.28 lb/cu in./386 in./sec^2 = 0.00072 lb sec^2 in.$^{-4}$

Of the six possible stress components only two exist: the tangential stress s_t and the radial stress s_r. The stress perpendicular to the disk s_{long} and the three possible components of shear stress are all zero by reason of symmetry. The two tangential forces on the element of Fig. 40 thus are $s_t\,dr$; they are exactly equal in magnitude because of rotational

49

symmetry, but they do not have the same direction, including the angle $d\theta$ between them. The radial force on the face $r\,d\theta$ is $s_r\,r\,d\theta$. On the opposite face $r + dr$ the force differs from this for two reasons: (1) the stress is probably different, and (2) the area is larger. Now we write that the sum of the radially outward components of all these forces is zero:

$$\omega^2 \rho r^2\,dr\,d\theta + \left[s_r\,r\,d\theta + \frac{d}{dr}\,(s_r\,r\,d\theta)\,dr \right] - s_r\,r\,d\theta - (s_t\,dr)\,d\theta = 0$$

The last term is the resultant (radially inward) of the two tangential forces. The symbol d/dr is not written $\partial/\partial r$, because all stresses are dependent on r only: they do not vary with θ or with the distance perpendicular to the disk. Cleaning up, this *equilibrium equation* gives

$$\frac{d}{dr}\,(rs_r) - s_t + \rho\omega^2 r^2 = 0 \qquad (35)$$

Now we turn to the displacements and deformations. Owing to the rotation any point in the disk will move elastically outward in the r direction only, and it will not move tangentially or longitudinally. Thus the displacements are described by a single function $u(r)$. It is clear that at the center of the disk u must be zero and that u will grow with r, being of the order of $1/1{,}000$ part of r at the most. The strains ϵ_r radially and ϵ_t tangentially are found from u by

$$\epsilon_r = \frac{du}{dr}$$

$$\epsilon_t = \frac{u}{r}$$

The reader should derive these equations for himself if he does not know them already. The first one is fairly obvious, and the second one refers to the feelings of a middle-aged gentleman who lets out one notch of his belt after his daily good dinner.

Next we apply Hooke's law to the strain expressions just found:

$$\frac{du}{dr} = \frac{1}{E}\,(s_r - \mu s_t)$$
$$\frac{u}{r} = \frac{1}{E}\,(s_t - \mu s_r) \qquad (36)$$

Now the three equations (35) and (36) contain the three unknowns s_r, s_t, and u. These equations with the boundary conditions are sufficient to solve the problem completely. We first eliminate two of the variables; it does not matter which two. Since the boundary conditions usually are expressed in terms of the radial stress s_r, we retain it and eliminate s_t

and u. We start by differentiating the second of Eqs. (36) and then substitute the first of (36) as well as the second of (36) into the result, to get rid of u. This leads to

$$s_t' - \mu s_r' + \frac{1+\mu}{r}(s_t - s_r) = 0 \qquad (37)$$

Then we solve Eq. (35) for s_t, find s_t' by differentiating, and substitute the values so found into Eq. (37). We then find an equation in which the combinations $(rs_r)'$ and $(rs_r)''$ appear, as well as s_r' separately. We bring everything into the combination (rs_r) and its derivatives by noting that

$$(rs_r)' = s_r + rs_r'$$

so that

$$s_r' = \frac{1}{r}[(rs_r)' - s_r]$$

The result of these operations is

$$r^2(rs_r)'' + r(rs_r)' - (rs_r) + (3+\mu)\rho\omega^2 r^3 = 0 \qquad (38)$$

This is a differential equation in the variable (rs_r) as a function of r. The equation is linear, but the coefficients are not constant: they are such powers of the independent variable r as correspond to the order of the derivative. The solution to this type of equation is a power of the variable,

$$(rs_r) = r^n$$

where n is an as yet unknown exponent.

Assuming this and entering with it into Eq. (38) where the "right-hand member," i.e., the last term, is made zero for the time being, we find

$$[n(n-1) + n - 1]r^n = 0$$

or $n^2 = 1$ with $n = \pm 1$.

Thus the general solution of the "reduced" equation is

$$(rs_r) = C_1 r + \frac{C_2}{r}$$

The "particular" solution is assumed to be of the form Ar^3. Substituting this into Eq. (38) and solving for A gives the particular solution, which is to be added to the previous result. Thus

$$rs_r = C_1 r + \frac{C_2}{r} - \frac{3+\mu}{8}\rho\omega^2 r^3$$

is the general solution of Eq. (38), subject to two integration constants, to be determined from the boundary conditions. From Eq. (35) we can write s_t in terms of the above expression differentiated. Then with s_r and

s_t written out, we can write u with the last of Eqs. (36). The result is

$$s_r = C_1 + \frac{C_2}{r^2} - \frac{3 + \mu}{8} \rho\omega^2 r^2$$

$$s_t = C_1 - \frac{C_2}{r^2} - \frac{1 + 3\mu}{8} \rho\omega^2 r^2 \qquad (39)$$

$$u = \frac{r}{E}\left[(1 - \mu)C_1 - (1 + \mu)\frac{C_2}{r^2} - \frac{1 - \mu^2}{8}\rho\omega^2 r^2\right]$$

If the disk does not contain a central hole, *i.e.*, if the point $r = 0$ is actually a part of the material of the disk, then Eqs. (39) state that both stresses become infinite at the center if the constant C_2 exists. Physically the stresses cannot be infinite, and hence for a solid disk $C_2 = 0$. The other constant is found from the stress or load applied to the outer boundary r_0. This load sometimes is the centrifugal loading of turbine blades; in other cases the solid disk under consideration is the shaft inside another disk; then the load is a shrink pressure. We shall write the equations for the latter case. Hence we substitute into the first of Eqs. (39)

$$r = r_0 \qquad s_r = -p_0$$

and calculate

$$C_1 = \frac{3 + \mu}{8}\rho\omega^2 r_0^2 - p_0$$

With this we have the final *result for a solid disk (no central hole) with an external pressure p_0 on the periphery at radius r_0*:

$$s_r = -p_0 + \frac{3 + \mu}{8}\rho\omega^2(r_0^2 - r^2)$$

$$s_t = -p_0 + \frac{3 + \mu}{8}\rho\omega^2\left(r_0^2 - \frac{1 + 3\mu}{3 + \mu}r^2\right) \qquad (40)$$

$$u = -p_0 r\frac{1 - \mu}{E} + \frac{1 - \mu}{8E}\rho\omega^2 r[(3 + \mu)r_0^2 - (1 + \mu)r^2]$$

An obvious but nonetheless important remark on these equations is that they consist of the sum of two terms, one proportional to p_0 and another one proportional to $\rho\omega^2$. Thus we see that the stresses due to the external pressure p_0 are independent of the centrifugal stresses. When the disk rotates and has external pressure (or tension) at the same time, the total stress is the sum of the two constituent cases. In the more complicated formulae that will follow, for disks with central holes, we shall remember that fact and shall present the results separately for each effect, thus making the formulae less cumbersome [Eqs. (41) to (43)].

The centrifugal stresses (as distinguished from the p_0 stresses) are seen in Eqs. (40) to be largest for $r = 0$, that is, at the center of the disk, and moreover $s_t = s_r$ at that point ("two-dimensional hydrostatic tension"). The stress is

$$s_{\text{center}} = \frac{3 + \mu}{8} \rho(\omega r_0)^2 \quad \text{or} \quad s_{\text{center}} = \frac{3 + \mu}{8} \rho V_0^2$$

where V_0 is the peripheral speed of the disk. For *steel* this becomes

$$s = 3V_0^2 \times 10^{-4}$$

The reader should check this figure, and he should also verify that when we allow a stress at the center $s = 30,000$ lb/sq in. in a 3,600-rpm flat turbine disk and ask for the allowable diameter, the answer is $D = 52$ in.

From Eqs. (40) the reader should deduce that the stress distribution diagrams, Fig. (41), are parabolas.

The p_0 part of the stress, as given by Eqs. (40), is extremely simple. We see that in a non-rotating disk, subjected to an external pressure p_0 at the periphery, the stress in the entire disk is a constant two-dimensional hydrostatic compression of magnitude p_0. This, of course, is a known result which can be found in the first chapter of every elementary text on hydrostatics.

Now we are ready to tackle the more general case of a disk r_0 with a central hole of radius r_i, the subscripts i and o indicating "inner" and "out-

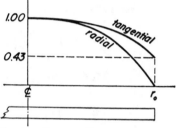

Fig. 41. Stress distribution diagram for a solid (non-holed) flat disk r_0 rotating at speed ω without radial stress at its rim ($p_0 = 0$). The ordinates are $s/(3 + \mu)$ $\rho\omega^2 r_0^2/8$. The curves are parabolas determined by the second terms of Eqs. (40), and both stresses are tensile. An outside radial load causes a "hydrostatic stress" in the disk which has to be superposed on the stress shown in this figure.

er." Instead of determining the constants C_1 and C_2 in Eqs. (39) for the complete case of a rotating disk with external pressures p_i and p_0 on the inner and outer boundaries, we remember the remark made right after Eqs. (40) and deduce the formulae for the three cases separately. First then we take an inner pressure p_i only on the non-rotating disk or

$$s_r = -p_i \text{ for } r = r_i \qquad s_r = 0 \text{ for } r = r_0 \qquad \omega^2 = 0$$

Substituting this into the first of Eqs. (39) and solving for the constants, we find

$$C_1 = \frac{p_i r_i^2}{r_0^2 - r_i^2} \qquad C_2 = -\frac{p_i r_0^2 r_i^2}{r_0^2 - r_i^2}$$

Substituting these values into Eqs. (39) gives *the result for a non-rotating flat disk r_0 with a hole r_i, subject only to an internal pressure p_i:*

$$s_r = p_i \frac{r_i^2}{r_0^2 - r_i^2} \left(1 - \frac{r_0^2}{r^2}\right)$$

$$s_t = p_i \frac{r_i^2}{r_0^2 - r_i^2} \left(1 + \frac{r_0^2}{r^2}\right) \tag{41}$$

$$u = p_i \frac{r}{E} \frac{r_i^2}{r_0^2 - r_i^2} \left[(1 - \mu) + (1 + \mu)\frac{r_0^2}{r^2}\right]$$

Next we take the case

$$\omega^2 = 0 \qquad s_r = 0 \text{ for } r = r_i \qquad s_r = -p_0 \text{ for } r = r_0$$

By substitution of these conditions into Eqs. (39), solving for C_1 and C_2, and insertion of the values so found into (39) we find *the result for a non-rotating flat disk r_0 with a hole r_i, subject only to an external pressure p_0*:

$$s_r = -p_0 \frac{r_0^2}{r_0^2 - r_i^2} \left(1 - \frac{r_i^2}{r^2}\right)$$

$$s_t = -p_0 \frac{r_0^2}{r_0^2 - r_i^2} \left(1 + \frac{r_i^2}{r^2}\right) \tag{42}$$

$$u = -p_0 \frac{r}{E} \frac{r_0^2}{r_0^2 - r_i^2} \left[(1 - \mu) + (1 + \mu)\frac{r_i^2}{r^2}\right]$$

Finally we consider the third partial case of the disk without boundary loadings at all, but just rotating:

$$\omega^2 = \omega^2 \qquad s_r = 0 \text{ for } r = r_i \text{ and for } r = r_0$$

By the same algebraic process as the two previous cases we obtain *the result for the rotating flat disk r_0 with a hole r_i without any radial loading on either boundary*:

$$s_r = \rho\omega^2 \frac{3 + \mu}{8} \left(r_0^2 + r_i^2 - \frac{r_0^2 r_i^2}{r^2} - r^2\right)$$

$$s_t = \rho\omega^2 \frac{3 + \mu}{8} \left(r_0^2 + r_i^2 + \frac{r_0^2 r_i^2}{r^2} - \frac{1 + 3\mu}{3 + \mu} r^2\right) \tag{43}$$

$$u = \rho\omega^2 \frac{r}{E} \frac{(3 + \mu)(1 - \mu)}{8} \left(r_0^2 + r_i^2 + \frac{1 + \mu}{1 - \mu}\frac{r_0^2 r_i^2}{r^2} - \frac{1 + \mu}{3 + \mu} r^2\right)$$

Equations (40) to (43) enable us to answer all questions of stress and deformations on spinning flat disks, singly or in combinations shrunk over each other.

In the general discussion of these formulae we start by examining the stresses in a spinning disk without peripheral load for the case of a very small central hole. Then $r_i \ll r < r_0$, and we see in Eqs. (43) that the maximum stresses occur at the hole $r = r_i$. For negligible r_i with respect to r_0, Eqs. (43) give for the stress at the hole

$$s_r = 0$$

naturally, because that boundary condition was imposed; and

$$s_t = \rho\omega^2 \frac{3 + \mu}{8} 2r_0^2$$

This tangential stress is *twice* the stress in the center of a solid disk [Eqs. (40)]. Hence the influence of a small hole, even of a pinhole, in a disk is to double the stress over the case of no hole. This result is not entirely surprising because a hole, even of infinitesimally small diameter, prevents a pull between two points 180 deg apart on its periphery, *i.e.*, prevents a

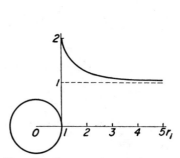

Fig. 42. Concentration of the tangential tensile stress near the *small* central hole of a spinning flat disk. The stress at the hole is twice that for no hole, but at one hole diameter from the edge of the hole it is only 1.11 times as large.

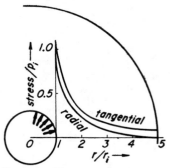

Fig. 43. Flat, non-rotating disk with $r_0/r_i = 5$ loaded by an internal pressure p_i only. The tangential stress is tensile, and the radial stress is compressive. Illustrates Eqs. (41).

radial stress. In the center of the solid disk this radial stress equals the tangential stress; in the small-holed disk the radial stress is zero, and the tangential stress is doubled. The region in which this stress concentration occurs is very limited, as can be seen from the second of Eqs. (43), in which r_i^2 is neglected with respect to r_0^2 and in which r^2 is considered of the same order of magnitude as r_i, restricting the result to the close neighborhood of the small hole:

$$s_t = \rho\omega^2 \frac{3 + \mu}{8} \left(r_0^2 + \text{small} + r_0^2 \frac{r_i^2}{r^2} - \text{small} \right)$$

$$= \rho\omega^2 \frac{3 + \mu}{8} r_0^2 \left(1 + \frac{r_i^2}{r^2} \right)$$

This stress is the solid-disk center stress, multiplied by the factor $1 + (r_i^2/r^2)$, which is 2 at the hole and diminishes to 1 at some distance from the hole, as shown in Fig. 42. The reader should check a few points on this curve numerically.

Figures 43, 44, and 45 show the stress distributions for a spinning disk for the case that $r_0 = 5r_i$, and these figures are interpretations of Eqs. (41),

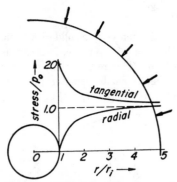

FIG. 44. Flat disk with $r_0/r_i = 5$ under the influence of external pressure p_0 only, at standstill. Illustrates Eqs. (42). The tangential as well as the radial stress is compressive.

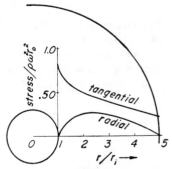

FIG. 45. Stress distribution in a spinning flat disk with a central hole r_i of one-fifth of the outer radius r_0. Both the radial and tangential stresses are tensile. The reader should calculate by Eqs. (40) the case of no central hole ($p_0 = 0$) and sketch in the result, which is instructive.

(42), and (43). The reader should again check numerically at least one point on each of these figures.

We conclude this section with a *numerical example* involving most of the formulae. Let a flat steel disk of 30 in. outside diameter with a 6-in.-diameter hole be shrunk around a solid steel shaft. The shrink allowance is 1 part per 1,000. We ask four questions:

1. At what rpm will the shrink fit loosen up as a result of the rotation?

2. What are the stresses when spinning at the speed calculated in the first question?

3. What are the stresses at standstill?

4. What are the stresses at half the speed of question 2?

To answer the first question, we remark that, when spinning at the required rpm, the shaft as well as the disk has no radial pressure on any boundary surface. We must calculate the u displacements for each one and then state that the increase in inner radius of the disk less the increase in outer radius of the shaft, both as functions of the unknown rpm, must be equal to the radial difference at standstill, *i.e.*, to the shrink allowance of 0.003 in. at 3 in. radius.

FORMULAE FOR THE CALCULATION OF FLAT DISKS

	Load	Radial stress s_r	Tangential stress s_t	Displacement u
Solid disk	External pressure p_0 + rotation (ω^2)	$-p_0 + \dfrac{3+\mu}{8}\rho\omega^2(r_0^2 - r^2)$	$-p_0 + \dfrac{3+\mu}{8}\rho\omega^2\left(r_0^2 - \dfrac{1+3\mu}{3+\mu}r^2\right)$	$-p_0 r\dfrac{1-\mu}{E} + \dfrac{1-\mu}{8E}\rho\omega^2 r[(3+\mu)r_0^2 - (1+\mu)r^2]$
Disk with hole in center	Internal pressure p_i	$p_i\dfrac{r_i^2}{r_0^2-r_i^2}\left(1-\dfrac{r_0^2}{r^2}\right)$	$p_i\dfrac{r_i^2}{r_0^2-r_i^2}\left(1+\dfrac{r_0^2}{r^2}\right)$	$p_i\dfrac{r}{E}\dfrac{r_i^2}{r_0^2-r_i^2}\left[(1-\mu)+(1+\mu)\dfrac{r_0^2}{r^2}\right]$
Disk with hole in center	External pressure p_0	$-p_0\dfrac{r_0^2}{r_0^2-r_i^2}\left(1-\dfrac{r_i^2}{r^2}\right)$	$-p_0\dfrac{r_0^2}{r_0^2-r_i^2}\left(1+\dfrac{r_i^2}{r^2}\right)$	$-p_0\dfrac{r}{E}\dfrac{r_0^2}{r_0^2-r_i^2}\left[(1-\mu)+(1+\mu)\dfrac{r_i^2}{r^2}\right]$
Disk with hole in center	Rotating with ω^2	$\rho\omega^2\dfrac{3+\mu}{8}\left(r_0^2+r_i^2-\dfrac{r_0^2 r_i^2}{r^2}-r^2\right)$	$\rho\omega^2\dfrac{3+\mu}{8}\left(r_0^2+r_i^2+\dfrac{r_0^2 r_i^2}{r^2}-\dfrac{1+3\mu}{3+\mu}r^2\right)$	$\rho\omega^2\dfrac{r}{E}\dfrac{(3+\mu)(1-\mu)}{8}\left(r_0^2+r_i^2+\dfrac{1+\mu}{1-\mu}\dfrac{r_0^2 r_i^2}{r^2}-\dfrac{1+\mu}{3+\mu}r^2\right)$

Equations (43) give for the disk

$$u_{disk} = \frac{\rho\omega^2}{E} \times 3 \times \frac{3.3 \times 0.7}{8}\left(225 + 9 + \frac{1.3}{0.7} \times 225 - \frac{1.3}{3.3} \times 9\right)$$

$$= 562\,\frac{\rho\omega^2}{E}$$

By Eqs. (40)

$$u_{shaft} = \frac{0.7}{8}\frac{\rho\omega^2}{E} \times 3(3.3 \times 9 - 1.3 \times 9) = 5\,\frac{\rho\omega^2}{E}$$

We see that the shaft expansion is very small with respect to the disk expansion, and in future cases we can save the trouble of calculating the shaft expansion. However, to be exact, we now write

$$(562 - 5)\,\frac{\rho\omega^2}{E} = 0.003 \text{ in.}$$

or:

$$\omega^2 = \frac{0.003}{557}\frac{30 \times 10^6 \times 386}{0.28} = 227{,}000 \text{ (radians/sec)}^2$$

$$\omega = 471 \text{ radians/sec} \quad\text{and}\quad \text{rpm} = 4{,}500$$

For the second question we glance at Fig. 45 and then take from Eqs. (43)

$$s_t = \rho\omega^2\frac{3.3}{8}\left(225 + 9 + 225 - \frac{1.9}{3.3} \times 9\right) = 187\rho\omega^2$$

$$s_t = \frac{187 \times 0.28 \times 227{,}000}{386} = 31{,}000 \text{ lb/sq in.}$$

In the third question there is an unknown pressure p between the disk and the shaft, which has to be calculated first from the deformations. Using Eqs. (41) for the disk and Eqs. (40) for the shaft,

$$u_{disk} = p\,\frac{3}{30 \times 10^6}\frac{9}{225 - 9}\left(0.7 + 1.3\,\frac{225}{9}\right) = 1.36p \times 10^{-7}$$

$$u_{shaft} = -p \times 3\,\frac{0.7}{30 \times 10^6} = -0.70p \times 10^{-7}$$

$$u_{disk} - u_{shaft} = \Delta r_{shrink}$$

$$(1.36 + 0.70)p \times 10^{-7} = 0.003$$

$$p = 14{,}600 \text{ lb/sq in.}$$

The tangential disk stress at the hole certainly will be the largest stress in the system, Fig. 43. Hence, by Eqs. (41)

$$s_t = 14,600 \frac{9}{225 - 9} \left(1 + \frac{225}{9}\right) = 15,600 \text{ lb/sq in.}$$

In the fourth question there is a mixture of centrifugal loading and pressure loading. At first thought we might be clumsy, calculate the radial deformation u under the influence of 2,250 rpm and an unknown p, write the shrink geometry equation, solve for p, etc. However, this can be done much more neatly by remarking that the stresses as well as the u deformations vary linearly with whatever loading there may be, either of the p kind or of the $\rho\omega^2$ kind. Thus at half speed the $\rho\omega^2$ stresses and deformations will be one-quarter of those in question 2. This leaves three-quarters of the required u deformation to be accounted for by the shrink pressure p. The answer to question 4 thus is

$$s_t = \tfrac{1}{4} \times 31,000 + \tfrac{3}{4} \times 15,600 = 19,500 \text{ lb/sq in.}$$

In general, for any intermediate speed, the conditions will be as shown in Fig. 46, where the stresses caused by $\rho\omega^2$ and p separately are shown as dotted lines, and their sum, the total actual stress, as a full line.

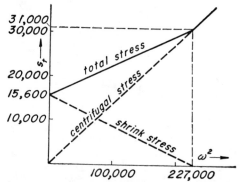

Fig. 46. Numerical answers for the hoop stress at the hole of the disk in the above example, showing that the stress is the sum of the pressure stress and the centrifugal stress, the latter being proportional to the square of the speed.

10. Disks of Variable Thickness. Turbine disks seldom are made flat; they usually are thick near their hub and taper down to a smaller thickness toward the periphery. The good practical reason for this is immediately apparent from Figs. 43 to 45 and even from Fig. 41: for a flat disk there is a pronounced stress concentration near the center, even for the solid disk; hence designers attempt to be more efficient by strengthening (thickening) the disk at the hub. The disk is still a body of revolution so that the thickness t is a function of r only. The calculation of such disks of variable thickness is much more complicated than that of disks of constant thickness. In the analysis of the disk of constant thickness, the principal equation was the equilibrium equation (35). It was found (page 50) by writing all the forces acting on the element of "unit thickness." Now we must call the thickness t instead of unity, and all forces are multiplied by t. We should remember that t varies with r, so that we must *not* bring t outside a d/dr operation. The new equilibrium equation then is

$$\frac{d}{dr}\,(trs_r) \,-\, ts_t \,+\, t\rho\omega^2r^2 = 0 \qquad (44)$$

On page 50 we then proceeded to investigate the strain and to write Hooke's law [Eqs. (36)]. If we reread that argument, we shall see that the thickness never enters into it, and therefore these equations apply without change. Also, if u is eliminated between them, leading to the "compatibility equation" (37), this equation still holds for variable thickness. Hence the problem is determined by Eqs. (44) and (36) for the three unknowns s_t, s_r, u [for a given prescribed thickness function $t(r)$], or also it is determined by Eqs. (44) and (37) for the two unknowns s_t and s_r only. For convenience the old equations are reprinted:

$$\frac{du}{dr} = \frac{1}{E}\,(s_r \,-\, \mu s_t)$$

$$\frac{u}{r} = \frac{1}{E}\,(s_t \,-\, \mu s_r) \qquad (36)$$

$$\frac{d}{dr}\,(s_t) \,-\, \mu\frac{d}{dr}\,(s_r) \,+\, \frac{1+\mu}{r}\,(s_t \,-\, s_r) = 0 \qquad (37)$$

We now proceed in the same manner as on page 51; we eliminate s_t from between (44) and (37), obtaining as a result an equation in the variable s_r only. From (44) we write s_t, then differentiate it to get $(s_t)'$; then we substitute both results into Eq. (37). In the process we should never forget that t is a variable, depending on r. Also, as on page 51, it has been found more convenient to work with a combination (trs_r) rather than with the radial stress s_r itself. The algebra of this is long and tedious; the reader should do it for himself and obtain the result:

$$r^2(trs_r)'' \,+\, r(trs_r)' \,-\, (trs_r) \,-\, \frac{rt'}{t}\,[r(trs_r)' \,-\, \mu(trs_r)]$$

$$+\, (3+\mu)\rho\omega^2r^3t = 0 \qquad (45)$$

This is the differential equation of the unknown dependent variable $(trs_r) =$ (thickness $\times$ radius $\times$ radial stress) as a function of r. The thickness t, being also a function of r, is supposed to be known. We see that for constant thickness, *i.e.*, for $t' = dt/dr = 0$, the formidable square-bracket term disappears; the constant t can be divided out, and Eq. (45) reduces to Eq. (38), for which we know the solution. However, it has been found by Stodola (who first published the result in his famous book "Steam and Gas Turbines") that another thickness function, the "hyperbolic" one, also leaves Eq. (45), in the same fundamental form which can be integrated. That thickness function is

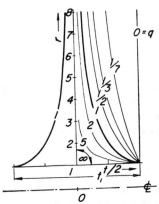

$$t = \frac{t_1}{r^q} \qquad (46)$$

where q is any positive number. The curves are "hyperbolas of order q," and they are shown in Fig. 47. For $q = 0$ the thickness is constant, and the theory of flat disks applies. For $q = 1$ the curve is an ordinary hyperbola. All profiles (except $q = 0$) have infinite thickness at the origin, and hence the theory which follows is useless for solid disks, but quite useful for disks with a central hole. The quantity t_1 is the thickness at unit radius. Since we shall obtain a complete solution for any value of q, we shall be able to handle disks of any profile in Fig. 47; we can give t_1 any value we want and we can place r_i any-where we want by choosing the proper "unit" for the unit radius where $t = t_1$. Thus, we can choose the disk thicknesses at $r = r_i$ and $r = r_0$ arbitrarily, and the intervening profile curve is a nice smooth one.

FIG. 47. Disks of "hyperbolic profiles," given by Eq. (46), for which an exact solution is available in Eqs. (48) and (49).

The first move toward a solution is to substitute Eq. (46) into Eq. (45), and from Eq. (46) we see that

$$t' = -\frac{q}{r}\,t \qquad \text{or} \qquad \frac{rt'}{t} = -q$$

Thus Eq. (45) becomes

$$r^2(trs_r)'' + r(1+q)(trs_r)' - (1+\mu q)(trs_r) + (3+\mu)\rho\omega^2 r^3 t = 0 \qquad (47)$$

This equation is linear in (trs_r); its coefficients are variable exactly in the same manner as was explained with Eq. (38), so that a solution of the "reduced equation," *i.e.*, of the equation with $\rho\omega^2 = 0$, takes the form of a power,

$$trs_r = r^n$$

where n is to be determined. Substitution of this assumption into the reduced equation (47) gives

$$n(n - 1) + n(1 + q) - (1 + \mu q) = 0$$

or

$$n^2 + qn - (1 + \mu q) = 0$$

which has two roots n:

$$n_1, n_2 = -\frac{q}{2} \pm \sqrt{\frac{q^2}{4} + \mu q + 1} \tag{48}$$

The general solution of the reduced equation (47) thus is

$$trs_r = C_1 r^{n_1} + C_2 r^{n_2}$$

To this has to be added a particular solution of the complete equation (47), which is usually found by inspection. Inspecting (47), we note that the right-hand member is a constant times $r^3 t$, which by (46) is constant r^{3-q}, a power of r. The rest of the equation is so built that the same power of r appears everywhere. Thus we try for the particular solution,

$$trs_r = A r^3 t$$

and substitute it into (47). In doing this we should not forget that t is variable, so that $(trs_r)' = 3A r^2 t + A r^3 t'$, etc. The algebra of the substitution is again fairly involved, and we come out with the result

$$A = -\frac{(3 + \mu)\rho\omega^2}{8 - (3 + \mu)q}$$

Therefore, the general solution of Eq. (47) is

$$trs_r = C_1 r^{n_1} + C_2 r^{n_2} - \frac{(3 + \mu)\rho\omega^2}{8 - (3 + \mu)q} r^3 t \tag{49}$$

where t and q are defined by Eq. (46) and where n_1 and n_2 have the values of Eq. (48). This determines the radial stress at any point, subject to the calculation of the integration constants C_1 and C_2 from the boundary conditions. The hoop stress s_t can then be found from Eq. (44) and the displacement u from the second of Eqs. (36).

Looking back to the developments of page 52 for the disk of constant thickness, our next job seems to be to work out general formulae for the three principal cases of boundary condition, corresponding to Eqs. (41) to (43). But, whereas these formulae for the flat disk were manageable, although a bit complicated, for the hyperbolic disk the corresponding results become so involved as to be practically useless. In an actual numerical case it is less work to start from the general (49) with its auxiliaries (46) and (48) than it would be to substitute into the very large counterparts of Eqs. (41) to (43).

Therefore we now proceed to an *illustrative numerical case*, and we take the example of page 56, asking the same four questions, but now applying them to a disk which we want to be 5 in. thick at the bore and 1 in. thick at the periphery. Applying the definition, Eq. (46), to the inner and outer radii of the disk, we have

$$\frac{t_i}{t_0} = \left(\frac{r_0}{r_i}\right)^q \quad \text{or} \quad 5 = (5)^q \quad \text{or} \quad q = 1$$

the "ordinary" hyperbola of Fig. 47.

The exponents n_1 and n_2 become with Eq. (48)

$$n_1, n_2 = -\tfrac{1}{2} \pm \sqrt{\tfrac{1}{4} + 0.3 + 1} = -0.50 \pm 1.25$$

$$n_1 = +0.75 \qquad n_2 = -1.75$$

Before entering with this into Eq. (49) we note that $tr = t_i$, a constant, by which we divide all four terms of Eq. (49). For the terms with C_1 and C_2 this simply gives a different meaning to the integration constants, but these constants are still floating. Thus

$$s_r = C_1 r^{0.75} + \frac{C_2}{r^{1.75}} - 0.70 \rho \omega^2 r^2$$

The boundary conditions for question 1 (spinning with a just loosened shrink fit) are

$$s_r = 0 \text{ for } r_i = 3 \text{ in. and for } r_0 = 15 \text{ in.}$$

or

$$0 = C_1 \sqrt[4]{3^3} + \frac{C_2}{3\sqrt[4]{3^3}} - 0.70 \rho \omega^2 9$$

$$0 = C_1 \sqrt[4]{15^3} + \frac{C_2}{15\sqrt[4]{15^3}} - 0.70 \rho \omega^2 225$$

or

$$0 = 2.28 C_1 + 0.146 C_2 - 6.3 \rho \omega^2$$

$$0 = 7.60 C_1 + 0.0088 C_2 - 157 \rho \omega^2$$

From these we solve for C_1 and C_2:

$$C_1 = +20.8 \rho \omega^2 \qquad C_2 = -283 \rho \omega^2$$

Thus the radial stress distribution in the disk as a function of the radius is

$$s_r = \left(20.8 r^{0.75} - \frac{283}{r^{1.75}} - 0.70 r^2\right) \rho \omega^2$$

which is plotted in Fig. 48.

The hoop stress s_t is calculated from the equilibrium equation (44), in which we again remember that tr is a constant, which can be brought outside the differential operator and then divided out:

$$s_t = rs_r' + \rho\omega^2 r^2$$

$$s_t = \left[15.6r^{0.75} + \frac{495}{r^{1.75}} - 0.40r^2 \right]\rho\omega^2$$

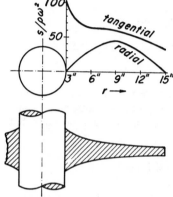

again plotted in Fig. 48. The maximum hoop stress occurs at the hub, as before, but now it is $104\rho\omega^2$, as compared with $187\rho\omega^2$ found on page 58 for the disk of uniform thickness. From a strength standpoint, therefore, the tapered disk is much to be preferred.

The radial displacement u follows from the second of Eqs. (36) (page 50):

$$u = \frac{r}{E}(s_t - 0.3s_r)$$

$$u = \left[9.4r^{0.75} + \frac{580}{r^{1.75}} - 0.19r^2 \right]\frac{\rho\omega^2 r}{E}$$

Fig. 48. Stress distribution in a "hyperbolic" disk rotating with zero shrink pressure at the bore.

which we don't care to plot. This function is of practical importance at the bore only: $r = 3$ in.:

$$(u)_{r=3 \text{ in.}} = (9.4 \times 2.28 + 580 \times 0.146 - 0.19 \times 9)\frac{\rho\omega^2 3}{E}$$

$$(u)_{r=3 \text{ in.}} = 310\frac{\rho\omega^2}{E}$$

This figure compares with the value 562 found on page 58 for the disk of constant thickness. Ordinarily we would neglect the centrifugal expansion of the 6-in.-diameter shaft, but we have the answer ready for us on page 58, at $5\rho\omega^2/E$. Thus the differential expansion of disk and shaft is $305\rho\omega^2 E$, and

$$305\frac{\rho\omega^2}{E} = 0.003 \text{ in.}$$

so that

$$\omega^2 = \frac{0.003 \times 30 \times 10^6 \times 386}{305 \times 0.28} = 406{,}000 \qquad \omega = 632 \qquad \text{rpm} = 6{,}000$$

This answers the first question. It shows that our tapered disk again is better than the flat one, in that it loosens its shrink fit at a speed roughly

30 per cent higher than the flat disk does, and hence the tapered design can be safely operated at a higher speed than the flat one.

The answer to the second question then is taken from Fig. 48. The hoop stress at the bore is

$$s_t = 104\rho\omega^2 = \frac{104 \times 0.28 \times 406,000}{386} = 31,000 \text{ lb/sq in.}$$

This answer is the same as that for the flat disk, which on afterthought we could have seen immediately, and thus it constitutes a check on our calculation. The answer differs by a few per cent from 30,000, which is the single stress s_t (s_r being zero at the hub then), corresponding to a strain 0.001 in./in., the shrink allowance. The small difference is caused by the small centrifugal expansion of the shaft.

The further treatment of this problem, leading to a linear diagram like Fig. 46, is left to the reader.

11. Disk of Uniform Stress. In view of the considerable complications in the design of flat or hyperbolic rotating disks, it is remarkable that a simple solution has been found to the question of designing the thickness variation $t(r)$ of the disk so as to make its stresses equal over the entire area. The solution was found, about 1900, by engineers of the de Laval Company in Sweden and was first published in Stodola's famous book "Steam and Gas Turbines."

We return to the general equations for a disk of variable thickness: Eq. (44) (page 60), the "equilibrium equation," and Eq. (37) (page 60), the "compatibility equation." The latter has its name because it results from the elimination of u from between Eqs. (36), and thus it expresses nothing but the fact that the displacement function u must be a continuous function. If we should set up an expression for the stresses that would satisfy Eq. (44) but should violate Eq. (37), it would mean that if we chopped up the unstressed disk into annular elements $dr \cdot 2\pi r$, and if we then stressed these elements with the stresses assumed, then the deformed rings would no longer fit together into a continuous plane: some would overlap, others would show clearance between each other. But if we find a set of stresses that satisfies both equilibrium *and* compatibility, and in addition the boundary conditions of the problem, then we have the true solution. Looking at Eqs. (44) and (37), suppose we ask if there exists a possibility of a solution for s_r and s_t, which is constant, *i.e.*, which makes s_r' and s_t' zero. If such a solution exists, then Eq. (37) tells us in addition that s_r and s_t must be equal to each other, so that we must have a condition of "two-dimensional hydrostatic stress." Suppose this to be the case with $s_r = s_t = s_0$; then Eq. (37) is satisfied, and the equilibrium equation (44) becomes

$$s_0 t' r + s_0 t - t s_0 + t\rho\omega^2 r^2 = 0$$

or

$$\frac{dt}{dr} + \frac{\rho\omega^2}{s_0} rt = 0$$

In this (non-linear) differential equation of the first order we can separate the variables and then integrate:

$$\frac{dt}{t} = -\frac{\rho\omega^2}{s_0} r\, dr$$

$$\log_e t = -\frac{\rho\omega^2}{2s_0} r^2 + \log_e C$$

$$t = Ce^{-\frac{\rho\omega^2}{2s_0} r^2} \tag{50}$$

This is the law of thickness variation for which the stress $s_t = s_r$ is constant over the entire disk. In order to visualize its meaning, we note that the exponent of an e function must be a pure number; hence

$$\sqrt{\frac{2s_0}{\rho\omega^2}} = \lambda \tag{51}$$

must have the dimension of a length, which we shall call λ. Also the constant C must be of the same dimension as t, because the e function is dimensionless. We see that for $r = 0$ the e function equals unity, so that C means the thickness at $r = 0$; we might as well call C by the new name t_0. Then Eq. (50) can be written as

$$t = t_0 e^{-(r/\lambda)^2} \tag{50a}$$

The function is plotted (non-dimensionally) in Fig. 49. We notice from the shape that there seems to be an inflection point in the curve, which we can calculate as follows,

$$\frac{d(t/t_0)}{d(r/\lambda)} = -2\frac{r}{\lambda} e^{-(r/\lambda)^2} = -2\frac{r}{\lambda}\frac{t}{t_0}$$

which is the slope of the curve, zero for $r/\lambda = 0$ and also zero for $t/t_0 = 0$ occurring at $r/\lambda = \infty$. The curvature is

$$\frac{d^2(t/t_0)}{d(r/\lambda)^2} = -2\frac{t}{t_0} - 2\frac{r}{\lambda}\frac{d(t/t_0)}{d(r/\lambda)} = -2\frac{t}{t_0} + 4\left(\frac{r}{\lambda}\right)^2 \frac{t}{t_0}$$

This curvature is zero, *i.e.*, we have an inflection point when $(r/\lambda)^2 = \frac{1}{2}$, or when $r/\lambda = 0.707$. Although Fig. 49 shows apparently but one shape of disk, in reality there are a great many disk forms included in it. We can make t_0 anything we please, and the same is almost true of λ, if we have some freedom of choosing the design stress s_0. Thus we can at will take any portion of the curve, Fig. 49, for our disk shape. For example, if we take from the center line to point A and then reduce t_0 to about one-twentieth of its value, we have a flat disk. We see that for this flat disk r/λ is small, *i.e.*, for a given r the quantity λ is large, which by Eq. (51) means either an enormously large design stress or a rather small rpm. The meaning of this is shown by Eqs. (40); at slow speed (standstill) the design stress $s_0 = -p_0$, which is constant, as required. If, in Fig. 49, we take the portion to point B, we have a case where the rim thickness is about half the hub thickness; if we go to point C, the rim thickness is small compared with the hub thickness.

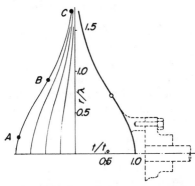

Fig. 49. Shape of rotating disk of equal stress, expressed by Eqs. (50a) and (51). Disks of this shape are often employed in the high-speed single-disk deLaval type of steam turbines with a shaft connection as shown sketched at right.

From the very statement of our original question it can be seen that *no answer can be found for a disk with a central hole.* This is because at the hole boundary $s_r = 0$, which would mean zero constant stress all over. The only solution is for disks without central hole, such as are commonly used in small single-wheel steam turbines. The shaft connection then is somewhat like that sketched in Fig. 49. The radial stress at the outer radius r_0 again has the constant value s_0, and this stress is usually supplied by the centrifugal force of turbine buckets, which do impose a radial loading on the disk but do not contribute to its strength.

We shall now discuss some *numerical examples.* First consider a disk of the same type as the hyperbolic one of page 63, taking $r_0 = 15$ in.; $r_i = 0$, because our new disk is solid; t at 15 in. to be 1 in. and t_0 at the center 5 in. We shall spin this disk at the same 6,000 rpm of our previous example and ask for the stress.

From Fig. 49 or, better, from Eq. (50a) we calculate that for $t/t_0 = \frac{1}{5}$ we must have $r/\lambda = 1.29$, which with $r = 15$ in. gives $\lambda = 11.7$ in. and $\lambda^2 = 136$ sq in. Substituting this into Eq. (51), with $\omega^2 = 406,000$ of the previous example, gives for the stress

$$s_0 = \frac{\rho\omega^2\lambda^2}{2} = \frac{0.28 \times 406{,}000 \times 136}{2 \times 386} = 20{,}000 \text{ lb/sq in.}$$

The hyperbolic disk had 31,000 lb/sq in. We see that the equal-strength disk has a stress greater than 50 per cent of the hyperbolic one, and we might expect 50 per cent on account of the property of Fig. 42. However, our present disk has a 20,000 lb/sq. in. radial stress everywhere, including the outside periphery. This means that for each inch of periphery (which is also a square inch) the new disk can carry 20,000 lb of centrifugal force from turbine blades. The stress can also be written as

$$s_0 = \frac{\rho\omega^2\lambda^2}{2} = \rho\omega^2\frac{136}{2} = 68\rho\omega^2 = 4\frac{1}{2}\rho\omega^2 r_0$$

This means that on each inch of periphery we must hang $4\frac{1}{2}$ cu in. of turbine blading of the same material as the disk.

In the hyperbolic example there was *no* radial stress at the *outside* periphery, and the imposition of a blade centrifugal load would increase the hub stress greatly.

For our second numerical example we propose to look at the shapes of the disk for three cases:

a. $s_0 = 30{,}000$ lb/sq in. at 1,800 rpm; $r_0 = 24$ in.
b. $s_0 = 30{,}000$ lb/sq in. at 3,600 rpm; $r_0 = 24$ in.
c. $s_0 = 7{,}500$ lb/sq in. at 3,600 rpm; $r_0 = 24$ in.

For these cases all necessary information is given to calculate λ from Eq. (51), with the result that

$$\lambda_a = 48 \text{ in.} \qquad \lambda_b = 24 \text{ in.} \qquad \lambda_c = 12 \text{ in.}$$

Hence, for $r_0 = 24$ in.

$$\left(\frac{r_0}{\lambda}\right)_a = \frac{1}{2} \qquad \left(\frac{r_0}{\lambda}\right)_b = 1 \qquad \left(\frac{r_0}{\lambda}\right)_c = 2$$

and, with the help of Fig. 49, roughly

$$\left(\frac{t_{\text{rim}}}{t_{\text{center}}}\right)_a = 78\% \qquad \left(\frac{t_r}{t_o}\right)_b = 39\% \qquad \left(\frac{t_r}{t_o}\right)_c = 3\%$$

Case *a* will be a stubby, almost flat disk; case *b* has a medium taper; and case *c* is too extreme to be a practical design.

In this connection it is interesting to write Eq. (51) in a somewhat different form

$$\omega r = \frac{r}{\lambda}\sqrt{\frac{2s_0}{\rho}}$$

in terms of the peripheral speed ωr of the wheel. If we want to run the wheel fast, we run the stress s_0 up high and make r/λ as large as possible. Figure 49 shows that the largest practical value of r/λ is about 1.3; with this and with ρ for steel the equation becomes

$$\omega r = 5.7 \sqrt{s_0}$$

where ωr is in feet per second and s_0 is in pounds per square inch, with numerical values as follows:

Stress s_0, lb/sq in.	5,000	10,000	20,000	40,000
Speed ωr, ft/sec	285	570	800	1,140

This shows that it is easy to ask a draftsman to design a wheel with 2,000 ft/sec peripheral speed, but not so easy to find the draftsman who can do it.

Thus, in conclusion, we see that a disk of constant stress is the best design, if it can be applied. For multidisk turbines the constructional complications are so severe that disks with a central hole are usually applied. Then a hyperbolic disk is better than a flat one. Flat disks are used for simplicity only in cases of low rpm or of low stress. With these three general types almost all design problems can be answered. Sometimes, however, disks are designed "by eye," and one is asked to calculate the stresses in such a prescribed shape. In practice it is sufficiently accurate to fit a hyperbola to the shape by Eq. (46) or Fig. 49, but if greater accuracy is desired, the shape can be broken up by intermediate radii into two or more annular disks. Each of these is approximated as well as possible by a hyperbola or by a flat disk, and all these disks then are joined together by proper boundary conditions. This, for one case, is a tremendous job, but if the reader is called upon to spend his life calculating turbine disks, several short cuts have been devised by various authors to lessen his burden.

Problems 33 to 60.

CHAPTER III

MEMBRANE STRESSES IN SHELLS

12. General Theory. The word "shell" is used in mechanics for a thin curved plate, *i.e.*, for a curved structure of which one dimension, the thickness, is "small" in comparison with the other two dimensions. When such a structure is flat, it is called a "plate." Shells and plates are capable of taking bending moments and shear forces, perpendicular to their own plane, as well as forces lying in their own plane. A "membrane," either flat or curved, is defined as a body of the same geometry as a plate or shell, but one incapable of transmitting transverse bending moments or shear forces. A "beam" is a body of which two dimensions are "small" with respect to the third dimension, and a "string" or "strut" is a body of the same geometry as a beam, but incapable of taking bending or shear. Thus a membrane is a two-dimensional string; a plate can be looked upon as a two-dimensional straight beam, and a shell is the two-dimensional counterpart of a curved beam.

Straight strings or struts can withstand only forces or loads directed along their center line; they cannot take loads perpendicular to themselves. Curved strings or curved struts (which are called "arches") are capable of taking loads perpendicular to themselves. The main cables of suspension bridges are curved strings loaded principally perpendicular to their center line, and the main arch in a bridge or building is in the same state of stress with a negative sign. As a two-dimensional generalization, a flat membrane can take only forces in its own plane. Usually such forces and stresses are tensile; if they become compressive, we must consider the possibility of buckling, just as we do that in a truss. A curved membrane can take loadings perpendicular to its surface. Examples are rubber balloons, inner tubes for automobiles, and blow-up rubber boats; in all cases the load is the internal air pressure, which is perpendicular to the surface.

The shells of technical importance to be discussed in this chapter are oil and water tanks, pipe lines, and steam boilers, made of steel or some other metal; obviously these structures are shells and not membranes, because they are all capable of taking bending stresses. However, if we think of a truss, we know that all its constituent bars are beams, because they are capable of taking bending stresses. Just the same, a calculation of the truss on the assumption that these beams are strings (or struts for the

70

compression members) gives results in very satisfactory agreement with fact. The agreement would be perfect if the nodal points of the truss were ideal hinges, and only the fact that these "hinges" are welded or riveted gusset-plate connections accounts for the presence of some bending in the bars. These bending stresses are usually much smaller than the tensile stresses and are called "secondary stresses." A completely similar situation exists with respect to shells. If these shells are really thin-walled, so that they can bend comparatively easily, they will try to take the loads imposed on them by tensile or compressive stresses only (like the balloons, tubes, and boats), and if the boundary conditions do not interfere with this natural wish of the shell, these stresses will be all that actually occur. If the boundary conditions do not allow the deformations called for in the shell by these tensile-compressive stresses, then local bending will occur, of the same nature as that in the bars of a truss. In trusses we have developed the habit of talking about "primary" and "secondary" stresses. This usage has not been transferred to thin shells, but here we talk of "membrane stresses" and "bending stresses." The knowledge of the membrane stresses in a shell is usually of much greater practical importance than the knowledge of the bending stresses. Besides, the membrane stresses are far easier to calculate. In this chapter we shall discuss membrane stresses in curved shells only; in the next chapter we shall take up flat plates, in which membrane stresses mean nothing, because they cannot help carry the loads. Necessarily the flat plates have to do this with bending stresses. The next subject in logical sequence should be that of bending stresses in shells. This, however, is extremely complicated, the solution of the first cases dating back only to 1920, and we shall limit ourselves only to the most important case: that of a cylinder with rotationally symmetrical loading, which will be discussed on page 164.

Before setting up equations for the membrane stresses one more remark is in order about the differences between strings, beams, membranes, and shells. Imagine someone constructing a large suspension bridge by first setting up the towers and then stringing the main cable across freely turning pulleys at the tops in a straight line without sag. If then the first loads of the bridge deck were suspended from the cable, it would sag considerably even under light loads. In the final construction the sag of that cable is so large that it changes the entire geometry of the situation and entirely changes the stresses in the cable imposed by those loads. Now imagine a *beam* spanned across the tower tops as in London Bridge. The service loads put on this beam will deform it only a little, and that deformation is of no effect on the manner in which the loads are carried. We conclude that strings or cables sometimes deform greatly under the loads and that their geometry depends greatly on the loading, while this is not true for beams. Now let us generalize this for membranes and shells.

There are cases where slight loads on a membrane cause great deformations. Imagine a straight garden hose made of fairly thick rubber that can retain a shape without internal air pressure. Let the cross section of the hose be an ellipse. Then if pressure is put into the hose, a relatively small pressure will suffice to deform the cross section to a pure circle and then a much greater pressure increase can be carried by hoop tension in the circular hose. It is clear that in this example the first mild pressure will put bending stresses in the hose walls until they are circular. From there on tensile stresses will hold the pressure. In the theory to follow we shall limit ourselves to shells of such initial shape that if they were true membranes without any bending stiffness, their shape would not change appreciably as a result of the loading. This limitation includes the usual round garden hose, but it excludes elliptical or rectangular hose, because all of these will turn circular first. All shells of revolution (including those of the most complicated meridian shapes, Fig. 54 or 59) are reasonably within our limitation provided that they are loaded in a rotationally symmetrical manner, and it is for this type of membrane that we now start to set up a theory.

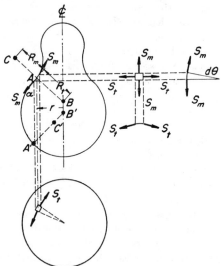

Fig. 50. For the derivation of Eqs. (52) and (53). A shell of revolution with a small square element $ds\ ds$ at point A. On it act the stresses s_m in the meridional plane and s_t in a direction tangent to the circular cross section. These two pairs of forces have resultants perpendicular to the shell, and they serve to hold the internal pressure force in check.

Derivation of Equilibrium Equations. Figure 50 shows the membrane. From symmetry we conclude that the principal stresses at each point lie in the meridional and tangential directions. The meridional stress s_m then lies in a plane with the rotational center line of the membrane, and it acts on a cross section through the membrane perpendicular to that center line. The tangential stress s_t is directed tangent to a circular cross section perpendicular to the center line. The first equation to be derived is the equilibrium equation of a small square $ds\ ds$ of the shell, in a direction perpendicular to itself. The derivation is almost the same as that of Eq. (11) (page 12), but here the stresses s_m and s_t in general differ from each other, while on page 12 the stress T was the same in both directions. Also, the curvatures in our new problem are the existing curvatures of the unloaded shell, and we have assumed that the shell does not materially change its shape during the loading. On page 12, on the other hand, the curvatures were caused by the loading, because the membrane there was originally flat. Looking first at the two sides ds on which the meridional stress s_m is acting, the forces are $s_m t\ ds$, where t is the local thickness. These two forces include a small angle $d\theta_m$ between them, and we have the relation $ds = R_m\ d\theta_m$, where R_m is the radius of curvature in the meridional plane. The resultant of the two forces, perpendicular to the surface, then is

$$(s_m t\ ds)\ d\theta_m = \frac{s_m t (ds)^2}{R_m}$$

In the same way the resultant of the forces on the other two faces is

$$\frac{s_t t (ds)^2}{R_t}$$

If these radii of curvature R_m and R_t are called positive when they are on the inside of the shell, then these two resultant forces, as written, also point to the inside. They balance the outward force of the internal pressure p,

$$\frac{s_m t (ds)^2}{R_m} + \frac{s_t t (ds)^2}{R_t} = p(ds)^2$$

or

$$\frac{s_m}{R_m} + \frac{s_t}{R_t} = \frac{p}{t} \tag{52}$$

The two letters on the right-hand side, p and t, may be functions of the location on the shell and do not need to be constant all over the place. In Eq. (52) they merely are the local values of the internal pressure and the shell thickness. The radii of curvature R_m and R_t can be easily visualized, by erecting a normal to the element $(ds)^2$ locally. The upper half of Fig. 50 is a meridional cut through the membrane; hence R_m is the radius of curvature of the plane curve of the figure, it is negative at A pointing outward AC, positive at $A'C'$, and infinite at the inflection point between

A and *A'*. For the radius R_t, also lying along the normal line *CAB*, we have to cut the shell with a plane normal to the meridian, *i.e.*, a plane normal to the paper, passing through the line *CAB*. The center of curvature then is that point on the line *CAB* which is at equal distance from all points of the intersecting curve close to point *A*. Now if we imagine ourselves located at point *B*, we can see all the points *A* on the horizontal circle at equal distance from us lying on a cone with *B* as apex. For small distances from *A* below and above the paper the cone and the normal plane coincide, being tangent to each other. Hence *B* is also the center of curvature for the intersection of the normal plane *CAB* with the shell. Thus R_t is the normal distance *AB* between the point *A* on the shell and the point *B* on the center line. In Fig. 50 all values of R_t are positive, pointing to the inside; for other shapes, such as the one in Fig. 54, negative R_t values may occur.

Equation (52), the condition of equilibrium normal to the surface, is a relation between two unknowns: s_m and s_t. To solve for them, one more equation is required: the condition of equilibrium of a finite part of the shell in the direction of the center line. In Fig. 50 we isolate the upper part of the shell above the circle containing all the points *A*. This part is pushed up by the internal pressure and pulled down by vertical component of the s_m stress at the cut:

$$s_m t 2\pi r \cos \alpha = p\pi r^2 \tag{53}$$

We shall not take the trouble of cleaning up this equation, because it does not have the universal application of Eq. (52). That equation applied to an element only, and *p* or *t* were local values. The new result (53) applies to a finite piece of shell, and the pressure *p* is the integrated or average value over the whole piece, while *t*, s_m, *r*, and α are local values. Equation (53) takes a different form depending on the nature of the pressure. For example, in the water tank of Fig. 51 we isolate the body of revolution *ABCDE*. The water pressures on the water cylinder *ABDE* are horizontal only and have no component along the center line. Hence the vertical equilibrium is

$$s_m t 2\pi r \cos \alpha = W_{ABCDE} \tag{53a}$$

where *W* is the weight of the entire isolated water body. We note that this weight is *not* $p\pi r^2$, because $p\pi r^2$ is the weight of the cylinder *ABDE* only, not including the cone *BCD*. A formal application of Eq. (53) or (53a) therefore may lead to errors. Thus in each individual case we apply Eq. (52) and then write the axial equilibrium equation of a suitably isolated portion of the shell. Between these two equations the stresses s_m and s_t can be solved.

The problem of the membrane stresses in shells therefore is a statically determined one, because we have used only equations of equilibrium (equations of statics) and nowhere have we used Hooke's law or any other law of deformation. We note in passing that this is also true for all of the simple (statically determined) trusses, which are solved by equations of equilibrium only and in which the stresses are entirely independent of the deformations, provided only that these deformations are small. It is *not* true for bent beams; there the usual linear bending stress distribution depends on Hooke's law; if the stress-strain law were different, the stress distribution in a bent beam would be different, but the stress distribution in the usual truss or thin-curved shell would still be the same. This argument makes the determination of the deformations in shells rather less important, because we hardly ever care about the deformations in themselves. They become of importance only if the truss or shell is made indeterminate by the addition of an extra bar or of some other stiffener. Then the deformations become vital and must be calculated. For our shells the local strains are easily found from Hooke's law after the stresses have been determined:

$$\epsilon_m = \frac{1}{E}\left(s_m - \mu s_t\right)$$
$$\epsilon_t = \frac{1}{E}\left(s_t - \mu s_m\right)$$

(54)

13. Applications. Our first example is the *cylinder r_0 under internal pressure*: the center portion of any pressure vessel. The meridional picture consists of two parallel straight lines, so that (Fig. 50) $R_m = \infty$ and $R_t = r_0$. With this Eq. (52) becomes

$$\frac{s_m}{\infty} + \frac{s_t}{r_0} = \frac{p}{t} \qquad \text{or} \qquad s_t = \frac{pr_0}{t}$$

a familiar elementary result. The longitudinal equilibrium equation takes the form of Eq. (53) with $\alpha = 0$ and

$$s_m = \frac{pr_0}{2t}$$

also a familiar result. With this simple example the meridional stress s_m is usually called longitudinal stress.

Next we again consider a *cylinder r_0*, this time *filled with a liquid*, say the cylindrical portion of an oil storage tank of 100 ft diameter and 30 ft height. The cylinder must stand *vertical*; only then is the pressure loading rotationally symmetrical, and only then does the theory of the previous section apply. If the cylinder lies horizontal, like an overland oil pipe line, the loading is not rotationally symmetrical: the case then becomes considerably more complicated, and its discussion will come along on page 92.

The application of Eq. (52) to our vertical oil tank is the same as that for a steam boiler (see the remark on page 74); hence the tangential stress still is $s_t = pr_0/t$. Now, however, p is a function of the height, and s_t increases linearly when going down from the liquid surface (for constant thickness t at least). In case we want to construct the cylindrical part of the tank with *constant* hoop stress, we must make the thickness increase toward the bottom, proportional to the distance down from the liquid surface.

In finding the meridional stress of the cylindrical oil or water tank we distinguish two cases: either the tank is supported at the bottom of the

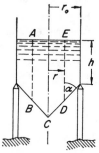

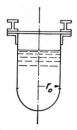

Fig. 51. Water tank with a conical bottom and cylindrical top supported ringwise from the bottom of the cylinder. The meridional stress in the circular section BD must be large enough to support the weight of the body of water $ABCDE$.

Fig. 52. Water tank suspended from the top. In this type of tank the meridional stress in each horizontal cross section of the cylinder must be sufficient to carry the weight of all the water; in a tank supported from below, like Fig. 51, the meridional stress in the cylinder is zero.

cylindrical part (Fig. 51 or the 100-ft-diameter oil tank resting on the ground) or the tank is suspended from the top of the cylindrical part (Fig. 52).

If in Fig. 51 we isolate a portion of the cylinder above a horizontal circular cut, then the water-pressure forces on this part are radial only, having no vertical component. The upper portion is in equilibrium without any vertical forces whatever, and hence the meridional stress is zero in the entire cylindrical part. In Fig. 52 we first make a horizontal cut through the cylinder above the water level; then clearly the vertical equilibrium of the bottom part requires a meridional stress,

$$s_m = \frac{W}{2\pi r_0 t}$$

where W is the weight of *all* the water, including that in the half sphere below the cylinder. (In all these calculations we neglect the weight of the shell itself; any stresses caused by the shell weight itself have to be added to the results obtained in this chapter.) Next we isolate a section of the cylindrical shell between two horizontal cuts, one above the water level, and one somewhere through the water. The water presses on the shell in a horizontal direction only, and hence vertical equilibrium requires that the meridional stress in the cylinder is the same at any level.

The next example is that of the *conical water-tank bottom* of Fig. 51. We have seen on page 74 that the meridional stress is

$$s_m = \frac{W_{ABCDE}}{2\pi r t \cos \alpha} = \frac{\gamma \{\pi r^2 [h + (r_0 - r) \cot \alpha] + \pi r^3 \cot \alpha/3\}}{2\pi r t \cos \alpha}$$

$$s_m = \frac{\gamma r}{2t} \left[\frac{h}{\cos \alpha} + \frac{r_0 - \frac{2}{3}r}{\sin \alpha} \right]$$

We conclude from this that the meridional stress at the apex of the cone is always zero. We also conclude that when the cone becomes a flat plate ($\alpha = 90$ deg; hence $\cos \alpha = 0$) then the stress becomes infinite if there is any water height h at all. Turning to Eq. (52) we first have to find the radii of curvature. Applying the discussion of Fig. 50 to our new case (Fig. 51), we see that $R_m = \infty$ and $R_t = r/\cos \alpha$. Thus Eq. (52) becomes

$$s_t = \frac{pr}{t \cos \alpha}$$

again showing zero stress at the apex, and again becoming infinitely large when the cone flattens out to a plate. The latter fact verifies that a flat membrane cannot take loads perpendicular to itself.

A very simple case is that of a *spherical shell* r_0 *under constant internal gas pressure*, like a *balloon*. If we draw two great circles on it, intersecting each other at right angles, we may call either one of them a meridian and then the other one is a tangent circle. From this symmetry it follows that the stresses s_m and s_t are equal. Also, the two principal radii of curvature R_m and R_t are equal to r_0. From Eq. (52) we then conclude

$$\frac{s}{r_0} + \frac{s}{r_0} = \frac{p}{t}$$

so that

$$s = \frac{pr_0}{2t}$$

The result can be verified by applying Eq. (53) to the half sphere:

$$s2\pi r_0 t = p\pi r_0^2$$

The situation is more complicated for a *spherical tank, filled wholly or partly with liquid* (Fig. 53). First we write the vertical equation (53) for a section AA, isolating the top slice of tank with its oil. Assuming tensile s_m stresses at A, we find that the upper assembly is pulled down by those stresses; it is also pulled down by the weight of the oil in that part, and it is pushed up by the hydraulic pressure $p\pi r^2$ on the circle AA. This latter quantity is equal to the weight of a cylinder of oil $AABB$. Hence the downpull of the s_m stress accounts for only the weight of the shaded volume in Fig. 53, which we designate as W^*:

$$W^* = 2\pi r t s_m \sin\,\theta$$

From this s_m can be calculated numerically in each case. Applying Eq. (52), we find

$$s_t + s_m = \frac{pr_0}{t} = \frac{\gamma h r_0}{t}$$

or

$$s_t = \frac{1}{2\pi t r \sin\,\theta}\,[2\pi r^2 h\gamma - W^*]$$

The first term in the square bracket is twice the weight $W_{\rm cyl}$ of the cylinder of fluid $AABB$ in Fig. 53, so that the entire square bracket is the sum of that cylinder $AABB$ and the actual fluid above line AA:

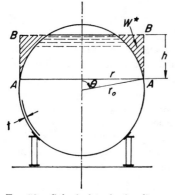

$$s_t = \frac{W_{\rm cyl} + W_{\rm fluid}}{2\pi t r_0 \sin^2\,\theta}$$

These expressions for s_t and s_m are good only in the region above the supporting ring. Inspecting s_m first, we see that the tensile meridional stress increases when we go down from the oil surface until we reach the center of the tank. When going down still farther ($\theta > 90$ deg), part of the shaded W^* area in Fig. 53 falls inside the tank, so that W^* decreases and with it the meridional stress. At some distance below the center W^* becomes zero, and below this level the s_m stress is compressive. On the other hand, the s_t stress is always tensile. The strength of a tank is usually judged by the maximum

Fig. 53. Spherical tank of radius r_0 and thickness t, partially filled with oil of specific weight γ lb/cu in.; supported by a ring near the bottom.

shear theory, and we see that the shear becomes large just above the supporting ring, because s_m and s_t have opposite signs.

For the region below the supporting ring the condition is the same as that for the conical tank bottom of Fig. 51, with the same analysis as given on page 77 for that case. Thus

$$s_m = \frac{W^{**}}{2\pi r t \sin\,\theta}$$

$$s_t = \frac{pr_0}{t} - s_m$$

where W^{**} is the weight of a body of water bounded by a cylinder r from the top surface down and by the spherical tank bottom below. The working out of numerical cases shows that the stress in the shell just above the supporting ring often is very much greater than below the supporting ring (Problem 61).

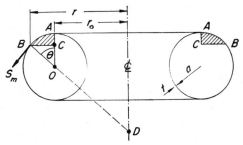

FIG. 54. Toroidal shell, having approximately the shape of a pump or turbine housing, subjected to constant internal pressure p.

Our next example (Fig. 54) is *a shell in the shape of a torus or doughnut,* a shape which resembles closely the "scroll case" of a Francis hydraulic turbine or centrifugal pump. The waterhead on these turbines or pumps usually is many times the height of the torus, so that the pressure p is sensibly constant inside. In order to apply Eq. (53), we isolate a ring-shaped piece of shell and water as indicated by shading in the figure. The stress s_m acting on the circle AA has no vertical component. Neither has the water pressure on the cylindrical surface AC a vertical component. Thus balance must occur between the water pressure on the annular plane surface BC and the s_m stress at B. (Be careful to note that this stress is s_m, meridional, in spite of the fact that it happens to be tangent to the circle a; the stress s_t is perpendicular to the paper of Fig. 54.) Equation (53) thus is

$$s_m 2\pi r t \sin \theta = p\pi(r^2 - r_0^2)$$

From the geometry we see that $r - r_0 = a \sin \theta$, so that

$$s_m = \frac{pa}{t} \frac{r + r_0}{2r}$$

From the discussion with Fig. 50, we have for the radii of curvature at point B

$$R_m = BO = a \qquad R_t = BD = \frac{r}{\sin \theta}$$

Substituting this into Eq. (52) gives

$$\frac{p}{t}\frac{r + r_0}{2r} + \frac{s_t \sin \theta}{r} = \frac{p}{t}$$

and, when worked out, remembering that $r - r_0 = a \sin \theta$, this becomes simply

$$s_t = \frac{pa}{2t}$$

a result which is the same for the straight cylinder ($r_0 \rightarrow \infty$), except that the meaning of s_t and s_m is reversed between the torus and the straight cylinder. The s_t stress in a straight cylinder follows from the s_m stress in the torus by letting r and r_0 go to infinity with respect to a, with the result pa/t, as it should be.

It is seen that both s_m and s_t stresses in the scroll case are tensile and that the s_t stress is fairly small everywhere. The s_m stress becomes a maximum at the inside point, where r is a minimum, and this stress becomes large for a doughnut with a small hole, where r_0 is only little larger than a.

The last example of this section is *a thin-walled dome of a building*, of spherical shape and equal thickness all over and loaded by its own weight only [or by a snow load which is assumed to be the same everywhere per unit actual area, not vertically projected area (Fig. 55)]. If γ is the weight

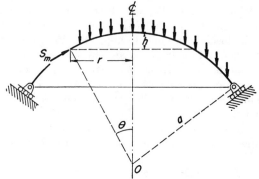

FIG. 55. Spherical dome of constant thickness, and hence constant weight per unit area, loaded by its own weight only.

per unit area of the dome, including its snow load, if the dome radius is a, and its thickness is t, then Eq. (53) for the compressive stress s_m gives

$$-s_m 2\pi r t \sin \theta = \gamma A$$

The area A of a spherical segment can be found in handbooks as being

$$A = 2\pi ah = 2\pi a(a - a \cos \theta) = 2\pi a^2(1 - \cos \theta)$$

From the figure we see that $r = a \sin \theta$, so that

$$s_m = -\frac{\gamma a}{t}\frac{1 - \cos \theta}{\sin^2 \theta} = \frac{-\gamma a}{t(1 + \cos \theta)}$$

The second stress is found from Eq. (52), where we remember that in a sphere $R_m = R_t = a$:

$$s_m + s_t = \frac{pa}{t}$$

The pressure p is the normal component of the weight, or $p = -\gamma \cos \theta$, negative because it acts inward (see Fig. 50):

$$s_t = \frac{\gamma a}{t}\left(-\cos \theta + \frac{1}{1 + \cos \theta}\right)$$

We see that the meridional stress is always negative, *i.e.*, compressive, as expected. The tangential stress is also compressive for small angles θ; at the top $\theta = 0$ the two stresses s_m and s_t are equal, which they must be from symmetry. For large angles θ the tangential stress becomes tensile; it is zero at an angle, where $1 + \cos \theta = 1/\cos \theta$, which occurs at $\theta = 52$ deg, and for $\theta > 52$ deg s_t is tensile. In thin-walled tanks made of metal we like tensile stresses and dislike compressive ones for the reason that buckling will occur sooner or later. Domes, however, are usually made of bricks, stone, or concrete, where we like compressive stresses but dislike tensile ones, because the material has practically no strength in tension.

Now we shall *review all the examples of this section for difficulties with boundary conditions*, and before drawing general conclusions we start with the case of a cylindrical boiler with two semispherical heads at the ends (Fig. 56).

The hoop stress s_t in the cylinder is pr/t, and the hoop stress in the half sphere is $pr/2t$ as we have seen (in the sphere the curvature in *both* directions carries the pressure load, while in the cylinder one of the two curvatures, being zero, is useless for that purpose). The meridional stress s_m is the same in both. The hoop strain ϵ_t then, by Eqs. (54), is more than twice as large in the cylinder as it is in the sphere, and, if these stresses as calculated by Eqs. (52) and (53) actually existed, the radial deformations would produce the situation of Fig. 56a. This, of course, does not occur, and the cylinder will pull the sphere outward, while the sphere will pull the cylinder inward by means of mutual transverse shear forces as indicated in Fig. 56b. The magnitude of these forces will be so that the gap is closed. But then the tangents to the two curves may not be the same, and to take care of that, mutual bending moments may occur between the two parts.

Thus in the case of Fig. 56, secondary bending and shear stresses exist, and the question arises in which of the other examples this is so, and in which others the membrane stresses alone are the whole story. If we look critically at Fig. 56, we see the answer to the question. The membrane

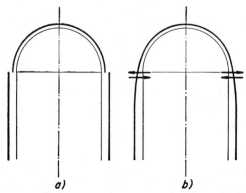

a)   *b)*

FIG. 56. A cylindrical boiler with hemispherical heads subjected to internal pressure. Under the influence of unadulterated membrane stresses [(Eqs. (52) and (53)], the deformation [(Eq. (54)] would be as shown in (a); in reality (b) takes place with additional local bending moments and transverse shear forces in both sphere and cylinder. These stresses will be calculated in detail on page 169.

deformations, Eqs. (54), must not be discontinuous; hence it follows that the membrane stresses s_t and s_m must not be discontinuous either. Now, if we examine Eqs. (52) and (53), we see that there must be no discontinuities in the thickness t, the pressure p, or the radii of curvature R_m and R_t. The pressure p is almost always continuous. The thickness t is often constant and mostly continuous, but still oil tanks are constructed in which the plates near the bottom are thicker than at the top to take care of the larger pressure there. In that case there will be a discontinuity in the stress at the joints and with it a situation like Fig. 56a, necessitating bending stresses. But most of all discontinuities occur in the radius of curvature, and this was responsible for the plight of Fig. 56a.

There is still another form of discontinuity which is not apparent in Eqs. (52) and (53), and that is a discontinuity in slope such as is shown in Fig. 51. The meridional membrane stress s_m in the cylinder, if any, is directed tangent to the cylinder, and the s_m stress in the cone is tangent to the cone. Let us for a moment imagine that the support in Fig. 51 is not at the joint between cylinder and cone, but somewhere else. Then the s_m of the cone will have a component perpendicular to the cylinder center line, pulling in on the bottom edge of the cylinder (as in Fig. 56b) and hence causing secondary stresses.

Still another cause for bending stresses occurs at a support. The membrane stresses at the support cause a certain deformation there, and if the support is ring-shaped and interferes with that deformation, secondary bending stresses are set up.

Summarizing, we find that secondary stresses are caused by supports, by discontinuities in slope or curvature in the membrane, or by discontinuities in the thickness or the loading of the membrane. For example, in Fig. 53 there will be secondary stress at the supporting ring, because it causes a concentrated loading there with consequent discontinuity in the stress; there is no secondary stress, however, at the free surface of the oil, because the discontinuity there is only in the rate of change of loading and not in the loading itself. In Fig. 54 there is practically no secondary stress, because everything is completely continuous, so that the membrane solution for that case will agree very well with the experimental fact. The secondary stress in the torus is "practically" zero, and not absolutely zero, because it slightly violates the condition of page 72 of no deformation of the shell due to the loading. In other words, a torus of circular section subjected to internal pressure will not quite retain its circular section. In still other words, a toroidally shaped soap bubble has a cross section slightly different from a circle; and if we start with a pure circular section the internal pressure will first tend to deform the section to that non-circle with consequent bending stresses. These, however, are small in comparison to bending stresses caused by discontinuities.

In the dome of Fig. 55 there will be secondary stress only if the support reaction differs from a purely tangential force. This will almost always be the case, because roller supports as shown in the figure are not common in building construction.

We shall see later, on page 169, that these bending stresses are usually local in character and that quite often they diminish the membrane stresses locally. For this reason the theory of membrane stresses in thin shells is of great practical importance, in spite of the fact that in almost every example of this section the membrane theory does not tell the whole story.

14. Shells of Uniform Strength. A few interesting solutions exist to the practical problem of how to shape a shell in order to give it uniform strength, and we shall discuss here three such cases: a boiler or pressure vessel head (Fig. 57), a "fluid-drop" gasoline storage tank (Fig. 59), and a building dome (Fig. 62). Before we start on these, we remark that almost all of the applications on pages 74 to 82 can be designed for constant maximum shear stress by adopting a variable plate thickness t. The only exception to this statement is the dome, where the loading depends on the thickness; in all the other examples the loading is independent of the thickness. Equations (52) and (53) are so built that if locally the thickness t is doubled, both stresses at that point are reduced to half, because in both equations the variables t, s_m, and s_t occur only in the two combinations $s_m t$ and $s_t t$. All we have to do then is to calculate the maximum shear stress (for constant t) as a function of location and then thicken the shell locally where that shear stress is large. Thus by making the thickness t inversely proportional to the calculated shear stress for constant t, we achieve constant shear stress distribution over the entire shell. We chose to make the maximum *shear* stress constant because that is a good criterion for yielding in steel plate. But we could have chosen any other criterion as well, such as maximum principal tensile stress (for concrete constructions) or maximum strain. In any case the demand to make this *one* criterion constant all over can be met by choosing the *one* variable, the thickness t, in an appropriate distribution.

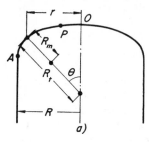

a)

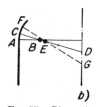

b)

Fig. 57.   Biezeno's construction for a boiler head of constant thickness and constant maximum shear based on the membrane stresses in the head and in the cylinder. Discontinuities in the curvatures occur at A and at P, so that near these points secondary bending stresses are to be expected.

This particular way of making a shell of constant strength is interesting mathematically, but it is hardly practical. Approximations to it are in daily use: large cylindrical bulk storage tanks for gasoline (100 ft in diameter) are usually constructed with several thicknesses of plate, stepping down in thickness toward the top where the s_t stress is less. Doing this sets up secondary bending stresses at the jumps in plate thickness, as we have seen on page 82.

The first practical question of equal strength was solved by Biezeno in 1922, who designed the *shape of a boiler drum head* so that with equal thickness t the maximum shear due to "membrane stress" is constant all over the head and over the cylindrical part as well. The construction is shown in Fig. 57, and the radius of curvature R_m near the cylindrical part is smaller than the cylinder radius R, and certainly smaller than R_t. We have in the head

$$\frac{s_t}{R_t} + \frac{s_m}{R_m} = \frac{p}{t} \tag{52}$$

$$2\pi r t s_m \sin\ \theta = \pi r^2 p \tag{53}$$

From this we solve for the two stresses in the head, remembering that $r = R_t \sin \theta$:

$$s_m = \frac{pR_t}{2t} \qquad s_t = \frac{pR_t}{2t}\left(2 - \frac{R_t}{R_m}\right)$$

Thus the meridional stress is always tensile, but the tangential stress will be compressive when $R_t > 2R_m$. We shall assume this to be the case (subject to later verification); then the maximum shear stress, by Mohr's circle, is half the difference between the two principal stresses:

$$(s_s)_{max} = \frac{1}{2}\frac{pR_t}{2t}\left(\frac{R_t}{R_m} - 1\right)$$

For the cylindrical part of the tank we found on page 75 $s_t = pR/t$ and $s_m = pR/2t$, both tensile, so that here the maximum shear stress is half the difference between the two extreme principal stresses s_t and "zero," or

$$(s_s)_{max} = \frac{1}{2}\frac{pR}{t}$$

Setting the shear stress in the cylinder and in the head equal to each other everywhere gives the criterion for constant strength,

$$R_t\left(\frac{R_t}{R_m} - 1\right) = 2R$$

which determines the shape of the head. From the figure we can easily see the values of R and R_t at each point, while R_m is more elusive; thus we solve the above for R_m:

$$R_m = \frac{R_t^2}{R_t + 2R}$$

At the junction between cylinder and head we see that $R_t = R$, so that the formula requires $R_m = R/3$, which satisfies our previous requirement at this point. Now we are ready to construct the shape of the head graphically with the formula as a recipe. We start in Fig. 57b by plotting point B at one-third of the cylinder radius and draw arc AC with B as center for a small angle. Then we draw CB until it intersects at D, with CD being the new value of R_t. Putting that into the recipe, we calculate R_m (which comes out somewhat larger than $R/3$), and we lay that off as CE; then describe a small arc CF with E as center, and so on. The construction continues from point to point, and R_m grows at a faster rate than R_t, until a point is reached where $R_m = \frac{1}{2}R_t$, somewhere near point P in Fig. 57a. Beyond this our recipe is no longer valid, because the s_t stress becomes tensile instead of being compressive as it was from A to P. Beyond P then the new maximum shear criterion is half the maximum stress, which is half s_m or $pR_t/4t$. Comparing this with the maximum shear stress in the cylinder, we recognize that $R_t = 2R$ at this point. We now jump with our value of R_m from $R_m = R$ at the left of P to $R_m = R_t = 2R$ at the right of P and complete the head with a spherical cap over the center from P to O. The two stresses here are $s_t = s_m = p(2R)/2t = pR/t$, so that the maximum shear is $pR/2t$, satisfying our criterion of constant maximum shear stress. Thus the shape is entirely determined.

We notice that in this solution there are two places (A and P) in which discontinuities occur in the radius of curvature R_m, and hence secondary bending and shear stresses will appear near those points. First let us investigate point A. By Eqs. (54) the increase in radius of the cylinder there calculates to $1.7pR/2Et$, and the decrease in radius of the head at A is $1.3pR/2Et$. This means that, as a result of the internal pressure p, shear forces appear, tending to pull in on the cylinder and to pull out on the head. The total discrepancy between the radii is $\frac{3}{2}(pR/Et)$. The reader should verify that in case the assembly is designed for $(s_s)_{max} = 10{,}000$ lb/sq in., and hence for $pR/t = 20{,}000$ lb/sq in., the discrepancy in radius is $0.001R$. Now this can be eliminated by proper assembly before the pressure is put on. If we make the radius at A in the head 0.001 in./in. greater than that of the cylinder and rivet or weld them together in that condition, we set up a residual bending stress in the case of $p = 0$; but this bending stress then disappears when the pressure is brought on (Fig. 58). No such procedure seems possible for removing the effect of the discontinuity in strain at point P, Fig. 57.

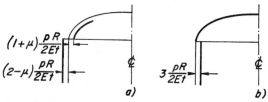

$(1+\mu)\dfrac{pR}{2Et}$

$(2-\mu)\dfrac{pR}{2Et}$

$3\dfrac{pR}{2Et}$

a)   *b)*

Fig. 58.   (a) The deformations caused by pressure in the cylinder and head of a boiler if each were subjected to pure membrane stresses only, without secondary bending. (b) Proposed unstressed shape of the drum and head before assembly. When internal pressure is put on the two parts individually, the gap closes up, so that if they are assembled with a shrink fit as shown, the secondary stresses under application of pressure will be much diminished.

Our second example is that of a *drop-shaped oil storage tank* (Fig. 59). This construction was suggested by the shape of a drop of water lying on a flat, waxed horizontal surface or of a drop of mercury on a horizontal table. There are two actions at work: capillary tension in the surface of the drop, which alone tends to make it purely spherical, and gravity of the liquid in the drop, which tends to flatten it out completely. The actual shape is a compromise between those two actions. Now the capillary tension in the surface of liquid is a property of that surface and is constant all over. Hence if we have a tank full of liquid encased in a steel skin of constant thickness and of constant tension in all directions, that tank should have the same shape as the drop. For this analogy it is necessary not only that the tank be entirely full of liquid, but that the liquid at the top point have a definite pressure. The parallel does not apply therefore to a tank which is vented to the atmosphere at the top. A graphical construction for the shape has been worked out which is practically the same as that of the previous example. Here, however, we demand in advance that the two stresses s_m and s_t are *individually* constant and equal to each other and to s_0, which is different from the situation in the boiler head. Referring to Fig. 59, we write

$$\frac{1}{R_m} + \frac{1}{R_t} = \frac{p}{s_0 t} \qquad (52)$$

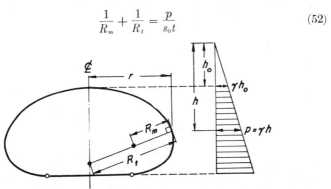

FIG. 59.   Oil tank in the shape of a drop; the oil is contained within a steel skin of constant thickness, having a stress s_0 which is the same in all directions at each point and also is the same at all points.

Here t and s_0 are constants, while the pressure p increases linearly toward the bottom of the tank. We shall use this equation as our recipe for constructing the shape, starting at the top. At the top the surface of revolution has the same radius of curvature in any direction, so that there (and there alone) $R_m = R_t$. Hence

$$R_{\text{top}} = \frac{2s_0 t}{p_{\text{top}}} = \frac{2s_0 t}{\gamma h_0}$$

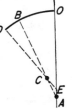

FIG. 60. Graphical construction of the drop-shaped tank by stepwise application of Eq. (52), starting at O, then proceeding to A, B, C, D, E, etc.

With this known radius we start the construction from the top of the tank, as shown in Fig. 60. The first step, from O to B, can be made quite large, because in Eq. (52) the pressure $p = \gamma h$ hardly changes on a horizontal tangent, and this pressure change is the only cause for a change in R_m or R_t. At point B we calculate the new pressure, which is slightly higher than at the top O, and with this in Eq. (52), with $R_t = AB$, we calculate R_m, which comes out somewhat smaller than before. The answer is laid out as BC in the diagram, and the new arc BD is described with C as center. This arc is made shorter than OB to give about the same height change. The new R_t then is DE, etc. The construction must be continued with approximately equal steps Δh in height until we come to a horizontal tangent of the tank on the ground.

We see that we have obtained a complete solution of the problem using Eq. (52) alone and without mentioning the other equilibrium equation (53). This is an interesting point to which we shall return on page 90; here we only state that with this construction the equilibrium along the vertical center line is automatically satisfied.

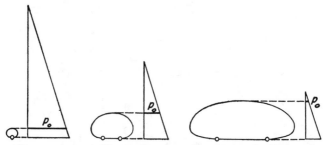

FIG. 61.   Mercury drops of different sizes on a table, showing the different shapes the tank of Fig. 59 assumes for various ratios of pressure between the top and bottom of the tank. The flat shape at the right is most advantageous if the tank is to be vented to atmosphere at the top.

The shape of the tank depends on the ratio of top and bottom pressures $h_{\text{top}}/h_{\text{bottom}}$, or, what is more easily seen when starting the construction, Fig. 60, it depends on the ratio $h_0/R_{t\ \text{top}}$. Suppose we make this ratio large, *i.e.*, a small R_t compared with h_0; then the first step of Fig. 60 can be made 180 deg, and the tank can be made purely spherical, resting on its bottom point, without ever getting an appreciable change in the pressure p. If, however, we start with $R_{\text{top}} = 10h_0$, then the tank becomes a flabby pancake. This can be visualized by thinking of drops of mercury of various sizes on a flat table, as shown in Fig. 61. The pressure at the top p_0 by Eq. (52) is proportional to $1/R_t$ so that p_0 decreases with increasing size, as shown. The slopes of the pressure-diagram lines must be the same, as they are all for the same mercury, gripped by the same g.

The third and last example of a shell of uniform stress is that of *a dome loaded by its own weight*. When that dome is made spherical and of constant thickness t, we have seen on page 81 that the stresses show appreciable variation over the surface. Now we ask what shape (of revolution) the dome must be given in order to make $s_t = s_m = -s_0$, compressive, and everywhere the same. The statement of the problem is entirely the same as that for the tank of Fig. 59. But whereas with the tank we succeeded in finding a shape satisfying our requirement with constant plate thickness t, we shall not be able to do this with the dome; here the shape as well as t must satisfy a definite law for making the stress constant. The reason for this will be explained at the end of the construction (page 90), when we shall be in a better position to understand it.

Let the dome be as shown in Fig. 62; the equilibrium perpendicular to the surface, as expressed by Eq. (52), is

$$\frac{1}{R_m} + \frac{1}{R_t} = \frac{p}{-s_0 t} = \frac{-\gamma t \cos \theta}{-s_0 t} = \frac{\gamma}{s_0} \cos \theta$$

where γ is the weight of the dome per unit volume and p is that component of the unit weight γt which is perpendicular to the surface of the dome, pointing outward.

It is seen that the thickness cancels out of the equation, which is practically the same as that for the drop-shaped tank. Again, at the top the radius of curvature is the same for all meridian cuts throughout the 360-deg compass, so that $R_m = R_t$ and $R_{\text{top}} = 2s_0/\gamma$. Thus, once we choose a working stress s_0 and a material γ, we have the radius at the top and can start the graphical construction of Fig. 60. In the oil tank the pressure head h increased when going down; here the angle θ increases; the construction is the same even if the cookbook recipe calls for different condiments. The construction is continued as far as we wish; the farther we go down, the higher our dome becomes in proportion to the base diameter.

So far there has been no significant difference between the dome and the oil tank, but now it comes. In the oil tank the p loading was entirely perpendicular to the skin, having no tangential component, while in the dome there is a meridional component of load $\gamma t \sin \theta$ per unit area. Now if we look at a square element $ds\, ds\, t$ of the shell (Fig. 63) and examine the equilibrium in the direction of one of the sides ds (in the plane of the shell), then we see that for constant stress s_0, for constant thickness, and for absence of a loading along the plane (as in our oil tank) the equilibrium is assured. We choose the two sides ds along a meridian and along a tangential circle. This means that for the oil tank of Fig. 59 a small

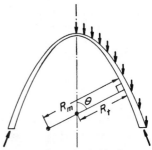

FIG. 62. Dome loaded by its own weight only, designed to such shape and thickness variation that the stress is everywhere the same: $s_t = s_m = -s_0$.

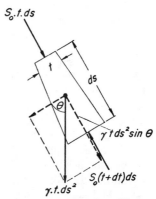

FIG. 63. Meridional equilibrium of an element $ds\, ds\, t$ of the shell. The presence of a component of loading in the direction of the meridian requires a compensating force, which for constant stress s_0 means an increased thickness $t + dt$.

element is in equilibrium in the tangential and meridional directions. If the latter equation is integrated along a meridian, we arrive at Eq. (53). Thus Eq. (53) is an expression for the meridional equilibrium of an element; the tangential equilibrium of such an element is automatically assured by the rotational symmetry.

Now in our dome there is a loading acting in the meridional direction (Fig. 63), so that the meridional equilibrium equation becomes

$$s_0 t \, ds + \gamma t (ds)^2 \sin \theta = s_0 (t + dt) \, ds$$

or

$$s_0 \, dt = \gamma t \, ds \sin \theta$$

But we see in Fig. 63 that $ds \sin \theta = dh$, the difference in vertical height across our element. Separating variables, we write

$$\frac{dt}{t} = \frac{\gamma}{s_0} \, dh$$

Integrated,

$$\log t = \frac{\gamma}{s_0} h + \text{const}$$

or

$$t = C e^{\gamma h / s_0} = t_0 e^{h/(s_0/\gamma)}$$

where h is measured downward (see Fig. 63).

The integration constant t_0 has the meaning of the thickness of the shell at the top $h = 0$. The quantity s_0/γ appearing in the exponent, and having the dimension of a length, means the height of a column of material so that the gravitational compressive stress at its bottom equals s_0. For almost any building material this height is a very great one. The thickness t of the dome is multiplied by a factor $e = 2.7$ when we go down from the top by this height s_0/γ. This length s_0/γ also is half of the radius of curvature at the top. Therefore the thickness of the dome increases by the factor 2.7 between the top and a point halfway down to the level of the center of curvature of the top. Since s_0/γ is very large, even for an extremely conservative stress, the possible size of a dome loaded by its own weight is very large.

15. Non-symmetrical Loading. The cases we have considered so far in this chapter were shells of revolution with loadings rotationally symmetrical about the axis of revolution. This symmetry enabled us to conclude that the principal directions of stress at each point were meridional and tangential, so that the state of stress at each point was described by two numbers s_m and s_t. At a point of the shell three equations of equilibrium could be written: one normal to the surface, Eq. (52), one in a meridional direction, which when integrated is equivalent to Eq. (53), and a third one in the tangential direction, which is automatically satisfied on account of the rotational symmetry.

Suppose now that we drop the symmetry and consider a thin-walled shell of any shape or a shell of revolution with a non-symmetrical loading. Then the principal stresses at a point of the shell are no longer meridional and tangential: in fact we do not know in which direction they are. The membrane stress at a point then can no longer be described by two numbers s_m and s_t; we need three numbers: the two principal stresses s_a, s_b and an angle α describing their direction, or two normal stresses s_1, s_2 on two given perpendicular directions with the shear stress s_s, as shown in Fig. 64. In a non-symmetrical case, therefore, we have one more un-

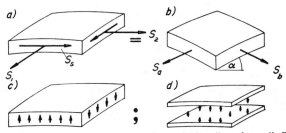

Fig. 64. (a) or (b) Stresses that are assumed to exist in a "membrane." The sets (a) and (b) are identical: they are just two different ways of describing the same thing, Mohr's circle furnishing the connection. The cases (c) and (d) show the other three possible stress components at a point, consisting of the two shear stresses (c) and a compressive or tensile stress between various thin sublayers of the shell as shown in (d). The definition of a "membrane" is that the stresses (c) and (d) are zero.

known than in the symmetrical case. But we also have one more equation of statics, because the equilibrium equation in the "tangential" direction now is an honest equation, and not an identity $A = A$ as it is in the symmetrical case. Looking over the derivation of Eq. (52) (page 73) for the equilibrium in the direction normal to the element, we see that that equation still holds here in the more complicated non-symmetrical case, because what is new here, the shear stress s_s of Fig. 64a, has no component in the normal direction. Hence the entire derivation of Eq. (52) and its end result remain in force. The two remaining equilibrium equations are along two perpendicular directions in the plane of the small element of shell, which is the tangent plane to the shell at that point. For a general shell we cannot always call these directions meridional and tangential, so that we shall call them x and y (Fig. 65). On the two faces dx, dy of the element, meeting in the corner A, we shall call the stresses s_x, s_y, and s_s. On the opposite faces the stresses then have different values as indicated in the figure. For the equilibrium in the x direction the difference between the two s_x forces on the dy faces must balance the difference between the two s_s forces on the dx faces,

$$\left(s_x + \frac{\partial s_x}{\partial x}\,dx\right)dy - s_x\,dy + \left(s_s + \frac{\partial s_s}{\partial y}\,dy\right)dx - s_s\,dx = 0$$

or

$$\frac{\partial s_x}{\partial x} + \frac{\partial s_s}{\partial y} = 0$$

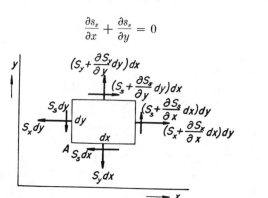

Fig. 65. A plane element $dx\,dy$ with the stresses acting on it. All three stresses s_x, s_y, and s_s vary from place to place, so that they assume slightly different values on opposite faces of the element. From this the second and third equilibrium equations (55) are derived.

In the same way the equilibrium in the y direction is found. Assembling all three equations together, we thus have

$$\frac{s_x}{R_x} + \frac{s_y}{R_y} = \frac{p}{t}$$

$$\frac{\partial s_x}{\partial x} + \frac{\partial s_s}{\partial y} = 0 \tag{55}$$

$$\frac{\partial s_y}{\partial y} + \frac{\partial s_s}{\partial x} = 0$$

To repeat: These are three equilibrium equations in the three unknowns s_x, s_y, and s_s, valid for the most general case of a thin-walled shell in which no bending or shear across the thickness t occurs. Thus *the problem of membrane stresses in the most general unsymmetrical shell is again statically determined.*

The *first example* we discuss is the best and most useful solution found so far of Eq. (55). It is that of *a long, horizontal, cylindrical water conduit* (Fig. 66) completely filled and supported on many points, all equally spaced apart. The non-symmetry in this case is not in the shell itself but in its loading: the pressure varies with the angle θ. For coordinates we choose θ and z, as shown in the figure. The third coordinate r is constant all over the shell. The water pressure is expressed by

$$p = \gamma h = \gamma r(1 - \cos \theta)$$

This is for the case of a pipe "just full" without excess pressure. In practice there usually is excess pressure (penstocks in hydraulic installations or oil-transport pipe lines), but that can be taken care of by superposing the constant-pressure solution of page 75 on what we are about to find. The principal radii of curvature at any point in the shell are r and ∞. Substituting this into the first of Eqs. (55), we have

$$\frac{s_t}{r} + \frac{s_l}{\infty} = \frac{\gamma r}{t} (1 - \cos \theta)$$

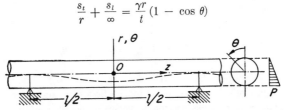

Fig. 66. Long, horizontal water pipe line, supported at equal distances l, just full of water. The solution of the general membrane equations (55) for this case leads to the stress distribution equations (56). This solution is due to Thoma (1920).

where the subscripts t and l mean tangential and longitudinal, corresponding to x and y, respectively in Eqs. (55). This can be solved immediately for the tangential stress:

$$s_t = \frac{\gamma r^2}{t} (1 - \cos \theta)$$

With this we enter into the second of Eqs. (55) and remember that $dx = r\,d\theta$ and $dy = dz$ in this case:

$$\frac{\partial}{r\partial \theta} \left[\frac{\gamma r^2}{t} (1 - \cos) \right] + \frac{\partial s_s}{\partial z} = 0$$

or

$$\frac{\partial s_s}{\partial z} = \frac{-\gamma r}{t} \sin \theta$$

In integrating this we remember that the ∂ sign means that θ is constant during the integration,

$$s_s = \frac{-\gamma r z}{t} \sin \theta + f_1(\theta)$$

where $f_1(\theta)$ is a "constant" of integration. Looking at Fig. 66, we see that the origin of z has been chosen at the center of the span, where for reasons of symmetry the shear stress must be zero (why?). At $z = 0$ the first term on the right side is zero, so that

$$0 = 0 + f_1(\theta)$$

and the "constant" $f_1(\theta)$ must vanish. Thus

$$s_s = \frac{-\gamma r z}{t} \sin \theta$$

With this we enter into the third of Eqs. (55),

$$\frac{\partial s_l}{\partial z} + \frac{\partial s_s}{r \partial \theta} = 0$$

$$\frac{\partial s_l}{\partial z} = + \frac{\gamma z}{t} \cos \theta$$

$$s_l = + \frac{\gamma z^2}{2t} \cos \theta + f_2(\theta)$$

where $f_2(\theta)$ is another "constant" of integration, to be found from the boundary conditions. Now, looking at the first term of s_l, we see that in any normal (circular) cross section it varies as cos θ, that is, linear with the vertical distance from the center of the circle, like the usual bending stress distribution. The second term $f_2(\theta)$ may represent any bending stress distribution, linear or non-linear. Now it appears highly improbable that we should find here a non-linear bending stress distribution, and we could *assume* it to be linear. In that case $f_2(\theta)$ should have the form C cos θ, and the constant C could be found from the bending moment by beam theory either at $z = 0$ or at $z = \pm l/2$. But we do not have to assume anything: the linear bending stress distribution can be proved, as follows: In Fig. 66 the deformed shape of the center line is indicated by a dotted curve. The deflection in the center of this curve is small of the first order with respect to the length l, and the rectified length of the dotted curve differs from l only by a quantity small of the second order, which is habitually neglected in strength of materials or elasticity. Hence we state that one full span of the center line of the pipe does not change its length. The same is true for any longitudinal fiber of the pipe, because above each support no point of the pipe moves to the right or to the left. Now the elastic extension of a fiber at location θ is

$$\int_{-l/2}^{+l/2} \frac{1}{E} (s_l - \mu s_t)\, dz$$

and we have just seen that this must be zero. We now substitute the obtained expressions for s_t and s_l [including the unknown $f_2(\theta)$] into this integral, set it equal to zero, and solve for f_2, with the result

$$f_2(\theta) = \frac{\gamma}{t} \left[-\frac{l^2}{24} \cos \theta + \mu r^2 (1 - \cos \theta) \right]$$

With this the longitudinal stress s_l becomes

$$s_l = \frac{\gamma}{t}\left(\frac{z^2}{2} - \frac{l^2}{24}\right) \cos\,\theta + \mu s_t$$

This result can be interpreted in a familiar manner. The second term μs_t is a tensile longitudinal stress caused by the fact that the natural Poisson contraction of l by the hoop stress s_t is prevented. The first term of s_l can be rewritten in the usual bending stress notation, if we verify that

$$y = r \cos\,\theta \qquad w = \gamma\pi r^2 \qquad I = \pi r^3 t$$

Then the first term is

$$\left[w\!\left(\frac{z^2}{2} - \frac{l^2}{24}\right)\right]\frac{y}{I}$$

The square bracket has the value $-wl^2/24$ at mid-span and $+wl^2/12$ above the supports, and the reader should check that the square bracket is the bending moment distribution obtained by the usual (statically indeterminate) beam theory for a beam I, l, loaded with uniform w and built in at both ends. Thus, recapitulating, the stress distribution in the pipe of Fig. 66 is

$$s_t = \frac{\gamma r^2}{t}(1 - \cos\,\theta)$$

$$s_s = -\frac{\gamma rz}{t}\sin\,\theta \tag{56}$$

$$s_l = \frac{\gamma}{t}\left(\frac{z^2}{2} - \frac{l^2}{24}\right)\cos\,\theta + \mu s_t$$

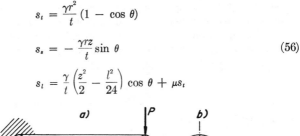

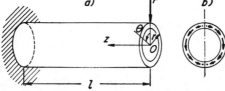

FIG. 67. Thin-walled pipe loaded as a cantilever. By membrane theory the stresses are as given in Eqs. (57). The load P is taken by the free-end section in the form of a shear stress distribution (b).

There are no discontinuities in the system, except at the concentrated reaction loads. The membrane solution (56) therefore will agree with fact very well at distances of about r from the bearings. The detail of the distribution of the bearing reaction load is, of course, not included in the result.

The *second example* we take up is *a pipe cantilevered into a wall with a concentrated end load P* (Fig. 67). Since there is no pressure load p at all, the first of Eqs. (55) reads

$$\frac{s_t}{r} + \frac{s_l}{\infty} = 0$$

so that $s_t = 0$. Substituting this into the second of Eqs. (55), it becomes

$$0 + \frac{\partial s_s}{\partial z} = 0$$

or, integrated, $s_s = f_1(\theta)$. Substituting this into the third equilibrium equation, we find

$$\frac{\partial s_l}{\partial z} + \frac{\partial}{r\partial \theta} f_1(\theta) = 0$$

or

$$s_l = -\int \frac{1}{r} f_1'(\theta) \, dz = -\frac{z}{r} f_1'(\theta) + f_2(\theta)$$

At the free end $z = 0$ the longitudinal stress is stated to be zero for all values of θ. We conclude that $f_2(\theta) = 0$. For the other integration "constant" $f_1(\theta)$ there is no readily discernible criterion, except that the shear force must be P and the bending moment must be Pz. This is not sufficient information from which we can calculate $f_1(\theta)$ without doubt, so that we now assume (in line with the result of the previous example) that the bending stress distribution s_l is linear, or

$$s_l = C_1 \cos \theta = -\frac{z f_1'(\theta)}{r}$$

Integrated,

$$f_1(\theta) = -\frac{rC_1}{z} \int \cos \theta \, d\theta = -\frac{rC_1}{z} \sin \theta + C_2$$

The function f_1 is the shear stress s_s, and, from symmetry, we see that s_s must be zero at $\theta = 0$ and at $\theta = \pi$. Thus $C_2 = 0$. The vertical component of the shear stress integrated over the annular cross section must equal $-P$†, or

$$\int_0^\pi s_s \sin \theta \, t \, rd\theta = \frac{-P}{2}$$

$$\frac{-r^2 C_1 t}{z} \int_0^\pi \sin^2 \theta \, d\theta = \frac{-\pi r^2 C_1 t}{2z} = \frac{-P}{2}$$

† The − sign is necessary because the shear stress as shown in Fig. 67 is negative by the definition of Fig. 65 (page 92), in connection with the fact that the x coordinate of Fig. 65 corresponds to the θ coordinate of Fig. 67 and the z coordinate of Fig. 67 is equivalent to the y coordinate of Fig. 65.

so that $C_1 = Pz/\pi r^2 t$. With this the solution of the problem is

$$s_t = 0$$

$$s_s = \frac{-P}{\pi r t} \sin \theta \qquad (57)$$

$$s_l = \frac{Pz}{\pi r^2 t} \cos \theta$$

The manner in which the shear stress is distributed over the cross section is shown in Fig. 67b. The solution (57) coincides with the one obtained by elementary beam theory. There are two discontinuities: at the free end and at the built-in end. At the free end the solution (57) requires that P be applied in the form of Fig. 67b; if it is put on in any other way, a local discrepancy results. At the built-in end the tube should be free to undergo such deformations as Eqs. (57) demand. In general the constraint there is different, so that another deviation from Eqs. (57) takes place. However, for long beams these equations describe the situation perfectly well in the central region, about one diameter removed from either end (Saint-Venant's principle, see page 183).

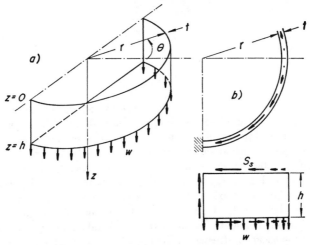

FIG. 68. Balcony beam. The membrane solution is given by Eqs. (58) and is illustrated in (b). The bending moment is taken not by the built-in end as required by practice but by (non-existing) shear forces at the top and bottom edges.

Our third and *last example* (Fig. 68) is a *semicircular balcony beam* of dimensions r, h, t built into a vertical wall at both ends and loaded at its bottom edge with a loading w lb/sq in. Choosing for the coordinates θ

and z as shown, the successive steps in Eqs. (55) are

$$\frac{s_t}{r} + \frac{s_l}{\infty} = 0 \qquad \therefore s_t = 0$$

$$0 + \frac{\partial s_s}{\partial z} = 0 \qquad \therefore s_s = f_1(\theta)$$

$$\frac{\partial s_l}{\partial z} + \frac{\partial f_1}{r \partial \theta} = 0 \qquad \therefore s_l = -\frac{z}{r} f_1' + f_2(\theta)$$

At the top edge $z = 0$, the longitudinal stress is prescribed to be zero, so that $f_2 = 0$. At the bottom edge $z = h$, we have $s_l = w$, or

$$w = -\frac{h}{r} f_1'$$

so that

$$f_1 = -\int \frac{rw}{h} d\theta = -\frac{rw\theta}{h} + C$$

This is the shear stress s_s, and it must be zero at the center $\theta = 0$, for reasons of symmetry; hence $C = 0$, and the final solution is

$$s_t = 0$$

$$s_s = -\frac{rw}{h} \theta \tag{58}$$

$$s_l = +\frac{w}{h} z$$

So far the mathematics. When we start to inspect this solution, our eyebrows go up. We expect bending moments at the built-in ends, and we are accustomed to see those moments in the form of linearly distributed bending stresses, which are s_l stresses in this case. But our solution states flatly that $s_l = 0$ everywhere, including the built-in ends.

Furthermore, Eqs. (58) say that there is a shear stress independent of the height z, so that it exists on the upper and lower edges, where it was supposed to be absent. Figure 68b illustrates the solution, and we see that the bending moment of w about the wall is taken not by the wall but rather by the shearing stresses on the upper and lower edges. The reader may verify by integration that everything is in order as far as moment equilibrium goes.

The solution (58) can be interpreted by modifying Fig. 68a. Suppose we add flanges to the top and bottom edges, making the cross section I-shaped instead of rectangular ht. Then the shear stresses of Fig. 68b can be transmitted to those flanges, and they in turn are anchored to the wall. That wall takes the bending moment in the form of two concentrated push-pull forces of the flanges.

This example shows that often it is easy enough to find a solution of Eqs. (55), but that the solution may show unexpected behavior at the boundaries. To find a solution conforming to given boundary conditions is usually impossible, because no "membrane" solution exists. The actual structure does develop bending stresses and shear stresses across the thickness to carry the load, but our Eqs. (55) are not powerful enough to describe that kind of stress.

Problems 61 *to* 75.

CHAPTER IV

BENDING OF FLAT PLATES

16. General Theory. The most important equation in the bending of straight beams states that the bending moment is the stiffness times the curvature d^2y/dx^2 of the "neutral line" of that beam. Plates are a two-dimensional generalization of beams, and we shall soon derive a pair of similar equations for plates, but before we can do that we must be clear about what we mean by the "curvature" of the neutral plane (the middle plane) of a flat plate. This is a little more complicated than might be supposed at first sight, so that we start from the beginning.

Geometry of Curved Surfaces. The middle plane of the unloaded flat plate becomes slightly curved when loaded. This slightly curved surface is conveniently described as $w = f(x, y)$, where x, y are the coordinates in the originally flat plane and w is the (small) elevation above it. The letter z is not used for this elevation, because z will mean the vertical distance of a plate particle from the neutral middle plane. Therefore, the plate extends in the unbent condition from $z = -t/2$ to $z = +t/2$, and, when bent, the material runs vertically from $(-t/2) + w$ to $(+t/2) + w$. Since $w(x, y)$ is a function of *two* variables, its derivatives must be written with ∂ instead of with d to avoid misunderstandings. The symbols $\partial w/\partial x$ and $\partial w/\partial y$ then are the slopes of the w surface when proceeding in the x and y directions, respectively. Likewise $\partial^2 w/\partial x^2$ and $\partial^2 w/\partial y^2$ are the "curvatures" of plane curves found by intersecting the w surface with vertical planes parallel to the x and y axes, respectively. [We remember that this is true only for surfaces deviating but little from a flat plane, in which the square of the slope is negligible; because the true expression for curvature is $w''/(1 + w'^2)^{3/2}$, which is only approximately equal to w''.] The reciprocals of the curvatures are the radii of curvature:

$$\frac{1}{R_x} = \frac{\partial^2 w}{\partial x^2} \qquad \frac{1}{R_y} = \frac{\partial^2 w}{\partial y^2} \tag{59}$$

The mixed second derivative is called the "twist" of the surface and is designated as $1/T_{xy}$:

$$\frac{1}{T_{xy}} = \frac{\partial^2 w}{\partial x \, \partial y} \tag{59a}$$

The reason for the name twist is seen in Fig. 69, because a sheet of paper can be given this property by twisting it with a torque, as shown. The designation $1/T_{xy}$ is chosen to bring it in line with $1/R_x$ and $1/R_y$ for the radii of curvature; it is clear that T_{xy} (the reciprocal of the twist) has the dimension of a length like R_x or R_y.

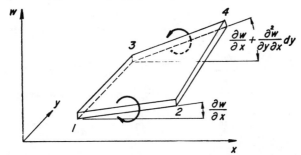

FIG. 69. Geometrical interpretation of $\dfrac{\partial^2 w}{\partial x\,\partial y}$ as the local "twist" of an element of surface. If the sides dx, dy of this element are made equal to "unity" and if the heights of the four corners are called w_1, w_2, w_3, w_4, then we have $w_3 - w_1 = \dfrac{\partial w}{\partial y}$; $w_4 - w_2 = \dfrac{\partial w}{\partial y}$ $+ \dfrac{\partial}{\partial x}\left(\dfrac{\partial w}{\partial y}\right)$ and hence, by subtraction, $\dfrac{\partial^2 w}{\partial x\,\partial y} = (w_1 + w_4) - (w_2 + w_3)$. Similarly $w_2 - w_1 = \dfrac{\partial w}{\partial x}$; $w_4 - w_3 = \dfrac{\partial w}{\partial x} + \dfrac{\partial}{\partial y}\left(\dfrac{\partial w}{\partial x}\right)$, and hence $\dfrac{\partial^2 w}{\partial y\,\partial x} = (w_4 + w_1) - (w_2 + w_3)$. This shows that $\dfrac{\partial^2 w}{\partial x\,\partial y} = \dfrac{\partial^2 w}{\partial y\,\partial x}$ for a continuous surface.

Now that we have analytical expressions for the curvatures in the x and y directions at a point, we ask the question of how to find the curvature at that same point in some other direction, at angle α with respect to the x direction. In Fig. 70 we look down on the xy plane, and the heights of the various points above the paper are $w = f(x, y)$. Going from one point to the next, we have in general

$$dw = \frac{\partial w}{\partial x}\,dx + \frac{\partial w}{\partial y}\,dy$$

Applying this in particular to going from A to B through a distance dl, we write

$$\frac{\partial w}{\partial l} = \frac{\partial w}{\partial x}\frac{dx}{dl} + \frac{\partial w}{\partial y}\frac{dy}{dl}$$

We see that $dx/dl = \cos\alpha$ and $dy/dl = \sin\alpha$, so that we can rewrite this to

$$\frac{\partial w}{\partial l} = \cos \alpha \, \frac{\partial w}{\partial x} + \sin \alpha \, \frac{\partial w}{\partial y}$$

and since the angle α is arbitrary, this is true for any value of α. If we now increase α by 90 deg, we reach the n or normal direction and the above becomes

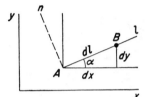

$$\frac{\partial w}{\partial n} = \cos (\alpha + 90) \, \frac{\partial w}{\partial x} + \sin (\alpha + 90) \, \frac{\partial w}{\partial y}$$

$$\frac{\partial w}{\partial n} = -\sin \alpha \, \frac{\partial w}{\partial x} + \cos \alpha \, \frac{\partial w}{\partial y}$$

Abstracting ourselves, we can write

Fig. 70. Plan view of an element of curved surface, for the derivation of the formulae for curvature and twist, leading to Mohr's-circle representation.

$$\frac{\partial}{\partial l} = \cos \alpha \, \frac{\partial}{\partial x} + \sin \alpha \, \frac{\partial}{\partial y}$$

$$\frac{\partial}{\partial n} = -\sin \alpha \, \frac{\partial}{\partial x} + \cos \alpha \, \frac{\partial}{\partial y}$$

which are equations in terms of differential "operators."

To find the curvature from the slope in the x direction, we did:

$$\frac{\partial}{\partial x} \left(\frac{\partial w}{\partial x} \right)$$

Similarly, the curvature in the l direction is

$$\frac{1}{R_l} = \frac{\partial}{\partial l} \left(\frac{\partial w}{\partial l} \right)$$

$$= \left(\cos \alpha \, \frac{\partial}{\partial x} + \sin \alpha \, \frac{\partial}{\partial y} \right) \left(\cos \alpha \, \frac{\partial w}{\partial x} + \sin \alpha \, \frac{\partial w}{\partial y} \right)$$

$$\frac{1}{R_\alpha} = \cos^2 \alpha \, \frac{\partial^2 w}{\partial x^2} + \sin^2 \alpha \, \frac{\partial^2 w}{\partial y^2} + \sin 2\alpha \, \frac{\partial^2 w}{\partial x \, \partial y}$$

To find the "twist" in the pair of directions x, y, we did:

$$\frac{1}{T_{xy}} = \frac{\partial}{\partial y} \left(\frac{\partial w}{\partial x} \right)$$

where y is a direction 90 deg counterclockwise from x. Similarly for the pair of directions l, n, we write

$$\frac{1}{T_\alpha} = \frac{\partial}{\partial n} \left(\frac{\partial w}{\partial l} \right)$$

$$= \left(-\sin \alpha \, \frac{\partial}{\partial x} + \cos \alpha \, \frac{\partial}{\partial y} \right) \left(\cos \alpha \, \frac{\partial w}{\partial x} + \sin \alpha \, \frac{\partial w}{\partial y} \right)$$

$$\frac{1}{T_\alpha} = \frac{1}{2} \sin 2\alpha \left(\frac{\partial^2 w}{\partial y^2} - \frac{\partial^2 w}{\partial x^2} \right) + \cos 2\alpha \, \frac{\partial^2 w}{\partial x \, \partial y}$$

Looking at this expression, we may recognize that by varying α it sometimes is positive and sometimes negative; hence there are some values of α for which the twist is zero. (If we don't see that now, it will be clear a little later, from Fig. 71.) To simplify the analysis, we now assume that our original x, y axes in Fig. 70 have been so chosen that the twist $1/T_{xy}$ is zero. Later we shall say that we have laid our x, y system "along the principal directions of curvature at the point A." With this choice of coordinate axes the formulae simplify to

$$\frac{1}{R_\alpha} = \cos^2 \alpha \frac{\partial^2 w}{\partial x^2} + \sin^2 \alpha \frac{\partial^2 w}{\partial y^2}$$

$$\frac{1}{T_\alpha} = \frac{1}{2}\sin 2\alpha\left(\frac{\partial^2 w}{\partial y^2} - \frac{\partial^2 w}{\partial x^2}\right)$$

The educated reader who has worked with stresses, strains, and moments of inertia will now sense the presence of Mohr's spirit and rewrite the results:

$$\frac{1}{R_\alpha} = \frac{1}{2}\left(\frac{1}{R_x} + \frac{1}{R_y}\right) + \frac{1}{2}\left(\frac{1}{R_x} - \frac{1}{R_y}\right)\cos 2\alpha$$

$$-\frac{1}{T_\alpha} = \frac{1}{2}\left(\frac{1}{R_x} - \frac{1}{R_y}\right)\sin 2\alpha$$

(60)

Thus the curvatures in all 360-deg compass directions at a point of a surface can be represented by the Mohr-circle diagram (Fig. 71). [Incidentally, Eqs. (60) apply to *any* continuous surface; they become restricted to nearly flat surfaces only when we write $\partial^2 w/\partial x^2$, etc., for the curvatures, instead of $1/R_x$, etc. The previous derivation still holds; we must assume that we were clever enough to choose the w axis of Fig. 70 perpendicular to the tangent plane of our highly curved surface at the point A being considered.]

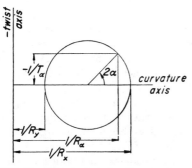

FIG. 71. Mohr's circle for the curvature and twist at a point of a curved surface.

From Fig. 71, we at once see several properties. First there is at any point a pair of mutually perpendicular directions for which the twist is zero; in these directions the curvatures are a maximum and a minimum, and of course we call these the "directions of principal curvature." We also see *Euler's theorem that the sum of the two curvatures in perpendicular directions at a point is constant*, independent of α:

$$\frac{1}{R_x} + \frac{1}{R_y} = \frac{1}{R_\alpha} + \frac{1}{R_{\alpha+90}}$$

(61)

If the two principal curvatures are the same, then the Mohr circle shrinks
to a point, the curvature is the same in all directions, and there is no twist
in any direction: the surface is purely spherical at that point.

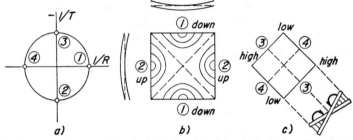

FIG. 72.   An element of surface at a "saddle point" (*b*) with the Mohr's circle (*a*).   The
dashed lines in Fig. 72*b* and *c* are lines of constant level.   Cutting the element out along
faces 1 and 2 (Fig. 72*b*) shows no twist; cutting it out at 45 deg, faces 3 and 4 (Fig. 72*c*)
remain straight, although they become tilted.   Compare this with the case of "pure
shear" in two-dimensional stress.

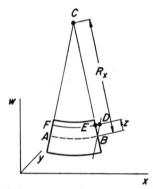

FIG. 73.   Element $t \, dx \, dy$ of
plate bent with radius of curva-
ture $R_x = 1/(\partial^2 w/\partial x^2)$ in the x
direction.   The middle-plane
fiber AB is neutral; hence the
fiber FD shortens by the amount
DE.   This leads to Eqs. (62).
The radius R_x has been so drawn
that $\partial^2 w/\partial x^2$ is positive, and z,
being in the $+w$ direction, is
also drawn positive.

An interesting case occurs when the two
principal curvatures are equal and of opposite sign.   The sum of the curvatures by
Euler's theorem [Eq. (61)] is then zero in all
directions.   The situation is illustrated in
Fig. 72.   It is interesting to look at Eq. (11)
(page 12), together with Eq. (61) and Fig.
72.   We conclude that in a membrane without normal pressure p, every point is a "saddle point," or, in different words, every surface element of such a membrane is in "pure
twist."

With this we finish our study of the geometrical properties of curvature and twist of
a surface, and we begin our main problem:
the bending of originally flat plates.   Analogous to what we know about beams, we start
with a *fundamental assumption: the middle
plane of our plate remains a neutral plane
during bending;* in other words, there is no
stress in the middle plane, and the stresses in
the fibers of the bent plate all occur as a
result of their normal distance from the neutral plane.   With beams this
assumption did not lead us into any trouble; with plates, however, we
shall see later, on page 138, particularly in Fig. 91, that *the assumption*

of a neutral middle plane restricts the results (in general) *to plate deflections which are small with respect to the plate thickness t.*

Strains. The middle surface then is deformed into a surface $w = f(x, y)$ because of the load, and our next objective is to find expressions for the strains, expressed in terms of this function w. For the strains ϵ_x or ϵ_y in the plane of the plate this is easy, as shown in Fig. 73. The line BD has been drawn parallel to CA, so that $AB = FD$. The stretch AB is "neutral," and before bending the two faces FA and EB were parallel. Then DE represents the shortening of fiber FD. The triangles BDE and CAB are similar, so that

$$-\epsilon_x = \frac{DE}{AB} = \frac{EB}{BC} = \frac{z}{R_x} = z\frac{\partial^2 w}{\partial x^2}$$

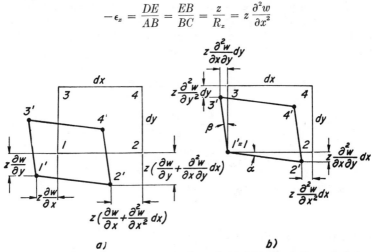

FIG. 74. An elemental area $dx\,dy$ of a plate located at height z above the neutral plane. In the unloaded state 1 2 3 4 its projection coincides with the corresponding $dx\,dy$ rectangle in the neutral plane. When bent, it veers off to the position $1'2'3'4'$ in Fig. 74a. Figure 74b is the same as (a), but now the figure $1'2'3'4'$ has been displaced parallel to itself to make $1'$ coincide with 1. From this figure we deduce the strain equations (62).

Here the letter z denotes the normal distance of the fiber in question from the neutral plane. Similarly we find in the y direction $\epsilon_y = -z(\partial^2 w/\partial y^2)$. The determination of the shear strain γ_{xy} in the xy plane of the plate is a little more difficult. Figure 74a shows a $dx\,dy$ rectangle of the plate at distance z above the neutral plane. When undeformed, this rectangle coincides in the projection shown with the corresponding $dx\,dy$ rectangle below it on the neutral plane. When bent, the normals on the neutral plane do not come up vertically, but at certain angles, which places the the points 1, 2, 3, 4 at z above the neutral plane in the new positions $1'$, $2'$, $3'$, $4'$. Consider point 1. The line element dx will have a slope $\partial w/\partial x$, and so will the normal on 1. Thus point $1'$ moves to the left through a distance $z(\partial w/\partial x)$. Now look at point 2. Its angle will not be quite the same: it will be $\dfrac{\partial w}{\partial x} + \dfrac{\partial}{\partial x}\left(\dfrac{\partial w}{\partial x}\right) dx$, and its movement to the left will be z times as large. Figure 74a carries these results and also those for the y movements of points 1 and 2. The reader should fill in for himself the displacements of point 3. Now strains are relative displacements; if points 1 and 2 were to move over by the same amounts, there would be no strain. Thus we redraw Fig. 74a in Fig. 74b, by subtracting the movements of point 1 from all the other movements. Figure 74b shows the displacements of points 2, 3, and 4 relative to point 1. The elongation in the x direction is 12′ less 12, or $-z(\partial^2 w/\partial x^2)\,dx$ on a base length dx. Hence again the strain $\epsilon_x = -z(\partial^2 w/\partial x^2)$, as found before. But the angle α now is seen to be $z(\partial^2 w/\partial x\,\partial y)\,dx$ divided by the base length dx, and similarly the angle β. The shear strain $\gamma_{xy} = \alpha + \beta$ so that, finally, we have

$$\epsilon_x = -z\frac{\partial^2 w}{\partial x^2} = -\frac{z}{R_x}$$

$$\epsilon_y = -z\frac{\partial^2 w}{\partial y^2} = -\frac{z}{R_y} \qquad (62)$$

$$\gamma_{xy} = 2z\frac{\partial^2 w}{\partial x\,\partial y} = \frac{2z}{T_{xy}}$$

Next, we *find the stresses by Hooke's law*:

$$E\epsilon_x = s_x - \mu s_y \qquad E\epsilon_y = s_y - \mu s_x$$

Solving this pair for the stresses s_x and s_y gives

$$s_x = \frac{E}{1 - \mu^2}(\epsilon_x + \mu\epsilon_y) \qquad s_y = \frac{E}{1 - \mu^2}(\epsilon_y + \mu\epsilon_x)$$

Substitution of Eqs. (62) into the above results leads to

$$s_x = \frac{-E}{1 - \mu^2}z\left(\frac{\partial^2 w}{\partial x^2} + \mu\frac{\partial^2 w}{\partial y^2}\right)$$

$$s_y = \frac{-E}{1 - \mu^2}z\left(\frac{\partial^2 w}{\partial y^2} + \mu\frac{\partial^2 w}{\partial x^2}\right) \qquad (63)$$

$$(s_s)_{xy} = 2Gz\frac{\partial^2 w}{\partial x\,\partial y}$$

We see that these stresses are all proportional to z, the distance from the neutral plane: we thus have linear bending stress distributions, just as in a bent beam, only now we have *two* bending moments, in the x and y directions (Fig. 75). In addition the shear stresses result in twisting couples on the plate element. In a beam we deal with the bending moment for the entire cross section. Here the plate extends indefinitely so that we introduce moments per unit length of cut through the plate, designated with a subscript 1. In this manner we have (Fig. 75b)

$$M_{1x} = - \int s_x z \, dA = \text{[substituting Eqs. (63)]}$$

$$+ \frac{E}{1 - \mu^2} \left(\frac{\partial^2 w}{\partial x^2} + \mu \frac{\partial^2 w}{\partial y^2} \right) \int z^2 \, dA$$

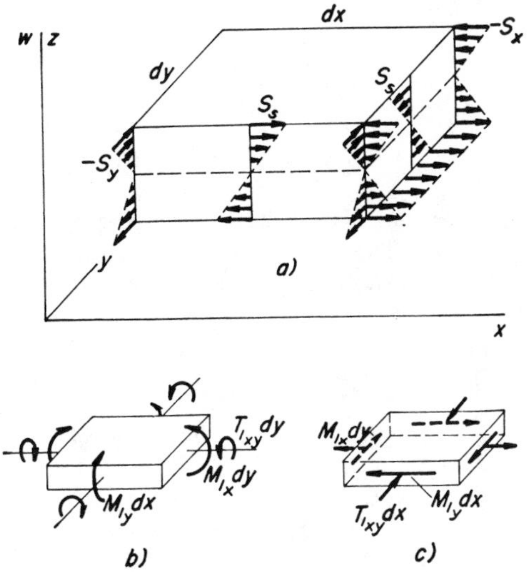

FIG. 75. (a) The stresses of Eqs. (63) shown on an element $t \, dx \, dy$; (b) the moments caused by these stresses, represented in the usual way; (c) the same moments, represented by the right-handed screw convention.

We now calculate $\int z^2 \, dA$ over a rectangular area of unit length and height t. We know that $I = bh^3/12$, so that here the integral is $t^3/12$ and

$$M_{1x} = \frac{E}{1 - \mu^2} \frac{t^3}{12} \left(\frac{\partial^2 w}{\partial x^2} + \mu \frac{\partial^2 w}{\partial y^2} \right)$$

Now this unit moment has a $+$ sign in front of it, because we define it positive in the direction shown in Fig. 75b or c. Equations (63) carry a $-$ sign, signifying that the stress for $+z$ is negative, or compressive, as shown in Fig. 75a.

In the above expression we see the factor

$$\frac{Et^3}{12(1 - \mu^2)} = D \tag{64}$$

which we denote by the single letter D, because it will appear from now on in almost every formula. It is called the *plate stiffness*, and it corresponds to EI in beam theory. (It is designated in the literature by a different letter by almost every author; the notation D adopted here is that of Timoshenko.) In a completely similar manner the unit bending moment in the y direction M_{1y} and the unit twisting torque T_{1xy} are calculated, with the result

$$M_{1x} = D\left(\frac{\partial^2 w}{\partial x^2} + \mu \frac{\partial^2 w}{\partial y^2}\right)$$

$$M_{1y} = D\left(\frac{\partial^2 w}{\partial y^2} + \mu \frac{\partial^2 w}{\partial x^2}\right) \qquad (65)$$

$$T_{1xy} = 2G \frac{t^3}{12} \frac{\partial^2 w}{\partial x \, \partial y} = D(1 - \mu)\left(\frac{\partial^2 w}{\partial x \, \partial y}\right)$$

because we remember that $E = 2G(1 + \mu)$ is the relation between the three elastic constants. The set of Eqs. (65) is equivalent to the single equation $M = EIy''$ in beam theory.

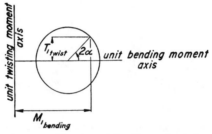

FIG. 76.   Mohr's circle representing the unit bending and twisting moments at a point of a plate. Once these moments are known for two perpendicular directions through that point, the diagram tells us how to find the moments in any other direction through that point.

Now, if we compare Eqs. (63) for the stresses with Eqs. (65) for the unit moments, we see that they are practically the same. If the z in (63) is replaced by $t^3/12$ (and the signs of the first two are reversed), we obtain Eqs. (65). But Eqs. (63) represent three stresses on a plane element, and these quantities are related to each other by the Mohr-circle construction. If we multiply everything by $t^3/12z$, Mohr's circle will still apply (with a reversed sign for the T_{1xy} torque). Thus we find in Fig. 76 still another application for the very versatile Mohr construction. It states that if we have once calculated the unit bending and twisting moments for a point of a plate in certain directions, we then can find the unit bending and twisting moment for cuts in any direction through that point. It also states that there are two perpendicular principal directions where the twisting moment is zero. Furthermore the sum of two unit bending moments in two perpendicular directions $M_{1x} + M_{1y}$ is a constant for all directions at that point.

The *next step* in our long story *is to derive the equivalent of the beam formula*

$$S = \frac{dM}{dx} = EIy'''$$

for the plate. Looking at Fig. 75c, we see four moment vectors parallel to the x axis and likewise four vectors parallel to the y axis. These vectors are almost equal and opposite to each other, but not quite. The vectors parallel to the x axis in Fig. 75c have a resultant to the right (tending to rotate the element about the x axis) of a magnitude

$$-M_{1y}\, dx + \left(M_{1y} + \frac{\partial M_{1y}}{\partial y}\, dy\right) dx - T_{1xy}\, dy + \left(T_{1xy} + \frac{\partial T_{1xy}}{\partial x}\, dx\right) dy$$

$$= \left(\frac{\partial M_{1y}}{\partial y} + \frac{\partial T_{1xy}}{\partial x}\right) dx\, dy$$

This torque can be held in equilibrium by vertical (z-direction) shear forces acting on the fore and aft dx faces with the moment arm dy between them. The compensating moment must be such that the shear force must be acting upward on the front face, downward on the back face. If this shear force per unit length be designated as S_{1x}, then the force on the front face is $S_{1x}\, dx$ and its moment is $S_{1x}\, dx\, dy$. Equating that to the above expression gives

$$S_{1x} = \frac{\partial M_{1y}}{\partial y} + \frac{\partial T_{1xy}}{\partial x} \qquad (66)$$

$$S_{1y} = \frac{\partial M_{1x}}{\partial x} + \frac{\partial T_{1xy}}{\partial y}$$

The second equation of this pair is to be derived by the reader in the same manner as the first. The force S_{1y} is upward on the left face, downward on the right face, as indicated in Fig. 77.

Finally we want the counterpart of

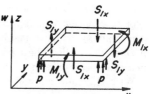

FIG. 77. Definition of positive signs of unit bending moments, shear forces, and distributed pressure loading to fit Eqs. (65), (66), and (67).

$$p = \frac{dS}{dx} = EIy^{(4)}$$

of beam theory. This one is found by remarking that in Fig. 77 the shear forces are not exactly equal and opposite but almost so. The (upward) vertical equilibrium of the plate element is expressed by

$$+S_{1x}\,dx - \left(S_{1x} + \frac{\partial S_{1x}}{\partial y}\,dy\right)dx + S_{1y}\,dy$$

$$- \left(S_{1y} + \frac{\partial S_{1y}}{\partial x}\,dx\right)dy + p\,dx\,dy = 0$$

where p is the pressure loading force in the direction of the deflection w. Cleaned up, this equation becomes

$$\frac{\partial S_{1x}}{\partial y} + \frac{\partial S_{1y}}{\partial x} = p$$

If we first substitute Eqs. (66) into this, and then Eqs. (65), reducing everything to the function w, we find, after some algebra,

$$\left(\frac{\partial^2}{\partial x^2} + \frac{\partial^2}{\partial y^2}\right)\left(\frac{\partial^2 w}{\partial x^2} + \frac{\partial^2 w}{\partial y^2}\right) = \frac{p}{D} \tag{67}$$

The differential operator $\dfrac{\partial^2}{\partial x^2} + \dfrac{\partial^2}{\partial y^2}$, which we have met before in Eq. (11) (page 12), of the membrane is called the Laplace operator, or the "harmonic" operator; it is often denoted as ∇^2 (pronounced "del squared") or also as Δ (delta). With the ∇ (del) notation the *differential equation* (67) of the flat plate is written

$$\nabla^4 w = \frac{p}{D} \tag{67a}$$

The membrane equation $\nabla^2 w = 0$ is often called the "harmonic" equation; the membrane shape w is then a "harmonic" function. (This nomenclature came about historically because the first problems to which this type of equation was applied were strings and drumheads: musical instruments giving off presumably harmonious tones.) Similarly Eq. (67) for $p/D = 0$ is called the *biharmonic differential equation*, and an unloaded plate can bend only in a *biharmonic function* w.

With this new symbolism some of the previous results can be written in a somewhat simpler manner. For example, when we substitute Eqs. (65) into Eqs. (66), the latter can be written as

$$S_{1x} = D\,\frac{\partial}{\partial y}\,(\nabla^2 w)$$

$$S_{1y} = D\,\frac{\partial}{\partial x}\,(\nabla^2 w) \tag{66a}$$

where D, of course, is the plate stiffness [Eq. (64)]. The geometrical meaning of the Laplace operator is the sum of the curvatures in two perpendicular directions, which we have seen [Fig. 71 or Eq. (61)] to be constant at a point and independent of the direction chosen at that point. The expression $\nabla^2 w$ therefore is sometimes called "twice the average curvature of the w surface at that point." If that average curvature is constant from point to point, then there can be no shear forces, as Eqs. (66a) inform us.

The unit shear forces S_{1x} and S_{1y} are taken by the plate cross section in the form of parabolically distributed shear stresses, just as is the case in a *beam* of rectangular cross section.

The problem of bent plates consists in finding a solution of Eq. (67) which fits all boundary conditions. When such a solution has been found, then the unit shear forces are found from Eqs. (66a) and the unit moments from Eqs. (65). The maximum bending stresses are found from the unit bending moments by the simple relation

$$s_{\text{max}} = \frac{M_1}{Z_1} = \frac{M_1}{\frac{1}{6}t^2 \times 1} = \frac{6M_1}{t^2} \tag{68}$$

which follows from comparing Eqs. (63), (64), and (65) with each other.

17. Simple Solutions; Saint-Venant's Principle. The general procedure in finding answers to plate problems is not straightforward but somewhat roundabout. We try to find some solution, any solution, to the plate equation (67) and examine afterward what it means and to what boundary conditions it applies. It is not too difficult to find such solutions, and with luck some of them have practical meaning. Most of them, however, are so strange that they never occur in practice, which nevertheless does not make them useless. With a large number of miscellaneous solutions known we can build up others by superposition, because equation (67) is *linear*. In this way we can build up all manner of cases and the most powerful method known in this direction is the Fourier series, where, once a solution has been found for sinusoidal loading, any other loading can be handled by infinite series.

Starting on this general program, the simplest solutions of Eq. (67) for zero pressure are quadratic functions: $w = x^2$, or $w = y^2$, or $w = xy$. The first function we try is $w = Cx^2$. Applying the harmonic operator ∇^2 to it, we find $\nabla^2 w = 2C$, a constant, and hence $\nabla^2(\nabla^2 w) = \nabla^2(2C) = 0$, satisfying the plate equation for zero pressure. The shape of the deformed plate, shown in Fig. 78, is a flat parabolic trough; its two principal curvatures by Eq. (59) (page 100) are

$$\frac{1}{R_x} = 2C \qquad \frac{1}{R_y} = 0$$

everywhere the same on the entire plate. The unit bending moments [Eqs. (65)] are

$$M_{1x} = 2CD \qquad M_{1y} = 2\mu CD \qquad T_{1xy} = 0$$

and, by Eq. (68), the stresses are $6/t^2$ times these unit moments. Since $\nabla^2 w = 2C$, a constant, we find from Eqs. (66a) that the unit shear forces are zero everywhere. Thus, if we cut out from the infinite plate a rectangle ab, as in Fig. 78, the outside loading consists of a uniformly distributed bending moment $2CD$ along the straight b edges and a moment 30 per cent as large along the curved a edges. It is interesting to note the presence of this latter moment, even when the b lines remain straight during the bending process. This, of course, is due to the Poisson-ratio effect; if the bending moments along the a edges were omitted, the b lines would bend by the so-called "anticlastic" effect.

The function $w = Cy^2$ does not present anything new, and next we investigate the superposition of Fig. 78 on the same case turned through 90 deg:

$$w = C(x^2 + y^2) = Cr^2$$

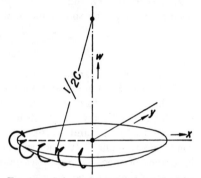

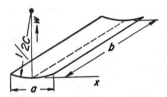

FIG. 78. Bending into a flat parabolic (circularly cylindrical) trough by bending moments at the plate edges only, and without pressure loading p. The surface is described by $w = Cx^2$.

FIG. 79. Spherical (or flat paraboloidal) bending of a plate, described by $w = Cr^2$, caused by bending moments on the outside edge only, and without pressure loading p.

Substitution of this into the various equations, as in the previous example, gives

$$\nabla^2 w = 4C \qquad \nabla^4 w = 0 \qquad \frac{1}{R_x} = \frac{1}{R_y} = 2C$$

Hence by Fig. 71

$$\frac{1}{R_\alpha} = 2C \qquad M_{1x} = M_{1y} = 2CD(1 + \mu)$$

Hence by Fig. 76

$$M_{1\alpha} = 2CD(1 + \mu) \qquad \text{and} \qquad T_{1\alpha} = 0 \text{ for any } \alpha$$
$$S_{1x} = S_{1y} = 0$$

The case is called "spherical bending" and is illustrated in Fig. 79.

The next function we take up is $w = Cxy$, for which we find successively

$$\nabla^2 w = 0$$

and, of course,

$$\nabla^4 w = 0$$

$$\frac{1}{R_x} = \frac{1}{R_y} = 0$$

but [Eq. (59a)]

$$\frac{1}{T_{xy}} = C \qquad \text{(see Fig. 69)}$$

$$M_{1x} = M_{1y} = 0$$

but

$$T_{1xy} = CD(1 - \mu)$$

$$S_{1x} = S_{1y} = 0$$

The case is illustrated in Fig. 80 and is called "uniformly distributed pure twist." There are no bending moments on x or y lines, only torques.

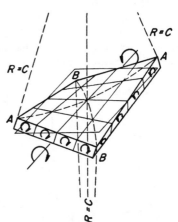

Fig. 80. Pure uniform twist of a plate. All lines parallel to the sides remain straight while tilting. The diagonal AA is curved holding water; the diagonal BB sheds water. The corners A are higher than normal; the corners B are lower than normal.

All x and y lines remain straight, but 45-deg lines curve, either up or downward, and there are unit bending moments $\pm C$ in those directions. The reader should carefully compare Fig. 80 with Fig. 72a, b, and c (page 104).

We could follow up this general trend of procedure and investigate $w = x^3$, $w = x^2 y$, and higher power functions, but that does not lead us anywhere in particular. The next example is that of a plate which bends in one direction only, somewhat like Fig. 78, but now with an arbitrary load on it, which can be a function of x only, not of y. We thus assume

$$w = f(x)$$

and substituting this into Eqs. (65) and (67) find

$$M_{1x} = D\frac{d^2 w}{dx^2} \qquad \left[M_{1y} = \mu D\frac{d^2 w}{dx^2} \qquad T_{1xy} = 0 \right]$$

$$D\frac{d^4 w}{dx^4} = p$$

These are seen to be ordinary beam equations for a beam in the x direction (and of height t and unit width in the y direction), with the notable exception that EI_1 of the beam has been replaced by $D = EI_1/(1 - \mu^2)$

and that there *is* a crosswise bending moment M_{1y}. Thus, because $1/(1 - \mu^2)$ is about 1.10, a plate bent like a beam in one plane only is about 10 per cent stiffer than it would be by pure beam action. The reason for this is illustrated in Fig. 81. Only near the unsupported ends of the plate, where there is no M_{1y} moment applied, does the plate curve down somewhat, escaping the s_y stresses. But in the center portion the plate cannot escape the s_y stresses by changing its cross section anticlastically like the beam, Fig. 81a.

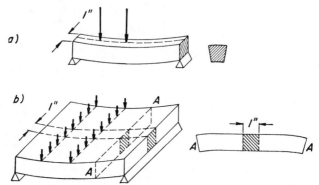

FIG. 81. A beam (*a*) and a unit width strip of plate (*b*) under identical bending loads. Because in case *b* the anticlastic curvature is prevented, the stiffness *b* is greater than the stiffness *a* by a factor $1/(1 - \mu^2)$, which amounts to about 10 per cent.

The last example to be discussed in this section is historically the most important case in plate bending, dating back to Navier in 1820. It is that of a plate of infinite extent in both the x and y directions being bent into a sinusoidal wave shape,

$$w = w_0 \sin \frac{\pi x}{a} \sin \frac{\pi y}{b}$$

illustrated by Fig. 82, consisting of rectangular fields a, b alternately bent up and down to a central height w_0. With this shape we enter into the various equations of the general theory as follows:

$$\frac{1}{R_x} = -\frac{\pi^2}{a^2} w \qquad \frac{1}{R_y} = -\frac{\pi^2}{b^2} w$$

$$\frac{1}{T_{xy}} = w_0 \frac{\pi^2}{ab} \cos \frac{\pi x}{a} \cos \frac{\pi y}{b} \qquad \text{[Eqs. (59)]}$$

$$\nabla^2 w = -\pi^2 \frac{a^2 + b^2}{a^2 b^2} w$$

$$D\nabla^4 w = p = +D\pi^4 \left(\frac{a^2 + b^2}{a^2 b^2}\right)^2 w \qquad \text{[Eq. (67)]}$$

$$S_{1x} = -D\frac{a^2 + b^2}{a^2 b^2}\pi^3 \frac{w_0}{b}\sin\frac{\pi x}{a}\cos\frac{\pi y}{b}$$

$$S_{1y} = -D\frac{a^2 + b^2}{a^2 b^2}\pi^3 \frac{w_0}{a}\cos\frac{\pi x}{a}\sin\frac{\pi y}{b} \qquad \text{[Eqs. (66a)]}$$

$$M_{1x} = -D\pi^2 w\left(\frac{1}{a^2} + \frac{\mu}{b^2}\right) \qquad M_{1y} = -D\pi^2 w\left(\frac{\mu}{a^2} + \frac{1}{b^2}\right)$$

$$T_{1xy} = D(1 - \mu)\frac{\pi^2}{ab}w_0 \cos\frac{\pi x}{a}\cos\frac{\pi y}{b} \qquad \text{[Eqs. (65)]}$$

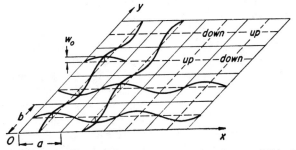

FIG. 82. Trigonometrically undulating surface of wave lengths $2a$ and $2b$ in the x and y directions, respectively, and of wave height w_0.

From this array of formulae we see that the loading diagram p has the same shape as the deflection diagram w, so that at all points of the plate there is the same ratio $p/w = D\pi^4(a^2 + b^2)^2/a^4 b^4$. Also the bending-moment diagrams distribute in the same manner. At any point the ratio between the M_{1x} and M_{1y} unit bending moments is the same. Thus we have a complete solution for the large plate with many undulations. This plate does not need any support, because its upward and downward loads p even out. Before we enter into the complicated case of cutting a rectangle out of this large plate, we may note that it is now possible to find a solution for a large plate with *any* alternate loading on a, b rectangles by breaking up the loading into a (double x and y) Fourier series of sine components. The answers for the deflection w, and the bending moments, shear forces, etc., come out in the form of double Fourier series, and in the standard treatises on flat plates (Nadai or Timoshenko) many pages covered with formidable $\sum \sum$ signs appear. Historically this is interesting, because the problem was solved by Navier in 1820, within a few years after the discovery of the differential equation (67) in 1811 by Lagrange, and the publication of the trigonometric series in 1819 by Fourier.

Now then we are ready to cut out of the plate of Fig. 82 a simply supported single rectangle a, b. On the edges of this rectangle we have $w = 0$,

$M_{1x} = M_{1y} = 0$, but the shear forces S_{1x} and S_{1y} and the twisting torque T_{1xy} do *not* disappear. We are safe in concluding that we now possess a solution for a rectangular plate under a sinusoidal hill loading (or under any other loading if we are not afraid of big black $\sum \sum$ signs) if we subject the edges to the proper lateral shear forces S_{1x}, S_{1y} and a properly distributed twisting moment T_{1xy} (Fig. 83). But we are *not* safe in stating

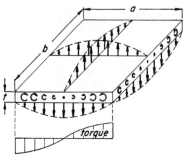

that we have a solution for a plate so loaded and simply supported at its edges, because it is easy enough to see how we can take care of the shear forces by a reaction from the supports, but not at all easy to understand how such supports can furnish a gradually varying twisting couple to the edge. In fact this point remained obscure for half a century until it was cleared up by Lord Kelvin in 1870. He knew that the twisting couple T_{1xy} of Fig. 83 was taken by the edge in the manner shown in Fig. 75a, by shearing stresses lying in the (horizontal) direction of the plane. Now the shear stresses trans-

FIG. 83. Rectangular plate of dimensions a, b, and t, loaded on its ab face with a sinusoidal pressure distribution and on its at and bt sides with shear forces (half sine waves) and torques (half cosine waves).

mitted by a small rectangle $t\,dx$ of the edge are statically equivalent to the same torque transmitted by the same shear stresses arranged vertically, as in Fig. 84b. These, however, cancel each other: entirely when the T_{1xy} remains constant along the edge, and partially when T_{1xy} varies. On one of the rectangles of Fig. 84a the torque is $T_{1xy}\,dx$. Then the forces shown in

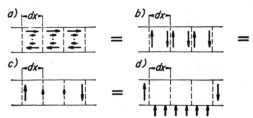

FIG. 84. Kelvin's observation that twisting moments transmitted by horizontal shear forces (*a*) are statically equivalent to twisting moments transmitted by vertical shear forces (*b*). These vertical forces cancel each other for the most part; only their small differentials remain (Fig. 84c and d).

Fig. 84b must be T_{1xy} in order to provide the same torques, and the little differential forces shown in Fig. 84c must be $(\partial T_{1xy}/\partial x)\,dx$. Hence the torque distribution of Fig. 84a is statically equivalent to a shear loading of $\partial T_{1xy}/\partial x$ per unit length of edge with finite reactions at the plate corners.

In this argument Kelvin made use of a common-sense proposition, known as *Saint-Venant's principle*, which states that: *If the loading on a small part of the boundary of an elastic system is replaced by a different loading, which is statically equivalent to the original loading, then the stress distribution in the system will be sensibly changed only in the neighborhood of the change; the stresses at a distance from the disturbance equal to the size of the disturbance itself will be changed by a few per cent only.* We have already used this principle tacitly off and on in this text, and it will be discussed more fully on page 118 and again on page 183, but now we apply it to our plate and say that if the torques on the edges are supplied by vertical reactions $(\partial T_{1xy}/\partial x)$ along the x edge (and by $\partial T_{1xy}/\partial y$ along the y edge) instead of by the horizontal shear forces of Fig. 84a or Fig. 75a, then no important change will take place in the stress distribution at a distance farther than t away from the edge. The same is true for replacing the actual parabolic distribution of the S_{1x} and S_{1y} unit shear force across the edge by some other distribution of the vertical-edge support forces S_{1x} and S_{1y}.

With this then we have the solution to the problem of a sinusoidally loaded rectangle a, b on simple supports along all edges: the edge reaction per unit length is $S_{1x} + (\partial T_{1xy}/\partial x)$ along the x edge and the corresponding quantity along the y edge. Looking at Fig. 84c, we suspect that this may be incorrect when we come to the ends of the edges, *i.e.*, to the corners of the plate. We now calculate the total value of the reaction on one side a, where $y = 0$ and $\cos \pi y/b = 1$:

$$
\begin{aligned}
R_a &= \int_{x=0}^{x=a} \left(S_{1x} + \frac{\partial T_{1xy}}{\partial x} \right) dx \\
&= -Dw_0 \frac{\pi^3}{a^2 b} \left[\frac{a^2 + b^2}{b^2} + (1 - \mu) \right] \int_0^a \sin \frac{\pi x}{a} \, dx \\
&= -Dw_0 \frac{\pi^3}{a^2 b} \left[\frac{a^2 + b^2}{b^2} + (1 - \mu) \right] \frac{2}{\pi} a
\end{aligned}
$$

Here the first term in the square bracket is caused by the shear force, and the second term is caused by the twisting couple. The reaction on a b side is found in the same manner, and the answer is of course the same as above, in which the letters a and b are reversed. The total reaction on four sides thus is

$$
-Dw_0 \frac{4\pi^2}{ab} \left[\left(\frac{a^2 + b^2}{ab} \right)^2 + 2(1 - \mu) \right]
$$

This reaction is downward, because the load p was acting upward (Fig. 83). The upward p force is

$$
\begin{aligned}
\iint p \, dx \, dy &= D\pi^4 \left(\frac{a^2 + b^2}{a^2 b^2} \right)^2 w_0 \int_0^a \sin \frac{\pi x}{a} \, dx \int_0^b \sin \frac{\pi y}{b} \, dy \\
&= Dw_0 4\pi^2 ab \left(\frac{a^2 + b^2}{a^2 b^2} \right)^2
\end{aligned}
$$

which is equal to the first term of the support reaction only, the one due to shear forces. The extra reaction due to twisting couples is compensated for by four equal concentrated upward forces R at the four corners of the plate of magnitude

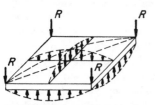

$$R = \frac{2\pi^2}{ab}(1 - \mu)Dw_0 \qquad (69)$$

FIG. 85. Rectangular plate ab on simple supports loaded by a sinusoidally distributed loading p. The edge-support reactions are also sinusoidal, but they are larger than necessary to compensate for the p loading. In order to keep the corners down on the foundation, concentrated forces R are required [Eq. (69)].

as shown in Fig. 85. Once this has been derived, the physical reason for it can be appreciated intuitively. If a square or rectangular plate, placed loosely on a rectangular foundation, is loaded in the center, it tends to become dish-shaped and the four corners tend to lift off the frame, contact being made only in the middle of the sides. If we demand contact all over the frame, the corners will have to be pressed down. For a square plate the above formulae show that the downward push on the four corners combined is 35 per cent of the original downward push in the center.

This finishes the story of the rectangular plate, and we now return to Saint-Venant's principle. It was used tacitly with the case of Fig. 67 (page 95) in the vicinity of the end of the pipe. The solution, as stated there, strictly applies only if the end of the tube is subjected to a set of shear forces (Fig. 67b). If we just put a load P on it any old way, we replace the distribution of Fig. 67b by a statically equivalent one. Saint-Venant's principle states that the difference caused by this does not extend sensibly beyond one diameter of the tube from the free end. A similar remark can be made in connection with Fig. 66 (page 93). The solution, Eqs. (56), for this case holds only when the support reactions are applied in the form of shear stresses across the section, as described by Eqs. (56). The actual support is different, although statically equivalent; hence the solution, Eqs. (56), will apply 99 per cent correctly at distances one pipe diameter or more from the supports. Still another example is furnished by Fig. 56a and b on page 82. The outside loading on each part of Fig. 56a is zero. If we replace that zero by a statically equivalent loading in the form of one balanced star of shear forces, then the influence of this will have died down one pipe diameter (or less) down the cylinder. Hence the cylinder there will be completely unloaded. The long analysis with the torsion case of Fig. 36 (page 44) is strictly true only if the end torques to the shaft are applied in the form of tangential shear stresses proportional to the radial distance from the center. If the torque comes out of a sleeve coupling and goes to the shaft either by friction or through a key, the local stresses are completely different, but by Saint-Venant's principle, one diameter below the coupling the streamlines of Fig. 36 hold true. The electrical analogue of this is in Fig. 38 (page 47). If the copper blocks are small and the current comes into the razor-test piece through a wire, the current distribution near the wire connection will be different from the pattern of Fig. 36, but one diameter downstream no detectable difference will remain.

Because the principle of Saint-Venant does not state that an *exact* coincidence takes place at a certain distance, but only a 99 per cent coincidence, no mathematical "proof" can be given for it. It is based on a large collection of mathematical experiences like the ones just cited, and it is of supreme practical importance to us, because without it no mathematical treatment of the subject would have meaning.

A proposition very similar to Saint-Venant's principle is that the influence of small local disturbances in *shape* does not extend sensibly beyond a distance of the order of the size of the disturbance. Examples of this are small holes or fillets, which do not affect the stress distributions at a distance but are of local interest only, even if they are extremely important there (Figs. 36 or 17).

18. Circular Plates. The deflections w and hence the stresses of a circular plate, with circular-symmetrical loading, depend on one variable r only, instead of on two x, y, because the symmetry implies that nothing changes with the angle θ or that $\partial/\partial\theta = 0$. This simplifies the general plate equations considerably. In Fig. 86, let A be a point of the plate at distance r from the center, and let us erect a perpendicular at A on the deflected middle surface of the plate. From symmetry this normal must intersect the vertical center line of the plate, and we have seen on page 72, Fig. 50, that the distance AC_t is R_t: the tangential radius of curvature at point A. The other radius of curvature R_m, the meridional one, is AC_m, where the point C_m may be anywhere on the line AC_t. Again, from symmetry, we recognize that these two are the principal radii of curvature at that point A and that there can be no "twist" in the r, θ directions in the plate at any point A. The angle OC_tA, designated as φ, is also the angle between the tangent to the plate at A and the horizontal, so that $\varphi = dw/dr = w'$, where w is the (upward) deflection of the middle surface. On page 74 we have seen, and now we should understand once more clearly, that

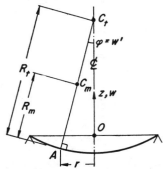

FIG. 86. Circular plate with definitions of the symbols r, R_t, R_m, w and $\varphi = w'$.

$$R_t = \frac{r}{\varphi} \quad \text{and} \quad R_m = \frac{dr}{d\varphi}$$

or

$$\frac{1}{R_t} = \frac{w'}{r} \quad \text{and} \quad \frac{1}{R_m} = \varphi' = w''$$

The Laplace operator ∇^2 was used first with Eq. (67) (page 110); it was there defined in terms of an x, y-coordinate system. The "transformation" of this into a polar r, θ-coordinate system is found in most texts on advanced calculus and is very unpleasant and tedious algebraically. Here we remark that Eq. (67) states that ∇^2 means the sum of the curvatures in the x and y directions and that by Eq. (61) (page 103) this equals the sum of the curvatures in any two perpendicular directions, for instance, in the tangential and meridional directions. Hence

$$\nabla^2 w = \frac{1}{R_t} + \frac{1}{R_m} = \frac{w'}{r} + w''$$

and generally

$$\nabla^2 = \frac{1}{r}\frac{d}{dr} + \frac{d^2}{dr^2}$$

Thus the plate equation (67) becomes

$$\frac{p}{D} = \nabla^2(\nabla^2 w) = \left(\frac{1}{r}\frac{d}{dr} + \frac{d^2}{dr^2}\right)\left(\frac{w'}{r} + w''\right)$$

$$= \frac{1}{r}\left(\frac{w''}{r} - \frac{w'}{r^2} + w'''\right) + \text{(previous parentheses differentiated)}$$

$$= \frac{1}{r}\left(\frac{w''}{r} - \frac{w'}{r^2} + w'''\right) + \left(\frac{w'''}{r} - \frac{w''}{r^2} - \frac{w''}{r^2} + \frac{2w'}{r^3} + w^{(4)}\right)$$

Cleaned up and multiplied by r^4, this is

$$r^4 w^{(4)} + 2r^3 w''' - r^2 w'' + rw' = \frac{pr^4}{D} \tag{70}$$

the equation of the deflection w of the middle surface of a circular plate of stiffness D [Eq. (64)] under a rotationally symmetrical loading p. To complete this we still have to "transform" the expressions for the moments, shear forces, and stresses from rectangular x, y to polar r, θ coordinates. Again, an algebraic transformation is laborious, and we do better to translate the x, y analytic expressions into English and from that into the r, θ symbolism. The unit moment equations (65) are "the stiffness D multiplied by the sum of the curvature in its own direction and μ times the curvature in the across direction," or

$$M_{1m} = D\left(w'' + \mu \frac{w'}{r}\right)$$

$$M_{1t} = D\left(\frac{w'}{r} + \mu w''\right)$$

(71)

while the unit twisting moment T_{1mt} is zero because there is no twist $\partial^2 w/(\partial r \cdot r \partial \theta)$ on account of symmetry. Furthermore, by Eqs. (66a) "the unit transverse shear force is the stiffness multiplied by the partial derivative in the across direction of the Laplacian function of the deflection," or

$$S_{1m} = D \frac{\partial}{r \partial \theta} (\nabla^2 w) = 0 \qquad \text{by symmetry}$$

and

$$S_{1t} = D \frac{\partial}{\partial r} (\nabla^2 w) = D \frac{\partial}{\partial r} \left(\frac{w'}{r} + w''\right)$$

(72)

As a useful exercise the reader should derive this last result independently, from the rotational equilibrium of a plate element $dr \cdot rd\theta$ subjected to the bending moments (71).

The solution to any symmetrically loaded circular plate, with or without central hole, consists of a solution of Eq. (70), fitting the boundary conditions of the case. Then Eqs. (71), (72), and (68) furnish the bending moments, shear forces, and bending stresses.

A very simple solution of Eq. (70) for the case of no load p is $w = Cr^2$, as can be easily verified. This is the case of spherical bending by edge moments, discussed on page 112, Fig. 79.

Now we proceed to solve Eq. (70) in general. We notice that it is an ordinary linear differential equation of the fourth order with variable coefficients (which are powers of the variable r with exponents equal to the grade of derivative) and with a right-hand member. The type is the same as encountered previously [Eq. (38), page 51, or Eq. (47), page 61], and the solution of the "reduced" equation has the form $w = r^p$, where p is to be determined from

$$p(p-1)(p-2)(p-3) + 2p(p-1)(p-2) - p(p-1) + p = 0$$

Taking terms 1 and 2 together, and likewise terms 3 and 4 together, gives

$$p(p-1)^2(p-2) - p(p-2) = 0$$
$$p(p-2)[(p-1)^2 - 1] = p(p-2)(p^2 - 2p) = p^2(p-2)^2 = 0$$

Thus there are four roots: $p = 0, 0, 2, 2$.

Double roots lead to logarithmic solutions, as the reader should verify by consulting a text on differential equations. Hence the general solution of the reduced equation (70) is

$$w = C_1 + C_2 \log_e r + C_3 r^2 + C_4 r^2 \log_e r$$

The particular solution of the complete equation (70) depends on the shape of the loading p, so that we can give no general expression for it. Now then we restrict ourselves to *uniform loading*, $p = p_0$, constant all over. Then we try for the particular solution,

$$w = Ar^4$$

where A is found by substitution into Eq. (70):

$$r^4 A(4 \cdot 3 \cdot 2 \cdot 1 + 2 \cdot 4 \cdot 3 \cdot 2 - 4 \cdot 3 + 4) = \frac{p_0 r^4}{D}$$

or

$$A = \frac{p_0}{64D}$$

Hence the general solution of the circular-plate equation (70) for uniform loading p_0 is

$$w = C_1 + C_2 \log_e r + C_3 r^2 + C_4 r^2 \log_e r + \frac{p_0 r^4}{64D} \tag{73}$$

The constants C are determined from the boundary conditions for each specific case. These boundary conditions often involve the bending moments, Eqs. (71), or shear forces, Eq. (72), for which we need derivatives of w,

$$w' = \frac{C_2}{r} + 2C_3 r + C_4(r + 2r \log_e r) + \frac{p_0 r^3}{16D}$$

$$w'' = -\frac{C_2}{r^2} + 2C_3 + C_4(3 + 2 \log_e r) + \frac{3p_0 r^2}{16D}$$

$$w''' = +\frac{2C_2}{r^3} + \frac{2C_4}{r} + \frac{3p_0 r}{8D}$$

so that, from Eqs. (71) and (72),

$$M_{1m} = D\left\{ \frac{C_2}{r^2}(-1 + \mu) + 2C_3(1 + \mu) \right.$$

$$\left. + C_4[3 + \mu + 2(1 + \mu) \log r] \right\} + \frac{3 + \mu}{16D} p_0 r^2 \tag{74}$$

$$S_{1t} = D\left(\frac{4C_4}{r} + \frac{p_0 r}{2D} \right)$$

First we investigate disks without central hole so that $r = 0$ is actually a part of the material of the disk. We see that for $r = 0$ two terms in the expression for the moment M_{1m} become infinite, namely, C_2/r^2 and

$C_4 \log r$. An infinite bending moment in the middle of a disk for finite loading is of course impossible, so that we conclude that for no hole $C_2 = C_4 = 0$.

Then Eqs. (73) and (74) simplify to

$$w = C_1 + C_3 r^2 + \frac{p_0 r^4}{64D}$$

$$M_{1m} = 2(1 + \mu)C_3 D + \frac{3 + \mu}{16} p_0 r^2$$

$$M_{1t} = 2(1 + \mu)C_3 D + \frac{1 + 3\mu}{16} p_0 r^2$$

$$S_{1t} = \frac{p_0 r}{2}$$

uniform load; no hole

Now we are ready to tackle the outside boundary condition where $r = R$. In case of a built-in edge we have $w = w' = 0$ at $r = R$, or

$$C_1 + C_3 R^2 + \frac{p_0 R^4}{64D} = 0$$

$$2C_3 R + \frac{p_0 R^3}{16D} = 0$$

from which we can solve for C_1 and C_3:

$$C_1 = +\frac{p_0 R^4}{64D} \qquad C_3 = -\frac{p_0 R^2}{32D}$$

Substituting this into the above expressions, we obtain the final solution (*no hole, uniform load, clamped edge*):

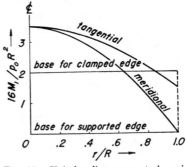

FIG. 87. Unit bending moments in uniformly loaded circular plates with clamped edge (upper base line) and simply supported edge (lower base line). The curves are parabolas expressed by Eqs. (75) and (78).

$$w = \frac{p_0 R^4}{64D} \left(1 - \frac{r^2}{R^2}\right)^2$$

$$M_{1m} = \frac{p_0 R^2}{16} \left[-(1 + \mu) + (3 + \mu)\frac{r^2}{R^2}\right]$$

$$M_{1t} = \frac{p_0 R^2}{16} \left[-(1 + \mu) + (1 + 3\mu)\frac{r^2}{R^2}\right]$$

$$S_{1t} = \frac{p_0 r}{2}$$

(75)

These results are shown graphically in Fig. 87.

The maximum deflection in the center $r = 0$ is

$$w_{max} = \frac{p_0 R^4}{64D} \quad \text{(clamped edge)} \tag{76}$$

and the maximum stress, Eq. (68), occurring at the outside edge $r = R$ in the meridional direction is

$$s_{max} = \frac{3}{4} p_0 \frac{R^2}{t^2} \quad \text{(clamped edge)} \tag{77}$$

Now we turn to a simply supported edge. The boundary conditions there are

$$r = R \qquad w = 0 \qquad M_{1m} = 0$$

We do not encounter the complication of Figs. 83 and 84 here, because the circular boundary coincides everywhere with a direction of principal curvature, so that there is no twisting couple on the edge. Thus there is no necessity for extra downward forces (like those of Fig. 85) to hold the edge down on its foundation; from symmetry alone we can conclude that the edge must press down on the foundation uniformly. The boundary conditions thus are

$$C_1 + C_3 R^2 + \frac{p_0 R^4}{64D} = 0$$

$$2(1 + \mu)C_3 D + (3 + \mu) \frac{p_0 R^2}{16} = 0$$

from which we solve for C_3 and C_1:

$$C_1 = \frac{5 + \mu}{1 + \mu} \frac{p_0 R^4}{64D}$$

$$C_3 = -\frac{6 + 2\mu}{1 + \mu} \frac{p_0 R^2}{64D}$$

Substituting this back, we find the final solution for the case of *no hole, uniform load, simply supported outside edge*:

$$w = \frac{p_0 R^4}{64D} \left(\frac{5 + \mu}{1 + \mu} - \frac{6 + 2\mu}{1 + \mu} \frac{r^2}{R^2} + \frac{r^4}{R^4} \right)$$

$$M_{1m} = -\frac{3 + \mu}{16} p_0 R^2 \left(1 - \frac{r^2}{R^2} \right)$$

$$M_{1t} = \frac{p_0 R^2}{16} \left[-(3 + \mu) + (1 + 3\mu) \frac{r^2}{R^2} \right] \tag{78}$$

$$S_{1t} = \frac{p_0 r}{2}$$

The maximum deflection at the center of the plate is

$$w_{\text{max}} = \frac{5 + \mu}{1 + \mu} \frac{p_0 R^4}{64D} \qquad \text{(supported edge)} \qquad (79)$$

The maximum stress occurs at the center, and it is the same in all directions:

$$s_{\text{max}} = \frac{3}{8} (3 + \mu) p_0 \frac{R^2}{t^2} \qquad \text{(supported edge)} \qquad (80)$$

All of these results are shown also in Fig. 87. It is seen that the bending moments, meridional as well as tangential, differ by the constant addition of $p_0 R^2/8$ between the clamped and freely supported cases, and we note that this amount $p_0 R^2/8$ is the meridional moment M_{1m} at the built-in edge of the plate. We see then that the freely supported case (under load p_0) can be considered as the superposition of a clamped case under load p_0 and a case of spherical bending (Fig. 79, discussed on page 112 and again on page 121). The reader should check that the entire deflected shape $w = f(r)$ in the simply supported case also is the sum of those two constituent cases.

One last remark about the results (75) and (78) deals with the shear stress due to the unit shear force S_{1t}. If that force were uniformly distributed across the section $1 \times t$ on which it acts, the shear stress would be S_{1t}/t. But we know from beam theory that a shear force distributes itself parabolically across the height with a maximum value of $\frac{3}{2}$ the average value in the neutral plane. Hence the maximum shear stress due to shearing (there are also shear stresses due to the bending on 45-deg spirals with respect to the radius, about which we do not talk now) occurs at the outside edge and is $\frac{3}{4} p_0 R/t$. The bending stresses are all proportional to $(R/t)^2$, so that for actual "plates," in which by definition t is much smaller than R, *the shear stress*, proportional to R/t itself, *is insignificant in comparison with the bending stress* $(R/t)^2$. This is just the same as in beam theory.

The next case to be discussed is the plate without hole, loaded only by a single concentrated force P at the center. This is more difficult, as might be suspected, because we can easily see, by isolating a small central cylinder $2\pi \, dr \, t$ and examining its vertical equilibrium, that the unit shear force S_{1t} must become infinitely large:

$$S_{1t} 2\pi \, dr = P \qquad \therefore \ S_{1t} = \frac{P}{2\pi} \frac{1}{dr}$$

When physical quantities that cannot be ignored become mathematically infinite, the analysis is apt to become complicated. We start with the general solution (73), which, by setting $p_0 = 0$, applies to our case everywhere except at the center point itself (where $p_0 = \infty$). We suspect that a solution exists with finite deflections w (from physical experience), and then the slope at the center must be zero. Hence from page 122 we find

$$w'_{r=0} = 0 = \frac{C_2}{r} + C_3 \times 0 + C_4 \times 0 + 0$$

If the constant C_2 exists, we get a steep slope at the center, so that we conclude $C_2 = 0$.

The second condition to be met is that the unit shear force S_{1t}, immediately adjacent to the center, becomes infinite in the proper manner: in the manner we have just seen:

$$\lim_{r \to 0} S_{1t} = \frac{P}{2\pi r}$$

From Eqs. (74), for the case that $p_0 = 0$, we have, on the other hand,

$$\lim_{r \to 0} S_{1t} = 4D \frac{C_4}{r}$$

so that

$$C_4 = \frac{P}{8\pi D}$$

The remaining two boundary conditions are on the outside of the plate and are the same ones we saw before. We pursue the case for a clamped outside edge:

$$r = R: \quad w = 0 = C_1 + C_3 R^2 + \frac{P}{8\pi D} R^2 \log R = 0$$

$$r = R: \quad w' = 0 = 2C_3 R + \frac{PR}{8\pi D} (1 + 2 \log R) = 0$$

From these we solve for C_1 and C_3:

$$C_1 = \frac{PR^2}{16\pi D} \qquad C_3 = -\frac{P}{16\pi D} (1 + 2 \log R) \qquad C_4 = \frac{P}{8\pi D}$$

Substituting this into the general result, Eq. (73), with $C_2 = 0$ and $p_0 = 0$, we finally obtain for the *circular plate R with clamped outer edge loaded by a central concentrated force P*

$$w = \frac{PR^2}{16\pi D} \left(1 - \frac{r^2}{R^2} + 2 \frac{r^2}{R^2} \log \frac{r}{R} \right)$$

$$M_{1m} = \frac{P}{4\pi} \left[1 + (1 + \mu) \log \frac{r}{R} \right]$$

$$M_{1t} = \frac{P}{4\pi} \left[\mu + (1 + \mu) \log \frac{r}{R} \right]$$
(81)

$$S_{1t} = \frac{P}{2\pi r}$$

The maximum deflection in the center is

$$w_{\max} = \frac{PR^2}{16\pi D} \qquad \text{(clamped edge)} \qquad (82)$$

and the bending moments are plotted in Fig. 88. They become "logarithmically infinite" near the concentrated load. This makes the stress likewise infinite, which should not surprise us, because if we prescribe an impossible loading ("concentrated" P),
we shall get an impossible stress
("infinite" stress). This, however,
does not make our result useless. By
Saint-Venant's principle (page 117)
Fig. 88 gives the stress distribution
correctly at some distance from the
concentrated load if that load is
replaced by another one, distributed
over some small central area and
having a total resultant P.

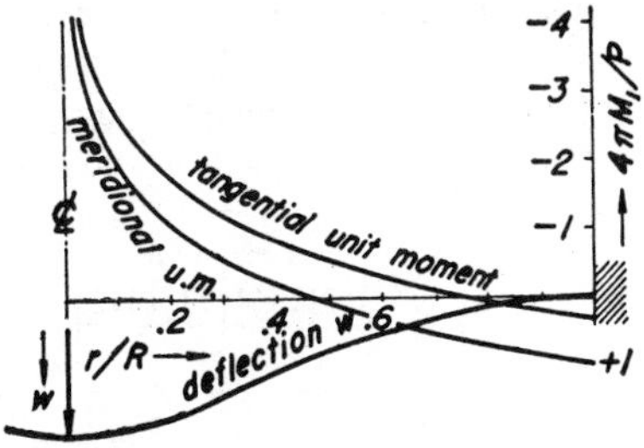

Disks with a central hole under
various loadings and with various
edge conditions can be calculated by
the same method. Much work has been expended on this, and some of the
results are given in the next section.

FIG. 88.   Deflection and bending-moment curves for a solid circular plate, clamped at the edge and loaded by a concentrated central load P. This illustrates Eqs. (81).

19. Catalogue of Results. In the last two sections we have seen that the calculation of plate deflections and stresses is a very laborious process, even in the simplest cases of circular plates without central hole. When a hole is present or when the plate is rectangular, the work of computation becomes so large that no one is justified in performing it for use on a given practical case. In the course of time many cases have been worked out: the fundamental theory principally by Navier and later by Levy, both in France, the numerical computations by Galerkin in Russia, by Wahl in the United States, and by others.[1]

The results are here listed for practical application. With them comes the oft-repeated warning that they are valid only for plates, which means $t \ll R$, and, moreover, only for small deflections $w < t$, as will be shown later in Fig. 91. The stresses are found from the bending moments listed, by Eq. (68), reprinted below:

$$s_{\max} = \frac{6}{t^2} M_1 \qquad (68)$$

[1] The sources and details of these results can be found in the two standard works on plates: Nadai, "Elastische Platten," Verlag Julius Springer, Berlin, 1925; Timoshenko, "Theory of Plates and Shells," McGraw-Hill Book Company, Inc., New York, 1940.

The symbol D appearing in the formulae below is the plate stiffness defined by Eq. (64), reprinted:

$$D = \frac{Et^3}{12(1 - \mu^2)} \approx 0.091Et^3 \qquad (64)$$

Here μ has been taken as 0.3, usual for steel and for practically all other materials. In the tabulations that follow, sometimes μ has been absorbed in the numerical coefficients, and in those cases it has been taken as $\mu = 0.3$.

The shear stresses due to transverse shear are negligible, as was discussed on page 125. All results listed are to be interpreted in the light of Saint-Venant's principle (page 117). Here they are:

Case 1.   Circular plate R, no hole, uniform load p_0, clamped edge:

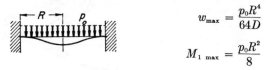

$$w_{max} = \frac{p_0 R^4}{64D}$$

$$M_{1\ max} = \frac{p_0 R^2}{8}$$

Case 2.   Circular plate R, no hole, uniform load p_0, simply supported edge:

$$w_{max} = 0.063\,\frac{p_0 R^4}{D}$$

$$M_{1\ max} = 0.206 p_0 R^2$$

Case 3.   Circular plate R, no hole, central concentrated force P, clamped edge:

$$w_{max} = \frac{PR^2}{16\pi D}$$

$$M_{1\ max} = \infty \quad \text{(see case 8)}$$

Case 4.   Circular plate R, no hole, central concentrated force P, simply supported edge; $\mu = 0.3$:

$$w_{max} = 0.05\,\frac{PR^2}{D}$$

$$M_{1\ max} = \infty \quad \text{(see case 9)}$$

Case 5.   Circular plate R, no hole, loaded with a total force P distributed uniformly over a circular line of radius a, so that $p_1 = P/2\pi a$; clamped edge:

$$w_{max} = \frac{P}{16\pi D}\left(R^2 - a^2 + 2a^2 \log_e \frac{a}{R}\right)$$

$$M_{1\ max} = \infty$$

Case 6. Circular plate R, no hole, with total load P distributed over a circular line a, simply supported edge:

$$w_{max} = \frac{P}{16\pi D}\left[\frac{3+\mu}{1+\mu}(R^2 - a^2) + 2a^2 \log_e \frac{a}{R}\right]$$

$$M_{1\ max} = \infty$$

Case 7. Circular plate R, no hole, with a single concentrated load P placed *eccentrically* at distance a from the center; various edge conditions.

The results of cases 5 and 6 apply here, except that the w_{max} listed there must be interpreted here as the deflection of the center, which in this case is *not* the maximum deflection, although quite close to it. This is based on a remark by the great Saint-Venant that a load element $p_1 a\ d\theta$ of cases 5 or 6 causes the same central deflection as another load $p_1 a\ d\theta$, placed elsewhere on the same circle, on account of symmetry. Hence if the circularly distributed load of cases 5 or 6 is shifted in any manner around the a circle, the center deflection of the plate does not change.

Case 8. Circular plate R, no hole, with a total load P, distributed uniformly over an inner circle of radius a, so that $p = P/\pi a^2$, clamped edge:

$$w_{max} = \frac{P}{16\pi D}\left(R^2 - \frac{3}{4}a^2 + a^2 \log \frac{a}{R}\right)$$

$$M_{1\ max} = \frac{P}{4\pi}\left(1 - \frac{a^2}{2R^2}\right) \quad \text{for } \frac{a}{R} > 0.57$$

$$M_{1\ max} = \frac{P}{4\pi}(1 + \mu)\left(\frac{a^2}{4R^2} - \log_e \frac{a}{R}\right) \quad \text{for } \frac{a}{R} < 0.57$$

Note that this reduces to case 1 for $a = R$ and to case 3 for $a = 0$.

Case 9. Circular plate R, no hole, with a total load P distributed uniformly over an inner circle of radius a, so that $p = P/\pi a^2$, simply supported edge:

$$w_{max} = \frac{P}{16\pi D}\left(\frac{3+\mu}{1+\mu}R^2 - \frac{7+3\mu}{4+4\mu}a^2 + a^2 \log_e \frac{a}{R}\right)$$

$$M_{1\ max} = \frac{P}{4\pi}\left[1 - \frac{1-\mu}{4}\frac{a^2}{R^2} - (1+\mu)\log \frac{a}{R}\right]$$

Note that this case reduces to case 2 for $a = R$ and to case 4 for $a = 0$.

Case 10.   Circular plate R with hole r, built in at the inside edge r, free at the outer edge R, uniformly loaded with pressure p_0 ("umbrella" plate),

$$w_{max} = \alpha \frac{p_0 R^4}{E t^3}$$

$$s_{max} = \beta \frac{p_0 R^2}{t^2}$$

where the values of α and β as functions of the ratio R/r are given in the table below.

Case 11.   Circular plate R, with hole r, built in and supported at the inner edge r, the outer edge being prevented from rotating, but not contributing to the reaction F, loaded uniformly with pressure p_0,

$$w_{max} = \gamma \frac{p_0 R^4}{E t^3}$$

$$s_{max} = \delta \frac{p_0 R^2}{t^2}$$

where the values of γ and δ are given in the table below.

Case 12.   Circular plate R with hole r, loaded uniformly with p_0 over the annular portion only, freely supported at the outer edge R, the inner edge being prevented from rotation, but not contributing to the reaction F,

$$w_{max} = \epsilon \frac{p_0 R^4}{E t^3}$$

$$s_{max} = \zeta \frac{p_0 R^2}{t^2}$$

where ϵ and ζ are to be taken from the table below.

Case 13.   Circular plate R, with hole r, simply supported at the inside edge r; free outer edge R, uniformly loaded with p_0,

$$w_{max} = \eta \frac{p_0 R^4}{E t^3}$$

$$s_{max} = \theta \frac{p_0 R^2}{t^2}$$

where η and θ are shown in the table below.

Case 14.   Circular plate R, with hole r, simply supported at the outer edge R; free inner edge r, loaded with a uniform p_0,

$$w_{max} = \kappa \frac{p_0 R^4}{E t^3}$$

$$s_{max} = \lambda \frac{p_0 R^2}{t^2}$$

where κ and λ are shown in the table below.

VALUES OF COEFFICIENTS FOR STRESS AND DEFLECTION FOR CASES 10 TO 14 OF PLATES
WITH A CENTRAL HOLE UNDER UNIFORMLY DISTRIBUTED LOADING p_0 OVER THE ENTIRE
ANNULAR AREA

R/r		1.25	1.50	2	3	4	5
Deflection	10, α	0.0023	0.018	0.094	0.293	0.448	0.564
	11, γ	0.0008	0.006	0.033	0.110	0.179	0.234
	12, ϵ	0.0034	0.031	0.125	0.291	0.417	0.492
	13, η	0.202	0.491	0.902	1.22	1.30	1.31
	14, κ	0.184	0.414	0.664	0.824	0.830	0.813
Stress	10, β	0.135	0.410	1.04	2.15	2.99	3.00
	11, δ	0.090	0.273	0.71	1.54	2.23	2.80
	12, ζ	0.122	0.336	0.74	1.21	1.45	1.59
	13, θ	0.66	1.19	2.04	3.34	4.30	5.10
	14, λ	0.59	0.976	1.44	1.88	2.08	2.19

Case 15. Circular plate R with hole r, clamped and supported at the inside edge r, the outer edge R being prevented from rotation and loaded with a total load P, linearly distributed around the periphery R.

$$w_{max} = \mu \frac{PR^2}{Et^3}$$

$$s_{max} = \nu \frac{P}{t^2}$$

where μ and ν are to be taken from the table below.

Case 16. Circular plate R with hole r, clamped and supported at the inner edge r, loaded by a total force P, linearly distributed along the free periphery R,

$$w_{max} = \xi \frac{PR^2}{Et^3}$$

$$s_{max} = \rho \frac{P}{t^2}$$

where ξ and ρ are to be taken from the table below.

VALUES OF COEFFICIENTS FOR STRESS AND DEFLECTION FOR CASES 15 TO 17 OF PLATES
WITH A CENTRAL HOLE, LOADED WITH A TOTAL FORCE P LINEARLY DISTRIBUTED
ALONG A CIRCULAR PERIPHERY

R/r		1.25	1.50	2	3	4	5
Deflection	15, μ	0.0013	0.0064	0.024	0.062	0.092	0.114
	16, ξ	0.0051	0.025	0.088	0.209	0.293	0.350
	17, σ	0.34	0.52	0.67	0.73	0.73	0.70
Stress	15, ν	0.115	0.220	0.405	0.703	0.933	1.13
	16, ρ	0.227	0.428	0.753	1.21	1.51	1.75
	17, τ	1.10	1.26	1.48	1.88	2.17	2.34

Case 17. Circular plate R with hole r, simply supported at the inner edge r, and loaded with a total force P linearly distributed along the free outer periphery R,

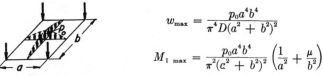

$$w_{\max} = \sigma \frac{PR^2}{Et^3}$$

$$s_{\max} = \tau \frac{P}{t^2}$$

where σ and τ are to be taken from the preceding table.

Case 18. (*Navier's Original Case*). Rectangular plate ab, with $b > a$, loaded sinusoidally $p = p_0 \sin (\pi x/a) \sin (\pi y/b)$ on simply supported edges with corner forces to hold it down:

$$w_{\max} = \frac{p_0 a^4 b^4}{\pi^4 D (a^2 + b^2)^2}$$

$$M_{1\ \max} = \frac{p_0 a^4 b^4}{\pi^2 (a^2 + b^2)^2} \left(\frac{1}{a^2} + \frac{\mu}{b^2} \right)$$

Case 19. Rectangular plate ab, with $b > a$, simply supported at the edges, under uniform pressure loading p_0 with sufficient corner forces to hold it down on the foundation,

$$w_{\max} = \alpha \frac{p_0 a^4}{Et^3}$$

$$M_{1\ \max} = \beta p_0 a^2$$

with the values of α and β in the table below:

b/a	1	1.2	1.4	1.6	1.8	2	3	4	5	∞
α	0.044	0.062	0.077	0.091	0.102	0.111	0.134	0.140	0.142	0.142
β	0.048	0.063	0.075	0.086	0.095	0.102	0.119	0.124	0.125	0.125

Case 20. Rectangular plate ab, simply supported on all four sides, subjected to a linearly increasing hydraulic pressure along the a sides, one

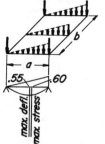

b side having zero pressure, the opposite b side having p_0. The maximum deflection occurs just off the middle of the plate toward the p_0 side (at about $0.55a$), the maximum stress somewhat farther off side (at about $0.60a$).

$$w_{\max} = \gamma \frac{p_0 a^4}{Et^3}$$

$$M_{1\ \max} = \delta p_0 a^2$$

where γ and δ are to be taken from the table below:

b/a	∞	4	3	2	1.5	1	0.75	0.50	0.25
γ	0.071	0.070	0.067	0.055	0.042	0.022	0.012	0.0037	0.0004
δ	0.064	0.063	0.061	0.053	0.043	0.026	0.021	0.0139	0.0051

Case 21. Rectangular plate ab, on four simply supported edges loaded with a single concentrated force P in its exact center,

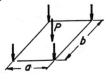

$$w_{max} = \epsilon \frac{Pa^2}{Et^3}$$

$$M_{1\ max} = \infty$$

where ϵ is given in the table below:

b/a	1	1.1	1.2	1.4	1.6	1.8	2	3	∞
ϵ	0.127	0.138	0.148	0.162	0.171	0.177	0.180	0.185	0.185

Case 22. Rectangular plate ab, under uniform load p_0, with the a edges clamped and the b edges simply supported,

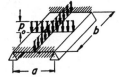

$$w_{max} = \zeta \frac{p_0 a^4}{Et^3}$$

$$M_{1\ max} = \eta p_0 a^2$$

where ζ and η are to be taken from the table below:

b/a	∞	3	2	1.6	1.3	1	0.75	0.50	0.25
ζ	0.142	0.128	0.099	0.066	0.042	0.021	0.0081	0.00177	0.00011
η	0.125	0.125	0.119	0.109	0.094	0.070	0.045	0.021	0.0052

Case 23. Rectangular plate ab, under uniform loading p_0, clamped along one a edge, and simply supported along the three remaining edges,

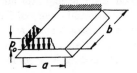

$$w_{max} = \kappa \frac{p_0 a^4}{Et^3}$$

$$M_{1\ max} = \lambda p_0 a^2$$

where κ and λ are in the following table:

b/a	∞	2	1.5	1.2	1	0.75	0.50	0.25
κ	0.142	0.101	0.070	0.047	0.030	0.0133	0.0033	0.0002
λ	0.125	0.122	0.112	0.098	0.084	0.058	0.031	0.0077

Case 24. Rectangular plate *ab* under uniform loading p_0, clamped along all edges (section of a continuous floor slab in a building, supported by beams on all sides):

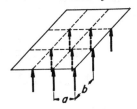

$$w_{\max} = \mu \frac{p_0 a^4}{E t^3}$$

$$M_{1\,\max} = \nu p_0 a^2$$

b/a	1	1.2	1.4	1.6	1.8	2	∞
μ	0.0138	0.0188	0.0226	0.0251	0.0267	0.0277	0.0285
ν	0.0513	0.0639	0.0726	0.0780	0.0812	0.0829	0.0833

Case 25. Rectangular plate *ab*, under uniform load p_0, being a section of a large continuous concrete building floor slab and supported at the corners of the sections *ab* by columns:

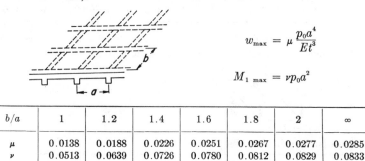

$$w_{\max} = \xi \frac{p_0 a^4}{E t^3}$$

At the columns: $M_1 = \infty$
In the center of each field: $M_1 = \rho p_0 a^2$

b/a	1	1.1	1.2	1.3	1.4	1.5	2	∞
ξ	0.063	0.053	0.047	0.042	0.039	0.037	0.032	0.028
ρ	0.036	0.037	0.038	0.039	0.039	0.039	0.041	0.042

In concluding this catalogue we mention an interesting reciprocal theorem. It is contended by some enthusiastic proponents of classical education that if a person has had a good training in Latin and Greek, he is then ready to tackle anything else, such as the theory of flat plates. The reciprocal of this point of view is that if a student has mastered the use of these 25 plate formulae, he has incidentally learned the Greek alphabet and hence is quite ready to start reading and enjoying Attic poetry.

20. Large Deflections. We now have to make good on our promise to show that all previous formulae on plates are true in general *only* if the deflection $w_{\max}$ is small in comparison with the thickness t of the plate. This is due to the fact that for larger deflections the middle surface of the plate (which was assumed to be stressless, page 104) becomes stretched, like a membrane, and in that state can carry the loading p_0 or P partly as a curved membrane. This limitation in general does not apply to beams, and in order to explain it, we start with the case (Fig. 89) of a beam, built in at both ends and loaded with a central force P. The simple beam theory for this case tells us that the deflection is

$$\delta = \frac{Pl^3}{192EI}$$

Now we make the preposterous assumption that the two side walls do not move *at all*; they do not move together by an amount of order δ, or by an amount of order δ^2/l even. Such immovable walls hardly exist, but if the wall were really

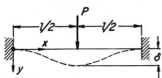

Fig. 89. Beam clamped at both ends between *immovable* walls. This causes a tension in the beam, which then carries part of the load P by string action.

immovable, then the beam center line would be in tension under the load P, because the curved deflected line is longer than the straight distance between the walls. Tension in the beam will cause a certain portion of the load P to be carried by string action, as in a suspension bridge, and if the load P^* so carried becomes comparable with P itself, then of course all our beam theory becomes inapplicable to the case. We shall now pursue this numerically. The length of the deflected beam is

$$s = \int ds = \int_0^l \sqrt{1 + y'^2}\, dx = \int_0^l \left(1 + \frac{y'^2}{2}\right) dx$$

$$s = l + \frac{1}{2}\int_0^l y'^2\, dx = l + \Delta l$$

The strain in the center line then is $\Delta l/l$, and the tensile force T of the string is

$$T = AE\,\frac{\Delta l}{l} = \frac{AE}{2l}\int_0^l y'^2\, dx$$

This tension T is mostly horizontal, but its maximum vertical component is

$$T_{\text{vert}} = y'_{\text{max}}\,\frac{AE}{2l}\int_0^l y'^2\, dx$$

Now we should calculate the deflected shape y by beam theory, but for simplicity of integration we assume reasonably that it is a displaced sine wave:

$$y = \frac{\delta}{2} - \frac{\delta}{2}\cos\frac{2\pi x}{l}$$

Then

$$y' = \frac{\pi \delta}{l} \sin \frac{2\pi x}{l} \quad \text{and} \quad y'_{max} = \frac{\pi \delta}{l}$$

The integral is

$$\int_0^l y'^2 \, dx = \frac{\pi^2 \delta^2}{l^2} \int_0^l \sin^2 \frac{2\pi x}{l} \, dx = \frac{\pi^2 \delta^2}{l^2} \frac{l}{2}$$

so that

$$T_{vert} = AE \frac{\pi^3}{4} \left(\frac{\delta}{l}\right)^3$$

If this force becomes as large as $P/2$, the entire load P is carried by string action. Let us see for what deflection this occurs.

$$AE \frac{\pi^3}{4} \left(\frac{\delta}{l}\right)^3 = \frac{P}{2}$$

The beam formula states that

$$P = \frac{192EI \delta}{l^3}$$

so that

$$AE \frac{\pi^3}{4} \left(\frac{\delta}{l}\right)^3 = \frac{96EI}{l^2} \left(\frac{\delta}{l}\right)$$

or

$$\delta^2 = \frac{96 \times 4}{\pi^3} \frac{I}{A}$$

For a rectangular cross section bh we have $I/A = bh^3/12bh = h^2/12$, and, substituted,

$$\frac{\delta}{h} = \sqrt{\frac{32}{\pi^3}} \approx 1$$

Thus we conclude that if the beam of Fig. 89 between *immovable* walls deflects as much as its own height or thickness, then the string action alone is sufficient to carry the load without any necessity of transverse shear forces in the beam. Obviously then the bending theory of simple beams does not apply any more. But *immovable* walls do not exist, so that this limitation does not apply to beams.

There are two other limitations to the deflection of beams which are much less severe than the (imaginary) one we just saw. One is, of course, that the stress should be less than the yield stress, and the other is that the slope should be small, so that we can write d^2y/dx^2 for the curvature instead of the more accurate $(d^2y/dx^2)/(1 + y'^2)^{3/2}$. If we apply this to a cantilever beam of rectangular cross section bh of length $l = 100h$, with an end load P, we can verify that the yield stress of $E/1,000$ is reached for $\delta = 7h$ and that in this condition the end slope is 0.1, so that the error in the curvature then is 1.5 per cent—entirely satisfactory. Deflections in beams which are several times the height thus are quite common and can be predicted accurately by beam theory, because in beams nothing resists the free stressless flexing of the neutral plane.

When we come to plates, we must distinguish between plates of which the middle neutral surface deforms into either a "developable" or a "non-developable" surface. A developable surface can be bent back to a plane without any strains, *i.e.*, without a change in length of any line of the surface. Cylinders and cones are developable. A sphere or a saddle surface is not developable. All 25 cases of the previous section are non-developable, with the exception of $b/a = \infty$ in cases 20 to 25, when the plate bends in a cylindrical shape. In that case tension in the middle, neutral surface can be caused only by immovable foundations, which do not exist in practice. Therefore *the limitation $w_{max} < t$ does not apply to cases where the plate bends into a cylinder or into a developable surface generally*, and the formulae are good until the yield stress appears. However, if a circular plate bends into a spherical dish shape, points on opposite ends of a diameter cannot move closer together without putting the entire outside periphery into a compressive hoop stress, which is a very powerful method of preventing these points from coming together. Therefore, a plate which bends into a non-developable surface must experience strains in its neutral plane, which is in violation of the fundamental assumption of page 104, on which all further results are based. Only when the deflections are small with respect to t are these tensions in the neutral plane negligible with respect to the bending stresses in the rest of the plate.

If a plate is so highly loaded that $w_{max} = 5t$ or larger (which can occur without yield stress only in very thin plates), then the tensile stresses in the neutral plane are large in comparison with the bending stresses, so that we may neglect the bending stresses and treat the plate as a "membrane" with the methods of Chap. III. This can be done without too much difficulty in each case, although it is not quite as simple as it might seem at first. A "flat" membrane can carry no load, and its load-carrying capacity develops only with the deflection. Then the load, instead of being proportional to the deflection, will vary with δ^3, as in the beam example just discussed.

Now then we possess two satisfactory theories: one for small deflections in which the membrane stress is neglected with respect to the bending stress and another one for large deflections in which the bending stress is neglected with respect to the membrane stress. The first theory is linear; the second one is not. But we have as yet no theory for the intermediate case where the two kinds of stress are of the same order of magnitude. An exact theory for this mixed case does exist, but it is extremely involved, and it is of course non-linear. One or two simple plate cases have been worked out with it to a complete conclusion: among others, the uniformly loaded circular plate with clamped edges. There is, however, a very simple approximate procedure which agrees well with the exact theory for the circular plate. In it we solve separately the plate problem and the membrane problem with the two extreme theories just mentioned. We write the answers in the form: load = f(deflection). Then we say that the load actually carried by the plate equals the sum of the two partial loads, carried membrane-wise and bending-wise, respectively.

We now proceed to carry this out in detail in an *example: the clamped circular plate with uniform loading.* The plate solution is given by Eq. (76) (page 124) or again as case 1 (page 128). The membrane solution is as yet unfamiliar and will now be derived.

The theory of pages 70 to 75 cannot be directly applied, because there we dealt with membranes of which the radii of curvature R_t and R_m were given. Here these radii are infinite on the unloaded membrane and assume definite values only when loaded. On page 73 Eqs. (52) and (53) were sufficient to solve for the two stresses s_t and s_m; here we have four unknowns: s_t, s_m, R_t, and R_m. However, the case is simple, because the pressure is constant all over; hence every element of the membrane is in the same state as every other element; the total shape must be a shallow spherical segment, and the stresses s_m and s_t must be equal; let us call them s.

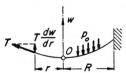

Fig. 90. A circular membrane of radius R, loaded with a uniform pressure p_0.

Now we apply Eq. (53) (page 74) to the vertical equilibrium of a circle r (Fig. 90):

$$st2\pi r \frac{dw}{dr} = p_0 \pi r^2 \qquad \text{or} \qquad \frac{dw}{dr} = \frac{p_0 r}{2st}$$

Integrated,

$$w = \frac{p_0 r^2}{4st} + \text{const} \qquad \text{or} \qquad w_{\max} = \frac{p_0 R^2}{4ts} \quad (a)$$

a relation between the two unknowns $w_{\max}$ and s. In order to solve the problem we must consider the deformations.

Now we calculate the elongation of a radius caused by the deformation:

$$\Delta l = \int ds - \int dr = \int \sqrt{dw^2 + dr^2} - \int dr$$

$$= \int dr \sqrt{1 + \left(\frac{dw}{dr}\right)^2} - \int dr \approx \int dr \left[1 + \frac{1}{2}\left(\frac{dw}{dr}\right)^2\right] - \int dr$$

$$= \frac{1}{2} \int_0^R \left(\frac{dw}{dr}\right)^2 dr = \frac{1}{2} \int_0^R \left(\frac{p_0 r}{2ts}\right)^2 dr$$

$$\Delta l = \frac{p_0^2 R^3}{24 t^2 s^2}$$

The strain is

$$\epsilon = \frac{\Delta l}{R} = \frac{p_0^2 R^2}{24 t^2 s^2}$$

Because this strain is the same in all directions (two-dimensional hydrostatic tension), we have for the stress $s = \epsilon E/(1 - \mu)$, so that

$$s = \frac{E}{1 - \mu} \frac{p_0^2 R^2}{24 t^2 s^2} \qquad (b)$$

We now eliminate the stress s from between Eqs. (a) and (b) with the result

$$p_0 = \frac{8}{3} \frac{E}{1 - \mu} \frac{t}{R} \left(\frac{w_{\max}}{R}\right)^3$$

This is the membrane solution. We see that the load is proportional to $w_{\max}^3$, as mentioned before. The bending solution from page 128 can be written as

$$p_0 = \frac{64D}{R^3} \left(\frac{w_{\max}}{R}\right)^1 \qquad (76)$$

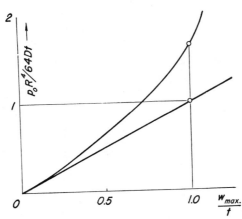

FIG. 91. Load-deflection curve for a uniformly loaded circular plate with clamped edges. The straight line represents the plate bending theory; the curve gives the complete theory for large deflection. It is seen that the plate theory is satisfactory for $w_{\max} < t/2$ but that for larger deflections the error becomes appreciable.

Now we say that in the mixed case the total load is partly carried by membrane action and partly by bending action,

$$p_0 = \frac{64D}{R^3} \left(\frac{w_{\max}}{R}\right)^1 + \frac{8}{3} \frac{E}{1 - \mu} \frac{t}{R} \left(\frac{w_{\max}}{R}\right)^3$$

or, written somewhat differently, remembering Eq. (64) (page 107),

$$\frac{p_0 R^4}{64 Dt} = \frac{w_{max}}{t} + \frac{1 + \mu}{2}\left(\frac{w_{max}}{t}\right)^3$$

$$\frac{p_0 R^4}{64 Dt} = \frac{w_{max}}{t}\left[1 + 0.65\left(\frac{w_{max}}{t}\right)^2\right]$$

(83)

We recognize from the development that the first term in the square brackets represents the plate bending solution and the second term, the membrane solution. We see that for $w_{max} = t$ the error in the load by the plate theory alone is 65 per cent. For large deflections (deflections of the order of the thickness) the plate gets much stiffer than the bending theory of this chapter indicates.

The result, Eq. (83), illustrated in Fig. 91, although approximate, agrees very well with the outcome of the exact theory and is also in good agreement with tests.

Problems 76 to 90.

CHAPTER V

BEAMS ON ELASTIC FOUNDATION

21. General Theory. The subject of this chapter grew out of the practical problem of railroad track. A long rail is a beam of small bending stiffness, and in order to sustain the large wheel loads placed on it, the rail must be supported almost along its entire length, by closely spaced crossties. The investigation of this problem led (about 1880) to a theory of interaction between a beam of moderate bending stiffness and an "elastic" foundation which imposes reaction forces on the beam that are proportional to the deflection of the foundation. This theory then was of great importance to civil engineers only, but later it was found that the fundamental theory applied not only to railroad track but to many other situations as well. An example is a bridge deck or floor structure consisting of a "grillage," or rectangular network of beams, closely spaced. Each individual beam of this network is supported by the many beams crossing it at right angles, and these crossbeams assert reactions on the first beam proportional to the local deflection. Each individual beam in the network thus is placed on an elastic foundation consisting of all the crossbeams. This line of thinking has proved to be very useful in the design of ship's bottoms and similar structures.

A second example is a thin-walled cylindrical shell loaded by pressures which vary with the longitudinal coordinate z only and which are constant with θ, circumferentially. If we cut out of this shell a longitudinal strip of width $rd\theta$, then this strip is a "beam," subjected to some radial loading along the length z. The beam then finds its reaction forces from the remaining part $(2\pi - rd\theta)$ of the shell in the form of hoop stresses on the two sides, having the small angle $d\theta$ between them and thus having a resultant in the radial direction, *i.e.*, in the direction of the load. This will be discussed on page 164.

Returning to the railroad track, the assumption made regarding the behavior of the elastic foundation is

$$q = -ky \qquad (84)$$

where y is the local downward deflection of the foundation under the rail; q is the downward (and $-q$ the upward) force from the foundation on the rail per unit length of rail, and k is the "foundation modulus," measured in units of $q/y = \text{lb/in./in.} = \text{lb/sq in.}$ For the usual railroad track this constant has a value of the order of $k = 1,500$ lb/sq in., which means that if the long rail is uniformly loaded with $q = 1,500$ lb per running inch, then the whole rail is pushed uniformly 1 in. into the foundation. The assumption (84) has the great advantage of being mathematically as simple as can be; it also is in fairly good agreement with the facts, although it can be criticized on two points. The first and most important is that an actual soil behaves non-linearly, becoming gradually stiffer for greater deflections. Therefore the $q = f(y)$ relation is represented by a curve rather than a straight line, and the slope k depends on the deflection y, becoming larger with increasing y. The mathematics of such non-linear phenomena is extremely complicated and unsatisfactory, so that here as well as in other cases we work out a linear theory, use it as far as it goes, and discuss deviations from it in a qualitative manner only. The second objection to Eq. (84) is illustrated in Fig. 92. The assumption (84) describes a soil entirely without continuity; the deflection at any point is caused by the load on that point only and is completely independent of other loads nearby. This, of course, is not in agreement with the actual behavior of most soils, but the objection is not as serious as it would seem at first sight. We do not consider cases of loads placed directly on the soil; there always is a rail in between, and if we place a rectangularly dis-

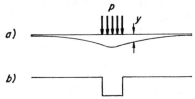

Fig. 92. A loading p, of the rectangular diagrammatic shape shown, placed directly on the soil (without a rail in between) will cause a soil deflection somewhat like that shown in (a), while the mathematical assumption (84) demands a deflection diagram (b).

continuous loading p (Fig. 92a) on the rail, then the deflection of the rail will be quite smooth and the reaction from the ground is also smoothly distributed over a comparatively great length.

Now we are ready to *set up the differential equation of the rail.* If p is the downward loading per unit length on the rail and q is the downward reaction force from the foundation, then the rail will obey the classical beam equation (which the reader has to look up in some elementary text),

$$EI \frac{d^4y}{dx^4} = p + q$$

where EI is the bending stiffness of the rail. Substituting the assumption (84),

$$\frac{d^4y}{dx^4} + \frac{k}{EI}\, y = \frac{p}{EI} \tag{85}$$

The remainder of this chapter deals with the solution, interpretation, and discussion of this differential equation. We note that it is a linear equation of the fourth order with a right-hand member. First we solve the "reduced" equation ($p = 0$) by the usual substitution,

$$y = e^{ax}$$

where a is an as yet unknown exponent. Then $y^{(4)} = a^4 y$, and

$$\left(a^4 + \frac{k}{EI}\right)y = 0$$

so that

$$a = \sqrt[4]{-\frac{k}{EI}} = \sqrt[4]{\frac{k}{EI}}\,\sqrt[4]{-1}$$

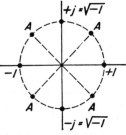

Fig. 93. The complex-number plane, showing the two square roots of -1 and the four fourth roots of -1 as the points A. The point -1 can be considered at angular distance π, 3π, 5π, 7π, 9π, etc., from the point $+1$; then the fourth roots are at angular distances $\frac{1}{4}\pi$, $\frac{3}{4}\pi$, etc., from that point, by De Moivre's theorem.

Fourth roots of negative numbers are found by De Moivre's theorem in the complex plane, as shown in Fig. 93. The four fourth roots of -1 are

$$\sqrt[4]{-1} = \frac{1}{\sqrt{2}}\,(\pm 1 \pm j)$$

as can be verified by arithmetic. The factor $\sqrt{2}$ can be absorbed with the k/EI, and, writing

$$\beta = \sqrt[4]{\frac{k}{4EI}} \tag{86}$$

the four solutions of the reduced differential equation become

$$y = e^{\beta x + i\beta x} \qquad y = e^{\beta x - i\beta x} \qquad y = e^{-\beta x + i\beta x} \qquad y = e^{-\beta x - i\beta x}$$

The general solution of this equation, containing four integration constants A, B, C, D is

$$y = e^{\beta x}[Ae^{i\beta x} + Be^{-i\beta x}] + e^{-\beta x}[Ce^{i\beta x} + De^{-i\beta x}]$$

In books on differential equations the square brackets are shown to be expressible in terms of trigonometric functions, thus:

$$y = e^{\beta x}[C_1 \cos \beta x + C_2 \sin \beta x] + e^{-\beta x}[C_3 \cos \beta x + C_4 \sin \beta x] \tag{87}$$

in which the constants C_1, C_2, C_3, C_4 are related to the previous A, B, C, D in some manner which is of no interest to us. The solution (87) with its definition equation (86) of the symbol β is the most general solution of the beam in those sections where it carries no load p. Most of our examples will be of beams with concentrated force loadings P; then Eq. (87) holds in the stretches between the forces. We first remark that the combination βx must be dimensionless (we have never yet seen the cosine of 5 in.), so that β is an inverse length, of which we shall see the physical significance later. Next we notice that Eq. (87) describes "damped sine waves," the C_1, C_2 terms being damped when going to the left (in the $-x$ direction), the C_3, C_4 terms being damped when going to the right. Thus if our beam is very long, then the C_1, C_2 terms show very large deflections to the right and the C_3, C_4 terms very large deflections to the left.

22. The Infinite Beam. Now we apply Eq. (87) to our first specific case: a beam or rail of infinite length both to left and right, loaded with a single concentrated force P in the middle $x = 0$. Then Eq. (87) applies everywhere, except at the load itself, but the constants $C_1 \cdots C_4$ will have different values at left and at right. [If they had the same values at left and right, then the entire beam would be expressible in terms of Eq. (87), which is not true on account of the presence of the load P]. Considering the half beam to the right $(x > 0)$, we see that the C_1, C_2 terms lead to infinite deflections y at infinite x, which is obviously contrary to the boundary conditions. If we make $C_1 = C_2 = 0$, then only the second half remains, which gives zero deflection at $x \to \infty$ in accordance with fact. Thus we say that $C_1 = C_2 = 0$ is necessitated by the boundary conditions at $x = \infty$, and we shall always see that there will be two conditions for each "end" of the beam, totaling four conditions. There remains the end at $x = 0$. We know nothing about the deflection or about the bending moment at the load P, but we can say something about the slope and about the shear force there. Unless the beam cracks, the slope must be horizontal, from symmetry. Also, making two cuts, immediately to the left and to the right of the load P, equilibrium of the short center piece requires that the two shear forces together equal P, and symmetry requires that each is $P/2$. Thus the conditions immediately to the right of the load are

$$x = 0 \qquad y' = 0 \qquad S = EIy''' = \frac{P}{2}$$

To evaluate these, we need the various derivatives of y, which, after making $C_1 = C_2 = 0$ in Eq. (87), are

$$y = e^{-\beta x}[C_3 \cos \beta x + C_4 \sin \beta x]$$

$$y' = \beta e^{-\beta x}[(-C_3 + C_4) \cos \beta x + (-C_3 - C_4) \sin \beta x]$$

$$y'' = \beta^2 e^{-\beta x}[-2C_4 \cos \beta x + 2C_3 \sin \beta x]$$

$$y''' = \beta^3 e^{-\beta x}[2(C_3 + C_4) \cos \beta x + 2(-C_3 + C_4) \sin \beta x]$$

The reader will do well to carry this series one line further and to verify that it then checks Eq. (85). Substituting $x = 0$ into the above expressions, the boundary conditions become

$$C_3 = C_4$$

$$EI\beta^3 2(C_3 + C_4) = \frac{P}{2}$$

from which

$$C_3 = C_4 = \frac{P}{8EI\beta^3} = \frac{P\beta}{2k}$$

by Eq. (86). Thus we find for the solution of the infinite beam, loaded with a force P at the center (Fig. 94),

$$y = \frac{P\beta}{2k} e^{-\beta x}(\cos \beta x + \sin \beta x)$$

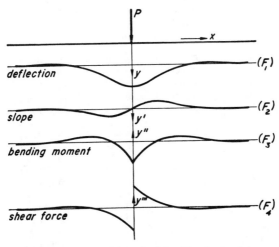

FIG. 94. Infinite beam with central force load P. The shapes of the curves are given numerically by the table of page 146, and the magnitudes are determined by Eqs. (89) and the table on page 146.

This function with its various derivatives will occur time and again in this chapter, so that it becomes convenient to give them shorter notations:

$$F_1(\beta x) = e^{-\beta x}(\cos \beta x + \sin \beta x)$$

$$F_2(\beta x) = e^{-\beta x} \sin \beta x = -\frac{1}{2\beta} F_1'$$

$$F_3(\beta x) = e^{-\beta x}(\cos \beta x - \sin \beta x) = \frac{1}{\beta} F_2' = -\frac{1}{2\beta^2} F_1''$$

$$F_4(\beta x) = e^{-\beta x} \cos \beta x = -\frac{1}{2\beta} F_3' = -\frac{1}{2\beta^2} F_2'' = \frac{1}{4\beta^3} F_1'''$$

$$F_1(\beta x) = -\frac{1}{\beta} F_4'$$

$$(88)$$

NUMERICAL VALUES OF THE F FUNCTIONS

βx	$F_1(\beta x)$	$F_2(\beta x)$	$F_3(\beta x)$	$F_4(\beta x)$	βx
0.0	1.000	0.000	1.000	1.000	0
0.2	0.965	0.163	0.640	0.802	0.2
0.4	0.878	0.261	0.356	0.617	0.4
0.6	0.763	0.310	0.143	0.453	0.6
0.8	0.635	0.322	−0.009	0.313	0.8
1.0	0.508	0.310	−0.111	0.199	1.0
1.2	0.390	0.281	−0.172	0.109	1.2
1.4	0.285	0.243	−0.201	0.042	1.4
1.6	0.196	0.202	−0.208	−0.006	1.6
1.8	0.123	0.161	−0.199	−0.038	1.8
2.0	0.067	0.123	−0.179	−0.056	2.0
2.2	0.024	0.090	−0.155	−0.065	2.2
2.4	−0.006	0.061	−0.128	−0.067	2.4
2.6	−0.025	0.038	−0.102	−0.064	2.6
2.8	−0.037	0.020	−0.078	−0.057	2.8
3.0	−0.042	0.007	−0.056	−0.049	3.0
3.2	−0.043	−0.002	−0.038	−0.041	3.2
3.4	−0.041	−0.009	−0.024	−0.032	3.4
3.6	−0.037	−0.012	−0.012	−0.024	3.6
3.8	−0.031	−0.014	−0.004	−0.018	3.8
4.0	−0.026	−0.014	0.002	−0.012	4.0
4.2	−0.020	−0.013	0.006	−0.007	4.2
4.4	−0.016	−0.012	0.008	−0.004	4.4
4.6	−0.011	−0.010	0.009	−0.001	4.6
4.8	−0.008	−0.008	0.009	0.001	4.8
5.0	−0.005	−0.007	0.008	0.002	5.0

With this new F notation the solution of the bothway infinite beam with central force P is:

Deflection $\qquad y = \dfrac{P\beta}{2k} F_1$

Slope $\qquad y' = -\dfrac{P\beta^2}{k} F_2$

$$(89)$$

Moment $\qquad EIy'' = -\dfrac{P}{4\beta} F_3$

Shear force $EIy''' = \dfrac{P}{2} F_4$

The most notable property of the solution, Fig. 94, is that the rail is pushed up above the original ground level at some distance from the load P. By Eq. (84) this of course means that the ground is supposed to pull down on the rail, with a force of an intensity about 4 per cent of that of the main pressure under the load. If the rail lifts off from the ground, the above equations do not apply strictly speaking, although they are a good approximation even then. Equations (89) apply only to the right half of Fig. 94; the left half of that figure is symmetrical with the right half in y and y'' and antisymmetrical in y' and y'''.

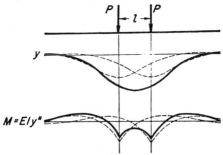

Fig. 95. Deflection and bending-moment diagrams for an infinite beam under two identical loads.

The general solutions (89) with the numerical values of the table of page 146 can be used for solving problems of infinite beams loaded with more than one force by superposing the various individual solutions. For example, Fig. 95 shows *a beam with two equal forces P* at distance l apart. The deflections caused separately by the individual loads are drawn in dashes, and the total deflection at each point is the sum of the two separate contributions. Numerical values for this come out of the table. We might ask for what distance l between the loads the deflection midway between loads becomes equal to or less than that under each load. The answer is $2F_1(\beta l/2) = F(0) + F(\beta l)$, and by trying several values of the table in this relation we see that for $\beta l = 2.00$ and $\beta l/2 = 1.00$ the two deflections are almost the same. Thus if βl is slightly larger than 2.00, we have the desired relation and $l = 2.00/\beta$. This length depends on the relative stiffness of the rail and the ground [Eq. (86)]; for a given ground k the length $l = 2/\beta$ is larger for a stiff rail than for a flexible one. For the usual roadbed $k = 1,500$ lb/sq in., and for a heavy 130 lb/yd rail of $I = 88$ in.[4] we calculate $1/\beta = 51$ in. The table shows that for a single load the deflection extends to $\beta x = 2.36$, which means that it extends to a distance $x = 2.36/\beta = 2.36 \times 51$ in. $= 10$ ft on either side of the load. If then adjacent wheels in a train are spaced closer than 20 ft, the rail will nowhere lift from the ground between wheels.

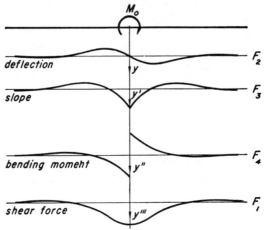

FIG. 96.   Infinite beam with a concentrated bending moment M_0 in the middle, described by Eqs. (90).

Another case of loading of fundamental importance is that of Fig. 96: *an infinite beam, loaded by a concentrated bending moment M_0 in the center $x = 0$.* We shall solve this problem in three different ways: by boundary conditions; by superposition of the two solutions in Fig. 94; and finally by Maxwell's reciprocal theorem.

For the first method we return to Eq. (87) and remark that for $x = \infty$ the deflection y must remain finite so that $C_1 = C_2 = 0$. Then at $x = 0$ the boundary conditions are, from symmetry,

$$x = 0 \qquad y = 0 \qquad M = EIy'' = -\frac{M_0}{2}$$

Substituting this into the four general expressions of pages 144 to 145, we find

$$C_3 = 0 \qquad \text{and} \qquad EI\beta^2 2C_4 = +\frac{M_0}{2}$$

so that

$$y = \frac{M_0}{4EI\beta^2} e^{-\beta x} \sin \beta x = \frac{M_0}{k} \beta^2 F_2(\beta x)$$

By successive differentiations, using the results obtained previously in Eqs. (88) and Eq. (86), we find for the infinite beam with central bending moment M_0 (Fig. 96)

$$y = \frac{M_0}{k} \beta^2 F_2(\beta x)$$

$$y' = \frac{M_0}{k} \beta^3 F_3(\beta x)$$

$$M = EIy'' = -\frac{M_0}{2} F_4(\beta x) \tag{90}$$

$$S = EIy''' = \frac{M_0\beta}{2} F_1(\beta x)$$

We see that the same four functions of page 146 reappear, but they are shifted down one notch. The reason for this is brought out clearly by the second method of derivation. We subject the rail (Fig. 97) to a push-pull pair of forces P at distance δ apart, a positive one, $+P$, at the origin and a negative one, $-P$, at $x = -\delta$. Then the deflection, by Eqs. (89), is

$$y = \frac{P\beta}{2k} [+F_1(\beta x) - F_1(\beta x + \beta \delta)]$$

which, following the habits of mathematicians who are about to give birth to a differentiation, is rewritten as

$$y = -\frac{(P\delta)\beta}{2k} \frac{F_1[\beta(x + \delta)] - F_1[\beta x]}{\delta}$$

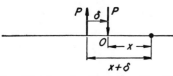

Fig. 97. A push-pull load system $P\delta$ becomes a concentrated momnet $M_0 = P\delta$ when δ is shrunk down to zero while P simultaneously grows to infinity.

Now we let the distance δ shrink and the forces P grow, so that the product $P\delta$ remains constant. In the limit $\delta \to 0$ the product $P\delta$ is a moment which we call M_0, and we have

$$y = -\frac{M_0\beta}{2k} \lim_{\delta \to 0} \frac{F_1[\beta(x + \delta)] - F_1[\beta x]}{\delta}$$

$$= -\frac{M_0\beta}{2k} \frac{dF_1(\beta x)}{dx} = [\text{Eqs. (88)}] = +\frac{M_0\beta^2}{k} F_2(\beta x)$$

which is the result, Eqs. (90). Thus the series of functions in Fig. 96 are the derivatives of those of Fig. 94.

The third manner of deriving the same result, Eqs. (90), from Fig. 94 is equally instructive. Maxwell's reciprocal theorem tells us that the (work-absorbing component of the) deflection at location 2 caused by a unit load at location 1 equals the "deflection" at 1 due to a unit "load" at 2. We apply this to the situation of Fig. 98, where a load P and a

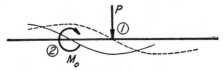

Fig. 98.   The deflection at 1 caused only by a unit moment M_0 at 2 equals the slope at 2 caused only by a unit load at 1. This statement of Maxwell's reciprocal theorem ties together the cases of Fig. 94 and Fig. 96.

moment M_0 are applied simultaneously, but at different locations 1 and 2. Then the work-absorbing component of deflection at location 2 is a slope in the direction of rotation of M_0, while the deflection at location 1 is a displacement parallel to force P in direction.   Assuming Eqs. (89) known, the first deflection, *i.e.*, the slope at 2, is $+P\beta^2 F_2(\beta x)/k$, and the slope distribution is sketched in Fig. 98 as a dotted line.   By Maxwell, the slope at 2 (for $P = 1$ lb) equals the deflection at 1, caused by a bending moment $M_0 = 1$ in.-lb.   The deflection distribution due to M_0 (as yet unknown to us) is sketched in Fig. 98 as a full line.   Now if the height of the dotted line above M_0 is equal to the depth of the full line at P, and if this is to be true for any location of M_0 relative to P, then the two curves must be of the same shape, merely horizontally displaced with respect to each other.   By pulling M_0 farther away from P it carries its full-line curve with it, while the dotted line stays at P.   To finish the argument we say then that the deflection at 1, due to a moment M_0 at 2, is $+M_0\beta^2 F_2(\beta x)/k$, which differs from the previous expression $+P\beta^2 F_2(\beta x)/k$ only in that P has been replaced by M_0, which makes no difference if both P and M_0 are unity.   Thus the first of Eqs. (90) is derived by differentiation.

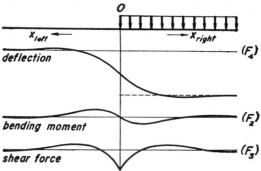

Fig. 99.   Infinite rail, loaded with a constant loading p_0 on its right half only.

Now we proceed to a few examples in which the distributed load p on the rail is not zero.   First *let the right half of the rail (Fig. 99) carry a con-*

stant loading p_0, and let the left half be free of loading. For the right half we must complete the general solution (87) with a particular integral of Eq. (85) in which p is constant $= p_0$. Such a particular integral is simple; it is

$$y = \frac{p_0}{k}$$

Since our beam still extends to infinity at right, no terms with $e^{+\beta x}$ can occur, so that

$$y_{\text{right}} = e^{-\beta x}(A \cos \beta x + B \sin \beta x) + \frac{p_0}{k}$$

To the left the general solution, Eq. (87), holds without change. If we now count x positive toward the *left* (Fig. 99), then we write

$$y_{\text{left}} = e^{-\beta x}(C \cos \beta x + D \sin \beta x)$$

The boundary conditions are now somewhat different from the previous cases; we do not know anything about y, y', y'', or y'''; all we know is that these quantities are the same just to the left as just to the right of the origin. Since the abscissa x reverses at O, we have there (using the derivative expressions of pages 144 to 145)

$$y_{\text{left}} = +y_{\text{right}} \qquad \text{or} \qquad C = A + \frac{p_0}{k}$$

$$y'_{\text{left}} = -y'_{\text{right}} \qquad \text{or} \qquad -C + D = +A - B$$

$$y''_{\text{left}} = +y''_{\text{right}} \qquad \text{or} \qquad D = B$$

$$y'''_{\text{left}} = -y'''_{\text{right}} \qquad \text{or} \qquad C + D = -A - B$$

Solving these, we find $B = D = 0$ and $C = -A = p_0/2k$. Then with the notation of Eqs. (88) we have the solution

$$y_{\text{right}} = \frac{p_0}{k}\left[1 - \frac{1}{2}F_4(\beta x)\right]$$

$$y_{\text{left}} = \frac{p_0}{k}\left[\frac{1}{2}F_4(\beta x)\right]$$

The deflection diagram, shown in Fig. 99, thus is the same as the lowest curve of Fig. 94 with the right-hand branch pushed down. The bending-moment and shear-force diagrams then are two and three steps down Eqs. (88), respectively, as shown in the figure.

The next example is an infinite beam loaded sinusoidally,

$$p = p_0 \sin \frac{2\pi x}{l}$$

with "peak intensity" p_0 and "wave length" l. This load pushes down and pulls up on the rail alternately: it has no practical significance in itself, but with Fourier's help can be made very useful (Fig. 100). The particular integral of Eq. (85) in this case we assume as

$$y = A \sin \frac{2\pi x}{l}$$

Substituting this into Eq. (85) gives

$$\left(\frac{2\pi}{l}\right)^4 A + \frac{k}{EI} A = \frac{p_0}{EI}$$

or

$$A = \frac{p_0}{k + (16\pi^4 EI/l^4)}$$

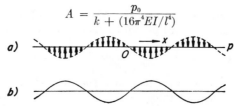

FIG. 100. A sinusoidally varying load (a) on a long beam causes a similar sinusoidal deflection (b) and hence also a sinusoidal bending-moment distribution (b). The deflections are given by Eq. (91). This solution can be made useful as the tool by which Fourier series can be built up.

Since, again, the beam can have no infinite deflections at $x = \infty$ the $e^{+\beta x}$ terms of Eq. (87) must disappear, so that the general solution for this case is

$$y = e^{-\beta x}(C_3 \cos \beta x + C_4 \sin \beta x) + \frac{p_0}{k + (16\pi^4 EI/l^4)} \sin \frac{2\pi x}{l}$$

Now we can reason that both C_3 and C_4 must be zero, because the loading pattern repeats itself indefinitely, so that, for symmetry, the deflection pattern also must repeat itself with the same wave length l. The β terms, however, do not repeat themselves, being damped waves. Hence $C_3 = C_4 = 0$, and the solution, rewritten with Eq. (86), is

$$y = \frac{p_0}{k} \frac{1}{1 + (\pi \sqrt{2}/\beta l)^4} \sin \frac{2\pi x}{l} \tag{91}$$

a sine wave of the same shape as the loading diagram. The "amplitude," or maximum deflection (in the middle of each load field), is seen to depend on the quantity βl, which we shall now interpret. In Eq. (87) we say that we progress "one natural wave length λ" along the bar when βx increases by 2π, or $\lambda = 2\pi/\beta$. Hence the combination $\beta l = 2\pi l/\lambda$ is 2π times the ratio of the load wave length l to the natural wave length λ. When βl is large, i.e., when the load wave length is relatively long, then Eq. (91) tells us that the maximum deflection is p_0/k; the deflection is the same as if the load were placed on the ground directly without rail in between. If, however, βl is very small, *i.e.*, if the load varies rapidly along the beam, then Eq. (91) tells us that y is small throughout, so that the beam hardly bends. The functional relationship is shown in Fig. 101.

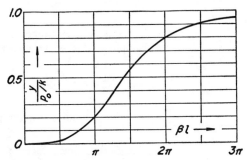

FIG. 101. Relation between the deflection at mid-span of the sinusoidally loaded beam of Fig. 100 and the wave-length ratio $l/\lambda = \beta l/2\pi$.

The relation (91) can be made the basis of calculating the deflections of a long beam under any kind of periodic loading along it. For example, if patches of constant loading p_0 of length $l/2$ alternate with patches $l/2$ free of pressure (Fig. 102), then that loading can be thought of as the

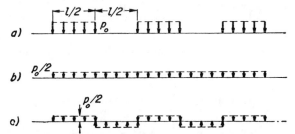

FIG. 102. A rectangular patch loading (*a*) is the sum of a constant loading (*b*) and a rectangular alternating loading (*c*). Each Fourier component term of this loading causes a deflection by Eq. (91). The deflection caused by the higher harmonics is small because their wave lengths are short (Fig. 101). Hence only a few of the lower harmonics of the loading determine the deflection.

sum of the average loading $p_0/2$ over the entire beam and a rectangular alternating loading of intensity $p_0/2$ and wave length l. By Fourier analysis this loading can be written as

$$\frac{p_0}{2} + \frac{p_0}{2}\frac{4}{\pi}\left(\sin\frac{2\pi x}{l} + \frac{1}{3}\sin 3\frac{2\pi x}{l} + \frac{1}{5}\sin 5\frac{2\pi x}{l} + \cdots\right)$$

Each one of these terms gives a deflection that can be calculated easily, the constant term giving $y = p_0/2k$, the others sinusoidal deflections with amplitudes according to Eq. (91). The maximum of all these terms occurs in the middle of a field; hence the maximum deflection is

$$y_{max} = \frac{p_0}{2k} + \frac{p_0}{2k}\frac{4}{\pi}\left[\frac{1}{1 + (\pi\sqrt{2}/\beta l)^4} + \frac{1}{1 + (3\pi\sqrt{2}/\beta l)^4} + \cdots\right]$$

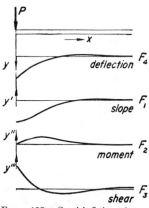

FIG. 103. Semi-infinite beam with an end load P. The solution here illustrated is described by Eqs. (92).

This series is very rapidly convergent; for example, if $\beta l = \pi$, the deflection is

$$y_{max} = \frac{p_0}{2k}\left[1 + \frac{4}{\pi}(0.2000 + 0.0031 + 0.0004 + 0.0001)\right]$$

23. Semi-infinite Beams. Consider the rail of Fig. 103, which extends to infinity at right, but which has one end at $x = 0$, and carries a concentrated load P at that end. The general solution, Eq. (87), with $C_1 = C_2 = 0$ applies here as in all previous cases. The conditions at the left-hand end are

$$x = 0 \quad \frac{M}{EI} = y'' = 0 \quad S = EIy''' = P$$

With this substituted into the expressions of pages 144 to 145 we have

$$C_4 = 0 \quad \text{and} \quad EI\beta^3 2C_3 = P$$

so that the general solution [remembering Eq. (86)] is

$$y = \frac{2\beta P}{k} e^{-\beta x} \cos \beta x = \frac{2\beta P}{k} F_4(\beta x)$$

Differentiating this three times by the rules of Eqs. (88) leads to the result for the *semi-infinite beam with end load P*:

Deflection $\quad y = \dfrac{2\beta P}{k} F_4(\beta x)$

Slope $\quad y' = -\dfrac{2\beta^2 P}{k} F_1(\beta x)$

Moment $\quad EIy'' = \dfrac{P}{\beta} F_2(\beta x)$ $\qquad\qquad$ (92)

Shear $\quad EIy''' = PF_3(\beta x)$

Next we solve the case of Fig. 104: the semi-infinite beam with an end moment M_0. Here the end conditions are

$$x = 0 \qquad EIy'' = M_0 \qquad S = EIy''' = 0$$

which leads to

$$-EI\beta^2 2C_4 = M_0 \qquad C_3 + C_4 = 0$$

or

$$C_4 = -\frac{M_0}{2EI\beta^2} \qquad C_4 = -C_3$$

With Eq. (86), and carrying out the differentiations with Eqs. (88), the final result for the *semi-infinite beam with end moment M_0* is

Deflection $\qquad y = \dfrac{2\beta^2 M_0}{k} F_3(\beta x)$

Slope $\qquad y' = -\dfrac{4\beta^3}{k} M_0 F_4 = -\dfrac{M_0}{EI\beta} F_4(\beta x)$

(93)

Moment $\quad EIy'' = M_0 F_1(\beta x)$

Shear $\quad EIy''' = -2\beta M_0 F_2(\beta x)$

These two cases, Figs. 103 and 104, are often useful; they can also be derived from Eqs. (89) and (90) for the bothway infinite beam, and vice versa, as will now be shown. Consider a bothway infinite beam loaded in the middle by a couple M_0 and a force P_0 simultaneously. The bending moment in the beam just to the right of the loads, by Eqs. (89) and (90), is

$$M = -\frac{P_0}{4\beta} - \frac{M_0}{2}$$

and the shear force at that place is

$$S = \frac{P_0}{2} + \frac{M_0 \beta}{2}$$

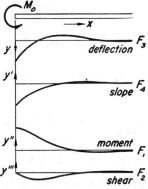

Fig. 104. Illustrates Eqs. (93) for the semi-infinite beam with an end moment M_0.

Now we adjust the relative values of P_0 and M_0 so that the bending moment M in the beam just to the right of the loads is zero, or $P_0 = -2\beta M_0$. Then the shear force there is $S = (P_0/2) - (P_0/4) = P_0/4$. If we now cut off from the bothway infinite beam the whole left half including the origin containing the loads P_0 and M_0, we have left a semi-infinite beam loaded with a shear force $P_0/4$ and without end moment. But that semi-infinite beam deflects just as the bothway infinite one under the loads P_0 and $M_0 = -P_0/2\beta$. Multiply by 4, and the semi-infinite beam of Fig. 103 under load P_0 has the same characteristics as the sum of the beam of Fig. 94 under load $4P_0$ and the beam of Fig. 96 under load $M_0 = -4P_0/2\beta$, or

$$y = 4P_0 \frac{\beta}{2k} F_1 - \frac{4P_0}{2\beta} \frac{\beta^2}{k} F_2$$

$$= \frac{2P_0\beta}{k} (F_1 - F_2) = \frac{2P_0\beta}{k} F_4$$

because of the definition equations (88) for the F function. These are the results (92), which were derived differently before. To find the results (93), we adjust P_0 and M_0 so as to make the shear force S zero, leaving only a bending moment. This is left as an exercise to the reader.

Now we shall do the opposite: derive Fig. 94 from a combination of Figs. 103 and 104. The beam of Fig. 94 carries its load P by splitting it into two shear forces $P/2$ each, one on each side of the load. Therefore we take a semi-infinite beam and load it with $P_0/2$ and with a moment M_0 simultaneously. Then we adjust the moment M_0 to such a value as to make the end slope zero, which gives us half the bothway infinite beam:

$$y = \frac{2\beta(P_0/2)}{k} F_4 [\text{Eqs. (92)}] + \frac{2\beta^2 M_0}{k} F_3 [\text{Eqs. (93)}]$$

$$y' = -\frac{\beta^2 P_0}{k} F_1 - \frac{4\beta^3}{k} M_0 F_4 \qquad [\text{by Eqs. (88)}]$$

At the origin both F_1 and F_4 are 1.00, and y' must be zero. Hence

$$\frac{\beta^2 P_0}{k} = -\frac{4\beta^3}{k} M_0 \qquad \text{or} \qquad M_0 = -\frac{P_0}{4\beta}$$

Then

$$y = \frac{P_0\beta}{k} \left(F_4 - \frac{1}{2} F_3 \right) = \frac{P_0\beta}{k} \left(\frac{1}{2} F_1 \right) \qquad [\text{by Eqs. (88)}]$$

This is the result, Eqs. (89), we set out to derive.

As an example of the application of the general results, Eqs. (92) and (93), to other cases of loading we take *Fig. 105: a semi-infinite beam subjected to a uniform loading p_0 all along its length and "freely" supported at its end.* The "free" support is considered to be a hinge, which results in a vertical reaction force X only, with zero end moment. Far to the right of this hinge the beam under the influence of the steady load p_0 will deflect to an amount p_0/k, and if the hinge force X were absent, the entire beam would go down parallel to itself by this distance p_0/k. The total deflection then can be looked upon as the superposition of this constant deflection p_0/k and an upward deflection caused by X of the shape shown in Fig. 103. The resulting deflection at the hinge must be zero, so that we have from Eqs. (92)

$$\frac{p_0}{k} = \frac{2\beta X}{k} F_4(0) = \frac{2\beta X}{k}$$

or

$$X = \frac{p_0}{2\beta}$$

and the deflection as a function of x is

$$y = \frac{p_0}{k} [1 - F_4(\beta x)]$$

as illustrated in Fig. 105.

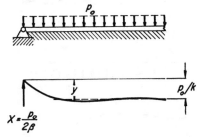

FIG. 105. Deflection diagram of a semi-infinite beam under uniform loading p_0 supported by an elastic foundation k and by a vertically immovable hinge at the left end.

As another example we ask for the end deflection (*Fig.* 106) *of a semi-infinite beam on an elastic foundation, loaded only by a loading p_0 over a stretch l adjacent to the free end.* A solution of this problem can be found by using many of the previous results. The general attack is as follows: First we consider a beam stretching to infinity in both directions (Fig. 106b) loaded by the load p_0 over a stretch l. We find the deflection of an arbitrary point A of this beam (outside the loaded stretch l) by using the result Fig. 94, integrated over the stretch l in the manner of Fig. 95, but now for many loads $p_0\,dx$ instead of for the two loads P of Fig. 95. Having this solution, we calculate the bending moment M_0 and the shear force S_0 in the bothway infinite beam at point B, the edge of the loading p_0. We then cut off the beam at the edge of the loading and impose on it at that point a force and a moment equal and opposite to the two quantities just calculated. This leaves the semi-infinite beam, loaded by p_0 over the stretch l, by $-M_0$ and $-S_0$, with zero moment and shear force at its ends. Thus all boundary conditions are satisfied, and the solution to the problem consists of the superposition of three cases: the bothway infinite beam under loading p_0l, the semi-infinite beam under loading $-P_0$, and the semi-infinite one under loading $-M_0$.

The mathematical steps of this process now follow:

The deflection at A due to a load element $p_0\,dx$ is by Eqs. (89)

$$dy_A = \frac{(p_0\,dx)\beta}{2k}\,F_1[\beta(a+x)]$$

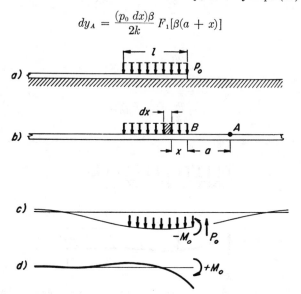

Fɪɢ. 106. Semi-infinite beam with constant loading p_0 over a finite portion l only. The solution is a superposition of the cases b, d, and e.

because point A is at distance $a + x$ from the load. The deflection at A of the bothway infinite beam due to the total stretch l of loading is

$$y_A = \frac{p_0\beta}{2k} \int_{x=0}^{x=l} F_1[\beta(a+x)]\,dx$$

$$= \frac{p_0\beta}{2k} \int_{x=0}^{x=l} F_1[\beta(a+x)]\,d(a+x)$$

$$= \frac{p_0\beta}{2k} \int_{x_1=a}^{x_1=a+l} F_1(\beta x_1)\,dx_1$$

By Eqs. (88) we have $F_1 = -(1/\beta)F_4'$, so that

$$y_A = -\frac{p_0}{2k} \int_{a}^{a+l} \frac{dF_4(\beta x_1)}{dx_1}\,dx_1 = \frac{p_0}{2k}\{F_4(\beta a) - F_4[\beta(a+l)]\}$$

The distance a, which was held constant so far, can now be made variable, **and then the above** expression is the deflection curve of the portion of the bar to the right of the load. The bending-moment, and shear-force curves follow by differentiation (with respect to a) with the help of Eqs. (88):

$$M_A = EIy''_A = \frac{\beta^2 p_0 EI}{k} \{F_2(\beta a) - F_2[\beta(a + l)]\}$$

$$S_A = EIy'''_A = \frac{\beta^3 p_0 EI}{k} \{F_3(\beta a) - F_3[\beta(a + l)]\}$$

In particular, for the point $B(a = 0)$ these quantities become

$$M_0 = - \frac{\beta^2 p_0 EI}{k} F_2(\beta l)$$

$$S_0 = \frac{\beta^3 p_0 EI}{k} [1 - F_3(\beta l)]$$

They are shown in Fig. 106c with their actual directions for small values of βl. The solution to our problem is the superposition of the cases, Fig. 106c, d, and e. We have no analytical expression as yet for the curve Fig. 106c to the left of point B (the above formula for y_A only holds to the right of B). But we asked only for the deflection at B, not for the deflection curve as a whole. The answer is found by superposing the above result and those of Eqs. (92) and (93),

$$y_B = \frac{p_0}{2k} [1 - F_4(\beta l)] + \frac{2\beta^2}{k} \frac{p_0}{4\beta^2} F_2(\beta l) + \frac{2\beta}{k} \frac{p_0}{4\beta} [1 - F_3(\beta l)]$$

or

$$y_B = \frac{p_0}{2k} (2 + F_2 - F_3 - F_4) = \frac{p_0}{k} [1 - F_3(\beta l)]$$

We see that this answer for the end deflection checks the two special cases $\beta = 0$ and $\beta = \infty$ for which the case is simple.

24. Finite Beams. The calculation of beams of finite length on an elastic foundation is no more difficult in principle than that of infinite beams. The same general solution, Eq. (87) (page 143), applies, and the four integration constants can be determined from the four boundary conditions, two at each end. This, however, is simple "in principle" only; in actual practice the labor involved in carrying it out is very large. Many cases have been worked out by patient calculators, and their results have been assembled and tabulated in a very useful book by M. Hetenyi entitled "Beams on Elastic Foundation."[1] We shall discuss only a single

[1] University of Michigan Press, Ann Arbor, 1946.

example here: that of a beam of total length l, loaded by a concentrated force P_0 in its center (Fig. 107).

The deformation is symmetrical, and for the right half of this beam the boundary conditions are

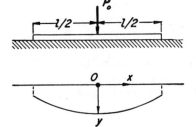

$$x = 0 \qquad y' = 0 \qquad EIy''' = \frac{P_0}{2}$$

$$x = \frac{l}{2} \qquad EIy'' = 0 \qquad EIy''' = 0$$

FIG. 107. Beam of length l, loaded in its center.

All the reader has to do now is to differentiate Eq. (87) three times and to substitute these conditions, thus obtaining four linear algebraic equations in terms of C_1, C_2, C_3, C_4. Anyone can solve linear algebraic equations, but in the process many pages of good blank paper are spoiled forever, and the answer for the deflection $y = f(x)$ occupies three full lines of print in Hetenyi's book: too large and cumbersome even for reprinting it here. We do reprint only the much simpler answers for the deflection at the center and at the end:

$$y_{\text{center}} = \frac{P_0 \beta}{2k} \frac{2 + \cos \beta l + \cosh \beta l}{\sin \beta l + \sinh \beta l}$$

$$y_{\text{end}} = \frac{2P_0 \beta}{k} \frac{\cos (\beta l/2) \cosh (\beta l/2)}{\sin \beta l + \sinh \beta l} \tag{94}$$

These results are well worth examining. From Eq. (86), the table on page 146, and Figs. 94 to 106 we remember the physical meaning of β: it is the reciprocal of a length, so that when βl becomes as large as 5 the deflection of the infinite beam has petered down to nothing. The character of the deflection curve, Fig. 107, depends on the value of βl: for small values of βl the beam is stiff and goes down like a rigid body, for large βl it goes down like Fig. 94, for intermediate values of βl the deflection curve is between those two extremes. In Eqs. (94), for $\beta l = \infty$, the denominator $\sinh \beta l = \infty$, and in the numerator $\cosh \beta l = \infty$. The reader should refresh his memory on hyperbolic functions and see that for $\beta l = \infty$ the end deflection becomes zero and the center deflection becomes $P_0 \beta / 2k$, as they should. Also, for the other extreme of $\beta l = 0$ the end and center deflections both become equal to P_0/kl, which they should. For a beam of finite length, between these extremes, we have

$$\frac{y_{\text{end}}}{y_{\text{center}}} = \frac{4 \cos (\beta l/2) \cosh (\beta l/2)}{2 + \cos \beta l + \cosh \beta l}$$

a relation which is shown plotted in Fig. 108. We see that for a beam shorter than $\beta l = 1$ the end deflection practically equals the center deflection (at $\beta l = 1.00$ the above ratio is 0.98) and that for a beam longer than $\beta l = \pi$ the end deflection is negligible. This confirms our physical intuition, that when the beam is sufficiently short it is relatively so stiff that it is a rigid body, and the theory is extremely simple. On the other hand if the beam is so long that the corresponding infinite beam of Fig. 94 would extend to the region of small deflections, then by cutting the infinite beam off at the ends we do not destroy shear forces or bending moments of any consequence and hence can use Fig. 94 for the finite beam as well. Only for the intermediate cases are we obliged to go into serious complications, and then we should refer to Hetenyi's book. However, in many practical cases a good approximation is obtained by using either the stiff-beam theory ($\beta l < 1$) or the long-beam theory ($\beta l > 3$), or by interpolating in between. This remark is not limited to the special case of loading of Fig. 107; it applies generally.

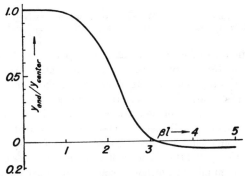

FIG. 108. The finite beam of total length l, loaded with P_0 in the center (Fig. 107). "Short" beams ($\beta l < 1$) are practically inflexible; for "long beams" ($\beta l > 3$) the infinite-length picture of Fig. 94 applies with decent accuracy; for "intermediate" beams ($1 < \beta l < 3$) this figure shows the ratio of the end deflection to the central deflection.

As an example, suppose the load P in Fig. 107 were offset to apply at the end instead of at the center (Fig. 109). The reader should verify that when the EI of the beam is so large that $\beta l < 1$, so that the short-beam theory applies, then the end deflection is $4P/kl$, while the other end comes up by an amount $2P/kl$. In case the beam is so flexible that βl is large (> 3), then Fig. 103 applies and the end deflection is $2\beta l P/kl$. In any case the load P is ultimately carried by the ground, so that the net areas of the shaded figures, Fig. 109b and c, must be equal.

In case the load in Fig. 109 were applied at the one-quarter-length point, we might resolve that load P statically into a component $P/2$ in the center and a component $P/2$ at the end. For the stiff beam the deflection curve would then be a superposition of Fig. 109*b* with a steady deflection. It is *not* permissible to apply this procedure to the flexible beam, *i.e.*, the deflection curve of a flexible beam under the load P at $l/4$ is *not* the sum of the curves for $P/2$ at $l/2$ and for $P/2$ at zero. Why not?

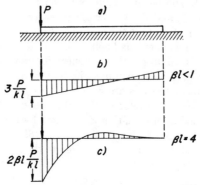

FIG. 109. Beam with end load (*a*). When the beam is comparatively stiff, it is "short" and deflects rigidly (*b*); when it is relatively flexible, it is "long" and deflects like (*c*).

25. Applications; Cylindrical Shells. Historically the first application of the theory of this chapter was to railroad track. An actual rail is not continuously supported; it rests on crossties some 15 in. apart. When the tie spacing is small with respect to the general aspect of the curves Figs. 94 to 106, the series of finite tie reaction loads can be replaced by the continuous loading indicated in these figures without changing anything much. From the table of page 146 we see that if the spacing c between ties is such that $\beta c \leq 0.2$ the theory will apply nicely. For larger spacings the theory is still applicable, although some errors must then be expected.

Another application for the general theory, which was discovered soon after its original derivation for railroad track, is to grid works of beams, which we shall now illustrate by the example shown in Fig. 110. A single concentrated load P is placed in the middle of a rectangular factory floor. We want to know the central deflection, and also the distribution of the load over the various crossbeams supporting the central longitudinal. The set of crossbeams, spaced at distance c apart, forms an "elastic foundation" for the longitudinal. The central deflection of a single crossbeam by itself under a load p_1c, by simple beam theory, is

$$\delta = \frac{p_1 c a^3}{48EI}$$

Then we can write

$$k = \frac{p_1}{\delta} = \frac{48EI}{a^3 c}$$

which is the uniform loading p_1 (pounds per running inch) to be placed on the (middle portion of the long) longitudinal in order to deflect the crossbeams 1 in. and hence is the "foundation constant" by the definition of page 141. Assuming the longitudinal to be "long," which is subject to later verification, we can find the central deflection from Eqs. (89). First we calculate β. If the stiffness EI of the longitudinal is the same as that of the crossbeams, we obtain on substitution into Eq. 86 (page 143)

$$\beta = \sqrt[4]{\frac{k}{4EI}} = \frac{1}{a}\sqrt[4]{48\frac{a}{c}} = \frac{5.25}{a}$$

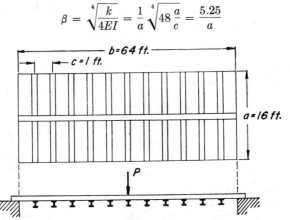

Fig. 110. Factory floor of 16 by 64-ft area having 63 beams spaced 1 ft apart across the short span with a single 64-ft central backbone. For this example we assume that EI is the same for the long and for the short beams.

for our case where $a = 16c$. Our longitudinal has a length $b = 4a$, so that $\beta b = 21$, so that we verify that the beam really is "long." The spacing of the cross girders is $\beta c = 5.25c/a = 5.25/16 = 0.33$. This is not as closely spaced as one might wish, but the theory will still be roughly applicable. The central deflection, by Eqs. (89) (page 147), is

$$y_P = \frac{P\beta}{2k}\cdot 1 = \frac{P5.25}{2a}\cdot\frac{a^3c}{48EI} = \frac{2.62Pa^2c}{48EI}$$

The deflections of the crossbeam n distances c from the central one are found from the F_1 table on page 146:

$n =$	0	1	2	3	4	5	6
$y =$	1.00	0.90	0.72	0.51	0.31	0.18	0.07

The load Q carried by the central crossbeam is calculated from

$$y_{central} = \frac{Qa^3}{48EI} = \frac{2.62Pa^2c}{48EI}$$

so that

$$Q_{\text{central}} = 2.62P\frac{c}{a} = 0.165P$$

The other beams carry loads proportional to their deflections as listed above. Adding up the loads carried by 13 beams, the central one and 6 on each side gives a total of $1.04P$, which checks our theory, because we know that the beams beyond these will be pulled *up* by the central loading.

By far the most important application of the theory of beams on elastic foundation is to *thin-walled cylindrical tubes* subjected to a loading which is rotationally symmetrical, but variable along the length: the load depends on z only and is independent of θ.

We have seen on page 75 that if a tube is subjected to a uniform external pressure p, a hoop stress occurs, which is

$$s_t = \frac{pr}{t}$$

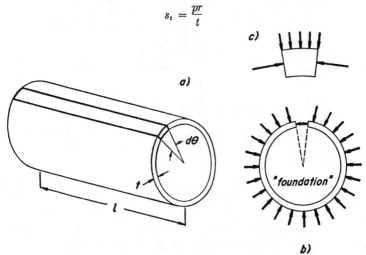

Fig. 111. A thin-walled tube subjected to uniform external pressure p will experience an elastic shrinking of its radius by an amount δ. A long, thin section of this tube can be looked upon as a "beam" (c) resting on an "elastic foundation" (b). This "beam" deflects by an amount δ under the influence of the load p.

If we now isolate from that tube a long longitudinal sliver $l \cdot rd\theta \cdot t$, as shown in Fig. 111, the two hoop stresses s_t acting on this piece are not quite in opposite directions, but include a small angle $d\theta$ between them. Each force, acting on an area lt is $s_t lt$, and the resultant of the two forces is $s_t lt\, d\theta$. If no longitudinal stress occurs, the hoop strain is s_t/E, and the change in radius, or the radial deflection, δ is

$$\delta = \frac{rs_t}{E} = \frac{pr^2}{Et}$$

Now think of the sliver of Fig. 111 as a "beam" of width $rd\theta$, which rests on an "elastic foundation" consisting of the rest of the pipe (covering an angle of $2\pi - rd\theta$). That beam deflects a distance $\delta = pr^2/Et$, when the beam is loaded with an external load per unit length $p\ rd\theta$. This means that the elastic foundation has a modulus k as defined by Eq. (84) of

$$k = \frac{p\ rd\theta}{\delta} = \frac{p\ rd\theta}{pr^2/Et} = \frac{Et}{r^2}rd\theta$$

If we make *the width of our beam equal to unity*, instead of $rd\theta$, the foundation modulus is

$$k = \frac{Et}{r^2} \tag{95}$$

Now we can drop the assumption of uniform external pressure p on our tube and proceed to the case of Fig. 112: a pipe loaded by a ring-shaped load at one location $z = 0$ only. Isolating a long beam of unit width from

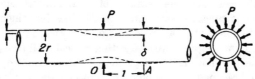

Fig. 112. A long, thin-walled tube subjected to a ring load of intensity P lb per circumferential inch. The reader should verify that the radial deflection δ under the load is

$$\delta = 0.64 \frac{P}{E}\left(\frac{r}{t}\right)^{3/2}$$

this pipe, this bothway infinite beam is loaded with a single central force P in the center, and it is held in radial equilibrium by hoop stresses all along its z length, which all together act as if the beam were resting on an elastic foundation of the stiffness of Eq. (95). Then the entire theory of this chapter applies; in particular, let us calculate the quantity β [Eq. (86), page 143]. Our beam has a width unity and a height t; we might think then that its bending stiffness would be

$$EI = \frac{Et^3}{12}$$

This would be the case if our beam would be free to expand sidewise, "anticlastically"; but the rest of the tube prevents that, so that we have the case of Fig. 81 (page 114), and the stiffness is about 10 per cent greater: by a factor $1/(1 - \mu^2)$. Thus the stiffness is

$$\frac{Et^3}{12(1 - \mu^2)}$$

and by Eq. (86) we have

$$\beta = \sqrt[4]{\frac{3(1 - \mu^2)}{t^2 r^2}} = \frac{1.28}{\sqrt{rt}} \tag{96}$$

From this formula we see that the "wave length" on such cyclinders usually is quite short: for example, if a concentrated ring load P is placed on a tube (Fig. 112), then its meridian will deform from a straight line to the shape of Fig. 94 and the F_1 table of page 146 tells us that the distance OA is found from $\beta l = 2.35$, so that

$$l = \frac{2.35}{\beta} = \frac{2.35}{1.28} \sqrt{rt} = 1.83r \sqrt{\frac{t}{r}}$$

A ratio $t/r = 1/25$ is not uncommon, and for such a pipe the length in Fig. 112 is $0.36r$, or only 18 per cent of the diameter. The "elastic foundation" of a thin cylindrical pipe thus is very "stiff" as compared with the "beam" which "rests on that foundation." This fact of the quick dying out of disturbances along the length is of great practical importance: it means that most practical cases are "long" tubes for which the theory of pages 144 to 158 holds. As we shall soon see, we can go even further in our generalization. Suppose we deal with a conical shell instead of with a cylindrical one. Following the same reasoning, we can cut out of this cone a "beam," resting on a "foundation," but now the beam is of variable width $rd\theta$ (variable EI) along its length, and also the foundation stiffness k is variable. The exact theory of this case has been worked out; it is frightfully complicated. But since the "wave length" is so short, we may say that for a short length along the cone, that cone is practically cylindrical and the theory of the cylinder (of infinite length) applies approximately. We can go even further and treat spherical shells (the problem of Fig. 56, page 82) in that manner, replacing the sphere locally by a cylinder of equal diameter.

As a first *numerical example* of this we take *an oil storage tank (Fig. 113)*, of 100 ft diameter, ¾ in. plate thickness at the bottom, and 30 ft head of oil of 0.9 specific gravity. By the membrane theory of page 82 we have seen that a discontinuity of deformation appears at the bottom corner; hence in addition to the membrane stresses there is a ring-shaped tensile force pulling *inward* on the cylinder and *outward* on the base plate. This alone would cause an angle of the cylinder at the bottom (Fig. 103, page 154), so that, in addition, there must be a local bending moment between the cylinder and the base plate. Before going into much detail we calculate the value of β to see whether or not our vertical tank wall is "long." We have by Eq. (96)

$$\beta = \frac{1.28}{\sqrt{50 \times 12 \times \tfrac{3}{4}}} = \frac{1}{16\tfrac{1}{2} \text{ in.}}$$

The cylinder length $l = 30$ ft, so that $\beta l = (30 \times 12)/16\frac{1}{2} = 22$. A glance at the table on page 146 tells us that the beam on elastic foundation is very "long" indeed; in fact most of the deformation takes place in the region $0 < \beta x < 2$, which is the lowest 10 per cent of the height. This permits us to say that the oil pressure is substantially constant in those lower 3 ft, so that the cylinder there remains a cylinder and does not become a cone. The tangential stress of the cylinder at the bottom, by membrane theory, is

$$s_t = \frac{pr}{t} = \frac{30 \times 0.9 \times 62.4}{144} \frac{600}{\frac{3}{4}} = 9,350 \text{ lb/sq in.}$$

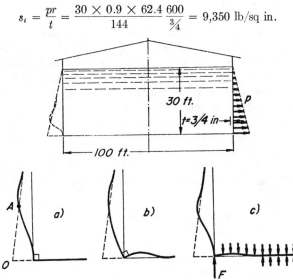

Fig. 113. Large oil storage tank. The membrane theory calls for hoop stresses in the cylinder only, increasing proportionally to the head of oil. The consequent radial swelling of the cylinder at the bottom is much larger than the radial swelling of the bottom base plate; hence bending of the shell occurs according to the pattern of Fig. 94 as sketched in the top figure. In the corner details (a), (b), (c), the unstressed tank is shown in thin outline; the deformed shape by membrane theory is shown dotted, and the presumed actual deformed shape in heavy line. Case a assumes the bottom to remain flat; case b assumes zero bending moment in the corner. The actual truth (c) lies between the extremes a and b.

The radial expansion at the base of the cylinder (if it were not attached to the bottom plate) would be

$$\Delta r = \frac{s_t}{E} r = \frac{9,350}{30 \times 10^6} 600 = 0.187 \text{ in.}$$

By membrane theory the bottom plate is without stress (the compressive pinching between oil and ground of about 12 lb/sq in. is negligible), and hence without radial expansion. To bring the bottom plate and the cylinder together, we must apply a ring distribution of radial force between them and possibly also some distributed bending moment. We shall soon find that in applying such a force the radial deformation in the cylinder is very much greater than that of the bottom flat plate, so that we can neglect the plate expansion. Now we examine Fig. 113a, b, c. Case a assumes that the bottom remains flat, the heavy curve then is the F_1 function of Fig. 94, and of course there is a bending moment at the corner. This moment is taken by the bottom plate, which must show a local curvature and cannot remain flat. On the other hand, case b assumes no bending moment at all in the corner; then the cylinder deforms like Fig. 103 with an F_4 function. Without bending moment the bottom plate cannot curve, but the geometry requires it. Hence neither case a nor case b will occur. The actual deformation will be intermediate between these two extremes, as shown in case c, where there is a ring force as well as some bending moment between the two. This necessitates a concentrated reaction F and a lifting off the ground of the floor plate. The further development of this is very complicated; we therefore are satisfied by assuming case a, which corresponds to Eqs. (89) and Fig. 94. Remembering that the force P is taken by the two halves in Fig. 94, so that the shear force is $P/2$, we now write the inward radial displacement of the shell, Fig. 113, at the base caused by a pull Q lb/in. [see Eqs. (89), (95), and (96)]:

$$y_{\text{cyl}} = \frac{2Q\beta}{2k} F_1(0) = \frac{2Q1.28}{2E} \left(\frac{r}{t}\right)^{\frac{3}{2}} \times 1$$

$$= \frac{1.28}{30 \times 10^6} \left(\frac{600}{\frac{3}{4}}\right)^{\frac{3}{2}} Q = 970Q \times 10^{-6} \text{ in.}$$

The bottom plate (which is of the same thickness t as the cylinder) under two-dimensional hydrostatic tension Q expands radially by

$$y_{\text{plate}} = \frac{Q}{Et} (1 - \mu)r = \frac{0.7}{30 \times 10^6} \left(\frac{600}{\frac{3}{4}}\right)^1 Q = 19Q \times 10^{-6} \text{ in.}$$

This verifies that the plate expansion is negligible with respect to the cylinder contraction. By Eqs. (89) the bending moment M in the shell at the bottom is

$$\frac{M}{y} = \frac{PF_3}{4\beta} \frac{2k}{P\beta F_1} = \frac{k}{2\beta^2}$$

With the numerical values of $y = 0.187$ in. and $1/\beta = 16.5$ in. already calculated, we have

$$M = \frac{Ebt}{2r^2} (0.187) \cdot (16.5)^2 = 1,600b \text{ in.-lb}$$

or the bending moment per unit circumferential length is

$$M_1 = 1{,}600 \text{ in.-lb/in.}$$

The stress is $6M_1/t^2$ (see page 111), or

$$s_{\text{bending}} = 17{,}000 \text{ lb/sq in.}$$

This stress occurs in the cylinder at the bottom in a vertical direction; it is tensile inside the tank and compressive on the outside. The membrane hoop stress that would have been there (without bottom) would be 9,350 lb/sq in. and directed tangentially, 90 deg from the bending stress just found. However, Fig. 113a shows us that the membrane hoop stress at the bottom is completely absent because the hoop strain has been prevented. Only at point A in Fig. 113a does the hoop stress come to its full value. The value of 17,000 lb/sq in. just calculated for the "secondary" bending stress is larger than the truth, because the bending moment in the actual case, Fig. 113c, is smaller than in our assumption, Fig. 113a.

For our *second numerical example we take the pressure vessel of Fig.* 56 (*page* 82), consisting of a cylinder and a half sphere of the same plate thickness t. We take for our dimensions $r = 48$ in. and $t = \frac{1}{2}$ in. Then, by Eq. (96),

$$\beta = \frac{1.28}{\sqrt{24}} = \frac{1}{3.83 \text{ in.}}$$

The curve in Fig. 113a is half the F_1 curve of Fig. 94, by symmetry. Hence the distance $OA = l$ of Fig. 113 is

$$l = \frac{1.58}{\beta} = 1.58 \times 3.83 = 6 \text{ in.}$$

This length is quite small compared with the radius of the sphere, 48 in., so that the first 6 in. of sphere adjacent to the cylinder do not deviate much from a cylindrical shape. We assume then that the half sphere locally will act like a cylinder, and the problem reduces itself to the fitting together of two cylinders (Fig. 56a) of slightly different diameters by appropriate shear forces (Fig. 56b). No bending moment will appear at the joint by reason of symmetry. The radial gap between the two cylinders, from membrane theory, is, by Eqs. (54) (page 75),

$$\Delta r = \frac{r}{E} \left[s_{t \text{ cyl}} - s_{t \text{ sph}} - \mu(s_{m \text{ cyl}} - s_{m \text{ sph}}) \right]$$

$$\Delta r = \frac{pr^2}{Et} \left[1 - \frac{1}{2} - \mu\left(\frac{1}{2} - \frac{1}{2}\right) \right] = \frac{pr^2}{2Et}$$

Half of this difference is to be taken up by the cylinder and the other half by the sphere in the manner of Fig. 103, Eqs. (92) (page 154). The bending stress is zero at the joint, and it reaches a maximum (see page 146) at $\beta x = 0.8$ or at a distance $x = 0.8/\beta = 3.1$ in. from the joint. The value of that stress is

$$s_{\text{bending max}} = \frac{6}{t^2} M_{\text{max}} = \frac{6}{t^2} \frac{P}{\beta} F_2(\beta x)_{\text{max}}$$

$$= \frac{6}{t^2} \frac{P}{\beta} 0.322 = \frac{6 \times 0.322}{t^2} \frac{k y_{\text{max}}}{2\beta^2}$$

$$= \frac{6 \times 0.322}{t^2} \frac{(Et/r^2) \times (pr^2/4Et)}{2/(3.83)^2} = 0.148 \frac{pr}{t}$$

by Eqs. (95) and (96) and $y_{\text{max}} = \frac{1}{2} \Delta r$ above. The maximum membrane stress occurs in the cylinder and is pr/t, very much larger than the bending stress.

Problems 91 *to* 112.

CHAPTER VI

TWO-DIMENSIONAL THEORY OF ELASTICITY

26. The Airy Stress Function. In this chapter we shall discuss a number of cases of plane stress in a more rigorous and general manner than we have done heretofore. The names "theory of elasticity" and "strength of materials" refer to the same subject; the first name is usual when that subject is treated by a mathematician, who insists on rigor, while the second name is traditional when the engineer comes to a solution, which may be rigorously exact if it happens to come out that way, but which just as well may be a good, useful approximation.

The accepted approach in theory of elasticity starts with the *displacements*, named u and v. Imagine an unstressed thin flat plate at rest in the xy plane, and "adequately" supported in that plane so that it can take loads and remain at rest. If that plate is subjected to loads and forces *in its own plane*, each point x, y of the plate will be displaced by a small amount. The coordinates of the point x, y of the unstressed plate become $x + u$ and $y + v$ in the stressed plate. Thus u, v are the components of displacement in the x, y direction, respectively. For the two-dimensional case, both u and v are functions of x and y. The functions $u(x, y)$ and $v(x, y)$ must be continuous in a mathematical sense: if they showed discontinuities, it would mean cracks or overlappings in the deformed plate, which are physically untenable. Although this requirement of continuity of u and v sounds trite, it is of the utmost importance, and it will be made the basis of the "compatibility equations" (101) (pages 175 and 176).

Now we proceed to deduce *the strains* ϵ_x, ϵ_y, and γ from the displacements u, v by means of Fig. 114, which shows a small rectangle $dx\,dy$ of the plate, drawn in full outline for the unstressed state and in dotted outline for the stressed state. The corner point 1 is our base of operations; hence by definition the horizontal distance $11'$ is u, and the vertical distance $11'$ is v. Corner 2 differs from corner 1 by the distance dx; hence the u of point 2 differs from the u of point 1 by the quantity du, which in this case is $(\partial u/\partial x)\,dx$. Subtracting distances, we have for the elongation of the length $dx = 12$:

$$1'2' - 12 = 22' - 11' = \left(u + \frac{\partial u}{\partial x}\,dx\right) - u = \frac{\partial u}{\partial x}\,dx$$

Hence the strain is

$$\epsilon_x = \frac{1'2' - 12}{12} = \frac{(\partial u/\partial x)\,dx}{dx} = \frac{\partial u}{\partial x}$$

In a similar manner, using point 3 instead of point 2, we find $\epsilon_y = \partial v/\partial y$.

The expression for the shear strain γ is somewhat more complicated. The shear angle $\gamma = \alpha + \beta$ in the figure. The horizontal distance $11' = u$ by definition. The horizontal distance $33'$ is $u + (\partial u/\partial y)\,dy$, because

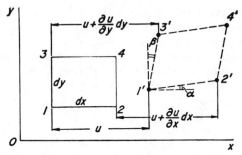

Fig. 114. An element $dx\,dy$, shown in the unstrained state 1234 and in the strained state $1'2'3'4'$. From this figure the strain equations (97) are derived.

point 3 differs from point 1 by an amount dy. Subtracting, we have for the horizontal distance between $1'$ and $3'$ the amount $(\partial u/\partial y)\,dy$. The vertical distance $1'3' = dy$, so that $\beta = \partial u/\partial y$, an angle smaller than 0.001 radian for mild steel. By an entirely similar analysis (involving points 1, $1'$, 2, and $2'$), the reader should find for the vertical distance $1'2'$ the expression $(\partial v/\partial x)\,dx$ and hence $\alpha = \partial v/\partial x$.

Then

$$\gamma = \alpha + \beta = \frac{\partial u}{\partial y} + \frac{\partial v}{\partial x}$$

Thus the three strain equations are

$$\epsilon_x = \frac{\partial u}{\partial x}$$

$$\epsilon_y = \frac{\partial v}{\partial y} \tag{97}$$

$$\gamma = \frac{\partial u}{\partial y} + \frac{\partial v}{\partial x}$$

The relation between these strains and the stresses is expressed by Hooke's law:

$$\epsilon_x = \frac{1}{E}\,(s_x - \mu s_y)$$

$$\epsilon_y = \frac{1}{E}\,(s_y - \mu s_x) \tag{98}$$

$$\gamma = \frac{s_s}{G}$$

The Equilibrium Equation. The stresses acting on an element $dx\,dy$ at a point must form a set of forces that leave the element in equilibrium. If these stresses do not vary from point to point (*i.e.*, if s_x, s_y, s_s are constant, independent of x or y), that equilibrium is automatically satisfied,

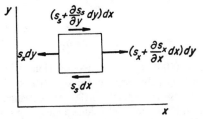

FIG. 115.   Forces acting on a small element $dx\,dy$ of a plate in which stresses vary from point to point. Only the forces in the x direction are shown. From this figure we derive the first of the equilibrium equations (99).

but if, as in Fig. 115, the stress varies from point to point, this condition gives rise to a pair of equations.   In the figure only the force components in the x direction are shown; there are four other forces in the y direction as well.   The resultant in the $+x$ direction of the four forces of Fig. 115 must be zero, or

$$\left(s_x + \frac{\partial s_x}{\partial x}\,dx\right)dy - s_x\,dy + \left(s_s + \frac{\partial s_s}{\partial y}\,dy\right)dx - s_s\,dx = 0$$

Of the six terms in this equation, four are small of the first order (being proportional to dx or dy), while two are small of the second order (being proportional to $dx\,dy$).   The first-order terms are seen to cancel each other off, so that equilibrium is expressed by the second-order terms only.   A similar expression can be derived for the equilibrium between the four forces in the $+y$ direction, not shown in Fig. 115, with the result

$$\frac{\partial s_x}{\partial x} + \frac{\partial s_s}{\partial y} = 0$$

$$\frac{\partial s_y}{\partial y} + \frac{\partial s_s}{\partial x} = 0 \tag{99}$$

The Airy Stress Function. In Eqs. (99) the state of stress is described by a set of three "dependent" variables s_x, s_y, s_s, each depending on two "independent" variables x, y. This makes the problem extremely complicated, and a great step forward was made by *Airy* (Astronomer Royal of Britain, about 1860) by assuming that the stresses could be described by a *single* function Φ of x, y, instead of by the three functions s_x, s_y, s_s. The stresses are derived from the "Airy stress function" Φ by differentiation, as follows:

$$s_x = \frac{\partial^2 \Phi}{\partial y^2}$$

$$s_y = \frac{\partial^2 \Phi}{\partial x^2} \tag{100}$$

$$s_s = - \frac{\partial^2 \Phi}{\partial x \, \partial y}$$

This definition, Eq. (100), of the stress function Φ has been so cleverly contrived that for *any* arbitrary continuous (three times differentiable) function Φ, the equilibrium equations (99) are satisfied, which the reader should verify by substitution. Besides being a very large analytical simplification, the Airy stress function offers the important advantage that it can be visualized. We can think of Φ plotted vertically on an xy base, forming a surface, and (if we choose the scale so as to make the heights Φ small enough to keep the slopes $\partial \Phi / \partial x$ small), then Eqs. (100) tell us that the normal stress in the x direction is the curvature of the Φ surface in the y direction, or, more generally, that the normal stress in any direction at each point equals the Φ curvature in a normal direction at the same point. The shear stress s_s can be visualized as the "twist" (page 101) of the Φ surface at that point. As an example, consider the Airy surface of Fig.

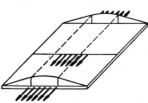

Fig. 116. Surface of an Airy stress function consisting of plane and cylindrical pieces. By the definition, Eq. (100), this leads to a constant stress in the center portion, causing non-compatible deformation. This Φ function does not satisfy the compatibility equation (101) and hence is not a true Airy stress function.

116, consisting of a circular cylinder in its center part and two tangent planes on the sides. By Eqs. (100) the stresses in the plate consist of a constant longitudinal stress in the center portion of the plate only, with zero stress in the side parts. It is seen that any one particle of the plate is in equilibrium, verifying the automatic relation between Eqs. (100) and (99). Still there is something wrong with this example, which we recognize when we examine the deformations. If the plate were really stressed as Fig. 116 indicates, then the center portion would stretch [Eqs. (98)], while the side portions would retain their original length. Hence if the plate was continuous in the unstressed state, it would not be continuous when stressed: the three pieces would not fit together. The stress distribution of Fig. 116 satisfies equilibrium, but it violates the equally necessary condition of continuity of deformation, which in this branch of science is called the condition of *compatibility*.

The Compatibility Equation. The mathematical requirement for such compatibility is that the displacement functions u, v be continuous, without cracks or overlappings, which again means that u and v must be differentiable. Looking at Eqs. (97), we see that

$$\frac{\partial^2 \epsilon_x}{\partial y^2} + \frac{\partial^2 \epsilon_y}{\partial x^2} = \frac{\partial^3 u}{\partial x \, \partial y^2} + \frac{\partial^3 v}{\partial y \, \partial x^2}$$

and also

$$\frac{\partial^2 \gamma}{\partial x \, \partial y} = \frac{\partial^3 u}{\partial x \, \partial y^2} + \frac{\partial^3 v}{\partial x^2 \, \partial y}$$

These are seen to be equal, so that

$$\frac{\partial^2 \epsilon_x}{\partial y^2} + \frac{\partial^2 \epsilon_y}{\partial x^2} = \frac{\partial^2 \gamma}{\partial x \, \partial y} \tag{101a}$$

is *the compatibility equation in terms of the strains.*

We shall now proceed to rewrite this result, first in terms of stress, resulting in Eq. (101b), and then in terms of the Airy function, giving Eq. (101c). First we substitute Eqs. (98) into (101a):

$$\frac{\partial^2 s_x}{\partial y^2} - \mu \frac{\partial^2 s_y}{\partial y^2} + \frac{\partial^2 s_y}{\partial x^2} - \mu \frac{\partial^2 s_x}{\partial x^2} = \frac{E}{G} \frac{\partial^2 s_s}{\partial x \, \partial y}$$

With the known relation $E = 2G \, (1 + \mu)$ between the elastic constants, the right-hand side of this can be written as

$$(1 + \mu)\left(\frac{\partial^2 s_s}{\partial x \, \partial y} + \frac{\partial^2 s_s}{\partial x \, \partial y}\right)$$

Now we introduce the equilibrium equations (99) and with them get rid of the shear stress in the above expression. To make the result symmetrical, we rewrite the first of the $\partial^2 s_s / \partial x \, \partial y$ terms in parentheses with the first equilibrium equation (99) and the second $\partial^2 s_s / \partial x \, \partial y$ with the second Eq. (99):

$$-(1 + \mu)\left(\frac{\partial^2 s_x}{\partial x^2} + \frac{\partial^2 s_y}{\partial y^2}\right)$$

We notice that the μ terms of this are the same as those of the left-hand side above, so that they cancel out, and the remaining four terms can be written as

$$\left(\frac{\partial^2}{\partial x^2} + \frac{\partial^2}{\partial y^2}\right)(s_x + s_y) = 0 \tag{101b}$$

This result is known as *the compatibility equation in terms of stress*, although we recognize from the derivation that it really is a mixture of the true compatibility equation (101a) and the equilibrium equations (99).

Finally, by substituting Eqs. (100) into the above, we obtain *the compatibility equation in terms of the stress function* Φ:

$$\left(\frac{\partial^2}{\partial x^2} + \frac{\partial^2}{\partial y^2}\right)\left(\frac{\partial^2}{\partial x^2} + \frac{\partial^2}{\partial y^2}\right)\Phi = 0 \tag{101c}$$

or, worked out,

$$\frac{\partial^4 \Phi}{\partial x^4} + 2\frac{\partial^4 \Phi}{\partial x^2\,\partial y^2} + \frac{\partial^4 \Phi}{\partial y^4} = 0 \tag{101c}$$

Discussion of the Harmonic and Biharmonic Equations. An equation of almost the same form as (101b) was seen previously: Eq. (11) (page 12). Also by Mohr's circle for stress we know that the sum $(s_x + s_y)$ at a point has the same value for *any* set of two perpendicular stresses at that same point, independent of their angle with respect to the x axis. In particular, that sum $(s_x + s_y)$ is equal to the sum of the two principal stresses at that point. Then, with Eq. (11) in mind, we can visualize Eq. (101b) as follows:

If the sum of the two principal stresses at a point x, y is plotted vertically above that point, then the curved surface so formed above the xy base has the shape of a stretched membrane with equal air pressures on both sides. Equation (101b) is known among mathematicians as the "Laplace" differential equation, or the "harmonic" differential equation. A function, such as $(s_x + s_y)$, which satisfies that differential equation is called a "harmonic" function. Extending the terminology, Eq. (101c) is known as the "biharmonic" equation, and the stress function Φ satisfying it is called a "biharmonic function." The visualization of the Φ surface is much more difficult than that of the harmonic $(s_x + s_y)$ surface. The Φ surface is so constituted that if at a point we take the sum of two perpendicular radii of curvature and plot this value z on xy as a base, we then get a new surface

$$z = \left(\frac{\partial^2}{\partial x^2} + \frac{\partial^2}{\partial y^2}\right)\Phi$$

This new z surface has the property [Eq. (101c)] that the sum of two perpendicular curvatures at any point is zero; in other words, the z surface can be represented by a membrane with equal air pressures on the two sides. The Φ surface itself is much more general. Verify by looking at Eq. (101c) that any harmonic function is also a biharmonic one; but conversely, a biharmonic function generally is not a harmonic one. As we soon shall see in the next twenty pages, there is no difficulty at all in finding biharmonic functions [*i.e.*, in finding solutions of Eq. (101c)]; we could write down hundreds of them without thinking too much. Each such solution, when differentiated by Eqs. (100), gives us a state of stress which is in equilibrium and at the same time gives consistent or "compatible" deformations; in other words, each biharmonic function Φ gives the solution to *some* stress problem. However, this does us little good: usually we want the solution to a special stress problem that comes up; and to find the stress function Φ belonging to *that* particular problem is quite another matter; it is so difficult that in general nobody is able to do it. In the next twenty pages we shall see that the problem has been tackled by entering the back door: we write down many biharmonic functions, differentiate them by Eqs. (100), and inspect the solutions so found. Some such solutions turn out to be practically important; others are too artificial and hence useless. Thus quite a catalogue of results is built up, and then by clever superposition of these cases others are found.

Before starting on this program, it is well to state what the mathematicians call a "uniqueness theorem." If we have a stressless thin plate of a certain shape and then subject that plate to a definite set of loads (in its own plane), we expect to find one definite answer for the stresses in the plate, and not two or three different answers which all are correct. This fact, which appeals to our intuition, is expressed by the mathematicians as follows: If for a given problem we have succeeded in finding a biharmonic stress function Φ, so that the stresses derived from it satisfy the boundary conditions of the problem, then that function Φ is "unique," *i.e.*, it furnishes *the* only correct solution to the stress problem. The mathematical proof to this proposition is complicated and will not be given here.

Plane Stress and Plane Strain. The general theory given so far and expressed by Eqs. (97) to (101) has been derived for a *thin* plate, not loaded perpendicularly to its plane, *i.e.*, for $s_z = 0$. The case is called one of *plane stress*. As a result there will be a strain in the z direction,

$$\epsilon_z = -\frac{\mu}{E}(s_x + s_y)$$

so that the plate will change its thickness. Hence the plane stress problem is *not* a plane strain problem. Suppose we now consider not a thin plate but an infinitely thick one, *i.e.*, a cylinder in which the length l in the z direction is much larger than the x and y dimensions. This cylinder is loaded by forces in the x and y directions only, evenly distributed all along the z length. Then the plane cross sections must remain plane; and a thin plate dz cut from this cylinder must remain of constant thickness. This is a case of *plane strain*, but when this occurs, the third stress s_z is not zero:

$$\epsilon_z = 0 = \frac{1}{E}[s_z - \mu(s_x + s_y)] \qquad \therefore s_z = \mu(s_x + s_y)$$

Thus, in general, a problem of *plane strain* (a long cylinder) cannot be a problem of plane stress at the same time. We now go over the entire previous analysis (which was for plane stress), this time for plane strain, in which a third stress s_z does appear. Equations (97) are unchanged, but Eqs. (98) become

$$\epsilon_x = \frac{1}{E}\,[s_x - \mu(s_y + s_z)]$$

$$\epsilon_y = \frac{1}{E}\,[s_y - \mu(s_x + s_z)] \qquad (98a)$$

$$\gamma = \frac{s_s}{G}$$

Continuing to follow the analysis of pages 173 to 176 for this new case, we see that the equilibrium equations (99) are not changed, and Eqs. (100) also can be kept without change. The compatibility equation (101a) also remains the same, because in its derivation the third direction z was never mentioned. In the next step, however, something new comes up. In substituting the new equations (98a) into (101a), we do get two extra terms on the left-hand side:

$$- \mu\,\frac{\partial^2 s_z}{\partial x^2} - \mu\,\frac{\partial^2 s_z}{\partial y^2}$$

The right-hand side of the equation remains without change, so that we find, instead of (101b), the result

$$\left(\frac{\partial^2}{\partial x^2} + \frac{\partial^2}{\partial y^2}\right)(s_x + s_y - \mu s_z) = 0$$

But, since $\epsilon_z = 0$ (plane strain), we have $s_z = \mu(s_x + s_y)$ which, when substituted into the above, leads again to (101b), except that the entire equation is multiplied by a factor $1 - \mu^2$, which can be divided out. Therefore Eq. (101b) remains unchanged after all, and (101c) as well.

Thus we conclude that if we have two plates of identical x, y shape, one of them very thin and the other very thick, and if these two plates are loaded in their own planes by external forces which have the same value per unit thickness, then the s_x, s_y, s_s distribution is the same in both. The only difference is that for the thin plate (plane stress; $s_z = 0$) the thickness changes according to

$$\epsilon_z = - \frac{\mu}{E}\,(s_x + s_y)$$

whereas for the thick plate (infinitely long cylinder; plane strain; $\epsilon_z = 0$) a third stress occurs, expressed by

$$s_z = \mu(s_x + s_y)$$

Incidentally, this conclusion holds for *external* forces only: it is not true when body forces, such as gravity or centrifugal force, come in. For rotating disks the case of plane strain differs from that of plane stress (see Problem 39).

27. Applications to Polynomials in Rectangular Coordinates. Equations (100) state in words that the stresses are the curvatures of the Airy surface, or Φ surface. Thus we see immediately that the surfaces

$$\Phi = \text{const} \qquad \Phi = Ax \qquad \Phi = By \qquad \Phi = Ax + By$$

all correspond to zero stress, because they are all planes without curvatures. The simplest Φ function with a stress is

$$\Phi = Ax^2$$

Substituting this into the right-hand side of the biharmonic equation (101c) gives a zero result, which means that $\Phi = Ax^2$ is admissible as an Airy function. From Eqs. (100) we see that the stress is

$$s_y = 2A \qquad s_x = 0 \qquad s_s = 0$$

which means a stress in the y direction, constant over the entire surface.

Similarly the function $\Phi = By^2$ means a constant stress $2B$ in the x direction. These two stress functions can be superposed on each other,

$$\Phi = Ax^2 + By^2$$

giving a field with a stress $2A$ in the y direction and $2B$ in the x direction. A special case of this occurs when $B = -A$, which is a push-pull field in the x and y directions, and, by Mohr's circle, we understand that it can also be described as a pure shear condition along axes at 45 deg with respect to the x, y axes.

The function

$$\Phi = Cxy$$

upon substitution into Eq. (101c) is seen to satisfy that condition, so that it is a permissible function. By Eqs. (100) we see that $s_x = s_y = 0$ and $s_s = C$. This then is a system of constant shear stress parallel to the x and y axes all over the plate. By Mohr's-circle construction this is equivalent to a push-pull stress system along lines at 45 deg with respect to the x and y axes.

The next function we investigate is

$$\Phi = Ax^3$$

Substitution into the biharmonic (101c) shows it to be satisfied, so that the function is a permissible Airy function. The stresses are

$$s_x = 0 \qquad s_y = 6Ax \qquad s_s = 0$$

illustrated by Fig. 117.   If we consider a rectangular piece of plate, placing the origin of coordinates in its center, then this is the case of a (flat) beam subjected to pure bending.

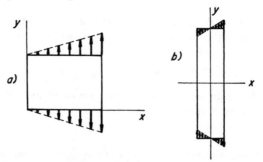

FIG. 117.   Stress field described by the Airy function $\Phi = Ax^3$, representing the case of "pure bending" (b), or bending with superposed tension (a) or compression, depending on which portion of the plane we look at.

This means that if a beam of rectangular cross section is subjected to external loads such as shown in Fig. 117b, then the exact stress distribution *inside* the beam also is linear, coinciding with the solution obtained long ago in simple strength of materials.   If the beam ends are loaded by a pure bending moment, which is *not* linearly distributed (Fig. 118a), then we

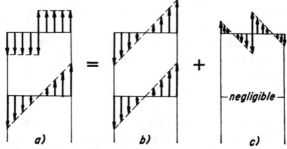

FIG. 118.   A non-linearly distributed bending moment on the end of a beam can always be resolved into a linearly distributed load and a residual load, which in itself is statically balanced.   By Saint-Venant's principle the latter causes negligibly small stresses at a distance from the end of the beam about equal to its height.   Hence any non-linear bending-moment distribution imposed on the ends becomes practically linear one beam height from the end.

can resolve that loading into the sum of a linearly distributed bending moment (b) and a residual loading (c), the latter being statically equivalent to zero.   By Saint-Venant's principle (page 117) this latter distribution dies down fast when going into the beam.   The distribution, Fig. 118b, being the exact solution $\Phi = Ax^3$, remains unchanged when going into the beam. Hence, when we compound together again the cases of Fig. 118*b* and *c* at some distance from the end, we find in Fig. 118*a* that the originally non-linear distribution applied to the end of the beam soon becomes linear when going inside the beam.

The stress function $\Phi = Ay^3$ gives the same distribution as Ax^3, turned around through 90 deg. The functions $\Phi = x^2y$ and its 90-deg equivalent $\Phi = xy^2$ lead to stress distributions of no particular interest and are left as exercises to the reader.

This finishes off all algebraic Φ functions of powers 1, 2, and 3. Turning now to fourth-power expressions, we start with $\Phi = Ax^4$. When substituting that into Eq. (101*c*), we find that it gives us the value $24A$ instead of zero. Hence the function is not "compatible" and is useless for our purpose. We can use it only in combinations with other terms, such as, for example,

$$\Phi = A(x^4 - y^4) \qquad \text{or} \qquad \Phi = A(x^4 - 6x^2y^2)$$

which *do* satisfy the biharmonic equation (101*c*). The stress distributions corresponding to the above Φ functions are of no particular interest and will not be pursued further.

Cantilever Beam. Many other stress functions consisting of powers of x and y in various combinations have been investigated, and a few have been found to be of practical significance. One of these is

$$\Phi = A(xy^3 - \tfrac{3}{4}xyh^2)$$

The reader should first verify that this *is* a biharmonic function, and hence is permissible as an Airy function. Then by Eqs. (100) the stresses come out as

$$s_x = 6Axy \qquad s_y = 0 \qquad s_s = 3A\left(\frac{h^2}{4} - y^2\right)$$

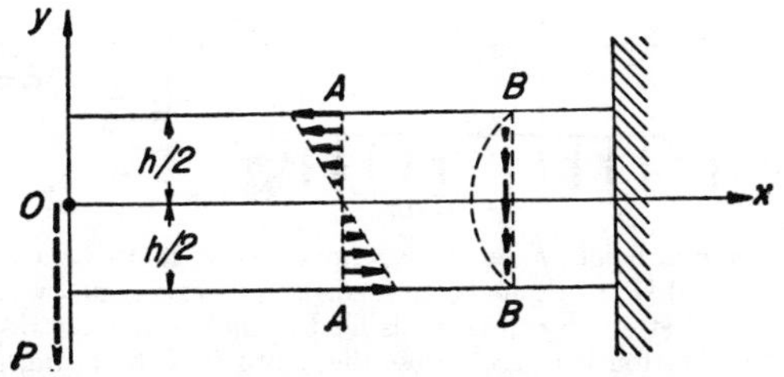

Fig. 119. Stress field expressed by the Airy function $\Phi = A(xy^3 - \tfrac{3}{4}xyh^2)$. This can be interpreted as a flat cantilever beam of height h, loaded by a force $P = Abh^3/2$, where b is the thickness of the beam perpendicular to the paper.

If we apply this (Fig. 119) to a rectangular area of height h, symmetrically distributed about the horizontal x axis, we can interpret it as the well-known solution of the cantilever beam. The shear stress is seen to be parabolically distributed, and its intensity is independent of x, that is, independent of the location along the beam. On the other hand, the bending stress s_x is seen to be proportional to x, to the distance from the origin O along the beam. Assume an end load P on the cantilever beam, giving a bending moment Px along the beam, and a shear force P along the beam. The reader should write down the known expressions from strength of materials for a flat cantilever beam and compare them with the above exact result, verifying that they coincide completely if the constant A is interpreted as $A = 2P/bh^3$, where b is the thickness of the beam. The above expression for the stress function was originally found by its author by trying many expressions and retaining only such as made practical sense. In this case it is seen that the exact solution leads to the same result as the one previously found by strength of materials on the basis of equilibrium alone, not considering compatibility.

Uniformly Loaded Beam on End Supports. The last example we give in this section is that of a fifth-power algebraic Φ function, which undoubtedly was found originally after much trial and error:

$$\Phi = A(-4y^5 + 20x^2y^3 - 15x^2yh^2 - 20y^3l^2 + 2y^3h^2 + 5x^2h^3)$$

The reader should first substitute this into the biharmonic equation (101c) and verify that it is indeed a permissible Airy function. Then, substitution into Eqs. (100) gives for the stresses

$$s_x = A[-80y^3 + 120y(x^2 - l^2) + 12h^2y]$$
$$s_y = A(+40y^3 - 30yh^2 + 10h^3)$$
$$s_s = A(-120xy^2 + 30xh^2)$$

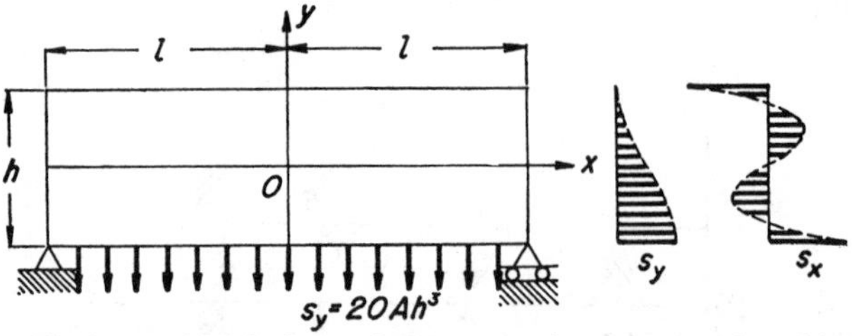

FIG. 120. Flat beam of height h, length $2l$, supported on its two ends and loaded with a uniform load $s_y = 20Ah^3$ along its bottom edge. The exact theory of elasticity gives the known solution of strength of materials for the shear-stress distribution across the beam; it states the distribution of s_y across the depth h of the beam, about which the strength-of-materials solution gives no information whatever, and for the bending stress s_x the exact solution furnishes some additional terms, which are neglected in strength of materials.

We interpret this in Fig. 120 on a rectangular area of height h and length $2l$, symmetrically arranged about the x, y origin O. We notice first that on the top side $y = h/2$ the s_y stress is zero, whereas on the bottom side

$y = -h/2$ it is constant, equal to $20Ah^3$. The shear stress is zero on the vertical center line, the y axis, and is proportional to the distance x from that axis. In any vertical section $x =$ constant the shear-stress distribution is parabolic. It thus appears that we have the case of a beam uniformly loaded with $20Ah^3$ along its bottom edge, supported on its two ends $x = \pm l$. The reader should verify that the shear-stress distribution, as given, coincides with the simple solution from strength of materials for this case, which shows a parabolic distribution of shear stress across a vertical cross section. The s_y stress is constant along horizontal lines and decreases from its maximum amount at the bottom edge to zero at the top edge in the manner shown in Fig. 120. The expression for the longitudinal bending stress shows three terms, of which the middle one, $120Ay(x^2 - l^2)$, should be verified to be the known one from strength of materials. The two additional terms

$$-80Ay^3 + 12Ah^2y$$

are new: they have been plotted in the sketch s_x of Fig. 120, and they constitute an additional longitudinal stress which the exact solution provides and which strength of materials neglects. They are not important for long beams, because we see that the additional terms do not contain x: they are constant along the beam, whereas the usual middle term $120y(x^2 - l^2)$ becomes large in the center of the beam and there is very much larger than the new terms for beams of some length.

Strictly speaking, the ends $x = \pm l$ of the beam should be stressless, and they are not, having the s_x distribution of Fig. 120 on them. But this s_x stress has a zero resultant force over the entire end section h and also a zero moment $\int s_x y \, dy$, so that it is statically equivalent to zero. By Saint-Venant's principle (page 117), the effect of this stress on the ends will have died down at a short distance from the ends, so that the stress distribution of page 182 does represent the actual stresses in the large center portion of the beam.

Here we see for the first time an example of a solution where the theory of elasticity gives us a more exact answer than simple strength of materials. Other polynomials for Φ have been discovered which pertain to practical cases, but in general this development does not hold much promise for further success, so that it will not be pursued further.

Saint-Venant's Principle. On several occasions this principle has been mentioned. It can be stated as follows: The stresses in a structure caused by a certain load distribution at a distance from the load of the order of magnitude of the size-extent of the loading is independent of the details of the load and determined only by the static resultant of that load. For example, suppose a beam rests on a knife-edge. If the knife-edge is sharp, the stress right under it will be greater than if it were blunt, but if the total force on the knife-edge is the same in both cases, the stress in the beam at some distance from the knife-edge is independent of its degree of sharpness. As a second example, consider Fig. 120, which is shown supported on knife-edges. The force P on each knife-edge is $P = s_v l$, half the total load on the beam. If there were really knife-edges as shown, the stress in the beam just above them would be infinite. The analysis gave us a load P carried in the form of a shear stress distributed parabolically across the end sections h, which is quite different from a load P carried as a concentrated force on a knife-edge. However, these two are *statically* equal to P, and by Saint-Venant's principle, the stress distribution at some distance from the end is the same for the two cases. The distance at which this takes place is somewhat indefinite; we say that it is a distance of the same order as the size-extent of the load, in this case h. Thus if we exclude from the beam of Fig. 120 two square pieces $h \times h$ at the ends, the center piece of the beam has stresses independent of the manner of application of the end loads P.

From these examples we see that the "principle" is not an exact mathematical theorem, but rather a practical or common-sense proposition which is of great utility because it enables us to deduce stresses in a structure independent of the details of the manner of application of the loads.

28. Polar Coordinates.   In many cases involving plates with circles or circular arcs in their peripheries, it is much more natural to work with polar coordinates r, θ than with rectangular ones x, y. We therefore now proceed to rewrite the principal equations of the preceding section into polar coordinates, starting with *the conditions of equilibrium* [Eqs. (99), page 173].

In Fig. 121 we consider an element $dr \, rd\theta$, on which are acting the tangential stress s_t, the radial stress s_r, and the shear stress s_s. Taking the height of the element perpendicular to the paper as unity, the various forces are found from the stresses by multiplication with the respective sides: dr, $rd\theta$, and $(r + dr)d\theta$. First we write the equilibrium in the radial direction. The principal forces are $s_r \, rd\theta$ directed inward and $s_r \, rd\theta + \dfrac{\partial}{\partial r} \left(s_r \, rd\theta \right) dr$ outward, giving a net outward resultant of

$$\frac{\partial}{\partial r} \left(s_r \, rd\theta \right) dr = \frac{\partial(rs_r)}{\partial r} \, dr \, d\theta = \left[s_r + r \frac{\partial s_r}{\partial r} \right] dr \, d\theta$$

Of the two terms inside the brackets the first one expresses the fact that the outer stress acts on a larger area than the inner one, whereas the second term states that the stress itself may have a larger value. Returning to Fig. 121, we next look at the shear forces on the two radial faces. The first one at θ is inward, $s_s \, dr$; the other one on the face $\theta + d\theta$ is outward, $[s_s + (\partial s_s/\partial \theta) \, d\theta] \, dr$, giving a net outward resultant of

$$\frac{\partial s_s}{\partial \theta}\, dr\, d\theta$$

This takes care of four out of the eight forces shown on Fig. 121, and the remaining four are directed primarily in a tangential direction. However, even these forces have small radial components that we cannot neglect. The force $s_t\, dr$ and its mate $[s_t + (\partial s_t/\partial\theta)\, d\theta]\, dr$ are not in line but enclose the small angle $d\theta$ between them. The two forces differ from each other by a small quantity only; they are substantially equal to $s_t\, dr$ and their resultant then is $(s_t\, dr)\, d\theta$, directed radially inward. Taking all of this together and dividing by $dr\, d\theta$, the equation of radial equilibrium is

$$s_r - s_t + r\,\frac{\partial s_r}{\partial r} + \frac{\partial s_s}{\partial \theta} = 0$$

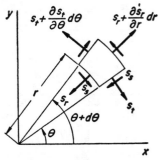

Now turning to the *tangential direction* in Fig. 121, we first take the principal forces $s_t\, dr$ and $[s_t + (\partial s_t/\partial\theta)\, d\theta]\, dr$, giving a difference of $(\partial s_t/\partial\theta)\, d\theta\, dr$ in the $+\theta$ direction. Next are the shear forces on the two curved faces. That on the inside face is $s_s\, rd\theta$, and the one on the outside face is

$$s_s\, rd\theta + \frac{\partial}{\partial r}\,(s_s\, rd\theta)\, dr$$

The net resultant of these two in the $+\theta$ direction is

FIG. 121. An element $r\, d\theta\, dr$ in polar coordinates with the stresses acting on it. From this figure the radial and tangential equilibrium equations (102) are derived.

$$\frac{\partial}{\partial r}\,(s_s\, rd\theta)\, dr = \left[s_s + r\,\frac{\partial s_s}{\partial r} \right] dr\, d\theta$$

again with two terms in the square brackets, one caused by the change in shear stress and the other one by the fact that even if $\partial s_s/\partial r$ were zero, the stress would be acting on two different areas. As before the remaining four forces are almost radial in direction, but not quite. The two shear forces on the straight faces dr are not parallel but include an angle $d\theta$ between them. Their sizes are almost equal, being $s_s\, dr$. The resultant of the two then is $(s_s\, dr)\, d\theta$, directed tangentially in the $+\theta$ direction. Putting all these together and dividing by $dr\, d\theta$ gives the tangential *equation of equilibrium*, printed below together with the radial one:

$$\frac{\partial s_t}{\partial \theta} + 2s_s + r\,\frac{\partial s_s}{\partial r} = 0 \qquad \text{(tangential)}$$

$$\tag{102}$$

$$s_r - s_t + r\,\frac{\partial s_r}{\partial r} + \frac{\partial s_s}{\partial \theta} = 0 \qquad \text{(radial)}$$

Next we turn to the equivalent of Eqs. (100) (page 174), where the Airy stress function is defined. The normal stresses are the curvatures of the Airy surface in a direction perpendicular to the direction of stress. This property should be expressible in polar as well as in rectangular coordinates, but the actual process of calculation, the "transformation of coordinates," is a surprisingly complex algebraic operation, which can be found in books on advanced calculus and which will not be reproduced here. It leads to Eqs. (103) below, which we shall now make plausible geometrically without pretending to "prove" them. The simplest one, the only one of the three without complication, is the one for the tangential stress, which should be equal to the curvature of the Airy surface $\Phi = f(r, \theta)$ along a cut in the radial direction, or

$$s_t = \frac{\partial^2 \Phi}{\partial r^2}$$

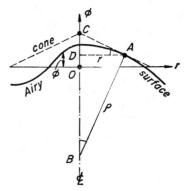

FIG. 122. An Airy surface Φ with a point A where the tangential slope $\partial\Phi/r\partial\theta$ happens to be zero. At point A a tangent cone is described with apex at C. The tangential radius of curvature of the cone at A is $AB = \rho$ as was explained on page 74 in connection with Fig. 50.

The radial stress is the curvature of the Airy Φ surface along a cut in the tangential direction, and this is more complicated. The slope of the Φ surface in the tangential direction is $\partial\Phi/rd\theta$, and we might start to write for the curvature

$$\frac{\partial}{r\partial\theta}\left(\frac{\partial\Phi}{r\partial\theta}\right) = \frac{1}{r^2}\frac{\partial^2\Phi}{\partial\theta^2}$$

This, however, is not correct, as can be seen from Fig. 122. Suppose the Airy surface to be a shallow symmetrical cone above the origin as center. In that case Φ is independent of θ, so that $\partial^2\Phi/\partial\theta^2 = 0$, but the curvature in the tangential direction is not zero. The radius of curvature ρ in Fig. 122 is found from

$$\frac{r}{\rho} = \frac{CD}{AC} \approx \frac{CD}{AD} = \frac{\partial\Phi}{\partial r}$$

so that the local curvature of the cone is

$$\frac{1}{\rho} = \frac{1}{r}\frac{\partial\Phi}{\partial r}$$

This has to be added to the other term derived above so that

$$s_r = \frac{1}{r}\frac{\partial\Phi}{\partial r} + \frac{1}{r^2}\frac{\partial^2\Phi}{\partial\theta^2}$$

Finally, the shear stress is the negative "twist" or mixed second derivative of Φ. We could write either

$$-\frac{\partial}{\partial r}\left(\frac{\partial \Phi}{r\partial \theta}\right) \quad \text{or} \quad -\frac{\partial}{r\partial \theta}\left(\frac{\partial \Phi}{\partial r}\right)$$

which are not the same. The first of these expressions is the correct one, as the full derivation shows. Thus we have for the equivalent of Eqs. (100)

$$s_r = \frac{1}{r}\frac{\partial \Phi}{\partial r} + \frac{1}{r^2}\frac{\partial^2 \Phi}{\partial \theta^2}$$

$$s_t = \frac{\partial^2 \Phi}{\partial r^2} \tag{103}$$

$$s_s = -\frac{\partial}{\partial r}\left(\frac{\partial \Phi}{r\partial \theta}\right)$$

As a check we should verify that these equations, substituted into the equilibrium equations (102), are satisfied for *any* function $\Phi(r, \theta)$ with no other restriction than that Φ has to be differentiable several times.

The *compatibility condition* for Airy's function [Eq. (101c), page 176] is that the sum of two perpendicular curvatures, twice applied, is zero. We saw on page 103 that the sum of the curvatures in two perpendicular directions at a point of a surface is the same for any set of such directions through that point. Therefore, the sum of the curvatures in the x and y directions equals the sum of those in the radial and tangential directions. Hence, using the result, Eqs. (103),

$$\frac{\partial^2}{\partial x^2} + \frac{\partial^2}{\partial y^2} = \frac{\partial^2}{\partial r^2} + \left(\frac{1}{r}\frac{\partial}{\partial r} + \frac{1}{r^2}\frac{\partial^2}{\partial \theta^2}\right)$$

and the compatibility equation in polar coordinates is

$$\left(\frac{\partial^2}{\partial r^2} + \frac{1}{r}\frac{\partial}{\partial r} + \frac{1}{r^2}\frac{\partial^2}{\partial \theta^2}\right)\left(\frac{\partial^2}{\partial r^2} + \frac{1}{r}\frac{\partial}{\partial r} + \frac{1}{r^2}\frac{\partial^2}{\partial \theta^2}\right)\Phi = 0 \tag{104}$$

Rotationally Symmetrical Stress Function. The first solution of these equations to be discussed is the case where Φ is independent of θ and depends on the radius r only. Then Airy's biharmonic equation reduces to

$$\left(\frac{d^2}{dr^2} + \frac{1}{r}\frac{d}{dr}\right)^2 \Phi = 0$$

or, worked out,

$$\left(r^4\frac{d^4}{dr^4} + 2r^3\frac{d^3}{dr^3} - r^2\frac{d^2}{dr^2} + r\frac{d}{dr}\right)\Phi = 0 \tag{105}$$

This equation is the same as Eq. (70) (page 120) with zero right-hand member, and its general solution was derived in detail on page 121:

$$\Phi = C_1 + C_2 \log_e r + C_3 r^2 + C_4 r^2 \log_e r \qquad (106)$$

Applying Eqs. (103) to this general solution, we find for the stresses

$$s_t = -\frac{C_2}{r^2} + 2C_3 + C_4(3 + 2 \log_e r)$$

$$s_r = +\frac{C_2}{r^2} + 2C_3 + C_4(1 + 2 \log_e r) \qquad (107)$$

$$s_s = 0$$

showing a stress distribution in which the radial and tangential stresses are *principal* stresses, since $s_s = 0$. For the special case that $C_4 = 0$, we find a familiar result: Lamé's stress distribution for hollow non-rotating cylinders under internal or external pressure, which was discussed in detail on pages 50 to 54, the principal results being given in Eqs. (41) and (42).

Pure Bending of a Curved Bar.   Another interesting solution is obtained when we consider the part C_4 of Eqs. (107). To be sure, we cannot just take C_4 and leave $C_2 = C_3 = 0$, because we then run afoul of dimensions: we cannot take the logarithm of the length r. The constant C_4 occurs in conjunction with C_3 in the derivation of the equation, and C_3 must contain a part equal to $-C_4 \log r_i$, where r_i, the inside radius, is a constant. Then we have the solution

$$s_t = C_4\left(3 + 2 \log_e \frac{r}{r_i}\right)$$

$$s_r = C_4\left(1 + 2 \log_e \frac{r}{r_i}\right)$$

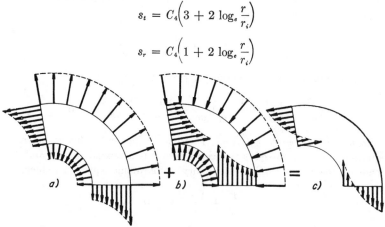

Fɪɢ. 123.   The C_4 term of Eqs. (107) is shown in (*a*). On it we superpose (*b*), which is a Lamé thick cylinder case with internal and external pressures equal and opposite to those of (*a*). The resultant (*c*) is free from stress on the curved contours, and it represents the case of pure bending of a flat curved beam.

which can be interpreted on a curved bar of inner radius r_i and outer radius r_0 (Fig. 123a). The radial stress on the inside radius $r = r_i$ equals C_4, and on the outside radius $s_r = C_4 [1 + 2 \log (r_0/r_i)]$. On the two radial boundaries of the curved bar we have tangential stresses s_t given by the above equation. This stress distribution of Fig. 123a in itself is not interesting: we can make it so by superposing on it a Lamé thick cylinder stress (Fig. 123b) with internal pressure $p_i = C_4$ and with external pressure $p_0 = C_4 [1 + 2 \log (r_0/r_i)]$. Then the curved edges of the bar become stressless, and we are left only with certain tangential stresses on the straight ends. The stress system (Fig. 123c) then is found from a combination of the above equations with Eqs. (41) and (42) (page 54):

$$s_t = C_4\left[3 + 2 \log_e \frac{r}{r_i} + \frac{r_i^2}{r_0^2 - r_i^2}\left(1 + \frac{r_0^2}{r^2}\right) \right.$$
$$\left. - \left(1 + 2 \log_e \frac{r_0}{r_i}\right) \frac{r_0^2}{r_0^2 - r_i^2}\left(1 + \frac{r_i^2}{r^2}\right) \right]$$

$$s_r = C_4\left[1 + 2 \log_e \frac{r}{r_i} + \frac{r_i^2}{r^2 - r_i^2}\left(1 - \frac{r_0^2}{r^2}\right) \right.$$
$$\left. - \left(1 + 2 \log_e \frac{r_0}{r_i}\right) \frac{r_0^2}{r_0^2 - r_i^2}\left(1 - \frac{r_i^2}{r^2}\right) \right]$$

This can be reduced algebraically to the somewhat simpler form

$$s_t = \frac{2C_4}{r_0^2 - r_i^2}\left(-r_0^2 \log_e \frac{r_0}{r} - r_i^2 \log_e \frac{r}{r_i} - \frac{r_0^2 r_i^2}{r^2} \log_e \frac{r_0}{r_i} + r_0^2 - r_i^2 \right)$$

$$s_r = \frac{2C_4}{r_0^2 - r_i^2}\left(-r_0^2 \log_e \frac{r_0}{r} - r_i^2 \log_e \frac{r}{r_i} + \frac{r_0^2 r_i^2}{r^2} \log_e \frac{r_0}{r_i} \right)$$

(108)

This system of stresses must be in equilibrium, because it was derived on the basis of an Airy stress function, which always gives stresses in equilibrium [Eqs. (100), page 174]. Looking at Fig. 123c, we recognize that the resultant force acting on each straight radius must be zero; otherwise the whole curved bar could not be in equilibrium. Hence if we apply to the previous result the operation

$$\int_{r_i}^{r_0} s_t \, dr$$

we must get zero for answer, and the reader should verify this. On the other hand, if we perform

$$\int_{r_i}^{r_0} s_t r \, dr = M$$

we obtain the bending moment on the bar, as represented by the stress distribution of Fig. 123c. This distribution is shown numerically accurate for the case $r_0/r_i = 3$ in Fig. 124. The ratio between the tangential stress at $r = r_0$ and $r = r_i$ in this case is 2.03. In strength of materials the case of a curved bar in bending is usually treated on the basis of the assumption that plane cross sections remain plane, which leads to a hy-

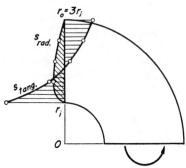

perbolic stress distribution with an inside-outside stress ratio 2.09. Therefore the error of the approximate solution in terms of tangential stresses is about 3 per cent only. The principal difference between the present exact solution, Eqs. (108), and the approximate solution in strength of materials lies in the presence of a radial stress, which is assumed to be absent in the simpler solution. The reader is advised to read again the derivation of this result in his elementary books on strength of materials and note that the derivation is based on equilibrium considerations

Fig. 124. Accurate plot of the stress distribution, Eqs. (108), for a flat curved bar of $r_0 = 3r_i$ loaded in pure bending in its own plane.

plus the assumptions of (a) plane cross sections remaining plane and (b) absence of radial stress. The solution so obtained is adequate for practical purposes, but it violates the radial-equilibrium as well as the compatibility condition.

Curved Cantilever Beam. The last example in this section concerns a stress function of the form

$$\Phi = f(r) \sin \theta$$

where $f(r)$ is as yet an undetermined function. The first requirement is that Φ must satisfy the biharmonic equation (104), so that we substitute our stress function into (104). The $\sin \theta$ can be divided out, and the partial differential equation (104) reduces to the ordinary one,

$$\left(\frac{d^2}{dr^2} + \frac{1}{r}\frac{d}{dr} - \frac{1}{r^2}\right)\left(\frac{d^2 f}{dr^2} + \frac{1}{r}\frac{df}{dr} - \frac{f}{r^2}\right) = 0$$

or, worked out,

$$\left(r^4 \frac{d^4}{dr^4} + 2r^3 \frac{d^3}{dr^3} - 3r^2 \frac{d^2}{dr^2} + 3r \frac{d}{dr} - 3\right)f(r) = 0$$

This equation is of the same general type as Eq. (105) or as Eq. (70); its solutions are powers of r, say r^p, and the values of p must be determined by the process employed on page 121. This leads to a fourth-degree equation in p of which the roots are $p = 3, 1, 1, -1$, and hence the general solution is

$$f(r) = C_1r^3 + C_2r + C_3r \log_e r + \frac{C_4}{r}$$

which can be verified by substitution into the above differential equation. The stress function is

$$\Phi = \left(C_1r^3 + C_2r + C_3r \log_e r + \frac{C_4}{r}\right) \sin \theta$$

By means of Eq. (103) (page 187) we deduce the stresses as follows:

$$s_t = \left(6C_1r + \frac{C_3}{r} + 2\frac{C_4}{r^3}\right) \sin \theta$$

$$s_r = \left(2C_1r + \frac{C_3}{r} - 2\frac{C_4}{r^3}\right) \sin \theta$$

$$-s_s = \left(2C_1r + \frac{C_3}{r} - 2\frac{C_4}{r^3}\right) \cos \theta$$

On account of the three arbitrary constants C_1, C_3, C_4, this set of equations can represent many stress distributions. We select the one of most practical interest by demanding that no radial stress s_r or shear stress s_s occur on the inner $r = r_i$ and outer $r = r_0$ edges of a curved bar:

$$s_s = s_r = 0 \qquad (\text{for } r = r_i \text{ and for } r = r_0)$$

This gives us the condition equations

$$2C_1r_i + \frac{C_3}{r_i} - \frac{2C_4}{r_i^3} = 0$$

$$2C_1r_0 + \frac{C_3}{r_0} - \frac{2C_4}{r_0^3} = 0$$

from which we can solve for C_3/C_1 and for C_4/C_1, leaving C_1 in the expressions as a size factor. The result of this operation is

$$\frac{C_3}{C_1} = -2(r_i^2 + r_0^2) \qquad \frac{C_4}{C_1} = -r_i^2r_0^2$$

Substituting this into the expressions for the stresses, we obtain

$$s_t = 2C_1 \sin \theta \left(3r - \frac{r_i^2 + r_0^2}{r} - \frac{r_i^2r_0^2}{r^3}\right)$$

$$s_r = 2C_1 \sin \theta \left(r - \frac{r_i^2 + r_0^2}{r} + \frac{r_i^2r_0^2}{r^3}\right) \tag{109}$$

$$s_s = -2C_1 \cos \theta \left(r - \frac{r_i^2 + r_0^2}{r} + \frac{r_i^2r_0^2}{r^3}\right)$$

The constant C_1 has no particular meaning: it determines the size of the stresses, but it does not affect their distribution pattern. It is seen that when we proceed along the bar, the tangential stress becomes zero every 180 deg, and at those spots the shear stress reaches its maximum. Halfway in between the situation is reversed. Figure 125 shows the quarter bar between $\theta = 0$ and $\theta = 90$ deg for the case $r_0/r_i = 3$.

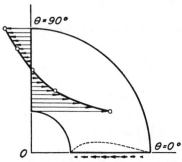

Again, as in all previous cases, these stresses must constitute an equilibrium system. The reader should verify that everything is correct by carrying out the two following integrations:

$$\left[\int_{r_i}^{r_0} s_t \, dr \right]_{\theta=90°} + \left[\int_{r_i}^{r_0} s_s \, dr \right]_{\theta=0°} = 0$$

FIG. 125. Curved cantilever bar of $r_0 = 3r_i$ loaded by a distributed shear force at the lower edge $\theta = 0$. The bending moment at the upper edge $\theta = 90$ deg has the distribution shown. These stresses are expressed by Eqs. (109).

which states that there is force equilibrium in the horizontal, or $\theta = 0$, direction, and

$$\left[\int_{r_i}^{r_0} s_t r \, dr \right]_{\theta=90°} = 0$$

which states that the s_t stresses have zero moment about O, or that the resultant of the s_t forces is in line with the equilibrizing shear force at $\theta = 0$.

Now we are ready to get some more solutions by superposing the stresses of Fig. 124 (pure bending) on those of Fig. 125 (cantilever). This is shown in Fig. 126, of which a is the case of Fig. 125. The forces at the top, $\theta = 90°$, are equivalent to either a single force equal, opposite, and in line

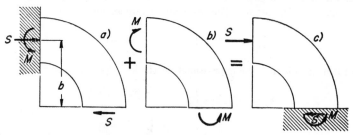

FIG. 126. The superposition of a cantilever (a), being loaded with a force S perpendicular to the local center line of the bar, on the case of pure bending (b) gives a cantilever (c) loaded by a force along the local center line. By varying the amount of the moment M and hence by varying the distance b in (a), the force S in (c) can be shifted up and down to any desired location.

with S at $\theta = 0$ or, as indicated here, to the combination of a force S plus a bending moment $M = Sb$. We can think of the $\theta = 90$ deg end as built into a wall, and we have a curved cantilever. Superposing onto this Fig. 126b, pure bending, we can compensate for the bending moment of Fig. 126a. The result, Fig. 126c, can be thought of as built in at the bottom, and we have a cantilever loaded by a force along the center line.

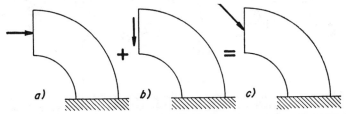

Fig. 127.   The superposition of (*a*) (which is the same as Fig. 126*c*) on top of (*b*) (which is the same as Fig. 126*a* mirrored and turned) leads to (*c*), a curved cantilever loaded by an oblique load.

Still another superposition is suggested in Fig. 127. The stresses in all these cases can be calculated by adding appropriate amounts of Eqs. (109) to Eqs. (108); the algebra of this is quite involved but presents no particular difficulty.

29. Kirsch, Boussinesq, and Michell.   In this section we shall deal with three important solutions of Airy's stress function in polar coordinates, found by a German, a Frenchman, and an Englishman, all just before the year 1900.

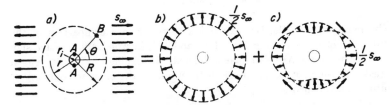

Fig. 128.   The case of a plate under uniform uniaxial tension s_∞ having a small circular hole r_i, as shown in (*a*) above, was treated by Kirsch as the superposition of a Lamé thick cylinder case with half the stress s_∞ as in (*b*) and a new case, shown in (*c*), obeying $\Phi = f(r) \cos 2\theta$.

Stress Concentration at a Circular Hole.   The first of these is the solution of Kirsch (1898) in Germany, giving the stress distribution around a small circular hole in a flat plate subjected to uniform tension s_∞ (Fig. 128). The principal result of the analysis is that the stress at the points A at the periphery of the hole is $3s_\infty$, or, in other words, that the stress-concentration factor of the small hole is 3.

In finding the solution we first remark that by Saint-Venant's principle the small central hole will not affect the stress distribution at a considerable distance from that hole ($r > 3r_i$). Thus, on a circle of large radius R in the plate, we have uniform tension s_∞ in the direction of x, or $\theta = 0$.

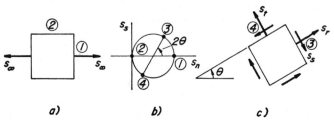

FIG. 129. The element (a) is located at the point B of Fig. 128a. Its stresses are represented in (b) by points 1 and 2 on the Mohr's circle. (c) is the same element cut out in the radial and tangential directions. The stresses on its faces 3 and 4 are represented by the corresponding points in (b).

This is translated into radial and tangential components by a Mohr's-circle construction (Fig. 129), from which we read by the usual Mohr procedure

$$s_r = \frac{s_\infty}{2}(1 + \cos 2\theta)$$

$$s_t = \frac{s_\infty}{2}(1 - \cos 2\theta) \qquad (a)$$

$$s_s = -\frac{s_\infty}{2}\sin 2\theta$$

The minus sign in the last expression comes from a comparison of the directions of the arrows in Figs. 129c and 121, in which the positive sign of s_s for use in the Airy formulae is defined. Returning to Fig. 128, Kirsch breaks up the above total stress distribution on the circular boundary R into two components,

(a) $\qquad s_r = \frac{s_\infty}{2} \qquad\qquad s_s = 0$

(b) $\qquad s_r = \frac{s_\infty}{2}\cos 2\theta \qquad s_s = -\frac{s_\infty}{2}\sin 2\theta$

of which part a represents a uniform radial tension, to be treated with the Lame formulae of page 57, and in which contribution b is shown in Fig. 128c. Kirsch tried and succeeded in representing this latter part by a stress function

$$\Phi = f(r)\cos 2\theta$$

This function is very similar to that of page 190; it is investigated by the same method, and the main difference consists in the appearance of factors 2 when differentiating the double angle $\cos 2\theta$. The equation for $f(r)$ thus becomes

$$\left(\frac{d^2}{dr^2} + \frac{1}{r}\frac{d}{dr} - \frac{4}{r^2}\right)\left(\frac{d^2f}{dr^2} + \frac{1}{r}\frac{df}{dr} - \frac{4f}{r^2}\right) = 0$$

or, worked out,

$$\left(r^4\frac{d^4}{dr^4} + 2r^3\frac{d^3}{dr^3} - 9r^2\frac{d^2}{dr^2} + 9r\frac{d}{dr}\right)f(r) = 0$$

By the process of page 121, assuming solutions of the form r^p, the algebraic equation for p is

$$p^4 - 4p^3 - 4p^2 + 16p = 0$$

with the four roots $p = 4, 2, 0, -2$.
The general solution thus is

$$\Phi = \left(C_1r^4 + C_2r^2 + C_3 + \frac{C_4}{r^2}\right)\cos 2\theta$$

and with Eqs. (103) this corresponds to the stresses

$$s_r = \left(-2C_2 - \frac{4C_3}{r^2} - \frac{6C_4}{r^4}\right)\cos 2\theta$$

$$s_t = \left(12C_1r^2 + 2C_2 + \frac{6C_4}{r^4}\right)\cos 2\theta \qquad (b)$$

$$s_s = \left(6C_1r^2 + 2C_2 - \frac{2C_3}{r^2} - \frac{6C_4}{r^4}\right)\sin 2\theta$$

In order to make this general case fit the special one of Fig. (128c) and the formulae (a), we must impose four conditions:

At $r = r_i$: $s_r = 0$ and $s_s = 0$

At $r = R = \infty$: $s_r = \dfrac{s_\infty}{2}\cos 2\theta$ and $s_s = \dfrac{-s_\infty}{2}\sin 2\theta$

Substituting the general stresses (b) into these conditions, we find

$$-2C_2 - \frac{4C_3}{r_i^2} - \frac{6C_4}{r_i^4} = 0$$

$$6C_1r_i^2 + 2C_2 - \frac{2C_3}{r_i^2} - \frac{6C_4}{r_i^4} = 0$$

$$-2C_2 = \frac{s_\infty}{2}$$

$$6C_1 \cdot \infty + 2C_2 = -\frac{s_\infty}{2}$$

From the last of these we conclude that $C_1 = 0$; from the next last that $C_2 = -s_\infty/4$; and from the remaining two that $C_3 = (s_\infty/2)r_i^2$ and $C_4 = -(s_\infty/4)r_i^4$. Thus the stresses of Fig. 128c are given by

$$s_r = \frac{s_\infty}{2}\left(1 - 4\frac{r_i^2}{r^2} + 3\frac{r_i^4}{r^4}\right)\cos 2\theta$$

$$s_t = \frac{s_\infty}{2}\left(-1 - 3\frac{r_i^4}{r^4}\right)\cos 2\theta \tag{c}$$

$$s_s = \frac{s_\infty}{2}\left(-1 - 2\frac{r_i^2}{r^2} + 3\frac{r_i^4}{r^4}\right)\sin 2\theta$$

The Lamé stresses of Fig. 128b are found in Eq. (42) (page 54), in which $r_0 = R \to \infty$ and p_0 is negative:

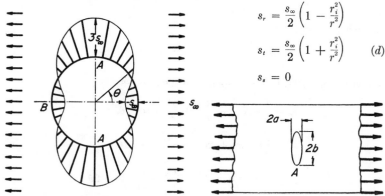

$$s_r = \frac{s_\infty}{2}\left(1 - \frac{r_i^2}{r^2}\right)$$

$$s_t = \frac{s_\infty}{2}\left(1 + \frac{r_i^2}{r^2}\right) \tag{d}$$

$$s_s = 0$$

FIG. 130. Tangential-stress distribution along the periphery of a circular hole in a large flat plate subjected to uniform tension s_∞, showing a stress-concentration factor 3 at points A.

FIG. 131. A plate under uniform tension with an elliptical hole of dimensions a and b which are small in comparison with the plate itself. The stress-concentration factor is given by Eq. (111), and it illustrates the great danger of sharp cracks in a material.

The sum of the stresses (c) and (d) is Kirsch's solution for the stress distribution near a small circular hole in a flat plate in tension. At the edge of the hole itself, where $r = r_i$, we verify that the stresses s_r and s_s are zero, as they should from the boundary conditions. The tangential stress along the edge of the hole $r = r_i$ is, from (c) and (d),

$$s_t = s_\infty(1 - 2\cos 2\theta) \tag{110}$$

which is shown graphically in Fig. 130. At the points A the stress is tensile and three times that at infinity, while at B the tangential stress is compressive, equal to s_∞ in magnitude.

A similar but much more complicated analysis has been made for a hole of elliptical shape, as shown in Fig. 131. This analysis will not be given here: its result for the stress-concentration factor at points A is

$$\frac{s_A}{s_\infty} = 1 + 2\frac{b}{a} \tag{111}$$

Applying this to a crack in the material, which can be approximated by an ellipse of, say, $b/a = 20$, it is seen that, if the crack is located *along* the direction of the stress s_∞, the stress-concentration factor is 1.10, about equal to unity, but when the crack is *across* the direction of the stress, that factor becomes 41.0. This illustrates the fact that once a sharp crack has started in a structure, a fairly small stress is sufficient to propagate it further.

Concentrated Load P on Edge of Plate or on Wedge. Another interesting solution, due to Boussinesq (1885), is contained in the function

$$\Phi = Cr\theta \sin \theta \tag{112}$$

First we must substitute this expression into the biharmonic equation (104) and verify that it does satisfy that equation, which it does. Then we find the stresses from Eqs. (103), as follows:

$$s_r = 2C\frac{\cos \theta}{r}$$

$$s_t = 0 \qquad s_s = 0 \tag{112a}$$

This is a remarkable stress field: all stresses are purely radial with respect to the origin of coordinates O. In Fig. 132 the stress is shown at an arbitrary point A. If we draw a dotted circle through A, tangent at O to the axis

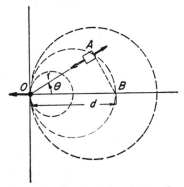

FIG. 132. Boussinesq's solution, described by Eqs. (112) and (112a). The dotted circles are loci of constant radial-stress intensity; large stresses occur on small circles.

$\theta = \pi/2$, and if the diameter of that circle OB is called d, then we notice that $r = d \cos \theta$, so that the stress can be written as

$$s_r = \frac{2C}{d}$$

Thus the loci of constant stress intensity are circles, as shown in Fig. 132, but the direction of the only existing principal stress at each point is always radial with respect to the origin O. We now can cut out from the plane certain portions bounded by straight radii through O, as is done in Fig. 133. First we look at the region between $\theta = -\alpha$ and $\theta = +\alpha$ (Fig. 133a), and we reverse the sign of all stresses, by multiplying the stress function by -1. The stress at A is $-(2C\cos\theta)/r$, and it operates on a small section $rd\theta$, radially toward O. This radial force can be resolved into components parallel and perpendicular to the center line PB. When integrated from $\theta = -\alpha$ to $\theta = +\alpha$, the resultant force perpendicular to PB becomes zero from symmetry, but the force parallel to PB (which for equilibrium $= P$) is

$$P = -2C \int_{-\alpha}^{+\alpha} \frac{\cos\theta}{r} \cos\theta \, rd\theta = -2C\left[\frac{\theta}{2} + \frac{1}{4}\sin 2\theta\right]_{-\alpha}^{+\alpha}$$

$$P = -C(2\alpha + \sin 2\alpha)$$

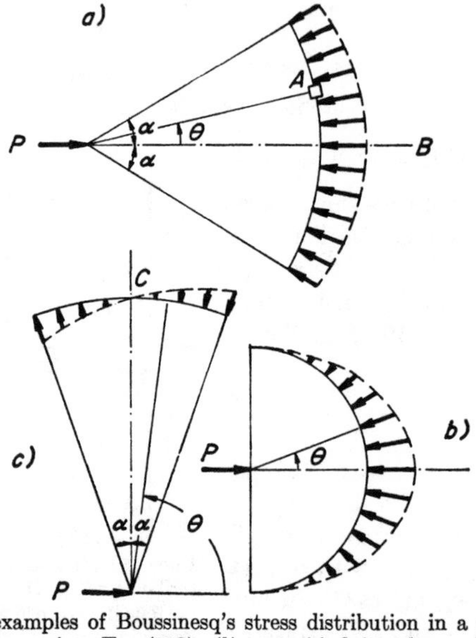

FIG. 133. Three examples of Boussinesq's stress distribution in a part of the plane: (a) a wedge in compression, Eq. (113); (b) a semi-infinite plane with a concentrated load, Eq. (113a); (c) a cantilever wedge in bending, Eq. (114).

This gives the relation between the force P and the constant C, and we conclude that the stress in the wedge of Fig. 133a is given by

$$s_r = -\frac{P}{\alpha + \frac{1}{2}\sin 2\alpha}\frac{\cos\theta}{r} \tag{113}$$

When the wedge angle 2α becomes 180 deg, we have the case of a semi-infinite plane loaded by a force P and its stress becomes

$$s_r = -\frac{2P}{\pi}\frac{\cos\theta}{r} \tag{113a}$$

which is shown in Fig. 133b.

Finally we cut out of the plane a wedge between $\theta = (\pi/2) - \alpha$ and $\theta = (\pi/2) + \alpha$, as shown in Fig. 133c. This represents a cantilever beam of wedge shape, and the stress distribution is again given by the general formulae (112a). To find the relation between the load P and the constant C in the stress, we again write an equation of equilibrium of the object Fig. 133c. The force equilibrium in the direction PC, as well as the moment equilibrium about the apex P, is automatically satisfied by symmetry. The force equilibrium in the direction θ, perpendicular to PC, is expressed by

$$P = -\int_{(\pi/2)-\alpha}^{(\pi/2)+\alpha} \left(2C \frac{\cos\theta}{r}\right)\cos\theta \cdot r d\theta$$

$$= -2C\left[\frac{\theta}{2} + \frac{1}{4}\sin 2\theta\right]_{(\pi/2)-\alpha}^{(\pi/2)+\alpha} = -2C\left(\alpha - \frac{1}{2}\sin 2\alpha\right)$$

so that the stress for the case, Fig. 133c, is

$$s_r = -\frac{P\cos\theta}{r(\alpha - \tfrac{1}{2}\sin 2\alpha)} \tag{114}$$

The results Eqs. (113) and (114) for the special case that the wedge angle 2α becomes 360 deg become identical, representing the stress caused in a full infinite plane by a force P acting in the plane at an interior point. That stress is

$$s_r = -\frac{P\cos\theta}{\pi r} \tag{114a}$$

where the angle θ is measured from the direction of the force P.

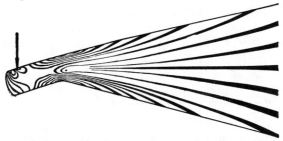

Fig. 134. Photograph of a bakelite specimen representing Fig. 133c taken with photoelastic test apparatus. The black lines are those of equal shear-stress intensity.

In all the cases of Fig. 133 the loci of equal radial-stress intensity are those of Fig. 132: circles passing through O and tangent to a line perpendicular to the load P. Lines of equal radial-stress intensity, by Mohr's circle, are also lines of equal shear-stress intensity (explain why), and those are the lines obtained in a photoelastic test. Figure 134 shows a photograph so obtained for the case Fig. 133b.

Cylinder Compressed by Diametrically Opposite Forces. In 1900 Michell in England found a solution of a circular disk or cylinder subjected to a pair of compressive forces along a diameter by an ingenious superposition of two Boussinesq solutions and a hydrostatic stress. Consider in Fig. 135 the half infinite plane *under* the line AA, and put into it a Boussinesq stress field caused by the force P_1. Then consider the half infinite plane *above* the line BB, and put into that a P_2 Boussinesq stress field, letting P_2 be the same as P_1. Then in the horizontal strip between AA and BB we have two superimposed stress fields. At a point C on the periphery the first stress field causes a stress [Eq. (113a)] of $-\dfrac{2P}{\pi}\dfrac{\cos\theta_1}{r_1}$ in the direction P_1C with zero stress in the perpendicular direction P_2C, while the second stress field causes $-\dfrac{2P}{\pi}\dfrac{\cos\theta_2}{r_2}$ in that perpendicular direction and nothing in the P_1C direction. These two are directly superimposable without any Mohr-circle complication, and moreover the two stresses are equal, because $\cos\theta_1/r_1 = \cos\theta_2/r_2 = 1/d$. Thus an element on the periphery of the circle of Fig. 135 is in a state of "two-dimensional hydrostatic compression" of intensity $2P/\pi d$, and this state of stress is depicted by a Mohr's circle reduced to point size, so that the same stress holds in any direction through the element. Now we superimpose a third stress field on top of the previous two, this time a *uniform* hydrostatic *tension* $2P/\pi d$ in the entire field. Then, of course, elements on the periphery of the circle are entirely without stress.

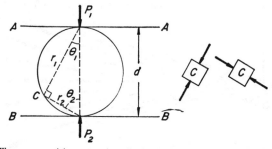

Fig. 135. The superposition at point C of two Boussinesq stress fields leads to a two-dimensional hydrostatic compression. The point C is then made stressless by the further superposition of an equal hydrostatic tension, uniformly distributed over the entire field.

Now we cut out the circle of Fig. 135 and find zero stresses on the periphery and two concentrated forces P diametrically opposite to each other. Inside the circle we have the superposition of two Boussinesq compressions, emanating from P_1 and P_2, plus a hydrostatic tension $2P/\pi d$. This then is the stress field inside a thin circular disk or inside a thick circular cylinder (reread page 178 to see that both these cases are included in the analysis.)

The superposition of these three stresses must be effected by a Mohr's-circle construction, and as an example we consider in Fig. 136a point A on the horizontal diameter at distance x from the center. The Boussinesq stress from the bottom is $-2P \cos \theta/\pi r$, but $\cos \theta = d/2r$ and $\cos \theta/r = d/2r^2 = d/2[x^2 + (d^2/4)]$, so that the stress of the first Fig. 136b is

$$s_1 = -\frac{4P}{\pi}\frac{d}{d^2 + 4x^2}$$

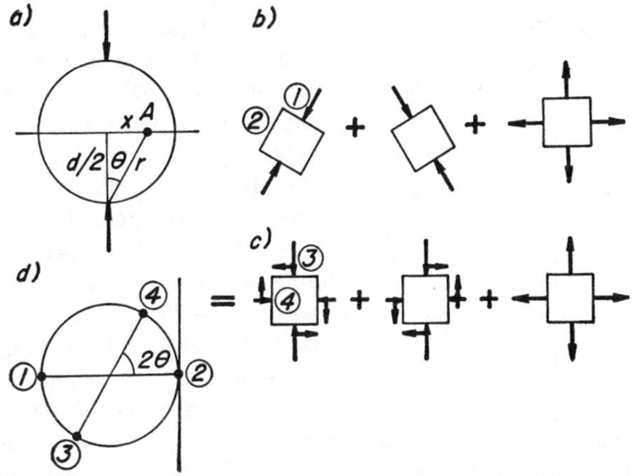

FIG. 136. The stress at an element A consists of the superposition of the three cases (b). Two of these are turned through an angle θ by means of a Mohr circle (d) with the result (c). Since the faces of all three cases are in line, the stresses can be added algebraically.

By Mohr's circle (Fig. 136d) this is turned through angle θ, and the stress s_3 becomes

$$s_3 = \frac{s_1}{2}(1 + \cos 2\theta) = s_1 \cos^2 \theta = s_1 \frac{d^2}{d^2 + 4x^2}$$

$$s_3 = \frac{-4P}{\pi}\frac{d^3}{(d^2 + 4x^2)^2}$$

The Boussinesq stress from the top force P has the same value, by symmetry. The hydrostatic stress is $+2P/\pi d$. Hence the total stress (Fig. 136c) in a direction parallel to PP is $2s_3 + s_{\text{hydro}}$,

$$s_x = \frac{2P}{\pi d}\left[1 - \frac{4d^4}{(d^2 + 4x^2)^2}\right]$$

a result which is plotted in Fig. 137. A special case of this general result is at the center of the cylinder, $x = 0$. Then the stress $s_x = -6P/\pi d$, compressive in the direction of the forces P. Also there is a tension $2P/\pi d$ there in the direction perpendicular to that of the forces P. The determination of the stress in any other interior point of the cylinder must be done by Mohr's construction and is fairly cumbersome if no advantage can be taken of symmetry.

30. Plasticity. In two-dimensional elasticity the stress at a point is described by three quantities s_x, s_y, s_s, or s_1, s_2, α, where s_1 and s_2 are the principal stresses and α is their angle with respect to a fixed direction.

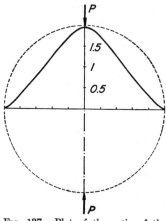

FIG. 137. Plot of the ratio of the actual compressive stress to the average compressive stress P/d across the central diameter of a cylinder between two forces P.

For solving these three quantities we have available three equations: the two equilibrium equations (99) or (102) and the compatibility equation (101b) or (101c) or (104). Solutions to these equations, as they have been discussed in the last 20 pages, are valid only while the material remains elastic. When the stresses are too large, the material becomes plastic, and we have seen a few simple solutions of that plastic state already (page 20).

In 1920 *Prandtl* in Germany opened up a new field by remarking that in general *two-dimensional* plasticity the three stresses s_x, s_y, s_s can be solved from three equations also: the two old equilibrium equations, which of course must be true for any material, and as a third equation the "condition of plasticity," to take the place of the compatibility equation. We remember that the compatibility equation expressed the fact that the small *elastic* strains of a small element $dx\,dy$ deform that element so that it still fits continuously in the pattern of all neighboring elements. When we go to a plastic state, Hooke's law no longer holds and the expressions for the elastic strains no longer hold, so that the compatibility equation is not valid any more. However, in the plastic regions there is a definite relation expressing plasticity and found as the result of experiment. Two such relations are being used, both expressing the test results reasonably well, and hence differing but little from each other numerically:

a. The maximum shear theory: $s_{s\ max}$ = const
b. The distortion energy theory: $s_1^2 - s_1 s_2 + s_2^2$ = const

We shall here proceed only with the maximum shear theory, which is the simpler one of the two, leaving the distortion energy to more elaborate treatises on the subject.

The plasticity criterion, according to the maximum shear theory, is expressed by

$$\frac{s_1 - s_2}{2} = \text{const} = s_{\text{yield}} \tag{115}$$

where s_1 and s_2 are the principal stresses in the plane of plastic flow. In case the stresses are not expressed in principal stresses, but in s_x, s_y, s_s, the criterion becomes

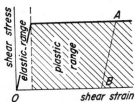

FIG. 138. The commonly accepted idealization of the stress-strain diagram for a ductile material such as steel. In the plastic range the maximum shear stress remains constant while the material strains indefinitely (up to 20 or more parts per 1,000). In the elastic range the stress and strain are proportional. The yield point occurs for a strain of the order of 1 part per 1,000. If an element is deformed from point O to point A and the stress is then released, it moves back elastically to B, leaving a permanent set OB in the element.

$$\left(\frac{s_x - s_y}{2}\right)^2 + s_s^2 = \text{const} = s_{s\ \text{yield}}^2 \tag{115a}$$

as the reader should verify by sketching a Mohr circle. Now Eq. (115a), together with the equilibrium equations (99) (page 173), determines the state of stress in the plastic region. A whole theory with many solutions has been built up on this; here we shall give only two important illustrative examples: the thick cylinder and the blunt knife-edge.

Thick Cylinder. If a thick-walled cylinder is subjected to internal pressure, the Lamé formulae (41) (page 54) describe the stress distribution when the internal pressure is sufficiently small, and the maximum shear stress occurs on the inside radius. When that stress reaches the yield point, plastic flow starts at the inside bore of the tube, and when the internal pressure is made still greater, the inner region of the cylinder becomes plastic (Fig. 140).

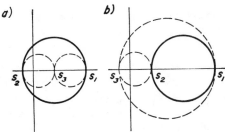

FIG. 139. The Mohr's-circle diagram about the stresses at a point was derived on equilibrium principles only and does not depend at all on Hooke's law or any other law of deformations; hence it applies to the plastic state as well. In *two-dimensional* plasticity, where the material flows in a plane, the plasticity criterion is Eq. (115), where s_1 and s_2 are the principal stresses in the plane of flow. Therefore the Mohr's circles (a) and (b) of this figure both represent the plastic state: we do not have to inquire about the value of the third stress s_3, perpendicular to the plane of flow.

This problem is somewhat simpler than the general two-dimensional case on account of its rotational symmetry. Instead of three unknown stresses, there are only two, s_t and s_r, while s_s is zero, because the radial and tan-

gential directions are principal directions. With one less unknown we also have one less equilibrium equation: tangential equilibrium is automatic and does not lead to an equation. Thus for the two unknowns s_t and s_r we have two equations: one radial equilibrium equation (35) (page 50) (in which $\rho\omega^2 = 0$, because there is no rotation) and one other equation. For the elastic portion that second equation is the compatibility equation (37) (page 51), which was derived from the two deformation equations (36). For the plastic portion the second equation is the condition of plasticity [Eq. (115)]. On the boundary between the two regions (at the unknown radius r_{pl}) we must demand that the radial stress s_r is the same in the elastic and plastic regions. With this the problem is completely determined as follows.

FIG. 140. Thick cylinder under large internal pressure. In the inner portion $r_i < r < r_p$ the material is plastic, and in the outer region the material is elastic. In both regions the equilibrium equation (35) (page 50) applies; in the plastic region the second equation is the plastic condition, Eq. (115) (page 203), while in the elastic region it is the compatibility equation (37) (page 51).

In the plastic region:

$$rs_r' + s_r - s_t = 0 \qquad \text{(equilibrium)}$$

$$s_t - s_r = 2s_{s\,\text{yield}} \qquad \text{(plasticity)}$$

Substitute the second equation into the first one, and integrate, remembering that $s_{s\,\text{yield}}$ is constant:

$$s_r = 2s_{s_y} \log_e r + \text{const}$$

At the inner boundary $r = r_i$ the radial stress is $s_r = -p_i$, from which we find the constant:

$$\left.\begin{aligned} s_r &= -p_i + 2s_{s_y} \log_e \frac{r}{r_i} \\ s_t &= -p_i + 2s_{s_y}\left(1 + \log_e \frac{r}{r_i}\right) \end{aligned}\right\} \qquad \text{(plastic region)}$$

The last equation is found from the previous one by means of the condition of plasticity $s_t - s_r = 2s_{s_y}$.

For the elastic region between $r = r_{pl}$ and $r = r_0$ (Fig. 140) we apply Eqs. (41) (page 54), remembering that r_i and p_i of that equation are called r_{pl} and p_{pl} in our new case:

$$s_r = p_{pl} \frac{r_{pl}^2}{r_0^2 - r_{pl}^2} \left(1 - \frac{r_0^2}{r^2}\right) \left.\begin{array}{c} \\ \\ \end{array}\right\}$$

$$s_t = p_{pl} \frac{r_{pl}^2}{r_0^2 - r_{pl}^2} \left(1 + \frac{r_0^2}{r^2}\right) \quad\text{(elastic region)}$$

In the elastic region we have $s_t - s_r < 2s_{sy}$, except right at the edge $r = r_{pl}$, where $<$ becomes $=$:

$$(s_t - s_r)_{r=r_{pl}} = p_{pl} \frac{r_{pl}^2}{r_0^2 - r_{pl}^2} 2 \frac{r_0^2}{r_{pl}^2} = 2s_{sy}$$

or

$$p_{pl} = s_{sy} \frac{r_0^2 - r_{pl}^2}{r_0^2}$$

Substituting this into the elastic-region equations,

$$s_r = s_{sy} \frac{r_{pl}^2}{r_0^2} \left(1 - \frac{r_0^2}{r^2}\right) \left.\begin{array}{c} \\ \\ \end{array}\right\}$$

$$s_t = s_{sy} \frac{r_{pl}^2}{r_0^2} \left(1 + \frac{r_0^2}{r^2}\right) \quad\text{(elastic region)}$$

We could solve for r_{pl} and find it as a function of p_i, but this leads to more algebra than the result is worth. It is more practical to ask for the value of the internal pressure p_i for two conditions: (a) at the start of yielding when $r_{pl} = r_i$ and (b) at the completion of yielding when $r_{pl} = r_0$. For condition a, just at the start of yielding, the entire tube is elastic, and from the above elastic equation we find

$$(s_r)_{r=r_i} = s_{sy} \frac{r_i^2}{r_0^2} \left(1 - \frac{r_0^2}{r_i^2}\right) = -s_{sy} \frac{r_0^2 - r_i^2}{r_0^2}$$

By definition of the "radial stress at the inside edge" this equals p_i, so that

$$(p_i)_{\text{yield just starts}} = s_{sy} \frac{r_0^2 - r_i^2}{r_0^2} \tag{116a}$$

For the condition b the entire cylinder is plastic, and the radial stress on the *outside* $r = r_0$ must be zero. From the plastic equation we thus find

$$(s_r)_{r=r_0} = 0 = -p_i + 2s_{sy} \log_e \frac{r_0}{r_i}$$

$$\therefore (p_i)_{\text{tube fully plastic}} = s_{sy} \log_e \left(\frac{r_0}{r_i}\right)^2 \tag{116b}$$

These results are shown plotted in Fig. 141. For thin tubes there is little margin of safety: no sooner has yield started than the whole tube yields and gives way. For a tube of great wall thickness, however, say $r_0/r_i = 5$,

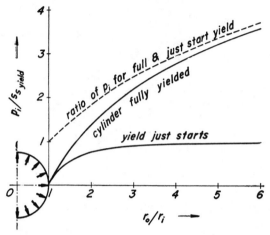

Fɪɢ. 141.   Internal pressure in a thick cylinder which will just start yielding at the inside radius, and that pressure required for full yielding of the entire cylinder.   The dashed curve gives the ratio of these two pressures, illustrating Eqs. (116a) and (116b).

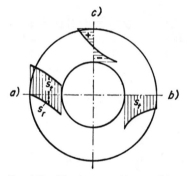

Fɪɢ. 142.   Plastic stress (a) caused by internal pressure sufficient to cause plastic flow throughout the cylinder. The tangential stress is tensile, and the radial stress is compressive.   Diagram (b) shows the elastic compressive tangential stress caused by removal of the internal pressure.   Diagram (c) is the sum of (a) and (b): it is the residual, or locked-up, tangential stress after removal of the pressure; it is compressive near the bore, tensile at the outside.

yield starts when the pressure equals s_{sy} approximately, but then that pressure can be made more than three times as large before the whole tube gives way.   We see that a thick-walled tube can thus withstand internal pressures which are far greater than the yield stress of the containing tube.

These relations allow us to follow numerically the process of hydraulically upsetting big guns for the purpose of giving them favorable locked-up stresses.   This is illustrated in Fig. 142 for a gun of $r_0/r_i = 2$.   The stressless and roughly premachined gun is subjected to internal hydraulic pressure so high that it yields all over, giving the stress pattern, Fig. 142a.   Then the pressure is removed, which by itself means superimposing a radial tension on the inside.   This causes the pattern, Fig. 142b, *elastically* (see points A, B on Fig. 138).   When the pressure is entirely removed, the gun fibers have tangential stresses in them equal to the sum of (a) and (b), which means compression near the bore. The gun is then finish-machined, and when it is fired afterward, the firing stresses are tangentially *tensile* near the bore. They first have to overcome the locked-up compressive stresses before they reverse sign. In this manner it is possible for the gun to withstand firing pressures up to twice as large as without this treatment and still remain entirely elastic, *i.e.*, without permanent changes in the bore diameter due to firing.

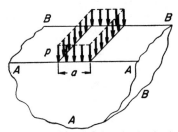

FIG. 143. Semi-infinite elastic-plastic body constrained between two stiff and immovable flat plates *AAA* and *BBB*, loaded with a uniform pressure *p* along width *a*.

Blunt Knife-edge. This problem is stated in Fig. 143, and the load can be regarded as the pressure exerted by a blunt knife-edge of width *a*. The elastic solution of this problem is known: either it can be found by integrating the Boussinesq forces of Fig. 132 along the edge over a length *a*, or it can be found by some manipulations on the stress function of Problem 117. This we shall not do here but shall remark only that in the elastic solution the maximum compressive stress occurs right under the loading *p*, all along *a*, and has the value *p*,

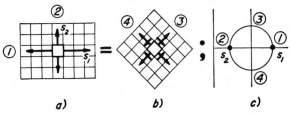

FIG. 144. Uniformly plastic field. (*a*) shows lines along the directions of the principal stresses; (*b*) shows lines along the directions of maximum shear stress (slip lines); (*c*) is the Mohr's circle for this case. The maximum shear stress is $(s_1 - s_2)/2 = s_{s\,yield}$; the normal stress along the faces 3 and 4 is the same and equal to $(s_1 + s_2)/2$.

while the other principal stress at those points is zero. Therefore as soon as *p* reaches the value s_{yield} (which by Mohr's circle equals $2s_{s\,yield}$), then plastic flow will start under the knife-edge. The question is how much larger *p* can be made before the knife-edge sinks way into the material. In solving the problem of Fig. 143 we shall find that the plastic region has the shape of Fig. 146 and that the plastic stress distribution in it can be expressed by two simple solutions of the plastic problem. The first solution, valid in the triangular regions I and III of Fig. 146, is simple indeed: the stresses are the same at all points of the region, the directions of the principal stress s_1 and s_2 are everywhere the same, and $s_1 - s_2 = 2s_{s\,yield}$.

This *uniform field of plastic stress* is illustrated in Fig. 144; the plastic flow of such a field is visualized as a slipping of the lines 3 and 4 of maximum shear stress: they are called the slip lines.

The second solution, governing region II in Fig. 146, is the solution of the *plastic sector*, expressed most easily in polar coordinates (Fig. 121). The two equations of equilibrium are Eqs. (102) (page 185), reprinted:

$$\frac{\partial s_t}{\partial \theta} + 2s_s + r\frac{\partial s_s}{\partial r} = 0$$

$$(s_r - s_t) + r\frac{\partial s_r}{\partial r} + \frac{\partial s_s}{\partial \theta} = 0 \tag{102}$$

and the plasticity condition is (page 203)

$$\left(\frac{s_t - s_r}{2}\right)^2 + s_s^2 = s_{s\,\text{yield}}^2 \tag{115a}$$

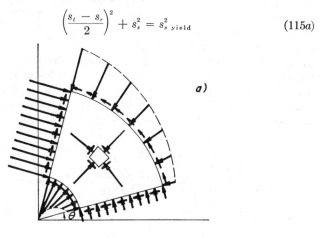

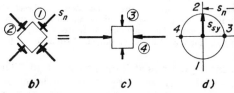

FIG. 145.   The plastic circular sector. (*b*) is an element cut out radially-tangentially, with normal stress s_n on *both* faces and maximum shear stresses; (*c*) is the same element cut out at 45 deg with respect to the radius, the principal stresses being $s_n \pm s_{sy}$; (*d*) is the Mohr's circle governing the stress.

Prandtl and Hencky noted that a solution of these equations could be found by assuming that $s_t = s_r$ at each point. Call this stress the normal stress $s_n(= s_t = s_r)$. The normal stress s_n is not the same everywhere; it is assumed to vary with θ only, but to be constant with r. With these assumptions the stresses at each point are described by s_n and s_s, but by Eq. (115a) $s_s = s_{s\ yield}$, constant everywhere. The equilibrium equations (102) simplify to

$$\frac{ds_n}{d\theta} + 2s_{sy} + 0 = 0$$

$$0 + 0 + 0 = 0$$

Integrating,

$$s_n = -2s_{sy} \int d\theta = -2s_{sy}\theta$$

The field of stress is illustrated in Fig. 145. A study of this figure reveals that the lines of maximum shear stress (*i.e.*, the slip lines) are radii and concentric circles, whereas the principal stress trajectories are spirals cutting the radii at 45 deg. The maximum shear stress is constant in magnitude all over the field, while the normal stress radially and tangentially s_n grows with the angular location θ,

$$s_n = -2s_{sy}\theta \qquad (117)$$

and the principal stresses are

$$s_{1,2} = s_n \pm s_{sy} = s_{sy}(\pm 1 - 2\theta)$$

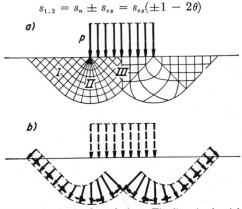

Fig. 146. The plastic blunt-knife-edge solution. The lines in the right half of (*a*) are principal stress trajectories; those in the left half are slip lines or lines of maximum shear stress, located at 45 deg with respect to the principal stress trajectories. (*b*) shows the loads transmitted by the plastic region to the underlying elastic region.

In this case (Fig. 145) the normal stress s_n grows with θ counterclockwise, but another solution where s_n grows clockwise with $-\theta$ also exists, of course. When proceeding with θ or $-\theta$ in the direction of growing s_n, the Mohr's circle (Fig. 145d) displaces itself to the left, but its size remains constant.

Now we are ready to build up Fig. 146 for the blunt-edge solution. When plasticity is fully developed, the plastic region is as shown, consisting of three triangles I, III with a uniformly plastic state and two quarter circles II in which we have the stress distribution of Fig. 145. To construct that figure, we start with region I, and we see (Fig. 146a) that the stress on the upper vertical boundary is zero. Since the region is plastic, the other stress must be $2s_{sy}$, as shown in the top figure of Fig. 147. This state of stress is the same all over the region I and also at the left boundary of region II. When we look at an element of region II, the normal stress (radial and tangential) depends on the distance θ, growing at the rate $2s_{sy}\theta$. For example, if we look at an element in the center of sector II, we have turned 45 deg $= \pi/4$ from region I, and the normal stress will be $2(\pi/4)s_{sy}$ larger than in region I. In region I it was s_{sy}, so that in the center of II it is $[1 + (\pi/2)]s_{sy}$. The shear stress remains s_{sy}. This is shown in the middle line of Fig. 147. If we now go to a point at the right boundary of region II, we have turned through 90 deg $= \pi/2$ since we left region I; hence the third line of Fig. 147. The latter state of stress is

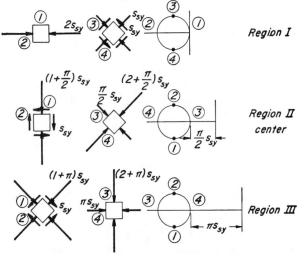

Region I

Region II center

Region III

FIG. 147. Stresses on an element in three different locations in the plastic region of Fig. 146 with their Mohr's circles. The diameter of all Mohr's circles is always equal to $2s_{sy}$.

uniform all over the region III. We end up with the result that the pressure p of the knife-edge is $(2 + \pi)s_{sy} = [1 + (\pi/2)]2s_{sy} = 2.57 \times 2s_{sy}$, or 2.57 times the pressure required to start the yield in the first place.

This completes the discussion of two examples in *plane* plasticity. It is remarked once more that both were solved by using the two equilibrium equations and the condition of plasticity between the stresses. Thus the two-dimensional plastic problem is statically determined. Recently this entire subject has been in a state of active development, and interested readers are referred to a book by R. Hill, entitled "Plasticity" (Oxford University Press, New York, 1950).

Problems 113 *to* 138.

CHAPTER VII

THE ENERGY METHOD

31. The Three Energy Theorems. Three propositions or theorems related to elastic energy are often used. They are known as the theorems of "virtual work," "Castigliano," and "least work," and they are sufficiently similar to be often confused with each other by beginners, but there are distinct differences between them.

The *theorem of work*, or "virtual work," states that if an elastic body or system in equilibrium is given a small displacement or deformation, then the work done by all external forces acting on the body equals the increase in elastic energy U stored in the body. If the small displacement (or "virtual" displacement as it is sometimes called) happens to be a displacement $d\delta_n$ in a direction to absorb work from one of the external forces P_n, while the other external forces do not do any work, then the theorem is expressed by

$$dU = P_n \, d\delta_n$$

or

$$\frac{\partial U}{\partial \delta_n} = P_n \tag{118}$$

in which U is expressed in terms of the displacements δ of the body, so that the loads P do not appear in the expression for U.

The *theorem of Castigliano* states that if the energy U stored in a sufficiently supported elastic system is expressed in terms of the loads P acting on it (and hence does not contain the displacements δ), then the change in energy caused by a small unit change in one of the loads equals the work-absorbing component of displacement under that load, or

$$\frac{\partial U}{\partial P_n} = \delta_n \tag{119}$$

The *theorem of least work* states that among all stress distributions in an elastic body or system which satisfy equilibrium, but which do not necessarily satisfy compatibility, the true or compatible stress distribution has the least elastic energy in the system, all other non-compatible stress distributions having greater energy than the true one.

Before giving any proofs for these theorems we shall illustrate their

operation on some examples, and we start with a simple cantilever beam
(Fig. 148). The bending moment is Px, and hence the curvature in the
beam is

$$y'' = \frac{Px}{EI}$$

The stored energy is

$$U = \frac{EI}{2} \int_0^l (y'')^2 \, dx = \frac{EI}{2} \left(\frac{P}{EI}\right)^2 \int_0^l x^2 \, dx = \frac{P^2 l^3}{6EI}$$

The energy is now expressed in terms of the
load, and thus it is in a form fit for the application of Castigliano's theorem [Eq. (119)]:

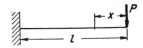

$$\frac{\partial U}{\partial P} = \frac{\partial}{\partial P} \left(\frac{P^2 l^3}{6EI}\right) = \frac{Pl^3}{3EI}$$

Fig. 148. Simple cantilever
for explaining the difference
between Eqs. (118) and (119).

which, by Castigliano, is the work-absorbing
deflection under P, that is, the vertical deflection under P.

In order to apply the virtual-work theorem [Eq. (118)], we must express
U in terms of the end deflection, which we pretend not to know. We
have elasticity so that $\delta = kP$, where k is a proportionality constant.
Then the energy can be written as

$$U = \frac{P^2 l^3}{6EI} = \frac{\delta^2 l^3}{6EIk^2}$$

in terms of the end deflection. By Eq. (118) we have

$$\frac{\partial U}{\partial \delta} = \frac{\delta l^3}{3EIk^2} = P \quad \text{or} \quad \frac{l^3}{3EIk} \frac{\delta}{k} = P$$

But $\delta/k = P$, so that $l^3/3EIk = 1$ and

$$k = \frac{\delta}{P} = \frac{l^3}{3EI}$$

the same result as before. In this illustration the theorem of Castigliano
is simple and direct, while the theorem of virtual work leads to more algebra
than the result is worth.

Castigliano's theorem is often applied to statically indeterminate systems, such as that of Fig. 149. We name the redundant support reaction
X and write the bending moments in the beam, then calculate the energy
U, which comes out as a function of the loads P and X. Castigliano then
says

$$\frac{\partial U(P, X)}{\partial X} = \delta_X$$

and this end deflection was required to be zero by the setup. From

$$\frac{\partial U(P, X)}{\partial X} = 0 \qquad (a)$$

we can calculate the support reaction X and further solve the problem. With the theorem of least work we again use the same Eq. (a), but our reasoning is different. We note that the cantilever of Fig. 149 is in equilib-

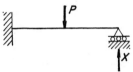

FIG. 149. Cantilever with end support, subjected to a single load. For this example the theorem of Castigliano and that of least work show the same formula (a), but with different explanations in the two cases.

rium for *any* values of P and X, so that all stress distributions in the system for the given load P and for all possible values of X are statically correct. All of these stress distributions give different end deflections δ_X, and only one among them gives $\delta = 0$, which is the one stress distribution compatible with the geometry of the system. In the expression $U(P, X)$ of the energy we can now regard X as an algebraic parameter defining the various energies. Among these the smallest or that having least energy is the correct one, and Eq. (a) expresses

that for variable X the energy U is extreme: either maximum or minimum. Physically we can recognize that for $\delta = 0$ the energy is a minimum and not a maximum, because for $X = 0$ the beam sags far down and has much energy, while for a large X the beam is bent up and again has much energy. For the correct in-between value the energy certainly is smaller than for the two extreme cases just described. But it can easily be proved that the energy from Eq. (a) is a minimum and not a maximum for this case, as follows: Using influence numbers on Fig. 149, we write for the downward deflection under P

$$\delta_P = \alpha_{11}P - \alpha_{12}X$$

and for the upward deflection at X

$$\delta_X = \alpha_{22}X - \alpha_{21}P$$

The work stored is the sum of the work performed by P and by X, both growing gradually from zero to their full value,

$$U = \tfrac{1}{2}P\,\delta_P + \tfrac{1}{2}X\,\delta_X$$
$$= \tfrac{1}{2}\alpha_{11}P^2 + \tfrac{1}{2}\alpha_{22}X^2 - \alpha_{12}XP$$

because we remember from Maxwell's theorem that $\alpha_{12} = \alpha_{21}$. All influence numbers in this expression are positive numbers, which can be recognized from their definition and physical meaning. Now, keeping P constant and varying X, we find

$$\frac{\partial U}{\partial X} = \alpha_{22}X - \alpha_{12}P$$

and

$$\frac{\partial^2 U}{\partial X^2} = \alpha_{22}$$

which is positive. From the calculus and from Fig. 150 we see that a positive second derivative (for a zero first derivative) means a minimum.

Each of the three theorems has a field of application for which it is useful. *Castigliano's* theorem is appropriate when deflections of beams or other structures are required or for finding the redundant reactions of statically indeterminate systems, as in the examples Figs. 148 and 149. In the latter case Castigliano's theorem is practically the same as the theorem of least work.

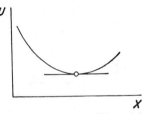

FIG. 150. The energy U is a minimum when $dU/dX = 0$ and when d^2U/dX^2 is positive.

The theorem of *least work*, however, is much more far-reaching than this, and it is most useful in rather complicated cases of stress distribution when an approximate solution is wanted. We shall see several examples of this in the next few pages, of which the crowning one is the curved steam pipe of pages 235 to 245.

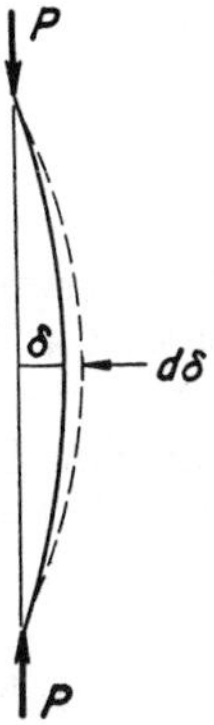

The theorem of *virtual work* does duty particularly in complicated cases of buckling, discussed in the next chapter. The principle is best explained by means of the familiar Euler column (Fig. 151). Let that column be straight originally, and let us consider it while slightly buckled with a central deflection δ under the buckling load P_{crit}. Then the column is given a small displacement increasing the deflection from δ to $\delta + d\delta$. This causes greater curvature and hence greater energy. Also it causes the two points of application of P_{crit} to move closer together, so that the pair of forces does work. Equating this work (which is proportional to P_{crit}) to the increment in elastic energy (which is independent of P_{crit} and depends on $d\delta$ only) gives an equation from which the critical load can be calculated.

FIG. 151. An Euler column is in a state of indifferent equilibrium under the buckling load P_{crit}. This load can be found by applying the theorem of virtual work to a small displacement being an increment $d\delta$ of the buckled shape.

The details of this process are shown on page 252, and the general procedure is repeated in many places in the next chapter.

Non-linear Elastic Materials. To show that there is a substantial difference between the theorems of virtual work and of Castigliano, we apply them to a cantilever beam (Fig. 148) in which the material does not obey Hooke's law, so that the relation between force and deflection is as in Fig. 152. The material is assumed to be still "elastic," *i.e.*, when the

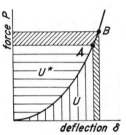

force P is diminished it goes back along the same $P\delta$ curve as it went up on, without enclosing a hysteresis loop. No energy is converted into heat; work done by the force is stored in elastic energy, which is recoverable without loss. The work done by the force in increasing from zero to P_A is

Fig. 152. Force-deflection curve for a cantilever of a non-Hooke's-law elastic material. The stored energy is U, the area under the curve; the area U^* to the left of the curve is called the "complementary energy." The principle of virtual work holds for the energy U; Castigliano's theorem holds only for the complementary energy U^*. The material is said to be "elastic" if, when slacking off the load, the deflection δ goes back along the same curve as it went up on, without enclosing a "hysteresis loop."

$$U = \int P \, d\delta$$

It is stored as elastic energy U and is indicated by the vertically shaded area of Fig. 152. Another integral can be formed:

$$U^* = \int \delta \, dP$$

It is shown by horizontal shading in the figure, and it has been given the name "complementary energy" by Westergaard, because it is not an energy although it has the same dimension as one. Now from the above definitions we see, purely mathematically, that $dU = P \, d\delta$, shown by the strip vertically under AB in Fig. 152, and $dU^* = \delta \, dP$, shown by the strip horizontally to the left of AB. From the first we conclude that

$$\frac{dU}{d\delta} = P$$

which is the theorem of virtual work. Hence that theorem holds for our cantilever beam even for non-linear material. Indeed the theorem is based on the very definition of work and is always true so long as no energy is dissipated in heat. On the other hand, from the horizontal strip in Fig. 152 we have

$$\frac{dU^*}{dP} = \delta$$

Castigliano states that $dU/dP = \delta$, and since U and U^* are different, we see that *Castigliano's theorem does not hold for non-linear materials.* For a material obeying Hooke's law, the curve of Fig. 152 is a straight line, and $U = U^*$, so that we can say that Castigliano's theorem [Eq. (119)] is true for linear materials only, while for non-dissipative, non-linear materials it is true only if applied to the complementary energy U^*, instead of to the energy U itself. Since we have seen on the example of Fig. 149 that the theorem of least work sometimes is expressed by the same equation as Castigliano's theorem, it follows that the theorem of least work also is restricted to Hooke's-law materials, and does not hold for non-linear materials. All of this is of no great practical importance, because we are unable to calculate much with non-linear materials anyhow, but it serves to illustrate the fact that the theorem of virtual work is quite different from that of least work or Castigliano.

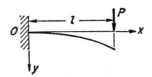

FIG. 153. The deflection curve of a cantilever or other beam can be represented by a Fourier series with unknown coefficients. By applying the theorem of virtual work these coefficients can be calculated, and the shape of the deflection curve can be determined.

Timoshenko's Method of Trigonometric Series. The theorem of virtual work has been applied by Timoshenko in connection with Fourier series, as will now be shown on the example of a cantilever beam (Fig. 153). Suppose that we did not know the shape of the deflection curve, we might try to represent it by a Fourier series, and we would fit each individual term of the Fourier series to the known boundary conditions:

$$y = b_1\left(1 - \cos\frac{\pi x}{2l}\right) + b_3\left(1 - \cos\frac{3\pi x}{2l}\right) + b_5\left(1 - \cos\frac{5\pi x}{2l}\right) + \cdots$$

$$= \sum_{1,3,5,\ldots} b_n\left(1 - \cos\frac{n\pi x}{2l}\right)$$

Any one of the terms has zero amplitude at O, is tangent at O, and has zero curvature y'' at the load P. The size of the various coefficients b_1, b_3, b_5, etc., determines the shape of the curve, and we pretend that we do not know the curve. Now we calculate the energy in the beam:

$$U = \frac{EI}{2}\int_0^l (y'')^2\, dx$$

The curvature y'' is found by differentiating twice:

$$y'' = \sum_{1,3,5} b_n\left(\frac{n\pi}{2l}\right)^2 \cos\frac{n\pi x}{2l}$$

In squaring this expression we get all the square terms $\cos^2 (n\pi x/2l)$ and also all the mixed terms $\cos (n\pi x/2l) \cos (m\pi x/2l)$. Readers familiar with Fourier series know that

$$\int_0^l \cos\frac{n\pi x}{2l} \cos\frac{m\pi x}{2l}\, dx = 0 \qquad \text{(for } n \neq m)$$

and that

$$\int_0^l \cos^2 \frac{n\pi x}{2l}\, dx = \frac{l}{2}$$

Thus the energy becomes

$$U = \frac{EI}{2} \sum_{1,3,5} \int_0^l b_n^2 \left(\frac{n\pi}{2l}\right)^4 \cos^2 \frac{n\pi x}{2l}\, dx$$

$$= \frac{EI}{2} \sum_{1,3,5} b_n^2 \left(\frac{n\pi}{2l}\right)^4 \frac{l}{2} = \sum_{1,3,5} b_n^2 \frac{n^4 \pi^4}{64 l^3} EI$$

Now this energy is expressed in terms of the b_n's, which are *deflections*. The load P does not appear in it, so that U is in the form fit for an application of the theorem of virtual work [Eq. (118)]. The small displacement we give the beam now consists in changing one coefficient b_n to $b_n + db_n$ and in leaving all other coefficients b unchanged. Because of this change the end deflection $(x = l)$ of the beam changes by

$$db_n \left(1 - \cos n \frac{\pi l}{2l}\right) = db_n$$

because $\cos n(\pi/2) = 0$ for $n = 1, 3, 5$, etc. The work done by the "external forces" is $P\, db_n$, and this work equals the change in U due to the increment db_n:

$$P = \frac{\partial U}{\partial b_n} = 2b_n \frac{n^4 \pi^4}{64 l^3} EI$$

We note that of all the terms in the $\sum$ of U only one term, b_n, changes; hence $\partial U/\partial b_n$ has only one term. Now from the above result we find

$$b_n = \frac{P l^3}{EI} \frac{32}{\pi^4 n^4}$$

which gives us the coefficient b_n, and this result is true of course for any value $n = 1, 3, 5$, etc. Hence the deflection curve of the cantilever beam is

$$y = \frac{P l^3}{EI} \frac{32}{\pi^4} \sum_{1,3,5} \frac{1}{n^4} \left(1 - \cos n \frac{\pi x}{2l}\right)$$

and in particular the end deflection is

$$\delta = (y)_{x=l} = \frac{P l^3}{EI} \frac{32}{\pi^4} \left[1 + \frac{1}{3^4} + \frac{1}{5^4} + \frac{1}{7^4} + \cdots\right]$$

Taking the first three terms of the series we find $\delta = P l^3/3.001 EI$, while the exact solution has the coefficient 3. In fact the *infinite* series is an exact answer, so that we have

$$\frac{\pi^4}{96} = 1 + \frac{1}{3^4} + \frac{1}{5^4} + \frac{1}{7^4} + \cdots$$

which is of curious interest mathematically. By taking beams of other support conditions and applying the same procedure, other similar series have been found. The practical value of the procedure lies in cases of beams of variable cross section EI, in which the integrations of the beam equation $EIy'' = M$ may be difficult and this method offers a new approach.

32. Examples on Least Work. The theorem of least work, for which a proof will be given on pages 230 to 234 is a powerful tool often applied in publications on elasticity and strength of materials these days, but it is not a simple tool. The amount of algebraic work involved usually is discouragingly large even for the simpler cases. However, some important results, such as the curved steam pipe of page 243, have been obtained with it that cannot be reproduced conveniently with any other method of attack, which makes the method very much worth while. In this section we shall apply the theorem by way of illustration to three cases of which the exact solution is already known, before embarking on the case of page 235, for which no answer is known except the one obtained by least work.

Distribution of Bending Stress in a Straight Beam of Rectangular Cross Section. We know that the answer for this case is a linear stress distribution, proportional to the distance from the neutral line through the center of gravity. Now we pretend not to know this, but we can reason that the distribution at least must be symmetrical about the center line. The simplest expression for such a symmetrical distribution, containing one arbitrary parameter, is (Fig. 154)

$$s_x = C_1(y + C_2 y^3)$$

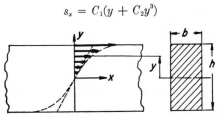

Fig. 154. A straight beam of rectangular section in pure bending. The bending stress is assumed to consist of a linear and a cubic term $s = C_1(y + C_2 y^3)$, and then the parameter C_2 is determined by the method of least work. The answer, of course, is $C_2 = 0$.

Here C_1 is a size constant, and C_2 is a parameter determining the type of distribution. The other stresses s_y and s_s are supposed to be zero throughout. First we verify that these stress distributions all satisfy the equilibrium equations (99) (page 173), independent of the values of C_1 and C_2.

The size constant C_1 is determined by the size of the bending moment M_0 on the beam as follows:

$$M_0 = \int_{-h/2}^{+h/2} s_x y \, dA = bC_1 \int_{-h/2}^{+h/2} (y + C_2 y^3) y \, dy$$

$$M_0 = bC_1 \left[\frac{h^3}{12} + C_2 \frac{h^5}{80} \right] \tag{a}$$

Solving for C_1 and substituting into the expression for the stress:

$$s_x = \frac{12M_0(y + C_2 y^3)}{bh^3(1 + \frac{3}{20}C_2 h^2)} \tag{b}$$

From Fig. 154 we see the meaning of the parameter C_2: if $C_2 = 0$, the stress distribution is purely linear; if $C_2 = \infty$, it is purely cubic; and for other values of C_2 it is mixed. We pretend not to know whether or not the exact stress distribution is present among the ones contained in Eq. (b), but we shall calculate the energy involved and find the value of C_2 for which that energy becomes a minimum. Then, if the exact solution happens to be contained in Eq. (b), we have found it; if not, we have a solution which is a decent approximation to the truth, as decent an approximation as can be obtained with *one* parameter at our disposal.

The energy of the beam of length l is

$$U = \frac{1}{2E} \int s_x^2 \, d \, \text{vol} = \frac{bl}{2E} \int_{-h/2}^{+h/2} s_x^2 \, dy = \text{by Eq. (a)}$$

$$= \frac{72M_0^2 l}{bh^6 E(1 + \frac{3}{20}C_2 h^2)^2} \int_{-h/2}^{+h/2} (y + C_2 y^3)^2 \, dy$$

$$= \left(\frac{72M_0^2 l}{bh^6 E} \frac{h^3}{12} \right) \frac{1 + \frac{3}{10}C_2 h^2 + \frac{3}{112}C_2^2 h^4}{(1 + \frac{3}{20}C_2 h^2)^2}$$

$$U = (\text{const}) \left(\frac{\text{Num}}{\text{Den}} \right)$$

This energy depends on the parameter C_2. It becomes extreme (either maximum or minimum) for

$$\frac{d}{dC_2} \frac{\text{Num}}{\text{Den}} = 0 = \text{Num} \frac{d}{dC_2} \text{Den} - \text{Den} \frac{d}{dC_2} \text{Num}$$

The reader should work out the algebra on a sheet of paper and note that a factor $1 + \frac{3}{20}C_2 h^2$ can be divided out. The remaining expression assumes the form $a_1 C_2^2 + a_2 C_2 + a_3$, in which the coefficients a_1 and a_3 are zero, so that we find $C_2 = 0$, a purely linear stress distribution, as expected, because we knew the answer to start with. The other root C_2 arising from the factor $1 + \frac{3}{20}C_2 h^2$ which was divided out, means that the square brackets in Eq. (a) becomes zero, and for a finite bending moment this means an infinite C_1, hence an infinite stress and infinite energy U. This then obviously is a maximum for the energy, instead of a minimum, and it must be ruled out by the statement of the theorem of *least* work.

Thick Cylinder with Internal Pressure. Our second example is the stress distribution in a cylinder r_i, r_0 under internal pressure p_i. The solution to this case is known and given in Eqs. (41) (page 54). We pretend not to know this, and write a solution for the stresses which satisfies equilibrium and which contains one arbitrary parameter. There are two equilibrium conditions to be satisfied: first, radial equilibrium of an element, expressed by Eq. (35) (page 50) (in which $\rho\omega^2 = 0$; no rotation); second, the tangential

Fig. 155. The tangential stress in a thick cylinder must keep equilibrium with the prescribed internal pressure p_i or

$$p_i r_i = \int_{r_i}^{r_0} s_t \, dr$$

equilibrium of Fig. 155. In order then to have an extra free parameter we must start with three and assume for the tangential stress

$$s_t = C_1 + C_2 r + C_3 r^2 \tag{c}$$

Then, satisfying the two equilibrium conditions, we can derive expressions for the stresses s_t and s_r in terms of a single parameter, and we can proceed

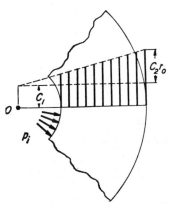

Fig. 156. Thick cylinder with an assumed linear tangential-stress distribution. The radial stress is arbitrarily assumed to be zero.

as in the previous example. The algebra involved in this process is very large in amount, although not difficult, and the process leads to a very good answer. We shall not apply it now but shall proceed in a simpler but much cruder manner. We say that of the two stresses s_t and s_r the tangential one s_t is more important, especially for reasonably thin-walled tubes. Now we take $s_r = 0$ for simplicity and work with s_t only. Then we need one parameter less, and we write

$$s_t = C_1 + C_2 r$$
$$s_r = 0$$

as illustrated in Fig. 156. Applying the equilibrium criterion of Fig. 155,

$$p_i r_i = \int_{r_i}^{r_0} (C_1 + C_2 r) \, dr = C_1(r_0 - r_i) + \frac{C_2}{2}(r_0^2 - r_i^2)$$

from which we determine C_1,

$$C_1 = \frac{p_i r_i}{r_0 - r_i} - \frac{C_2}{2}(r_0 + r_i)$$

and the stress distribution is

$$s_t = \frac{p_i r_i}{r_0 - r_i} + C_2\left(r - \frac{r_0 + r_i}{2}\right) \tag{d}$$

$$s_r = 0$$

Now this contains an arbitrary parameter C_2; it does satisfy the equilibrium condition of Fig. 155, but it violates the equilibrium equation (35) (page 50). Strictly speaking, therefore, the theorem of least work should not be applied, and any answer we may get will be out of equilibrium radially. But since s_t is the more important stress, we proceed anyhow.

The energy U is

$$U = \frac{1}{2E}\int s_t^2 \, d\text{vol} = \frac{1}{2E}\int s_t^2 \, r d\theta \, dr \, dl$$

$$= \frac{2\pi l}{2E}\int_{r_i}^{r_0} s_t^2 r \, dr$$

A slight simplification can be obtained by differentiating before integrating:

$$0 = \frac{\partial U}{\partial C_2} = \int_{r_i}^{r_0} s_t \frac{\partial s_t}{\partial C_2} r \, dr$$

$$0 = \int_{r_i}^{r_0}\left[\frac{p_i r_i}{r_0 - r_i} + C_2\left(r - \frac{r_0 + r_i}{2}\right)\right]\left(r - \frac{r_0 + r_i}{2}\right)r \, dr$$

Splitting this up into terms with and without C_2, we have

$$C_2 = -\frac{\dfrac{p_i r_i}{r_0 - r_i}\int\left(r - \dfrac{r_0 + r_i}{2}\right)r \, dr}{\int\left(r - \dfrac{r_0 + r_i}{2}\right)^2 r \, dr}$$

$$C_2 = -\frac{p_i r_i}{r_0 - r_i}\frac{\dfrac{r_0^3 - r_i^3}{3} - \dfrac{(r_0 + r_i)(r_0^2 - r_i^2)}{4}}{\dfrac{r_0^4 - r_i^4}{4} - \dfrac{(r_0 + r_i)(r_0^3 - r_i^3)}{3} + \dfrac{(r_0 + r_i)^2(r_0^2 - r_i^2)}{8}}$$

There is not much point in simplifying this expression: we do better to look at it numerically for a certain case. Take first $r_0/r_i = 2$, for which it becomes $C_2 = -\frac{2}{3}(p_i/r_i)$, and the stresses at the inside and outside radii are, by Eq. (d),

$$\frac{r_0}{r_i} = 2 \qquad (s_t)_{\text{inside}} = \frac{4}{3}p_i \qquad (s_t)_{\text{outside}} = \frac{2}{3}p_i$$

The exact solution for this case, by Eqs. (41) (page 54), is

$$\frac{r_0}{r_i} = 2 \qquad (s_t)_{\text{inside}} = \frac{5}{3}\, p_i \qquad (s_t)_{\text{outside}} = \frac{2}{3}\, p_i$$

For a cylinder of smaller wall thickness the agreement is even better:

Least work: $\qquad \dfrac{r_0}{r_i} = \dfrac{3}{2} \qquad (s_t)_{\text{inside}} = \dfrac{12}{5}\, p_i \qquad (s_t)_{\text{outside}} = \dfrac{8}{5}\, p_i$

Exact: $\qquad\quad \dfrac{r_0}{r_i} = \dfrac{3}{2} \qquad (s_t)_{\text{inside}} = \dfrac{13}{5}\, p_i \qquad (s_t)_{\text{outside}} = \dfrac{8}{5}\, p_i$

These cases are shown in Fig. 157. We note that the least-work solution agrees closely with the exact one but does not follow it precisely. The one is linear, and the other is curved. The solution is necessarily approximate because the assumptions (d) do not include the exact stress distribution. In view of the fact that we fudged the radial-equilibrium condition, the agreement of Fig. 157 is remarkably good.

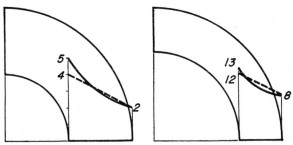

Fig. 157. Tangential-stress distribution in thick cylinders under internal pressure. The full lines give the exact solution, and the dashed ones the approximate solution with the method of least work. The area under the exact curve always equals that under the approximate one because of the equilibrium requirement of Fig. 155.

Bending-stress Distribution in a Curved Bar. The third example to be discussed is the bending of a curved bar in its own plane (Fig. 158) of which we know that the stress distribution is not linear. We write for the bending stress

$$s_t = C_1 z + (C_0 + C_2 z^2)$$

of which the first term is a linear bending distribution (Fig. 158a) and the term in the parentheses is a parabolic stress, symmetrical about the center line of the bar. For pure bending the total tangential force over a section between r_i and r_0 should be zero; the first term $C_1 z$ does that automatically, and now we adjust C_0 and C_2 so that the net force of the parabolic distribution also is zero,

$$\int_{-h/2}^{+h/2} (C_0 + C_2 z^2)\, dz = 0 = C_0 h + C_2 \frac{h^3}{12}$$

or

$$C_2 = -\frac{12 C_0}{h^2}$$

and the stress distribution is

$$s_t = C_1 \left[z + \frac{C_0}{C_1}\left(1 - 12\,\frac{z^2}{h^2}\right)\right]$$

The size constant C_1 determines the bending moment M_0:

$$M_0 = b \int_{-h/2}^{+h/2} s_t z\, dz = C_1 \frac{bh^3}{12} \qquad \text{or} \qquad C_1 = \frac{12 M_0}{bh^3}$$

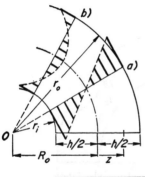

The term $1 - 12(z^2/h^2)$ does not give any bending, as is obvious from looking at b in Fig. 158. Renaming $C_0/C_1 = A$ for short, the bending stress is

$$s_t = \frac{12 M_0}{bh^3}\left[z + A\left(1 - 12\,\frac{z^2}{h^2}\right)\right] \qquad (e)$$

This contains one parameter A, which makes the stress distribution vary from type a, Fig. 158, for $A = 0$ to type b for $A = \infty$. Now this set of stresses s_t by itself is *not* in equilibrium, which we recognize by considering a thin curved string element about O as center. The ends are pulled and are not in line, so that a radial stress is necessary to hold the string. Mathematically this is expressed by the equilibrium equation (35) (page 50) (for $\omega^2 = 0$), from which s_r can be calculated. But when we do that and specify that $s_r = 0$ on $r = r_i$ and $r = r_0$, we find that the parameter A in Eq. (e) becomes fixed instead of floating. Just as in the previous example, we should have started off with one extra parameter in expression (e) to get a good solution. This is a great labor, so that here, as previously, we assume the comparatively unimportant radial stress to be zero, so that Eq. (e) represents the complete stress picture,

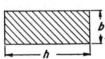

Fig. 158. Curved beam of rectangular cross section bh and mean radius of curvature R_0. The tangential-stress distribution is assumed to be the superposition of a linear one (a) and a parabolic one (b) which is so adjusted that the total tangential force is zero. This is expressed by Eq. (e).

even if it is somewhat out of equilibrium. Then

$$U = \frac{1}{2E} \int s_t^2 \, dvol = \frac{1}{2E} \int s_t^2 \, rd\theta \, b \, dr$$

$$= \frac{b\theta}{2E} \left(\frac{12M_0}{bh^3}\right)^2 \int \left[z + A\left(1 - 12\frac{z^2}{h^2}\right)\right]^2 r \, dr$$

But $r = R_0 + z$ (Fig. 158) so that

$$U = \text{const} \int_{-h/2}^{+h/2} \left[z + A\left(1 - 12\frac{z^2}{h^2}\right)\right]^2 (R_0 + z) \, dz$$

For least work

$$\frac{\partial U}{\partial A} = 0 = \int_{-h/2}^{+h/2} \frac{\partial}{\partial A}(s_t^2) \, dvol$$

$$0 = \int_{-h/2}^{+h/2} \left[z + A\left(1 - 12\frac{z^2}{h^2}\right)\right]\left(1 - 12\frac{z^2}{h^2}\right)(R_0 + z) \, dz$$

Splitting this into terms containing A and independent of A, we find

$$-A = \frac{I_1}{I_2} = \frac{\displaystyle\int_{-h/2}^{+h/2} z\left(1 - 12\frac{z^2}{h^2}\right)(R_0 + z) \, dz}{\displaystyle\int_{-h/2}^{+h/2} \left(1 - 12\frac{z^2}{h^2}\right)^2 (R_0 + z) \, dz}$$

These integrals are easily evaluated. We recognize that

$$\int_{-h/2}^{+h/2} z^{2n+1} \, dz = 0$$

for when the power of z in the integrand is odd, the integrand curve is symmetrical about the center of the z system and the integral is zero. Therefore we calculate only even powers of z in the integrands. Worked out, we find for I_1, the numerator integral,

$$I_1 = \int z^2\left(1 - 12\frac{z^2}{h^2}\right) dz = \frac{z^3}{3} - \frac{12}{5}\frac{z^5}{h^2} \bigg|_{-h/2}^{+h/2} = h^3\left(\frac{1}{12} - \frac{3}{20}\right) = -\frac{h^3}{15}$$

and the denominator integral

$$I_2 = \int \left(1 - 12\frac{z^2}{h^2}\right)^2 R_0 \, dz = R_0\left[z - 8\frac{z^3}{h^2} + \frac{144}{5}\frac{z^5}{h^4}\right]_{-h/2}^{+h/2}$$

$$= R_0 h\left(1 - 2 + \frac{9}{5}\right) = \frac{4}{5}R_0 h$$

so that

$$A = -\frac{I_1}{I_2} = \frac{h^2}{12R_0}$$

The stress distribution is, by Eq. (*e*),

$$s_t = \frac{12M_0}{bh^3}\left(z + \frac{h^2}{12R_0} - \frac{z^2}{R_0}\right) \qquad (f)$$

The exact solution for this case is given by the complicated Eqs. (108) (page 189). Also in elementary books of strength of materials we find a "hyperbolic" stress distribution, based on the arbitrary assumption that plane cross sections remain plane (which they don't). The result (*f*) just obtained by the method of least work, even in its faulty form violating one equilibrium equation, is closer to the exact solution than the hyperbolic one. As an example consider the numerical case shown in Fig. 124 (page 190), where $r_0 = 3r_i$ or in our present notation $R_0 = h$. For that case the ratio between the tangential stress inside and outside (r_i and r_0 or in our present notation $z = -h/2$ and $+h/2$) is

-2.00 for the least-work solution, (*f*)

-2.03 for the exact solution, Eq. (108)

-2.09 for the "hyperbolic" solution

33. Proofs of the Theorems. *Maxwell's Reciprocal Relations.* Before embarking on the proofs of our three energy theorems we review Maxwell's reciprocity theorem, which states in symbols

$$\alpha_{12} = \alpha_{21} \qquad (120)$$

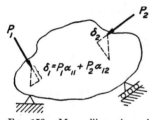

FIG. 159. Maxwell's reciprocal property $\alpha_{12} = \alpha_{21}$ is proved by equating the energy of this system, calculated in two ways: first, by putting on P_1 and then P_2; second, by putting on P_2 first and P_1 afterward.

and in words: In an elastic system obeying Hooke's law, the (work-absorbing component of the) deflection at location 1 caused by a unit force at location 2 equals the deflection at location 2 caused by a unit force at 1. For the proof we consider Fig. 159, a Hooke elastic system, just sufficiently supported. We put onto this system the load P_1. Since α_{11} and α_{21} are defined as the deflections at the location of the first subscript, caused by a unit force at the location of the second subscript, the load P_1 causes a deflection of $P_1\alpha_{11}$ at location 1 and of $P_1\alpha_{21}$ at location 2. The work done by this is $\frac{1}{2}P_1(P_1\alpha_{11})$ at location 1 and zero at location 2. Now we put on load P_2, causing additional deflections at 1 and 2 of $P_2\alpha_{12}$ and $P_2\alpha_{22}$, respectively. On the first of these deflections force P_1 is acting full strength and performs an amount of work $P_1(P_2\alpha_{12})$, while on the second deflection the force P_2 acts, growing from zero to full strength and hence performing work of $\frac{1}{2}P_2(P_2\alpha_{22})$. The total work on the system done thus far is $U = \frac{1}{2}P_1^2\alpha_{11} + P_1P_2\alpha_{12} + \frac{1}{2}P_2^2\alpha_{22}$. Now we start all over again from the unloaded system, and put on *first* P_2, then P_1, reversing the previous order. The work done is derived by the same argument, only now the subscripts 1 and 2 are reversed, so that $U = \frac{1}{2}P_2^2\alpha_{22} + P_2P_1\alpha_{21} + \frac{1}{2}P_1^2\alpha_{11}$. The work stored is a function of the final loads only, and not of the manner in which these loads are put on; and hence the above two amounts of work are equal, and by comparing the expressions we conclude that $\alpha_{12} = \alpha_{21}$, which completes the proof.

Three remarks are in order. First, the above argument is not restricted to locations 1 and 2 but holds generally so that $\alpha_{23} = \alpha_{32}$ and $\alpha_{mn} = \alpha_{nm}$.

The second remark is that in the proof all "deflections" were "work-absorbing components" of the actual deflections. If under a vertical load the point of support moves away partly horizontally, this horizontal displacement absorbs no work and is disregarded. The entire argument holds true if some of the "loads" are not forces but moments; in that case the corresponding "deflection" is the angle of rotation of the body at the point of application of the moment.

The third remark is that the proof holds true only for systems obeying Hooke's law. The very idea of influence number α implies deflections proportional to their forces, which is Hooke's law. Then again, when we say that the deflection due to P_2 is the same, whether or not P_1 was there first, we imply Hooke's law. Finally the factor $\frac{1}{2}$ before some of the expressions for work done implies Hooke's law, because for a case as shown in Fig. 152 that factor is not equal to $\frac{1}{2}$.

The Theorem of "Virtual" Work. Consider in Fig. 160 an elastic system, just sufficiently supported and subjected to a number of loads $P_1, P_2, \ldots, P_n$. The reactions at the supports automatically take such values that the system is in equilibrium. Call $\delta_1, \delta_2, \ldots, \delta_n$ the work-absorbing components of the displacements under those forces, *i.e.*, displacement components in the direction of a force P, or angles of rotation under a moment, as indicated in the figure. Now apply a (virtual) displacement to the system consisting of a change $d\delta_2$ in one of the displacements δ_2 only. all other dis-

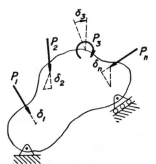

Fig. 160. The theorem of virtual work is proved by giving this system a displacement $d\delta_2$ and leaving all other δ's unchanged.

placements $\delta_1, \delta_3, \ldots, \delta_n$ being kept constant (this, of course, is not easy; in order to do it we have to change *all* the forces $P_1, P_2, \ldots, P_n$ by small amounts in a complicated way; however, we are not interested now in finding these force variations). In applying this "virtual" displacement the forces $P_1, P_3, \ldots, P_n$ do no work at all, because their points of application do not displace (at least not in the "work-absorbing" direction). The only force doing work is P_2, by an amount $P_2 \, d\delta_2$, plus a fraction of $dP_2 \, d\delta_2$, caused by the change in P_2. This latter amount is small of the second order and hence is negligible. The work $P_2 \, d\delta_2$, done by P_2 and hence by *all* external forces, is stored as extra elastic energy dU in the body, because we assumed the body to be "elastic." If that energy is expressed in terms of the displacements $\delta_1, \delta_2, \ldots, \delta_n$, and hence does not contain $P_1, \ldots, P_n$, then we can say

$$dU = P_2 \, d\delta_2 \quad \text{or} \quad \left(\frac{dU}{d\delta_2}\right)_{d\delta_1, d\delta_3, \ldots, d\delta_n = 0} = P_2$$

or in the usual shorthand notation of partial derivatives:

$$\frac{\partial U}{\partial \delta_2} = P_2$$

which is the theorem of virtual work. It holds true for all "elastic," *i.e.*, frictionless, materials, not only for those obeying Hooke's law, but also for those of the characteristic of Fig. 152.

For the special case of Hooke's law, there are certain linear relationships between the P's and the δ's which can be expressed best by influence numbers α. The deflection at location 1 caused by all the forces is

$$\delta_1 = \alpha_{11}P_1 + \alpha_{12}P_2 + \cdots + \alpha_{1n}P_n$$

Similarly we have

$$\delta_2 = \alpha_{21}P_1 + \alpha_{22}P_2 + \cdots + \alpha_{2n}P_n$$

$$\delta_3 = \alpha_{31}P_1 + \alpha_{32}P_2 + \cdots + \alpha_{3n}P_n$$

$$\cdots\cdots\cdots\cdots\cdots\cdots\cdots\cdots\cdots\cdots\cdots\cdots$$

$$\delta_n = \alpha_{n1}P_1 + \alpha_{n2}P_2 + \cdots + \alpha_{nn}P_n$$

This is a system of n linear relations between the δ's and the P's. If the α numbers are known and the deflections $\delta_1, \ldots, \delta_n$ are known, they can be considered as n linear algebraic equations in the unknowns $P_1, \ldots, P_n$, and they can be solved for the P's. The result can be written in the form

$$P_1 = \beta_{11}\delta_1 + \beta_{12}\delta_2 + \beta_{13}\delta_3 + \cdots + \beta_{1n}\delta_n$$

$$P_2 = \beta_{21}\delta_1 + \qquad \cdots \qquad + \beta_{2n}\delta_n$$

$$\cdots\cdots\cdots\cdots\cdots\cdots\cdots\cdots\cdots\cdots\cdots\cdots$$

$$P_n = \beta_{n1}\delta_1 + \qquad \cdots \qquad + \beta_{nn}\delta_n$$

where the β numbers have certain relations with the α numbers. These relations are quite complicated algebraically.

The meaning of α_{mn} is the deflection at location m caused by unit force at location n, all other forces being zero, while incidentally there are some deflections at other points as well. Vice versa, the meaning of β_{mn} is the force at location m necessary to cause unit deflection at location n, all other deflections being zero, while incidentally some forces are required at other points to bring about this desired state of deflections. The two definitions are completely reciprocal: the words "force" and "deflection" are interchanged between them. Without proving it in detail, we state that for the β's also we have

$$\beta_{mn} = \beta_{nm}$$

Now we write the work stored in the system Fig. 160. We apply first 1 per cent of P_1, 1 per cent of P_2, P_3, . . . , P_n, and then again 1 per cent of each, letting all forces grow gradually to their maximum value at the same rate. Since Hooke's proportionality law holds, all deflections also grow proportionally and the work done is

$$U = \tfrac{1}{2}P_1\delta_1 + \tfrac{1}{2}P_2\delta_2 + \cdots + \tfrac{1}{2}P_n\delta_n$$

In order to make this expression fit for the theorem of virtual work, it must be in terms of deflections only, while the forces must be out of it. We substitute the corresponding expressions for the forces:

$$U = \tfrac{1}{2}\delta_1(\beta_{11}\delta_1 + \beta_{12}\delta_2 + \cdots + \beta_{1n}\delta_n) + \tfrac{1}{2}\delta_2(\beta_{21}\delta_1 + \cdots + \beta_{2n}\delta_n)$$
$$+ \cdots + \tfrac{1}{2}\delta_n(\beta_{n1}\delta_1 + \cdots + \beta_{nn}\delta_n)$$

This is the form required: exclusively written in δ's, no P's appearing. Now

$$\frac{\partial U}{\partial \delta_2} = \frac{1}{2}\,\delta_1\beta_{12} + \frac{1}{2}\,(\beta_{21}\delta_1 + \beta_{23}\delta_3 + \cdots + \beta_{2n}\delta_n) + \beta_{22}\delta_2$$
$$+ \frac{1}{2}\,\delta_3\beta_{32} + \frac{1}{2}\,\delta_4\beta_{42} + \cdots + \frac{1}{2}\,\delta_n\beta_{n2}$$

By virtue of the fact that $\beta_{mn} = \beta_{nm}$ this becomes

$$\frac{\partial U}{\partial \delta_2} = \beta_{21}\delta_1 + \beta_{22}\delta_2 + \beta_{23}\delta_3 + \cdots + \beta_{2n}\delta_n$$

which we see is P_2, proving the theorem.

Proof of Castigliano's Theorem. This proof is simpler than the previous one: it is true only for linear systems obeying Hooke's law. Using the same Fig. 160 of the previous proof, we have for the energy again

$$U = \tfrac{1}{2}P_1\delta_1 + \tfrac{1}{2}P_2\delta_2 + \cdots + \tfrac{1}{2}P_n\delta_n$$

Whereas in the theorem of virtual work we needed U in terms of the displacements δ, we now need it in terms of the loads P. We thus substitute the expression of δ in terms of P:

$$U = \quad \tfrac{1}{2}P_1(\alpha_{11}P_1 + \alpha_{12}P_2 + \cdots + \alpha_{1n}P_n)$$
$$+ \tfrac{1}{2}P_2(\alpha_{21}P_1 + \alpha_{22}P_2 + \cdots + \alpha_{2n}P_n)$$
$$+ \cdots\cdots\cdots\cdots\cdots\cdots\cdots$$
$$+ \tfrac{1}{2}P_n(\alpha_{n1}P_1 + \alpha_{n2}P_2 + \cdots + \alpha_{nn}P_n)$$

Now we differentiate with respect to one of the P's, say P_3, leaving all other P's constant:

$$\frac{\partial U}{\partial P_3} = \frac{1}{2}P_1\alpha_{13} + \frac{1}{2}P_2\alpha_{23} + \frac{1}{2}(\alpha_{31}P_1 + \alpha_{32}P_2 + \alpha_{34}P_4 + \cdots + \alpha_{3n}P_n)$$
$$+ \alpha_{33}P_3 + \frac{1}{2}P_4\alpha_{43} + \frac{1}{2}P_5\alpha_{53} + \cdots + \frac{1}{2}P_n\alpha_{n3}$$

With the relations $\alpha_{mn} = \alpha_{nm}$, we can rearrange the terms,

$$\frac{\partial U}{\partial P_3} = \alpha_{31}P_1 + \alpha_{32}P_2 + \alpha_{33}P_3 + \alpha_{34}P_4 + \cdots + \alpha_{3n}P_n$$

which, by the definition of the α numbers, equals δ_3 and proves Castigliano's theorem.

Proof of the Theorem of Least Work. On page 214 it was shown that the application of Castigliano's theorem to statically indeterminate structures can be interpreted in terms of the theorem of least work. There the system consisted of beams, twisted bars, and such like, in which the stress distribution is entirely known, except for the few statically indeterminate quantities of the problem. The applications of the theorem of least work to the examples of pages 219 to 225, however, are to cases where the number of statically indeterminate quantities can be said to be infinity, because the stress distribution can vary infinitely within the limitations of equilibrium. The general proof of the property that in a Hooke elastic system the one true compatible stress distribution has less energy than all other equilibrium stress distributions is too complicated to be given here, and we shall restrict the proof to two-dimensional stress systems.

On page 174 we have seen that if plane stresses are derived by Eq. (100) from any arbitrary Φ function (not necessarily satisfying the biharmonic equation), we have a set of stresses satisfying the equilibrium equations. Now we shall calculate the energy stored in a flat disk by stresses due to an arbitrary Φ function, then minimize that energy by the methods of variational calculus, and find the biharmonic equation (101c) for Φ as an answer. This then will prove that among all possible equilibrium stress distributions (*i.e.*, among those derived from all possible Φ functions) the one true compatible stress distribution has the least energy.

First we must have an expression for the energy stored in an element

$dA = dx\,dy$ in the plane subject to stresses s_x, s_y and a shear stress s_s (Fig. 161). The strain in the x direction is $\epsilon_x = (s_x - \mu s_y)/E$, and the elongation of the element is $(s_x - \mu s_y)\,dx/E$. The force $s_x\,dy$ does work to the amount

$$\frac{1}{2} \cdot \text{force} \cdot \text{elongation} = \frac{1}{2}(s_x^2 - \mu s_x s_y)\frac{dA}{E}$$

Similarly the force $s_y\,dx$ in the y direction contributes

$$\frac{1}{2}(s_y^2 - \mu s_x s_y)\frac{dA}{E}$$

The work by the shear stresses is

$$\frac{1}{2}s_s\,dx\,\gamma\,dy = \frac{1}{2}s_s^2\frac{dA}{G} = \frac{1+\mu}{E}s_s^2\,dA$$

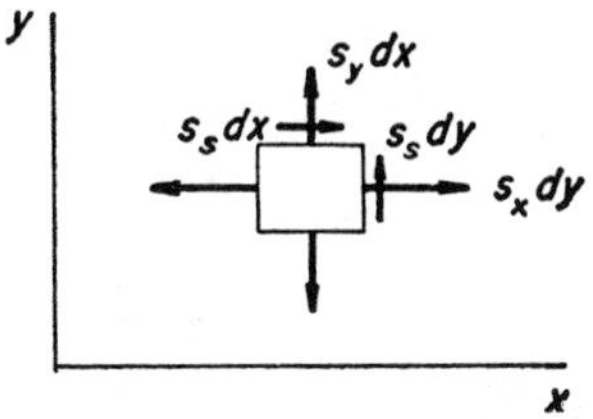

FIG. 161. An element $dx\,dy$ subjected to the stresses s_x, s_y, and s_s contains the strain energy given by Eq. (121).

Hence the energy stored in the element is

$$dU = \frac{dA}{2E}\left[s_x^2 + s_y^2 - 2\mu s_x s_y + 2(1+\mu)s_s^2\right] \tag{121}$$

With the definition equation (100) (page 174) of Airy's function the total energy of the plate is

$$U = \iint \frac{dx\,dy}{2E}\left[\left(\frac{\partial^2\Phi}{\partial x^2}\right)^2 + \left(\frac{\partial^2\Phi}{\partial y^2}\right)^2 - 2\mu\frac{\partial^2\Phi}{\partial x^2}\frac{\partial^2\Phi}{\partial y^2} + 2(1+\mu)\left(\frac{\partial^2\Phi}{\partial x\,\partial y}\right)^2\right] \tag{a}$$

which for short we shall call

$$U = \iint F\left(\frac{\partial^2\Phi}{\partial x^2},\,\frac{\partial^2\Phi}{\partial y^2},\,\frac{\partial^2\Phi}{\partial x\,\partial y}\right)dx\,dy$$

or still shorter

$$U = \iint F(\Phi_{xx},\,\Phi_{yy},\,\Phi_{xy})\,dx\,dy \tag{b}$$

Here Φ is an arbitrary function of x and y, but we now write

$$\Phi(x,y) = \Phi_0(x,y) + uf(x,y) \tag{c}$$

where Φ_0 is the correct, compatible, Airy stress function and $uf(x,y)$ is the variation from that function. This is a standard procedure in the "calculus of variations," for which the reader is referred to texts on advanced calculus. The function $f(x,y)$ is almost completely arbitrary; its only limitations are that f itself and its two slopes $\partial f/\partial x$ and $\partial f/\partial y$ have to be zero on the boundary of the plate (Fig. 162); in the interior of the plate $f(x,y)$ is entirely arbitrary. This function is multiplied by a very small real number u. By varying u and keeping $f(x,y)$ the same for the time being, we can make $\Phi(x, y)$ vary about the neighborhood of the true value $\Phi_0(x, y)$, and by this procedure we have reduced the variation of all these functions to the variation of a single number u. Now in forming the minimum energy we calculate dU/du or by Eqs. (b) and (c)

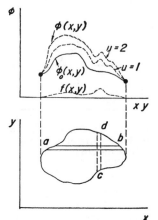

$$0 = \frac{dU}{du} = \iint \frac{dF}{du} \, dx \, dy$$

$$= \iint \left(\frac{\partial F}{\partial \Phi_{xx}} \frac{\partial \Phi_{xx}}{\partial u} + \frac{\partial F}{\partial \Phi_{yy}} \frac{\partial \Phi_{yy}}{\partial u} \right.$$

$$\left. + \frac{\partial F}{\partial \Phi_{xy}} \frac{\partial \Phi_{xy}}{\partial u} \right) dx \, dy$$

From Eq. (c) we have

$$\Phi_{xx} = \Phi_{0_{xx}} + u f_{xx}$$

and $\partial \Phi_{xx}/\partial u = f_{xx}$, which is shorthand for $\partial^2 f/\partial x^2$. Hence

$$0 = \iint \frac{\partial F}{\partial \Phi_{xx}} f_{xx} \, dx \, dy + \iint \frac{\partial F}{\partial \Phi_{yy}} f_{yy} \, dx \, dy$$

$$+ \iint \frac{\partial F}{\partial \Phi_{xy}} f_{xy} \, dx \, dy \qquad (d)$$

Fig. 162. The stress function and its variation. $\Phi_0(x, y)$ is the correct function we are looking for. Its deviations are expressed by Eq. (c), where $f(x, y)$ is an arbitrary function and u is a small real number, a parameter.

We shall start working out the first one of these three double integrals (see Fig. 162 for the limits):

$$\iint \frac{\partial F}{\partial \Phi_{xx}} f_{xx} \, dx \, dy = \int dy \int_a^b \frac{\partial F}{\partial \Phi_{xx}} f_{xx} \, dx = \int dy \left[\int_a^b \frac{\partial F}{\partial \Phi_{xx}} \, d(f_x) \right]$$

Integrating the inside bracketed integral by parts gives

$$\int dy \left[\frac{\partial F}{\partial \Phi_{xx}} f_x \, \Big|_a^b - \int_a^b f_x \frac{d}{dx} \left(\frac{\partial F}{\partial \Phi_{xx}} \right) dx \right]$$

Now the first term within square brackets is zero, because we have assumed our function f with zero slopes at the boundary, so that $f_x = \partial f/\partial x$ is zero at a and at b. On the second term within the square brackets we perform once more a partial integration:

$$- \int dy \int_a^b \frac{d}{dx} \left(\frac{\partial F}{\partial \Phi_{xx}} \right) df = - \int dy \left[\frac{d}{dx} \frac{\partial F}{\partial \Phi_{xx}} f \, \Big|_a^b - \int_a^b f \left(\frac{d^2}{dx^2} \frac{\partial F}{\partial \Phi_{xx}} \right) dx \right]$$

Again the first term within square brackets is zero because the function f itself is supposed to be zero at the boundary, *i.e.*, at points a and b, so that we finally find for the first one of the three integrals in Eq. (d)

$$+ \iint \left(\frac{d^2}{dx^2} \frac{\partial F}{\partial \Phi_{xx}} \right) f(x,\,y)\ dx\ dy$$

Now we proceed to the second integral in Eq. (*d*). It is treated in the same manner as the first integral, only x and y reversed, so that the partial integrations within the square brackets are on a vertical strip of width dx between c and d in Fig. 162, instead of on the horizontal strip of width dy between a and b as shown. The answer is

$$\iint \frac{\partial F}{\partial \Phi_{yy}} f_{yy}\ dx\ dy = \iint \left(\frac{d^2}{dy^2} \frac{\partial F}{\partial \Phi_{yy}} \right) f(x,\,y)\ dx\ dy$$

The third integral of Eq. (*d*) is mixed: we repeat the calculation as follows:

$$\iint \frac{\partial F}{\partial \Phi_{xy}} f_{xy}\ dx\ dy = \int dy \int \frac{\partial F}{\partial \Phi_{xy}}\ df_y$$

$$= \int dy \left[\underbrace{\frac{\partial F}{\partial \Phi_{xy}} f_y \Big|_a^b}_{\text{zero}} - \int_a^b \left(\frac{d}{dx} \frac{\partial F}{\partial \Phi_{xy}} \right) f_y\ dx \right]$$

$$= - \iint \left(\frac{d}{dx} \frac{\partial F}{\partial \Phi_{xy}} \right) (f_y\ dy)\ dx = - \int dx \int_c^d \left(\frac{d}{dx} \frac{\partial F}{\partial \Phi_{xy}} \right) df$$

$$= - \int dx \left[\underbrace{\left(\frac{d}{dx} \frac{\partial F}{\partial \Phi_{xy}} \right) f \Big|_c^d}_{\text{zero}} - \int_c^d \left(\frac{d^2}{dx\ dy} \frac{\partial F}{\partial \Phi_{xy}} \right) f(x,\,y)\ dy \right]$$

$$= + \iint \left(\frac{d^2}{dx\ dy} \frac{\partial F}{\partial \Phi_{xy}} \right) f(x,\,y)\ dx\ dy$$

Finally Eq. (*d*) becomes

$$0 = \iint \left[\frac{d^2}{dx^2} \frac{\partial F}{\partial \Phi_{xx}} + \frac{d^2}{dy^2} \frac{\partial F}{\partial \Phi_{yy}} + \frac{d^2}{dx\ dy} \frac{\partial F}{\partial \Phi_{xy}} \right] f(x,\,y)\ dA$$

integrated over the entire area of the plate Fig. 162. Now we remember that our function $f(x,\,y)$ [Fig. 162 or Eq. (*c*)] is entirely arbitrary in the interior of the plate. If then the above integral (visualized as a volume under a hill on the base, Fig. 162) is to be zero for any arbitrary function $f(x,\,y)$, that can only be if the large square bracket is zero. Hence

$$\frac{d^2}{dx^2} \frac{\partial F}{\partial \Phi_{xx}} + \frac{d^2}{dy^2} \frac{\partial F}{\partial \Phi_{yy}} + \frac{d^2}{dx\ dy} \frac{\partial F}{\partial \Phi_{xy}} = 0 \qquad (e)$$

is the condition that the energy [Eq. (*a*)] is either a maximum or a minimum when the stress function Φ is varied arbitrarily. Equation (*e*) is known to mathematicians as the "Euler differential equation of the variational problem making the integral (*a*) an extremum," and it can be found in texts on advanced calculus. The function F is the large square bracket of Eq. (a), except for a factor $2E$ which we divide out, since Eq. (e) is zero. We thus have

$$F = \Phi_{xx}^2 + \Phi_{yy}^2 - 2\mu\Phi_{xx}\Phi_{yy} + 2(1 + \mu)\Phi_{xy}^2$$

$$\frac{\partial F}{\partial \Phi_{xx}} = 2\Phi_{xx} - 2\mu\Phi_{yy}$$

$$\frac{\partial F}{\partial \Phi_{yy}} = 2\Phi_{yy} - 2\mu\Phi_{xx}$$

$$\frac{\partial F}{\partial \Phi_{xy}} = 4(1 + \mu)\Phi_{xy}$$

Substituting this into the Euler equation (e), we find

$$\frac{d^2}{dx^2}(2\Phi_{xx} - 2\mu\Phi_{yy}) + \frac{d^2}{dy^2}(2\Phi_{yy} - 2\mu\Phi_{xx}) + 4(1 + \mu)\frac{d^2}{dx\,dy}\Phi_{xy} = 0$$

$$2\Phi_{xxxx} - 2\mu\Phi_{xxyy} + 2\Phi_{yyyy} - 2\mu\Phi_{xxyy} + 4\Phi_{xxyy} + 4\mu\Phi_{xxyy} = 0$$

The terms with μ drop out, so that, independent of Poisson's ratio, we have:

$$\Phi_{xxxx} + \Phi_{yyyy} + 2\Phi_{xxyy} = 0 \qquad\qquad (f)$$

This is a differential equation which the function Φ of Eq. (c) must satisfy. As a particular case $u = 0$, and the Φ function becomes the Φ_0 function. Thus the Φ_0 function also must satisfy Eq. (f). Thus the Φ_0 function is the stress function which makes the energy a minimum, and Eq. (f) is the biharmonic equation (101c) (page 176), so that our theorem of least work is proved.

Strictly speaking we have proved only that if Φ_0 is the Airy function, the energy is an extremum: either maximum or minimum. The fact that the energy is a minimum and not a maximum could be proved as well by going on to the next differentiation. This, however, is a large job, and it is physically evident that the energy in the true state cannot be a maximum because it is easy enough to make that energy greater by locking some extra internal stresses in the plate.

34. Bending of Thin-walled Curved Tubes. If a curved tube, such as a steam pipe in a power plant, is subjected to bending moments in its own plane at the ends of the tube, the increase or decrease in curvature of the pipe and its deflections can be calculated by ordinary curved-beam theory, usually by the theory of slightly curved beams because r/R is of the order of $\frac{1}{10}$ in a practical case. Bending experiments on such pipes have shown deflections many times greater than the calculation would indicate, so that curved thin-walled pipes actually are several times (up to 10 times) as flexible as is predicted by simple beam theory. This was explained by von Kármán in 1911 on the basis of the theory of least work, and his derivation will be the subject of the next 10 pages.

Let the pipe of Fig. 163 be built in at the right end and subjected to a bending moment M_0 at the left end. That end will turn through some angle φ_0, and according to the old beam theory the cross sections will not distort, remaining thin-walled circles. This means that the outside fiber

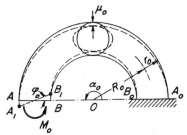

Fig. 163. Shows how the longitudinal fibers of a curved beam can avoid being extended (A_0A_1) or compressed (B_0B_1) by moving closer toward the center of the cross section, thus flattening the cross section to the dotted elliptical shape. The extra energy involved in bending the cross section to an elliptical shape is less than the saving in energy from preventing the longitudinal fibers from stretching. The final results of the analysis are given by Eqs. (127) and (125). Incidentally we see that for a *straight* pipe in bending the fibers cannot escape elongation by going somewhere else, because the shortest distance between two points is a straight line already. For the straight pipe the old simple bending theory is applicable.

of the tube, from A_0 to A, will be distorted to run from A_0 to A_1, but it will still follow the full line, just being extended by an amount AA_1. Similarly the inside fiber B_0B will be distorted to B_0B_1, being shortened by BB_1. All of this will involve a certain amount of stored energy. However there exists a means for the fibers to escape being extended and compressed. The fiber A_0A can go from A_0 to A_1 without any elongation by going down somewhat, following the dashed line, and similarly the compression fiber B_0B_1 can avoid shortening by going up a little. This behavior would certainly diminish the energy stored, but the escape of the fibers necessarily means a distortion of the cross section: a flattening of the circle. Flattening the circular cross section requires energy: to make that energy as small as possible, we do it by pure bending, leaving the length of the originally circular neutral fiber unchanged so that no hoop compression takes place. This requires the pipe to swell sidewise and acquire an ellipse-like cross section. In the analysis the flattening is expressed by a number u_0 shown in Fig. 163, and the bending deformation is expressed by φ_0. If u_0/φ_0 is made zero, then there is much energy in extending the fibers A_0A and B_0B longitudinally and none in distorting the section; on the other hand, if u_0/φ_0 is made so large that the dotted line A_0A_1 is equal in length to the full line A_0A, then all the energy is in distortion of the cross section. We now determine analytically a value of u_0/φ_0 between the two extremes just mentioned in which the total energy from longitudinal extension and from distortion of the cross section becomes a minimum.

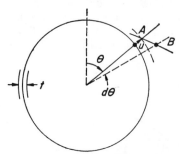

Distortion of Cross Section. The analysis is long, and we start with investigating the distortion of the cross section, as shown in Fig. 164. The original shape of the center line is a circle of radius r_0; the distortion is expressed by the radial displacement u, positive outward: $u = f(\theta)$. The slope of the distorted shape with respect to the tangent of the dotted circle at point A of Fig. 164 is

Fig. 164. The deformed shape of the cross section is described by the outward radial displacement u as a function of θ.

$$\text{Slope relative to tangent} = \frac{du}{rd\theta} = \frac{u'}{r}$$

Now $r = r_0 + u$, and developing in a Taylor series,

$$\frac{1}{r} = \frac{1}{r_0 + u} = \frac{1}{r_0[1 + (u/r_0)]} = \frac{1}{r_0}\left(1 - \frac{u}{r_0} + \frac{u^2}{r_0} + \cdots\right)$$

Then the slope is

$$\frac{u'}{r} = \frac{u'}{r_0}\left(1 - \frac{u}{r_0} + \cdots\right) = \frac{u'}{r_0} - \frac{uu'}{r_0^2} + \cdots$$

The displacement u is considered small with respect to r, and we shall retain only quantities of first order of smallness. Hence uu'/r_0^2 is small of second order, and we neglect it. The slope thus is simply u'/r_0 at point A (Fig. 164). At the next point B the slope, relative to the tangent there, is

$$\frac{u'}{r_0} + \frac{d}{d\theta}\left(\frac{u'}{r_0}\right) d\theta = \frac{u'}{r_0} + \frac{u''}{r_0} d\theta$$

The difference in slope between points B and A, both with respect to a *fixed* direction, is

$$d\theta - \text{slope at } B + \text{slope at } A = \left(1 - \frac{u''}{r_0}\right) d\theta$$

The local curvature of the distorted shape is

$$\text{Curvature} = \frac{\text{change in slope}}{\text{length of arc}} = \frac{[1 - (u''/r_0)] \, d\theta}{rd\theta}$$

$$= \frac{1 - (u''/r_0)}{r_0 + u} = \frac{1 - (u''/r_0)}{r_0[1 + (u/r_0)]}$$

$$= \frac{1 - (u''/r_0)}{r_0} \left(1 - \frac{u}{r_0} + \cdots \right)$$

$$= \frac{1}{r_0} - \frac{u''}{r_0^2} - \frac{u}{r_0^2} + \text{ terms of higher order}$$

The original curvature of the non-distorted cross section was $1/r_0$ so that the increase in curvature due to the deformation is

$$\text{Increase in curvature } = -\frac{u + u''}{r_0^2} \qquad (a)$$

This, incidentally, is an important general result, which is made the starting point for other problems in the bending of rings, such as will be encountered later on page 276. The differential equation of a ring, bent in its own plane, thus is

$$EI \frac{u + u''}{r_0^2} = M \qquad (122a)$$

where M is the bending moment, positive when it tends to *decrease* the curvature of the ring. For long tubes where anticlastic curvature is prevented, the equation is

$$\frac{EI}{1 - \mu^2} \frac{u + u''}{r_0^2} = M \qquad (122b)$$

for the reason explained on page 114.

Now, returning to Fig. 163, we must write an expression for u to simulate the flattening of the cross section. We do not know the shape the cross section takes, so that strictly speaking we should write an expression with many parameters. This, however, is too complicated, and we do as best we can with a single parameter. Looking at Fig. 163 and Fig. 164, we write

$$u = -u_0 \cos 2\theta \qquad (b)$$

which is a reasonable flattened ellipse-like curve. The single parameter u_0 tells the amount of flattening. From this assumption we deduce

$$u'' = +4u_0 \cos 2\theta$$

and substituting into Eq. (a),

$$\text{Increase in curvature } = -\frac{3u_0 \cos 2\theta}{r_0^2}$$

Now we turn to Fig. 165 showing a short piece ds of the undistorted circular center line of the cross section. Curvature is defined as $d\alpha/ds$, and the increase in curvature is $\Delta(d\alpha/ds)$. The elongation of a fiber at distance y from the neutral center line is seen to be $y \, \Delta(d\alpha)$; its length is ds (provided that y is small with respect to r_0, which is the case for a "thin-walled" tube); hence the strain is $y \cdot \Delta(d\alpha/ds)$, or y times the increment in curvature. The value of y runs from $-t/2$ to $+t/2$ across the thickness of the tube.

Applying this to the result just obtained, we have

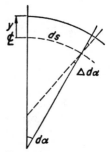

$$\epsilon_1 = -\frac{3u_0}{r_0^2}\cos 2\theta\, y \qquad (c)$$

Fig. 165. To prove that the strain ϵ equals y (the distance from the neutral fiber) times the increase in curvature of the bar [Eq. (c)].

for the strain in a direction tangent to the cross section. Other strains will occur in the longitudinal direction along the pipe (perpendicular to ϵ_1), and since these strains will have a cross effect on each other in connection with energy, we must leave Eq. (c) for the time being and calculate the longitudinal strain first.

Rayleigh's Inextensibility Property. When the circular cross section is changed into an elliptical one, this does not take place by *radial* displacements u only, because that would entail local elongations of the center line. For example, near the top of Fig. 163 the cross section moves closer to its center, and its radius r is less than r_0. If all points moved purely radially, without any tangential movement, the displaced piece $rd\theta$ would be shorter than the original one $r_0 d\theta$. Similarly 90 deg further the cross section bulges out, and the displaced fiber would be elongated by purely radial displacements. This is not allowable for two reasons. First, tensions in the center line mean more energy, which is unnecessary and hence undesirable ("least work"). Second, a local tension in a curved piece is out of equilibrium without internal pressure in the tube, which is supposed

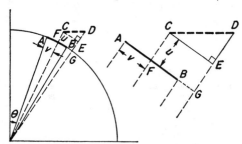

Fig. 166. Derivation of Rayleigh's equation (122), expressing the fact that a line element AB retains its original length while moving to a new position CD.

to be zero. Hence we must provide tangential displacements v (Fig. 166) in addition to the radial ones u, so related to each other that each line element ds retains its length. Let $AB = r_0 d\theta$ be such an element, which moves to the new position CD. We draw CE parallel to AB and remark that the lengths of CD and CE differ from each other by a second-order quantity only,

$$CE = CD \cos \alpha = CD \left(1 - \tfrac{1}{2}\alpha^2 + \cdots\right)$$

so that we neglect $-\tfrac{1}{2}\alpha^2$, because $\alpha = \angle\, DCE$ is a small angle. We demand that the length CE equals the length AB as far as first-order quantities are concerned. The tangential distance between A and C is called $AF = v$, the radial distance $FC = u$. The tangential distance between B and D is $BG = v + dv = v + (dv/d\theta)\, d\theta$. Therefore $FG - AB = (dv/d\theta)\, d\theta$. Also, CE is longer than FG in ratio $(r_0 + u)/r_0 = 1 + (u/r_0)$. Hence $CE - FG = (u/r_0)FG = (u/r_0)r_0 d\theta = u\, d\theta$. Adding, we find

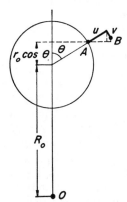

$$CE - AB = u\, d\theta + \frac{dv}{d\theta}\, d\theta = \left(u + \frac{dv}{d\theta}\right) d\theta$$

This quantity we demand to be zero, so that

$$u = -\frac{dv}{d\theta} \tag{122}$$

This is Rayleigh's condition for "inextensible deformation of a ring," and it is used in many places other than the present analysis. Applying it to our present case, we find by integrating Eq. (b)

$$u = -u_0 \cos 2\theta \tag{d}$$

$$v = +\frac{u_0}{2} \sin 2\theta$$

Fig. 167. A fiber at A, designated by the value θ, moves away from the pipe-bend center O by an amount $u \cos \theta - v \sin \theta$.

Calculation of Longitudinal Strain. We now return to Fig. 163 and remember that our present objective is to calculate the strain in the longitudinal fibers AA_0 and BB_0. The most important step in that calculation is to find out how much closer that fiber gets to the center O of the pipe bend. In Fig. 167 we consider the fiber designated by θ and note that that fiber moves from A to B. It moves radially away from the bend center O by an amount

$$\Delta R = u \cos \theta - v \sin \theta$$

and substituting Eqs. (d) this becomes

$$\Delta R = -u_0 \cos 2\theta \cos \theta - \frac{u_0}{2} \sin 2\theta \sin \theta$$

$$= -u_0(\cos^2 \theta - \sin^2 \theta) \cos \theta - \frac{u_0}{2} 2 \sin \theta \cos \theta \sin \theta$$

$$= -u_0 \cos^3 \theta$$

The radius of this fiber θ (Figs. 163 and 167) is $R = R_0 + r_0 \cos \theta$ so that the unit elongation due to this effect alone is $\epsilon = (-u_0 \cos^3 \theta)/R$. The total length of the fiber (Fig. 163) is $R\alpha_0$, where α is the total angle of the bend, so that the total elongation of the fiber (due to the flattening of the cross section) is

$$\Delta l = \frac{-u_0 \cos^3 \theta}{R} R\alpha_0 = -u_0\alpha_0 \cos^3 \theta$$

Now this fiber elongates not only because of the u_0 or flattening effect, but primarily because of the φ_0 or bending effect of Fig. 163. The total elongation from the latter cause is (Figs. 163 and 167)

$$\varphi_0 \cdot r_0 \cos \theta$$

Hence the combined tangential elongation of the fiber is

$$\Delta l = \varphi_0 r_0 \cos \theta - u_0\alpha_0 \cos^3 \theta$$

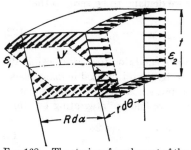

FIG. 168.   The strains of an element of the tube wall of dimensions t, $rd\theta$, and $R\ d\alpha$. The ϵ_1 strain [Eq. (c)] is caused by the bending of the pipe wall incident to the deformation of a circular section to an ellipse-like section. The ϵ_2 strain [Eq. (e)], directed along the longitudinal lines of the pipe, is caused by elongation (or shortening) of the longitudinal fibers due to bending of the pipe as a whole.

The original length of the fiber is $\alpha_0 R = \alpha_0 R_0 + \alpha_0 r_0 \cos \theta$, and the tangential strain ϵ_2 would be $\Delta l/\alpha_0 R$.

Here von Kármán makes an important simplification. Subsequent integrations with the above expression become extremely involved, and they would be much simplified if the denominator $\alpha_0 R$ were constant. Now for tubes with $R_0 > 5r_0$, no great error is made in replacing the radius R by R_0; for the upper fibers the radius so taken is too small, for the lower fibers it is too large, and as far as energy is concerned later on, the errors cancel each other to a great extent, but not entirely. Thus we say

$$\epsilon_2 = \frac{\Delta l}{R_0\alpha_0} = \frac{r_0}{R_0} \frac{\varphi_0}{\alpha_0} \cos \theta - \frac{u_0}{R_0} \cos^3 \theta \qquad (e)$$

Calculation of Energy.   This result, together with Eq. (c), determines the two principal strains in any element of the tube, as shown in Fig. 168. In the third direction, perpendicular to the tube wall, the stress is zero. We now need an expression for the energy stored, and for it we refer to Eq. (121) (page 231), in which we set the shear stress $s_s = 0$. This is in terms of two *stresses*, the third stress being zero, as in our case. In order to convert this to strains, we use Hooke's-law expressions (98) (page

173). The reader should solve Eqs. (98) for s_x and s_y and substitute the answers into Eq. (121), obtaining as a result

$$dU = \frac{E \, dvol}{2(1 - \mu^2)} (\epsilon_1^2 + \epsilon_2^2 + 2\mu\epsilon_1\epsilon_2) \tag{123}$$

for the case of plane *stress* ($s_3 = 0$) and ϵ_1, ϵ_2 being the principal strains. This expression has to be integrated over the entire volume of the tube. One simplification can be made by looking in Fig. 168 at two slices dy at equal distances above and below the center of the wall. For these slices ϵ_2 is the same and ϵ_1 has opposite signs, so that the products $\epsilon_1\epsilon_2$ also are equal with opposite signs. Hence the third term of Eq. (123) reduces to zero when integrated over the tube, and the energies due to ϵ_1 and ϵ_2 can be calculated separately and then added.

First we calculate the energy U_1 of flattening the section:

$$U_1 = \frac{E}{2(1 - \mu^2)} \int_{-t/2}^{+t/2} dy \int_0^{2\pi} r_0 d\theta \int_0^{\alpha_0} \epsilon_1^2 R_0 \, d\alpha$$

$$= \frac{Er_0}{2(1 - \mu^2)} \frac{9u_0^2}{r_0^4} \int_{-t/2}^{+t/2} y^2 \, dy \int_0^{2\pi} \cos^2 2\theta \, d\theta \int_0^{\alpha_0} R_0 \, d\alpha$$

$$= \frac{Er_0}{2(1 - \mu^2)} \frac{9u_0^2}{r_0^4} \cdot \frac{t^3}{12} \cdot \pi \cdot R_0\alpha_0$$

$$U_1 = \frac{3\pi}{8} \frac{E}{1 - \mu^2} \frac{u_0^2 t^3 R_0\alpha_0}{r_0^3} \tag{f}$$

The reader will have noticed that in integrating along the longitudinal $R \, d\alpha$ direction we have taken the average length $R_0 \, d\alpha$ of the fibers instead of their individual lengths $R \, d\alpha$. This is in line with the simplifications made previously.

Incidentally the result (f) is of general importance for other problems as well, and we shall have occasion to use it later, on page 281. Since $R_0\alpha_0 = l$ is the length of the tube, we can say generally that the energy stored in a pipe, which is made ellipse-like by Eq. (b), is

$$U = \frac{3\pi}{8} \frac{E}{1 - \mu^2} \frac{u_0^2 t^3 l}{r_0^3} \tag{124}$$

Now the energy due to longitudinal stretch or bending of the tube as a whole is

$$U_2 = \frac{E}{2(1 - \mu^2)} \int dy \int r_0 d\theta \int \epsilon_2^2 R_0 \, d\alpha$$

$$= \frac{Er_0}{2(1 - \mu^2)} tR_0\alpha_0 \left[\left(\frac{r_0}{R_0}\frac{\varphi_0}{\alpha_0}\right)^2 \int_0^{2\pi} \cos^2 \theta \, d\theta - \frac{2r_0u_0}{R_0^2}\frac{\varphi_0}{\alpha_0} \int_0^{2\pi} \cos^4 \theta \, d\theta \right.$$

$$\left. + \left(\frac{u_0}{R_0}\right)^2 \int_0^{2\pi} \cos^6 \theta \, d\theta \right]$$

The three trigonometric integrals should be looked up in a table, or the reader can work them out without difficulty by first reducing to the double angle

$$\cos^2 \theta = \frac{1}{2}(1 + \cos 2\theta)$$

The results are

$$\int_0^{2\pi} \cos^2 \theta \, d\theta = \pi \qquad \int_0^{2\pi} \cos^4 \theta \, d\theta = \frac{3}{4}\pi \qquad \int_0^{2\pi} \cos^6 \theta \, d\theta = \frac{5}{8}\pi$$

With this we find

$$U_2 = \frac{\pi E r_0 t R_0 \alpha_0}{2(1 - \mu^2)}\left[\left(\frac{r_0}{R_0}\frac{\varphi_0}{\alpha_0}\right)^2 - \frac{3}{2}\frac{r_0}{R_0}\frac{u_0}{R_0}\frac{\varphi_0}{\alpha_0} + \frac{5}{8}\left(\frac{u_0}{R_0}\right)^2\right] \tag{g}$$

The total energy stored in the pipe is the sum of U_1 and U_2. We see that the terms are proportional to u_0^2 or to $u_0\varphi_0$ or to φ_0^2. We now bring φ_0^2 outside the brackets and rearrange the terms so that they appear in the form of dimensionless ratios:

$$U = U_1 + U_2 = \frac{\pi E}{1 - \mu^2} \, t R_0 r_0 \alpha_0 \varphi_0^2 \left[\left(\frac{u_0}{\varphi_0 R_0}\right)^2\left(\frac{5}{16} + \frac{3}{8}\frac{t^2 R_0^2}{r_0^4}\right)\right.$$
$$\left. - \left(\frac{u_0}{\varphi_0 R_0}\right)\left(\frac{3}{4}\frac{r_0}{R_0\alpha_0}\right) + \frac{1}{2}\left(\frac{r_0}{R_0\alpha_0}\right)^2\right] \tag{h}$$

Application of the Theorem of Least Work. The expression (h) is proportional to the square of the angle of bending φ_0, and it contains in the square bracket the parameter $u_0/\varphi_0 R$, which is dimensionless and expresses the ratio between flattening and bending. By varying that parameter the state of stress in the tube is varied; the various states of stress represented by the various values of $u_0/\varphi_0 R$ are all more or less in equilibrium, although not completely so. In saying that the theorem of least work requires the energy (h) to be a minimum for varying values of $u_0/\varphi_0 R$ we commit an error of the same character as in the examples of page 222 and page 224. (See Problem 170.) Being aware of this, we nevertheless write

$$\frac{dU}{d(u_0/\varphi_0 R_0)} = 0$$

In calculating this out we can disregard the multipliers before the square brackets of (h) and work with the bracket by itself, so that

$$2\frac{u_0}{\varphi_0 R_0}\left(\frac{5}{16} + \frac{3}{8}\frac{t^2 R_0^2}{r_0^4}\right) - \frac{3}{4}\frac{r_0}{R_0\alpha_0} = 0$$

or, worked up in dimensionless ratios,

$$\frac{u_0\alpha_0}{r_0\varphi_0} = \frac{6}{5 + 6\lambda^2} \tag{i}$$

where

$$\lambda = \frac{tR_0}{r_0^2} \qquad (125)$$

The ratio λ is characteristic for the pipe: it is a small number for greatly curved pipes with very thin walls, and it is a large number for slightly curved thicker walled pipes, being ∞ for straight pipes. From Eq. (i) we can see that a straight pipe ($\lambda = \infty$) does not flatten its cross section, $u_0 = 0$, and that the maximum possible flattening for a very thin walled and greatly curved pipe is

$$\left(\frac{u_0}{r_0}\right)_{\text{max}} = \frac{6}{5}\frac{\varphi_0}{\alpha_0}$$

Substituting the result (i) for the flattening parameter into the energy (h) and rewriting in terms of the pipe characteristic λ of Eq. (125), we find

$$U = \frac{\pi}{2}\frac{E}{1-\mu^2}\frac{tr_0^3}{R_0}\frac{\varphi_0^2}{\alpha_0}\frac{12\lambda^2+1}{12\lambda^2+10} \qquad (k)$$

On the other hand, if in Eq. (h) we set $u_0 = 0$, that is, if we take the old-fashioned theory, disregarding flattening, we have

$$(U)_{u_0=0} = \frac{\pi}{2}\frac{E}{1-\mu^2}\frac{tr_0^3}{R_0}\frac{\varphi_0^2}{\alpha_0} \qquad (l)$$

We notice that the energy in both these expressions is in terms of φ_0^2, the "displacement," and that the "load" M_0 does not appear in them. Thus they are in the form fit for applying the "virtual" work theorem [Eq. (118), page 212]:

$$M_0 = \frac{\partial U}{\partial \varphi_0} = \pi\frac{E}{1-\mu^2}\frac{tr_0^3}{R_0}\frac{\varphi_0}{\alpha_0}\frac{12\lambda^2+1}{12\lambda^2+10} \qquad (126)$$

For the old, discarded theory we have in the same way, operating on Eq. (l),

$$(M_0)_{\text{no flattening}} = \pi\frac{E}{1-\mu^2}\frac{tr_0^3}{R_0}\frac{\varphi_0}{\alpha_0} \qquad (m)$$

Thus we find for the factor decreasing the stiffness of the pipe in the new theory as compared with the old one:

$$\frac{(\varphi_0/M_0)_{\text{true}}}{(\varphi_0/M_0)_{\text{no flattening}}} = \frac{12\lambda^2+10}{12\lambda^2+1} \qquad (127)$$

where λ is defined in Eq. (125). We see from it that for a pipe in which $t = \frac{1}{8}$ in., $r_0 = 12$ in., and $R_0 = 60$ in. the value of $\lambda = 0.052$ and the stiffness of the pipe is decreased by a factor 9.7, almost 10. This is an extreme case, but a steam pipe of 1 in. thickness, 20 in. diameter $= 2r_0$, and $R_0 = 6$ ft still is 2.25 times as flexible as simple beam theory would indicate. The relation (127) is shown in Fig. 169.

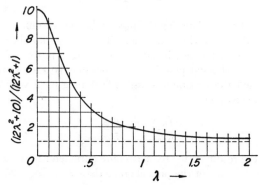

FIG. 169. Shows vertically the factor by which a thin-walled curved tube is more flexible than is predicted by simple beam theory, plotted horizontally against $\lambda = tR/r^2$, the tube characteristic. This illustrates Eq. (127).

Bending Perpendicular to the Plane of the Pipe. So far we have discussed the problem of the bending of a curved pipe in its own plane, increasing or decreasing its existing curvature. Now we ask what will happen when a bending moment is applied to such a pipe tending to bend it perpendicular to its own plane. The answer to that question was given by Vigness, who showed that the complete von Kármán theory of the last 10 pages holds in the new case almost without exception. This is shown in Fig. 170. The compression fiber is marked A, the tension fiber B, and the two

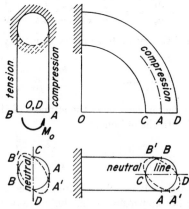

FIG. 170. Curved tube subjected to a bending moment in a plane perpendicular to that of the tube. The fibers again can escape compression or tension by moving away from and toward the center O, respectively. The circular cross section distorts to an ellipse-like curve at 45 deg with respect to the neutral line (Vigness).

neutral fibers C and D. The compression fiber can escape compression and shortening by moving away from the center O of the bend, from position A to A'. Similarly the tension fiber can escape tension and its consequent elongation by moving closer to the center O, from B to B'. The two neutral fibers C and D stay at the same radial distance from O. In general all fibers in the compression half of the section move away from O and all fibers in the tension half toward O. When this happens, we see that the distorted cross section is ellipse-like, as in Fig. 163, only now the ellipse is at 45 deg with respect to the neutral line of bending, instead of in line with it as in Fig. 163. The energy involved is the same as before and all formulae of the last 10 pages hold, only with slightly different words. The end result [Eq. (127)] is the same.

The analysis of this section refers to the case where the bending moment is constant along the length of the tube. When that moment varies along the beam, as is usual, then we assume that the local flattening u_0 also varies along it and is proportional to the bending moment. This certainly will be the case when the moment varies slowly and gradually along the beam, while the approximation will be less good for sudden jumps in bending moment. In any case the procedure in calculating beams of this kind is to replace the quantity EI of the section by

$$EI \frac{12\lambda^2 + 1}{12\lambda^2 + 10}$$

and then to calculate the structure by the usual methods, either by beam formulae or by Castigliano's energy theorem.

35. Flat Plates in Bending. We have seen that for applying the theorem of "virtual" work we need an expression of the stored energy of the system in terms of the *displacements*, independent of the loads. All the displacements of a flat x, y plate, bent perpendicular to its own plane, are given by the deflection function $w = f(x, y)$. Any displacements u and v in the middle plane of the plate itself are caused only by loadings in the plane of the plate, which are absent in our case of bending. (The u and v displacements are important for the different problem of two-dimensional stress imposed on the plate by forces in its own plane, as discussed in Chap. VI, and particularly on page 172.) We now propose to derive an expression for the energy stored in a plate element $t \, dx \, dy$ in terms of its vertical deflection w and the various derivatives of w.

On page 107, Fig. 75, we saw that such an element is subjected to two pairs of bending moments, $M_{1x} \, dy$ and $M_{1y} \, dx$, and to a double pair of twisting couples, $T_{1xy} \, dx$ and $T_{1xy} \, dy$. The bending moments $M_{1x} \, dy$ do work on an angular displacement in the xz plane: the angle on one side is $\partial w / \partial x$, and on the other side it is

$$\frac{\partial w}{\partial x} + \frac{\partial}{\partial x}\left(\frac{\partial w}{\partial x}\right) dx$$

The relative angle of turn of one dy side of the element with respect to the other thus is $(\partial^2 w / \partial x^2)\ dx$. The work done by the pair of bending moments is

$$\frac{1}{2}\ M_{1x}\ dy\ \frac{\partial^2 w}{\partial x^2}\ dx = \frac{1}{2}\ M_{1x}\ \frac{\partial^2 w}{\partial x^2}\ dx\ dy$$

The factor $\frac{1}{2}$ is due to the fact that the moment grows together with the curvature $\partial^2 w / \partial x^2$, so that the average value of the moment during this growth is $\frac{1}{2} M_{1x}$. Similarly the work done by the other pair of bending moments is

$$\frac{1}{2}\ M_{1y}\ \frac{\partial^2 w}{\partial y^2}\ dx\ dy$$

The angle of twist of one dy side is $\partial w / \partial y$, and on the opposite dy side (at distance dx to the right of the first side) that angle is

$$\frac{\partial w}{\partial y} + \frac{\partial}{\partial x}\left(\frac{\partial w}{\partial y}\right) dx$$

Hence the relative angle of twist is $(\partial^2 w / \partial x\ \partial y)\ dx$, and the work by that pair of twisting moments is

$$\frac{1}{2}\ T_{1xy}\ dy\ \frac{\partial^2 w}{\partial x\ \partial y}\ dx$$

But there is another pair of twisting moments on the two dx faces, giving the same amount of work again. Now we are permitted to add these four contributions of work together, because any one of the four individual deformations does work only in conjunction with the moment in its own direction, and such a deformation absorbs no work out of the other three pairs of moments. Thus there are no cross terms, and the total energy stored in the plate element is

$$dU = \frac{dx\ dy}{2}\left(M_{1x}\ \frac{\partial^2 w}{\partial x^2} + M_{1y}\ \frac{\partial^2 w}{\partial y^2} + 2T_{1xy}\ \frac{\partial^2 w}{\partial x\ \partial y}\right)$$

This result is mixed: the displacements w *and* the loads M and T appear in it. In order to reduce it to the w form only, we must express the moments in terms of the deflections w. This was done in Eqs. (65) (page 108). Substitution of Eqs. (65) into the above result leads to

$$dU = \frac{D\ dx\ dy}{2}\left[\left(\frac{\partial^2 w}{\partial x^2}\right)^2 + \left(\frac{\partial^2 w}{\partial y^2}\right)^2 \right.$$
$$\left. + 2\mu\ \frac{\partial^2 w}{\partial x^2}\ \frac{\partial^2 w}{\partial y^2} + 2(1 - \mu)\left(\frac{\partial^2 w}{\partial x\ \partial y}\right)^2\right] \quad (128)$$

This important formula is derived here mainly for its application to the buckling problem of Fig. 202 (page 302), which is of practical importance. Now we shall give a few examples of its use in finding plate deflections by means of the theorem of virtual work.

Suppose we consider a rectangular plate ab (Fig. 171), simply supported on all edges and loaded perpendicularly to its plane by an arbitrary load distribution. The deflection can be expressed by a double Fourier series:

$$w = \sum_{m=1}^{\infty} \sum_{n=1}^{\infty} a_{mn} \sin \frac{m\pi x}{a} \sin \frac{n\pi y}{b} \quad (a)$$

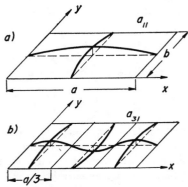

The first term of this series a_{11} $\sin (\pi x/a) \sin (\pi y/b)$ is illustrated in Fig. 171a, the term a_{13} will have one half sine wave in the x direction and three half sine waves in the y direction, etc. The coefficients a_{11}, a_{12}, a_{21}, etc., determine the shape of the deflected surface. We now want to calculate the energy stored in the plate ab, deformed according to Eq. (a). Our first step is to find the energy if w contains *one term* only, the general one a_{mn}, all other terms being zero. This is the case illus-

Fig. 171. Illustrates two terms of the double Fourier series (a) giving the deflection of a plate.

trated on page 115, Fig. 82, with m half waves in the x direction and n half waves in the y direction. The half wave lengths in our present case (different from Fig. 82) are a/m and b/n, and the height of the wave is a_{mn}, instead of the w_0 shown in the previous figure. Then the work in the entire plate, integrating Eq. (128), is calculated:

$$w = a_{mn} \sin \frac{m\pi x}{a} \sin \frac{n\pi y}{b} \quad (b)$$

$$\left(\frac{\partial^2 w}{\partial x^2}\right)^2 = a_{mn}^2 \left(\frac{m^2\pi^2}{a^2}\right)^2 \sin^2 \frac{m\pi x}{a} \sin^2 \frac{n\pi y}{b}$$

$$\iint \left(\frac{\partial^2 w}{\partial x^2}\right)^2 dx\, dy = a_{mn}^2 \frac{m^4\pi^4}{a^4} \int_0^a \sin^2 \frac{m\pi x}{a}\, dx \int_0^b \sin^2 \frac{n\pi y}{a}\, dy$$

Now the two integrals are squared sine waves, the area under which is "half the base length," $a/2$ for the first one, and $b/2$ for the second one, which can be calculated or seen more easily by sketching the integrand and looking at the area. Hence

$$\iint \left(\frac{\partial^2 w}{\partial x^2}\right)^2 dx\, dy = a_{mn}^2 \frac{m^4\pi^4}{a^4} \frac{ab}{4}$$

The other terms in Eq. (128) are integrated similarly, with the result

$$U = \frac{D}{2} a_{mn}^2 \pi^4 \frac{ab}{4} \left[\frac{m^4}{a^4} + \frac{n^4}{b^4} + 2\mu \frac{m^2 n^2}{a^2 b^2} + 2(1 - \mu) \frac{m^2 n^2}{a^2 b^2} \right]$$

$$U = a_{mn}^2 \pi^4 \frac{Dab}{8} \left(\frac{m^2}{a^2} + \frac{n^2}{b^2} \right)^2 \tag{129}$$

This is the work stored in a plate deflected according to the single-term expression (b). If we now deflect the plate more generally, with many terms [Eq. (a)], the complications become great, because in working out the squares $(\partial^2 w / \partial x^2)^2$ we get not only terms such as a_{mn}^2 but also all the double products $a_{mn} \cdot a_{pq}$. The square terms a_{mn}^2 give the integrated result (129), just derived, and luckily the integrated double-product terms $a_{mn} \cdot a_{pq}$ all become zero, because

$$\int_0^a \sin \frac{m\pi x}{a} \sin \frac{n\pi x}{a} \, dx = 0 \qquad \text{(for } m \neq n\text{)}$$

and similarly for the cosine integrals. This is the fundamental property which makes the Fourier series a workable proposition; without these integrals being zero the Fourier series would be impractically complicated. Thus, we can generalize Eq. (129), applying it to any arbitrary deflection [Eq. (a)]:

$$U = \pi^4 \frac{Dab}{8} \sum_{m=1}^{\infty} \sum_{n=1}^{\infty} a_{mn}^2 \left(\frac{m^2}{a^2} + \frac{n^2}{b^2} \right)^2 \tag{129a}$$

Uniformly Loaded Plate. We shall now use this result to derive from it (by the principle of "virtual" work) the central deflection of a uniformly loaded rectangular plate. Under the influence of such a load p (pounds per square inch) the plate will have a deflected shape expressible by a doubly infinite number of coefficients a_{mn}. We now give the plate a "virtual" or small displacement, by permitting *one* of the coefficients a_{mn} to increase to $a_{mn} + da_{mn}$, leaving all other coefficients at their old value. Physically this means that the plate deflection is increased by a small pattern (Fig. 82, page 115) with mn fields of size a/m and b/n and central height da_{mn}. Because of this extra displacement the energy is increased by

$$\frac{\partial U}{\partial a_{mn}} da_{mn} = \pi^4 \frac{Dab}{8} 2 a_{mn} \, da_{mn} \left(\frac{m^2}{a^2} + \frac{n^2}{b^2} \right)^2 \tag{c}$$

There is only *one* term in this expression, because all other terms in Eq. (129a) remain constant. This increment in energy must be equal to the work done by the pressure force p, which is p times the volume increase under it. The volume of one partial field of dimension a/m and b/n is

$$da_{mn} \frac{ab}{mn} \frac{2}{\pi} \frac{2}{\pi}$$

because the area under a sine wave is $2/\pi$ times the base. There are mn such areas, but looking at Fig. 82 we see that they mostly cancel each other. In fact if either m or n is an even number, the number mn is even and the fields, being alternately up and down, have zero total volume. Only when both m and n are odd does one field remain uncompensated, so that the work done by the pressure p on the entire plate ab is

$$\frac{4}{\pi^2} \frac{ab}{mn} \, da_{mn}$$

for m and n both odd. The equation of "virtual" work is

$$\pi^4 \frac{Dab}{8} 2a_{mn} \, da_{mn} \left(\frac{m^2}{a^2} + \frac{n^2}{b^2}\right)^2 = \frac{4p}{\pi^2} \frac{ab}{mn} \, da_{mn}$$

so that

$$a_{mn} = \frac{16p}{\pi^6 D} \frac{1}{mn\left(\dfrac{m^2}{a^2} + \dfrac{n^2}{b^2}\right)^2} \qquad \text{(for m and n odd)} \tag{d}$$

$$a_{mn} = 0 \qquad \text{(for either m or n even)}$$

This gives us the deflected surface of the plate. The center point of the plate (Fig. 171) is deflected in the positive direction for the term a_{11} and in the opposite or negative direction for the term a_{31} or more generally according to the schedule below:

$$a_{11} \quad a_{13} \quad a_{31} \quad a_{15} \quad a_{51} \quad a_{35} \quad a_{53} \quad a_{17}$$

$$+ \quad - \quad - \quad + \quad + \quad - \quad - \quad +$$

Taking a square plate, where $a = b$, the result (d) is

$$(a_{mn})_{\text{square}} = \frac{16pa^4}{\pi^6 D} \frac{1}{mn(m^2 + n^2)^2}$$

and the center deflection is

$$\delta_{\text{center, square}} = \frac{16pa^4}{\pi^6 D} (a_{11} - a_{13} - a_{31} + a_{15} + a_{51} - a_{35} - \cdots)$$

$$= \frac{16pa^4}{\pi^6 D} \left(\frac{1}{4} - \frac{1}{300} - \frac{1}{300} + \frac{1}{3,380} + \frac{1}{3,380} - \cdots\right)$$

$$= \frac{16pa^4}{\pi^6 D} \times 0.244 = 0.00405 \frac{pa^4}{D} = 0.0442 \frac{pa^4}{Et^3}$$

which is the result shown in the table on page 132, case 19.

Central Concentrated Force. As a second example we take a simply supported rectangular plate again, but now loaded by a single concentrated central force P. Its work on a virtual displacement da_{mn} is $P\,da_{mn}$, either positive or negative. We shall worry about the sign later and now equate this work to the increment in energy Eq. (c), with the result

$$a_{mn} = \frac{4P}{\pi^4 D}\,\frac{1}{ab\left(\dfrac{m^2}{a^2} + \dfrac{n^2}{b^2}\right)^2}$$

The signs are alternately positive and negative, always so that the individual deflection a_{mn} in the center of the plate is in the direction of the force P. (Why?) Again both m and n must be odd, because if one of them were even, the center of the plate would be on a line of zero deflection.

Thus we have for the center deflection of a rectangular plate $b/a = 2$

$$(\delta)_{b=2a} = \frac{2Pa^2}{\pi^4 D} \sum_m \sum_n \frac{1}{[m^2 + (n^2/4)]^2}$$

$$= \frac{2Pa^2}{\pi^4 D}\,(a_{11} + a_{13} + a_{31} + a_{15} + a_{51} + a_{35} + \cdots)$$

$$= \frac{2Pa^2}{\pi^4 D}\,(0.640 + 0.095 + 0.012 + 0.019 + 0.001 + 0.004 + \cdots)$$

$$= \frac{2Pa^2}{\pi^4 D} \times 0.771 = 0.0159\,\frac{Pa^2}{D} = 0.175\,\frac{Pa^2}{Et^3}$$

which is slightly less than the result 0.180 shown in the table on page 133. The difference is due to the slow convergence of the series; the contributions of many more very small terms will bring it up to 0.180.

Problems 139 *to* 175.

CHAPTER VIII

BUCKLING

36. Rayleigh's Method. On page 215 brief mention was made of the application of the method of "virtual" work to the buckling of beams. We shall now examine this in detail on a number of cases, starting with the simple Euler column.

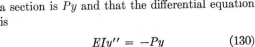

Column of Uniform Stiffness. Let the originally straight column of Fig. 172 be in a curved position $y = f(x)$ of indifferent equilibrium under the influence of end forces P. The classical, simple Euler theory states that the bending moment in a section is Py and that the differential equation is

$$EIy'' = -Py \qquad (130)$$

Fig. 172. Euler column in indifferent equilibrium under a pair of compressive loads P. The buckling load is $P = \pi^2 EI/l^2$, and the shape is half a sine wave.

The solution of this equation, as given in elementary textbooks, leads to the Euler buckling load or critical load

$$P_{\text{crit}} = \pi^2 \frac{EI}{l^2}$$

Let us now assume that the shape of the curve is $y = f(x)$, as yet unknown. Then the bending energy stored in the beam is

$$U = \int_0^l \frac{M^2}{2EI}\, dx = \int_0^l \frac{(EIy'')^2}{2EI}\, dx = \frac{1}{2}\int_0^l EI(y'')^2\, dx \qquad (a)$$

If the cross section is uniform, EI is a constant and can be brought before the integral sign. If we leave EI inside the integral, the equation applies to non-uniform cross sections as well. The energy of compression $U = P^2l/2AE$ has to be added to the bending energy, but when we increase the buckling deflection y, the bending energy increases, while the compression energy remains constant. This constant energy will not enter into the analysis, and we do not need to make further mention of it. Now we must calculate the small distance $\delta = AA_1$ (Fig. 172) through which the force P performs work. The rectified length of the arc OA_1 must be the same as the straight piece OA because the compressive stress

251

in the center line P/A is the same for both. [This is true for small deflections $y = f(x)$ only, which we suppose from now on.] We have for an element

$$ds = \sqrt{dx^2 + dy^2} = dx\sqrt{1 + y'^2}$$

$$l = \int_0^l ds = \int_0^{l-\delta} dx\sqrt{1 + y'^2} = \int_0^l dx\sqrt{1 + y'^2} - \int_{l-\delta}^l dx\sqrt{1 + y'^2}$$

The last integral equals δ, because $\sqrt{1 + y'^2} \approx 1$, since the slope y' is small. Thus

$$\delta = \int_0^l dx\sqrt{1 + y'^2} - l$$

The square root $\sqrt{1 + y'^2}$ is approximately

$$\sqrt{1 + y'^2} = 1 + \frac{y'^2}{2} + \frac{y'^4}{} + \cdots$$

so that, neglecting powers higher than 2 of the small slope,

$$\delta = \int_0^l dx\left(1 + \frac{y'^2}{2}\right) - l = l + \frac{1}{2}\int_0^l (y')^2\, dx - l$$

$$\delta = \frac{1}{2}\int_0^l (y')^2\, dx$$

and the work done by the force P is

$$\text{Work} = \frac{P}{2}\int_0^l y'^2\, dx \tag{b}$$

By the principle of virtual work this work, done by the outside forces, equals the increment Eq. (a) of elastic energy:

$$P\frac{1}{2}\int_0^l (y')^2\, dx = \frac{1}{2}\int_0^l EI(y'')^2\, dx \tag{131}$$

$$P_{\text{crit}} = \frac{\int_0^l EI(y'')^2\, dx}{\int_0^l (y')^2\, dx} \tag{131a}$$

Here $y(x)$ is the true shape of the buckling curve, which we do not know in advance. Rayleigh's method consists in assuming a reasonable curve $y = f(x)$, which approximates the true one, of substituting that shape into Eq. (131), and of so obtaining an approximate answer for the buckling load. It will be proved on page 267 that the *approximate* P_{crit} *so obtained is always greater than the true value for* P_{crit}.

We happen to know in this case (Fig. 172) that the exact shape is a sine wave:

$$y = y_0 \sin\frac{\pi x}{l}$$

Substituting this into Rayleigh's equation (131a), we have

$$y' = \frac{y_0\pi}{l} \cos \frac{\pi x}{l} \qquad y'' = - \frac{y_0\pi^2}{l^2} \sin \frac{\pi x}{l}$$

$$P_{\text{crit}} = EI \frac{(y_0\pi^2/l^2)^2 \int_0^l \sin^2 (\pi x/l) \, dx}{(y_0\pi/l)^2 \int_0^l \cos^2 (\pi x/l) \, dx}$$

Both integrals are square sines or cosines, whose value is "half the base length" $l/2$, so that

$$P_{\text{crit}} = \pi^2 \frac{EI}{l^2}$$

the *exact* answer, because we put in the *exact* curve to start with.

Now we deliberately put in a curve which we know is wrong: a shallow parabola or circular arc. Try in Fig. 172: $y = A + Bx + Cx^2$, and fit the boundary conditions $x = 0$, $y = 0$ and $x = l$, $y = 0$. We then find $y = Cx(x - l) = C(x^2 - xl)$. With this we enter Eq. (131):

$$y' = C(2x - l) \qquad y'' = 2C$$

$$\int y'^2 \, dx = C^2 \int_0^l (2x - l)^2 \, dx = \frac{C^2}{2} \int_0^l (2x - l)^2 \, d(2x - l)$$

$$= \frac{C^2}{6} (2x - l)^3 \Big|_0^l = \frac{C^2}{6} (l^3 + l^3) = \frac{1}{3} C^2 l^3$$

$$\int_0^l y''^2 \, dx = 4C^2 \int_0^l dx = 4C^2 l$$

$$P_{\text{crit}} = EI \frac{4C^2 l}{\frac{1}{3}C^2 l^3} = \frac{12EI}{l^2}$$

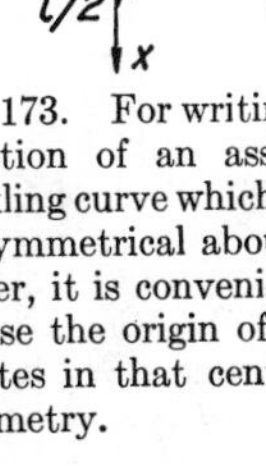

The factor 12 is greater than the exact one $\pi^2 = 9.87$, in accordance with Rayleigh's theorem. The error is more than 20 per cent, because the curve we chose was stupid. This curve has $y'' = 2C = $ constant, whereas physically we see that the bending moment or curvature must be zero at the ends $x = 0$ and $x = l$, because the force P there has no moment arm.

Let us now set up a shape without curvature at the two ends. We could do this with Fig. 172 by

FIG. 173. For writing the equation of an assumed buckling curve which must be symmetrical about the center, it is convenient to choose the origin of coordinates in that center of symmetry.

setting $y = A + Bx + Cx^2 + Dx^3$, etc., and fit the boundary conditions. However, this can be simplified by taking advantage of the fact that we want the curve to be symmetrical about the middle $x = l/2$. Let us take a new coordinate system (Fig. 173) with the origin in the middle. Then a symmetrical curve is given by

$$y = y_0\left[1 + A\left(\frac{x}{l/2}\right)^2 + B\left(\frac{x}{l/2}\right)^4\right]$$

We want $y = 0$ at $x = \pm l/2$, which is at $x^2 = l^2/4$, and also $y'' = 0$ at $x^2 = l^2/4$. Substituting this into the assumption,

$$y = 0 = 1 + A + B$$

$$y'' = 0 = \frac{2A}{(l/2)^2} + 12\frac{B}{(l/2)^2}$$

Solve for A and B, and substitute:

$$y = y_0\left[1 - \frac{6}{5}\left(\frac{x}{l/2}\right)^2 + \frac{1}{5}\left(\frac{x}{l/2}\right)^4\right]$$

$$y' = \frac{y_0}{l/2}\left[-\frac{12}{5}\left(\frac{x}{l/2}\right) + \frac{4}{5}\left(\frac{x}{l/2}\right)^3\right]$$

$$y'' = \frac{y_0}{(l/2)^2}\left[-\frac{12}{5} + \frac{12}{5}\left(\frac{x}{l/2}\right)^2\right]$$

We verify that this is symmetrical about the center of Fig. 173 and that $y = y'' = 0$ at both ends. Entering with this into Rayleigh's equation (131a),

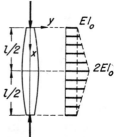

$$P_{\text{crit}} = \frac{EI}{(l/2)^2}\frac{\dfrac{144}{25}\displaystyle\int_{-l/2}^{+l/2}\left[1 - \left(\frac{x}{l/2}\right)^2\right]^2 dx}{\dfrac{144}{25}\displaystyle\int_{-l/2}^{+l/2}\left[\frac{x}{l/2} - \frac{1}{3}\left(\frac{x}{l/2}\right)^3\right]^2 dx}$$

$$= \frac{4EI}{l^2}\frac{\displaystyle\int_{-1}^{1}(1 - \xi^2)^2\, d\xi}{\displaystyle\int_{-1}^{1}\left(\xi - \frac{\xi^3}{3}\right)^2 d\xi}$$

Fig. 174. Strut of a cross section with a bending stiffness EI which tapers off linearly from a maximum value $2EI_0$ in the center to EI_0 at the ends.

The reader should work out these integrals and verify that the result is

$$P_{\text{crit}} = \frac{168EI}{17l^2} = 9.882\frac{EI}{l^2}$$

which is very close to the exact result $\pi^2 = 9.870$, but is a little *larger* than the exact answer, as it should be.

Column of Variable Cross Section. If the section varies along the length as in Fig. 174, we only have to keep EI inside the integral and apply

Rayleigh's formula (131a) without change. Assuming the half sine wave

$$y = y_0 \sin \frac{\pi x}{l}$$

for a shape, we have

$$\int_0^l E I y''^2 \, dx = 2 \int_0^{l/2} E I y''^2 \, dx = 2 \int_0^{l/2} E I_0 \left(1 + \frac{x}{l/2} \right) y''^2 \, dx$$

$$= 2 E I_0 \int_0^{l/2} y''^2 \, dx + \frac{4 E I_0}{l} \int_0^{l/2} x y''^2 \, dx$$

$$= 2 E I_0 y_0^2 \frac{\pi^4}{l^4} \left(\int_0^{l/2} \sin^2 \frac{\pi x}{l} \, dx + \frac{2}{l} \int_0^{l/2} x \sin^2 \frac{\pi x}{l} \, dx \right)$$

$$= 2 E I_0 y_0^2 \frac{\pi^4}{l^4} \left(\frac{l}{4} + \frac{2}{l} \frac{l^2}{\pi^2} \int_0^{\pi/2} \varphi \sin^2 \varphi \, d\varphi \right)$$

The last integral we look up in tables and find for it

$$\int_0^{\pi/2} \varphi \sin^2 \varphi \, d\varphi = \left[\frac{\varphi^4}{4} - \frac{\varphi \sin 2\varphi}{4} - \frac{\cos 2\varphi}{8} \right]_0^{\pi/2} = \frac{\pi^2}{16} + \frac{1}{4}$$

or

$$\int_0^l E I y''^2 \, dx = 2 E I_0 y_0^2 \frac{\pi^4}{l^4} \left[\frac{l}{4} + \frac{2l}{\pi^2} \left(\frac{\pi^2}{16} + \frac{1}{4} \right) \right]$$

The elongation integral is the same as for the uniform strut:

$$\int_0^l y'^2 \, dx = y_0^2 \frac{\pi^2}{l^2} \int_0^l \cos^2 \frac{\pi x}{l} \, dx = y_0^2 \frac{\pi^2}{2l}$$

Hence, by Eq. (131),

$$P_{\text{crit}} = \frac{\pi^2 E I_0}{l^2} \left(\frac{3}{2} + \frac{2}{\pi^2} \right) = \frac{\pi^2 1.70 E I_0}{l^2}$$

This answer is somewhat too large, by Rayleigh's rule, because although a half sine wave is the exact shape for a uniform column, it is only an approximation to the deformed shape for the column of Fig. 174.

Buckling of a Flagpole under Its Own Weight. Consider the case (Fig. 175) of a cantilever EI, l loaded by a sidewise force P at the top and loaded downward by its own weight $w_1 l$ where w_1 is the weight per unit length. To find the work done by $w_1 l$ on the deformation, we first find the work done by a small piece $w_1 \, dx$ of weight at A. The point A moves downward by

$$(\Delta h)_P = \int_0^x (ds - dx) = \int_0^x dx (\sqrt{1 + y'^2} - 1)$$

$$= \int_0^x dx \left(1 + \frac{y'^2}{2} + \cdots - 1 \right) = \frac{1}{2} \int_0^x y'^2 \, dx$$

The work done by $w_1\, dx$ is

$$\frac{w_1\, dx}{2} \int_0^x y'^2\, dx$$

and the work done by the entire weight is

$$\int_0^l \frac{w_1\, dx}{2} \int_0^x y'^2\, dx$$

The work done by the load P is $\frac{1}{2}Py_l$; the factor $\frac{1}{2}$ comes in because P grows proportionally to δ. The bending energy stored in the beam is

$$\int_0^l \frac{EI}{2}\, (y'')^2\, dx$$

Hence by the principle of work this energy equals the work done by the external forces, or

$$\int_0^l EI(y'')^2\, dx = Py_l + \int_0^l w_1\, dx \int_0^x y'^2\, dx \qquad (132)$$

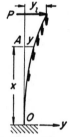

Fig. 175. Flagpole under its own gravity loading and a sidewise force P at the top.

This is the general energy of the flagpole. It is true strictly only for the exact shape $y(x)$ of the deformation, which we don't know, and this time we really don't know. In case of a uniform beam the quantities EI and w_1 can be brought outside the integrals. Also, when $P = 0$ we have the special case of buckling under gravity. We must now substitute for $y = f(x)$ a reasonable shape. It should have no curvature at the top $(M = EIy'' = 0$ at $x = l)$. The two simplest expressions we can pick are trigonometric and algebraic. We take the trigonometric one here and leave the others as Problems 186 and 187 for the reader. Suppose (Fig. 175)

$$y = y_l\left(1 - \cos\frac{\pi x}{2l}\right)$$

which is a displaced quarter cosine wave of amplitude y_l. The calculation of Eq. (132) now proceeds as follows:

$$y' = \frac{\pi}{2l}\, y_l \sin\frac{\pi x}{2l} \qquad y'' = \frac{\pi^2}{4l^2}\, y_l \cos\frac{\pi x}{2l}$$

$$\int_0^x y'^2\, dx = \frac{\pi^2}{4l^2}\, y_l^2 \int_0^x \sin^2\frac{\pi x}{2l}\, dx = \frac{\pi}{2l}\, y_l^2 \int_0^{\pi x/2l} \sin^2 \varphi\, d\varphi$$

The integral is looked up in tables,

$$\int_0^\varphi \sin^2 \varphi\, d\varphi = \frac{\varphi}{2} - \frac{1}{4}\sin 2\varphi$$

so that

$$\int_0^x y'^2\, dx = \frac{\pi}{8l}\, y_i^2\left(\frac{\pi x}{l} - \sin\frac{\pi x}{l}\right)$$

The last term of Eq. (132) is

$$w_1\frac{\pi}{8l}\, y_i^2 \int_0^l \left(\frac{\pi x}{l} - \sin\frac{\pi x}{l}\right) dx = \frac{w_1}{8}\, y_i^2 \int_0^\pi (\varphi - \sin\varphi)\, d\varphi$$

$$= \frac{w_1}{8}\, y_i^2\left(\frac{\pi^2}{2} - 2\right) = w_1 y_i^2\left(\frac{\pi^2}{16} - \frac{1}{4}\right)$$

The left-hand side of Eq. (132) is

$$EI\,\frac{\pi^4}{16l^4}\, y_i^2 \int_0^l \cos^2\frac{\pi x}{2l}\, dx = EI\,\frac{\pi^4}{16l^4}\, y_i^2\,\frac{l}{2}$$

Putting all terms together,

$$\frac{\pi^4 EI}{32l^3} - w_1\left(\frac{\pi^2}{16} - \frac{1}{4}\right) = \frac{P}{y_i} \tag{a}$$

We shall return to this result soon, but first we make $P = 0$ and look at the buckling under gravity alone:

$$(w_1)_{\text{crit}} = \frac{EI}{l^3}\,\frac{\pi^4}{32\left(\dfrac{\pi^2}{16} - \dfrac{1}{4}\right)} = 8.30\,\frac{EI}{l^3} \tag{b}$$

This is the critical weight under which the flagpole is in a state of indifferent equilibrium in the shape of Fig. 175 for $P = 0$. If we divide Eq. (a) by $(\pi^2/16) - \frac{1}{4}$, the first term becomes $(w_1)_{\text{crit}}$ so that Eq. (a) can be written

$$y_i = \frac{1}{\dfrac{\pi^2}{16} - \dfrac{1}{4}}\,\frac{P}{(w_1)_{\text{crit}} - w_1} = 2.76\,\frac{P}{(w_1)_{\text{crit}} - w_1} \tag{133a}$$

This tells us that if w_1 becomes as high as the critical loading, then y_i becomes infinity for finite load P: the cantilever has lost all resistance against sidewise push at the top. The result (b) should be greater than the exact truth: the *exact* buckling load has been found to be

$$(w_1)_{\text{crit}} = 7.84\,\frac{EI}{l^3} \tag{133b}$$

Exact Differential Equation of Flagpole. The exact solution of the flagpole problem (Fig. 175) with $P = 0$ is more difficult than the energy solution just given. To derive the differential equation we look (Fig. 176) at the equilibrium of a short piece dx. On top of it it carries the weight of the piece of rod above it:

$$F = \int_x^l w_1 \, dx = w_1(l - x)$$

and from below comes the force $F + dF$. Both forces are in the direction of gravity, *i.e.*, vertical parallel to the x axis. Between them they form a clockwise moment $F \, dy$.

For clockwise rotational equilibrium of the element dx we have

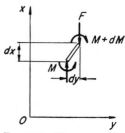

$$dM + F \, dy = 0$$

or

$$\frac{dM}{dx} = -F \frac{dy}{dx} = -w_1(l - x) \frac{dy}{dx}$$

But by the bending of beams we have

$$M = EIy'' \qquad \text{or} \qquad \frac{dM}{dx} = EIy'''$$

Fig. 176. Element of the cantilever of Fig. 175 for the case of zero side force P. The rotational equilibrium of this element is expressed by the differential equation (134).

Hence the differential equation of the flagpole under its own weight (without the force P of Fig. 175) is

$$y''' + \frac{w_1}{EI} (l - x)y' = 0 \qquad (134)$$

This is a non-linear differential equation (it contains the term xy'), which does not have a solution in finite form. Solutions have been found in the form of infinite power series, which can be expressed in terms of Bessel functions. For the details of this development, which are not easy, the reader is referred to more advanced books, for example, to Timoshenko's "Theory of Elastic Stability."[1]

37. Coil Springs; Beams on Elastic Foundation. When a common coil spring is subjected to compressive forces or to end bending moments, it behaves like any other ordinary "beam," except that it is a very "soft" beam and that it can take deformations very much larger than the usual beam. We can apply the usual Euler buckling formula to this case, but we have to interpret it in the light of "large deformations," *i.e.*, of deformations so large that the geometry of the loaded structure is markedly different from that of the unloaded structure. Consider the spring with "hinged" ends, *i.e.*, with ends that are free to rotate. The buckling load by Euler's formula then is:

$$P_{\text{crit}} = \frac{\pi^2 EI}{l^2} \qquad (135)$$

[1] McGraw-Hill Book Company, Inc., New York, 1936.

Here l is the length of the spring *in its compressed state* (different from the uncompressed length $l_0 = l + \Delta l$, the compression Δl being a substantial fraction of l_0); the quantity EI is the "bending stiffness" of the spring, regarded as a beam. The response of a spring to compression and to bending can be calculated by curved beam theory or by Castigliano's theorem (Problems 144 and 145), with the results (Fig. 177a and b)

$$\Delta l = \frac{P8nD^3}{Gd^4} \tag{136}$$

$$\varphi = M \frac{32nD}{Ed^4} (2 + \mu) \tag{137}$$

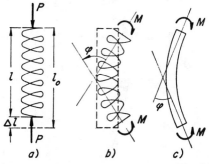

FIG. 177. Coil spring in compression P and in bending M. The deformations Δl and φ are expressed by Eqs. (136) and (137). An ordinary beam (c) in bending responds to $\varphi = Ml/EI$.

where D is the coil diameter, d the wire diameter, and n the number of turns of the "closely coiled" spring.

An ordinary beam (Fig. 177c) has an angle of bending

$$\varphi = M \frac{l}{EI}$$

Comparing this to Eq. (137), we conclude that the equivalent bending stiffness of a spring is

$$(EI)_{spring} = \frac{Ed^4l}{32nD(2 + \mu)} \tag{138}$$

This then is the meaning of EI in Eq. (135) when that equation is applied to a spring. Also in Eq. (135) we write $l = l_0 - \Delta l = l_0 - \delta_{crit}$, where δ_{crit} is the compression of the spring just when it buckles. Substituting (138) and the last result into (135), we find

$$P_{crit} = \frac{\pi^2 Ed^4l}{32nDl^2(2 + \mu)} = \frac{\pi^2 Ed^4}{32(2 + \mu)nD(l_0 - \delta_{crit})}$$

Now Eq. (136) enables us to eliminate P_{crit} from this:

$$(P_{\text{crit}} =)\ \frac{Gd^4 \delta_{\text{crit}}}{8nD^3} = \frac{\pi^2 E d^4}{32(2 + \mu)nD(l_0 - \delta_{\text{crit}})}$$

This is an equation with δ_{crit} as the unknown, and with some algebra it can be put into a cleaner form [remember that $E = 2G(1 + \mu)$]:

$$\left(\frac{\delta_{\text{crit}}}{l_0}\right)^2 - \left(\frac{\delta_{\text{crit}}}{l_0}\right) + \frac{\pi^2}{2}\frac{1 + \mu}{2 + \mu}\frac{D^2}{l_0^2} = 0$$

This is a quadratic equation in the unknown δ_{crit}/l_0 (the percentage compression before buckling), and it contains a parameter D/l_0, expressing the original slenderness of the spring. Taking $\mu = 0.3$, the solution is

$$\frac{\delta_{\text{crit}}}{l_0} = \frac{1}{2} - \frac{1}{2}\sqrt{1 - 11.2\left(\frac{D}{l_0}\right)^2} \qquad (139)$$

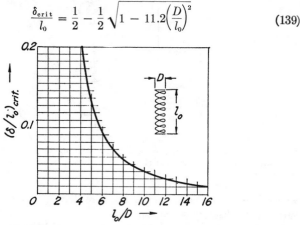

Fɪɢ. 178. Buckling of a coil spring with hinged ends (= freely rotatable ends). The abscissa is the slenderness of the unloaded spring, and the ordinate is the percentage decrease in length under the buckling load before buckling occurs. This is expressed by Eq. (139), and it agrees well with experiment in the range of this diagram.

a relation which is plotted in Fig. 178. It shows that a spring which is longer than five diameters buckles under a compressive load which decreases its length by less than 13 per cent. For springs shorter than $5D$ the figure and its equation (139) do not express the facts any more. More exact theories including the effect of the lateral shear force and the lateral shear deformation have been worked out recently, but these are much more complicated than what has been given here. Figure 178 covers the most practical part of the range covered by the usual springs. In order to find the critical *load* P_{crit} from the critical *deflection* of the figure, formula (136) has to be applied.

Beams on Elastic Foundation. Consider the beam of Fig. 179, being, for example, a rail on a track which is in compression due to temperature rise. Under what circumstances can such a rail buckle in the vertical plane? By the energy method the problem can be approached in two different manners, depending on whether we consider the reaction forces from the foundation as external forces on the rail, or whether we consider the foundation as part of our elastic system which can absorb elastic energy like the rail. We shall take the latter course and consider the rail plus the foundation as the elastic system, subjected to the external forces P only. The bending energy stored in the rail is given by Eq. (a) (page 251):

$$U_{\text{rail}} = \frac{1}{2} \int EI(y'')^2 \, dx \tag{a}$$

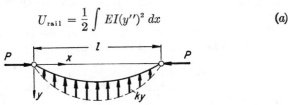

Fig. 179. A beam hinged at both ends, embedded in an elastic foundation of constant k, subjected to compressive end forces P, will buckle according to Eq. (141) if it is not too long.

The force acting on the foundation per length dx (exerted by the rail) is $ky \, dx$, and, the displacement being y, the work done on the foundation is $\frac{1}{2}ky^2 \, dx$. Hence the energy stored in the foundation is

$$U_{\text{foundation}} = \frac{1}{2} \int ky^2 \, dx \tag{b}$$

The work done by the external forces P on the shortening of the span is given by Eq. (b) (page 252):

$$\text{Work by } P = \frac{P}{2} \int y'^2 \, dx \tag{c}$$

The principle of work is expressed by

$$\frac{P}{2} \int y'^2 \, dx = \frac{1}{2} \int ky^2 \, dx + \frac{1}{2} \int EIy''^2 \, dx \tag{140}$$

The reader should now derive this same result by thinking of the rail by itself as the elastic system and letting the foundation act as a set of external forces.

Following Rayleigh's procedure, we now assume some reasonable shape $y(x)$, substitute it in (140), and solve for P, which then is the critical buckling load, because *only* when $P = P_{\text{crit}}$ is the beam *in equilibrium* in the deflected shape. We choose for the shape

$$y = y_0 \sin \frac{\pi x}{l}$$

and then the integrals in Eq. (140) are the same as those of page 253. The equation becomes

$$\frac{P}{2}\left(\frac{\pi}{l}\right)^2 y_0^2 \frac{l}{2} = \frac{k}{2} y_0^2 \frac{l}{2} + \frac{EI}{2}\left(\frac{\pi}{l}\right)^4 y_0^2 \frac{l}{2}$$

or

$$P_{\text{crit}} = k\left(\frac{l}{\pi}\right)^2 + EI\left(\frac{\pi}{l}\right)^2 \tag{141}$$

which is substantially greater than the Euler load. The Euler buckling load is the last term by itself; it is augmented by kl^2/π^2 due to the foundation.

With the notation used in elastic foundations [Eq. (86), page 143], this equation can be brought to a dimensionless form:

$$\frac{P_{\text{crit}}}{\sqrt{kEI}} = \left(\frac{\sqrt{2}\beta l}{\pi}\right)^2 + \left(\frac{\pi}{\sqrt{2}\beta l}\right)^2 \tag{142}$$

with

$$\beta = \sqrt[4]{\frac{k}{4EI}} \tag{86}$$

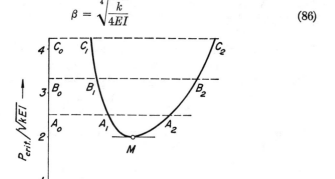

FIG. 180. The buckling load P_{crit} of a beam EI of length l with hinged ends on an elastic foundation k. This is a plot of Eq. (142).

In Eq. (142) all three terms are dimensionless, so that it has been made fit for plotting into a diagram (Fig. 180). The Euler critical load on an ordinary column (*not* on elastic foundation) decreases with increasing length. Here, however, we see that when the length increases above a certain minimum $l = \pi/2\beta$ (point M in the diagram), the buckling load increases with length. This, however, has to be taken with a grain of salt, because a long beam does not *have* to buckle out in a single half sine wave but can take two or more half sine waves if that happens to be "easier," *i.e.*, if that is associated with a smaller buckling load. Suppose we draw in Fig. 180 a line $A_0A_1A_2$ so chosen that $A_0A_1 = A_1A_2$; then the length corresponding to point A_2 is twice that of point A_1. Hence a bar of length A_2 [of length $(\sqrt{2}/\pi)\beta l = \sqrt{2}$; see Problem 188] can buckle with a single half wave, point A_2, or with two half waves, point A_1, for the same buckling load $P_{crit} = 2\frac{1}{2}\sqrt{kEI}$. If the length is greater than that corresponding to A_2 the load P_{crit} for two half waves is smaller than that for a single half wave. We can go further and draw the line $B_0B_1B_2$, so that $B_0B_2 = 3B_0B_1$, and a third line $C_0C_1C_2$, where $C_0C_2 = 4C_0C_1$, etc. The shapes corresponding to the smallest buckling load are shown in Fig. 180a.

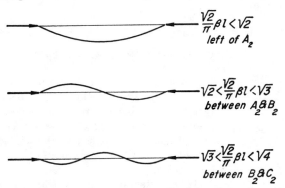

$$\frac{\sqrt{2}}{\pi}\beta l < \sqrt{2}$$
left of A_2

$$\sqrt{2} < \frac{\sqrt{2}}{\pi}\beta l < \sqrt{3}$$
between A_2 & B_2

$$\sqrt{3} < \frac{\sqrt{2}}{\pi}\beta l < \sqrt{4}$$
between B_2 & C_2

Fig. 180a. Various buckled shapes of bars on elastic foundation for various lengths, interpreting the graph of Fig. 180.

Suppose now we have a very long rail, so long that it will buckle most easily in a large number of half waves. We now ask what half wave length l the bar will choose for the purpose of making its buckling load as small as possible. This obviously takes place at point M in the diagram (Fig. 180) because that is the smallest load P_{crit} for any length. We have there $(\sqrt{2}/\pi)\beta l = 1$ or

$$\text{Half wave length } l = \frac{\pi}{\sqrt{2}\beta} = \pi\sqrt[4]{\frac{EI}{k}} \tag{143}$$

with

$$P_{crit} = 2\sqrt{kEI} = 2\frac{\pi^2 EI}{l^2} = 2P_{Euler}$$

This is the half wave length which will be assumed by a very long rail in an elastic foundation when subjected to a gradually increasing compressive end load. When the end load reaches the P_{crit} of Eqs. (143), the beam buckles in many half sine waves of length l, as indicated. If the P_{crit} so found comes out larger than the end load giving yield compression stress, Eqs. (143) obviously do not apply: in that case the beam yields before it buckles.

Longitudinally Compressed Thin-walled Tubes. On page 164 we have seen that the theory of elastic foundation had its principal application in tubes with rotationally symmetrical loading. Thus the case of Fig. 179 and Eqs. (143) can be applied to a thin-walled circular tube under longitudinal compression (without any radial loading on it). The formulae for translating the rail into a tube were given on page 165 [Eqs. (95) and (96)]. The beam on elastic foundation is a longitudinal strip of pipe of width $b = rd\theta$. To find the total load P_{crit} of the entire tube, we have to add the loads on all these strips, which amounts to making $b = 2\pi r$ in the formula for P_{crit}. With Eqs. (95) and (96), the results (143) modify for a thin-walled tube to

$$\text{Half wave length } l = 1.73 \sqrt{rt}$$
$$\text{Longitudinal buckling load } P_{crit} = 3.80Et^2 \tag{143a}$$

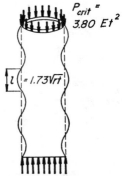

FIG. 181. Buckling of a thin-walled tube in a rotationally symmetrical form caused by end compression. The length of the half wave is extremely short, and the result [Eqs. (143a)] does not correspond with experiment. Actual test results show a buckling load P_{crit} of about 40 per cent of the calculated value shown in this figure.

The shape of the buckling is rotationally symmetrical, as shown in Fig. 181. This is a beautiful theory, but unfortunately it does not conform to the sordid facts. Experiments on the longitudinal compression of thin-walled circular struts have produced buckling at loads which are consistently about 40 per cent of that of Eqs. (143a). Repeated attempts have appeared in the literature to explain this discrepancy, so far, however, without complete satisfaction. Therefore, Eqs. (143a) should not be used for design purposes, for which we should rely on the published test results until a better theory is found.

38. Proof of Rayleigh's Theorem. Rayleigh's theorem, of which several examples were given on pages 252 to 262, states that if an approximate buckling shape $y(x)$ is inserted into the energy equation (131) of a bar, then an approximate critical load is found, which always errs on the high side, so that among all approximate values so found the smallest one is the best one. The proof of this theorem is based on "normal functions" and is quite the same as the proof for a similar proposition in the theory of vibration of bars. In that case we equate the kinetic and potential energies of the vibrating bar, both expressed in terms of the deformations, and the natural frequency comes out of it. Here again, if an approximate vibrating shape $y(x)$ is inserted into the energy equation, we get an approximate natural frequency, which is always somewhat too large.

We now start with the proof and begin by writing down the differential equation (page 251) and the energy equation (page 252) of the buckling column:

$$EIy'' = -Py \tag{130}$$

$$P \int_0^l (y')^2 \, dx = \int_0^l EI(y'')^2 \, dx \tag{131}$$

If the exact shape $y(x)$ is known and is substituted into these equations, they are both satisfied. Now we know that there is not one such solution for a bar but an infinite number of them: for a uniform bar, hinged at both ends, they are one, two, three, etc., half sine waves; for other bars and other end conditions, they have different shapes. Let these various exact solutions (not known to us at present) be denoted by

$$y_1(x), \ y_2(x), \ \ldots, \ y_n(x), \ \ldots$$

and their corresponding buckling loads by

$$P_1, P_2, \ \ldots, P_n, \ \ldots$$

The nth energy equation then is

$$P_n \int_0^l (y_n')^2 \, dx = \int_0^l EI(y_n'')^2 \, dx \tag{131a}$$

and it is *exactly* satisfied.

Now, Rayleigh substitutes into Eq. (131) a shape which is not $y_1(x)$ because he does not know exactly what $y_1(x)$ looks like, but he finds an approximation. Let us write that approximation $y(x)$ in terms of a series,

$$y(x) = a_1 y_1(x) + a_2 y_2(x) + \cdots + a_n y_n(x) + \cdots \tag{a}$$

in which the individual terms are the various exact buckling shapes. If the approximation is a good one, the coefficient a_1 is large compared with the other coefficients a_2, a_3, which represent the impurities in the assumed shape. The proof which is now coming is a generalization of the Fourier-series process. In Fourier series we have the fundamental formulae

$$\left. \begin{array}{l} \displaystyle\int_0^l \sin \frac{m\pi x}{l} \sin \frac{n\pi x}{l} \, dx = 0 \\[3mm] \displaystyle\int_0^l \cos \frac{m\pi x}{l} \cos \frac{n\pi x}{l} \, dx = 0 \end{array} \right\} \quad \text{(for } m \neq n\text{)}$$

Here, where we have the more general $y_m(x)$ function instead of $\sin (m\pi x/l)$, there are also two relations, which we shall now write down and use, while postponing their proof till later. They are

$$\int_0^l y'_m y'_n \, dx = 0 \qquad \text{(for } m \neq n) \tag{b}$$

$$\int_0^l EI y''_m y''_n \, dx = 0 \qquad \text{(for } m \neq n) \tag{c}$$

and they are true for any bar of variable cross section EI for either hinged or built-in ends. The y_m functions are the natural buckled shapes of the bar.

Rayleigh then substitutes the assumption (a) into his energy equation (131):

$$P = \frac{\int_0^l EI(y'')^2 \, dx}{\int_0^l (y')^2 \, dx} = \frac{\int_0^l EI(a_1 y''_1 + a_2 y''_2 + \cdots + a_n y''_n + \cdots)^2 \, dx}{\int_0^l (a_1 y'_1 + a_2 y'_2 + \cdots + a_n y'_n + \cdots)^2 \, dx}$$

The P in this expression is the approximate answer we expect to get. It would be the exact P_1 only if the impurity coefficients a_2, a_3, etc., were zero. Now in working out the squares in the two integrands above, we get square terms y''^2_n and double product terms $y''_m y''_n$. By virtue of the two auxiliary theorems (b) and (c), the double products integrated all become zero, so that we can write

$$P = \frac{\int_0^l EI(a_1^2 y''^2_1 + a_2^2 y''^2_2 + \cdots + a_n^2 y''^2_n + \cdots) \, dx}{\int_0^l (a_1^2 y'^2_1 + a_2^2 y'^2_2 + \cdots + a_n^2 y'^2_n + \cdots) \, dx}$$

$$P = \frac{a_1^2 \int_0^l EI y''^2_1 \, dx + a_2^2 \int_0^l EI y''^2_2 \, dx + \cdots}{a_1^2 \int_0^l y'^2_1 \, dx + a_2^2 \int_0^l y'^2_2 \, dx + \cdots}$$

Now we look at each term in the numerator of the above expression and consider the energy equation (131). This equation is exactly true for the various exact buckling shapes $y_1, y_2, \ldots, y_n$ [Eq. (131a)]. The first term in the numerator thus is

$$a_1^2 \int_0^l EI y''^2_1 \, dx = a_1^2 P_1 \int_0^l y'^2_1 \, dx$$

and similarly for the other terms:

$$P = \frac{a_1^2 P_1 \int_0^l y_1'^2 \, dx + a_2^2 P_2 \int_0^l y_2'^2 \, dx + \cdots}{a_1^2 \int_0^l y_1'^2 \, dx + a_2^2 \int_0^l y_2'^2 \, dx + \cdots}$$

$$P = P_1 \frac{a_1^2 \int_0^l y_1'^2 \, dx + \frac{P_2}{P_1} a_2^2 \int_0^l y_2'^2 \, dx + \frac{P_3}{P_1} a_3^2 \int \cdots}{a_1^2 \int_0^l y_1'^2 \, dx + a_2^2 \int_0^l y_2'^2 \, dx + a_3^2 \int \cdots}$$

Now P_1 is the smallest buckling load, so that P_2/P_1 and P_3/P_1 and all the following ratios are greater than 1. Thus we recognize that the complicated fraction in the above expression is greater than 1, because each term in the numerator is larger than the term below it in the denominator. Hence

$$P > P_1$$

which proves Rayleigh's proposition.

To make the proof complete, we still have to *prove the auxiliary propositions* (b) *and* (c). We start by writing the differential equation (130) twice:

$$EIy_m'' = -P_m y_m$$
$$EIy_n'' = -P_n y_n$$

Cross multiplying diagonally and dividing by $-EI$ gives

$$P_m y_m y_n'' = P_n y_n y_m''$$

Multiply by dx, and integrate:

$$P_m \int_0^l y_m y_n'' \, dx = P_n \int_0^l y_n y_m'' \, dx \qquad (d)$$

We take the first of these integrals and integrate it "partially" a couple of times:

$$\int_0^l y_m y_n'' \, dx = \int_0^l y_m \, dy_n' = y_m y_n' \Big|_0^l - \int_0^l y_n' \, dy_m$$

The first term is zero at both limits $y_m = 0$ at $x = 0, l$ because y_m is a natural buckling shape and the bar is supposed to be hinged at both ends. Thus

$$\int_0^l y_m y_n'' \, dx = -\int y_n' \, dy_m = -\int y_n' y_m' \, dx$$

$$= -\int y_m' \, dy_n = -\underbrace{y_m' y_n \Big|_0^l}_{\text{zero}} + \int y_n \, dy_m'$$

$$= \int y_n \, dy_m' = \int y_n y_m'' \, dx \qquad (e)$$

Substitute the last result into Eq. (d):

$$P_m \int_0^l y_n y_m'' \, dx = P_n \int_0^l y_n y_m'' \, dx$$

Now since $m \neq n$ and $P_m \neq P_n$, this can be true only if the integral is zero:

$$\int_0^l y_n y_m'' \, dx = 0 \qquad (f)$$

But, by Eq. (e), this means that

$$\int_0^l y_n' y_m' \, dx = 0 \qquad (b)$$

which proves proposition (b) of page 266. Now we return to (f), and in it substitute for y_n its value from the differential equation (130):

$$0 = \int_0^l y_n y_m'' \, dx = - \int_0^l \left(\frac{EI}{P_n} y_n'' \right) y_m'' \, dx = - \frac{1}{P_n} \int_0^l EI y_n'' y_m'' \, dx$$

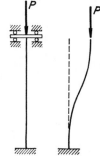

Fig. 182. Column built in at the bottom and constrained at the top to keep a vertical tangent. This type of end condition satisfies Rayleigh's theorem, so that an approximate buckling load found by that method comes out somewhat larger than the true value.

which proves proposition (c).

Twice in the proof we saw an expression of the form $y_m y_n'$ taken between the limits 0 and l, which gave us zero for the usual hinged or built-in ends, because there y is zero. However, the expression is zero at the end limits also if the slope y' is zero, even if y itself is permitted to have a value at the end. A case of this kind is illustrated in Fig. 182. Therefore, Rayleigh's theorem is true for columns of variable cross section with end points which either do not move sidewise or are not permitted to turn.

39. Vianello's or Stodola's Method. Rayleigh's method leads to an answer which we know is somewhat too large, but we have no way of estimating how much too large. This defect does not apply to another method, found by *Vianello* for buckling columns, and later discovered independently for the parallel problem of vibrating shafts by *Stodola*. This procedure enables us to improve our answer in successive steps, or successive "iterations," and ultimately leads us as close to the exact answer as we want by taking a sufficiently large number of iterations. The method is based on the differential equation (130) (page 251).

$$EI y'' = -Py \qquad (130)$$

Vianello assumes a reasonable approximate shape which we call $_Iy$. (We use a Roman subscript in front of y for this first approximation to distinguish it from y_1 by which we mean the exact first natural buckling shape, as before.) He then substitutes this $_Iy$ into the right-hand side of the differential equation:

$$EIy'' = -P_Iy$$

The right-hand side now is a definite function of x so that we can integrate twice:

$$_{II}y = -P \iint \frac{_Iy}{EI} \, dx \, dx$$

fixing the integration constants properly. The result so obtained we call $_{II}y$. If we had taken the true shape y_1 for $_Iy$, the differential equation tells us that the answer $_{II}y$ is the same as y_1, and if $_Iy$ differs from y_1, then $_{II}y$ is approximately like y_1. This is the first step, or first iteration. Now we put the new result $_{II}y$ into the right-hand side of the differential equation, integrate, and find a third approximation $_{III}y$. Vianello's theorem states that this process converges to the true solution y_1. Before giving the proof we shall illustrate it on the classical bothway-hinged uniform Euler column EI, l. In order to take advantage of symmetry, the origin of coordinates is laid in the center of the column (Fig. 173). As a first approximation we take a parabola, which we know to be wrong, because it has constant curvature:

$$_Iy = y_0\left[1 - \left(\frac{x}{l/2}\right)^2 \right] \tag{a}$$

Substituting this into the right-hand side of Eq. (130),

$$EI \,_{II}y'' = -P \,_Iy = -Py_0\left[1 - \left(\frac{x}{l/2}\right)^2 \right]$$

Integrate once:

$$_{II}y' = -\frac{Py_0}{EI} \int_0^l \left(1 - \frac{4x^2}{l^2} \right) dx$$

$$= -\frac{Py_0}{EI}\left(x - \frac{4x^3}{3l^2} + \text{const} \right)$$

The constant is to be found from boundary conditions. We know by symmetry that the slope y' must be zero at $x = 0$; hence the constant is zero.

Integrate a second time:

$$_{II}y = -\frac{Py_0}{EI} \int \left(x - \frac{4x^3}{3l^2} \right) dx$$

$$= -\frac{Py_0}{EI}\left[\frac{x^2}{2} - \frac{x^4}{3l^2} + \text{const} \right]$$

The boundary condition now is that $y = 0$ at $x = \pm l/2$ or at $x^2 = l^2/4$. Hence the constant is

$$\text{Const} = -\frac{l^2}{8} + \frac{l^4}{48l^2} = -\frac{5l^2}{48}$$

and

$$_{II}y = -\frac{P}{EI}\, y_0 \left[-\frac{5l^2}{48} + \frac{x^2}{2} - \frac{x^4}{3l^2} \right]$$

or, making the constant in the square brackets equal to 1 for comparison with Eq. (a),

$$_{II}y = \frac{5}{48}\frac{Pl^2}{EI}\, y_0 \left[1 - \frac{24}{5}\frac{x^2}{l^2} + \frac{16}{5}\frac{x^4}{l^4} \right] \qquad (b)$$

The square brackets of $_{I}y$ [Eq. (a)] and of $_{II}y$ [Eq. (b)] both have unit value in the center of the beam and zero value at the two ends $\pm l/2$. The shapes of the curves differ, but they are approximately the same. Then, since $_{II}y$ must be approximately $_{I}y$, the factors before the square brackets of Eqs. (a) and (b) also must be the same, and from that we find the first approximation of the buckling load:

$$_{I}P = \frac{48}{5}\frac{EI}{l^2} = 9.60\frac{EI}{l^2}$$

The exact answer is $\pi^2 = 9.87$, so that this is quite decent already. We note that the approximate answer is not larger than the exact one; there is no reason why this should be so, since we are not dealing with Rayleigh's method, and the answer with Vianello's method may be off on either side of the true value.

Now we proceed to the next iteration:

$$EI\,_{III}y'' = -P\,_{II}y = -\frac{5}{48}\frac{P^2}{EI}l^2 y_0 \left[1 - \frac{24}{5}\frac{x^2}{l^2} + \frac{16}{5}\frac{x^4}{l^4} \right]$$

Integrating once and fixing the integration constant properly,

$$_{III}y' = -\frac{5}{48}\left(\frac{P}{EI}\right)^2 l^2 y_0 \left[x - \frac{8}{5}\frac{x^3}{l^2} + \frac{16}{25}\frac{x^5}{l^4} \right]$$

Integrating again,

$$_{III}y = -\frac{5}{48}\left(\frac{P}{EI}\right)^2 l^2 y_0 \left[\frac{x^2}{2} - \frac{2}{5}\frac{x^4}{l^2} + \frac{8}{75}\frac{x^6}{l^4} - \frac{61l^2}{600} \right]$$

or, reducing the constant term in the square brackets to unity,

$$_{III}y = \frac{61}{120 \times 48}\left(\frac{Pl^2}{EI}\right)^2 y_0 \left[1 - \frac{300}{61}\frac{x^2}{l^2} + \frac{240}{61}\frac{x^4}{l^4} - \frac{64x^6}{61l^6} \right] \qquad (c)$$

Again the square brackets in this expression is unity in the center of the bar and zero at the ends, thus corresponding approximately to the square brackets of the previous iteration [Eq. (b)]. Since $_{III}y$ and $_{II}y$ also must be approximately equal, we equate the factors before the brackets of (b) and (c):

$$_{II}P = \frac{120 \times 48}{61} \times \frac{5}{48} \frac{EI}{l^2} = \frac{600}{61} \frac{EI}{l^2} = 9.84 \frac{EI}{l^2}$$

This is the second approximation for the buckling load, much closer to the exact value of $\pi^2 = 9.87$ than the first approximation. It is now of interest to compare the three consecutive shapes $_Iy$, $_{II}y$, and $_{III}y$ with the exact shape, which is a sine wave, and to that end we rewrite the expressions (a), (b), and (c) in terms of the new variable,

$$\varphi = \frac{\pi x}{l}$$

which has the dimension of an angle, being zero in the center and running to $\pm \pi/2$ at the ends. The reader should check the numbers and verify as follows:

$$_Iy = 1 - 0.405\varphi^2$$
$$_{II}y = 1 - 0.486\varphi^2 + 0.032\varphi^4$$
$$_{III}y = 1 - 0.498\varphi^2 + 0.040\varphi^4 - 0.001\varphi^6$$
$$y_{\text{exact}} = 1 - 0.500\varphi^2 + 0.042\varphi^4 - 0.001\varphi^6 + 0.000\varphi^8 - \cdots$$

The last expression is the Taylor series for a cosine. We see that the shape gets closer to the exact one with every iteration.

For columns with different end conditions or variable EI, the method works in the same manner. We shall now proceed to prove that Vianello's process converges to the true solution.

Proof of the Convergence of Vianello's Method. Let the first assumption $_Iy$ for the buckled shape be

$$_Iy = a_1y_1 + a_2y_2 + \cdots + a_ny_n + \cdots \qquad (d)$$

If the choice is a wise one, the coefficient a_1 is large, and the coefficients a_2, a_3, are relatively small. The functions y_1, y_2, . . . , are the natural buckling shapes of the bar, as explained on page 265, y_n consisting of n half sine waves for the special case of the uniform Euler column with hinged ends.

Following Vianello's procedure, we substitute (d) into the differential equation (130):

$$EI\,_{II}y'' = -P[a_1y_1 + a_2y_2 + \cdots + a_ny_n + \cdots]$$

or

$$_{II}y = -P\left[a_1 \iint \frac{y_1\,dx\,dx}{EI} + a_2 \iint \frac{y_2\,dx\,dx}{EI} + \cdots \right]$$

Now any one natural shape y_n satisfies the differential equation (130):

$$EIy_n'' = -P_n y_n$$

or

$$y_n = -P_n \iint \frac{y_n \, dx \, dx}{EI}$$

With this we can rewrite every term in the above square brackets:

$$_{11}y = P\left[\frac{a_1}{P_1} y_1 + \frac{a_2}{P_2} y_2 + \cdots + \frac{a_n}{P_n} y_n + \cdots \right] \qquad (e)$$

Here P is the approximate value of the buckling load, while $P_1 \ldots P_n$ are the various exact buckling loads. The equation can also be written as

$$_{11}y = \frac{P}{P_1}\left[a_1 y_1 + \frac{P_1}{P_2} a_2 y_2 + \frac{P_1}{P_3} a_3 y_3 + \cdots \right]$$

The square brackets of this series have the same first term as the original assumption (d), while all other terms are smaller, because they are multiplied by a ratio P_1/P_n, and the first buckling load is smaller than all the others. If $_{11}y$ is substituted into the differential equation, we find in the same way

$$_{111}y = \left(\frac{P}{P_1}\right)^2\left[a_1 y_1 + \left(\frac{P_1}{P_2}\right)^2 a_2 y_2 + \left(\frac{P_1}{P_3}\right)^2 a_3 y_3 + \cdots \right]$$

in which we see that the higher terms are smaller than in the previous approximation. If we carry out the process $N + 1$ times, the higher terms are multiplied by $(P_1/P_n)^N$, which becomes closer and closer to zero for growing N. Thus eventually we find for large N

$$\lim_{N \to \infty} {}_{N+1}y = \left(\frac{P}{P_1}\right)^N a_1 y_1$$

and the curve $_{N+1}y$ coincides in every detail with the exact curve y_1.

Vianello's Solution of the Flagpole Problem. The differential equation (134) of the collapsing flagpole was derived on page 258. In order to apply Vianello's procedure to it, we assume some sort of shape for the slope y'. To illustrate the method, we purposely make a stupid choice,

$$_1y' = \alpha$$

i.e., a constant slope and a linear deflection curve at angle α (Fig. 183). We could have done better by assuming $_1y' = Cx$, but we shall now go ahead with the less fortunate assumption to see how quickly the solution converges. Substitute $_1y' = \alpha$ into the differential equation (134) (p. 258):

$$_{11}y''' = \frac{w_1}{EI} (x - l) \, _1y' = \frac{w_1}{EI} (x - l)\alpha$$

Integrate:

$$_{II}y'' = \frac{w_1\alpha}{EI}\left(\frac{x^2}{2} - lx + \text{const}\right)$$

At the top of the pole $x = l$ there is no bending moment, and hence no y''. From this we find the constant to be $l^2/2$ and

$$_{II}y'' = \frac{w_1\alpha}{EI}\left(\frac{x^2}{2} - lx + \frac{l^2}{2}\right)$$

Integrate again:

$$_{II}y' = \frac{w_1\alpha}{EI}\left(\frac{x^3}{6} - \frac{lx^2}{2} + \frac{l^2 x}{2} + \text{zero}\right)$$

The integration constant is zero because the slope y' must be zero at the base $x = 0$. The deflection curve is found again by integration:

$$_{II}y = \frac{w_1\alpha}{EI}\left(\frac{x^4}{24} - \frac{x^3 l}{6} + \frac{x^2 l^2}{4} + \text{zero}\right)$$

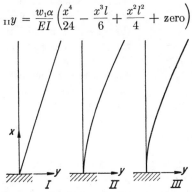

FIG. 183. Three consecutive Vianello iterations for the shape of a flagpole buckling under its own weight.

This shape is so much different from $_{I}y = \alpha x$ (see Fig. 183) that it is useless for comparison, and we must perform another iteration:

$$_{III}y''' = \frac{w_1}{EI}(x - l)\,_{II}y' = \left(\frac{w_1}{EI}\right)^2\alpha(x - l)\left(\frac{x^3}{6} - \frac{x^2 l}{2} + \frac{xl^2}{2}\right)$$

$$= \left(\frac{w_1}{EI}\right)^2\alpha\left[\frac{x^4}{6} - \frac{2}{3}x^3 l + x^2 l^2 - \frac{1}{2}xl^3\right]$$

Integrating three times with proper regard to the integration constants leads to

$$_{III}y = \left(\frac{w_1}{EI}\right)^2\alpha\left[\frac{x^7}{1,260} - \frac{x^6 l}{180} + \frac{x^5 l^2}{60} - \frac{x^4 l^3}{48} + \frac{x^2 l^5}{40}\right]$$

This curve looks much like the previous one, $_{II}y$ (Fig. 183). We match the two for size by calculating their amplitude at the tip $x = l$ and equating them:

$$(\text{III}y)_{x=l} = \left(\frac{w_1}{EI}\right)^2 \alpha l^7 \frac{9}{560} = (\text{II}y)_{x=l} = \frac{w}{EI}\alpha l^4 \frac{70}{560}$$

From this we conclude

$$\left(\frac{w_1 l^3}{EI}\right)_{\text{crit}} = \frac{70}{9} = 7.78$$

which is very close to the exact value 7.84 of Eq. (133b) (page 257).

40. Rings, Boiler Tubes, and Arches. Consider the ring of Fig. 184, of purely circular contour, subjected to uniform external pressure. Since the pressure is uniformly distributed, it tends to put hoop compression into the ring, but there is no tendency to deform it out of the circular shape.

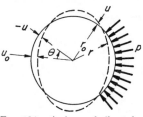

FIG. 184. A ring or boiler tube under external hydrostatic pressure p will collapse into a flattened, ellipse-like shape when the pressure reaches the critical value of Eqs. (146).

However, if by some chance the ring *were* flattened somewhat, then the pressure would tend to increase the flattening. It has been observed that there exists a critical value of the pressure p in which the originally circular ring is in a state of indifferent equilibrium when flattened. For the derivation of the differential equation of this effect we use the expression for the change in curvature [Eq. (122a), page 237]:

$$EI\frac{u + u''}{r_0^2} = M \qquad (122a)$$

The deformation of the ring is expressed by the radial displacement u, positive outward, u being a function of the angle θ and being small with respect to the radius of the ring. The value of u at angle $\theta = 0$ we call $-u_0$.

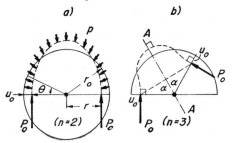

FIG. 185. To prove that the compressive force P_0, occurring in the ring at the locations where $u = -u_0$ and $u' = 0$, equals $p(r_0 - u_0)$ for deformations which are described by waves around the periphery: $2\alpha = 2\pi/n$, where $n = 1, 2, 3$, etc. This is Eq. (a).

In order to find the bending moment M in an arbitrary section θ of the ring, we first look at Fig. 185a. The pressure forces on the upper half of the ring are statically equivalent to that same pressure acting on a diameter. Hence the compressive force P_0 in the cross section $\theta = 0$ is found from the vertical equilibrium of that half ring:

$$2P_0 = p2r = p2(r_0 - u_0)$$

or

$$P_0 = p(r_0 - u_0) \tag{a}$$

If the ring collapses in a form different from the flattened shape of Fig. 185a (and later we shall see that it can do that: Fig. 187), we assume that it will again show $u = -u_0$ with $u' = 0$ at some angle $\theta = 2\alpha$ different from 180 deg, as in Fig. 185b. The equilibrium of the portion 2α cut out from the tube, taken along the line AA, gives

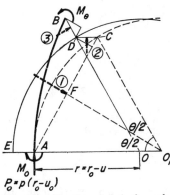

$$2P_0 \sin \alpha = p2r \sin \alpha$$

with the same result (a). Thus Eq. (a) is always true for the case that the tube collapses in a number of symmetrical waves around the periphery.

Now, in Fig. 186, we cut out from the ring the section between $\theta = 0$, point A, and $\theta = \theta$, point B, where θ is an arbitrary angle. At point A acts the normal force $P_0 = p(r_0 - u_0)$ and an unknown bending moment M_0. At point B there is a bending moment M_θ, which we like to calculate, as well as normal and shear forces P_θ and S_θ, which we don't care about. In order to find M_θ at B, we consider moment equilibrium about B, which is not affected by the P and S forces at B.

FIG. 186. The thin circle is the undeformed shape, the thick curve the deformed shape of the ring. The dashed circle is equal to the undeformed thin circle, displaced by u_0 to the right, so that O_1 is its center and $OO_1 = u_0$.

On the deformed, curved piece AB of Fig. 186 acts the pressure p, which gives a force statically equivalent to the force p acting on any other line connecting points A and B. For our derivation we find it convenient to draw through point A a dashed circle about center O_1, displaced from O by u_0 to the right. Now we draw OB, which produces the intersection D; then we go parallel to the right from D, producing point C, and connect A with C. We call $DB = u$, the general radial displacement, and $DC = u_0$. The pressure force of p on the curved line AB equals the force of p on the broken straight line $ACDB$. Now $OE = OD = r_0 = O_1 A = O_1 C$. The secant $AC = 2r_0 \sin(\theta/2)$, and the pressure force one on that portion is $p2r_0 \sin(\theta/2)$. The pressure forces on CD and BD, shown in the figure as two and three, are of the order of magnitude u; their moment arms about point B are also of order u, so that their moments are of order u^2. In this analysis we are interested in first-order quantities only, so that we can neglect the forces two and three. For the moment equilibrium about B, then, we have to consider four quantities: M_0, M_θ, and the moments from P_0 and force one. The moment arm of P_0 is the horizontal distance between A and B, which equals the horizontal projections of $AC + CD + BD$, or

$$r_0(1 - \cos \theta) - u_0 - u \cos \theta$$

The moment arm of force one about B is the projection of the distance FB on the line AC or the projection on AC of the lengths $FC + CD + DB$, which is

$$r_0 \sin \frac{\theta}{2} - u_0 \sin \frac{\theta}{2} + u \sin \frac{\theta}{2}$$

The equilibrium equation then is

$$M_\theta = M_0 + p(r_0 - u_0)[r_0(1 - \cos \theta) - u_0 - u \cos \theta]$$
$$- p2r_0 \sin \frac{\theta}{2} \left(r_0 \sin \frac{\theta}{2} - u_0 \sin \frac{\theta}{2} + u \sin \frac{\theta}{2}\right)$$

In working this out we first take the p terms of finite magnitude, not containing u or u_0, and find that they all cancel, because of the identity

$$1 - \cos \theta = 2 \sin^2 \frac{\theta}{2}$$

Next we take the first-order terms, $i.e.$, those proportional to pu and to pu_0, which combine to $-pr_0(u + u_0)$, as the reader should verify. Finally there are several terms of second order, proportional to u^2 or uu_0, etc., which we neglect, so that

$$M_\theta = M_0 - pr_0(u + u_0) \tag{b}$$

Referring to Eq. (122a) (page 237) and noting that M_θ as drawn in Fig. 186 tends to *decrease* the local curvature, we have

$$EI \frac{u + u''}{r_0^2} = M_0 - pr_0(u + u_0)$$

We remember that u_0, M_0, r_0 are constants, not depending on θ, and that $u = f(\theta)$. Taking the variable terms together on the left, we have

$$u'' + u\left(1 + \frac{pr_0^3}{EI}\right) = \frac{M_0 r_0^2}{EI} - \frac{pr_0^3 u_0}{EI} \tag{144}$$

This is the differential equation for the buckling of *a ring* of bending stiffness EI in its own plane. In case we want to apply it to a long boiler tube, we have to work with Eq. (122b) instead of Eq. (122a), and the general result (144) still holds per unit length of tube, but now we have to replace

$$EI \text{ by } \frac{EI}{1 - \mu^2} = \frac{Et^3}{12(1 - \mu^2)} = D$$

[see Eq. (64), page 107] to take care of the prevented anticlastic curvature of the long tube, thus:

$$u'' + u\left(1 + \frac{pr_0^3}{D}\right) = \frac{M_0 r_0^2}{D} - \frac{pr_0^3 u_0}{D} \tag{144a}$$

This is the buckling equation *for a unit length of a long tube.* The differential equation (144a) is linear, and it has a constant right-hand member. With the shorthand notation

$$k^2 = 1 + \frac{pr_0^3}{D} \tag{145}$$

its general solution is

$$u = C_1 \sin k\theta + C_2 \cos k\theta + \frac{(M_0 r_0^2/D) - (pr_0^3 u_0/D)}{1 + (pr_0^3/D)}$$

or

$$u = C_1 \sin k\theta + C_2 \cos k\theta + \frac{M_0 - pr_0 u_0}{pr_0 + (D/r_0^2)}$$

One of our boundary conditions is $u' = 0$ at $\theta = 0$, because we chose our origin of coordinates that way (Fig. 184). This makes $C_1 = 0$ and $u = C_2 \cos k\theta +$ (the above constant, independent of θ). When we go around the circle from $\theta = 0$ to $\theta = 2\pi$, we must end up at $\theta = 2\pi$ with the same $u(= -u_0)$ that we started with at $\theta = 0$. This means that

$$\cos (k \cdot 0) = \cos (k \cdot 2\pi) = 1 \quad \text{or} \quad k = 1, 2, 3, \ldots$$

The meaning of k thus is the number of full cosine waves around the periphery. By Eq. (145) we have

$$k^2 = 1 + \frac{pr_0^3}{D} = 1, 4, 9, \ldots$$

or

$$p_{\text{crit}} = (k^2 - 1) \frac{D}{r_0^3} = \frac{D}{r_0^3} \times (0, \quad 3, \quad 8, \quad 15, \ldots) \tag{146}$$

$$\text{for } k = 1, \quad 2, \quad 3, \quad 4, \ldots$$

This is the formula of *Levy*, published in France in 1884, a year after the basic differential equations (122a) and (122b) were found by *Boussinesq.* The formula is illustrated in Fig. 187. The lowest form is interesting mathematically: for $k = 1$ we have two nodes, and geometrically this means a small sidewise displacement of the undistorted circle, which ob-

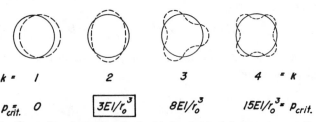

$$k = 1 \qquad 2 \qquad 3 \qquad 4 \ = k$$

$$p_{crit.} \ \ 0 \qquad \boxed{3EI/r_0^3} \qquad 8EI/r_0^3 \qquad 15EI/r_0^3 = p_{crit.}$$

FIG. 187. The various shapes of a ring buckled under the influence of external pressure p. The number k is the number of full sine waves around the periphery, and p_{crit} is the corresponding critical pressure to produce indifferent equilibrium in the shapes shown [Eqs. (146)]. For a long tube the quantity EI has to be replaced by $D = Et^3/12(1 - \mu^2)$.

viously is in equilibrium without any pressure at all. The first case of significance is for $k = 2$, when the tube or ring goes to an ellipse-like shape and the critical pressure is

$$p_{\text{crit}} = \frac{3EI}{r_0^3} \qquad \text{(ring)}$$

$$(146a)$$

$$p_{\text{crit}} = \frac{3Et}{12r_0^3(1 - \mu^2)} \qquad \text{(tube)}$$

For higher modes the critical pressures are higher.

Derivation of Tube-buckling Formula by Energy Method. The results (146a) can be derived by the method of work as well. If we have a round tube or ring and we imagine it distorted in the shape of Fig. 184, there is bending in it, and there will be a certain amount of elastic energy stored in the tube. It will not stay distorted by itself; we have to pinch it from the sides, and as soon as we remove these pinching forces, the tube snaps back elastically to the circular form. The necessary value of the pinching forces can be found by increasing the flattening somewhat, by finding the work the pinching forces do on this deformation, and by equating it to the increase in stored elastic energy. If the pinching is being done by a uniform external pressure force, we follow the same procedure. The work done by such a pressure p on the deformation is p times the decrease in area of the tube (per unit length). Now we must invent a decent approximation of the deformation to describe the situation of Fig. 184. We might write

$$u = -u_0 \cos 2\theta$$

and if we then try to find the difference in area between the ellipse-like tube and the circular one, we find

$$\frac{1}{2}\int_0^{2\pi}(r_0+u)^2\,d\theta - \frac{1}{2}\int_0^{2\pi}r_0^2\,d\theta = r_0\int_0^{2\pi}u\,d\theta + \text{second-order term}$$

$$= -r_0u_0\int_0^{2\pi}\cos 2\theta\,d\theta + \cdots$$

$$= \text{zero} + \text{second-order term}$$

Hence the work done by the pressure p is of second order in u only; the first-order effect disappears. This is always the case with the energy method: we have seen it before in the left side of Eq. 131 (page 252). But if we work with second-order terms, the expression for $u = -u_0\cos 2\theta$ is not good enough, because we shall soon see that the wavy line $u = -u_0\cos 2\theta$ has a length which differs from the circle $u = 0$ by a quantity of the order u_0^2. The buckled shape should have the same length as the original circle, and we assume

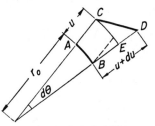

Fig. 188. To find the difference in length between a circular element $AB = r_0 d\theta$ and the deformed element CD. In the text this is shown to be

$$CD - AB = (u + u'^2/2r_0)\,d\theta.$$

$$u = -u_0\cos 2\theta + a \qquad (c)$$

where we shall determine the constant a so as to keep the same length of the circular center line of the pipe or ring. To find the change in length, we consider in Fig. 188 an element $AB = r_0 d\theta$ of the undeformed tube which goes to CD when deformed. Now

$$(CD)^2 = (CE)^2 + (ED)^2 = (r_0+u)^2(d\theta)^2 + (du)^2$$

$$= (r_0+u)^2(d\theta)^2 + u'^2(d\theta)^2$$

$$= (d\theta)^2(r_0^2 + 2r_0u + u^2 + u'^2)$$

$$= r_0^2(d\theta)^2\left(1 + 2\frac{u}{r_0} + \frac{u^2+u'^2}{r_0^2}\right)$$

so that

$$CD = r\,d\theta\sqrt{1 + 2\frac{u}{r_0} + \frac{u^2+u'^2}{r_0^2}}$$

In working out this root it is not good enough to say

$\sqrt{1+\epsilon} = 1 + \frac{1}{2}\epsilon$, but we have to take one more term,

$\sqrt{1+\epsilon} = 1 + \frac{1}{2}\epsilon - \frac{1}{8}\epsilon^2$ and

$$CD = r_0\,d\theta\left[1 + \frac{u}{r_0} + \frac{u^2+u'^2}{2r_0^2} - \frac{1}{8}\left(2\frac{u}{r_0}\right)^2 + \cdots\right]$$

We have written all terms up to order u^2, neglecting higher powers of u.

$$d(\Delta s) = CD - AB = d\theta\left(u + \frac{u^2}{2r_0} + \frac{u'^2}{2r_0} - \frac{u^2}{2r_0} + \cdots\right)$$

Integrated,

$$\Delta s = \int_0^{2\pi}\left(u + \frac{u'^2}{2r_0}\right) d\theta = 0$$

stating that the entire length of the deformed curve equals that of the original circle. Substituting the assumption (c) into this,

$$0 = \int_0^{2\pi}\left(-u_0 \cos 2\theta + a + \frac{4u_0^2}{2r_0}\sin^2 2\theta\right) d\theta$$

$$0 = 0 + 2\pi a + 2\pi\frac{u_0^2}{r_0}$$

so that

$$a = -\frac{u_0^2}{r_0}$$

and the deformed shape is

$$u = -u_0 \cos 2\theta - \frac{u_0^2}{r_0}$$

The area of the deformed tube, integrated from elemental triangles $d\theta$, is

$$\int_0^{2\pi}\frac{(r_0 + u)^2}{2} d\theta = \int_0^{2\pi}\left(\frac{r_0^2}{2} + r_0 u + \frac{u^2}{2}\right) d\theta$$

$$= \int_0^{2\pi}\frac{r_0^2}{2} d\theta - u_0\int_0^{2\pi} r_0 \cos 2\theta\, d\theta$$

$$+ u_0^2\int_0^{2\pi}\left(-1 + \frac{\cos^2 2\theta}{2}\right) d\theta + u_0^3\int \cdots$$

The first of these integrals is the area πr_0^2 of the original circle; the second one is zero; the third one is $-2\pi + (\pi/2) = -3\pi/2$; and the fourth and higher ones are negligible because they are proportional to higher powers of u_0. Hence

$$\Delta\text{area} = -\frac{3\pi u_0^2}{2}$$

and the work done by the external pressure p is:

$$+\tfrac{3}{2}\pi p u_0^2 \qquad\qquad (d)$$

This is for a complete ring if p is measured in pounds per inch of circumference, or it is for a unit length of pipe when p is measured in pounds per inch².

The work done in deforming a unit length of the tube to its bent form has been calculated before [Eq. (124), page 241]:

$$U_{\text{unit length}} = \frac{3\pi}{8} \frac{E}{1 - \mu^2} \frac{u_0^2 t^3}{r_0^3} \tag{124}$$

This was derived for a shape $u = -u_0 \cos 2\theta$ without the term u_0^2/r_0. But we recognize that the new term is a superposed extension of order u_0^2 and that the tension energy it represents is of order u_0^4, which we have neglected so far.

Finally, by the theorem of virtual work we equate Eqs. (*d*) and (124), from which we find

$$p_{\text{crit}} = \frac{Et^3}{4r_0^3(1 - \mu^2)} \tag{146a}$$

which is the result found previously on page 278.

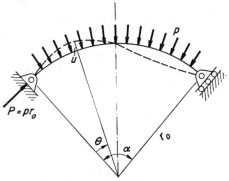

Fig. 189. Arch of central angle α and radius r_0, hinged at both ends, under uniform radial pressure p. It buckles with u a full sine wave at a critical pressure given by Eq. (148). This problem was solved by Timoshenko.

Buckling of a Circular Arch. Consider the thin arch α of Fig. 189, hinged at both ends, one of the hinges on rollers, subjected to a uniform radial load p lb/in. This problem was solved by Timoshenko, who remarked that it is very similar to that of the closed ring. First we see that the roller support at the right necessitates a tangential (*i.e.*, a compressive) reaction force without shear. Then, from an equilibrium analysis, as in Fig. 185*b*, we conclude that that force $P = pr_0$ and the same force must act at the left-hand hinge. If we now look at Fig. 186 and compare it with the left portion θ of Fig. 189, we see that Fig. 189 is a special case of Fig. 186 with $M_0 = 0$ and $u_0 = 0$. The fact that in Fig. 186 the tangent to the arc AB is perpendicular to OA was never used in the analysis. From Fig. 186 we concluded that the bending moment at θ was given by

Eq. (*b*) (page 276). Here then that result is simplified to

$$M_0 = -pr_0 u$$

The reader is advised to derive this result directly from Fig. 189, without the many complications of page 275. With the above expression for the bending moment the differential equation (144*a*) simplifies to

$$u'' + k^2 u = 0 \qquad (147)$$

in which the value of k^2 is, as before on page 77,

$$k^2 = 1 + \frac{pr_0^3}{EI} \qquad \text{(for a ring)} \qquad (145)$$

The solution of Eq. (147) is

$$u = C_1 \sin k\theta + C_2 \cos k\theta$$

At $\theta = 0$ we have $u = 0$, which makes $C_2 = 0$, so that the solution is $u = C_1 \sin k\theta$. At the other end $\theta = \alpha$, the bending moment is zero:

$$(u'')_{\theta=\alpha} = -C_1 k^2 \sin k\alpha = 0$$

Therefore $k\alpha = 0$, π, 2π, 3π, etc., the shape of buckling being 1, 2, 3, etc., *half* sine waves. From among these we rule out 1, 3, 5, etc., half sine waves because a quick sketch shows us that these shapes are associated with an elongation or shortening of the center line of the arch, which would involve a large energy of deformation. The shapes with 2, 4, 6, etc., half sine waves have the same length (up to first-order quantities) as the circular arch before buckling. Hence the lowest critical load occurs for $k\alpha = 2\pi$, in the shape shown in Fig. 189, and

$$4\pi^2 = k^2\alpha^2 = \left(1 + \frac{pr_0^3}{EI}\right)\alpha^2$$

$$p_{\text{crit}} = \left(\frac{4\pi^2}{\alpha^2} - 1\right)\frac{EI}{r_0^3} \qquad (148)$$

For the extreme case that $\alpha = 2\pi$ the critical load becomes zero and the arch becomes a 360-deg ring, hinged at the bottom. Such a ring can turn about the hinge indifferently, so that no pressure is required for that. The other extreme occurs when α becomes zero, and the arch degenerates to a straight line. Then of the two terms in the parentheses of Eq. (148) the first one overwhelms the second one, and we can write

$$p_{\text{crit}} = \frac{4\pi^2}{\alpha^2}\frac{EI}{r_0^3}$$

or

$$r_0 p_{\text{crit}} = \frac{4\pi^2 EI}{(\alpha r_0)^2}$$

Since $pr_0 = P$ and $\alpha r_0 = l$, this is Euler's hinged-column formula.

41. Twist-bend Buckling of Beams. If a beam is very stiff against bending in one plane and very flexible in a perpendicular plane, like a ruler or T square, and if that beam is loaded in the stiff plane, it has been observed to buckle out in the flexible direction, and this bending buckling in the flexible plane is always associated with a twist. Consider the case of Fig. 190, where the beam of cross section ht (the height h being many

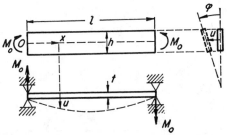

Fig. 190.   A beam with $h \gg t$, supported at its ends so that the angle φ is zero there, subjected to bending moments M_0 in its stiff plane. When M_0 reaches the critical value [Eq. (150)], the beam buckles out in a combination of bending u in the flexible plane and torsion φ.

times the thickness t) is simply supported on its ends between flat guides so that it cannot twist-turn at those ends. The beam is loaded by two equal and opposite bending moments at the ends in the stiff plane, which puts the upper fiber in compression and the lower fiber in tension. When these stresses get sufficiently high, the upper fiber can buckle out sidewise, while the lower fiber roughly remains straight. This means a sidewise bending u of the middle line $h/2$ of the beam together with a twist, because in the center of the span the h is no longer vertical, while at the ends h is held in place by the end guides.

A similar situation exists with the cantilever beam of Fig. 192 (page 286). The bending deflection in the stiff plane is very small, and when the load P gets large enough, the beam can be in indifferent equilibrium in a condition of sidewise bending combined with twist. This type of problem was solved in 1899 independently by Prandtl in Germany and by Michell in England.

Twist-bend Instability by Bending Moments.   This is the simplest case in this class of problems, and the system is shown in Fig. 190. We call u the sidewise displacement of the *center line* $h/2$ of the beam. If the angle φ were zero throughout, then this u would also be the sidewise displacement of the upper and lower fibers of the beam. In the buckled shape however, there will be an angle $\varphi = \varphi(x)$, and $u = u(x)$, so that then u is not the displacement of any fibers except the center one. [The top-fiber curve displaces by $u + (h\varphi/2)$.] The bending moments M_0 are represented in the plane sketch of Fig. 190 as double-headed straight arrows, related to the curved arrows by a right-hand screw convention.

The differential equations are found from considering the equilibrium of a piece of the beam from O to x (Fig. 191). In the plane view of Fig. 191a the moment exerted on the beam for equilibrium must be M_0, as shown. The M_0 at point O is called a bending moment in the stiff plane, but the same moment M_0 at x can no longer be called that. We first break up M_0 into two components in the horizontal plane, as shown. The moment $M_0(du/dx)$ is called a twisting moment, since it is directed along the center line. The magnitude of the other component M_0^- differs from M_0 only in quantities of the second order. Now we proceed to the other projection (Fig. 191b). The moment vector M_0^- in the horizontal plane is again

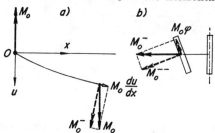

Fɪɢ. 191. Left-hand portion of the beam of Fig. 190 in the buckled state. The moment M_0 is resolved into three components: M_0^{--} in the stiff bending direction, $M_0\varphi$ in the flexible bending direction, and M_0u' in the twisting direction.

resolved into components; $M_0\varphi$ is called the bending moment in the flexible plane, and M_0^{--} (differing from the magnitudes of M_0 and M_0^- by second-order quantities only) is the true local bending moment in the stiff plane.

Now consider a small element dx of the beam at x and write the deformation equations in the flexible bending plane and in the twisting direction:

$$EI_f u'' = -M_0\varphi$$
$$C\varphi' = M_0 u' \tag{149}$$

Here C is the torsional stiffness $Ght^3/3$ (see page 15); EI_f is the flexible bending stiffness $Eht^3/12$. The bending moment $M_0\varphi$ is so directed as to tend to cause a negative curvature u'' in the beam; hence the negative sign in Eqs. (149). The twist moment M_0u' tends to increase φ locally, so that in the second equation the sign is positive. Here then we have a *pair* of equations in two variables u, φ, whereas in the simple Euler-column problem we had one equation,

$$EIy'' = -Py$$

We are now ready to solve Eqs. (149). Differentiating the second one, we find u'' from it and substitute into the first one, thus eliminating u:

$$\frac{EI_f \cdot C}{M_0} \varphi'' = -M_0\varphi$$

or

$$\varphi'' + \frac{M_0^2}{EI_f \cdot C} \varphi = 0$$

The general solution is

$$\varphi = C_1 \sin\left(x \frac{M_0}{\sqrt{EI_f \cdot C}}\right) + C_2 \cos\left(x \frac{M_0}{\sqrt{EI_f \cdot C}}\right)$$

At the left boundary $x = 0$, we have $\varphi = 0$, and as a consequence $C_2 = 0$:

$$\varphi = C_1 \sin\left(x \frac{M_0}{\sqrt{EI_f \cdot C}}\right)$$

At the other end $x = l$, we again have $\varphi = 0$. This can be done in two ways. One possibility is $C_1 = 0$, which gives us a true but uninteresting solution: a non-buckled straight beam. The other possibility is that C_1 has an arbitrary value φ_{max} and that the sine is zero or

$$\frac{M_0 l}{\sqrt{EI_f \cdot C}} = \pi, \, 2\pi, \, 3\pi, \, \text{etc.}$$

We are interested in the lowest buckling load only, which is

$$(M_0)_{crit} = \frac{\pi\sqrt{EI_f \cdot C}}{l} \tag{150}$$

The shape of the buckling then is $\varphi = \varphi_{max} \sin(\pi x/l)$, a half sine wave. From the second of Eqs. (149) we then conclude that

$$\varphi = \varphi_{max} \sin\frac{\pi x}{l}$$
$$u = \frac{C}{M_0} \varphi_{max} \sin\frac{\pi x}{l} = \frac{l}{\pi} \sqrt{\frac{C}{EI_f}} \, \varphi_{max} \sin\frac{\pi x}{l} \tag{151}$$

The reader is advised to work Problem 200 to get a better visualization of the deformed shape.

If the beam is not sufficiently flexible either in bending or in torsion [Eq. (150) contains the product of the two], then the critical bending moment becomes large and the possibility exists that the beam will yield before it buckles. Assuming $E = 2\frac{1}{2}G$ and a yield stress of $E/1,000$, this occurs when

$$\text{Yields before buckling for } \frac{hl}{t^2} \leq 2,000 \tag{152}$$

approximately. The derivation of this result is left to the reader as Problem 199.

Twist-bend Instability of Cantilever Beam. Consider the cantilever beam of Fig. 192, subjected to a vertical force P, acting in the center line $h/2$ of the end of the cantilever. As before, the height h of the beam is considerably larger than the thickness t. The x coordinate is supposed to start from the force P, that is, from the free end of the beam, which will give us the simplest possible expressions for the moments. Let u be the sidewise displacement and φ be the angle of rotation, both functions of x, and both zero for $x = l$. We now investigate the equilibrium of a piece of the beam between $x = 0$ and $x = x$, the latter an arbitrary section at point A, which is inclined at angle φ. We now resolve the end force P into components along and across the section at x (*not* along its own section at $x = 0$). These components are $P\varphi$ and P^-, where the $-$ sign indicates that P is smaller than P, but only in quantities of order φ^2, which we neglect. For equilibrium it is necessary to have shear forces at x of magnitude P^- in the stiff direction locally and of magnitude $P\varphi$ in the flexible direction locally. Also there are bending moments at x of magnitude P^-x in the stiff direction and $P\varphi x$ in the flexible direction.

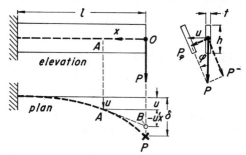

FIG. 192. Cantilever beam loaded by a force P in its stiff plane. When P reaches the value of Eq. (155), the beam can be in indifferent equilibrium in a deflected shape u, φ as shown, where the twist and flexible bending couples caused by P are in equilibrium with the elastic resisting couples $C\varphi'$ and $EI_f u''$. This equilibrium is expressed by Eqs. (153).

Now looking at the plan projection of Fig. 192, if the force P were located at point B on the tangent to the curve at A, then there would be no twisting of the section at A. Now, however, there is a twisting couple at A of magnitude P^- multiplied by a moment arm from P perpendicular to line AB, which is equal to the distance PB up to first-order quantities in terms of u. Thus the twisting couple is

$$P(\delta + u'x - u)$$

To understand the $+$ sign before the term $u'x$, it is well to remember that x counts positive to the left so that the slope u' shown in the plan of Fig. 192 is a negative slope.

The differential equations of bending and twist at a small section dz at point A are

$$P(\delta + u'x - u) = -C\varphi'$$
$$P\varphi x = +EI_f u'' \tag{153}$$

where again the signs are understood by remembering that x is positive toward the left. To solve the set (153), we eliminate u by differentiating the first equation,

$$P(u''x + u' - u') = -C\varphi''$$

so that $u'' = -C\varphi''/Px$. But from the second of Eqs. (153) we have another expression for $u'' = P\varphi x/EI_f$. Equating these two, we find

$$\varphi'' + \frac{P^2}{C \cdot EI_f}\, x^2\varphi = 0$$

or, shorter,

$$\varphi'' + k^2 x^2 \varphi = 0 \tag{154}$$

with

$$k^2 = \frac{P^2}{C \cdot EI_f}$$

This equation is a non-linear one on account of the $x^2\varphi$ term, and it has no simple solution. A solution exists in terms of Bessel functions, and for readers familiar with such functions, here it is:

$$\varphi = \sqrt{x}\left[C_1 J_{\frac{1}{4}}\!\left(\frac{kx^2}{2}\right) + C_2 Y_{\frac{1}{4}}\!\left(\frac{kx^2}{2}\right) \right]$$

But since most readers are not on speaking terms with Bessel functions of fractional order, the solution of Eq. (154) will now be worked out in series form. Let us assume that it can be written as

$$\varphi = a_0 + a_1 x + a_2 x^2 + \cdots + a_n x^n + \cdots$$

where the coefficients a_n are not known as yet. From this assumption we deduce

$$\varphi'' = 2a_2 + 6a_3 x + 12a_4 x^2 + \cdots + n(n-1)a_n x^{n-2} + \cdots$$
$$k^2 x^2 \varphi = \qquad\qquad\quad k^2 a_0 x^2 + \cdots + \quad k^2 a_{n-4} x^{n-2} + \cdots$$

Adding these two expressions, the answer must be zero by Eq. (154), so that

$$0 = 2a_2 + 6a_3 x + (12a_4 + k^2 a_0)x^2 + \cdots$$
$$+ [n(n-1)a_n + k^2 a_{n-4}]x^{n-2} + \cdots$$

Now this expression has to be zero, not only for $x = 0$ and $x = 0.01l$, but also for all possible values of x between 0 and l, millions of them. This can be possible only if all coefficients before the powers of x are zero, or

$$a_2 = 0 \qquad a_3 = 0 \qquad a_4 = -\frac{k^2}{12}a_0 \qquad \text{etc.}$$

In general,

$$a_n = -\frac{k^2}{n(n-1)}a_{n-4} \qquad (a)$$

This is a "recursion formula" from which we can calculate any coefficient if the coefficient four places below is known. Starting with a_0, we have

$$a_4 = -\frac{k^2}{12}a_0 \qquad a_8 = -\frac{k^2}{8 \times 7}a_4 = +\frac{k^2}{8 \times 7 \times 4 \times 3}a_0 \qquad \text{etc.}$$

Starting with a_1, we have

$$a_5 = -\frac{k^2}{5 \times 4}a_1 \qquad a_9 = +\frac{k^2}{9 \times 8 \times 5 \times 4}a_1 \qquad \text{etc.}$$

Starting with a_2, which we have seen to be zero, we find

$$a_6 = \text{const } a_2 = 0 \qquad \text{and} \qquad a_{10} = a_{14} = a_{18} = \cdots = 0$$

Starting with a_3, which is zero, we have

$$a_3 = a_7 = a_{11} = \cdots = 0$$

Hence all coefficients can be expressed in terms of a_0 and a_1, and these two quantities can now be regarded as integration constants; and the general solution for φ can be written as

$$\varphi = a_0\left(1 - \frac{k^2 x^4}{12} + \frac{k^4 x^8}{8 \times 7 \times 4 \times 3} - \frac{k^6 x^{12}}{12 \times 11 \times 8 \times 7 \times 4 \times 3}\right.$$
$$\left. + \frac{k^8 x^{16}}{} + \cdots\right) + a_1\left(x - \frac{k^2 x^5}{5 \times 4} + \frac{k^4 x^9}{9 \times 8 \times 5 \times 4}\right.$$
$$\left. - \frac{k^6 x^{13}}{13 \times 12 \times 9 \times 8 \times 5 \times 4} + \cdots\right)$$

One boundary condition requires that $\varphi' = 0$ for $x = 0$, because φ' is proportional to the twisting couple, which is zero at the free end. Now, if we differentiate the above expression and then set $x = 0$, we find that all terms disappear except one, which is a_1. Hence $a_1 = 0$, and the entire second series disappears. The first series is left, and a_0 now is a size multiplier, which is arbitrary in value, just as in Euler's-column analysis. Then in

$$\varphi = 1 - \frac{(kx^2)^2}{4 \times 3} + \frac{(kx^2)^4}{8 \times 7 \times 4 \times 3} - \frac{(kx^2)^6}{12 \times 11 \times 8 \times 7 \times 4 \times 3} + \cdots$$

we have the additional boundary condition that $\varphi = 0$ for $x = l$ at the built-in end, so that

$$0 = 1 - \frac{(kl^2)^2}{4 \times 3} + \frac{(kl^2)^4}{8 \times 7 \times 4 \times 3} - \cdots \qquad (b)$$

This is an equation with the unknown $kl^2 = Pl^2/\sqrt{C \cdot EI_f}$, [by Eq. (154)], and we must calculate kl^2 from it. However, algebraically it is an equation of infinite degree, having an infinite number of roots, which is complicated. We are interested in the smallest root of kl^2 only, and in order to find it, we make the numerical computations leading to Fig. 193. Looking at expression (b), we see that if kl^2 is sufficiently small, the terms become smaller and smaller, so that we get approximations by chopping off the series. Thus the first approximation is

$$0 = 1 - \frac{(kl^2)^2}{12} = 0 \qquad \text{or} \qquad kl^2 = \sqrt{12} = 3.47$$

A better approximation retains three terms:

$$0 = 1 - \frac{(kl^2)^2}{12} + \frac{(kl^2)^4}{672} = 0$$

With $k^2l^4 = x$, this is $x^2 - 56x + 672 = 0$ or

$$x = 28 \pm \sqrt{112}$$

with

$$kl^2 = \sqrt{17.4} = 4.17 \qquad \text{and} \qquad kl^2 = \sqrt{38.6} = 6.2$$

We have two roots, and the smallest one is 4.17. In Fig. 193 the first term of the series (which is 1), plotted against kl^2, gives a horizontal line; the first two terms give a parabola intersecting the positive abscissa axis

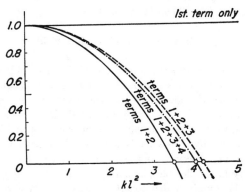

FIG. 193. Plots of the infinite series [Eq. (b)] chopped off at various points, showing that the first intersection of the kl^2 axis is approximated rapidly by retaining more and more terms of Eq. (b).

at $kl^2 = 3.47$; the first three terms give a curve of fourth order, intersecting at $kl^2 = 4.17$ and 6.2; the first four terms give a curve of sixth order with three positive intersections, etc. From the fact that the signs in Eq. (b) alternate, we see that we successively overshoot and undershoot the lowest root by retaining more terms. Thus the exact value lies *between* the last two approximations. Carrying this out numerically, we find successively

$$3.47 \qquad 4.17 \qquad 3.99 \qquad 4.01 \qquad 4.01$$

Thus the exact solution for the first buckling load is $kl^2 = 4.01$, or with the meaning of k given in Eq. (154)

$$P_{\text{crit}} = 4.01 \frac{\sqrt{C \cdot EI_f}}{l^2} \tag{155}$$

This solves the problem, and all we have to do now is to see under which circumstances the solution applies, *i.e.*, for which dimensions the beam buckles before it yields. The beam yields when

$$s_{\text{yield}} = \frac{Pl}{I_{\text{stiff}}} \frac{h}{2} = \frac{6Pl}{th^2} \qquad \text{or} \qquad P_{\text{yield}} = s_{\text{yield}} \frac{th^2}{6l}$$

It buckles when

$$P_{\text{crit}} = \frac{4.01}{l^2} \sqrt{G \frac{1}{3} ht^3 E \frac{ht^3}{12}} = \frac{0.67ht^3}{l^2} \frac{E}{\sqrt{2(1 + \mu)}}$$

Hence it buckles before yielding if

$$\frac{0.67ht^3}{l^2} \frac{E}{\sqrt{2(1 + \mu)}} \leq s_{\text{yield}} \frac{th^2}{6l}$$

which for $s_{\text{yield}} = E/1{,}000$ and $\mu = 0.3$ becomes

$$\frac{hl}{t^2} \geq 2{,}500 \qquad \text{(buckles before yielding)} \tag{c}$$

As an example for a cross section $h = 10t$, if the beam is longer than $25h$, it will buckle first, whereas if it is shorter than $25h$, it will yield before buckling if the load P is gradually increased from zero on up.

Solution of Twist-bend Cantilever by Energy Method. When applying the energy method, we first have to calculate the energy stored in the buckled structure as caused by a reasonably assumed deformation. Suppose this deformation to be $u = u(x)$ and $\varphi = \varphi(x)$. Then the energy is partly bending energy in the flexible plane and partly twist energy. These two energies may be simply added together, because a bending deformation does not absorb work from a twisting moment, and vice versa. Hence (Fig. 192):

$$U = \frac{EI}{2} \int_0^l u''^2 \, dx + \frac{C}{2} \int \varphi'^2 \, dx$$

This energy must then be equated to the work done by the external forces, in this case by P on the deformation incident to buckling. To find the downward motion of P, we look at a small element dx at point A in Fig. 192. We assume the entire beam to be rigid except the element dx at A, which is allowed to flex as it wants to. That element then acquires a curvature u'', and the outer portion of the beam, from A to P, rotates as a rigid body through the small angle $u'' \, dx$. This causes a sidewise horizontal displacement at the end O of $u'' \, dx \, x$. But at A the beam is not quite vertical; it is inclined at angle φ; therefore, the end point O moves downward through an amount $u'' \, dx \, x\varphi = u'' \varphi x \, dx$. This is the contribution to the downward motion of one element dx of the beam only: the total motion of P is

$$\int_0^l u'' \varphi x \, dx$$

With this, the energy equation for determining the critical load P becomes

$$\frac{EI}{2} \int_0^l u''^2 \, dx + \frac{C}{2} \int_0^l \varphi'^2 \, dx = P \int_0^l u'' \varphi x \, dx \qquad (156)$$

All we have to do now is to assume reasonable functions for u and φ, but this is difficult because we have no idea how many degrees of φ correspond to an inch worth of u. We can do something by looking at the second differential equation (153) and from it write $P\varphi x / EI_f$ for u''. Substituting this into Eq. (156) eliminates u entirely, and after some algebra we find

$$P_{\text{crit}} = C \cdot EI_f \frac{\int_0^l \varphi'^2 \, dx}{\int_0^l \varphi^2 x^2 \, dx} \qquad (d)$$

Now we have to assume something reasonable for φ. We know from Fig. 192 that at the free end $x = 0$ the torque is zero and hence $\varphi' = 0$, while at the fixed end $x = l$ we have $\varphi = 0$. This is satisfied by $\varphi = \varphi_0[1 - (x^2/l^2)]$, a parabola. The reader should now work Problem 201 and find for the buckling load

$$P_{\text{crit}} = 4.18 \frac{\sqrt{C \cdot EI_f}}{l^2} \qquad (e)$$

which is not a bad approximation.

42. Buckling of Shafts by Torsion. Consider a shaft simply supported at its ends, subjected to a pair of equal and opposite torsional couples at the ends. The ordinary configuration of the shaft is with a straight center line, but when the torque reaches a critical value, indifferent equilibrium of the shaft can exist with a curved center line. For this problem we cannot assume that the center-line curve is a plane curve, as in Euler's simple column, but it will be a space curve $y = f_1(x)$, $z = f_2(x)$ (Fig. 194).

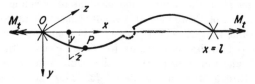

FIG. 194. Straight shaft of length l, subjected to equal and opposite torques M_t at the ends. When M_t reaches the critical value of Eqs. (157), indifferent equilibrium with the shaft center line in a space curve.

Consider now the equilibrium of a piece of shaft between $x = 0$ and $x = x$, or between the points O and P. At O acts the torque M_t, shown as the double-headed arrow in the figure. Equilibrium now requires that at P act a torque M_t with a vector equal, opposite, and parallel to M_t. This vector at P then no longer is directed along the center line of the shaft. In Fig. 195 this vector is shown as PA, and we now proceed to resolve it into three components: along the center line and parallel to the x and y axes. We assume, as usual, that the shaft buckles only slightly, so that dy and dz are small with respect to dx, and dx and ds are equal up to quantities of first order. Then from Fig. 195 we have

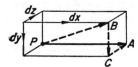

$$PA = M_t \quad PB = M_t^+ \quad BC = M_t \frac{dy}{dx} = M_t y'$$

and

$$CA = M_t z'$$

FIG. 195. Detail at point P of Fig. 194. The vectors PA, BC, CA, and PB can be considered first to represent the length elements dx, dy, dz, and ds, respectively, but they also may represent the torque M_t and its components along dy, dz, and ds. The component PB is along the shaft center line, while BC and CA are almost perpendicular to the center line.

The moment vector PB of length $M_t^+ = M_t$, being directed along the center line, is called a local torsion couple. The vectors BC and CA are not quite perpendicular to the center line, but almost so, and the differences between BC, AC, and the components of M_t perpendicular to the center line are small of second order, and hence negligible. Then BC and AC can be interpreted as bending moments, $BC = M_t y'$ lying in the xz plane and $CA = M_t z'$ in the xy plane. The differential equations of bending in these two planes of an element ds at P then are

$$
\begin{aligned}
M_t y' &= -EIz'' \\
M_t z' &= +EIy''
\end{aligned}
\tag{157}
$$

The signs occurring in these equations should be carefully verified by the reader.

To solve this set of equations, we can proceed as we did with Eqs. (149), eliminating one of the variables, etc. However, a solution can be obtained with considerably less algebra by using complex numbers.[1] Equations (157) are seen to be symmetrical in y and z, and crossed up: the slope in one direction causes curvature in the other direction. Real and complex numbers behave similarly; if a number, either real or imaginary, is multiplied by j, it turns through 90 deg in the complex plane (Fig. 93, page 143). Define a complex number

$$u = y + jz$$

This number u is a function of x: it is a vector representation of the space deflection, Fig. 194, at any point x.

Multiply the second of Eqs. (157) by j, and add it to the first one:

$$M_t(y' + jz') = EI(+jy'' - z'') = jEI(y'' + jz'')$$

or

$$u'' + \frac{jM_t}{EI} u' = 0 \qquad (a)$$

This is a *first*-order equation in terms of u', with the general solution

$$u' = C_1 e^{-\frac{jM_t}{EI} x}$$

$$u' = C_1 \cos\left(\frac{M_t}{EI} x\right) - jC_1 \sin\left(\frac{M_t}{EI} x\right)$$

$$u = C_1 \frac{EI}{M_t}\left[\sin\left(\frac{M_t}{EI} x\right) + j \cos\left(\frac{M_t}{EI} x\right) + C_2\right]$$

One boundary condition requires that $y = z = 0$ at the left end $x = 0$, which also means that $u = y + jz = 0$ at $x = 0$. From this condition we find the constant $C_2 = -j$ and

$$u = C^*\left\{\sin\left(\frac{M_t}{EI} x\right) - j\left[1 - \cos\left(\frac{M_t}{EI} x\right)\right]\right\}$$

At the other end $x = l$, again $y = 0$, $z = 0$, and hence $u = 0$. This can be met as usual by making $C^* = 0$, which gives the true but uninteresting result that the shaft can be in equilibrium straight. But C^* does not have to be zero: we can also satisfy the condition by making the quantity in the brackets zero at $x = l$:

[1] Equations (157) were derived and the problem was solved by Greenhill in 1895. The beautiful solution by complex numbers here reproduced is due to H. A. Webb and is taken from the English text "Strength of Materials" by John Case, Edward Arnold & Co., London, first published in 1925.

$$\sin\left(\frac{M_t}{EI}\, l\right) - j\left[1 - \cos\left(\frac{M_t}{EI}\, l\right)\right] = 0$$

which is satisfied by

$$\frac{M_t}{EI}\, l = 2\pi,\ 4\pi,\ 6\pi,\ \text{etc.}$$

Hence the lowest critical torque is

$$(M_t)_{\text{crit}} = \frac{2\pi EI}{l} \tag{158}$$

and for this torque the shape is given by

$$u = y + jz = C^*\left[\sin\frac{2\pi x}{l} + j\left(1 - \cos\frac{2\pi x}{l}\right)\right]$$

In the xy plane the shaft bows out in a full 2π sine wave, whereas in the xz plane it is $1 - $ a full 2π cosine wave, as shown in Fig. 196.

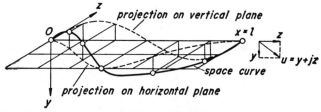

Fig. 196. Buckled space curve of a shaft subjected to end torques. In the vertical xy plane the curve is a sine wave; in the horizontal plane it is a $1 - $ cosine wave. The figure is constructed in skew projection, in which the vertical-plane sine wave appears undistorted; the horizontal $1 - $ cosine wave appears distorted, and the space curve is constructed point by point by skew parallelogram construction from the two projections.

As in all buckling cases, we now must still answer the question of the range in which this result applies, *i.e.*, find out for what dimensions the shaft buckles before it yields. Assuming $s_{\text{yield}} = E/1,000$, the yield shear stress to be half the yield tensile stress, and a solid circular shaft of radius r and length l, it

Buckles before yielding when $\dfrac{l}{r} \geq 2,000\pi$ (a)

This result is to be derived by the reader (Problem 204). We see that only extremely long and thin shafts run in danger of buckling; the question hardly is a practical one, except possibly for long, thin wires transmitting torque.

Shaft Buckling by Combined Torsion and Compression. Suppose the shaft of Fig. 194 to be subjected simultaneously to torques M_t and end thrusts P. The bending moments caused by the thrust P are Py and Pz in the xy plane and xz plane, respectively. The bending caused by the torque is given by Eq. (157). The combined differential equations then are

$$EIz'' = -Pz - M_t y'$$
$$EIy'' = -Py + M_t z' \tag{159}$$

Again we use the complex notation $u = y + jz$ for the deflection. Multiply the first equation by j, and add it to the second one:

$$EI(y'' + jz'') = -P(y + jz) - jM_t(y' + jz')$$

or

$$u'' + \frac{jM_t}{EI}u' + \frac{P}{EI}u = 0 \tag{b}$$

This linear equation has the general solution

$$u = C_1 e^{p_1 x} + C_2 e^{p_2 x}$$

where

$$p_{1,2} = \frac{-jM_t}{2EI} \pm j\sqrt{+\left(\frac{M_t}{2EI}\right)^2 + \frac{P}{EI}} = j(\alpha \pm \beta)$$

so that with the formula $e^{jpx} = \cos px + j \sin px$ the result can be written as

$$u = e^{j\alpha x}(A \sin \beta x + B \cos \beta x)$$

where A and B are complex constants of integration. For $x = 0$ this becomes

$$(u)_{x=0} = B$$

and the left boundary condition demands that at $x = 0$, both y and z are zero, so that also $u = 0$. Hence $B = 0$, and

$$u = Ae^{j\alpha x} \sin \beta x$$

At the other end $x = l$ the complex deflection u again must be zero, which we can satisfy uninterestingly by making $A = 0$, and hence $u = 0$ throughout, or interestingly by making $e^{j\alpha l} \sin \beta l = 0$. The e function cannot be zero, but the sine function can. Hence

$$\beta l = \pi, 2\pi, \text{ etc.}$$

The lowest buckling-load combination corresponds to the lowest root π, or

$$\sqrt{\left(\frac{M_t}{2EI}\right)^2 + \frac{P}{EI}} = \frac{\pi}{l} \tag{c}$$

This can be brought into a more understandable form by squaring and dividing by π^2/l^2:

$$\frac{M_t^2}{(2\pi EI/l)^2} + \frac{P}{\pi^2 EI/l^2} = 1$$

or

$$\left(\frac{M_t}{M_{t\,\text{Greenhill}}}\right)^2 + \frac{P}{P_{\text{Euler}}} = 1 \tag{160}$$

This beautiful result contains Eqs. (157) and Euler's simple column formula as special cases. The reason for the square with M_t and the first power with P is physically clear, because when P reverses its sign from a compressive thrust to a tensile pull, it stabilizes the system, while when M_t reverses its sign from clockwise to counterclockwise, it buckles the shaft with equal effectiveness.

Shaft Instability by End Thrust and Centrifugal Force. This is a problem in dynamics, that of the critical whirling speed of a uniform shaft, simply supported at both ends and subjected to an end thrust P. We quickly transform the dynamic problem into a static one by d'Alembert's principle, replacing the dynamic effect of the shaft rotation by the centrifugal force, $\mu_1\omega^2 y$ per unit length (Fig. 197). The bending moment at an arbitrary point x caused by the thrusts P is $-Py$, the sign being negative because in the figure the forces P tend to give the beam a negative curvature y''. We can write for this

$$EIy'' = -Py$$

or

$$EIy^{(4)} = -Py''$$

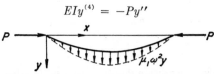

FIG. 197. A shaft of uniform mass per unit length μ_1 and uniform stiffness EI, rotating at speed ω, subjected to end thrusts P, can be in a state of indifferent (d'Alembert) equilibrium with a curved center line when ω and P satisfy the combination of Eq. (162).

The centrifugal force by itself (for $P = 0$) acts like a distributed loading $\mu_1\omega^2 y$, and for it the beam equation is

$$EIy^{(4)} = +\mu_1\omega^2 y$$

The total bending moment is the sum of that due to thrust and centrifugal force,

$$EIy^{(4)} = -Py'' + \mu_1\omega^2 y$$

or

$$y^{(4)} + \frac{P}{EI}\,y'' - \frac{\mu_1\omega^2}{EI}\,y = 0 \tag{161}$$

This is a linear differential equation of the fourth order with four characteristic roots:

$$p_{1,2,3,4} = \pm\sqrt{-\frac{P}{2EI} \pm \sqrt{\left(\frac{P}{2EI}\right)^2 + \frac{\mu_1\omega^2}{EI}}}$$

The further mathematical work on the solution is algebraically complicated, but not fundamentally difficult. The four integration constants are to be determined by the four boundary conditions:

$$y = y'' = 0 \qquad (\text{at } x = 0 \text{ and } x = l)$$

The details are left as an exercise to the reader, the result being very similar to Eq. (c) (page 295):

$$\frac{P}{2EI} + \sqrt{\left(\frac{P}{2EI}\right)^2 + \frac{\mu_1\omega^2}{EI}} = \frac{\pi^2}{l^2}$$

Now we eliminate the square root by bringing the small left-hand term to the right-hand side and by squaring and rearranging somewhat:

$$\frac{P}{\pi^2 EI/l^2} + \frac{\omega^2}{\pi^2 EI/\mu_1 l^2} = 1$$

or, written in a clear form,

$$\frac{P}{P_{\text{Euler}}} + \left(\frac{\omega}{\omega_{\text{crit}}}\right)^2 = 1 \qquad (162)$$

Here ω_{crit} is the shaft critical whirling speed without end thrust. The square is there because the shaft whirls equally well for clockwise as for counterclockwise ω.

Combination of Torque, End Thrust, and Rotation. The beautiful results (160) and (162) make one suspect that if a uniform rotating shaft is subjected to a thrust P and to a torque M_t, it should become unstable for

$$\frac{P}{P_{\text{Euler}}} + \left(\frac{M_t}{M_{t\,\text{Greenhill}}}\right)^2 + \left(\frac{\omega}{\omega_{\text{crit}}}\right)^2 = 1 \qquad (163)$$

This formula is a useful one, but it is not exactly correct, being only in the nature of a decent approximation. The exact answer is quite complicated and can be represented best in the form of a diagram containing a family of curves, not given here. The solution was published by Southwell in 1921.

43. Twist Buckling of Columns. The usual pin-ended column subjected to end compression forces P will either yield first or buckle in bending by the classical Euler formula

$$P_{\text{crit}} = \pi^2\frac{EI}{l^2} \qquad (a)$$

All structural beam sections, built-up box sections, and circular pipe columns behave in this way. However, if we have a column in which the twisting stiffness C is very small, and the bending stiffness EI comparatively large, then it may happen that an instability in which the column twists occurs at a lower P than the Euler buckling load. Such great torsional flexibility combined with good bending stiffness can occur only

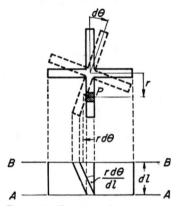

in very thin-walled open sections, such as those shown in Fig. 12 (page 16). This remark enables us to obtain the principal result by a very simple analysis, which is limited to thin-walled sections only and hence does not apply to substantial cross sections. For simplicity we consider a cross section with two perpendicular axes of symmetry, so that the center of twist and the center of gravity coincide, such as the cross of Fig. 198. The figure shows two cross sections of the column, somewhere between the ends, at distance dl apart longitudinally. Suppose these two sections, originally vertically above each other, twist by an angle $d\theta$ with respect to each other in the buckled state. Their relative rotation takes place about the center of twist, which in this case is the geometric center. Consider a fiber of cross section dA at

FIG. 198. Two normal cross sections AA and BB of the column, at distance dl longitudinally. The sections have an angle of twist $d\theta$ elastically with respect to each other in the buckled state. A point P at distance r from the center of twist moves through $rd\theta$ relative to its mate at distance dl below it.

an arbitrary point P, distance r from the center. This fiber in the unbuckled state is straight and vertical, and when in the buckled state of indifferent equilibrium, it is a piece of a spiral lying on a concentric cylinder of radius r. Then the displacement of P in the upper section relative to the lower one is $rd\theta$, directed perpendicular to the radius r. The spiral angle then is $rd\theta/dl$, as indicated in the lower part of Fig. 198. Now consider in Fig. 199 the equilibrium of that one fiber dA. For small twisting the total compressive force P will remain uniformly distributed over the total cross section, so that our fiber carries its portion $P\,dA/A$. But these two forces are not in equilibrium. We can resolve them into components along and across the fiber, as shown dotted in Fig. 199. The force components along the fiber equilibrize each other, but the cross components do not. These then must be neutralized by shear stresses or shear forces across the top and bottom of the fiber, Fig. 199. The shear force is

$$P\frac{dA}{A}\,r\,\frac{d\theta}{dl} = Pr\theta'\,\frac{dA}{A}$$

directed perpendicular to r, and it has a moment about the shaft center of

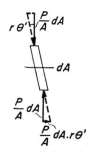

$$Pr^2\theta' \frac{dA}{A}$$

so that the total shear moment carried by the cross section is

$$\int Pr^2\theta' \frac{dA}{A} = \frac{P\theta'}{A} \int r^2\, dA = \frac{P\theta'}{A} I_p$$

where I_p is the polar moment of inertia of the cross section A. This moment or torque twists the bar and therefore must be equal to $C\theta'$, where C is the torsional stiffness. Equating the two expressions, we find

$$P_{\text{crit}} = \frac{C \cdot A}{I_p} \qquad (164)$$

FIG. 199. A fiber of section dA, buckled into a spiral angle $rd\theta/dl = r\theta'$ must carry its share $P\,dA/A$ of axial load. For equilibrium, the fiber can hold this only in the form of two forces along its own direction, shown dashed. The actual force $P\,dA/A$ is the vector sum of this force along the fiber and a skew force $P\,dA\,r\theta'/A$, also shown dashed. All the shear forces together for all the fibers of the cross section form a torque.

This is the axial load in which indifferent equilibrium in the twisted state can exist; hence we call it the critical load.

It is of interest to note that this result is entirely independent of the length of the bar or of its end conditions. It holds for clamped ends as well as for free ends, only the bar has to be sufficiently long so that it can twist for a portion of its length without interference with the warping of the cross sections. This means that the bar has to be many times longer than its greatest width dimension, because if not, the end conditions will prevent free warping, and the torsional stiffness will not be C (see page 35).

Application to a Cross-shaped Section. We now apply this result to the cross-shaped section of Fig. 200, for which we have from known formulae $(b \gg t)$

$$A = 2bt$$

$$I_{\text{bending}} = \tfrac{1}{12}b^3t + \text{negligible}$$

$$I_p = \tfrac{1}{6}b^3t$$

$$C = G\tfrac{1}{3} \times 2bt^3 \qquad \text{(page 15)}$$

FIG. 200. Cross-shaped section for numerical example. The results for beams of this section are shown in Fig. 201.

With the further usual assumptions for mild steel $E = 2\tfrac{1}{2}G$ and $S_{\text{yield}} = E/1,000$, we find the three results below, by substitution into formula (a) (page 297) and into Eq. (164):

$$P_{\text{crit twist}} = \frac{8Gt^3}{b}$$

$$P_{\text{Euler}} = \frac{\pi^2 E b^3 t}{12 l^2}$$

$$P_{\text{yield}} = \frac{E2bt}{1,000}$$

We now plot this in the diagram (Fig. 201), where the cross-sectional dimension b/t is plotted vertically against the length ratio, or column slenderness, l/b. Each point in this diagram represents a column of certain geometrical shape. First we find the locus where the yield load equals the Euler load. It is

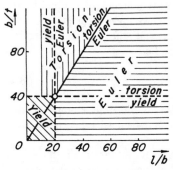

FIG. 201. Shows regions of slenderness l/b and wall-thickness ratio t/b, for which ordinary columns will first twist-buckle, bend-buckle, or yield. This figure applies to the cross section Fig. 200.

$$\frac{l}{b} = 20$$

a vertical line, to the left of which it yields first and to the right of which it Euler-buckles first. Next we calculate the locus of columns which buckle in twist at the same time as they yield. It is

$$\frac{b}{t} = 40$$

a horizontal line in Fig. 201, above which the column twist-buckles first and below which it yields first.

Third we find the locus of columns that Euler-buckle and twist-buckle at the same load P. It is

$$\frac{l}{b} = 2\frac{b}{t}$$

a diagonal of slope 2, above which the column twist-buckles first and below which it Euler-buckles first. These lines intersect in a triple point, representing the one column for which all three critical loads are the same. The various lines subdivide the figure in areas. The rectangle, of short columns with thick walls t, shaded at 45 deg, represents columns that will yield first. The area to the right, of long columns, shaded horizontally, shows columns that will Euler-buckle first. The third area, shaded vertically, represents columns of moderate length but with very thin walls t; these will twist-buckle before anything else happens. The vertical shading has not been carried out all the way to the left; there we would have short columns, where the influence of the ends affects the warping of the cross section, thus making the section stiffer against torsion (see page 35), so that for columns shorter than $l/b = 10$, say, the theory of Eq. (164) does not apply.

Application to Unsymmetrical Cross Sections. In an unsymmetrical cross section the center of gravity and the center of twist usually are two distinctly different points. The general analysis of page 298 still holds, but referring to Fig. 198 the point about which cross sections turn relative to each other is not the center of symmetry but the center of twist. No change whatever need be made in the words of the argument of page 298; the general result [Eq. (164)] still holds; only I_p has to be interpreted as the polar moment of inertia of the cross section *about the center of twist*, and not about another point, such as the center of gravity. In fact the center of gravity is of no importance at all in the twist-buckle analysis. It comes in only when we want to construct a diagram like Fig. 201; then for the Euler-bend-buckle calculation we need EI, where I is a diametral moment of inertia about a principal axis through the center of gravity. If the center of twist is far away from the center of gravity, the polar moment of inertia I_p about it becomes relatively large, so that by Eq. (164) the twist-buckle critical load is small. Thus unsymmetrical sections, like slit, thin-walled tubes, show a twist-buckle sensitivity even greater than that of Fig. 201 (see Problem 208).

As was said previously, twist buckle is of practical interest only when the torsional stiffness is small, *i.e.*, for open sections. For closed sections it is of no significance whatever. For example, a closed thin-walled tube or pipe still obeys Eq. (164), because it is thin-walled. For it we have

$$C = GI_p$$

so that Eq. (164) states that $P_{crit}/A = G$, which means that the compressive stress for which a thin-walled tube will twist-buckle is 12,000,000 lb/sq in. Other closed box sections are in a similar position. In general a designer will try to make his beams and columns fairly stiff against torsion, so that it is only very rarely that Eq. (164) becomes of practical significance.

44. Thin Flat Plates. The stability of thin flat plates is an important and difficult subject on which many papers have been written in the past half century. The first major contribution came in 1891 from G. H. Bryan in England, who solved the problem of a rectangular plate, freely supported along all four edges and compressed along *one* of the two sides. He showed that such a plate buckles into a number of doubly sinusoidal hills and cups with straight nodal lines dividing the main rectangle into a number of subrectangles, in the manner of Fig. 171 (page 247). At the time the paper was written its application was limited to the girders of bridge structures, but now the subject is of great importance in the aircraft industry as well. Figure 202 shows a box column made up of four thin side plates, held together by angles, which have to remain straight. In compression such a beam can buckle in the plates, leaving the four corner angles straight. Each side plate of this column, or girder, then is simply supported at all four edges and is described by Bryan's theory.

Assume then for the deflection (Fig. 203)

$$w = A_{mn} \sin m \frac{\pi x}{h} \sin n \frac{\pi y}{b} \qquad (a)$$

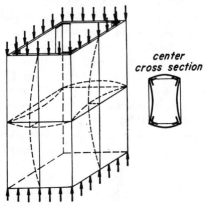

center cross section

Fig. 202. Box column made up of four corner angles and four thin side plates, under compression. It can buckle as shown, when the end rectangles remain undistorted, whereas the center of the column goes into a figure made up of four half sine waves. The corners remain straight, and the center vertical of each panel becomes a half sine wave. Other forms of buckling are possible with more than one half sine wave in each panel, which is then cut up into subrectangles along straight nodal lines. Each panel is a rectangular plate with simply supported edges, to which Bryan's equation (165) applies.

The energy stored in the plate due to this deflection was calculated before on page 248, Eq. (129):

$$U = A_{mn}^2 \pi^4 \frac{Dbh}{8} \left(\frac{m^2}{h^2} + \frac{n^2}{b^2} \right)^2 \qquad (b)$$

The symbol D here is the plate stiffness of Eq. (64) (page 107). Now we have to calculate the work done by the loading p, by thinking of the plate as a collection of vertical strips of width dy. The work done on one such strip is the same as that on a column [page 252 Eq. (b)]:

$$dW = p \, dy \int_0^h \frac{1}{2} \left(\frac{dw}{dx} \right)^2 dx$$

The slope is

$$\frac{dw}{dx} = \left(A_{mn} m \frac{\pi}{h} \sin n \frac{\pi y}{b} \right) \cos m \frac{\pi x}{h}$$

where the parentheses contain the factors remaining constant in the above integration. The integral of a squared cosine being equal to half the base length, we have for one strip

$$dW = p \, dy \, A_{mn}^2 \, \frac{m^2\pi^2}{h^2} \sin^2 \frac{n\pi y}{b} \frac{h}{4}$$

Now we integrate the strips dy from $y = 0$ to $y = b$:

$$W = pA_{mn}^2 \, \frac{m^2\pi^2}{h^2} \frac{b}{2} \frac{h}{4}$$

By the principle of virtual work this expression must be equal to the energy U for the critical loading of indifferent equilibrium; hence

$$p_{\text{crit}} = \frac{\pi^2}{m^2} Dh^2 \left(\frac{m^2}{h^2} + \frac{n^2}{b^2} \right)^2 \qquad (c)$$

This formula gives the critical load per unit length for the various possibilities m, n. We are interested only in the lowest value of the buckling load, and on examining Eq. (c) we see that the letter n occurs in one place only, in the parentheses, so that for all possible integer values of n, the load p_{crit} will be smallest for $n = 1$. We cannot draw the same conclusion for m, because that letter appears outside the parentheses as well. Thus we have

$$p_{\text{crit}} = \frac{\pi^2}{m^2} Dh^2 \left(\frac{m^2}{h^2} + \frac{1}{b^2} \right)^2$$

or

$$p_{\text{crit}} = \frac{\pi^2 D}{h^2} \left(m + \frac{h^2}{mb^2} \right)^2 \qquad (165)$$

This is the buckling load for one half sine wave across the plate width b and m half sine waves along the length. We note that if we retain only the first term of the parentheses we have Euler's classical column formula, which would describe the case if the two vertical edges of the plate of Fig. 203 were not supported. The presence of the second term in the parentheses then gives the increase in p_{crit} caused by the angle-iron supports of the vertical edges of the plate. Equation (c) shows us that the value of m required to give p_{crit} as low as possible a value depends on the plate dimensions h/b in an intricate manner. The simplest way to bring this out is by rewriting Eq. (c) once more,

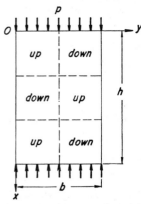

Fig. 203. A rectangular plate of height h and width b, with simply supported edges subjected to a pressure p (pounds per running inch) in the x direction, is assumed to buckle according to Eq. (a). The case shown here is for $m = 3$, $n = 2$.

$$p_{\text{crit}} = \frac{\pi^2 D}{b^2} \left(\frac{mb}{h} + \frac{h}{mb} \right)^2$$

or, in a dimensionless form, fit for plotting,

$$\frac{p_{\text{crit}} b^2}{\pi^2 D} = \left(\frac{mb}{h} + \frac{h}{mb} \right)^2$$

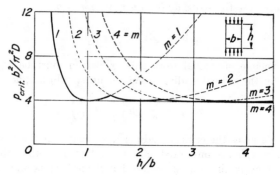

FIG. 204. Critical load per unit length on the side b of a plate of stiffness D and height h simply supported on all four edges. This causes buckling with one half sine wave across the width b and m half sine waves along the height h. Illustrates Eqs. (165) and (165a). The plate thickness t should be less than $b/60$ approximately; otherwise the plate will yield first.

Figure 204 shows a plot of this relation where vertically we have $p_{\text{crit}} b^2/\pi^2 D$ (call it y) and horizontally we have h/b (call it x). The curves then are

$$y = \left(\frac{m}{x} + \frac{x}{m} \right)^2 \tag{d}$$

one curve in the diagram for each integer value of m. The minimum of the dimensionless critical load y is found from

$$\frac{dy}{dx} = 0 = 2 \left(\frac{m}{x} + \frac{x}{m} \right) \left(-\frac{m}{x^2} + \frac{1}{m} \right)$$

The only real value for x satisfying this is $x = m$, and then the corresponding value for y [Eq. (d)] is $y = 4$. This is plotted in Fig. 204, and from it we see that a plate m times as high as it is wide will buckle in m half sine waves. A long plate ($h \gg b$) therefore will buckle in square fields of dimensions $b \times b$, and its critical load for all practical purposes is

$$p_{\text{crit}} = \frac{4\pi^2 D}{b^2} \qquad (h \gg b) \tag{165a}$$

This critical pressure is per unit length; hence p_{crit} is carried by an area $1 \times t$, where t is the plate thickness. The compressive buckling stress

s_{crit} thus is

$$s_{crit} = \frac{4\pi^2 D}{b^2 t} = \frac{4\pi^2 E t^3}{12(1 - \mu^2)b^2 t} = \frac{4\pi^2}{12(1 - \mu^2)} E \left(\frac{t}{b}\right)^2$$

The plate will yield when

$$s_{yield} = \frac{E}{1,000}$$

Equating these two, we find $b/t = 60$, approximately. This means that a long rectangular plate, supported on all four edges, will buckle before yielding under compression if its thickness is less than one-sixtieth plate width. For good utilization of material, therefore, box columns like Fig. 202 should be designed with a plate thickness not less than $b/60$. If we do that, we can dismiss the thought of buckling altogether and design on yield only.

Other Edge Conditions. Consider the angle of Fig. 205, loaded like an Euler strut. It can buckle as indicated with one or more half waves along the free sides B, whereas the corner edge A is "simply supported." A normal cross section remains undistorted in its own plane, merely turns about the corner, so that no bending moment appears between the two legs joined at the corner. This case has been worked out by Timoshenko; it is a very complicated analysis, and it leads to the following result for the critical compressive stress:

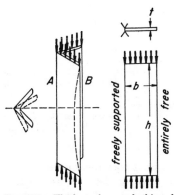

$$s_{crit} = \left(0.46 + \frac{b^2}{h^2}\right)\frac{\pi^2 D}{b^2 t} \quad (166)$$

which will not be proved in this text. Again the (steel) column will yield if

$$s_{yield} = \frac{E}{1,000}$$

Equating this to the above, we find

$$0.46\left(\frac{t}{b}\right)^2 + \left(\frac{t}{h}\right)^2 = \frac{1}{900}$$

For a reasonably long column $h > 10b$ the second term is negligible with respect to the first one, and we find approximately

$$b = 20t$$

FIG. 205. The legs of an angle, hinged at its end under a compressive load, can be considered as rectangular plates freely hinge-supported on three sides and unsupported along the fourth side h. For this case the buckling load is given by Eq. (166). However the (long) angle yields first when $t > b/20$.

Thus angles of a wall thickness less than $b/20$ will plate-buckle before they yield, but if the wall thickness t is greater than $b/20$, they will yield first. In ordinary structural steel profiles the thickness t is always larger than $b/20$, so that the case of Fig. 205 will never occur there. But for duralumin or alloy steels the yield stress is much greater than $E/1,000$, and when these materials are used in built-up angle constructions, instability according to Eq. (166) may occur before the yield stress is reached.

Many other cases of different edge supports for rectangular and circular plates have been investigated, and for these the reader is referred to the book by Timoshenko, "Theory of Elastic Stability."[1]

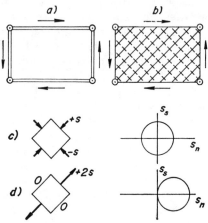

Fig. 206. (a) A panel consisting of a thin skin attached to four rigid bars, pin-jointed at the corners, subjected to shear. This is more or less equivalent to (b), where the skin is replaced by two perpendicular sets of strings, one of which becomes limp under the loading, and the other of which carries the load in the form of tension. If the skin in (a) had not buckled, an element of it would be stressed as in (c). In the actual case of shear buckling the state of stress in that element for the same shear load is about as shown in (d). The Mohr's circles for these two cases have the same diameter, *i.e.*, the same shear stress; hence the total shear load that can be carried with buckling is about equal to that without buckling.

Shear Buckling of Aircraft Panels. In aircraft construction thin aluminum skins attached to frameworks of beams or girders are used extensively. An element of such a construction is shown in Fig. 206, consisting of four beams forming a rectangle with a thin skin attached to the beams and covering the entire rectangle between them. The beams are often rigidly attached to each other at the corners, but suppose we are pessimistic and assume them to be pin-jointed at the four corners. We also assume the beams to be rigid in comparison with the sheet in between. Let this element be subjected to a shear load. The four pin-jointed bars offer no resistance whatever to this type of loading, and they would collapse

[1] McGraw-Hill Book Company, Inc., New York, 1936.

into a flat parallelogram without the skin in between. That skin then will be subjected to a uniform plane shear, and we can visualize its action by replacing it by two intersecting sets of strings or wires at 45 deg, in the directions of principal stress. One set of strings takes tension; the other takes compression. It does not require much of a shear force to make the compression strings buckle, and just before this happens, the tensile stress in the one set of strings equals the compressive stress in the other set. When the shear load is increased beyond this critical one, the system does not collapse; the tension strings take more tension, and the compression stress in the other set remains constant or diminishes. When the shear load has gone up to ten or twenty times the critical load, the tension stress is more than ten or twenty times larger than the compressive stress in the other set, and we can say that the compressive stress is then practically zero on a relative basis. This state of affairs has not really increased the stress at all, as compared with the non-buckled position, as

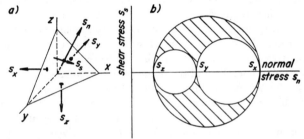

Fig. 207. Mohr's circle for stress. In (a) the axes x, y, z are principal axes at a point in the structure. The oblique plane has an arbitrary position. It will be proved on pages 308 to 313 that the normal s_n and shear stress s_s, when plotted on a Mohr diagram (b), are represented by some point within the shaded area.

can be seen from Fig. 207. Therefore this type of buckling is without danger and occurs all the time. It can be easily observed on the wings of an airplane while flying in bumpy weather. The buckling corrugations on the skin of the wing are changing with each variation in the wing loading from gusts in the wind.

Problems 176 *to* 213.

CHAPTER IX

MISCELLANEOUS TOPICS

45. Mohr's Circle for Three Dimensions. On many occasions in the past chapters we have made use of Mohr's circle for *stress*, and in all those cases the stress system was two-dimensional, so that we dealt with one Mohr's circle only. It was stated without proof that if in Fig. 207*a* we have three principal planes at a point with three principal stresses s_x, s_y, and s_z, and if we then draw an arbitrary oblique plane, find the normal and shear stress on that plane, and plot them in a Mohr diagram (Fig. 207*b*), then the stresses s_n and s_s are depicted by a point lying in the shaded area. As a consequence, if we take the Mohr's circle connecting the largest and the smallest of the three principal stresses, we then have the worst stresses that can occur at the point in question. This property has been used frequently, and the proof for it was postponed until "later." The reason for this (a usual practice in textbooks on strength of materials, many of which never give the proof at all) is a good one; the proof is long and tedious, and its study offers no great reward in better understanding of the principles. For completeness' sake it is now given.

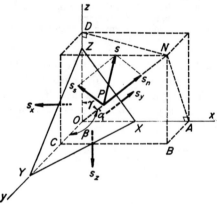

Fig. 208. The normal ON on the arbitrary oblique plane XYZ, piercing that plane at point P, and its three angles α, β, γ with the x, y, and z axes, respectively. These three angles satisfy the general relation (*a*). The stress s_n is directed along the normal ON; the shear stress s_s lies in the plane XYZ; the total stress s is the vector sum of s_n and s_s. These stresses satisfy the general relations (*b*) to (*e*).

308

General Relations. First we derive five general relationships which we shall need for the proof. The first of these is a geometrical proposition, having nothing to do with stress. In Fig. 208 the axes x, y, z are the principal axes at point O, and XYZ is the arbitrary oblique plane on which we propose to study the stresses. Rather than to work with this plane itself, it will be found easier to work with the normal ON to it because the directions in space of a radial line are easier to visualize than those of a plane. The angles of the normal ON with respect to the three axes are called α, β, γ. The parallelepiped $OABCD$ in Fig. 208 contains the normal as a diagonal. We see that the sides of this parallelepiped have the lengths $OA = ON \cos \alpha$, $OC = ON \cos \beta$, and $OD = ON \cos \gamma$. It will be convenient to think of ON as being of unit length; then its projections on the three axes are $\cos \alpha$, $\cos \beta$, $\cos \gamma$. Now by Pythagoras we have

$$1 = ON^2 = OA^2 + AN^2 = OA^2 + (AB^2 + BN^2)$$
$$= OA^2 + OC^2 + OB^2 = \cos^2 \alpha + \cos^2 \beta + \cos^2 \gamma$$

or

$$\cos^2 \alpha + \cos^2 \beta + \cos^2 \gamma = 1 \qquad (a)$$

This is our first relation. For the second one we first look at the areas of the various triangles in Fig. 208. The angle between two planes equals the angle between the normals on those planes. Hence the angle between the yz plane and the oblique XYZ plane is α, and if we think of triangle XYZ as having unit area, then triangle OYZ (which is the projection of triangle XYZ on the yz plane) has the area $\cos \alpha$. Now, if XYZ is of unit area and the three projected triangles have areas $\cos \alpha$, $\cos \beta$, $\cos \gamma$ and their stresses are s_x, s_y, s_z, the *forces* on these three projected triangles are $s_x \cos \alpha$, $s_y \cos \beta$, $s_z \cos \gamma$. There are no shear stresses on these three planes, because x, y, z were supposed to be principal axes. Now for equilibrium of the tetrahedron $OXYZ$ it is necessary that on the oblique triangle there act a force F equal and opposite to the vector resultant of the three other forces, and since these three forces are mutually perpendicular we have, by Pythagoras,

$$F = s_x^2 \cos^2 \alpha + s_y^2 \cos^2 \beta + s_z^2 \cos^2 \gamma$$

This is the *force* on the oblique triangle, and since its area is unity, this is also the total stress on that oblique plane. Such a *total* stress is a vector *not* perpendicular to the plane, but at some angle with respect to it. The total stress vector can be resolved into a component along the normal ON of Fig. 208 and a component lying in the plane XYZ. The total stress we shall call s; the two components s_n and s_s, normal stress and shear stress.

We thus have two relations at once:

$$s^2 = s_x^2 \cos^2 \alpha + s_y^2 \cos^2 \beta + s_z^2 \cos^2 \gamma \qquad (b)$$
$$s^2 = s_n^2 + s_s^2 \qquad (c)$$

The next relation is found from writing the equilibrium equation of the tetrahedron in the normal ON direction. There are five stresses acting on it: s_x, s_y, s_z on the three principal planes, s_n, s_s on the oblique plane. The *forces* of these five stresses are $s_x \cos \alpha$, $s_y \cos \beta$, $s_z \cos \gamma$, s_n, s_s. Of these five the force s_s has no component in the normal direction, being perpendicular to it. The force s_n is directed along the normal. The other three forces include certain angles with the normal; for example, the force $s_x \cos \alpha$, being parallel to the x axis, has the angle α with the normal. The projection of $s_x \cos \alpha$ on the normal thus is $(s_x \cos \alpha) \cos \alpha = s_x \cos^2 \alpha$ and similarly for the other two forces. Thus the equilibrium equation along the normal is

$$s_n = s_x \cos^2 \alpha + s_y \cos^2 \beta + s_z \cos^2 \gamma \qquad (d)$$

The fifth and last general relation is an expression for the shear stress s_s, to be derived from (c), because we know s and s_n from (b) and (d). This involves considerable algebra;

$$s_s^2 = s^2 - s_n^2 = s_x^2 \cos^2 \alpha + s_y^2 \cos^2 \beta + s_z^2 \cos^2 \gamma - s_x^2 \cos^4 \alpha - s_y^2 \cos^4 \beta$$
$$-s_z^2 \cos^4 \gamma - 2s_x s_y \cos^2 \alpha \cos^2 \beta - 2s_x s_z \cos^2 \alpha \cos^2 \gamma - 2s_y s_z \cos^2 \beta \cos^2 \gamma$$

In the first line of this we see expressions like $\cos^2 \alpha - \cos^4 \alpha$, which we transform:

$$\cos^2 \alpha - \cos^4 \alpha = \cos^2 \alpha(1 - \cos^2 \alpha) = \text{using relation } (a)$$
$$\cos^2 \alpha(\cos^2 \beta + \cos^2 \gamma)$$

With this we have:

$$s_s^2 = s_x^2 \cos^2 \alpha(\cos^2 \beta + \cos^2 \gamma) + s_y^2 \cos^2 \beta(\cos^2 \alpha + \cos^2 \gamma)$$
$$+ s_z^2 \cos^2 \gamma(\cos^2 \alpha + \cos^2 \beta) - 2s_x s_y \cos^2 \alpha \cos^2 \beta, \text{ etc.}$$

Rearranging,

$$s_s = \cos^2 \alpha \cos^2 \beta(s_x^2 + s_y^2 - 2s_x s_y) + \cos^2 \alpha \cos^2 \gamma(s_x^2 + s_z^2 - 2s_x s_z)$$
$$+ \cos^2 \beta \cos^2 \gamma(s_y^2 + s_z^2 - 2s_y s_z)$$

so that we have for our fifth and last relation

$$s_s^2 = (s_x - s_y)^2 \cos^2 \alpha \cos^2 \beta + (s_x - s_z)^2 \cos^2 \alpha \cos^2 \gamma$$
$$+ (s_y - s_z)^2 \cos^2 \beta \cos^2 \gamma \qquad (e)$$

For convenience we reprint them all together:

(a) $\qquad \cos^2 \alpha + \cos^2 \beta + \cos^2 \gamma = 1$

(b) $\qquad s^2 = s_x^2 \cos^2 \alpha + s_y^2 \cos^2 \beta + s_z^2 \cos^2 \gamma$

(c) $\qquad s^2 = s_n^2 + s_s^2 \qquad\qquad\qquad\qquad\qquad\qquad (167)$

(d) $\qquad s_n = s_x \cos^2 \alpha + s_y \cos^2 \beta + s_z \cos^2 \gamma$

(e) $\qquad s_s^2 = (s_x - s_y)^2 \cos^2 \alpha \cos^2 \beta + \text{two other terms, cyclic}$

Special Two-dimensional Cases. Suppose now that in a special case one of the angles α, β, γ becomes 90 deg, so that $\cos \alpha = 0$, say. Expressions (*d*), (*e*), and (*a*) then reduce to

$$s_n = s_y \cos^2 \beta + s_z \cos^2 \gamma$$

$$s_s = (s_y - s_z) \cos \beta \cos \gamma$$

$$\cos \beta = \sin \gamma$$

These are the familiar Mohr formulae for two-dimensional stress, which after some transformation are usually written as

$$s_n = \frac{s_y + s_z}{2} + \frac{s_y - s_z}{2} \cos 2\beta$$

$$s_s = \frac{s_y - s_z}{2} \sin 2\beta$$

and are represented by the usual Mohr's circle. There are three such special cases for α, β, γ = 90 deg, and hence there are three such two-dimensional circle representations, one for s_z, s_y, another for s_z, s_z, and a third for s_y, s_z, as shown in Fig. 210. It means then that the state of stress s_n, s_s on one of the special planes of Fig. 209 is represented on Fig. 210

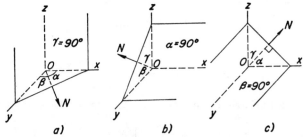

Fig. 209. Special positions of the oblique plane of Fig. 208 in which one of the normal angles is 90 deg, so that the oblique plane is parallel to one of the axes. These are cases of two-dimensional stress, depicted by the circles of Fig. 207*b*.

by a point lying on one of the circles. If the special plane of Fig. 209*a* turns about a vertical axis, changing its angle α, then the point in Fig. 210 representing the stress on that plane moves along the Mohr's circle connecting s_x and s_y. Also when the plane of Fig. 209*b* turns about the x axis, varying angle β, the Mohr picture point in Fig. 210 moves along the circle connecting s_y and s_z.

Three-dimensional Proof. Mohr's statement is that for any general value of α, β, γ, that is, for any general position of the oblique plane of Fig. 208, the values of normal and shear stress [Eqs. (*d*) and (*e*)] will plot on the $s_n s_s$ plane as a point within the shaded area of Fig. 210. This we shall now proceed to prove. In Fig. 210 plot $OB = s_n$ and $BC = s_s$, so that the point C depicts the stress. The point C may not fall within the circle; it might be at C'. To prove that it is within the larger circle, we have to

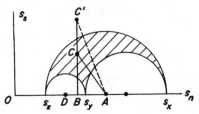

FIG. 210. Point C or C' represents the state of stress on an arbitrary oblique plane. From the five general relations (a) to. (e) we prove that the point C or C' must lie inside the large circle and outside the two smaller circles.

prove that AC is less than the radius of the large circle, of which the center is A. We choose the principal axes so that s_x is the largest principal stress:

$$s_x > s_y > s_z$$

Then

$$OA = \frac{s_x + s_z}{2} \qquad OB = s_n$$

Hence

$$AB = -s_n + \frac{s_x + s_z}{2} \qquad BC \text{ or } BC' = s_s$$

Hence

$$AC^2 = s_s^2 + \left(-s_n + \frac{s_x + s_z}{2}\right)^2$$

The radius of the larger circle is $(s_x - s_z)/2$. We now have to prove that

$$s_s^2 + \left(-s_n + \frac{s_x + s_z}{2}\right)^2 \leq \frac{(s_x - s_z)^2}{4}$$

and we proceed to simplify this inequality to such a point that its truth becomes evident. Working it out,

$$s_s^2 + s_n^2 - s_n(s_x + s_z) + \frac{(s_x + s_z)^2}{4} \leq \frac{(s_x - s_z)^2}{4}$$

Using proposition (c) and also working out the squares and seeing that two out of the three terms in them cancel,

$$s^2 - s_n(s_x + s_z) + \frac{s_x s_z}{2} \leq -\frac{s_x s_z}{2}$$

$$s^2 + s_x s_z \leq s_n(s_x + s_z)$$

Now substitute the expressions (b) and (d) for the total and normal stress:

$$s_x^2 \cos^2 \alpha + s_y^2 \cos^2 \beta + s_z^2 \cos^2 \gamma + s_x s_z$$
$$\leq s_x(s_x + s_z) \cos^2 \alpha + s_y(s_x + s_z) \cos^2 \beta + s_z(s_x + s_z) \cos^2 \gamma$$

Canceling some terms left and right,

$$s_y^2 \cos^2 \beta + s_x s_z \leq s_x s_z(\cos^2 \alpha + \cos^2 \gamma) + s_y(s_x + s_z) \cos^2 \beta$$

Apply Eq. (a) to the first term on the right side and then cancel the $s_x s_z$ term:

$$s_y^2 \cos^2 \beta \leq (-s_x s_z + s_y s_x + s_y s_z) \cos^2 \beta$$

Divide by $\cos^2 \beta$, and rearrange terms:

$$s_y(s_y - s_z) \leq s_x(s_y - s_z)$$

Dividing by $s_y - s_z$ finally reduces our inequality to

$$s_y \leq s_x$$

which evidently is true, because s_x was defined as the largest principal stress. Thus we recognize that our inequality is correct and that point C or C' of Fig. 210 must lie *within* the largest circle.

Now we must still prove that a general point C lies outside the smaller circles. Let D be the center of the $s_y s_z$ circle. Then we must prove that DC is larger than the radius of the $s_y s_z$ circle, or

$$DC^2 = DB^2 + BC^2 = (OB - OD)^2 + BC^2 \geq \left(\frac{s_y - s_z}{2}\right)^2$$

or

$$\left(s_n - \frac{s_y + s_z}{2}\right)^2 + s_s^2 \geq \frac{(s_y - s_z)^2}{4}$$

The steps in the proof of this inequality are the same as those previously given, so that we leave out some lines in the argument:

$$s^2 - s_n(s_y + s_z) + s_y s_z \geq 0$$

$$s_x^2 \cos^2 \alpha + s_y^2 \cos^2 \beta + s_z^2 \cos^2 \gamma - s_x(s_y + s_z) \cos^2 \alpha - s_y(s_y + s_z) \cos^2 \beta$$
$$- s_z(s_y + s_z) \cos^2 \gamma + s_y s_z \geq 0$$

$$\cos^2 \alpha(s_x^2 - s_x s_y - s_x s_z) - s_y s_z(\cos^2 \beta + \cos^2 \gamma - 1) \geq 0$$

$$s_x^2 - s_x s_y - s_x s_z + s_y s_z \geq 0$$

$$(s_y - s_x)(s_z - s_x) \geq 0$$

Since $s_x > s_y > s_z$, both factors on the left are negative and their product is positive, which proves the inequality.

The reader should now repeat this argument once more and prove that point C lies outside the third circle of $s_x s_y$, thus completing the proof.

Mohr's Circles for Strain. Figure 211 shows an infinitesimally small parallelepiped cut out of an elastic structure at point O, so that its sides are along the principal directions of strain. By this we mean that if in the unstrained state all corner angles of the parallelepiped are 90 deg, then

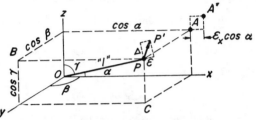

Fig. 211. An element with a diagonal length OP = unity and consequently with side lengths $\cos \alpha$, $\cos \beta$, $\cos \gamma$. The axes are principal axes of strain. When this element is strained, the point A moves to A' (in the zy plane) and P moves to P'. The total displacement PP' can be resolved into a longitudinal displacement ϵ and a crosswise displacement Δ. Sine OP is of unit length, ϵ is the strain, and Δ is the angle of turn of the direction OP.

after the straining they remain 90 deg. The size and shape of the parallelepiped are so chosen that the diagonal OP has an arbitrary direction with respect to the sides, *i.e.*, with respect to the principal axes x, y, z, and characterized by the angles α, β, γ, as shown. If we make the length of the diagonal OP equal to unity, then the sides of the parallelepiped are $\cos \alpha$, $\cos \beta$, and $\cos \gamma$. If we now strain the piece, it remains a parallelepiped and the three principal strains are called ϵ_x, ϵ_y, and ϵ_z. The point O is held in place, and the three axes are not allowed to rotate; then point A moves to A' with displacements $\epsilon_x \cos \alpha$ and $\epsilon_y \cos \beta$ in the x and y directions, respectively. Point P moves to another point P' with displacement components $\epsilon_x \cos \alpha$, $\epsilon_y \cos \beta$, and $\epsilon_z \cos \gamma$ in the three principal directions. In general the direction PP' will not be in line with OP. Let us call PP' the *total* displacement δ_{total} of P, and let us resolve this total displacement into a component along OP and into a component perpendicular to OP, which we may call the longitudinal displacement and the perpendicular displacement. Since OP = unit length, the longitudinal displacement is also equal to the strain ϵ in the OP direction and the perpendicular displacement is equal to the angle Δ through which the direction OP turns. Between the letters α, β, γ, δ_{total}, ϵ, and Δ we have relations completely identical with Eqs. (167):

(a) $$\cos^2 \alpha + \cos^2 \beta + \cos^2 \gamma = 1$$

(b) $$\delta_{\text{total}}^2 = (\epsilon_x \cos \alpha)^2 + (\epsilon_y \cos \beta)^2 + (\epsilon_z \cos \gamma)^2$$

(c) $$\delta^2_{\text{total}} = \epsilon^2 + \Delta^2 \tag{168}$$

(d) $$\epsilon = \epsilon_x \cos^2 \alpha + \epsilon_y \cos^2 \beta + \epsilon_z \cos^2 \gamma$$

(e) $$\Delta^2 = (\epsilon_x - \epsilon_y)^2 \cos^2 \alpha \cos^2 \beta + 2 \text{ cyclic terms}$$

The relations (a), (b), and (c) are Pythagoras' theorem for the distances OP, and PP', respectively. The relation (d) follows by resolving the three displacements $\epsilon_x \cos \alpha$, $\epsilon_y \cos \beta$, $\epsilon_z \cos \gamma$ of P into components along OP and across it. The sum of the OP components is the longitudinal displacement. Finally, (e) is calculated from (c), (b), and (d) with the help of (a), exactly as it was done on page 310, with the same result. Thus a Mohr-circle diagram for three-dimensional strains can be constructed in which we plot horizontally the strain of an arbitrary direction and vertically the angle of rotation of that arbitrary vector. By the proof given on page 312 we can conclude that the angle Δ always must lie inside the shaded area of Fig. 207b. The angles Δ have no particular practical significance; they are related to the shear strains, but in such a complicated manner as to be useless for the purpose except in two-dimensional cases. Then the parallelepiped of Fig. 211 degenerates into a flat plane; if $\gamma = 90$ deg, it is the xy plane and P coincides with C. Then the angle Δ lies in the xy plane; the difference between the Δ of OC and the Δ of a radius perpendicular to OC in the xy plane is the shear strain. For a three-dimensional case, however, the expression (168e) fails to disclose the plane in which the angle Δ is located, so that we cannot calculate any shear strain component from it directly. This makes the *three*-dimensional Mohr-circle diagram for strain of limited usefulness.

46. Torsion of Pretwisted Thin-walled Sections. Saint-Venant's theory of torsion, as given in Chap. I, applies to cylindrical bars of any cross section. For thin-walled sections, such as those of Fig. 12 (page 16), that theory becomes quite simple, and it has been applied not only to the straight cylindrical bars for which it was derived but also to slightly pretwisted ones, of which aircraft propeller blades are the most important practical example. Quite recently (in 1950), however, it was observed that a pretwisted bar, even a slightly pretwisted one, is considerably stiffer against torsion than the same straight bar. This was explained by Chen Chu to be caused by the appearance of secondary longitudinal stresses. Physically the reason is as follows: a longitudinal fiber, following the same element dA of the cross section, is not a straight line but a spiral about the center fiber of a symmetrical section. When the bar is twisted (keeping the length of the center fiber unchanged), the spiral becomes longer if the elastic twist is in the same direction as the pretwist, and shorter in the opposite case. Elongation of the spiral causes tension in it, following the spiral direction. This tension is mostly longitudinal (parallel to the center fiber), but it has a small component in the plane of the cross section and directed tangentially. All these horizontal components over a complete cross section form a torque, which must be added to the Saint-Venant torque caused by the shear-force distribution of Fig. 12, and this secondary torque can become substantially larger than the Saint-Venant torque itself. The result of the analysis, to which we now proceed, is shown in Fig. 213 for a rectangular cross section.

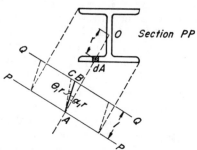

Fig. 212. Two sections PP and QQ at unit distance apart longitudinally of a pretwisted I beam. A fiber dA appears in vertical projection as a piece of spiral AB in the unstressed state. This spiral AB goes to the position AC when the section QQ is twisted elastically through angle θ_1 with respect to section PP.

Analysis. Consider in Fig. 212 a thin-walled H section or any other thin-walled symmetrical section with its center O. Let the angle of pretwist per unit length be α_1, that is, two sections at unit distance apart longitudinally are turned with respect to each other by the angle α_1 about point O in the unstressed state of the bar. Then we twist the bar elastically through angle θ_1 per unit length. A fiber dA, at distance r from O, then is a spiral of angle $\alpha_1 r$ in the unstressed state and of angle $(\alpha_1 + \theta_1)r$ in the stressed state. The angle $\theta_1 r$ is necessarily small, but we also assume $\alpha_1 r$ to be small, that is, $\alpha_1 r = \sin \alpha_1 r$; $\cos \alpha_1 r = 1$, which in practice limits the pretwist spiral angle to about 10 deg, as it is in aircraft propellers. If during this elastic twisting the two sections remain at unit distance apart, the fiber AB elongates to AC, the elongation being

$$\Delta l = AC - AB = \sqrt{1 + \sin^2 (\alpha_1 + \theta_1)r} - \sqrt{1 + \sin^2 \alpha_1 r}$$
$$\approx [1 + \tfrac{1}{2} \sin^2 (\alpha_1 + \theta_1)r] - [1 + \tfrac{1}{2} \sin^2 \alpha_1 r]$$
$$= \tfrac{1}{2} \sin^2 (\alpha_1 + \theta_1)r - \tfrac{1}{2} \sin^2 \alpha_1 r$$
$$\approx \tfrac{1}{2}(\alpha_1 r + \theta_1 r)^2 - \tfrac{1}{2}(\alpha_1 r)^2 \approx \alpha_1 r \theta_1 r + \tfrac{1}{2}(\theta_1 r)^2$$

The angle $\theta_1 r$ is an elastic shearing angle and hence must be of the order of 0.001 radian within the elastic limit, while $\alpha_1 r$ may be of the order of 0.1 radian. Hence we neglect the last term with respect to the first one, and $\Delta l = \alpha_1 \theta_1 r^2$ is the elongation for a unit length of spiral. For a thin-walled section this elongation must be caused by a tensile stress along the spiral, because a cross stress of comparable magnitude is excluded for reasons of equilibrium. Hence the spiral tensile stress would be $E\alpha_1 \theta_1 r^2$, but this integrates over the entire cross section into a total longitudinal pull on the bar, which is absent. To fix this, we must add a constant longitudinal stress (not dependent on r) over the section, so as to make the total pull zero.

$$0 = \int_A (E\alpha_1 \theta_1 r^2 + \text{const}) \, dA = E\alpha_1 \theta_1 I_p + \text{const } A = 0$$

The constant then is $-E\alpha_1 \theta_1 I_p / A$, and the spiral stress is

$$s_{\text{spiral}} = E\alpha_1 \theta_1 \left(r^2 - \frac{I_p}{A} \right) \qquad (a)$$

tensile in the outer fibers and compressive for the fibers near the center O of Fig. 212. In Eq. (a), of course, I_p is the polar moment of inertia about O, and A is the area of the cross section. Now the component of the spiral stress in the plane of the cross section is $\alpha_1 r$ times that stress, and it is directed perpendicular to r in the section. Hence it contributes to the torque an amount

$$dM_t = (\alpha_1 r s_{\text{spiral}} \, dA) r$$

and the torque is

$$M_t = E\alpha_1^2 \theta_1 \int_A \left(r^4 - \frac{I_p}{A} r^2 \right) dA \qquad (169)$$

Applying this general result to a bar of thin rectangular cross section bt, we have

$$\int_A r^4 \, dA = 2 \int_0^{b/2} x^4(t \, dx) = 2t \frac{(b/2)^5}{5} = \frac{b^5 t}{80}$$

$$\frac{I_p}{A} \int_A r^2 \, dA = \frac{b^3 t / 12}{bt} 2 \int_0^{b/2} x^2 t \, dx = \frac{b^5 t}{144}$$

and the torque from the longitudinal stresses is

$$\frac{b^5 t E \alpha_1^2 \theta_1}{180}$$

The Saint-Venant torque of the straight, non-pretwisted bar, in the manner of Fig. 12, is found from Eq. (12) (page 15):

$$\frac{bt^3 G \theta_1}{3}$$

The total torque is the sum of these two, and we can write it as follows:

$$M_{t\text{ total}} = \frac{bt^3G\theta_1}{3}\left[1 + \frac{E}{G}\frac{b^4\alpha_1^2}{60t^2}\right]$$

$$= \frac{bt^3G\theta_1}{3}\left[1 + \frac{1}{6}\left(\frac{b}{2}\alpha_1\right)^2\frac{b^2}{t^2}\right] \tag{170}$$

The factor in square brackets is that by which the pretwisted bar is stiffer than the straight one; the quantity $b\alpha_1/2$ appearing in it is the spiral angle of the outer fiber of the section (Fig. 212), the maximum spiral angle of the section. This relationship is plotted in Fig. 213, and from it we see that the effect is large: a thin rectangular bar of ordinary proportions, pretwisted to a reasonably small spiral angle, can be three or four times as stiff against torsion as the corresponding straight bar.

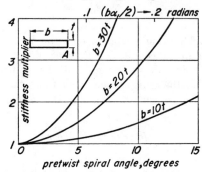

Fig. 213. Factor by which a pretwisted rectangular bar is stiffer torsionally than the same straight bar. This factor is plotted against the pretwist spiral angle of the fiber A, most remote from the center of the section. The figure illustrates Eq. (170). This effect was observed and explained by Chen Chu in the year 1950!

Straightening of a Pretwisted Bar by Longitudinal Tension. If a pretwisted bar, such as an aircraft propeller blade, is subjected to a tensile force, caused by centrifugal force, for example, it experiences a torque tending to untwist the original pretwist. Consider again (Fig. 212) a fiber of cross section dA having the shape of a spiral with spiral angle $\alpha_1 r$. If the total tensile force on the bar is P, then the portion carried by our fiber is $P\,dA/A$ and it is parallel to the center line of the twisted bar, as shown by the fully lined arrows of Fig. 214. These fully lined forces are now resolved into components longitudinally along the spiral and crosswise, both shown dotted in Fig. 214. The shear force $(P\,dA/A)\alpha_1 r$ is directed perpendicular to the radius r in a normal cross section of the bar, and hence its contribution to the torque is r times the force. Integrating over the cross section leads to the torque:

$$\int P\frac{dA}{A}\alpha_1 r^2 = \frac{P}{A}\alpha_1\int r^2\,dA = \frac{PI_p\alpha_1}{A}$$

or

$$M_t = \frac{PI_p\alpha_1}{A} \tag{171}$$

This is the torque which tends to straighten the pretwisted blade. For an aircraft propeller the force P, being caused by centrifugal action, varies along the blade, so that the torque also varies along the blade, being large near the root and zero at the tip.

Bending of Pretwisted Beams. Consider a pretwisted beam of a thin-walled cross section, such as shown in Fig. 198 (page 298) or Fig. 212. For simplicity let the dimensions of Fig. 212 be such that the two principal moments of inertia are equal, so that by the Mohr-circle theorem the beam section has the same bending stiffness in all directions. If such a beam, pretwisted, is subjected to bending, the accepted theory of strength of materials states that the pretwist has no effect whatever on the bending deflection. But it has been noticed experimentally that a pretwisted beam shows *considerably* larger deflections than a straight beam of the same cross section and length under the same bending load. So far no satisfactory explanation for this effect has been given. It is left as a challenge to the reader with the remark that in a subject as old-fashioned as strength of materials new effects of considerable numerical importance can still be discovered in the atomic age.

Fig. 214. The forces acting on a spiral-shaped fiber of a propeller blade are shown in full lines. These can be resolved into a pair of tensile forces which do not tend to untwist the fiber, and into a pair of small crosswise forces which do tend to straighten out the spiral. Note the similarity with Fig. 199 (page 299) and the fact that if the forces are reversed they tend to increase the spiral effect and may lead to instability.

47. The Theorems of Biezeno and Spielvogel. We shall now deal with two applications of Castigliano's theorem to structures of some practical importance, both of which appear very complicated at first but lead to surprisingly simple end results. The first is the problem of finding the bending and twisting moments in a circular ring, loaded by an arbitrary force distribution perpendicular to its own plane, and supported in a statically determinate manner, *i.e.*, generally on three supports. The second problem is that of determining the end reactions of a steam pipe of arbitrary plane shape, built in at both ends, caused by a rise in temperature of the structure. The first problem was solved by *Biezeno* and the second one by *Spielvogel.*

Biezeno's Theorem on the Transversely Loaded Ring. Let in Fig. 215 a ring be loaded with a number of forces $P_1, P_2, \ldots, P_n$, perpendicular to the plane of the ring. Taking an arbitrary point A on the ring, let these forces be located at angular distances α_1, α_2, ..., α_n from point A. Let the ring be supported on three points; the reactions R_1, R_2, and R_3 can be calculated by statics, and then they can be considered as loads (with

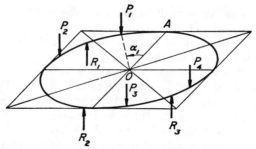

FIG. 215. A circular ring supported on three simple supports R_1, R_2, R_3 loaded by a number of vertical forces $P_1 \ldots P_n$ located at angular distances $\alpha_1 \ldots \alpha_n$ from a base point A. Biezeno multiplies all forces and reactions by the factor $\alpha/2\pi$, different for each force, and then calculates the shear force and the bending and twisting moments at A from these "reduced" forces by the rules of statics [Eqs. (172)]. The result is independent of the stiffness EI or GI_p of the ring.

negative signs). Now we proceed to multiply each load and reaction by the quantity $\alpha_n/2\pi$; that is, a load at 90 deg from A is multiplied by $\frac{1}{4}$; a load at 240 deg from A is multiplied by $\frac{2}{3}$, etc. These new loads and reactions are called the "reduced" loads, P_n^*, and obviously they do not necessarily constitute a system in equilibrium. Then Biezeno's theorem states that the three statically indeterminate quantities at the cross section A are found as follows:

$$S_0 = \sum_n P_n^*$$

$$M_{b0} = \sum_n P_n^* r \sin \alpha_n \qquad (172)$$

$$M_{t0} = \sum_n P_n^* r (1 - \cos \alpha_n)$$

or in words: *The shear force at the section A is the sum of all "reduced" loads and reactions; the bending moment at A is the moment of all "reduced" loads and reactions about the diameter through A, and the twisting moment at A is the moment of all "reduced" loads and reactions about the tangent to the circle at A.* It is remarkable that this answer is entirely independent of the stiffnesses EI or GI_p or even of their ratio.

For the proof of Biezeno's theorem (172) we calculate the three internal reactions at A by Castigliano's method, isolating the piece from $\theta = 0$ at A to $\theta = \theta$ (Fig. 216). The three unknown reactions at A are called S_0, M_{b0}, M_{t0}, where the zero subscript indicates that the angle θ is zero there. The shear force S_0 is designated as a cross, suggesting that the force goes into the paper. For equilibrium we need moments and a shear force at the other end $\theta = \theta$. In the intervening piece a number of loads or reactions act of which one, P_n, is shown, coming toward us out of the

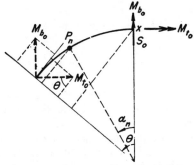

Fɪɢ. 216. A piece O of the ring of Fig. 215, drawn for the purpose of deriving the expressions (a) for the moments at the arbitrary section θ.

paper. To find the moments at θ, we shift the M_{bo} and M_{to} moments to that location and resolve their vectors radially and tangentially:

$$M_{b\theta} = M_{bo} \cos \theta - M_{to} \sin \theta + S_0 r \sin \theta + \sum_n P_n r \sin (\theta - \alpha_n)$$

$$M_{t\theta} = M_{bo} \sin \theta + M_{to} \cos \theta + S_0 r(1 - \cos \theta)$$
$$+ \sum_n P_n r[1 - \cos (\theta - \alpha_n)] \tag{a}$$

The energy in the entire ring then is

$$U = \frac{r}{2EI} \int M_{b\theta}^2 \, d\theta + \frac{r}{2GI_p} \int M_{t\theta}^2 \, d\theta$$

Now Castigliano's theorem requires that

$$\frac{\partial U}{\partial M_{b0}} = 0 \qquad \frac{\partial U}{\partial M_{t0}} = 0 \qquad \frac{\partial U}{\partial S_0} = 0 \tag{b}$$

or

$$\frac{1}{EI} \int_{\alpha_n}^{2\pi} M_{b\theta} \cos \theta \, d\theta + \frac{1}{GI_p} \int_{\alpha_n}^{2\pi} M_{t\theta} \sin \theta \, d\theta = 0 \tag{c}$$

$$-\frac{1}{EI} \int_{\alpha_n}^{2\pi} M_{b\theta} \sin \theta \, d\theta + \frac{1}{GI_p} \int_{\alpha_n}^{2\pi} M_{t\theta} \cos \theta \, d\theta = 0 \tag{d}$$

$$\frac{1}{EI} \int_{\alpha_n}^{2\pi} M_{b\theta} \sin \theta \, d\theta + \frac{1}{GI_p} \int_{\alpha_n}^{2\pi} M_{t\theta}(1 - \cos \theta) \, d\theta = 0 \tag{e}$$

The integrations extend from α_n to 2π, different for each load, with the understanding that for M_{b0}, M_{t0}, S_0 the angle $\alpha = 0$.

Adding Eq. (*e*) to Eq. (*d*), we find

$$\int_{\alpha_n}^{2\pi} M_{t\theta}\, d\theta = 0$$

or

$$S_0 r 2\pi + \sum_n P_n r[(2\pi - \alpha_n) - \sin(2\pi - \alpha_n)] = 0$$

$$S_0 + \sum_n P_n - \sum_n P_n \frac{\alpha_n}{2\pi} + \sum_n \frac{P_n}{2\pi} \sin \alpha_n = 0$$

Now we remember that the P_n symbol includes all the forces and all the reactions on the ring, so that for vertical static equilibrium the second term in the above expression is zero. Likewise the last term (multiplied by the radius r) represents the moment of all forces about the diameter OA of Fig. 215, which must be zero for equilibrium of the entire ring. Now the third term in the above expression is the sum of the "reduced" forces and reactions by Biezeno's definition, so that the first of the Eqs. (172) is proved.

Now we write the second of Eqs. (*b*):

$$\int \frac{\partial U}{\partial M_{t0}}\, d\theta = 0$$

$$-\frac{1}{EI} \int M_{b0} \sin \theta \, d\theta + \frac{1}{GI_p} \int M_{t0} \cos \theta \, d\theta = 0$$

$$-\frac{1}{EI}\left[-M_{t0}\pi + S_0 r\pi + \sum_n P_n r \int_{\alpha_n}^{2\pi} \sin(\theta - \alpha_n) \sin \theta \, d\theta \right]$$

$$+\frac{1}{GI_p}\left[+M_{t0}\pi - S_0 r\pi + \sum_n P_n r \int_{\alpha_n}^{2\pi} \{1 - \cos(\theta - \alpha_n)\} \cos \theta \, d\theta \right] = 0$$

Working out the integrals, we note that the quantities in the two square brackets come out identical except for a sign, so that each one must be zero, and the result is independent of EI or GI_p:

$$-M_{t0}\pi + S_0 r\pi + \sum_n P_n r\left[\frac{1}{2}\sin \alpha_n + \left(\pi - \frac{\alpha_n}{2}\right)\cos \alpha_n \right] = 0$$

There are three terms under the $\sum$ sign. The first one is half the moment of the forces about the diameter, which is zero as we have seen before. The second term is the sum of $P_n r \cos \alpha_n$, which is the moment about another diameter, again zero. In the third term we see the combination $P_n \alpha_n$, which can be written as $2\pi P_n^*$ in terms of the "reduced" forces. Thus

$$-M_{t0} + S_0 r - \sum_n P_n^* r \cos \alpha_n = 0$$

Now substitute into this the first of Eqs. (172), and find the third of Eqs. (172), which is thereby derived.

The second of Eqs. (172) follows from Eq. (c):

$$\frac{\partial U}{\partial M_{b0}} = 0$$

in the same manner; the details are left as an exercise to the reader.

As an example of the application of this result to a specific simple case

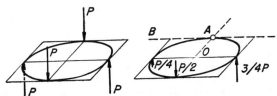

FIG. 217.   Application of Biezeno's theorem to a simple case. The true loads are shown in the left figure; the "reduced" loads in the right figure. These "reduced" loads are not an equilibrium system.

consider the ring loaded by two loads P, 180 deg apart, supported by two equal and opposite loads in between (Fig. 217). The shear force at A is $P/2$, being the sum of the reduced loads; the twisting couple is zero, being the moment of the reduced loads about the axis AB, and the bending moment at A is $Pr/2$, being the moment about OA.

Spielvogel's Theorem. A beam of arbitrary plane shape (Fig. 218) is built in at both ends A and O; it is subjected to a temperature rise. If

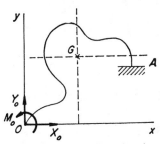

the constraint at O is removed and the pipe or beam is free to expand thermally from the fixed base A, the point O moves through distances Δx and Δy in the direction of the negative x and y axes, respectively. When these expansions are prevented by the built-in connection at O, reactions X_O, Y_O, and M_O will be exerted by the wall on the pipe, and Spielvogel has shown that these reactions can be found from

FIG. 218. A heated steam pipe, built in at both ends A and O; broken loose at O, where the wall reactions X_O, Y_O, and M_O are applied. For this problem Spielvogel derived the general formulae (173).

$$\Delta x = I_{xG}X_O - I_{xyG}Y_O$$

$$\Delta y = I_{yG}Y_O - I_{xyG}X_O \qquad (173)$$

$$M_O = x_G Y_O - y_G X_O$$

where x_G, y_G are the coordinates of the "center of gravity" of the pipe considered as a structure of "weight" $1/EI$ per unit length and I_{xG}, I_{yG},

I_{xyG} are the moments and products of inertia of the pipe (of weight $1/EI$ per unit length) about the x and y axes through the center of gravity G. These formulae considerably facilitate the calculation of thermal stresses in plane pipe systems as compared with the direct application of Castigliano's theorem.

For *the proof* we return to Fig. 218, assuming that the end O has been broken loose and is subjected to the three reactions shown. Then the bending moment at an arbitrary section x, y is

$$M = M_o + X_o y - Y_o x$$

and the energy in the pipe is

$$U = \frac{1}{2} \int \frac{M^2}{EI} \, ds$$

where the EI has been kept under the integral sign, because in most applications involving circular bends and straight sections EI differs in the various sections by von Kármán's factor (page 244). Under the influence of these three end reactions the end O of the hot pipe is pushed back from the position $-\Delta x$, $-\Delta y$ to the origin 0, 0, so that Castigliano's theorem states

$$\frac{\partial U}{\partial M_o} = 0 \qquad \frac{\partial U}{\partial X_o} = \Delta x \qquad \frac{\partial U}{\partial Y_o} = \Delta y$$

Written out fully, these equations are

$$\int \frac{M}{EI} \, ds = M_o \int \frac{ds}{EI} + X_o \int \frac{y \, ds}{EI} - Y_o \int \frac{x \, ds}{EI} = 0 \qquad (f)$$

$$\int \frac{M}{EI} y \, ds = M_o \int \frac{y \, ds}{EI} + X_o \int \frac{y^2 \, ds}{EI} - Y_o \int \frac{xy \, ds}{EI} = \Delta x \qquad (g)$$

$$-\int \frac{M}{EI} x \, ds = -M_o \int \frac{x \, ds}{EI} - X_o \int \frac{xy \, ds}{EI} + Y_o \int \frac{x^2 \, ds}{EI} = \Delta y \qquad (h)$$

Now if the "weight" per unit length of the pipe is $1/EI$, then the "weight" W of the entire pipe is

$$W = \int \frac{ds}{EI}$$

and the usual definition of "center of gravity" is

$$x_G = \frac{\int (x \, ds/EI)}{\int (ds/EI)} \qquad y_G = \frac{\int (y \, ds/EI)}{\int (ds/EI)}$$

With this notation Eq. (f) becomes the third of Eqs. (173). The other two equations (g) and (h) can be written

$$\Delta x = M_0 W y_G + X_0 I_{x0} - Y_0 I_{xy0}$$

$$\Delta y = -M_0 W x_G - X_0 I_{xy0} + Y_0 I_{y0}$$

Here the "moments of inertia" are about the x and y axes through the origin O and are so indicated by the subscript O. Substituting the third of Eqs. (173) for M_0 into these leads to

$$\Delta x = X_0(I_{x0} - y_G^2 W) - Y_0(I_{xy0} - x_G y_G W)$$

$$\Delta y = -X_0(I_{xy0} - x_G y_G W) + Y_0(I_{y0} - x_G^2 W)$$

But by the parallel-axis theorem of moments and products of inertia the parentheses are these moments about a set of axes parallel to x and y and passing through the center of gravity G, so that now the first two of Eqs. (173) are proved also.

As an example we take the pipe system shown in Fig. 219, for which we easily calculate

$$x_G = \frac{l}{2} \qquad y_G = \frac{2l}{3}$$

$$I_{xG} = \frac{l^3}{3EI} \qquad I_{xyG} = 0$$

$$I_{yG} = \text{(not necessary)}$$

$$\Delta x = \alpha T l \qquad \Delta y = 0$$

$$\therefore \ X_O = \frac{3EI\alpha T}{l^2} \qquad M_O = \frac{2EI\alpha T}{l}$$

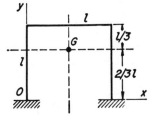

Fig. 219. Steam pipe heated to temperature T with expansion coefficient α, as an example of Spielvogel's procedure.

For cases where curved pieces of pipe occur in conjunction with straight ones of the same actual EI we multiply the stiffness of the curved pieces with von Kármán's factor [Eq. (127), page 243], which makes the curved pieces "heavier" than the straight ones for calculating the center of gravity and the moments of inertia. In his book "Piping Stress Calculations Simplified" (McGraw-Hill Book Company, Inc., New York, 1943), Spielvogel has extended this procedure to space pipes as well, but then the formulae are only approximately true.

Problems 214 *to* 217.

PROBLEMS

1. *a.* A 12-in. steel I beam with flanges and webb ½ in. thick is subjected to a torque of 35,000 in.-lb. Find the maximum shear stress and the twist per unit length, neglecting stress concentrations.

b. In order to reduce the stress and the angle of twist of this section, ½-in.-thick flat plates are welded onto the side of the section as shown by the dotted lines. Find the stress and the twist per unit length.

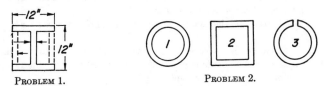

PROBLEM 1.   PROBLEM 2.

2. The three tubular sections shown all have the same wall thickness t and are made from the same width of plate, *i.e.*, they have the same circumference. Neglecting stress concentrations, find the ratio of the three shear stresses for

a. Equal twisting moments in all three cases.

b. Equal angles of twist in all three cases.

3. The formulae for twisting moment and stress for a thin rectangular section $M_t = Gbt^3\theta_1/3$ and $s_s = G\theta_1 t$ can be made to apply to an unsymmetrical section in which the thickness is small compared with the length, such as the cross section of a propeller blade. The cross section is divided as shown in the figure, and the formulae become

$$M_t = \frac{G\theta_1}{3} \sum t^3 \, \Delta b \qquad s_{s\,\text{max}} = G\theta_1 t_\text{max}$$

Calculate the maximum stress for the section shown in terms of the twisting moment.

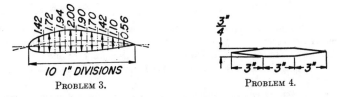

PROBLEM 3.   PROBLEM 4.

4. A bar having the tapered cross section shown is subjected to a twisting moment of 8,000 in.-lb. Find the maximum shear stress, using the method of the previous problem, but replacing the finite summations by integrations.

5. The specified dimensions of the cross section of a pipe were 4 in. mean diameter and 0.25 in. wall thickness. When the pipe was delivered, the wall thickness was found to vary according to the equation $t = 0.25 + 0.05 \cos \theta$ to a close enough approximation. The calculated torsional shear stress in the ideal tube was 9.500 lb/in.^{2}

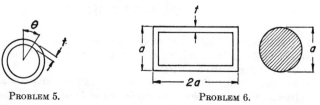

PROBLEM 5.   PROBLEM 6.

a. If subjected to the twisting moment for which it was designed, what would be the maximum shear stress in the actual tube?

b. What would be the calculated and actual angles of twist for a 5-ft length of tube?

6. A thin-walled box section of dimensions $2a \times a \times t$ is to be compared with a solid circle section of diameter a. Find the thickness t so that the two sections have

a. The same stress for the same torque.

b. The same stiffness.

7. A two-compartment thin-walled box section with one compartment slit open has constant wall thickness t. Write formulae for

a. The stress for a given torque.

b. The stiffness, that is, M_t / θ_1.

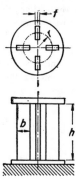

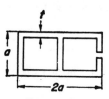

PROBLEM 7.   PROBLEM 8.

8. A modernistic table supported by four flat legs of height h and distance r from table center is subjected to a torque. At what ratio h/r does the twisting moment due to the Saint-Venant torsional stresses in the legs equal that due to bending of the legs? Assume Poisson's ratio $\mu = 0.3$, the legs to be built in at both ends, and $b \gg t$.

9. It is necessary to couple two tanks together so that the connection is gastight and still has some torsional flexibility. In order to do this, it is proposed to make a thin-walled connection with many convolutions as shown. There are 48 convolutions or fingers around the circle. The material is bronze with $G = 6 \times 10^6$.

Assume a working shear stress of 8,000 lb/sq in., which includes an allowance for stress concentration. Calculate the permissible angle of twist.

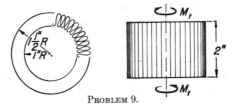

PROBLEM 9.

10. A torque tube has the shape of a thin-walled square of side a and wall thickness t. Compare this tube with a solid shaft of circular cross section and with diameter $2a/3$. Calculate the wall thickness t of the square tube in terms of a for the two following cases:

a. The square tube has the same torsional stiffness as the solid shaft.

b. It has the same stress for the same torque as the solid shaft. Neglect stress concentration at the corners.

11. A shaft of hollow square cross section, outside side 6 in., wall thickness ¼ in., and internal fillet radii ¼ in. fails in torsion. It is to be replaced by a solid circular shaft of the same torsional stiffness. Find the diameter of the circular shaft and the stresses in both shafts for a moment of 100,000 in.-lb.

12. A hollow shaft of ¹⁄₃₂ in. wall thickness with internal stiffeners is as shown. If the maximum allowable shear stress is 8,000 lb/sq in., what is the torsional moment the shaft can carry? Neglect stress concentration. If $G = 6 \times 10^6$ lb/sq in., what is the angle of twist permissible in a 2-ft length?

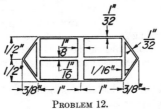

PROBLEM 12.

13. A hollow aluminum section is designed as in (*a*) of the figure for a maximum shear stress of 5,000 lb/sq in., neglecting stress concentrations. Find the twisting moment which can be taken by the section and the angle of twist on a 10-ft length. If then the section is made as in (*b*), find the allowable twisting moment for the same stress and the angle of twist.

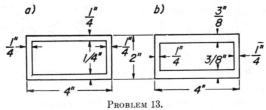

PROBLEM 13.

14. The stress for a given torque and the rigidity are calculated for a circular tube of mean radius r and thickness t. If the bore comes out eccentric by Δt, find the ratio of the actual maximum stress and rigidity to the calculated values. Assume as an expression for the thickness $t + \Delta t \cos \theta$.

15. An aluminum-alloy T section 6 by 6 by $\frac{3}{4}$ in. with a $\frac{3}{8}$-in. fillet radius is subjected to a twisting moment. What is the allowable angle of twist on a 6-ft length for a maximum shear stress of 6,000 lb/sq in.? Assume $G = 4 \times 10^6$ lb/sq in., and consider stress concentration. What is the effect on the angle of twist if one end is considered "built in," *i.e.*, if warping of the cross section is prevented at that end?

16. A steel girder has the cross section shown, all wall thicknesses being $\frac{1}{2}$ in. The stress due to twisting is not to exceed 10,000 lb/sq in. No stress concentrations.

  a. What is the maximum allowable torque?

  b. What is the angle of twist per foot length under that torque?

  c. Describe the stress distribution across the section.

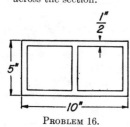

PROBLEM 16.

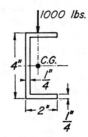

PROBLEM 17.

17. A steel channel section 4 by 2 by $\frac{1}{4}$ in. is used as a cantilever 2 ft long and has an end load of 1,000 lb. Using the theory of the center of twist, find the angle of twist at the end, assuming free warping of all cross sections.

18. A closely coiled helical spring can be made of wire of either square $d \times d$ or circular $\pi d^2/4$ section. Compare the stresses and deflections for the two cases under the same end load P.

19. A section subject to twisting is as shown. Find the allowable twisting moment for a maximum shear stress of 10,000 lb/sq in., and calculate the stresses in the different parts of the section. Neglect stress concentrations.

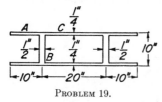

PROBLEM 19.

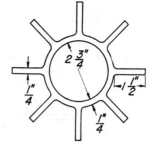

PROBLEM 20.

20. A hollow tube with longitudinal fins is subject to twisting. Find the percentage of the twisting moment which is taken by the fins and the stresses for a twisting moment of 20,000 in.-lb.

21. *a.* Show that the expression

$$\Phi = C\left(y^2 + x^2 - \frac{y^3}{a} + \frac{3x^2 y}{a} + A\right)$$

is a permissible Saint-Venant Φ function, C, A, and a being constants. Find the value of C in terms of the unit angle of twist θ_1.

b. Show that the above Φ function is the true solution for an equilateral triangle with axes as shown. Adjust the value of A to bring the Φ function into line with the boundary condition.

PROBLEM 21.

22. For reasons of symmetry the maximum height of the Φ hill for the equilateral triangle is located over the center of gravity of the section. Using the Φ function of the previous problem, sketch in the contour lines of one-fourth, one-half, and three-fourths maximum height by first finding the four points of intersection with the x and y axes and then deducing eight more points from symmetry.

23. *a.* From the Φ function of Prob. 21 find the stresses, and give an expression for the maximum shear stress. Its location is found by considering the contour lines of Prob. 22.

b. Obtain an expression for the torsional stiffness of the triangular shaft of the previous problems by integrating the stress function.

24. *a.* Verify that

$$\Phi = -\frac{G\theta_1}{2}\left(x^2 + y^2 - 2ax + \frac{2b^2 ax}{x^2 + y^2} - b^2\right)$$

where a and b are as shown and C is a constant, is the Saint-Venant Φ function for the torsion of a round shaft with a semicircular keyway.

b. Obtain an expression for the maximum stress in the section.

c. What is the ratio of the maximum stress to the maximum stress in a shaft without a groove when b gets very small?

PROBLEM 24.

25. *a.* Derive the expression

$$M_t = 2\pi s_y\left(\frac{R^3}{3} - \frac{r_0^3}{12}\right)$$

for the torque transmitted by a solid circular shaft of radius R in which plastic flow has occurred to some intermediate radius r_0. Make the usual assumption that at strains greater than the yield strain (*i.e.*, plastic strain) the stress remains constant and equal to the yield stress s_y.

b. Find the percentage increase in torque which can be carried when the solid shaft becomes entirely plastic as compared with the case of incipient plasticity.

c. Obtain the answer to question *b* by considering Nadai's extension of Prandtl's membrane analogy. NOTE: A shallow cone erected over a shallow paraboloid of revolution and tangent to it around the base has twice the height of the paraboloid.

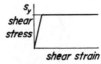

PROBLEM 25.

26. For a circular tube in torsion with outer and inner radii r_0 and r_i plot the ratio of the torques for just starting plasticity and completely developed plasticity against r_i/r_0.

27. Using the results of Prob. 23 for a triangular cross section, find the ratio between the torques for complete plasticity and just impending plasticity.

28. Find the ratio of the torques for fully developed plasticity to just starting plasticity for a shaft of narrow rectangular cross section.

29. Referring to Fig. 36a (page 44), calculate numerically the spacings of the various Φ lines in the left and right portions of the diagram.

30. Determine the percentage error in using Saint-Venant's approximate formula (16), page 20, for the torque in

a. A thin rectangular section.

b. A thin-walled slit tube.

c. An equilateral triangle (see Prob. 23).

31. A thin-walled section of uniform thickness t consists of a half circle of radius a and two straight pieces. If the center of gravity of the section is in the center of the semicircle,

a. Find the length of the straight piece.

b. Find the twisting stress caused by a moment M_t in terms of a and t.

c. Find the position of the center of twist.

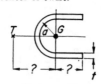

PROBLEM 31.

32. A tapered bar of rectangular cross section and length l carries a torque M_t. If the thickness t is constant and the width of the bar varies uniformly from b to $2b$, obtain the expression for the maximum shear stress and total angle of twist.

33. A solid steel shaft of 6 in. diameter has a steel cylinder of 16 in. diameter shrunk over it with a shrink allowance of 0.0005 in./in.

a. Calculate the external pressure p_0 on the outside of the cylinder which is required to reduce to zero the tangential tension at the inside of the cylinder.

b. Calculate the resultant radial pressure at the shaft surface due to the shrink fit and to that external pressure.

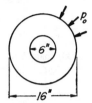

PROBLEM 33.

34. A steel shaft of 5 in. diameter has a steel disk shrunk on it of 25 in. diameter. The shrink allowance is 0.0008 in./in.

a. Find the radial and tangential stresses of the disk at standstill.

b. Find the rpm necessary to loosen the fit.

c. From (*a*) and (*b*) deduce quickly what the shrink pressure is at half the speed found in (*b*).

35. A steel disk of 20 in. outside diameter and 4 in. inside diameter is shrunk on a steel shaft so that the pressure between shaft and disk at standstill is 5,000 lb/sq in.

a. Assuming that the shaft does not change its dimensions because of its own centrifugal force, find the speed at which the disk is just free on the shaft.

b. Solve the problem without making the assumption *a* by considering the shaft and disk assembly as a single solid non-holed disk.

36. A steel disk of 30 in. diameter is shrunk onto a steel shaft of 3 in. diameter. The interference on the diameter is 0.0018 in.

a. Find the maximum tangential stress in the disk at standstill.

b. Find the speed in rpm at which the contact pressure is zero.

c. What is the maximum tangential stress at the speed found in (*b*)?

37. A flat steel turbine disk of 30 in. outside diameter and 6 in. inside diameter rotates at 3,000 rpm, at which speed the blades and shrouding cause a tensile rim loading of 600 lb/sq in. The maximum stress at this speed is to be 16,000 lb/sq in. Find the maximum shrinkage allowance on the diameter when the disk is put on the shaft.

38. The outward radial deflection at the outside of a thick cylinder subjected to an internal pressure p_i is

$$\frac{2p_i r_0 r_i^2}{E(r_0^2 - r_i^2)} \qquad \text{[by Eq. (41), page 54]}$$

By Maxwell's reciprocal theorem find the inward radial deflection at the inside of a thick cylinder subjected to external pressure.

39. A rotating flat disk is in a state of plane *stress*, *i.e.*, the stresses are all parallel to one plane, and the axial stress is zero. A rotating long cylinder is in a state of plane *strain*, *i.e.*, there is no distortion of the normal cross sections, but there will be an axial stress s_a. Derive the equations

$$s_n = C_1 + \frac{C_2}{r^2} - \frac{(3 - 2\mu)}{8(1 - \mu)} \rho \omega^2 r^2$$

$$s_t = C_1 - \frac{C_2}{r^2} - \frac{(1 + 2\mu)}{8(1 - \mu)} \rho \omega^2 r^2$$

which are the equivalent of Eqs. (39) (page 52), for the case of plain strain.

40. Using the results of Prob. 39, obtain the expression

$$s_a = \frac{\mu}{4(1 - \mu)} (r_0^2 - 2r^2) \rho \omega^2$$

for the axial stress in a rotating long solid cylinder with zero internal and external pressures and ends free from constraint.

41. From Eqs. (43) show that the ratio of the maximum tangential stress to the maximum radial stress for a rotating flat disk with no boundary loading is

$$\frac{2\left(r_0^2 + \dfrac{1 - \mu}{3 + \mu} r_i^2\right)}{(r_0 - r_i)^2}$$

Where do these maximum stresses occur?

42. A circular disk of outside and inside radii r_0 and r_i fits snugly without clearance or pressure around an incompressible core of radius r_i. It is then subjected to a compressive load of p_0 lb/sq in. uniformly distributed around the outer boundary.

Develop the approximate formulae

$$s_{r_i} = -\frac{2p_0}{1 + \mu} \qquad s_{t_i} = -\frac{2\mu p_0}{1 + \mu}$$

for the radial and tangential stresses at the radius r_i, assuming that r_i is small compared with r_0.

43. A steel turbine rotor of 30 in. outside diameter, 6 in. inside diameter, and 2 in. thickness has 100 blades 6 in. long, each weighing 1 lb. Assuming no expansion of the 6 in. shaft due to its *own* centrifugal force, calculate the initial shrink allowance on the diameter so that the rotor loosens on the shaft at 3,000 rpm.

44. A disk of thickness t and outside diameter $2r_0$ is shrunk onto a shaft of diameter $2r_i$ producing a radial interface pressure p in the non-rotating condition. It is then rotated with an angular velocity ω radians/sec. If f is the coefficient of friction between disk and shaft and ω_0 is that value of the angular velocity for which the interface pressure falls to zero, show that

a. The maximum horsepower is transmitted when $\omega = \omega_0/\sqrt{3}$.

b. This maximum horsepower is equal to $0.000365 r_i^2 t f p \omega_0$, where the dimensions are pounds and inches.

45. A steel gear is approximated by a disk 2.82 in. thick of 4 in. inside diameter and 30 in. outside diameter. The gear is shrunk onto a steel shaft with a diametral interference of 0.0024 in.; the coefficient of friction at the fit is $f = 0.3$.

a. What is the maximum horsepower which this gear can transmit?

b. At what rpm should the gear run in transmitting this maximum power?

c. What should the diametral shrink interference be if the power to be transmitted is double that possible with the 0.0024-in. interference?

d. At what speed should this new gear run?

PROBLEM 45.

PROBLEM 46.

46. A bronze ring of 16 in. outside diameter is shrunk around a steel shaft of 8 in. diameter. At room temperature the shrink allowance is 0.001 in./in. (that is, 0.004 in. on the radius). Calculate

a. The temperature above room temperature to which the entire assembly must be raised in order to loosen the shrink fit.

b. The rpm at room temperature which will loosen the shrink fit.

The constants are

For steel: $E = 30 \times 10^6$ lb/sq in.; $\mu = 0.3$; $\alpha = 6.67 \times 10^{-6}$ in./in./°F; $\gamma = 0.28$ lb/cu in.

For bronze: $E = 15 \times 10^6$; $\mu = 0.3$; $\alpha = 10 \times 10^{-6}$; $\gamma = 0.33$ lb/cu in.

47. A solid cast-iron disk of 12 in. diameter has a steel rim of 16 in. outside diameter shrunk on it. If at 10,000 rpm the pressure between the rim and the disk is zero, calculate the shrink allowance used.

$$\mu = 0.3 \text{ and } \gamma = 0.283 \text{ lb/cu in. for both materials}$$

$$E_{\text{cast iron}} = 15 \times 10^6 \qquad E_{\text{steel}} = 30 \times 10^6$$

48. A steel rim of 30 in. outside diameter is shrunk on an aluminum disk of 24 in. outside diameter and 4 in. inside diameter. At standstill the normal pressure between the disk and the rim in *p*. Assuming no pressure between the disk and the shaft, what is the magnitude of the normal pressure between the disk and the rim when the disk is rotating at 1,800 rpm?

$$E_{\text{aluminum}} = 10 \times 10^6 \text{ lb/sq in.} \qquad \gamma = 0.095 \text{ lb/cu in.} \qquad \mu = 0.3$$

49. A steel shaft of 4 in. diameter is shrunk inside a bronze cylinder of 10 in. outside diameter. The shrink allowance is 1 part per 1,000 (that is, 0.002 in. difference between the radii). Find the tangential stress in the bronze at the inside and outside radii and the stress in the shaft.

$$E_{\text{steel}} = 30 \times 10^6 \text{ lb/sq in.} \qquad E_{\text{bronze}} = 15 \times 10^6 \text{ lb/sq in.,}$$

$\mu = 0.3$ for both metals

50. A steel shaft of 3 in. diameter has an aluminum disk shrunk on it of 10 in.

outside diameter. The shrink allowance is 0.001 in./in. Calculate the rpm of rotation at which the shrink fit loosens up. Neglect the expansion of the shaft caused by rotation.

$$\mu = 0.3 \qquad E = 10 \times 10^6 \qquad \gamma = 0.095 \text{ lb/cu in.}$$

51. Show that when an aluminum disk of constant thickness and of radii r_i and r_0 is forced onto a steel shaft of radius $r_i + \delta$, the maximum stress in the disk (*i.e.*, at the inner radius) is given by

$$s_{t_i}\left[\left(\frac{1 - \mu_s}{E_s} + \frac{\mu_a}{E_a}\right)\frac{r_0^2 - r_i^2}{r_0^2 + r_i^2} + \frac{1}{E_a}\right] = \frac{\delta}{r_i}$$

52. A rod of constant cross section and of length $2a$ rotates about its center in its own plane, so that each end of the rod describes a circle of radius a. Find the maximum stress in the rod as a function of the peripheral speed V. At what speed is the stress 20,000 lb/sq in. in a steel rod?

53. A thick-walled spherical shell of radii r_i and r_0 is subjected to internal or external pressure. By symmetry the principal stresses are s_r radially and s_t tangentially (the same in all tangential directions).

a. Sketch Mohr's circle for the stresses at a point.

b. Derive the equilibrium equation

$$rs_r' + 2s_r - 2s_t = 0$$

by considering the stresses on a section of an elementary shell.

c. Derive the compatibility equation by eliminating u, the radial displacement, between the expressions for the radial and tangential strains $\epsilon_r = du/dr$; $\epsilon_t = u/r$; that is, derive the equation

$$s_t(1 + \mu) + rs_t'(1 - \mu) - s_r(1 + \mu) - \mu rs_r' = 0$$

d. Combining "compatibility" with "equilibrium," obtain the differential equation $rs_r'' + 4s_r' = 0$ for s_r, and show that the solutions for s_r and s_t are

$$s_r = A + \frac{B}{r^3} \qquad s_t = A - \frac{B}{2r^3}$$

e. Show that if the internal and external pressures are p_i and p_0, we have

$$A = \frac{p_i r_i^3 - p_0 r_0^3}{r_0^3 - r_i^3} \qquad B = \frac{(p_0 - p_i)r_0^3 r_i^3}{r_0^3 - r_i^3}$$

54. *Wound Cylindrical Pressure Vessel.* Cylindrical thick-walled pressure vessels have been made by starting from a comparatively thin-walled cylinder (say 56 in. diameter and 1 in. wall thickness), to which a thin sheet (say $\frac{1}{8}$ in. thickness) is welded all along a longitudinal line. This sheet is then wrapped around the vessel many times, under tension, so that finally the outer diameter (say 80 in.) is considerably larger than the inner one. The last wrap of the thin sheet is held in place by welding and by the end head pieces fitting over the cylinder. Assume that the tensile stress in the sheet during winding is constant $= s_0$; let $r_i =$ the inner radius of the central tube; $r_i + a =$ the outer radius of the central tube; $t =$ the thickness of the wrapping sheet, to be considered "small" calculus-wise; $r_0 =$ the outer radius of the assembly: $\rho =$ a variable radius between r_i and r_0.

a. Prove that the hoop stress locked up in the cylinder by this process is given by

$$(s_{\text{tang}})_{\text{at }\rho} = s(\rho) - \int_{r=\rho}^{r=r_0} s(\rho) \, \frac{r}{r^2 - r_i^2} \left(1 + \frac{r^2}{\rho^2}\right) dr$$

where $s(\rho) = s_0$ for $r_i + a < \rho < r_0$ and $s(\rho) = 0$ for $r_i < \rho < r_i + a$.

b. Now put an internal pressure p_0 into the vessel, which sets up a Lamé hoop-stress distribution in addition to the locked-up wrapping hoop stress. Write the condition that the *total* hoop stress at r_i is the same as that at r_0. This condition will contain as the only unknown the wrapping tension s_0.

c. Calculate the required wrapping tension s_0 for the case of $p_0 = 10,000$ lb/sq in., $r_i = 28$ in., $a = 1$ in., $r_0 = 40$ in.; and calculate the combined hoop stress at r_i and r_0 (which is the same value), as well as halfway between.

55. Finish the problem of page 65 of the text, by answering questions 3 and 4 of page 56 for the hyperbolic disk.

56. A disk of hyperbolic profile has diameters of 60 in. and 12 in. with corresponding disk thicknesses of 3 in. and 6 in. Find the maximum blade loading, expressed in pounds per inch of circumference permissible when the maximum stress at the bore is limited to 20,000 lb/sq in.

57. *a.* Prove that the maximum shear stress at the bore of a disk shrunk on a solid shaft of the same material, with a given interference, is independent of the shape of the disk (flat, hyperbolic, etc.)

b. Prove that the maximum stress at the bore of a disk shrunk on a solid shaft of the same material does not change as the speed varies from zero to the critical loosening speed (neglect the expansion of the *shaft* due to rotation).

58. A turbine blade is to be designed for constant tensile stress s_0 under the action of centrifugal force by varying the area A of the blade section. Consider the equilibrium of an element, and show that the condition is

$$\frac{A}{A_h} = e^{-\rho\omega^2 (r^2 - r_h^2)/2s_0}$$

where A_h and r_h are the cross-sectional area and radius at the hub (*i.e.*, base of the blade).

59. A steel turbine rotor of 30 in. outside diameter and 4 in. inside diameter carries 100 blades, each weighing 1 lb with centers of gravity lying on a circle of 34 in. diameter. At the outside diameter of the disk its thickness must be 2 in. to accommodate the blades. The rated speed is 4,000 rpm. Assume no pressure at the bore.

a. Find the maximum stress for a disk of uniform thickness.

b. Find the maximum stress for a disk of hyperbolic profile, the thickness at the hub being 15 in. and the tip thickness being 2 in. as before.

c. Find the thickness at the axis and the thickness just under the rim if a disk of constant stress (10,000 lb/sq in.) is used.

60. A turbine disk of constant stress is to be designed to suit existing blading. The design stress is to be 30,000 lb/sq in. with a maximum axial thickness of 4 in. Blading particulars are: pitch approximately 1 in.; weight of one blade and root

0.525 lb.; the center of gravity of the blades to lie at the rim of the disk; peripheral speed 1,000 ft/sec. From these data determine the wheel radius, the speed, and the disk thickness just under the blades.

61. A spherical oil tank of the type shown in Fig. 53 (page 78) is entirely full of oil of specific weight γ lb/cu in. The tank dimensions are r_0 and t. The supporting ring is placed at 30 deg from the bottom ($\theta = 150$ deg in Fig. 53). Find the maximum shear stress in the tank walls just above the supporting ring, just below the supporting ring, and at the bottom of the tank. Check that the difference of the vertical component of the meridional stresses above and below the ring when integrated round the tank equals the weight of the oil.

62. A shell has the shape of a doughnut with a square cross section of side a. Find the membrane stresses caused by internal pressure p, and point out where this membrane solution has to be supplemented by bending stresses.

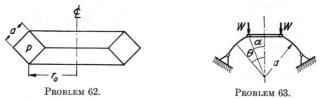

PROBLEM 62.   PROBLEM 63.

63. A spherical dome as in Fig. 55 is used in a structure with the upper portion removed. It carries a vertical load W lb per unit length as shown.

a. Ignoring the local bending at the upper ring, show that the stresses are given by

$$s_m = -\frac{a\gamma(\cos \alpha - \cos \theta) + W \sin \alpha}{t \sin^2 \theta}$$

$$s_t = \frac{a\gamma(\cos \alpha - \cos \theta - \cos \theta \sin^2 \theta) + W \sin \alpha}{t \sin^2 \theta}$$

b. Show also that the condition that no tensile stress exists is

$$\cos \theta(1 + \sin^2 \theta) \geq \frac{W}{a\gamma} \sin \alpha + \cos \alpha$$

64. A steam dome in a boiler has the shape of half an ellipsoid of revolution rotated about its semiminor axis. Show that for a uniform pressure p the stresses are given by

$$s_m = \frac{p}{2b^2 t}(a^4 y^2 + b^4 x^2)^{1/2}$$

$$s_t = \frac{p(a^4 y^2 + b^4 x^2)^{1/2}}{b^2 t}\left[1 - \frac{a^4 b^2}{2(a^4 y^2 + b^4 x^2)}\right]$$

where a is the semimajor axis in the x direction and b is the semiminor axis in the y direction.

65. A liquid container made from thin sheet metal of conical shape is supported from the top. Show that the maximum meridional stress occurs at three-fourths of the distance from the bottom apex to the liquid level and that the maximum tangential stress occurs at half the distance from the apex to the liquid level.

66. A steel conical tank of ⅛ in. wall thickness and 90 deg apex angle is supported from the top and filled to a central depth of 10 ft with water. Find the locations, expressed in feet vertically above the apex, where

a. The tangential strain is maximum.

b. The tangential strain is zero.

67. A plastic observation dome for a pressurized aircraft is made in the form of a paraboloid of revolution ⅛ in. thick, 12 in. in diameter, and 9 in. in height. Find the pressure differential the dome can withstand for a maximum stress of 1,000 lb/sq in.

68. Show that in a spherical tank of radius r_0 and thickness t, just full of liquid and supported by a ring near the bottom, the maximum shear stress is given by

$$\frac{\gamma r_0 h}{6t}\left(1 + \frac{1}{1 + \cos\theta}\right)$$

the notation being that of Fig. 53, page 78.

69. A spherical steel tank of 10 ft diameter just full of liquid is suspended as shown. If handles are attached to the tank when empty, in a tangential direction, at what distance below the center should they be placed in order to avoid secondary stresses when the tank is full? (Condition is $\epsilon_t = 0$.)

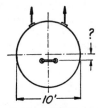

PROBLEM 69.

70. A pressure vessel is to be made from ½-in. steel plate. The pressure is 400 lb/sq in., and the maximum shear stress is to be 6,000 lb/sq in. The ends are to be designed so that the maximum shear stress is constant over the vessel. What should be the difference in diameters of the cylinder and the end pieces before assembly to have no bending stress at the junction when under pressure? (See page 86.)

Find graphically the radius (from the center line of the tank) at which there is discontinuity of strain, and the over-all length of the tank if the cylindrical part is 60 in. long.

71. A drop-shaped water tank is to be made from ½-in. steel plate, with a constant stress of 10,000 lb/sq in. The top of the tank is under a 50-ft head of water. Find graphically the over-all dimensions of the tank, *i.e.*, the height and maximum diameter.

72. An indoor baseball field is to be covered by a concrete dome which supports only its own weight and is required to be 100 ft high in the center. The concrete has a minimum thickness of 4 in., a weight of 150 lb/cu ft, and a design compressive stress of 200 lb/sq in. Design the dome for constant stress, and find the thickness of the material and the diameter at the base.

73. *a.* Show that Eqs. (55) (page 92) for cylindrical shells can be written as

$$s_t = \frac{R_t P}{t}$$

$$\frac{\partial s_l}{\partial z} + \frac{1}{r}\frac{\partial s_s}{\partial \theta} = -\frac{Q}{t}$$

$$\frac{\partial s_s}{\partial z} + \frac{1}{r}\frac{\partial s_t}{\partial \theta} = -\frac{R}{t}$$

where r, θ, and z are the coordinates as in Fig. 66 and P, Q, R are forces per unit surface area, directed in the positive radial, axial, and tangential directions, respectively. s_t, s_s, and s_l are the tangential, shear, and longitudinal stresses.

b. Apply the above equations to obtain expressions for the stresses in a semicircular roof of length $2b$ and radius r, simply supported at the ends $z = \pm b$, and loaded only by its own weight γ lb per unit area. Take the origin of coordinates at the center of the span as in Fig. 66, page 93.

Where does the solution behave unexpectedly?

74. Derive formulae similar to Eqs. (56) (page 95) for the stresses in a pipe line in the form of an open semicircular channel, running full of fluid, taking the origin as before in the center of the span.

In starting this problem do not consider, at first, the state of the top of the channel, whether it is closed off by a flat upper plate welded to the edges or whether it is open at the top with or without reinforcing steel sections at the upper edges. After you obtain the solution for the semicircular shell, examine it and interpret it for these various constructions.

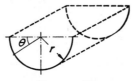

Problem 74.

75. A long horizontal water conduit is to be made of either circular pipe or semicircular channel. For a cross-sectional area of 7 sq ft, plate thickness of ½ in., and maximum stress of 5,000 lb/sq in., what are the permissible span lengths in either case? For the channel stresses modify Eqs. (56), or use the results of Prob. 74.

76. Derive the formula

$$w = \frac{PR^2}{16\pi D}\left[\left(1 - \frac{r^2}{R^2}\right)\frac{3+\mu}{1+\mu} + 2\frac{r^2}{R^2}\log_e\frac{r}{R}\right]$$

for the deflection of a simply supported circular plate with a central load P, by calculating appropriate values for the integration constants in the general solution of page 122 of the text.

77. Derive the formula of the previous problem (for the centrally loaded *freely supported* plate) by superposition of the case of a centrally loaded plate with *built-in* edges (page 126) on that of a plate loaded only by edge moments, without P (spherical bending).

78. Case 5 in the catalogue of results (page 128) can be used to obtain the central deflection for a circular plate with built-in edges, loaded by any arbitrary circularly symmetrical loading. To illustrate this, derive case 8 from case 5.

79. A circular plate of radius R with a central hole of radius a is simply supported at the outside edge and is loaded only by a moment M_1 per unit length at the outside edge. Derive the expression

$$\frac{M_1 R^2}{R^2 - a^2}\left[1 - \left(\frac{a}{r}\right)^2\right]$$

for the unit bending moment in a meridional direction at any point r between a and R.

PROBLEM 79.

80. Consider the plate of the previous problem, loaded only by shear forces along the inner edge, the total load being P. Find an expression for the deflection, and then let a tend to zero as a limit. By comparing with case 4 in the catalogue of results, show that the maximum deflection is not affected by a small hole at the center.

81. A flat circular plate of radius R built in at the edge is subjected to temperature difference ΔT between its two faces. Show that the stress in the plate is

$$s = \frac{\alpha E}{2(1 - \mu)}\,\Delta T$$

where α is the coefficient of thermal expansion of the material.

82. The construction for a circular platform on a tubular stepped mast for a ship is as shown in the figure. Assuming that a/R and ϵ/a are small, show that the stress in the central portion of the platform plate is given by

$$\frac{3}{2\pi}\frac{P\epsilon}{ar^2}$$

NOTE: The deflection curve inside the load circle for case 6 (page 129) is

$$w = \frac{P}{8\pi D}\left[(a^2 + r^2)\log\frac{a}{R} + (R^2 - a^2)\frac{(3 + \mu)R^2 - (1 - \mu)r^2}{2(1 + \mu)R^2}\right]$$

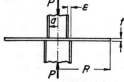

PROBLEM 82.

83. A solid circular plate carrying uniform load, with its outside edge either simply supported, built in, or somewhere between the two, has a small hole drilled through its center. Show without evaluating any constants that the stress concentration factor is 2.

84. Derive the numerical value of the coefficients $\alpha = 0.044$ and $\beta = 0.048$ for the deflection and moment of a simply supported, uniformly loaded *square* plate (case 19, page 132) for $b/a = 1$.

Do this by the method of Navier, discussed briefly on page 115, first expressing the uniform load in the form of a double Fourier series, then finding the deflection and the moment in the form of double series, and evaluating the first few terms of these numerically up to the third decimal place 0.001.

85. The equation of the contour of an ellipse is

$$\frac{x^2}{a^2} + \frac{y^2}{b^2} - 1 = 0$$

At the edge of an elliptical plate $w = 0$ and

$$1 - \frac{x^2}{a^2} - \frac{y^2}{b^2} = 0$$

Hence one might attempt to write for the deflection

$$w = C\left(1 - \frac{x^2}{a^2} - \frac{y^2}{b^2}\right)^2$$

Show that this satisfies the plate equation. What boundary and load conditions does it represent?

86. From the value of w obtained in the previous problem, find the unit bending moments at the ends of the minor axis ($2b$) and the major axis ($2a$) of an elliptical plate. Show that when $b = a$ the result reduces to that for a clamped circular plate with uniform load and when b/a is very small, the result reduces to that for a clamped beam with uniform load and length $2b$.

87. A plate in the side or bottom of a ship may be considered to be under uniform loading from the water pressure and clamped along all edges. A $\frac{1}{2}$-in. plate of 4 ft width is to be used as a bottom plate in a ship drawing $13\frac{1}{2}$ ft of water. For a maximum stress of 10,000 lb/sq in. what is the maximum plate length (*i.e.*, frame spacing), and what is then the maximum deflection? Salt water weights 64 lb/cu ft.

88. A floor slab in a building can be made continuous as in case 25 (page 134) or laid in separate sections as in case 19 (page 132). What thickness of material is required in each case for a maximum stress of 1000 lb/sq in. for a slab size of 5 by $2\frac{1}{2}$ ft and a maximum permissible loading of 1,500 lb/sq ft?

89. A pressure-control device which consists of a thin steel disk of 2 in. diameter clamped at the edge is to close an electric circuit by moving 0.04 in. at the center when the pressure reaches 410 lb/sq in. What should be the thickness of the disk?

90. A circular plate with a central hole is simply supported at the outer and inner edges and carries a uniform load over its surface. If the inner radius is one-third of the outer, what height should the outer support be below the inner if the loads carried by the two supports are to be equal?

91. A rail with cross section as shown rests on ballast having a modulus $k = 1,500$ lb/sq in. and is loaded by a single concentrated load of 40,000 lb. Find

a. The maximum rail deflection.

b. The maximum bending stress.

c. The bending moment 18 in. from the load.

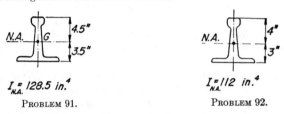

$I_{N.A.} = 128.5$ in.^{4}

PROBLEM 91.

$I_{N.A.} = 112$ in.^{4}

PROBLEM 92.

92. A rail with cross section as shown rests on a ballast foundation of modulus $k = 1,500$ lb/sq in. The rail is subjected to two concentrated loads each of 30,000 lb, 5 ft apart. What are the maximum stress and maximum deflection of the rail?

93. A long steel rail of $I = 88.5$ in.^{4} lies on a foundation of modulus $k = 1,500$ lb/sq in. The rail carries many concentrated loads of 30,000 lb, all equally spaced 20 ft apart along the rail. Find the deflection under the loads and also at points midway between loads.

94. A small locomotive weighing 75 tons with its weight distributed uniformly on three axles 7 ft apart runs on a light track of $k = 1,400$ lb/sq in., $I = 41$ in.^{4}, $Z_{min} = 15$ cu in., and $E = 30 \times 10^6$ lb/sq in. Find the maximum deflection and maximum stress produced by the locomotive in passing over the track.

95. The semi-infinite beam of Fig. 105 (page 157) has the left end clamped instead of hinged. Show that the deflection is now given by

$$y = \frac{p_0}{k} \left[1 - F_1(\beta x) \right]$$

96. A grid work of beams is as shown. I_T, I_L are the moments of inertia of the transverse and longitudinal beams, l is the length of the transverse beams, and a is their center-to-center spacing. If the transverse beams are considered "built in" at the ends, find the value of β for the longitudinal beam considered as a beam on an elastic foundation.

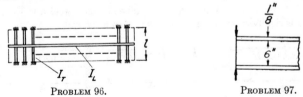

PROBLEM 96.

PROBLEM 97.

97. A bronze pipe of 6 in. diameter and $\frac{1}{8}$ in. wall thickness is subjected to a circumferential load as shown. At what distance from the end is the diameter unchanged by the load? What is the value of the load (pounds per inch) if the diameter under it changes by 0.006 in.? $E_{bronze} = 15 \times 10^6$ lb/sq in.

98. A long thin-walled steel pipe of radius r and wall thickness t has a steel ring shrunk over it in the middle of its length. Show that if the cross section of the ring is $A = 1.56 \sqrt{rt^3}$, then the shrink allowance is shared equally between the ring and the pipe (*i.e.*, the reduction in pipe diameter equals the increase in ring diameter during shrinkage).

99. A long steel pipe of 12 in. inside diameter, $\frac{1}{8}$ in. wall thickness, with an internal pressure of 300 lb/sq in., is to have a maximum radial deflection of 0.002 in. To do this, steel rings of $\frac{1}{2}$ by $\frac{1}{2}$ in. square cross section are shrunk on the pipe with an interference of 1/1,000. What is the maximum ring spacing under these conditions?

100. A steel pipe of 3 ft diameter, $\frac{1}{2}$ in. thickness, with an internal pressure of 500 lb/sq in., is joined to a pressure vessel. The connection is assumed to be rigid, *i.e.*, there is no expansion or angular rotation of the end of the pipe. At what distance from the end of the pipe does the pipe diameter reach its fully expanded value, and what is the maximum bending stress?

101. A long steel pipe of 48 in. outside diameter and $\frac{1}{2}$ in. thickness is used in a structure as a column. At the center of the column a thin platform prevents radial expansion. Under an axial load of 750,000 lb, what are the longitudinal and tangential stresses in the outer fibers under the constraint?

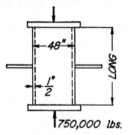

PROBLEM 101.

102. A steel pipe of 30 in. internal diameter and $\frac{1}{2}$ in. thickness is subjected to an internal pressure of 300 lb/sq in. A rigid circular support (assume a knife-edge) is located midway between the ends of the shell. Find the axial and tangential stresses in the outer fiber under the support for the three conditions below:

  a. The pipe takes no longitudinal thrust.

  b. The axial thrust of the internal pressure is taken by ends welded to the pipe.

  c. The shell is rigidly supported at the ends by two fixed walls.

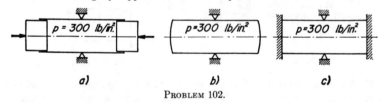

PROBLEM 102.

103. A long pipe of 30 in. outside diameter and $\frac{1}{2}$ in. thickness is subjected to radial loads of 1,500 lb/in. distributed around the circumference at two sections

2 in. apart, as shown in the figure. For the section midway between the loads determine

    a. The radial deflection.

    b. The longitudinal and tangential stresses in the outer fiber.

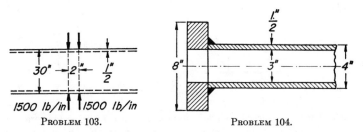

PROBLEM 103.   PROBLEM 104.

104. A long steel hollow shaft of 4 in. outside diameter and $\frac{1}{2}$ in. thickness rotates at 10,000 rpm and has steel flanges welded to the ends as shown. Using Eqs. (40) and (43), find the longitudinal bending stress in the shaft at the flange due to the difference in centrifugal expansion of the tube and the flange. Assume that no change of slope can take place at the end of the tube.

105. Steel boiler tubes of 4 in. outside diamater and $\frac{1}{4}$ in. wall thickness are full of water under 500 lb/sq in. pressure. They fit into a "header," where the radial support may be considered knife-edged, and protrude $\frac{1}{2}$ in. as shown.

    a. Show by superposition that the deflection under P is given by

$$y = \frac{P\beta}{2k}\left[1 + 2F_4^2(\beta\epsilon) + F_3^2(\beta\epsilon)\right]$$

where ϵ is the distance from the knife-edge to the end of the tube.

    b. Apply the above to find the load per inch of circumference in this case.

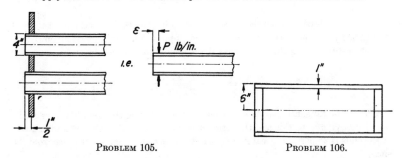

PROBLEM 105.   PROBLEM 106.

106. The body of an axial compressor rotor is constructed as shown by attaching a thin-walled hollow cylinder to two solid ends.

Assuming no change of slope at the ends, find the local bending stresses for 7,000 rpm, radius 6 in., and wall thickness 1 in.

107. A large 8-ft-diameter compressed-air vessel is to be made of $\frac{1}{2}$-in. plate and is to carry a pressure of 100 lb/sq in. Investigate the three types of end construction shown, for local bending stresses at the discontinuity. Assume that at the joint only shear forces exist and no bending moments. Also assume that in (b) and (c) the radial gap is shared equally between the cylinder and the head. At (a) the end is attached to a "solid" foundation, (b) is a hemispherical end, and (c) a head of constant stress (page 84).

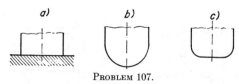

PROBLEM 107.

108. A long cylindrical shell supported as shown is raised in temperature by T degrees. Show that the maximum local bending stresses due to this expansion are given by $s = 0.588\alpha TE$, where α is the linear coefficient of thermal expansion. Thus the stresses for a given material depend only on the temperature rise and not on the shell dimensions.

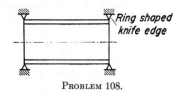

PROBLEM 108.

109. A cylindrical shell with no constraints has a radial temperature difference ΔT across the wall thickness, varying linearly across the wall.

a. Show that the maximum bending stresses away from the ends due to this temperature variation are $(\alpha E \Delta T)/2(1 - \mu)$ in both the axial and tangential directions.

b. At the ends of the shell there are no moments. Hence the condition at the end is obtained by superimposing an end moment opposite in sign to that given by the stresses in (a). Using this, show that the increase in radius at the end is

$$u = \frac{2\beta^2}{k} \frac{\alpha E\ \Delta T\ t^2}{12(1 - \mu)}$$

c. Find the tangential stress at the ends from (b), using the condition $u = (r/E)(s_t - \mu s_{\mathrm{axial}})$, and to this add the stress from (a) to show that the maximum stress at the ends is 25 per cent greater than the stress at a considerable distance from the ends.

110. A steel tank of 40 ft diameter and 30 ft height is full of oil of specific gravity 0.9. The upper half of the tank is made from $\frac{1}{4}$-in. plate and the lower half from $\frac{1}{2}$-in. plate. What are the values of the moment and shear force at the discontinuity?

111. A long steel pipe of 40 in. diameter and $\frac{1}{2}$ in. wall thickness carries water under 200 lb/sq in. pressure. At the joints spaced "far" apart it can be considered built in, *i.e.*, no expansion or rotation occurs there. What are the longitudinal and tangential stresses at the inside and outside of the pipe at these joints?

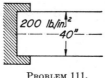

PROBLEM 111.

112. The theory of bending of beams is governed by the second-order differential equation $EIy'' = M$, while for torsion we have the much simpler first-order equation $GI_p\theta' = -M_t$. The theory of *torsion* of a bar embedded in an elastic foundation is likewise much simpler than that of bending. Develop such a theory, and carry it to the point of finding equations corresponding to Eqs. (84) to (89) and a result corresponding to Fig. 94.

113. Equation (105) (page 187) is the general solution of the compatibility equation in polar coordinates for stress functions which depend on r only and are independent of θ. Assuming the reverse, that is, $\Phi = f(\theta)$ independent of r,

a. Find the general solution of the compatibility equation in terms of four integration constants, and verify that one of these four gives zero stress everywhere so that three independent solutions remain.

b. Investigate the simplest of the three solutions, and recognize it as a case of some practical importance.

c. Sketch the stress fields of the other two solutions, which have no particular importance.

114. Following up the development leading to Fig. 125 (page 192), calculate the resultant shear force S across the top side $\theta = 0$, and thus evaluate the constant C_1 in Eqs. (109).

115. Refer to the wedge of Fig. 133a (page 198). The relation between the end force P and the constant C was calculated in the text by considering the equilibrium of the wedge bounded by two radii and by a circular arc about the apex P, the forces being directed radially on this circular arc.

Derive the same relation between P and C by considering the wedge as bounded by the same two radii and in addition by a straight line perpendicular to PB to replace the circular arc.

116. Refer to the cantilever wedge of Fig. 113c (page 198). In the text the relation between the load P and the constant C was found by considering the equilibrium of a sector bounded by a circular arc about the apex P as center. Replacing the circular arc by a straight line perpendicular to PC, derive the same relation between C and P by considering the equilibrium of the triangle thus formed. Find the shear-stress and bending-stress distributions across the straight line.

117. Prove that the expression $\Phi = Cr^2\theta$ is a legitimate Airy stress function, and deduce the stresses from it. Describe these with a sketch for a semi-infinite plane extending from $\theta = -\pi/2$ through $\theta = 0$ to $\theta = +\pi/2$.

118. From the result, Eq. (113a) (page 198), for the stress due to a concentrated load on a semi-infinite plane, deduce by integration the principal stresses at a depth

a below the center of a distributed load of intensity q on a semi-infinite plane as shown. The loading subtends an angle 2α.

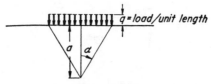

PROBLEM 118.

119. Derive the answer to Prob. 118, by using the result of Prob. 117. Superpose the loading given by $\Phi = Cr^2\theta$ upon that given by $\Phi = Cr^2\theta$ displaced along the plane through a distance l. Verify that the only resultant loading on the semi-infinite plane edge due to this combination is a distributed load of intensity $2C\pi$ over length l.

120. Figure 135 (page 200) outlines a method for finding the stress in a circular disk subjected to two radial forces P, spaced 180 deg apart. Derive the corresponding results for a disk subjected to *three* radial forces P, spaced 120 deg apart. Note that the radii r_1, r_2, r_3 from the three forces to an arbitrary point C on the periphery enclose angles of 60 deg with each other.

121. Generalize the method of the previous problem to the case of a circular disk subjected to n radial forces P spaced at angles $2\pi/n$ apart.

122. A flat circular disk is subjected to four loads P, each equal to 1,000 lb per inch thickness of the plate. They are arranged as shown, 45 deg apart. Calculate the maximum principal stress at the center point of the plate.

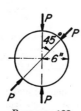

PROBLEM 122.

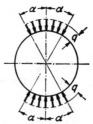

PROBLEM 123.

123. A cylinder (or circular disk) is loaded with compressive stress over two opposing arcs of 2α each as shown.

a. Find (by a process of integration) the state of stress in the center of the disk.

b. Write the answer down for the two special cases $\alpha = 90$ deg and $\alpha =$ very small, and see that the answers reduce to previously known results.

124. Investigate the expression $\Phi = (\cos^3 \theta)/r$ as a possible stress function.

a. Is it permissible as an Airy stress function?

b. Sketch the radial and shear stresses on the periphery of a circle of radius a.

125. To determine the displacements u and v in the xy plane, we proceed as follows:

1. From the stresses and Eqs. (98) (page 173), we find ϵ_x, ϵ_y, and γ.

2. By integration of Eqs. (97) (page 172), we obtain

$$u = \int \frac{\partial u}{\partial x}\, dx + f_1(y) \qquad v = \int \frac{\partial v}{\partial y}\, dy + f_2(x)$$

3. These expressions are then substituted (after differentiation) into the third of Eqs. (97), which is then set equal to s_s/G. From that equation the unknown functions f_1 and f_2 are solved.

Following the above procedure for the case of the cantilever of Fig. 119 (page 181),

$$\Phi = \frac{2P}{bh^3}\left(xy^3 - \frac{3}{4}\, xyh^2\right)$$

show that

$$v = -\frac{P}{EI}\left(\frac{x^3}{6} + \frac{l^3}{3} - \frac{l^2 x}{2} + \frac{\mu x y^2}{2}\right)$$

and

$$u = -\frac{P}{EI}\left(\frac{l^2 y}{2} - \frac{x^2 y}{2} - \frac{\mu y^3}{6}\right) - \frac{P}{GI}\left(\frac{y^3}{6} - \frac{h^2}{8}\, y\right)$$

Hence, verify that

  a. The end deflection is the same as in the elementary theory.

  b. Plane sections do *not* remain plane.

126. A square block of side a has tensile stresses in it described by $s_x = Cy$, $s_y = Cx$, and possibly some shear stresses in addition.

  a. Find the stress function by integration.

  b. Find the most general shear stresses which can be associated with these tensile stresses.

  c. Find the displacement functions u and v, proceeding as indicated in Prob. 125.

  d. Find the extension of the diagonal OB.

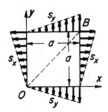

PROBLEM 126.

127. Using the method of Prob. 125 and the stresses obtained for Fig. 120 (page 182), show that the deflection at the center of a simply supported beam carrying uniform load w per unit length is

$$\delta_0\left[1 + \frac{3}{5}\frac{h^2}{l^2}\left(\frac{4}{5} + \frac{\mu}{2}\right)\right]$$

where $2l$ is the length of the beam, h the height and δ_0 the deflection given by strength of materials.

128. The stresses and deflections in rectangular beams with arbitrary load distributions along the upper or lower edge could be obtained by building up stress functions in the form of polynomials, which is mainly a matter of trial and error. A better method consists in the use of Fourier series, and for this we require the stress function for a beam with sinusoidal loading as shown in the figure. Assuming that

$$\Phi = \sin \frac{\pi x}{l} \, f(y)$$

where $f(y)$ is as yet an unknown function, show that in order to satisfy compatibility we must have

$$\Phi = \sin \frac{\pi x}{l} \left(C_1 \cosh \frac{\pi y}{l} + C_2 \sinh \frac{\pi y}{l} + C_3 y \cosh \frac{\pi y}{l} + C_4 y \sinh \frac{\pi y}{l} \right)$$

PROBLEM 128.

129. *a.* Apply the stress function of Prob. 128 to the case of a flat thin beam of infinite length and of height h, subjected to equal sinusoidal load distributions on both of its long sides, of half wave length l, as indicated. Solve the four integration constants by satisfying the conditions of sinusoidal normal stress and zero shear stress on these faces, and prove that the result for the normal stress *in the center line* of the beam is

$$(s_y)_{y=0} = 2A \frac{\dfrac{\pi h}{2l} \cosh \dfrac{\pi h}{2l} + \sin \dfrac{\pi h}{2l}}{\sinh \dfrac{\pi h}{l} + \dfrac{\pi h}{l}}$$

b. Plot the ratio $(s_y)_{y=0}/(s_y)_{y=h/2} = (s_y)_{y=0}/A$ against the ratio l/h.

130. The beam of Prob. 129 is subjected to edge stresses in the shape of rectangular waves instead of sinusoidal ones; *i.e.,* the stress is $+A$ for $0 < x < l$, and $-A$ for $l < x < 2l$ on the top as well as the bottom sides of the beam.

a. Expand this loading into a Fourier series of sinusoidal loadings.

b. Using the result of Prob. 129*b*, find the stress at point P of the beam by summing a series, for the particular case $l = 2h$.

PROBLEM 130.

131. *a.* It was shown in Eq. (110) (page 196) that the stress-concentration factor due to a small circular hole in a flat plate subject to tension (or compression) in one direction was 3. By superposition, find the stress-concentration factor due to a small hole in a flat plate subject to pure shear.

132. *a.* By appropriately superimposing two Kirsch solutions in the manner of Prob. 131, find the stress-concentration factor due to a small circular hole in a plate subjected to two-dimensional hydrostatic tension.

b. Show that the same result is obtained by considering the Lamé solution for a thick cylinder under external tension when the outer radius extends to infinity.

133. What are the stresses given by the stress function

$$\Phi = \frac{qr^2}{2\pi} \left(\frac{\sin 2\theta}{2} - \theta \right)$$

Interpret the loading described by these stresses on the semi-infinite plate from $\theta = 0$ to $\theta = \pi$.

134. Equation (112) (page 197) describes the stress function

$$\Phi = -P \frac{r}{\pi} \theta \sin \theta$$

for a semi-infinite plane, loaded by a single concentrated load P. If we consider now the case of two loads, P and $-P$, at a very small distance a apart, we have for its stress function, by superposition,

$$\Phi_{\text{total}} = \Phi_P + \Phi_{-P} = \Phi_P - \left(\Phi_P + \frac{\partial \Phi_P}{\partial y} a \right)$$

$$= -\frac{\partial \Phi_P}{\partial y} a = Pa \frac{\partial}{\partial y} \left(\frac{r}{\pi} \theta \sin \theta \right) = M_0 \frac{\partial}{\partial y} \left(\frac{r}{\pi} \theta \sin \theta \right)$$

Here the symbol $\partial/\partial y$ means that x is kept constant, the function Φ being considered to depend on x and y. It can also be considered to depend on r and θ. There are relations $r = f_1(x, y)$, $\theta = f_2(x, y)$ etc. In the calculus we have the following relation for a function, described as depending either on x, y or on r, θ:

$$\frac{\partial F}{\partial y} = \frac{\partial F}{\partial r} \cdot \frac{\partial r}{\partial y} + \frac{\partial F}{\partial \theta} \cdot \frac{\partial \theta}{\partial y}$$

Work this out and so find the stress function for a semi-infinite plane subjected to a concentrated moment M_0.

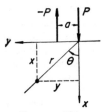

PROBLEM 134.

135. A beam of rectangular cross section bh is subjected to bending.

a. Find the maximum bending moment it can carry before yield starts.

b. Sketch the stress distribution for bending moments greater than (*a*), and find the bending moment required to plasticize the entire beam.

136. Repeat the previous problem for an I beam in which the flange area is much larger than that of the vertical web.

137. A thick cylinder of inside and outside radii r_i and r_0 is subjected to internal pressure until it is just completely yielded.

a. Find the pressure required and the tangential stress at the bore while under pressure.

b. The pressure is now relieved, superposing *elastic* stresses on the plastic ones of (*a*). Find the elastic tangential stress at the bore caused by release of the pressure.

c. By subtraction find the locked-up tangential compression at the bore after release of the pressure.

d. For thin tubes (*i.e.*, for $r_0/r_i \approx 1$), this locked-up stress is small; for very thick tubes, it comes out greater than the yield stress, which of course is impossible. Write the condition that the locked-up stress equals the yield stress, and from it find the ratio r_0/r_i of the tube. The answer represents the thickest tube for which it is profitable to be completely upset by hydraulic pressure.

138. (To be worked after Prob. 137.) Find the internal pressure required in a gun of $r_0/r_i = 3$ in order to get compressive tangential stress locked up in it (after release of pressure) equal to the yield stress.

139. A three-legged square frame is as shown; the three members are of the same cross section and are pin-jointed to a solid foundation. What percentage of the uniform load is carried by each joint?

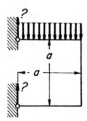

PROBLEM 139.   PROBLEM 141.

140. Two conditions must be satisfied by an ideal piston ring. (1) It should be truly circular when in the cylinder, and (2) it should exert a uniform pressure all around. Assuming that these conditions are satisfied by specifying the initial shape, the cross section EI being kept constant, show that the initial gap width must be $3\pi pr^4/EI$ if the ring is closed when in the cylinder. The uniform pressure is p lb per inch circumference; r and EI are the dimensions of the ring for bending in its own plane.

141. For a thin ring of radius r subjected to two diametrically opposite loads P in its own plane, show that the bending moment at any section is given by

$$M = Pr\left(\frac{\sin \theta}{2} - \frac{1}{\pi}\right)$$

142. Show that the ring of the previous question under the loads P changes in diameter by $0.149(Pr^3/EI)$ in the direction of the load and by $-0.137(Pr^3/EI)$ in a perpendicular direction. I is the moment of inertia of the ring section for bending in its own plane. Consider bending strain energy only.

143. A torque-measuring device is as shown; l is the length of each of the springs and I the moment of inertia of one spring for bending in the plane of the moment. Find the stiffness of the system, *i.e.*, the torque per unit angle at the shaft.

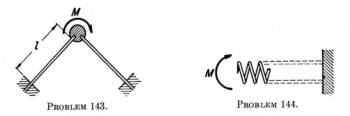

PROBLEM 143. PROBLEM 144.

144. A closely coiled helical spring is subjected to a bending moment which lies in the plane of the axis of the spring. Show that the stiffness (*i.e.*, the moment per unit angle) is given by

$$\frac{Ed^4}{64nD[1 + (\mu/2)]}$$

where d is the wire diameter, D the coil diameter, and n the number of coils.

145. *a.* The spring of the previous problem is subjected to an axial force P. Show that the change in length Δl is given by

$$\Delta l = \frac{P8nD^3}{Gd^4}$$

b. Show also that if the same spring is subjected to twisting moment M_t (that is, a moment lying in a plane perpendicular to the axis) the angle of twist of the spring is $\theta = \pi DnM_t/EI$.

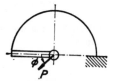

PROBLEM 146.

146. For a certain application it is desired to have a spring suspension with two qualities. (1) The deflection must be in the direction of the load only. (2) The spring constant P/δ must be independent of the direction of the load.

Considering bending strain energy only of the semicircular section shown, prove that this construction satisfies both requirements and find the spring constant.

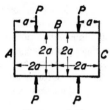

PROBLEM 147.

147. A framework as shown is loaded with four compressive loads P. If all joints are considered rigid and all bars are of equal cross section EI, what are the compressive forces in the three connecting bars A, B, and C? Consider bending energy only.

148. A semicircular beam (a balcony) is built in at both ends and carries a load W as shown. Find expressions for the bending and twisting moments.

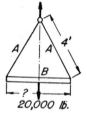

PROBLEM 148.   PROBLEM 149.

149. A framework as shown carries a load of 20,000 lb. The members A are 4 ft long, have a bending inertia $I = 1$ in.^{4}, are pin-jointed together at the top, and are fixed rigidly to the member B of $I = 40$ in.^{4} What is the maximum length for B if the bending moment in A is not to exceed 4,000 in.-lb?

150. The controlling element of a high-speed engine governor is a circular steel hoop of rectangular section. Show that the vertical deflection caused by rotation is given by

$$\delta = \left(\frac{2\rho}{E}\right)\frac{\omega^2 r^5}{t^2}$$

where r is the hoop radius, t the thickness of the cross section, ω the angular velocity, and ρ the mass density of the material.

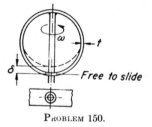

PROBLEM 150.   PROBLEM 151.

151. A body is supported by springs of rectangular cross section and thickness t. The springs are shaped as shown in a three-quarters circle of radius r, hinged at A and built in at B. Show that the deflection caused by a central vertical load on the body is $\delta = 4.93(sr^2/Et)$, where s is the maximum bending stress.

152. If the ring of Probs. 141 and 142 is used in a chain, it is often stiffened by a transverse member. Considering this new member to be infinitely stiff, *i.e.*, that it does not change its length and hence absorbs no strain energy, find the increase in diameter in the direction of the load.

PROBLEM 152.

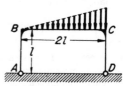

PROBLEM 153.

153. A structure consists of three members AB, BC, CD as shown, and carries a distributed load which varies uniformly as shown. Joints A and D are pinned, while B and C are rigid. If $I_{BC} = 2I_{AB} = 2I_{CD}$ and the length of $BC = 2CD$, what are the *horizontal* reactions at A and D in terms of the total load?

154. Apply the method of virtual work to find the deflection at the center of a simply supported beam of length l with a central load W. Proceed as on page 217; the symmetry of the case makes it simpler to take the origin in the center and to write for the deflection curve

$$y = \sum_{n=\text{odd}} b_n \cos \frac{n\pi x}{l}$$

Check that this expression for the deflection satisfies the end conditions, find the series for the deflection curve, and calculate the center deflection by taking the first two terms of the series.

155. Repeat the previous problem for a beam with a uniform loading of w lb per unit length.

156. Apply the method of virtual work to find the maximum deflection in a simply supported beam of length l and total loading W distributed as shown.

PROBLEM 156.

157. The method of virtual work can be used with the membrane analogy for torsion to obtain an approximation for the angle of twist and the stress due to a given twisting moment on a section.

For a rectangular section of sides a and b the height of the membrane can be expressed as

$$z = \sum_{m=\text{odd}} \sum_{n=\text{odd}} a_{mn} \cos \frac{m\pi x}{a} \cos \frac{n\pi y}{b}$$

The increase in strain energy in the membrane due to blowing up is the tension times the change in area

$$T \frac{1}{2} \int_{-a/2}^{+a/2} \int_{-b/2}^{+b/2} \left[\left(\frac{\partial z}{\partial x}\right)^2 + \left(\frac{\partial z}{\partial y}\right)^2 \right] dy \, dx$$

Thus the increase in strain energy due to change in a_{mn} of δa_{mn} is

$$\frac{\partial U}{\partial a_{mn}} \delta a_{mn} = T \frac{\pi^2 ab}{4} \left(\frac{m^2}{a^2} + \frac{n^2}{b^2} \right) a_{mn} \, \delta a_{mn}$$

The work done by the pressure on the displacement δa_{mn} is

$$p \int_{-a/2}^{+a/2} \int_{-b/2}^{+b/2} \delta a_{mn} \cos \frac{m\pi x}{a} \cos \frac{n\pi y}{b} \, dx \, dy = p \frac{4}{\pi^2} \delta a_{mn} \frac{ab}{mn} (-1)^{\frac{m+n}{2}-1}$$

which, when equated to the change in strain energy, gives the coefficients a_{mn}. Using the above and converting from the membrane to the twisted section by the methods of Chap. I, find the torsional stiffness M_t/θ, and the maximum stress for a square section of sides a. Take the first term of the expansion only, and compare the answer with the exact values from the table of page 16.

158. Repeat the previous problem for a rectangle with sides $2a$ and a, taking the first four terms in the expansion. Compare the values for M_t/θ and for maximum stress so found with the exact values as tabulated on page 16.

159. The method described in Prob. 157 can be modified by replacing the trigonometric series for the membrane height z by an appropriate algebraic expression. The simplest expression for the square membrane which satisfies the boundary conditions is

$$z = C\left(\frac{a^2}{4} - x^2\right)\left(\frac{a^2}{4} - y^2\right)$$

Show, following the discussion of Prob. 157, that C is obtained from

$$\frac{\partial U}{\partial C} \delta C = \frac{\partial}{\partial C} \int_{-a/2}^{+a/2} \int_{-a/2}^{+a/2} \frac{T}{2} \left[\left(\frac{\partial z}{\partial x}\right)^2 + \left(\frac{\partial z}{\partial y}\right)^2 \right] dx \, dy \cdot \delta C$$

$$= p \int_{-a/2}^{+a/2} \int_{-a/2}^{a/2} \delta C\left(\frac{a^2}{4} - x^2\right)\left(\frac{a^2}{4} - y^2\right) dx \, dy$$

Evaluate C, and hence find the stiffness M_t/θ and the maximum stress in a square of side a. Compare the result with the exact values of page 16 and with those obtained in Prob. 157.

160. To illustrate the method of least work, assume that the stress distribution in a straight bar of circular cross section subject to twisting moment M_t is unknown. Write $s_s = C_1 r^2 + C_2 r^3$ for the shear stress. Find one constant from the condition that

$$M_t = \int_0^R s_s 2\pi r^2 \, dr$$

and the other from the condition of minimum energy. Plot the actual linear stress distribution and the stress distribution given by the above approximation on the same graph.

161. An approximate solution for the torsion of a square section can also be obtained by least work. Consider a square of side $2a$, and assume an expression $A(x^2 - a^2)(y^2 - a^2) + B(x^4 - a^4)(y^4 - a^4)$ for the Saint-Venant Φ function. One condition for the coefficients A and B is

$$M_t = \iint (s_x y - s_y x) \, dx \, dy = 2 \iint \frac{\partial \Phi}{\partial x} \, x \, dy \, dx$$

(see page 9), the other condition being least work. Using this, obtain expressions for the torsional stiffness and the maximum stress.

162. A flat rectangular plate a, b is subjected to half-sinusoidal force distributions in its own plane on the two faces a only, while the faces b are free of stress:

$$s = s_0 \sin \frac{\pi x}{a} \qquad (\text{for } y = 0 \text{ and } y = b)$$

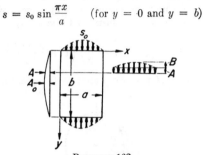

PROBLEM 162.

We want to calculate the internal stress distribution in an approximate manner by the method of least work. To that end we assume that the stress at some inside section $y = y$ consists of a constant plus a half sine wave $s_y = A + B \sin (\pi x/a)$, where A and B are both functions of y. It is clear that A must be zero at the ends and maximum A_0 in the middle $y = b/2$, while B must be s_0 at the ends and smaller in the middle. Assume then $A = A_0 \sin (\pi y/b)$, in which A_0 is the unknown parameter in the problem.

 a. For equilibrium in the y direction, B must be expressible in terms of A and s_0. Do this, and write s_y in terms of A_0, s_0, x, and y only, not containing the letters A and B.

The s_y system so written is *not* a system of equilibrium stresses; certain shear stresses s_s and cross stresses s_x are necessary to produce equilibrium.

 b. Using Eqs. (99) (page 173), find $s_s = f(x, y, A_0)$ and s_x necessary in conjunction with the above s_y to produce equilibrium.

 c. Of the stresses so found, the s_y and s_s stresses are more important than the s_x stresses. For simplicity the s_x stresses may be neglected. Calculate the energy stored in an element $dx \, dy$ of the plate, and from it write the integral U for the total plate energy (in terms of A_0 and s_0) knowing that the result is approximate only, because $s_x \neq 0$ although assumed so.

 d. Write the condition that this energy U must satisfy, and from it calculate A_0.

 e. For $\mu = 0.3$ and $\mu = 0$ plot the ratio

$$\frac{s_{y(x=a/2,\, y=b/2)}}{s_0}$$

as a function of a/b.

163. From the system

$$\delta_1 = \alpha_{11}P_1 + \alpha_{12}P_2$$

$$\delta_2 = \alpha_{21}P_1 + \alpha_{22}P_2$$

solve for P_1 and P_2, and express the β influence numbers in terms of the α numbers (page 228). Knowing that $\alpha_{12} = \alpha_{21}$, prove that $\beta_{12} = \beta_{21}$.

164. The system of two loads of the previous problem is replaced by one of three loads P_1, P_2, P_3. Prove the three reciprocal relations for the β influence numbers. The algebra of this problem is quite involved, and not particularly useful or instructive.

165. A piston ring of constant cross section must be truly circular when in the cylinder and must exert a uniform pressure on a cylinder. By using Eq. (122a) (page 237) show that the shape when unstrained is given by

$$(\text{Radius } R)_{\text{at } \theta} = r + \frac{pr^4}{EI}\left(1 + \frac{\theta \sin \theta}{2}\right)$$

From this, find an expression for the gap width, verifying that it is the same as that given by Prob. 140.

PROBLEM 165.

166. A steam-turbine crossover pipe of 18 in. outside diameter and ½ in. wall thickness is subjected to a temperature rise of 250°F. If it is considered built in at the ends, what are the values of the end moments and forces? The coefficient of thermal expansion for steel is 6.67×10^{-6} in./in./°F.

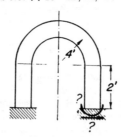

PROBLEM 166.

167. A curved steel pipe of 16 in. diameter is made in the form of a quarter circle of radius 4 ft; it is built in at one end and free at the other. The loading at the free end is equivalent to a direct load P and a twisting moment $6P$ ft lb as shown. If there is to be no displacement of the free end perpendicular to the plane of the circle, what should be the thickness of the pipe?

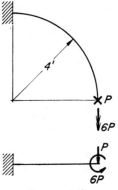

PROBLEM 167.

168. A section of oil pipe line of 30 in. outside diameter, $\frac{1}{2}$ in. wall thickness, and 2,800 ft length goes from a shore station over floats to a discharging station where it is firmly anchored. The possible temperature variation after assembly is 50°F. How many expansion bends of the type shown are required if the end thrust is to be limited to 10 tons? $\alpha = 6.67 \times 10^{-6}$ in./ in./deg F.

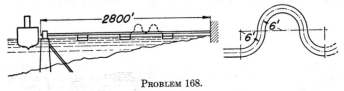

PROBLEM 168.

169. For a curved tube in which $\lambda = 0.41 = \sqrt{\frac{1}{6}}$, calculate the longitudinal strain ϵ_2 (page 240), and plot it across the section of the pipe, *i.e.*, plot ϵ_2 against the quantity $r_0 \cos \theta$ of Fig. 167. On the same graph plot the strain distribution given by the old theory.

170. Von Kármán's result [Eq. (127), page 243] for the flattening of a tube in bending can be derived in a manner quite different from that in the text, by considering the equilibrium of a piece $d\alpha$ of the pipe. Equation (e) (page 240) gives the longitudinal strains on this piece of pipe. Multiplied by E, this produces a longitudinal stress distribution. Looking at a single fiber $r d\theta$ of the cross section, the longitudinal stresses on the two ends enclose the small angle $d\alpha$ between each other and hence have a resultant directed toward or away from the center of curvature of the pipe. Plot these resultants as a function of θ, and recognize that they tend to pinch the cross section. Now assuming the cross section to be a ring of constant $EI (r \ll R)$, solve the ring problem by a Castigliano's method for the flattening of the diameter, and find for it the result

$$\frac{\alpha_0 u_0}{r_0 \varphi_0} = \frac{6}{10\frac{1}{20} + 6\lambda^2}$$

which is very close to Eq. (*i*) (page 242).

171. A steel pipe of 1 ft diameter and $\frac{1}{4}$ in. wall thickness is arranged in a semi-circle with 3 ft mean diameter. It is clamped at one end and subjected to a force $P = 500$ lb at the other end. Calculate the deflection in the direction of the force.

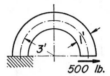

PROBLEM 171.

172. Using Eqs. (127), (c), (e), and (i) of pages 238 to 243, show that for the bending of a curved pipe the maximum *shear stress* at the outer fibers is multiplied by the factor

$$\frac{6\lambda^2 + 9\lambda - 1}{12\lambda^2 + 1} \frac{1}{1 + \mu}$$

as compared with the old, nonflattening theory.

Note that the maximum shear stress at these outer fibers is not the maximum shear stress in the pipe.

173. For the ring shown in Prob. 141 the moment was found to be

$$M_\theta = Pr\left(\frac{\sin\theta}{2} - \frac{1}{\pi}\right)$$

and the change in diameter under the load was $0.149 Pr^3/EI$. Obtain the same expression for the change in diameter by substituting the above expression for M_θ into Eq. (122a) (page 237) and integrating.

174. Apply the method of virtual work to determine the central deflection of a simply supported square plate under uniform load. Use a double cosine series, taking the origin at the center of the plate, instead of a sine series as in the text, the answer being the same in both cases.

175. Apply the method of virtual work to find the central deflection of a simply supported rectangular plate $b/a = 2$ under a concentrated central force, using a double cosine series. The result is the same as that obtained in the text using a double sine series.

176. A column of total length $2L + l$ has a short central piece l of bending stiffness EI, while the two long end pieces L are perfectly stiff ($EI = \infty$). By the energy method, find the buckling load for hinged ends.

PROBLEM 176.

177. Apply Rayleigh's method to find the critical load for a column built in at one end and free at the other, the moment of inertia of the cross section being given by $I = I_0 \cos^2(\pi x/2l)$. Assume for the deflection

$$y = y_0\left(1 - \cos\frac{\pi x}{2l}\right)$$

PROBLEM 177.   PROBLEM 178.

178. A cantilever column with a free upper end is known to buckle in a quarter sine wave. If now the sideways movement of the free end is opposed by a spring k, as shown, we assume that the buckled shape remains unaltered. Find the critical load.

179. *a.* Obtain the exact solution for the critical load for the column of Prob. 178 by setting up the differential equation. Leave the solution in the form $\tan\varphi = f(\varphi)$, from which the critical load can be determined graphically or numerically.

b. Calculate the load numerically, first drawing a graph for purposes of orientation, for the case that the spring stiffness is $k = 9EI/l^3$, and compare this exact result with the approximate answer of the previous problem.

180. *a.* Find the maximum height of a solid steel flagpole of circular cross section with a diameter of $2.82 = 2\sqrt{2}$ in.

b. A flagpole is made of steel tubing of 5 in. outside diameter and 4 in. inside diameter. It is 60 ft high. The wind load on the flag perpendicular to the pole is 48 lb. Calculate the deflection at the top of the pole. Use the exact formula (133*b*) (page 257) for the critical load.

181. For a column of constant solid circular cross section buckling under its own weight, find an expression for the critical length in terms of the radius of the cross section and E/γ, where γ is the weight per unit volume of the material. Apply this result to

a. The case of Prob. 180*a.*

b. A wood pole of 2 in. diameter with $E = 2 \times 10^6$ lb/sq in. and $\gamma = 50$ lb/cu ft.

182. The column of Fig. 175 (page 256) is loaded by its own weight and by a vertical load P. Using the energy method and assuming a deflection curve

$$y = C\left(x^2 - \frac{x^3}{3l}\right)$$

calculate the critical load P. Check the correctness of the general result for the two special cases $w = 0$ and $P = 0$.

183. Set up the differential equation for a column, loaded only by its own weight, with both ends hinged, the top end being free to move in the vertical direction. (See figure on next page.)

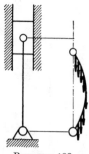

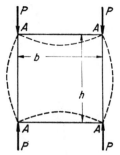

PROBLEM 183.   PROBLEM 184.

184. A rigid rectangular frame of height h, width b, and bar stiffness EI is loaded with four forces P as shown. Find the buckling load by proceeding as follows: Make cuts at A, and consider the statically indeterminate bending moments at these points. Then write the differential equation of the upright members, and solve. Leave the solution as a transcendental equation.

185. A column has hinged ends which are prevented from rotation by end moments, which are proportional to the angle of rotation $= k(dy/dx)_{x=\pm l/2}$.

a. Set up the differential equation and find an expression for the critical load. Leave it in the form $\tan \varphi = f(\varphi)$, from which the critical load can be obtained graphically. Take the origin of coordinates at the center of the column.

b. Calculate the coefficient numerically by trial and error (after an exploratory graphical intersection of a tangent curve with an algebraic one) for the special case that the end stiffness is $k = 2EI/l$.

186. The critical load for a column loaded only by its own weight was obtained on page 257 by Rayleigh's method, assuming a trigonometric expression for the deflected shape. Now find a similar approximation for the critical loading by taking a third-order algebraic expression for the deflection curve. The expression should satisfy $x = 0, y = 0, y' = 0$ and $x = l, y'' = 0$.

187. A still better approximation for the previous case of the column loaded by its own weight can be expected by fitting an algebraic expression which satisfies *all* the boundary conditions, that is, $x = 0, y = 0, y' = 0$ and $x = l, y'' = 0, y''' = 0$ (no bending moment or shear force at the free end). Find such an expression, and calculate the critical loading.

188. Referring to Fig. 180 and Eq. (142) (page 262), prove that the various dashed horizontal lines through that figure are as follows:

$$\frac{\sqrt{2}}{\pi} \beta l \text{ at } A_2 = \sqrt{2}, \text{ at } B_2 = \sqrt{3}, \text{ at } C_2 = \sqrt{4}, \text{ etc.}$$

$$\frac{P_{crit}}{\sqrt{kEI}} \text{ at } A = 2\tfrac{1}{2}, \text{ at } B = 3\tfrac{1}{3}, \text{ at } C = 4\tfrac{1}{4}, \text{ etc.}$$

From this, derive the details of Fig. 180a.

189. *a.* Prove that a railroad rail can buckle in the vertical plane before yielding if

$$\sqrt{\frac{E}{k}} \geq 2,000 \frac{\rho}{\sqrt{A}}$$

where ρ is the radius of gyration of the cross section $\rho^2 = I/A$, A is the area of the cross section, and k is the foundation constant, assuming as usual that the yield stress is 1,000 times smaller than the modulus E.

b. Investigate this formula for a standard rail of 130 lb/yd; $I = 88$ in.^{4}, $A = 13$ sq in., with the usual track constant $k = 1,500$ lb/sq in. Can it buckle in the vertical plane (before it yields) because of a large temperature rise?

c. What foundation modulus k would permit this standard rail to buckle before yield, and what temperature rise is required? Temperature coefficient for steel $= 6.67 \times 10^{-6}$ in./in./°F.

190. Derive a formula and a diagram similar to Fig. 178 (page 260) for the buckling of closely coiled helical springs with non-rotatable ends ("fixed" or "built-in" ends).

191. On page 252 Rayleigh's method is described for finding the buckling load by expressing the elastic energy in terms of the displacement y. The differential equation $EIy'' = M$ of the beam enables us to express the elastic energy in terms of the bending moment as well as in terms of the displacement.

a. Derive the following two variants of Rayleigh's theorem:

$$P_{\text{crit}} = \frac{\int y'^2 \, dx}{\int (y^2/EI) \, dx} \qquad P_{\text{crit}} = \sqrt{\frac{\int EIy''^2 \, dx}{\int (y^2/EI) \, dx}}$$

The first of these expressions does not contain y''. Now it is often easier to guess at the shape y itself than at a second derivative of it, so that the first of the above expressions often gives a better approximation than Eq. (131a) (page 252). This is most evident if our choice of curve is crude in regard to bending moment but fairly good in regard to displacement y as in the following example:

b. Assume for the simple Euler strut the shape $y = C(x^2 - xl)$ as in Fig. 173 (page 253). Calculate the buckling load with the two formulae of this problem, and compare the results with that of page 253.

192. Prove by a method parallel to that of page 266 that the two expressions of Prob. 191a give approximations for the buckling load that are larger than the exact value.

193. Find the critical load of the column in Prob. 177, using the first formula of Prob. 191a. Which answer gives the best approximation to the critical load, and why?

194. A column hinged at both ends has a variation in stiffness given by $I = I_0[1 - (4x^2/l^2)]$, the origin being taken at the center of the column.

a. Apply Rayleigh's method, assuming a parabola for the deflection curve to estimate the critical load.

b. Then with the same assumed deflection curve go through one step of Vianello's method, and obtain another estimate.

c. From the two results what conclusions can be drawn as to the assumed deflection curve and the critical load calculated from it?

195. Using Vianello's method, obtain an approximation for the buckling load of a column with hinged ends. The moment of inertia of the cross section varies linearly from I_0 at one end $x = 0$ to zero at the other end $x = l$.

Assume a deflection curve of the form $y = x(l - x)$, and apply the method once only. Compare terms on the basis of central deflections.

196. Repeat the previous problem with a column whose stiffness varies linearly from EI_0 at one end to $EI_0/2$ at the other.

197. Referring to page 269 in the text, calculate the buckling load of a flagpole of constant w_1/EI by Vianello's method, starting with a parabolic shape $y = ax^2$, carrying out one iteration first and then a second one.

198. What external pressure could the hull of a submarine (treated as a tube) take without buckling for a thickness of 1 in. and diameter of 30 ft?

199. *a.* In a twist-bend buckling case caused by bending moments (Fig. 190), find a general relation between the dimensions t, h, l, the elastic constants E, G, and the yield stress s_y, for which buckling and yielding occur at the same bending moment. Designate by an inequality under which condition yielding occurs first.

b. By substituting numbers verify Eq. (152) (page 285).

200. A beam of dimensions t, h, l is subjected to critical bending moments in the stiff plane, so that it buckles in the twist-bend manner (page 285).

a. Find the relation between the height h and the length l for which the bottom fiber (*i.e.*, the tension fiber) remains straight.

b. Find the relation between l and h for which the top and bottom fibers bow out in ratio 3:2 in the same direction.

c. For what l/h does the top fiber bow out n times as much as the bottom fiber in the same direction?

201. Finish the development of page 291 of the text, leading to Eq. (*e*) as an approximate result for the critical twist-bend load of a cantilever.

202. Instead of placing the load P in the center line of the beam as in Fig. 192 (page 286), place it on the top of the beam, or generally place it at a distance b above the origin O of Fig. 192. Modify the energy equation (156) (page 291) to take care of this change, and using the same assumption for φ as in the text, calculate the buckling load. The development leads to a quadratic equation in P, with a middle term proportional to b. Find that the order of magnitude of the middle term is small (of order b/l) with respect to the other two terms. In the solution for P retain only the first power of b, neglecting smaller effects, and so show that

$$(P_{crit})_{\text{load at } b} = (P_{crit})_{\text{load at } O}\left(1 - 1.57\frac{b}{l}\sqrt{\frac{EI_f}{C}}\right)$$

203. The beam of Fig. 190 (page 283) is subjected to an end thrust P in addition to end moments M. By adding the effect of P to Eqs. (149), show that the lowest buckling combination is given by

$$\frac{P}{P_{\text{Euler}}} + \left(\frac{M}{M_{crit}}\right)^2 = 1$$

Note that this is the same case as that of an eccentric end load.

204. Prove the result (*a*) of page 294, that a solid circular shaft subjected to torsion buckles before yielding if $l/r \geq 2,000\pi$.

205. The result for the buckling of a shaft by torsion [Eq. (158)] applies to a shaft with equal bending stiffness in all directions. Show that for a shaft having principal moments of inertia of the cross section I_1 and I_2 the critical torque is given by

$$M_t = \frac{2\pi E \sqrt{I_1 I_2}}{l}$$

206. Calculate the critical values for the three following cases:

a. Collapsing pressure on a brass condenser tube of 1 in. diameter, $\frac{1}{32}$ in. wall thickness, for which $E = 10 \times 10^6$ lb/sq in.

b. End buckling load on a cantilever of $h = 3$ in., $b = \frac{1}{16}$ in., $l = 3$ ft, made of wood, with $E = 1 \times 10^6$ lb/sq in. and $G = \frac{1}{16}E$.

c. Critical torque on a piano wire of $\frac{1}{16}$ in. diameter and 4 ft length.

207. *a.* The drilling rods in an oil well are of alloy steel 4 in. outside diameter, 3 in. inside diameter, and have a working shear stress of 20,000 lb/sq in. Calculate the critical length for torsional buckling, ignoring end loading.

b. For the same rod, calculate the critical length for Euler buckling if the buckling occurs when the compressive stress is 40,000 lb/sq in., ignoring the torque.

208. Derive a diagram similar to Fig. 201 (page 300) for a hollow split thin-walled tube of diameter d, wall thickness t, and length l. Make the usual assumptions $E/G = 2.5$ and $E = 1,000s_{yield}$.

Plot d/t vertically and l/d horizontally.

209. Plot a diagram similar to Fig. 201 (page 300) for the section shown in Prob. 31 (page 332). Make the usual assumptions $E/G = 2.5$ and $E = 1,000s_{yield}$. Information about the section can be obtained from the answer to Prob. 31. Plot a/t vertically against l/a horizontally.

210. A channel section is used as a column; the three sides of the channel are of equal length and thickness. If the column is 10 ft long and hinged at the ends, what are the limiting dimensions of the cross section?

$E/G = 2.5$, and $E = 1,000s_{yield}$, as usual.

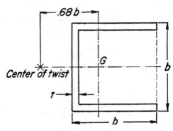

PROBLEM 210.

211. Plot a triple-point diagram like Fig. 201 for the case of a long square box column (Fig. 202), comparing plate buckling, Euler-column buckling, and yield. The material is structional steel with $E/1,000 = s_{yield}$.

212. With Eq. (166) for a very long rectangular plate supported on three edges and free on the fourth (long) edge, subjected to compression in its long direction, derive a triple-point diagram like Fig. 201, comparing plate buckling, Euler buckling of an angle like Fig. 205, and yielding. Plot the diagram for an alloy material with a high yield point $s_{yield} = E/500$.

213. Referring to Eq. (143a) and Fig. 181 (page 264), and assuming that it is a good formula (which it is not), construct a triple-point diagram like Fig. 201 for this kind of buckling, for Euler-column buckling, and for yielding by compression.

214. A propeller blade of rectangular cross section $b \cdot t$ has radii r_t at the top and r_h at the hub. It is made of a material with specific weight γ and shear modulus G. It is uniformly twisted with angle α over its entire length, or $\alpha = \alpha_1(r_t - r_h)$, and the propeller rotates with a tip peripheral speed V_t (so that $V_t = \omega r_t$).

Find an expression for the total angle θ of straightening due to a centrifugal force, for the simplified case that r_h is negligible with respect to r_t.

Substitute numbers for steel $\gamma = 0.28$ lb/cu in.; $G = 12 \times 10^6$ lb/sq in.; $V = 1,000$ ft/sec; $b = 10t$.

215. On page 320 Biezeno's theorem was discussed for forces in a direction perpendicular to the plane of a closed circular ring, supported in a statically determined manner. A similar theorem exists for the closed circular ring loaded with forces F_n *in the plane* of the ring and directed radially to and from the center. Derive formulae for the normal force, the shear force, and the bending moment in the ring, similar to the result (172) (page 320). In the derivation use bending energy in the ring only (neglecting shear and tension energy).

216. The same as Prob. 215, but now the forces on the periphery of the ring are directed *tangentially*, still in the plane of the ring.

217. A steam pipe, built in at both ends, consists of a semicircle and two straight pieces as shown. Its cross section is circular of radius r and thickness t. When the temperature of the pipe is raised, there will be forces and moments at the built-in ends as a result of the temperature rise.

Calculate the force on the foundation caused by a temperature rise of 600°F for the following dimensions:

$$R = 72 \text{ in.}; r = 6 \text{ in.}; t = \tfrac{1}{4} \text{ in.}; E = 30 \times 10^6 \text{ lb/sq in.}; \alpha = 6.5 \times 10^{-6} \text{ in./in./°F}$$

Do this for the actual case of the pipe, including the von Kármán flattening effect [Eq. (127), page 243]. Do it also, neglecting the flattening effect.

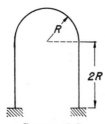

PROBLEM 217.

ANSWERS TO PROBLEMS

1. (a) 0.002 radian/in.; 12,000 lb/sq in. (b) 3.84×10^{-6} rad/in.; 265 lb/sq in.

2. (a) $1 : \dfrac{4}{\pi} : \dfrac{3L}{2\pi t}$; (b) $1 : \dfrac{\pi}{4} : \dfrac{2\pi t}{L}$. **3.** $0.147 M_t$. **4.** 9,500 lb/sq in.

5. 11,870 lb/sq in., 0.0237 radian, 0.0242 radian.

6. (a) $t = \dfrac{\pi a}{64}$; (b) $t = \dfrac{3}{4}\dfrac{\pi a}{64}$.

7. (a) $s_s = \dfrac{M_t}{2t(a^2 + t^2)} \approx \dfrac{M_t}{2a^2 t}$; (b) $\dfrac{M_t}{\theta_1} = Gat(a^2 + t^2) \approx Ga^3 t.$

8. $\dfrac{h}{r} = 2.79$. **9.** 1.41 deg. **10.** (a) $t = 0.0194a$; (b) $t = 0.029a$.

11. $D = 4.7$ in.; 10,500 lb/sq in. for square section; 4,900 lb/sq in. for circular section.

12. $M_t = 1,120$ in.-lb, $\theta = 1.98$ deg.

13. (a) $M_t = 16,400$ in.-lb; $\theta = 7.1$ deg.
(b) $M_t = 15,250$ in.-lb; $\theta = 5.85$ deg.

14. Stress ratio $\dfrac{\text{actual}}{\text{calculated}} = 1 + \dfrac{\Delta t}{t} + \cdots$.

Rigidity ratio $\dfrac{\text{actual}}{\text{calculated}} = 1 - \dfrac{1}{4\pi}\left(\dfrac{\Delta t}{t}\right)^2 + \cdots$.

15. $\theta = 3.77$ deg. Preventing warping at the "built-in" end does not change the rigidity, as the center of twist is at the junction of web and flange in a T section, and consequently only twisting, and no bending, is involved.

16. (a) 428,000 in.-lb. (b) 3.28×10^{-3} radian/ft. (c) No stress in center section.

17. $\theta = 3.66$ deg.

18. $\dfrac{\text{Stress(circular)}}{\text{Stress(square)}} = 1.06.$

$\dfrac{\text{Deflection(circular)}}{\text{Deflection(square)}} = 1.44.$

19. 10^6 in.-lb; stress at $A = 312$ lb/sq in.; at B $= 5,000$ lb/sq in.; at $C = 10,000$ lb/sq in.

20. 1.16%; s_s (tube) $= 5,600$ lb/sq in., s_s (fin) $= 928$ lb/sq in.

21. (a) $C = -\dfrac{G\theta_1}{2}$; (b) $A = -\dfrac{4a^2}{27}$.

22. The intersections of the curves for $\frac{1}{4}$, $\frac{2}{4}$, and $\frac{3}{4}$ height, respectively, with a bisector line of the triangle (the y-axis) occur at distances from the center of gravity of the triangle, as follows: $\frac{1}{4}$ height: $-0.292a$ and $+0.450a$; $\frac{2}{4}$ height: $-0.258a$ and $+0.335a$; $\frac{3}{4}$ height: $-0.177a$ and $+0.218a$.

The intersections with a line perpendicular to the bisector (the x-axis) are: $\frac{1}{4}$ height: $\pm0.333a$; $\frac{2}{4}$ height: $\pm0.273a$; $\frac{3}{4}$ height: $\pm0.193a$.

23. (a) $(s_s)_y = -\dfrac{G\theta_1}{2}\left(2x + \dfrac{6xy}{a}\right)$.

$(s_s)_x = \dfrac{G\theta_1}{2}\left(2y - \dfrac{3y^2}{a} + \dfrac{3x^2}{a}\right)$.

$(s_s)_{max} = -\dfrac{G\theta_1 a}{2}$.

(b) $\dfrac{M_t}{\theta_1} = \dfrac{Ga^4}{26}$.

24. (b) Maximum stress $G\theta_1(2a - b)$. (c) Ratio $\to 2$ as $b \to 0$.

25. (b) 33.3%.

26. When we plot the ratio of the plastic to the elastic torque versus the ratio r_i/r_0, we find an almost linear relationship. For $r_i/r_0 = 0$, the torque ratio $= 1.33$, and for $r_i/r_0 = 1.00$, the torque ratio $= 1.00$.

27. $\frac{5}{3}$. **28.** $\frac{3}{2}$.

29. The distances from the center line are in ratio of $0.47 : 0.67 : 0.80 : 0.88 : 0.95 : 1.00$.

30. (a) Error -10%; (b) $+195\%$; (c) $+13\%$.

31. (a) Straight section $= 1.41a$; (b) $s_s = \dfrac{0.5 M_t}{at^2}$; (c) $1.93a$ to the left of G.

32. $s_{max} = \dfrac{3M_t}{bt^2}$; $\theta = \dfrac{2.08 M_t l}{Gbt^3}$.

33. (a) $p_0 = 8{,}550$ lb/sq in.; (b) $p = 15{,}000$ lb/sq in.

34. (a) $s_r = -11{,}500$ lb/sq in., $s_t = 12{,}500$ lb/sq in.

(b) rpm $= 4{,}850$. (c) $\frac{3}{4} \times 11{,}500$ lb/sq in.

35. (a) rpm $= 3{,}960$.

36. (a) $s_t = 9{,}100$ lb/sq in.; (b) rpm $= 3460$; (c) $s_t = 18{,}000$ lb/sq in.

37. 0.00342 in. on the diameter.

41. Maximum radial stress at $r = \sqrt{r_0 r_i}$.

Maximum tangential stress at $r = r_i$.

43. 0.00372 in.

45. (a) 3,950 hp; (b) rpm $= 2{,}010$; (c) 0.0038 in.; (d) rpm $= 2{,}530$.

46. (a) 300°F; (b) rpm $= 5{,}420$. **47.** 0.015 in. on the diameter.

48. $(p - 668)$ lb/sq in.

49. Stress in shaft $-7{,}400$ lb/sq in.
Tangential stress inside $10{,}200$ lb/sq in.; outside $2{,}800$ lb/sq in.

50. rpm $= 13{,}200$. **52.** Maximum stress $= \dfrac{\rho V^2}{2}$; $\quad V = 615$ ft/sec.

54. (c) $s_0 = 2{,}200$ lb/sq in.; $(s_{\text{tang}})_{r_i} = (s_{\text{tang}})_{r_o} = 21{,}400$ lb/sq in.;
$(s_{\text{tang}})_{\text{midway}} = 25{,}000$ lb/sq in.

56. $w = 2.94$ lb per circumferential inch.

59. (a) $26{,}260$ lb/sq in. (b) $s_t = 11{,}700$ lb/sq in. at the bore.
(c) Thickness at tip $= 0.232$ in.; at axis $= 0.98$ in.

60. $r = 9.45$ in.; $t = 0.69$ in.; rpm $= 12{,}150$.

61. Maximum shear, just above ring $2.62\gamma r_0^2/t$; just below ring $0.485\gamma r_0^2/t$;
at the bottom $0.5\ \gamma r_0^2/t$.

62. $s_m = \dfrac{p(r^2 - r_0^2)}{\sqrt{2}\ rt}$; $\quad s_t = \dfrac{\sqrt{2}\ pr}{t}$.

Bending at the corners, where there is discontinuity of slope.

66. (a) 4.74 ft; (b) 9.45 ft. **67.** 7.8 lb/sq in. **69.** 5.2 in.

70. Difference in diameter 0.018 in.; radius $= 9.8$ in.; over-all length 74.8 in.

71. Height 44.5 ft; diameter 66 ft.

72. Base diameter 525 ft; base thickness $6\frac{3}{4}$ in.

73. (b) $s_t = -\dfrac{\gamma r\ \cos\theta}{t}$; $s_s = -\dfrac{2\gamma z\ \sin\theta}{r}$; $s_l = -\dfrac{\gamma\ \cos\theta}{rt}(b^2 - z^2)$.

74. $s_t = \dfrac{\gamma r^2}{t}\sin\theta$; $s_s = -\dfrac{\gamma rz\ \cos\theta}{t}$; $s_l = \dfrac{\gamma}{t}\left(\dfrac{l^2}{24} - \dfrac{z^2}{2}\right)\sin\theta + \mu s_t$.

75. Both cases $= 76$ ft.

84. $w = \dfrac{16p_0 a^4}{\pi^6 D}\displaystyle\sum_{m=1}^{\infty}\sum_{n=1}^{\infty}\dfrac{\sin\dfrac{m\pi x}{a}\sin\dfrac{n\pi y}{a}}{mn(m^2 + n^2)^2}$.

$M_x = \dfrac{16p_0 a^2}{\pi^4}\displaystyle\sum_{m=1}^{\infty}\sum_{n=1}^{\infty}\dfrac{(m^2 + \mu n^2)\sin\dfrac{m\pi x}{a}\sin\dfrac{n\pi y}{a}}{mn(m^2 + n^2)^2}$.

85. Elliptical plate, built in at the edges with uniform loading.

86. $M_{1x} = \dfrac{p/a^2}{(3/a^4) + (3/b^4) + (2/a^2 b^2)}$ at $x = a$;

$M_{1y} = \dfrac{p/b^2}{(3/a^4) + (3/b^4) + (2/a^2 b^2)}$ at $y = b$.

87. Frame spacing $2\frac{1}{2}$ ft; deflection 0.0325 in.

88. Thickness: separate sections $t = 2.4$ in., continuous $t = 2.16$ in.

89. 0.03 in. **90.** $0.198\ \dfrac{p_0 R^4}{E t^3}$.

91. (*a*) 0.236 in.; (*b*) −19,750 lb/sq in.; (*c*) −266,000 in.-lb.
92. Stress −12,600 lb/sq in. Deflection 0.29 in.
93. 0.192 in., 0.002 in.

94. $\delta_{\max} = 0.238$ in.; $s_{\max} = 14,700$ lb/sq in. **96.** $\beta = \sqrt[4]{\dfrac{48}{al^3}\dfrac{I_T}{I_L}}$.

97. ¾ in., 149 lb/in. **99.** 2.64 in.
100. Distance = 5.6 in.; maximum stress 34,100 lb/sq in.
101. $s_l = -15,500$ lb/sq in.; $s_{\text{tang}} = -4,650$ lb/sq in.
102. (*a*) $s_l = -16,300$ lb/sq in.; $s_t = -4,900$ lb/sq in.
    (*b*) $s_l = -9,400$ lb/sq in.; $s_t = -2,820$ lb/sq in.
    (*c*) $s_l = -12,200$ lb/sq in.; $s_t = -3,660$ lb/sq in.
103. (*a*) 0.00885 in. (*b*) $s_l = -10,500$ lb/sq in.; $s_t = -20,850$ lb/sq in.
104. $s = 10,400$ lb/sq in. **105.** $P = 475$ lb/in. **106.** Stress = 21,300 lb/sq in.
107. (*a*) 5,000 lb/sq in.; (*b*) 1,470 lb/sq in.; (*c*) 4,400 lb/sq in.
110. Moment = −31 in.-lb/in.
    Shear force = 11.25 lb/in.
111. $s_l = -3,270$ outside; 4,710 inside.
    $s_l = -10,900$ outside; 15,700 inside.
112. Hétényi (pp. 151–152).

$$M_{t_1} = -k_t\theta \tag{84}$$

$$GI_p\theta'' - k_t\theta = -M_{t_1} \tag{85}$$

$$\alpha = \sqrt{\frac{k_t}{GI_p}} \tag{86}$$

$$\theta = C_1e^{\alpha x} + C_2e^{-\alpha x} \tag{87}$$

$$\theta = \frac{M_0}{2\alpha GI_p}e^{-\alpha x} \qquad M_x = \frac{M_0}{2}e^{-\alpha x} \tag{89}$$

113. (*a*) $\Phi = C_1\cos 2\theta + C_2\sin 2\theta + C_3\theta + C_4$.
  (*b*) $s_t = s_r = 0$; $s_s = C_3/r^2$; a pulley in a state of plane twist; find the relation between the constant C_3 and the transmitted torque.

(*c*) $s_t = 0$; $s_r = -\dfrac{4C_1}{r^2}\cos 2\theta$; $s_s = -\dfrac{2C_1}{r^2}\sin 2\theta$ and the C_2 solution turned 45 deg with respect to the C_1 solution. Look at the equilibrium of a quarter pie.

114. $C_1 = \dfrac{S/2}{(r_0^2 + r_i^2)\log_e(r_0/r_i) + (r_i^2 - r_0^2)}$.

116. $s_s = P\cos^2\theta \sin\theta/r(\alpha - \frac{1}{2}\sin 2\alpha)$.
    $s_{\text{bending}} = -P\cos\theta\sin^2\theta/r(\alpha - \frac{1}{2}\sin 2\alpha)$.
117. $s_r = s_t = 2C\theta$; $s_s = -C$.

118. Stresses $= \dfrac{-2q}{\pi}\left(\alpha \pm \dfrac{\sin 2\alpha}{2}\right)$.

120. Three forces P on three semi-infinite planes rotated 120 deg with respect to one another, plus hydrostatic tension $3P/\pi d$.

121. Add hydrostatic tension $nP/\pi d$. **122.** 256 lb/sq in. at 22.5 deg.

123. (a) Stresses $= \dfrac{-2q}{\pi} (\alpha \pm \sin 2\alpha)$. (b) $-q$ and $\dfrac{-2q}{\pi} (\alpha \pm 2\alpha)$.

124. (a) Yes; (b) $s_r = \dfrac{2 \cos \theta}{r^3} (1 - 5 \cos^2 \theta)$; $s_{\bullet} = -6 \cos^2 \theta \sin \theta / r^3$.

126. (a) $\Phi = \dfrac{C}{6} (x^3 + y^3) + Axy$.

(b) Shear stresses const $= s_{\bullet}$.

(c) $u = \dfrac{C}{E} \left(yx - \dfrac{\mu x^2}{2} - \dfrac{y^2}{2} + \dfrac{Es_{\bullet}y}{2GC} \right)$

$v = \dfrac{C}{E} \left(xy - \dfrac{\mu y^2}{2} - \dfrac{x^2}{2} + \dfrac{Es_{\bullet}x}{2GC} \right)$.

(d) Extension $= \dfrac{Ca^2}{\sqrt{2}\,E} (1 - \mu) + \dfrac{s_{\bullet}a}{\sqrt{2}\,G}$.

129.

l/h........	0.2	0.4	0.6	0.8	1	2
Stress ratio	0.007	0.194	0.502	0.727	0.852	0.983

130. $s/A = 1.05$. **131.** 4. **132.** 2.

133. $s_t = \dfrac{-q}{\pi} \left(\theta - \dfrac{\sin 2\theta}{2} \right)$; $s_r = \dfrac{-q}{\pi} \left(\theta + \dfrac{\sin 2\theta}{2} \right)$;

$s_{\bullet} = \dfrac{q}{2\pi} (1 - \cos 2\theta)$.

Loading is uniform pressure over the part of the half infinite plane given by $\theta = \pi$.

134. $\Phi = -\dfrac{M_0}{\pi} [\theta + \sin \theta \cos \theta]$.

135. (a) $M = \dfrac{Is_{\text{yield}}}{y_{\max}}$.

(b) $M = s_{\text{yield}} aA$, where A is the cross-sectional area bh and a is the distance $h/4$ from the center of gravity of the area above the neutral line to the neutral line. For the rectangular section the bending moment at full yield is 1.50 times the bending moment at just start of yield.

136. If the web is neglected, the bending moment at full yield is the same as that at just start of yield.

137. (a) Eq. (116b) (page 205); $s_t = 2s_{sy}[1 - \log (r_0/r_i)]$.

(b) $s_t = -2s_{sy} \dfrac{r_0^2 + r_i^2}{r_0^2 - r_i^2} \log \dfrac{r_0}{r_i}$.

(c) $s_{t \text{ residual}} = 2s_{sy}\left(1 - \dfrac{2r_0^2}{r_0^2 - r_i^2} \log \dfrac{r_0}{r_i}\right)$.

(d) $\dfrac{r_0^2 - r_i^2}{r_0^2} = \log \dfrac{r_0}{r_i}$ or $\dfrac{r_0}{r_i} = 2.22$.

If a gun of $r_0/r_i > 2.22$ has to be upset by hydraulic pressure, that pressure should *not* be made so great as to yield the entire gun.

138. $(p_i)_{\text{yield starts}} = 0.89s_{sy}$; $(p_i)_{\text{full plas}} = 2.20s_{sy}$, and p_i required by problem = $1.78 s_{sy}$.

139. Top joint 72.5%; bottom joint 27.5%.

143. Stiffness $= \dfrac{8EI}{l}$.   **146.** $\dfrac{P}{\delta} = \dfrac{2}{\pi} \dfrac{EI}{r^3}$.

147. $A = C = \tfrac{3}{8} P$; $B = \tfrac{5}{4} P$.

148. $M_b = Wa\left(\dfrac{\cos \theta}{2} - \dfrac{\sin \theta}{\pi}\right)$; $M_t = Wa\left(\dfrac{\sin \theta}{2} + \dfrac{\cos \theta}{\pi} - \dfrac{1}{2}\right)$.

149. Maximum length of B is 46 in.   **152.** Change in diameter $= 0.03Wr^3/EI$.

153. Horizontal reactions $= \dfrac{\text{load}}{20}$.

154. $y_{\max} = \dfrac{Wl^3}{EI} \dfrac{2}{\pi^4}\left(1 + \dfrac{1}{3^4} + \dfrac{1}{5^4} + \cdots\right)$.

155. $y = \dfrac{wl^4}{EI} \dfrac{4}{\pi^5}\left(1 - \dfrac{1}{3^5} + \dfrac{1}{5^5} - \cdots\right)$.

156. $y = \dfrac{Wl^3}{106.2EI}$.

Deflection not accurately expressed by two sine components due to shape of loading.

157. $\dfrac{M_t}{\theta_1} = 0.1335Ga^4$; $s_{\max} = 3.87 \dfrac{M_t}{a^3}$.

158. $\dfrac{M_t}{\theta_1} = 0.454Ga^4$; $s_{\max} = 1.91 \dfrac{M_t}{a^3}$.

159. $\dfrac{M_t}{\theta_1} = 0.139Ga^4$; $s_{\max} = 4.5 \dfrac{M_t}{a^3}$.   **160.** $s_s = \dfrac{45}{8\pi} \dfrac{M}{R^5}\left(r^2 - \dfrac{2}{3} \dfrac{r^3}{R}\right)$.

161. $s_{\max} = 0.616 \dfrac{M_t}{a^3}$; exact value $= 0.600 \dfrac{M_t}{a^3}$.

162. (a) $s_y = A_0 \sin \dfrac{\pi y}{b} + \left(s_0 - \dfrac{\pi}{2} A_0 \sin \dfrac{\pi y}{b}\right) \sin \dfrac{\pi x}{a}.$

(b) $s_s = - A_0 \cos \dfrac{\pi y}{b} \left(\dfrac{\pi x}{b} - \dfrac{\pi a}{2b} + \dfrac{\pi a}{2b} \cos \dfrac{\pi x}{a}\right).$

$s_x = - A_0 \dfrac{\pi}{b} \sin \dfrac{\pi y}{b} \left(\dfrac{\pi x^2}{2b} - \dfrac{\pi a x}{2b} + \dfrac{a^2}{2b} \sin \dfrac{\pi x}{a}\right).$

(c) $U = \displaystyle\iint \left(\dfrac{s_y^2}{2E} + \dfrac{s_s^2}{2G}\right) dx\, dy.$

$U = \dfrac{1}{2E} \left[\dfrac{A_0^2 ab}{2} \left(\dfrac{\pi^2}{8} - 1\right) + A_0 s_0 ab\left(\dfrac{8}{\pi^2} - 1\right) + \dfrac{s_0 ab}{2}\right]$

$\qquad\qquad + \dfrac{1 + \mu}{2E} \left[\dfrac{A_0^2 a^3}{b} \left(\dfrac{5}{24} \pi^2 - 2\right)\right].$

(d) $\dfrac{\partial U}{\partial A_0} = 0, \quad \dfrac{A_0}{s_0} = \dfrac{1}{1.23 + 0.575(1 + \mu)(a/b)^2}.$

(e) For both $\mu = 0.3$ and $\mu = 0$ we find a rapid increase from

$$\dfrac{s_{y \text{ center}}}{s_0} = 0.54 \text{ for } \dfrac{a}{b} = 0$$

at the start. For $a/b > 5$ we are very close to the asymptote $s_{y \text{ center}}/s_0 = 1$. For all values of a/b, we find the curve for $\mu = 0.3$ slightly higher than the curve for $\mu = 0$.

163. $\beta_{11} = \dfrac{\alpha_{22}}{\Delta}, \ \beta_{22} = \dfrac{\alpha_{11}}{\Delta}, \ \beta_{12} = \beta_{21} = - \dfrac{\alpha_{12}}{\Delta},$

where $\Delta = \begin{vmatrix} \alpha_{11} & \alpha_{12} \\ \alpha_{21} & \alpha_{22} \end{vmatrix} = \alpha_{11}\alpha_{22} - \alpha_{12}^2.$

166. Moment $= 1.2 \times 10^6$ in.-lb, force $= 23,000$ lb.

167. 1 in. **168.** 3 expansion bends.

169. $\epsilon_2 = \dfrac{r_0 \varphi_0}{R_0 \alpha} \cos \theta(1 - \cos^2 \theta);$ old theory $\epsilon_2 = \dfrac{r_0 \varphi_0}{R_0 \alpha} \cos \theta.$

$\epsilon_2 = $ maximum at $54° 44'$ and $125° 16'$.

$\epsilon_2 = 0$ at $0°$, $90°$, and $180°$.

171. $= 0.044$ in. **176.** $P_{\text{crit}} = \dfrac{2EI}{Ll}.$

177. $P = \dfrac{3\pi^2}{16} \dfrac{EI_0}{l^2}.$

In view of the remarks on page 268 just before article 39, it might be concluded that this answer is not necessarily larger than the exact answer. It can, however, be considered as half of a hinged column of length $2l$ in which the critical load, as given, is greater than the exact value.

178. $P_c = \dfrac{\pi^2 EI}{4l^2} + \dfrac{8kl}{\pi^2}$.

179. (a) $\tan \sqrt{\dfrac{Pl^2}{EI}} = \sqrt{\dfrac{Pl^2}{EI}} \left(1 - \dfrac{P}{kl}\right)$; (b) $P = \dfrac{9.29EI}{l^2}$.

180. (a) 62 ft. (b) Deflection at top 14 in.

181. $l_{\mathrm{crit}} = 1.25r^{\frac{2}{3}} \left(\dfrac{E}{\gamma}\right)^{\frac{1}{2}}$.

　(a) See Prob. 180a. (b) 42 ft 10 in.

182. $P_{\mathrm{crit}} = \dfrac{2.5EI}{l^2} - \dfrac{5wl}{16}$.

183. $EIy^{(4)} + w_1(l - x)y'' - w_1 y' = 0$.

Constants from $y = 0$ and $y'' = 0$ for both $x = 0$ and $x = l$.

184. $\tan \dfrac{h}{2} \sqrt{\dfrac{P}{EI}} = -\dfrac{b}{2} \sqrt{\dfrac{P}{EI}}$.

185. (a) $\tan \dfrac{l}{2} \sqrt{\dfrac{P}{EI}} = -\dfrac{2EI}{kl} \cdot \dfrac{l}{2} \sqrt{\dfrac{P}{EI}}$; (b) $P = 4.12 \dfrac{EI}{l^2}$.

186. $w_{1\,\mathrm{crit}} = \dfrac{8EI}{l^3}$, by assuming $y = x^2 - \dfrac{x^3}{3l}$.

187. $w_{1\,\mathrm{crit}} = \dfrac{8EI}{l^3}$, by assuming $y = \dfrac{3}{2} x^2 - \dfrac{x^3}{l} + \dfrac{x^4}{4l^2}$.

189. (b) No; buckling before yielding is not possible.
　(c) $k \leq 15$ lb/sq in.; temperature rise 153°F.

190. $\dfrac{\delta_{\mathrm{crit}}}{l_0} = \dfrac{1}{2} - \dfrac{1}{2} \sqrt{1 - 44.8\left(\dfrac{D}{l_0}\right)^2}$.

Curve is above and to the right of the curve in Fig. 178.

191. $\dfrac{10EI}{l^2}$ and $\dfrac{10.96EI}{l^2}$, respectively.

193. $P = \dfrac{\pi^2}{8} \dfrac{EI_0}{l}$.

This is smaller and hence better than the answer found in Prob. 177.

194. (a)(b) $P = \dfrac{8EI}{l^2}$. (c) They are both exact values.

195. $P_{crit} = 4\dfrac{EI_0}{l^2}$, exact $3.67\dfrac{EI_0}{l^2}$.

196. $P_{crit} = 6.4\dfrac{EI_0}{l^2}$, exact $6.55\dfrac{EI_0}{l^2}$.

197. $w = 7.7\dfrac{EI}{l^3}$. **198.** 1.42 lb/sq in.

199. Yields first if $\dfrac{hl}{t^2} < \pi\sqrt{\dfrac{G}{E}}\dfrac{E}{s_y}$.

200. (a) $l = 1.25h$; (b) $l = 6.25h$; (c) $l = 1.25\dfrac{n+1}{n-1}h$.

206. (a) 670 lb/sq in.; (b) 0.096 lb; (c) 2.94 in.-lb.

207. (a) 785 ft; (b) 9 ft.

208. Diagram exactly the same shape as Fig. 201; triple point at $l/d = 35.1$, $d/t = 10.3$.

209. Triple point at $l/a = 75.8$, $a/t = 5.17$. Diagram as in Fig. 201.

210. $b = 4.68$ in.; $t = 0.345$ in.

211. Triple point at $b/t = 60$, $l/b = 40.5$ similar to Fig. 201.

212. Triple point at $b/t = 14.4$, $l/b = 14.3$. Diagram as in Fig. 201.

213. Diagram similar to Fig. 201. Triple point at $r/t = 605$, $l/r = 70.3$. The straight diagonal line of Fig. 201 is replaced by a parabola $r/t = 0.123\,(l/r)^2$. The shaded field of torsion is replaced by the field of buckling due to P_{crit}.

214. $\theta/\alpha = \gamma V^2 b^2/12Ggt^2$; $\theta/\alpha = 0.07$.

Note that for the case $b = 30t$ the formula would give $\theta/\alpha = 0.63$, and for $b = 40t$ even more than 1.00, which is obviously wrong. The analysis is good only for small θ/α, or for the case that the original geometry is not sensibly changed by θ.

215. Shear force: $S_0 = \displaystyle\sum_n F_n^* \cos \alpha_n$.

Normal force: $P_0 = \displaystyle\sum_n F_n^* \sin \alpha_n$.

Moment: $M_0 = r\left(P_0 + \dfrac{1}{2\pi}\sum F_n\right)$.

In words: The shear and normal force in a section equal the sum of the components of the "reduced" forces in their own direction. The expression for the bending moment contains the symbol F_n without star and cannot be put into words simply.

216. $S_0 = \displaystyle\sum_n T_n^* \sin \alpha_n$.

$P_0 = \displaystyle\sum_n T_n^* \cos \alpha_n$.

$M_0 = r(P_0 + \sum T_n^*)$.

The words for the normal and shear force are the same as in Prob. 215; for the bending moment we can say that the moment about the center of the circle caused by all reduced forces and by the statically indeterminate reactions in the cut $\theta = 0$ vanishes.

217. $$\frac{EI \, \Delta x}{R^3 X_0} = \frac{\frac{4}{3} k^2 + (4 + 1\frac{1}{6}\pi)k + \left(\frac{\pi^2}{8} - 1\right)}{\frac{2}{k} + \frac{\pi}{2} k}$$

For k = von Kármán factor = 4/13, X_0 = 790 lb actually. For $k = 1$ we have X_0 = 1,220 lb.

INDEX

A CATALOG OF SELECTED
DOVER BOOKS
IN SCIENCE AND MATHEMATICS

Astronomy

BURNHAM'S CELESTIAL HANDBOOK, Robert Burnham, Jr. Thorough guide to the stars beyond our solar system. Exhaustive treatment. Alphabetical by constellation: Andromeda to Cetus in Vol. 1; Chamaeleon to Orion in Vol. 2; and Pavo to Vulpecula in Vol. 3. Hundreds of illustrations. Index in Vol. 3. 2,000pp. 6⅛ x 9¼.
Vol. I: 0-486-23567-X
Vol. II: 0-486-23568-8
Vol. III: 0-486-23673-0

EXPLORING THE MOON THROUGH BINOCULARS AND SMALL TELESCOPES, Ernest H. Cherrington, Jr. Informative, profusely illustrated guide to locating and identifying craters, rills, seas, mountains, other lunar features. Newly revised and updated with special section of new photos. Over 100 photos and diagrams. 240pp. 8¼ x 11. 0-486-24491-1

THE EXTRATERRESTRIAL LIFE DEBATE, 1750–1900, Michael J. Crowe. First detailed, scholarly study in English of the many ideas that developed from 1750 to 1900 regarding the existence of intelligent extraterrestrial life. Examines ideas of Kant, Herschel, Voltaire, Percival Lowell, many other scientists and thinkers. 16 illustrations. 704pp. 5⅜ x 8½. 0-486-40675-X

THEORIES OF THE WORLD FROM ANTIQUITY TO THE COPERNICAN REVOLUTION, Michael J. Crowe. Newly revised edition of an accessible, enlightening book recreates the change from an earth-centered to a sun-centered conception of the solar system. 242pp. 5⅜ x 8½. 0-486-41444-2

A HISTORY OF ASTRONOMY, A. Pannekoek. Well-balanced, carefully reasoned study covers such topics as Ptolemaic theory, work of Copernicus, Kepler, Newton, Eddington's work on stars, much more. Illustrated. References. 521pp. 5⅜ x 8½.
0-486-65994-1

A COMPLETE MANUAL OF AMATEUR ASTRONOMY: TOOLS AND TECHNIQUES FOR ASTRONOMICAL OBSERVATIONS, P. Clay Sherrod with Thomas L. Koed. Concise, highly readable book discusses: selecting, setting up and maintaining a telescope; amateur studies of the sun; lunar topography and occultations; observations of Mars, Jupiter, Saturn, the minor planets and the stars; an introduction to photoelectric photometry; more. 1981 ed. 124 figures. 25 halftones. 37 tables. 335pp. 6½ x 9¼. 0-486-40675-X

AMATEUR ASTRONOMER'S HANDBOOK, J. B. Sidgwick. Timeless, comprehensive coverage of telescopes, mirrors, lenses, mountings, telescope drives, micrometers, spectroscopes, more. 189 illustrations. 576pp. 5⅝ x 8¼. (Available in U.S. only.)
0-486-24034-7

STARS AND RELATIVITY, Ya. B. Zel'dovich and I. D. Novikov. Vol. 1 of *Relativistic Astrophysics* by famed Russian scientists. General relativity, properties of matter under astrophysical conditions, stars, and stellar systems. Deep physical insights, clear presentation. 1971 edition. References. 544pp. 5⅝ x 8¼. 0-486-69424-0

Chemistry

THE SCEPTICAL CHYMIST: THE CLASSIC 1661 TEXT, Robert Boyle. Boyle defines the term "element," asserting that all natural phenomena can be explained by the motion and organization of primary particles. 1911 ed. viii+232pp. 5⅜ x 8½.
0-486-42825-7

RADIOACTIVE SUBSTANCES, Marie Curie. Here is the celebrated scientist's doctoral thesis, the prelude to her receipt of the 1903 Nobel Prize. Curie discusses establishing atomic character of radioactivity found in compounds of uranium and thorium; extraction from pitchblende of polonium and radium; isolation of pure radium chloride; determination of atomic weight of radium; plus electric, photographic, luminous, heat, color effects of radioactivity. ii+94pp. 5⅜ x 8½.   0-486-42550-9

CHEMICAL MAGIC, Leonard A. Ford. Second Edition, Revised by E. Winston Grundmeier. Over 100 unusual stunts demonstrating cold fire, dust explosions, much more. Text explains scientific principles and stresses safety precautions. 128pp. 5⅜ x 8½.   0-486-67628-5

THE DEVELOPMENT OF MODERN CHEMISTRY, Aaron J. Ihde. Authoritative history of chemistry from ancient Greek theory to 20th-century innovation. Covers major chemists and their discoveries. 209 illustrations. 14 tables. Bibliographies. Indices. Appendices. 851pp. 5⅜ x 8½.   0-486-64235-6

CATALYSIS IN CHEMISTRY AND ENZYMOLOGY, William P. Jencks. Exceptionally clear coverage of mechanisms for catalysis, forces in aqueous solution, carbonyl- and acyl-group reactions, practical kinetics, more. 864pp. 5⅜ x 8½.
0-486-65460-5

ELEMENTS OF CHEMISTRY, Antoine Lavoisier. Monumental classic by founder of modern chemistry in remarkable reprint of rare 1790 Kerr translation. A must for every student of chemistry or the history of science. 539pp. 5⅜ x 8½.   0-486-64624-6

THE HISTORICAL BACKGROUND OF CHEMISTRY, Henry M. Leicester. Evolution of ideas, not individual biography. Concentrates on formulation of a coherent set of chemical laws. 260pp. 5⅜ x 8½.   0-486-61053-5

A SHORT HISTORY OF CHEMISTRY, J. R. Partington. Classic exposition explores origins of chemistry, alchemy, early medical chemistry, nature of atmosphere, theory of valency, laws and structure of atomic theory, much more. 428pp. 5⅜ x 8½. (Available in U.S. only.)   0-486-65977-1

GENERAL CHEMISTRY, Linus Pauling. Revised 3rd edition of classic first-year text by Nobel laureate. Atomic and molecular structure, quantum mechanics, statistical mechanics, thermodynamics correlated with descriptive chemistry. Problems. 992pp. 5⅜ x 8½.   0-486-65622-5

FROM ALCHEMY TO CHEMISTRY, John Read. Broad, humanistic treatment focuses on great figures of chemistry and ideas that revolutionized the science. 50 illustrations. 240pp. 5⅜ x 8½.   0-486-28690-8

Engineering

DE RE METALLICA, Georgius Agricola. The famous Hoover translation of greatest treatise on technological chemistry, engineering, geology, mining of early modern times (1556). All 289 original woodcuts. 638pp. 6¾ x 11.   0-486-60006-8

FUNDAMENTALS OF ASTRODYNAMICS, Roger Bate et al. Modern approach developed by U.S. Air Force Academy. Designed as a first course. Problems, exercises. Numerous illustrations. 455pp. 5⅜ x 8½.   0-486-60061-0

DYNAMICS OF FLUIDS IN POROUS MEDIA, Jacob Bear. For advanced students of ground water hydrology, soil mechanics and physics, drainage and irrigation engineering and more. 335 illustrations. Exercises, with answers. 784pp. 6⅛ x 9¼.
0-486-65675-6

THEORY OF VISCOELASTICITY (Second Edition), Richard M. Christensen. Complete consistent description of the linear theory of the viscoelastic behavior of materials. Problem-solving techniques discussed. 1982 edition. 29 figures. xiv+364pp. 6⅛ x 9¼.   0-486-42880-X

MECHANICS, J. P. Den Hartog. A classic introductory text or refresher. Hundreds of applications and design problems illuminate fundamentals of trusses, loaded beams and cables, etc. 334 answered problems. 462pp. 5⅜ x 8½.   0-486-60754-2

MECHANICAL VIBRATIONS, J. P. Den Hartog. Classic textbook offers lucid explanations and illustrative models, applying theories of vibrations to a variety of practical industrial engineering problems. Numerous figures. 233 problems, solutions. Appendix. Index. Preface. 436pp. 5⅜ x 8½.   0-486-64785-4

STRENGTH OF MATERIALS, J. P. Den Hartog. Full, clear treatment of basic material (tension, torsion, bending, etc.) plus advanced material on engineering methods, applications. 350 answered problems. 323pp. 5⅜ x 8½.   0-486-60755-0

A HISTORY OF MECHANICS, René Dugas. Monumental study of mechanical principles from antiquity to quantum mechanics. Contributions of ancient Greeks, Galileo, Leonardo, Kepler, Lagrange, many others. 671pp. 5⅜ x 8½.   0-486-65632-2

STABILITY THEORY AND ITS APPLICATIONS TO STRUCTURAL MECHANICS, Clive L. Dym. Self-contained text focuses on Koiter postbuckling analyses, with mathematical notions of stability of motion. Basing minimum energy principles for static stability upon dynamic concepts of stability of motion, it develops asymptotic buckling and postbuckling analyses from potential energy considerations, with applications to columns, plates, and arches. 1974 ed. 208pp. 5⅜ x 8½.
0-486-42541-X

METAL FATIGUE, N. E. Frost, K. J. Marsh, and L. P. Pook. Definitive, clearly written, and well-illustrated volume addresses all aspects of the subject, from the historical development of understanding metal fatigue to vital concepts of the cyclic stress that causes a crack to grow. Includes 7 appendixes. 544pp. 5⅜ x 8½. 0-486-40927-9

ROCKETS, Robert Goddard. Two of the most significant publications in the history of rocketry and jet propulsion: "A Method of Reaching Extreme Altitudes" (1919) and "Liquid Propellant Rocket Development" (1936). 128pp. 5⅜ x 8½.   0-486-42537-1

STATISTICAL MECHANICS: PRINCIPLES AND APPLICATIONS, Terrell L. Hill. Standard text covers fundamentals of statistical mechanics, applications to fluctuation theory, imperfect gases, distribution functions, more. 448pp. 5⅜ x 8½.
0-486-65390-0

ENGINEERING AND TECHNOLOGY 1650–1750: ILLUSTRATIONS AND TEXTS FROM ORIGINAL SOURCES, Martin Jensen. Highly readable text with more than 200 contemporary drawings and detailed engravings of engineering projects dealing with surveying, leveling, materials, hand tools, lifting equipment, transport and erection, piling, bailing, water supply, hydraulic engineering, and more. Among the specific projects outlined-transporting a 50-ton stone to the Louvre, erecting an obelisk, building timber locks, and dredging canals. 207pp. 8⅜ x 11¼.
0-486-42232-1

THE VARIATIONAL PRINCIPLES OF MECHANICS, Cornelius Lanczos. Graduate level coverage of calculus of variations, equations of motion, relativistic mechanics, more. First inexpensive paperbound edition of classic treatise. Index. Bibliography. 418pp. 5⅜ x 8½.   0-486-65067-7

PROTECTION OF ELECTRONIC CIRCUITS FROM OVERVOLTAGES, Ronald B. Standler. Five-part treatment presents practical rules and strategies for circuits designed to protect electronic systems from damage by transient overvoltages. 1989 ed. xxiv+434pp. 6⅛ x 9¼.   0-486-42552-5

ROTARY WING AERODYNAMICS, W. Z. Stepniewski. Clear, concise text covers aerodynamic phenomena of the rotor and offers guidelines for helicopter performance evaluation. Originally prepared for NASA. 537 figures. 640pp. 6⅛ x 9¼.
0-486-64647-5

INTRODUCTION TO SPACE DYNAMICS, William Tyrrell Thomson. Comprehensive, classic introduction to space-flight engineering for advanced undergraduate and graduate students. Includes vector algebra, kinematics, transformation of coordinates. Bibliography. Index. 352pp. 5⅜ x 8½.   0-486-65113-4

HISTORY OF STRENGTH OF MATERIALS, Stephen P. Timoshenko. Excellent historical survey of the strength of materials with many references to the theories of elasticity and structure. 245 figures. 452pp. 5⅜ x 8½.   0-486-61187-6

ANALYTICAL FRACTURE MECHANICS, David J. Unger. Self-contained text supplements standard fracture mechanics texts by focusing on analytical methods for determining crack-tip stress and strain fields. 336pp. 6⅛ x 9¼.   0-486-41737-9

STATISTICAL MECHANICS OF ELASTICITY, J. H. Weiner. Advanced, self-contained treatment illustrates general principles and elastic behavior of solids. Part 1, based on classical mechanics, studies thermoelastic behavior of crystalline and polymeric solids. Part 2, based on quantum mechanics, focuses on interatomic force laws, behavior of solids, and thermally activated processes. For students of physics and chemistry and for polymer physicists. 1983 ed. 96 figures. 496pp. 5⅜ x 8½.
0-486-42260-7

Mathematics

FUNCTIONAL ANALYSIS (Second Corrected Edition), George Bachman and Lawrence Narici. Excellent treatment of subject geared toward students with background in linear algebra, advanced calculus, physics and engineering. Text covers introduction to inner-product spaces, normed, metric spaces, and topological spaces; complete orthonormal sets, the Hahn-Banach Theorem and its consequences, and many other related subjects. 1966 ed. 544pp. 6⅛ x 9¼. 0-486-40251-7

ASYMPTOTIC EXPANSIONS OF INTEGRALS, Norman Bleistein & Richard A. Handelsman. Best introduction to important field with applications in a variety of scientific disciplines. New preface. Problems. Diagrams. Tables. Bibliography. Index. 448pp. 5⅜ x 8½. 0-486-65082-0

VECTOR AND TENSOR ANALYSIS WITH APPLICATIONS, A. I. Borisenko and I. E. Tarapov. Concise introduction. Worked-out problems, solutions, exercises. 257pp. 5⅜ x 8¼. 0-486-63833-2

AN INTRODUCTION TO ORDINARY DIFFERENTIAL EQUATIONS, Earl A. Coddington. A thorough and systematic first course in elementary differential equations for undergraduates in mathematics and science, with many exercises and problems (with answers). Index. 304pp. 5⅜ x 8½. 0-486-65942-9

FOURIER SERIES AND ORTHOGONAL FUNCTIONS, Harry F. Davis. An incisive text combining theory and practical example to introduce Fourier series, orthogonal functions and applications of the Fourier method to boundary-value problems. 570 exercises. Answers and notes. 416pp. 5⅜ x 8½. 0-486-65973-9

COMPUTABILITY AND UNSOLVABILITY, Martin Davis. Classic graduate-level introduction to theory of computability, usually referred to as theory of recurrent functions. New preface and appendix. 288pp. 5⅜ x 8½. 0-486-61471-9

ASYMPTOTIC METHODS IN ANALYSIS, N. G. de Bruijn. An inexpensive, comprehensive guide to asymptotic methods–the pioneering work that teaches by explaining worked examples in detail. Index. 224pp. 5⅜ x 8½ 0-486-64221-6

APPLIED COMPLEX VARIABLES, John W. Dettman. Step-by-step coverage of fundamentals of analytic function theory–plus lucid exposition of five important applications: Potential Theory; Ordinary Differential Equations; Fourier Transforms; Laplace Transforms; Asymptotic Expansions. 66 figures. Exercises at chapter ends. 512pp. 5⅜ x 8½. 0-486-64670-X

INTRODUCTION TO LINEAR ALGEBRA AND DIFFERENTIAL EQUATIONS, John W. Dettman. Excellent text covers complex numbers, determinants, orthonormal bases, Laplace transforms, much more. Exercises with solutions. Undergraduate level. 416pp. 5⅜ x 8½. 0-486-65191-6

RIEMANN'S ZETA FUNCTION, H. M. Edwards. Superb, high-level study of landmark 1859 publication entitled "On the Number of Primes Less Than a Given Magnitude" traces developments in mathematical theory that it inspired. xiv+315pp. 5⅜ x 8½. 0-486-41740-9

CALCULUS OF VARIATIONS WITH APPLICATIONS, George M. Ewing. Applications-oriented introduction to variational theory develops insight and promotes understanding of specialized books, research papers. Suitable for advanced undergraduate/graduate students as primary, supplementary text. 352pp. 5⅜ x 8½.
0-486-64856-7

COMPLEX VARIABLES, Francis J. Flanigan. Unusual approach, delaying complex algebra till harmonic functions have been analyzed from real variable viewpoint. Includes problems with answers. 364pp. 5⅜ x 8½.
0-486-61388-7

AN INTRODUCTION TO THE CALCULUS OF VARIATIONS, Charles Fox. Graduate-level text covers variations of an integral, isoperimetrical problems, least action, special relativity, approximations, more. References. 279pp. 5⅜ x 8½.
0-486-65499-0

COUNTEREXAMPLES IN ANALYSIS, Bernard R. Gelbaum and John M. H. Olmsted. These counterexamples deal mostly with the part of analysis known as "real variables." The first half covers the real number system, and the second half encompasses higher dimensions. 1962 edition. xxiv+198pp. 5⅜ x 8½. 0-486-42875-3

CATASTROPHE THEORY FOR SCIENTISTS AND ENGINEERS, Robert Gilmore. Advanced-level treatment describes mathematics of theory grounded in the work of Poincaré, R. Thom, other mathematicians. Also important applications to problems in mathematics, physics, chemistry and engineering. 1981 edition. References. 28 tables. 397 black-and-white illustrations. xvii + 666pp. 6⅛ x 9¼.
0-486-67539-4

INTRODUCTION TO DIFFERENCE EQUATIONS, Samuel Goldberg. Exceptionally clear exposition of important discipline with applications to sociology, psychology, economics. Many illustrative examples; over 250 problems. 260pp. 5⅜ x 8½.
0-486-65084-7

NUMERICAL METHODS FOR SCIENTISTS AND ENGINEERS, Richard Hamming. Classic text stresses frequency approach in coverage of algorithms, polynomial approximation, Fourier approximation, exponential approximation, other topics. Revised and enlarged 2nd edition. 721pp. 5⅜ x 8½. 0-486-65241-6

INTRODUCTION TO NUMERICAL ANALYSIS (2nd Edition), F. B. Hildebrand. Classic, fundamental treatment covers computation, approximation, interpolation, numerical differentiation and integration, other topics. 150 new problems. 669pp. 5⅜ x 8½. 0-486-65363-3

THREE PEARLS OF NUMBER THEORY, A. Y. Khinchin. Three compelling puzzles require proof of a basic law governing the world of numbers. Challenges concern van der Waerden's theorem, the Landau-Schnirelmann hypothesis and Mann's theorem, and a solution to Waring's problem. Solutions included. 64pp. 5⅜ x 8½.
0-486-40026-3

THE PHILOSOPHY OF MATHEMATICS: AN INTRODUCTORY ESSAY, Stephan Körner. Surveys the views of Plato, Aristotle, Leibniz & Kant concerning propositions and theories of applied and pure mathematics. Introduction. Two appendices. Index. 198pp. 5⅜ x 8½. 0-486-25048-2

INTRODUCTORY REAL ANALYSIS, A.N. Kolmogorov, S. V. Fomin. Translated by Richard A. Silverman. Self-contained, evenly paced introduction to real and functional analysis. Some 350 problems. 403pp. 5⅜ x 8½. 0-486-61226-0

APPLIED ANALYSIS, Cornelius Lanczos. Classic work on analysis and design of finite processes for approximating solution of analytical problems. Algebraic equations, matrices, harmonic analysis, quadrature methods, much more. 559pp. 5⅜ x 8½. 0-486-65656-X

AN INTRODUCTION TO ALGEBRAIC STRUCTURES, Joseph Landin. Superb self-contained text covers "abstract algebra": sets and numbers, theory of groups, theory of rings, much more. Numerous well-chosen examples, exercises. 247pp. 5⅜ x 8½. 0-486-65940-2

QUALITATIVE THEORY OF DIFFERENTIAL EQUATIONS, V. V. Nemytskii and V.V. Stepanov. Classic graduate-level text by two prominent Soviet mathematicians covers classical differential equations as well as topological dynamics and ergodic theory. Bibliographies. 523pp. 5⅜ x 8½. 0-486-65954-2

THEORY OF MATRICES, Sam Perlis. Outstanding text covering rank, nonsingularity and inverses in connection with the development of canonical matrices under the relation of equivalence, and without the intervention of determinants. Includes exercises. 237pp. 5⅜ x 8½. 0-486-66810-X

INTRODUCTION TO ANALYSIS, Maxwell Rosenlicht. Unusually clear, accessible coverage of set theory, real number system, metric spaces, continuous functions, Riemann integration, multiple integrals, more. Wide range of problems. Undergraduate level. Bibliography. 254pp. 5⅜ x 8½. 0-486-65038-3

MODERN NONLINEAR EQUATIONS, Thomas L. Saaty. Emphasizes practical solution of problems; covers seven types of equations. ". . . a welcome contribution to the existing literature...."—*Math Reviews.* 490pp. 5⅜ x 8½. 0-486-64232-1

MATRICES AND LINEAR ALGEBRA, Hans Schneider and George Phillip Barker. Basic textbook covers theory of matrices and its applications to systems of linear equations and related topics such as determinants, eigenvalues and differential equations. Numerous exercises. 432pp. 5⅜ x 8½. 0-486-66014-1

LINEAR ALGEBRA, Georgi E. Shilov. Determinants, linear spaces, matrix algebras, similar topics. For advanced undergraduates, graduates. Silverman translation. 387pp. 5⅜ x 8½. 0-486-63518-X

ELEMENTS OF REAL ANALYSIS, David A. Sprecher. Classic text covers fundamental concepts, real number system, point sets, functions of a real variable, Fourier series, much more. Over 500 exercises. 352pp. 5⅜ x 8½. 0-486-65385-4

SET THEORY AND LOGIC, Robert R. Stoll. Lucid introduction to unified theory of mathematical concepts. Set theory and logic seen as tools for conceptual understanding of real number system. 496pp. 5⅜ x 8¼. 0-486-63829-4

TENSOR CALCULUS, J.L. Synge and A. Schild. Widely used introductory text covers spaces and tensors, basic operations in Riemannian space, non-Riemannian spaces, etc. 324pp. 5⅜ x 8¼. 0-486-63612-7

ORDINARY DIFFERENTIAL EQUATIONS, Morris Tenenbaum and Harry Pollard. Exhaustive survey of ordinary differential equations for undergraduates in mathematics, engineering, science. Thorough analysis of theorems. Diagrams. Bibliography. Index. 818pp. 5⅜ x 8½. 0-486-64940-7

INTEGRAL EQUATIONS, F. G. Tricomi. Authoritative, well-written treatment of extremely useful mathematical tool with wide applications. Volterra Equations, Fredholm Equations, much more. Advanced undergraduate to graduate level. Exercises. Bibliography. 238pp. 5⅜ x 8½. 0-486-64828-1

FOURIER SERIES, Georgi P. Tolstov. Translated by Richard A. Silverman. A valuable addition to the literature on the subject, moving clearly from subject to subject and theorem to theorem. 107 problems, answers. 336pp. 5⅜ x 8½. 0-486-63317-9

INTRODUCTION TO MATHEMATICAL THINKING, Friedrich Waismann. Examinations of arithmetic, geometry, and theory of integers; rational and natural numbers; complete induction; limit and point of accumulation; remarkable curves; complex and hypercomplex numbers, more. 1959 ed. 27 figures. xii+260pp. 5⅜ x 8½. 0-486-63317-9

POPULAR LECTURES ON MATHEMATICAL LOGIC, Hao Wang. Noted logician's lucid treatment of historical developments, set theory, model theory, recursion theory and constructivism, proof theory, more. 3 appendixes. Bibliography. 1981 edition. ix + 283pp. 5⅜ x 8½. 0-486-67632-3

CALCULUS OF VARIATIONS, Robert Weinstock. Basic introduction covering isoperimetric problems, theory of elasticity, quantum mechanics, electrostatics, etc. Exercises throughout. 326pp. 5⅜ x 8½. 0-486-63069-2

THE CONTINUUM: A CRITICAL EXAMINATION OF THE FOUNDATION OF ANALYSIS, Hermann Weyl. Classic of 20th-century foundational research deals with the conceptual problem posed by the continuum. 156pp. 5⅜ x 8½. 0-486-67982-9

CHALLENGING MATHEMATICAL PROBLEMS WITH ELEMENTARY SOLUTIONS, A. M. Yaglom and I. M. Yaglom. Over 170 challenging problems on probability theory, combinatorial analysis, points and lines, topology, convex polygons, many other topics. Solutions. Total of 445pp. 5⅜ x 8½. Two-vol. set. Vol. I: 0-486-65536-9 Vol. II: 0-486-65537-7

INTRODUCTION TO PARTIAL DIFFERENTIAL EQUATIONS WITH APPLICATIONS, E. C. Zachmanoglou and Dale W. Thoe. Essentials of partial differential equations applied to common problems in engineering and the physical sciences. Problems and answers. 416pp. 5⅜ x 8½. 0-486-65251-3

THE THEORY OF GROUPS, Hans J. Zassenhaus. Well-written graduate-level text acquaints reader with group-theoretic methods and demonstrates their usefulness in mathematics. Axioms, the calculus of complexes, homomorphic mapping, *p*-group theory, more. 276pp. 5⅜ x 8½. 0-486-40922-8

Math–Decision Theory, Statistics, Probability

ELEMENTARY DECISION THEORY, Herman Chernoff and Lincoln E. Moses. Clear introduction to statistics and statistical theory covers data processing, probability and random variables, testing hypotheses, much more. Exercises. 364pp. 5⅜ x 8½. 0-486-65218-1

STATISTICS MANUAL, Edwin L. Crow et al. Comprehensive, practical collection of classical and modern methods prepared by U.S. Naval Ordnance Test Station. Stress on use. Basics of statistics assumed. 288pp. 5⅜ x 8½. 0-486-60599-X

SOME THEORY OF SAMPLING, William Edwards Deming. Analysis of the problems, theory and design of sampling techniques for social scientists, industrial managers and others who find statistics important at work. 61 tables. 90 figures. xvii +602pp. 5⅜ x 8½. 0-486-64684-X

LINEAR PROGRAMMING AND ECONOMIC ANALYSIS, Robert Dorfman, Paul A. Samuelson and Robert M. Solow. First comprehensive treatment of linear programming in standard economic analysis. Game theory, modern welfare economics, Leontief input-output, more. 525pp. 5⅜ x 8½. 0-486-65491-5

PROBABILITY: AN INTRODUCTION, Samuel Goldberg. Excellent basic text covers set theory, probability theory for finite sample spaces, binomial theorem, much more. 360 problems. Bibliographies. 322pp. 5⅜ x 8½. 0-486-65252-1

GAMES AND DECISIONS: INTRODUCTION AND CRITICAL SURVEY, R. Duncan Luce and Howard Raiffa. Superb nontechnical introduction to game theory, primarily applied to social sciences. Utility theory, zero-sum games, n-person games, decision-making, much more. Bibliography. 509pp. 5⅜ x 8½. 0-486-65943-7

INTRODUCTION TO THE THEORY OF GAMES, J. C. C. McKinsey. This comprehensive overview of the mathematical theory of games illustrates applications to situations involving conflicts of interest, including economic, social, political, and military contexts. Appropriate for advanced undergraduate and graduate courses; advanced calculus a prerequisite. 1952 ed. x+372pp. 5⅜ x 8½. 0-486-42811-7

FIFTY CHALLENGING PROBLEMS IN PROBABILITY WITH SOLUTIONS, Frederick Mosteller. Remarkable puzzlers, graded in difficulty, illustrate elementary and advanced aspects of probability. Detailed solutions. 88pp. 5⅜ x 8½. 65355-2

PROBABILITY THEORY: A CONCISE COURSE, Y. A. Rozanov. Highly readable, self-contained introduction covers combination of events, dependent events, Bernoulli trials, etc. 148pp. 5⅜ x 8¼. 0-486-63544-9

STATISTICAL METHOD FROM THE VIEWPOINT OF QUALITY CONTROL, Walter A. Shewhart. Important text explains regulation of variables, uses of statistical control to achieve quality control in industry, agriculture, other areas. 192pp. 5⅜ x 8½. 0-486-65232-7

Math–Geometry and Topology

ELEMENTARY CONCEPTS OF TOPOLOGY, Paul Alexandroff. Elegant, intuitive approach to topology from set-theoretic topology to Betti groups; how concepts of topology are useful in math and physics. 25 figures. 57pp. 5⅜ x 8½. 0-486-60747-X

COMBINATORIAL TOPOLOGY, P. S. Alexandrov. Clearly written, well-organized, three-part text begins by dealing with certain classic problems without using the formal techniques of homology theory and advances to the central concept, the Betti groups. Numerous detailed examples. 654pp. 5⅜ x 8½. 0-486-40179-0

EXPERIMENTS IN TOPOLOGY, Stephen Barr. Classic, lively explanation of one of the byways of mathematics. Klein bottles, Moebius strips, projective planes, map coloring, problem of the Koenigsberg bridges, much more, described with clarity and wit. 43 figures. 210pp. 5⅜ x 8½. 0-486-25933-1

THE GEOMETRY OF RENÉ DESCARTES, René Descartes. The great work founded analytical geometry. Original French text, Descartes's own diagrams, together with definitive Smith-Latham translation. 244pp. 5⅜ x 8½. 0-486-60068-8

EUCLIDEAN GEOMETRY AND TRANSFORMATIONS, Clayton W. Dodge. This introduction to Euclidean geometry emphasizes transformations, particularly isometries and similarities. Suitable for undergraduate courses, it includes numerous examples, many with detailed answers. 1972 ed. viii+296pp. 6⅛ x 9¼. 0-486-43476-1

PRACTICAL CONIC SECTIONS: THE GEOMETRIC PROPERTIES OF ELLIPSES, PARABOLAS AND HYPERBOLAS, J. W. Downs. This text shows how to create ellipses, parabolas, and hyperbolas. It also presents historical background on their ancient origins and describes the reflective properties and roles of curves in design applications. 1993 ed. 98 figures. xii+100pp. 6½ x 9¼. 0-486-42876-1

THE THIRTEEN BOOKS OF EUCLID'S ELEMENTS, translated with introduction and commentary by Sir Thomas L. Heath. Definitive edition. Textual and linguistic notes, mathematical analysis. 2,500 years of critical commentary. Unabridged. 1,414pp. 5⅜ x 8½. Three-vol. set.
Vol. I: 0-486-60088-2 Vol. II: 0-486-60089-0 Vol. III: 0-486-60090-4

SPACE AND GEOMETRY: IN THE LIGHT OF PHYSIOLOGICAL, PSYCHOLOGICAL AND PHYSICAL INQUIRY, Ernst Mach. Three essays by an eminent philosopher and scientist explore the nature, origin, and development of our concepts of space, with a distinctness and precision suitable for undergraduate students and other readers. 1906 ed. vi+148pp. 5⅜ x 8½. 0-486-43909-7

GEOMETRY OF COMPLEX NUMBERS, Hans Schwerdtfeger. Illuminating, widely praised book on analytic geometry of circles, the Moebius transformation, and two-dimensional non-Euclidean geometries. 200pp. 5⅝ x 8¼. 0-486-63830-8

DIFFERENTIAL GEOMETRY, Heinrich W. Guggenheimer. Local differential geometry as an application of advanced calculus and linear algebra. Curvature, transformation groups, surfaces, more. Exercises. 62 figures. 378pp. 5⅜ x 8½. 0-486-63433-7

History of Math

THE WORKS OF ARCHIMEDES, Archimedes (T. L. Heath, ed.). Topics include the famous problems of the ratio of the areas of a cylinder and an inscribed sphere; the measurement of a circle; the properties of conoids, spheroids, and spirals; and the quadrature of the parabola. Informative introduction. clxxxvi+326pp. 5⅜ x 8½.
0-486-42084-1

A SHORT ACCOUNT OF THE HISTORY OF MATHEMATICS, W. W. Rouse Ball. One of clearest, most authoritative surveys from the Egyptians and Phoenicians through 19th-century figures such as Grassman, Galois, Riemann. Fourth edition. 522pp. 5⅜ x 8½.
0-486-20630-0

THE HISTORY OF THE CALCULUS AND ITS CONCEPTUAL DEVELOP-MENT, Carl B. Boyer. Origins in antiquity, medieval contributions, work of Newton, Leibniz, rigorous formulation. Treatment is verbal. 346pp. 5⅜ x 8½.   0-486-60509-4

THE HISTORICAL ROOTS OF ELEMENTARY MATHEMATICS, Lucas N. H. Bunt, Phillip S. Jones, and Jack D. Bedient. Fundamental underpinnings of modern arithmetic, algebra, geometry and number systems derived from ancient civilizations. 320pp. 5⅜ x 8½.
0-486-25563-8

A HISTORY OF MATHEMATICAL NOTATIONS, Florian Cajori. This classic study notes the first appearance of a mathematical symbol and its origin, the competition it encountered, its spread among writers in different countries, its rise to popularity, its eventual decline or ultimate survival. Original 1929 two-volume edition presented here in one volume. xxviii+820pp. 5⅜ x 8½.
0-486-67766-4

GAMES, GODS & GAMBLING: A HISTORY OF PROBABILITY AND STATISTICAL IDEAS, F. N. David. Episodes from the lives of Galileo, Fermat, Pascal, and others illustrate this fascinating account of the roots of mathematics. Features thought-provoking references to classics, archaeology, biography, poetry. 1962 edition. 304pp. 5⅜ x 8½. (Available in U.S. only.)
0-486-40023-9

OF MEN AND NUMBERS: THE STORY OF THE GREAT MATHEMATICIANS, Jane Muir. Fascinating accounts of the lives and accomplishments of history's greatest mathematical minds–Pythagoras, Descartes, Euler, Pascal, Cantor, many more. Anecdotal, illuminating. 30 diagrams. Bibliography. 256pp. 5⅜ x 8½.
0-486-28973-7

HISTORY OF MATHEMATICS, David E. Smith. Nontechnical survey from ancient Greece and Orient to late 19th century; evolution of arithmetic, geometry, trigonometry, calculating devices, algebra, the calculus. 362 illustrations. 1,355pp. 5⅜ x 8½. Two-vol. set.   Vol. I: 0-486-20429-4   Vol. II: 0-486-20430-8

A CONCISE HISTORY OF MATHEMATICS, Dirk J. Struik. The best brief history of mathematics. Stresses origins and covers every major figure from ancient Near East to 19th century. 41 illustrations. 195pp. 5⅜ x 8½.   0-486-60255-9

Physics

OPTICAL RESONANCE AND TWO-LEVEL ATOMS, L. Allen and J. H. Eberly. Clear, comprehensive introduction to basic principles behind all quantum optical resonance phenomena. 53 illustrations. Preface. Index. 256pp. 5⅜ x 8½. 0-486-65533-4

QUANTUM THEORY, David Bohm. This advanced undergraduate-level text presents the quantum theory in terms of qualitative and imaginative concepts, followed by specific applications worked out in mathematical detail. Preface. Index. 655pp. 5⅜ x 8½. 0-486-65969-0

ATOMIC PHYSICS (8th EDITION), Max Born. Nobel laureate's lucid treatment of kinetic theory of gases, elementary particles, nuclear atom, wave-corpuscles, atomic structure and spectral lines, much more. Over 40 appendices, bibliography. 495pp. 5⅜ x 8½. 0-486-65984-4

A SOPHISTICATE'S PRIMER OF RELATIVITY, P. W. Bridgman. Geared toward readers already acquainted with special relativity, this book transcends the view of theory as a working tool to answer natural questions: What is a frame of reference? What is a "law of nature"? What is the role of the "observer"? Extensive treatment, written in terms accessible to those without a scientific background. 1983 ed. xlviii+172pp. 5⅜ x 8½. 0-486-42549-5

AN INTRODUCTION TO HAMILTONIAN OPTICS, H. A. Buchdahl. Detailed account of the Hamiltonian treatment of aberration theory in geometrical optics. Many classes of optical systems defined in terms of the symmetries they possess. Problems with detailed solutions. 1970 edition. xv + 360pp. 5⅜ x 8½. 0-486-67597-1

PRIMER OF QUANTUM MECHANICS, Marvin Chester. Introductory text examines the classical quantum bead on a track: its state and representations; operator eigenvalues; harmonic oscillator and bound bead in a symmetric force field; and bead in a spherical shell. Other topics include spin, matrices, and the structure of quantum mechanics; the simplest atom; indistinguishable particles; and stationary-state perturbation theory. 1992 ed. xiv+314pp. 6⅛ x 9¼. 0-486-42878-8

LECTURES ON QUANTUM MECHANICS, Paul A. M. Dirac. Four concise, brilliant lectures on mathematical methods in quantum mechanics from Nobel Prize-winning quantum pioneer build on idea of visualizing quantum theory through the use of classical mechanics. 96pp. 5⅜ x 8½. 0-486-41713-1

THIRTY YEARS THAT SHOOK PHYSICS: THE STORY OF QUANTUM THEORY, George Gamow. Lucid, accessible introduction to influential theory of energy and matter. Careful explanations of Dirac's anti-particles, Bohr's model of the atom, much more. 12 plates. Numerous drawings. 240pp. 5⅜ x 8½. 0-486-24895-X

ELECTRONIC STRUCTURE AND THE PROPERTIES OF SOLIDS: THE PHYSICS OF THE CHEMICAL BOND, Walter A. Harrison. Innovative text offers basic understanding of the electronic structure of covalent and ionic solids, simple metals, transition metals and their compounds. Problems. 1980 edition. 582pp. 6⅛ x 9¼. 0-486-66021-4

CATALOG OF DOVER BOOKS

HYDRODYNAMIC AND HYDROMAGNETIC STABILITY, S. Chandrasekhar. Lucid examination of the Rayleigh-Benard problem; clear coverage of the theory of instabilities causing convection. 704pp. 5⅜ x 8¼. 0-486-64071-X

INVESTIGATIONS ON THE THEORY OF THE BROWNIAN MOVEMENT, Albert Einstein. Five papers (1905–8) investigating dynamics of Brownian motion and evolving elementary theory. Notes by R. Fürth. 122pp. 5⅜ x 8½. 0-486-60304-0

THE PHYSICS OF WAVES, William C. Elmore and Mark A. Heald. Unique overview of classical wave theory. Acoustics, optics, electromagnetic radiation, more. Ideal as classroom text or for self-study. Problems. 477pp. 5⅜ x 8½. 0-486-64926-1

GRAVITY, George Gamow. Distinguished physicist and teacher takes reader-friendly look at three scientists whose work unlocked many of the mysteries behind the laws of physics: Galileo, Newton, and Einstein. Most of the book focuses on Newton's ideas, with a concluding chapter on post-Einsteinian speculations concerning the relationship between gravity and other physical phenomena. 160pp. 5⅜ x 8½. 0-486-42563-0

PHYSICAL PRINCIPLES OF THE QUANTUM THEORY, Werner Heisenberg. Nobel Laureate discusses quantum theory, uncertainty, wave mechanics, work of Dirac, Schroedinger, Compton, Wilson, Einstein, etc. 184pp. 5⅜ x 8½. 0-486-60113-7

ATOMIC SPECTRA AND ATOMIC STRUCTURE, Gerhard Herzberg. One of best introductions; especially for specialist in other fields. Treatment is physical rather than mathematical. 80 illustrations. 257pp. 5⅜ x 8½. 0-486-60115-3

AN INTRODUCTION TO STATISTICAL THERMODYNAMICS, Terrell L. Hill. Excellent basic text offers wide-ranging coverage of quantum statistical mechanics, systems of interacting molecules, quantum statistics, more. 523pp. 5⅜ x 8½. 0-486-65242-4

THEORETICAL PHYSICS, Georg Joos, with Ira M. Freeman. Classic overview covers essential math, mechanics, electromagnetic theory, thermodynamics, quantum mechanics, nuclear physics, other topics. First paperback edition. xxiii + 885pp. 5⅜ x 8½. 0-486-65227-0

PROBLEMS AND SOLUTIONS IN QUANTUM CHEMISTRY AND PHYSICS, Charles S. Johnson, Jr. and Lee G. Pedersen. Unusually varied problems, detailed solutions in coverage of quantum mechanics, wave mechanics, angular momentum, molecular spectroscopy, more. 280 problems plus 139 supplementary exercises. 430pp. 6½ x 9¼. 0-486-65236-X

THEORETICAL SOLID STATE PHYSICS, Vol. 1: Perfect Lattices in Equilibrium; Vol. II: Non-Equilibrium and Disorder, William Jones and Norman H. March. Monumental reference work covers fundamental theory of equilibrium properties of perfect crystalline solids, non-equilibrium properties, defects and disordered systems. Appendices. Problems. Preface. Diagrams. Index. Bibliography. Total of 1,301pp. 5⅜ x 8½. Two volumes. Vol. I: 0-486-65015-4 Vol. II: 0-486-65016-2

WHAT IS RELATIVITY? L. D. Landau and G. B. Rumer. Written by a Nobel Prize physicist and his distinguished colleague, this compelling book explains the special theory of relativity to readers with no scientific background, using such familiar objects as trains, rulers, and clocks. 1960 ed. vi+72pp. 5⅜ x 8½. 0-486-42806-0

CATALOG OF DOVER BOOKS

A TREATISE ON ELECTRICITY AND MAGNETISM, James Clerk Maxwell. Important foundation work of modern physics. Brings to final form Maxwell's theory of electromagnetism and rigorously derives his general equations of field theory. 1,084pp. 5⅜ x 8½. Two-vol. set. Vol. I: 0-486-60636-8 Vol. II: 0-486-60637-6

QUANTUM MECHANICS: PRINCIPLES AND FORMALISM, Roy McWeeny. Graduate student-oriented volume develops subject as fundamental discipline, opening with review of origins of Schrödinger's equations and vector spaces. Focusing on main principles of quantum mechanics and their immediate consequences, it concludes with final generalizations covering alternative "languages" or representations. 1972 ed. 15 figures. xi+155pp. 5⅜ x 8½. 0-486-42829-X

INTRODUCTION TO QUANTUM MECHANICS With Applications to Chemistry, Linus Pauling & E. Bright Wilson, Jr. Classic undergraduate text by Nobel Prize winner applies quantum mechanics to chemical and physical problems. Numerous tables and figures enhance the text. Chapter bibliographies. Appendices. Index. 468pp. 5⅜ x 8½. 0-486-64871-0

METHODS OF THERMODYNAMICS, Howard Reiss. Outstanding text focuses on physical technique of thermodynamics, typical problem areas of understanding, and significance and use of thermodynamic potential. 1965 edition. 238pp. 5⅜ x 8½. 0-486-69445-3

THE ELECTROMAGNETIC FIELD, Albert Shadowitz. Comprehensive undergraduate text covers basics of electric and magnetic fields, builds up to electromagnetic theory. Also related topics, including relativity. Over 900 problems. 768pp. 5⅜ x 8¼. 0-486-65660-8

GREAT EXPERIMENTS IN PHYSICS: FIRSTHAND ACCOUNTS FROM GALILEO TO EINSTEIN, Morris H. Shamos (ed.). 25 crucial discoveries: Newton's laws of motion, Chadwick's study of the neutron, Hertz on electromagnetic waves, more. Original accounts clearly annotated. 370pp. 5⅜ x 8½. 0-486-25346-5

EINSTEIN'S LEGACY, Julian Schwinger. A Nobel Laureate relates fascinating story of Einstein and development of relativity theory in well-illustrated, nontechnical volume. Subjects include meaning of time, paradoxes of space travel, gravity and its effect on light, non-Euclidean geometry and curving of space-time, impact of radio astronomy and space-age discoveries, and more. 189 b/w illustrations. xiv+250pp. 8⅜ x 9¼. 0-486-41974-6

STATISTICAL PHYSICS, Gregory H. Wannier. Classic text combines thermodynamics, statistical mechanics and kinetic theory in one unified presentation of thermal physics. Problems with solutions. Bibliography. 532pp. 5⅜ x 8½. 0-486-65401-X

Paperbound unless otherwise indicated. Available at your book dealer, online at **www.doverpublications.com**, or by writing to Dept. GI, Dover Publications, Inc., 31 East 2nd Street, Mineola, NY 11501. For current price information or for free catalogues (please indicate field of interest), write to Dover Publications or log on to **www.doverpublications.com** and see every Dover book in print. Dover publishes more than 500 books each year on science, elementary and advanced mathematics, biology, music, art, literary history, social sciences, and other areas.